Madagascar & Comoros

Paul Greenway

>x0x0x0x0x0x0x0x0x0x0x(

D0201890

Madagascar & Comoros

3rd edition

Published by
Lonely Planet Publications
Head Office: PO Box 617, Hawthorn, Vic 3122, Australia
Branches: 155 Filbert St, Suite 251, Oakland, CA 94607, USA
10 Barley Mow Passage, Chiswick, London W4 4PH, UK
71 bis rue du Cardinal Lemoine, 75005 Paris, France

Printed by
SNP Printing Pte Ltd, Singapore

Photographs by

David Curl	Gilles Gautier	Paul Greenway
Peter Ptschelinzew	Paul Scott	Deanna Swaney
Robert Willox		

Front cover: A white lemur, also known as a sifaka, north-western Madagascar (David Curl)

First Published
November 1989

This Edition
November 1997

Although the authors and publisher have tried to make the information as accurate as possible, they accept no responsibility for any loss, injury or inconvenience sustained by any person using this book.

National Library of Australia Cataloguing in Publication Data

Greenway, Paul 1960-
Madagascar & Comoros

3rd ed.
Includes index.
ISBN 0 86442 496 5.

1. Madagascar – Guidebooks. 2. Comoros – Guidebooks.
I. Swaney, Deanna. II. Title.

916.91045

text & maps © Lonely Planet 1997
photos © photographers as indicated 1997
climate chart of Moroni compiled from information supplied by Patrick J Tyson, © Patrick J Tyson, 1997

Paul Greenway

Paul got his first tropical disease in 1985, and has had the 'travel bug' ever since. He has been to over 50 countries, and has learnt to say 'one beer, please' in just about every known language. Gratefully plucked from the security and blandness of the Australian Public Service, he is now a full-time traveller, writer, photographer and drifter. Paul has co-written the Lonely Planet *Indonesia* and *Indian Himalaya* guides. He was also recently seen eating mutton and riding yaks while researching the guide to *Mongolia*, and eating kebabs (but not drinking beer) and riding camels for the next update of the LP guide to *Iran*. Paul is based in Adelaide, in South Australia, where he eats and breathes Australian rules football, relaxes to tuneless heavy rock and will do anything (like going to Mongolia and Iran) to avoid settling down.

Deanna Swaney

After completing university studies, Deanna Swaney made a shoestring tour of Europe and has been addicted to travel ever since. She has written and co-authored many books for Lonely Planet, covering areas as diverse as *Bolivia*, Arctic and tropical island paradises, *Zimbabwe, Botswana & Namibia*, *Brazil* and *Mauritius, Réunion & Seychelles*. Deanna updated the second edition of *Madagascar & Comoros* and contributed to the shoestring guides to *Africa, South America* and *Scandinavia*.

From Paul

In Madagascar, plenty of thanks go to: Paul Saxton, from the American embassy, and his family, who invited me to my first Thanksgiving dinner; the many helpful staff at several ANGAP offices throughout the country whose names I never knew (nor could remember); the ever-smiling Samoela Andriankotonirina, the librarian at the WWF office in Tana; the lovely Jacky Andriamalala, from the American Cultural Centre; and Clare Wilkinson & Connie Boylan (UK) and Natasha Amor (Australia). In the Comoros, thanks also to Issouffou Oihabi, a Comoran English teacher on Mohéli, who helped with the Comoran language section, and continued to teach though he and his colleagues had not been paid for over nine months; Zaki Muhieddine from Tropic Tours & Travel in Moroni; and Marie Ali Saîd from the Tourism Office in Moroni.

I am extremely grateful to every reader who writes to Lonely Planet. Extra special thanks to those who go to the effort of typing and indexing their comments to the relevant pages (I love you all!); and to readers whose first language is not English but still write fluently in what Stan & Marja Tavenier from the Netherlands call 'charcoal English'. Of the many who have written, I'd particularly like to thank the following: Heike Alber &

Andreas Letto (Germany); Sanne Friedrich (Switzerland); John Kupiec (USA); Patrick Lachenmeier (Switzerland); Isabelle Loots & Uwe Hübler (Germany); Yves Périsse (France); and Benjamin Schmidt (Germany) for his comments about cycling around Madagascar.

I would also like to thank Deanna Swaney, the previous co-author of this book, for her comments and suggestions, and the editors, designers and cartographers at Lonely Planet's head office in Melbourne for their support and hard work.

This Book

The first edition of this book was researched and written by Robert Willox, who prepared the way for Deanna Swaney to update and expand the second edition. This third edition was thoroughly revised by Paul Greenway.

From the Publisher

David Andrew edited this third edition, ably assisted by Miriam Cannell, who also handled some of the proofing, and Michelle Coxall, to whom most of the proofing fell. David also helped with the special Wildlife section. Cathy Lanigan cast her expert eye over the Health chapter and Michelle Glynn helped with last minute proofing and corrections. Sarah Fee and Mohamed Ahmed-Chamanga wrote the language sections for Madagascar and the Comoros, respectively, which were then edited by Peter D'Onghia and Sally Steward. Kerrie Williams created the index.

Glenn van der Knijff was the design dynamo who handled mapping and layout, and created those neat chapter endings. Simon Bracken designed the cover, with cartographic assistance from Adam McCrow. Illustrations were provided by Indra Kilfoyle and Glenn. Thanks to David Curl for the use of his photos as reference material.

Thanks

Many thanks to the travellers who used the last edition and wrote to us with helpful hints, useful advice and interesting anecdotes:

Amani Ahrens, Heike Alber, Rachel Andrews, Istvan Barkanyi, Andrea & Stefanie Bedo, Sophie Bishop, Brian Chambers, G Choshen, John & Elizabeth Cox, Zsolt Cseke, Leif Dahl, J Day, Eveline der Maur, S Friedrich, H Fuhrmann, N Funk, Stephane Gagne, David Goedheer, Bruno Goldman, M Goodman, Clare & Johan Hermans, Darren Hincks, Uwe Hubler, Kirsten Inga Burt, E Iversen, J C Javet, Tristan Jeeves, Rosalind Knowlson/Willder, Kirros Kokkas, Michaela Kraut, Christian Kull, John Kupiec, Patrick Lachenmeier, Daniel Laurin, Kirsten Leong, Attilio Lestingi, Andreas Letto, Isabelle Loots, T Meier, Angela Miller, Anita Morav, Daniel Mueller, M Naud, Alex Oldroyd, R Osterreicher, Ross Patterson, Yves Perisse, Brigitte Poulet, Stephen Powell, Vince & Barbara Roth, J Schachter, Benjamin Schmidt, Stefan Schwarzer, Jim Sellars, James Sellers, V Stichweh, C Storme, Karen & Jan Strack, Stan & Marja Tavenier, Adam Taylor, Adriana Tedesco, T Tropen, G D Twigger, Silke Ubber, A van Hout, E Veraghert, F Vereecken, K Weber, Karl Werner Schmidt and Gretchen Young.

Warning & Request

Things change – prices go up, schedules change, good places go bad and bad places go bankrupt – nothing stays the same. So, if you find things better or worse, recently opened or long since closed, please tell us and help make the next edition even more accurate and useful.

We value all of the feedback we receive from travellers. Julie Young coordinates a small team who read and acknowledge every letter, postcard and email, and ensure that every morsel of information finds its way to the appropriate authors, editors and publishers.

Everyone who writes to us will find their name in the next edition of the appropriate guide and will also receive a free subscription to our quarterly newsletter, *Planet Talk*. The very best contributions will be rewarded with a free Lonely Planet guide.

Excerpts from your correspondence may appear in new editions of this guide; in our newsletter, *Planet Talk*; or in updates on our Web site – so please let us know if you don't want your letter published or your name acknowledged.

Contents

COMOROS

Map Legend

ROUTES

⊢⊢⊢⊢⊢⊢⊢○⊢⊢	Train Route, with Station
– – – – – –	Walking Track
– · – · – · – ·	Ferry Route

Country Maps

─────────	Highway
─────────	Major Road
– – – – –	Unsealed Road

Regional Maps

─────────	Highway
─────────	Major Road
=========	Unsealed Road
─────────	Minor Road

City Maps

─────────	Highway
─────────	Major Road
– – – – –	Unsealed Road
─────────	Street

AREA FEATURES

	National Park, City Park
	Building
	Pedestrian Square
	Market
+ + + + +	Cemetery
	Built-Up Area
	Reef

BOUNDARIES

▬▬ · ▬▬ · ▬▬	International Boundary
▬ – · ▬ – · ▬	Regional Boundary

HYDROGRAPHIC FEATURES

	River, Creek
	Intermittent River or Creek
⟩⟩ ─╫─ ⟨	Rapids, Waterfalls
⬭ ⬭	Lake, Intermittent Lake

SYMBOLS

✪ CAPITAL	National Capital	✈	Airport	☀	Lookout
◎ Capital	Regional Capital	⁂	Archaeological Site	⚑	Monument
● City	City	✪	Bank	◪	Mosque
● Town	Town	⋔	Beach	▲	Mountain
● Village	Village	▥	Castle, Fort	🏛	Museum
		▦ ⊞	Cathedral, Church	★	Police Station
■	Place to Stay	⌒	Cave	✉	Post Office
▲	Camping Ground	◩	Dive Site	⚓	Shipwreck
⏏	Caravan Park	○	Embassy	🏛	Stately Home
▼	Place to Eat	✿	Gardens	▣	Tomb
☗	Pub or Bar	✛	Hospital	❶	Tourist Information
☕	Café	☀	Lighthouse	●	Transport

Note: not all symbols displayed above appear in this book

Top Left:	Young Comoran women daub their faces with a beauty mask.
Top Right:	Village women in traditional dress, Comoros.
Bottom Left:	Friendly Malagasy children posing at Lac Andraikiba, central Madagascar.
Bottom Right:	A Malagasy girl in traditional dress in Fianarantsoa, central Madagascar.

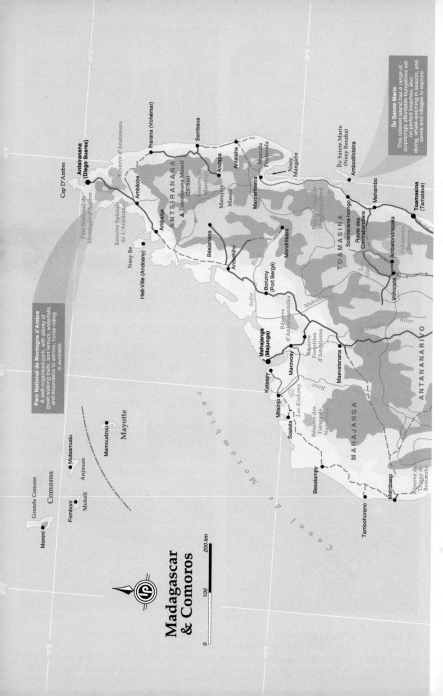

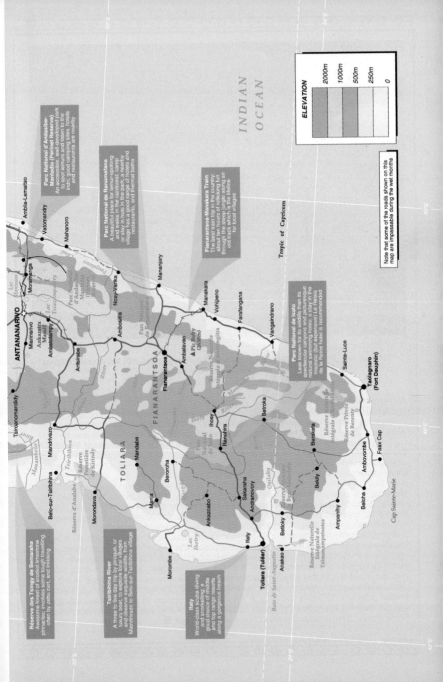

Réserve des Tsingy de Bemaraha
Awesome forest of eroded limestone pinnacles: involves some tough travelling, often by zebu cart, and trekking

Tsiribihina River
A three to five day trip by pirogue, or luxury boat, to explore local villages and observe organic wildlife, from Miandrivazo to Belo-sur-Tsiribihina village

Ifaty
World-class scuba diving and snorkeling; a good choice of middle and top range resorts along a gorgeous beach

Parc National d'Andasibe-Mantadia (Périnet Reserve)
An accessible, well-developed park to spot lemurs and listen to the indri; good camping sites, hotels and restaurants are nearby

Parc National de Ranomafana
A beautiful place for lemur-spotting and walks in the rainforest; camp or stay in huts in the park, a nearby village has a good range of hotels and restaurants, and thermal baths

Fianarantsoa-Manakara Train
The best train trip in the country: about ten hours of rolling along a steep mountain range on an old track which is the lifeline for local villages

Parc National de l'Isalo
Less known for its wildlife than its spectacular canyons and picturesque natural swimming holes; a stay in the much-photographed Canyon de la Reine Isabel is recommended

Note that some of the roads shown on this map are impassable during the wet months

ELEVATION

2000m
1000m
500m
250m
0

INDIAN OCEAN

ANTANANARIVO

Tropic of Capricorn

Tsaraotana
Mahanoro
Vatomandry
Ambila-Lemaitso
Moramanga
Mariarano
Ankaratra Massif
Ambatolampy
Antsirabe
Nosy Varika
Ambositra
Ambalavao
FIANARANTSOA
Fianarantsoa
▲ Pic Boby (2658m)
Mananjary
Ihosy
Ranohira
Manakara
Vohipeno
Faratangana
Betroka
Vangaindrano
Sainte-Luce
Taolagnaro (Fort Dauphin)
Faux Cap
Beloha
Amboyombe
Réserve Privée de Berenty
Réserve Spéciale de Kalambatritra
Beraketa
Ampanihy
Bekily
Betioky
Ampanihy
Andranovory
Sakaraha
TOLIARA
Toliara (Tuléar)
Anakao
Baie de Saint-Augustin
Réserve Naturelle Intégrale de Tsimanampetsotsa
Cap Sainte-Marie
Itampolo
Lac Ihotry
Ankazoabo
Morombe
Manja
Beroroha
Mandabe
Morondava
Belo-sur-Tsiribihina
Réserve d'Analabe
Réserve Forestière de Kirindy
Miandrivazo
Tsiroanomandidy

Sakalava women wearing colourful lambas on Nosy Be. Lambas with a myriad of patterns can be seen all over Madagascar.

A Garment for all Seasons

The *lamba* is a traditional all-purpose garment worn by men and women throughout Madagascar. It resembles a large shawl, measuring approximately 1m X 2.5m, that can be woven from cotton, white silk, raffia, hemp, wool and even banana leaves; today synthetic materials may be more commonly used. Western-style dress is becoming more common in Madagascar, though the lamba can still be seen all over the island. It is usually worn as a comfortable outer garment, wrapped around the shoulders and often draped over the head with one tail hanging behind. Other variants are as a dress, cloak or a hood to keep off the sun (or rain), and even as a loin cloth. But the lamba can be adapted to suit all sorts of purposes and in daily life among the Malagasy it is used in many and various ways. For example, a lamba makes a light cover for a sleeper; it can be wrapped around and used to carry a baby or small sacks of goods, such as rice or flour; some folk even use them to carry small livestock and you may see someone walking to market with a half a dozen struggling ducks or chickens wrapped in a lamba.

Women normally spin and weave the cloth to make a lamba. As with many aspects of Malagasy life, the wearing of lambas is loaded with superstitions. When it is worn with the tail falling on the right side of the body it signifies that the wearer is in mourning and is called a *lamba maitso* 'green cloth' (although it isn't necessarily green). A *lamba mena* ('red cloth', although it is rarely actually red) is a burial shroud that should never be worn by a living person since it could cause their death. A lamba's colour and material is believed to influence the wearer: a red lamba is worn on special occasions to signify authority; a silk lamba is supposed to cause drowsiness; indigo arouses passion, but makes the wearer militant; sorcerers also use indigo to create mischief. Some lambas have popular proverbs printed along the hem. ■

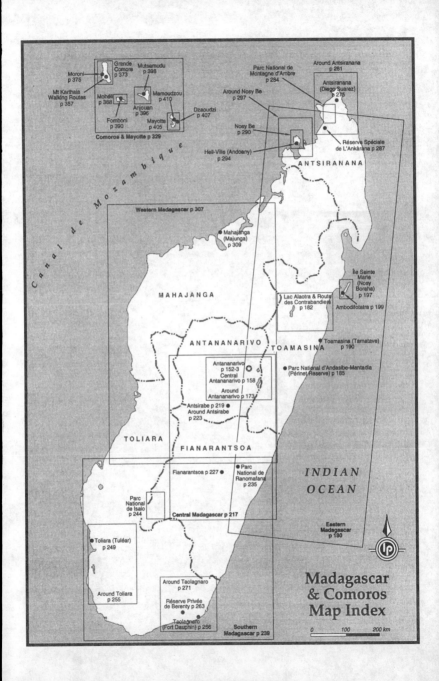

Moroni
p 375

Mt Karthala
Walking Routes
p 357

Grande
Comore
p 373

Mutsamudu
p 396

Mohéli
p 388

Mamoudzou
p 410

Anjouan
p 396

Fomboni
p 390

Mayotte
p 405

Dzaoudzi
p 407

Comoros & Mayotte p 329

Parc National de
Montagne d'Ambre
p 284

Around Antsiranana
p 281

Around Nosy Be
p 297

Antsiranana
(Diego Suarez)
p 275

Nosy Be
p 290

Réserve Spéciale
de L'Ankàrana p 287

Hell-Ville (Andoany)
p 294

ANTSIRANANA

Western Madagascar p 307

Mahajanga
(Majunga)
p 309

MAHAJANGA

Île Sainte
Marie
(Nosy
Boraha)
p 197

Lac Alaotra & Route
des Contrabandiers
p 182

Ambodifotatra p 199

ANTANANARIVO

TOAMASINA

Toamasina (Tamatave)
p 190

Antananarivo
p 152-3
Central
Antananarivo p 158

Around
Antananarivo p 173

Parc National d'Andasibe-Mantadia
(Périnet Reserve) p 185

Antsirabe p 219
Around Antsirabe
p 223

TOLIARA

FIANARANTSOA

Fianarantsoa p 227

Parc
National de
Ranomafana
p 235

Parc
National
de Isalo
p 244

Central Madagascar p 217

INDIAN
OCEAN

Toliara (Tuléar)
p 249

Eastern
Madagascar
p 180

Around Toliara
p 255

Around Taolagnaro
p 271

Réserve Privée
de Berenty p 263

Taolagnaro
(Fort Dauphin) p 256

Southern
Madagascar p 239

Madagascar
& Comoros
Map Index

0   100   200 km

Canal de Mozambique

Introduction

In describing Madagascar the tourist brochures and travel agencies tend to trot out phrases such as 'a unique travel experience', 'a strange and exotic land', or 'a diverse country of mystery, beauty and adventure ... with warm and friendly people'. These descriptions could apply to a lot of countries in the world – and Madagascar is different. Really!

Madagascar is the world's fourth-biggest island; it stands only ankle-high alongside the hulking mass of Africa, but stretches 1600km from north to south and spans 650km at its widest point. However, Madagascar shouldn't be considered a part of Africa in anything but the geographical sense, though it does participate in African political affairs.

The Malagasy, as Madagascar's people (and language) are known, are descended primarily from Malay-Polynesian mariners who first settled the island around 1500 years ago. The 'ruling' tribe of Madagascar, the Merina, are based in the central highlands. There are 17 other officially recognised tribes and each has their own territory, customs and traditions.

The terrain is equally varied and unlike Africa, and there are some amazing natural features. The centre of the island is composed of a spine of mountains backed by a high plateau which descends into tropical forest in the east and north, and into stark desert in the south and south-west. The landscape is punctuated by geological and geographical oddities, including whale-back

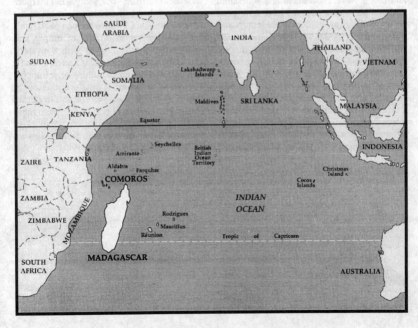

domes south of Fianarantsoa; the maze formations of the Isalo National Park; the labyrinthine rock forests *(tsingy)* in the north and west; and the semi-natural Pangalanes canal, which extends nearly half the length of the east coast.

Wildlife is another matter. Madagascar's plants and animals evolved separately from those on mainland Africa. The island seems to have been a testing ground for evolution – 'nature's design laboratory', somebody called it – and most of Madagascar's creatures and vegetation are found nowhere else on earth. Many of these unique forms are critically endangered because their natural habitat – the forest – is rapidly being burnt and logged, then converted into grazing lands, rice paddies and townships.

Thankfully, some recent impressive efforts by Malagasy and foreign environmental and aid agencies have helped halt the destruction of some forests, and protect the vast array of endemic and endangered flora and fauna. Several excellent and accessible national parks and reserves have now been set up which allow visitors to see lemurs and other animals in the wild (or domesticated and banana-grabbing), and to walk among the rainforests. These parks are now a major attraction and rate as a highlight for many visitors, along with two beautiful islands: Nosy Be and Île Sainte Marie.

Madagascar seems to be a land that travellers and tourists have largely ignored; although tourism is making gains, it isn't nearly as popular as nearby Mauritius, the Seychelles or eastern and southern Africa. Madagascar is an ideal destination for adventurous travellers and those inspired by fascinating history, traditional culture and unique wildlife. Organised packaged tours for sun-worshippers, divers and ecotourists are becoming increasingly popular as well.

So, now is your chance. Having read this far, you're probably either packing to leave or seriously considering a trip. If you're the sort of independent traveller who craves something different and isn't put off by a bit of discomfort, Madagascar is definitely for you. On this huge island, every journey is an adventure, whether it's by foot, ox-cart, boat, bus, train or *taxi-brousse* ('bush taxi'). We hope this book will help introduce travellers to this superb and affordable destination.

If Madagascar seems mysterious, you should see the Comoros, made up of three islands which form the Federal Islamic Republic of the Comoros, and one, Mayotte, which opted to stick with France. They are quite distinct from – but, sadly, a fair bit more expensive than – their big neighbour to the south-east. The Comoros are one of Africa's big surprises, with dozens of empty and spectacular beaches, towns with a mysterious ambience reminiscent of Zanzibar, and a friendly and colourful culture as yet uncorrupted by tourism. If that's not enough, you'll also find an active volcano to climb, lots of great hiking opportunities, even more wildlife and only two international class hotels. Visitors may get the feeling they've sailed off the edge of the world.

Facts about the Region

HISTORY

The following section gives an overview of the histories of Madagascar and the Comoros before the French colonisation during the late 19th century. For a subsequent colonial and post-colonial history refer to the Facts about Madagascar and Facts about the Comoros chapters.

Madagascar

Although it lies a relatively short sail from the African mainland, Madagascar apparently remained uninhabited until around 1500 to 2000 years ago. And the first settlers came not from Africa but from the distant shores of Indonesia and Malaysia, 6400km away. The majority of the current population has descended from these Malay-Polynesian migrants. They began arriving from the 6th century onwards and particularly during the 9th century, when the powerful Hindu-Sumatran Empire of Srivijaya controlled much of the maritime trade in the Indian Ocean.

How these first Indonesian settlers reached the 'Great Red Island' (as Madagascar is often called) isn't clear, but the blend

Chronology of Madagascar & The Comoros

circa 1st century: probable settlement of the Comoros by Malay-Polynesians

circa 2nd century: settlement of Madagascar by Malay-Polynesians

circa 700: the Comoros converts to Islam

circa 13th-15th centuries: Shirazis from Persia settle in the Comoros

1529: probable first arrival of Europeans on the Comoros

1599: first Europeans arrive on Madagascar

circa 1700: the Menabe tribe spreads its power in Madagascar

circa 1790: the Merina becomes the major tribe in Madagascar

circa 1800: the Merina capital moves to Antananarivo

1820: Britain recognises Madagascar under Merina rule

1843: Mayotte cedes to France

1886: Anjouan cedes to France; Mohéli becomes a French protectorate

1890: Britain recognises French sovereignty over Madagascar

1908: France annexes Grande Comore

1947: first unsuccessful insurrection against French; the Comoros gain autonomy from French rule in Madagascar

1960: Madagascar becomes independent

1974: Grande Comore, Anjouan and Mohéli seek independence after referendum; Mayotte votes to remain part of France

1975: France recognises the independence of the Comoros (without Mayotte)

1978: first coup attempt by Bob Dénard in the Comoros

1989: the re-election of President Ratsiraka in Madagascar sparks riots

1996/97: rounds of presidential elections in Madagascar between November 1996 and February 1997 return former communist, Ratsiraka; there is another unsuccessful coup in the Comoros led by Dénard ■

of Asian and African elements that comprise the Malagasy culture, along with other anthropological and ethnographical clues, suggest they may well have colonised Madagascar after migrating in a single voyage by way of the East African coast.

However, the distribution of Indonesian-style sailing boats along the northern shores of the Indian Ocean suggests that the first settlers took a round-about rather than direct route. These boats were coastal vessels rather than ocean-going craft so it's possible they followed the coastline of the Indian Ocean, trading and perhaps even settling along the shores of India, Arabia and Africa before finally arriving in uninhabited Madagascar.

These first Malagasy brought with them the food crops of South-East Asia, and even today the island's agricultural areas bear more resemblance to those of Oriental countries than to the African mainland. It has been suggested that the food surpluses resulting from the gradual spread of these crops to the mainland permitted the Bantu tribes of the African interior to migrate to the coasts of Kenya and Tanzania.

Over the years, after a series of wars and confederation, the population evolved into 18 tribes (or 'ethnic groups', as some prefer to call them). In what became the ruling tribe, the Merina of the central highlands, Asian features predominate (as they do in the neighbouring Betsileo tribe). The largest coastal tribes, the Sakalava of the west coast and the Bara of the southern central region, appear to have more African origins.

European Discovery The first Europeans, in a Portuguese fleet under the command of Diego Dias, arrived on the island in 1500 and named it Ilha de São Lourenço, although this name lasted only briefly. The origins of the name Madagascar are still unclear. The existence of the island had been reported by Marco Polo and was known to Arab cartographers long before Europeans added it to their maps. It has been suggested that the name could be a variation on anything from Mogadishu (the capital of Somalia, with

which it might have been confused) to the names of various Malagasy tribes, perhaps with an Arabic suffix. It could also be a corruption of the word Malagasy itself, the name used by the people to refer to themselves.

Whatever its origins, the name 'Madagascar' stuck and became widely accepted. The centuries following its discovery by Europeans saw repeated attempts by the Portuguese, Dutch and British to establish permanent bases on the island. However, some of the most successful were distinctly non-governmental organisations: for several decades from the end of the 17th century onwards, bands of pirates established their Indian Ocean bases in Madagascar, especially on and around Île Sainte Marie. They made significant genetic, as well as financial, contributions to local communities.

Unification Increasing trade with Europeans in slaves and arms eventually brought about the development of Malagasy kingdoms. Around the island, three small states emerged: the kingdom of Menabe in the west; the Zana-Malata on the east coast, composed primarily of people of mixed Malay-Polynesian and European (especially pirate) ancestry; and the Merina, who inhabited the highlands.

At the end of the 16th century, the Menabe kingdom spread its power northward along the coast as far as the mouth of the Tsiribihina River and then, under King Andriamisara I, eastward into the highlands. He established a capital at Bengy on the banks of the Sakalava River, which eventually gave its name to the united peoples of Menabe.

Andriamisara's successor, Andriandahifotsy, had ambitions of uniting the whole of southern and eastern Madagascar under his rule; he never quite reached the goal and after his reign the expansion stopped. Later, during the reign of Andriamandisoarivo (1685-1712), the Sakalava sub-kingdom of Boina was created near Mahajanga by his disinherited son, also called Andriamandisoarivo. It lasted until the early 19th century, when clans and groups began to break away and formed autonomous states.

In the early 18th century Île Sainte Marie became the pirate headquarters in the Indian Ocean and attracted buccaneers and ruffians from such diverse places as France, The Netherlands, North America, Portugal and Britain. Ratsimilaho, son of the English pirate Thomas White and a Malagasy princess, Antavaratra Rahena, was largely responsible for unifying the Zana-Malata (the *mulattos*, or offspring of foreign pirates and Malagasy women) and other rival east coast tribes into the empire of Betsimisaraka.

For several years the region saw continuous power struggles, but the one that led to the eventual unification of eastern Madagascar was started by the chief of the small Tsitambala clan, Ramanano, whose armies took control of all the east coast ports.

In 1712 Ratsimilaho and his armies managed to stop the Tsitambala advance at Fenoarivo (also known as Fénérive) and sent them fleeing across the rice paddies. Since then, the Tsitambala have borne the nickname Betanina (The Muddy Ones).

Having created a unified state of his own, Ratsimilaho assumed the throne and called the new state Betsimisaraka (Those Who Stand Together).

In 1750 Ratsimilaho's daughter Bety married a French corporal, Jean-Onésime Filet, better known as 'La Bigorne'. As a wedding gift, Ratsimilaho presented them with the island of Île Sainte Marie. Upon the king's death, Princess Bety ascended the throne and ceded the island to France. Their son Zanahary eventually took over the kingdom, but he was unable to control clan uprisings and the Betsimisaraka kingdom dwindled until only the port of Fenoarivo remained.

As with the tribes of the west coast, friction and nationalist feeling emerged on the east coast and resulted in fragmentation. During the late 18th century, one character, a Hungarian-French slave trader called Maurice-Auguste Comte de Beniowski, installed himself at Antongila and proclaimed himself emperor of all Madagascar.

He was overthrown in 1786 by French troops sent from Réunion.

Merina Rule The late 18th century saw the start of Merina domination of the whole of Madagascar, which lasted well into the 19th century.

Andrianampoinimerina In 1787, after forcefully wresting the Merina kingdom from four of his cousins (who had been co-inheritors), Chief Ramboasalama ascended the throne of Ambohimanga and took the name of Andrianampoinimerina, or 'The Hope of Imerina' (that's the shortened version – his whole title contains 53 letters!).

In the 1790s he managed to unify the Merina tribe of the highlands using weapons acquired through long-established trade networks and advisers from the European maritime nations. This new power soon became the dominant tribe in Madagascar, controlling nearly half the island.

Radama I & Ranavalona I Andrianampoinimerina's son Laidama became king upon his father's death in 1810 and took the name Radama I. With his help, the disparate Malagasy tribes began to coalesce.

Radama I established a highly organised army of 35,000 with which he put down Betsileo insurrections in the south; conquered Boina, the northern Sakalava kingdom in the west; and in 1817 managed to subdue and enslave the tribes of the east. With the help of the conquered Betsimisaraka king Jean-Réné of Toamasina (aka Tamatave), he expanded right down the coast all the way to present-day Taolagnaro (Fort Dauphin).

He finally added the kingdom of Antakàrana, in the far north, whose princes chose suicide or exile over surrender. Unable to take the Sakalava kingdom of Menabe, Radama married the princess Rasalimo, daughter of the Menabe king Ramitraho, in order to ensure sovereignty over that region as well. Thereby, he fulfilled his father's vow: 'my kingdom shall have no frontier but the sea'.

Radama I also worked to foster relations with European powers. He appointed a French army sergeant, Robin, as general in command of his army. An Englishman, James Hastie, with whom he'd signed a treaty halting the slave trade, was appointed as his personal adviser. The first Merina capital was established at Ambohimanga but was moved to Antananarivo before 1800, leaving the former capital as the nation's ritual centre.

The Merina were so isolated in the highlands that when the kingdom was opened to European businesspeople and representatives of foreign powers, they were forced to trek many days from the ports into the once forbidden highlands to conduct business with the king. In 1820 Britain signed a treaty recognising Madagascar as an independent state under Merina rule; British aid and influence remained strong until well into the 19th century.

During this period missions of various denominations, most notably the London Missionary Society (LMS), arrived with a contingent made up mainly of Welsh missionaries to spread the word and the Merina court was converted to Christianity. The first school was set up at Toamasina on the east coast and others followed around the country. Subsequently, a system of phonetics was developed and the Malagasy language was written down for the first time. By 1835 the Bible had been printed in Malagasy.

When Radama died in 1828 at the age of 36 his widow and successor, the xenophobic Ranavalona I, strengthened the army and declared the Christian faith illegal. Those missionaries and 200 of their flock who refused to abandon Christianity or flee the island were martyred.

Radama II In 1861 the queen died and her son Radama II ascended the throne. He immediately reversed many of her policies: he abolished forced labour, instituted freedom of religion, reformed the judicial system, reopened the kingdom to outsiders and granted foreign trading concessions.

With Europeans back in favour, Christianity became more or less official in Madagascar, but the king himself was unable to decide between British Protestantism and French Catholicism. Numerous missionary groups, including Catholics, were gaining footholds in other areas of the island. Despite Ranavalona I's efforts to squash it, Christianity endured and Madagascar became one of the world's most successful Christian missions.

After Radama II had been in power one year a mysterious plague struck Antananarivo and many people perished. The malady was attributed to the ancestors' discontent over Radama II's cosy relations with foreign powers – and the growing power of outsiders in Madagascar. A deep rift appeared among the Merina elite. As a result, on 11 May 1862 the king was assassinated by the brother of his prime minister.

The Queens The assassination seriously undermined the monarchy. The Malagasy could not abandon either the will of the ancestors or royal lineage so Radama II was replaced by his widow, who took the name Rasoherina. Following tradition, she married the prime minister.

Her powers were restrained by an edict which stated she could act only with the consent of the ministers and, in effect, the real power fell to the prime minister. There was a hitch when the brother of the prime minister and commander in chief of the army, Rainilaiarivony, staged a rebellion against his brother, usurped his office and (of course) married his brother's wife, the queen.

Rasoherina survived until 1868, at which time Ranavalona II was crowned (and was in turn married by Rainilaiarivony). After her death, in 1883, she was succeeded by Ranavalona III, who also married the wily prime minister. Seven years later, after an agreement with the British which resulted in Britain's sovereignty over Zanzibar, France became the recognised and sole European power in Madagascar

Her Majesty's Displeasure

Much has been written about the social and political upheaval caused by the French colonial presence, but it was positively benign compared to the excesses of Madagascar's own Queen Ranavalona I. Although often dismissed as merely 'wicked' and no more than a footnote to history, Ranavalona was a despot and tyrant who inflicted genocide, privation and torture on her subjects on a scale that rivals the worst excesses of the 20th century.

Ranavalona ascended the throne upon the death of her consort King Radama I, and quickly reversed his enlightened policies. The xenophobic queen declared Christianity illegal and outlawed its practitioners. Several hundred of her subjects who refused to disavow, along with a number of missionaries, were hurled to their death from the cliffs at Ambohipotsy. Ranavalona rebuffed the overtures of French and British envoys, who were seeking to extend their countries' strategic influence in the region; diplomats were often treated poorly and even imprisoned. Incarceration and slavery were usually the fate of any outsider unfortunate enough to be shipwrecked. And they were not the only ones to feel the brunt of the queen's paranoia.

Ranavalona ordered her highly disciplined Hova guardsmen to systematically subjugate rival tribes, enslave her enemies and slaughter the remainder. Her armies would descend like locusts, stripping the countryside bare of provisions as they swept through and using slaves to construct roads and fortifications. Those who didn't die in battle or perish in slavery slowly starved in the ravished countryside. Even the works of engineering were allowed to fall into disuse since the deeply paranoid queen thought they would help her enemies to invade. There are no accurate estimates of the death toll; contemporary writers estimated that tens of thousands were executed annually and that 10,000 slaves died in the making of one road alone.

Nobody knows for sure just what troubled the royal mind, but numbers alone did not satisfy her; her methods of dispatch were as inventive as they were sadistic. Prisoners would be yoked by the neck to an iron wheel and turned loose to wander in the countryside, the living literally supporting the dead until they all died of starvation or broken necks. A favourite among the Merina aristocracy, who treated it as a sporting event, was the boiling pits below the cliffs at Ambohipotsy. Scores of people were staked in long, narrow waist-high pits with great cauldrons at the end of each sitting over a roaring fire. Each pit in turn was slowly filled with boiling water until the prisoners were par-boiled alive. This spectacle was always a crowd-pleaser; other prisoners were dangled from the cliffs in a Malagasy precursor to bungee-jumping before being cut loose, delighting the assembled crowds even more if they landed in the boiling pits below.

The Queen survived many plots against her life. Anyone she suspected of treason – including Rakotobe, her nephew and heir to the throne, and sometimes her lovers – was subjected to an horrific trial by ordeal. They were forced to swallow three pieces of chicken skin with shavings from the extremely poisonous fruit of the tanguin, a tree that grows in Madagascar. Violent spasms and cramps, convulsions and vomiting quickly followed, but to be proved innocent the accused had to regurgitate the three bits of chicken in an auspicious manner, as judged by her shamans. If only two pieces were coughed up it was a sign of guilt and met with torture and death. This could mean being sawn in half, or having limbs amputated then being sewn into a buffalo hide and left to rot.

These excesses are well documented in writings of Europeans like Ida Pfeiffer and the French adventurer Jean Laborde. The mistreatment of European envoys led a combined French and British force to bombard Tamatave in June 1848, but Ranavalona eventually died of natural causes and was succeeded by her son Prince Rakota. ■

Comoros

Legend has it that 1000 years before the birth of Christ, King Solomon searched the Comoros for the throne (some say it was a ring) he'd given to the Queen of Sheba. It had been tossed into the crater of Mt Karthala by vengeful *djinns* (evil genies) who had been expelled from Solomon's realm by his merchant navy.

Like the Malagasy, the earliest settlers in the Comoros were probably of Malay-Polynesian origin. Tradition has them arriving somewhere between the 5th and 6th centuries AD, but the latest evidence indicates that perhaps it was as early as the 1st century BC. Although these origins are still visible in nearby Madagascar, particularly among the dominant Merina tribe, the Comoran lines have blended with later waves of African, Arab and Shirazi immigrants.

The Muslims today like to believe the islands were already inhabited at the time of the Prophet Mohammed's birth in 570 AD. After being told by Arab sailors of the Prophet's birth, the Comorans sent an ambassador, Mitsuamuvindja, to Arabia, but the founder of Islam died before the emissary arrived. Around the year 642 AD Mitsuamuvindja returned home, bringing with him an Arabian caliph, Mohammed Athoumai Kouba, who converted his countryfolk to the faith.

For the next 1000 years, the islands were ruled by rival and warring sultanates whose wealth was based on the slave and spice trades. The slave trade, which was not abolished in the Comoros until 1904, was the source of most African immigration.

The most powerful and numerous of the immigrants were the Shirazis who came to East Africa after their community in Persia was invaded by the Mongols. They settled along the coast of Tanzania and eventually in the Comoros between the 13th and 15th centuries. Most arrived from the Tanzanian city of Kilwa, which was eventually overrun by the Portuguese in the early 16th century. The Shirazi princesses married local Comoran chiefs and thereby established rival royal lines which would cause untold conflict in the years to come.

European Discovery It's thought that the first Europeans to arrive in the Comoros were the Parmentier brothers, French navigators who stopped briefly at Grande Comore in 1529. However, details of their voyage aren't certain; the first reliable account was provided by the Portuguese sailors Diego Dias and Ferdinand Soares, who came across Mayotte early in the 16th century en route to or from Antsiranana (Diego Suarez) at the northern tip of Madagascar. An English sailor, James Lancaster, and Dutch seafarers also called in at the end of the century, although they didn't remain.

The Portuguese traders who followed largely ignored the islands in their 16th and 17th century voyages up and down the coast of East Africa, except for the occasional revictualling stop. Early in the 17th century, King Charles I of England fitted out the vessel *Seahorse* and sent it to the Indian Ocean under the command of Captain Quaid with orders to attack any ship encountered south of the equator. Captain Quaid based himself at Mohéli and remained there for the rest of his life.

Apart from that, the most outside interference until the mid-19th century was to come from Madagascar. Mayotte and Mohéli, in particular, were repeatedly raided by Sakalava and Betsimisaraka pirates from *Le Grande Île*.

Thus the island sultans were generally left to their own devices. At one stage, Grande Comore had 12 sultans squabbling for the title of *tibé* (grand sultan). Anjouan had two sultans, and Mayotte and Mohéli had one each. Between 1740 and 1841, the conflicts regarding changes of power (and wealth) became so heated that the islands seemed to be permanently embroiled in civil war and came to be regarded as *L'Archipel aux Sultans Batailleurs* (Islands of the Warring Sultans).

The French colonialists were soon able to manipulate the sultans into fighting each other, rather than their new European rulers. By the early 20th century the French managed to control all islands of the Comoros, including Mayotte, with little effort or bloodshed.

CLIMATE

The climate of Madagascar and the Comoros can generally be described as tropical: it is either hot and dry, or hot and wet. There are some climatic differences between the two, however, and Madagascar is large enough to have significant variations across the island.

Many Comorans and Malagasy, especially in southern Madagascar, complain that the wet season starts later and later; this is mainly the result of continuing deforestation. You could travel to either country from April to as late as Christmas and rain is unlikely to significantly affect your visit.

From January to March, the wet season will almost certainly disturb your trip: you won't be able to avoid bucket loads of rain; flooded rivers and damaged roads will make some overland travel impossible; and the rough seas will make inter-island boat travel dangerous or delayed. Also, every year or so some part of either country is wrecked by a serious cyclone, usually resulting in loss of life. Try to avoid this time of the year.

For more information about the climate of either country, refer to the Facts about Madagascar and Facts about the Comoros chapters.

FLORA & FAUNA

A peculiar assortment of plants and animals evolved in the Comoros, and in great abundance in Madagascar, when the islands split from Africa as the supercontinent of Gondwana broke up. Many have since disappeared, but with recent efforts from conservationists the vast array of endemic lemurs, bats, chameleons, frogs, orchids and baobabs, to name just a few, will hopefully survive.

The special Wildlife of Madagascar & the Comoros section in this chapter provides a lot more detail about the region's special plants, mammals, birds, reptiles, fish and insects.

Endangered Species

According to the World Wide Fund for Nature (WWF) Madagascar has the dubious distinction of being 'one of the world's highest conservation priorities'. The extraordinary range of endemic flora and fauna is under threat from the seemingly ceaseless destruction of the island's rainforests.

In the past, large animals that roamed the forests of Madagascar included a giant ground-dwelling lemur, *Megaladopis*, the Aldabra tortoise, a pygmy hippo and a flightless, ostrich-like bird, *Aepyornis* (also known as the 'elephant bird'), which stood more than 3m tall. Crushed Aepyornis egg shells still carpet remote areas of the southwest, particularly around Faux Cap. A few years ago, an Aepyornis egg was actually found buried in dunes on the shore of faraway Western Australia.

Continued deforestation, poaching, hunting and urban sprawl still threaten many species of animals. Some lemurs, such as the mongoose lemur, are highly endangered. Others, like the broad-nosed gentle lemur, were thought to be extinct, but have been rediscovered and are now protected in national parks and reserves. Some of the fish under threat of extinction include the black bass and the prehistoric-looking coelacanth. Of the 100 or so species of unique birdlife, the Madagascar fish-eagle is very rare.

According to the WWF, 12 endemic plants used for medicinal purposes are endangered, including the Madagascar periwinkle. The main threats to Madagascar's plant life are from overgrazing; clearing forests to feed animals and grow rice; increased numbers of livestock which eat native plants; and fires caused by *tavy*, the slash-and-burn method of farming.

The Malagasy government has been forced to give conservation a high priority, although resources and funds will always be very low. It is now highly illegal to export, hunt and collect lemurs, tortoises, snakes, crocodiles, most birds, Aepyornis eggs and shells, and the plant known as the 'elephant's foot' (*Pachypodium*). Thanks to the help of many local and international development and environmental agencies it may not be too late to save what is left.

If you want more information about Madagascar's endangered species, refer to the definitive study, *Madagascar: Profil de L'Environnement*, edited by MD Jenkins and printed by the WWF. It is mostly written in French, but has interesting passages in English.

Environmental Organisations

A multitude of Malagasy and international organisations have taken a strong interest in the environment of Madagascar (although interest in the nearby Comoros is negligible!). If you have a specific interest, the best place to find a more complete list is on the Internet (especially the site http://www.duke.edu/web/primate/links.html). A few more general organisations are listed below:

ANGAP
> This Malagasy non-government organisation is responsible for most national parks and reserves in Madagascar; 1 Rue Naka Rabemanantsoa, BP 1424, Anatanimena, Antananarivo, Madagascar (☎ (261-2) 305 18; fax (261-2) 319 94; email ANGAP@bow.dts.mg)

Earthwatch
> 680 Mt Auburn St, PO Box 9104, Watertown, MA, USA 02272-9104 (☎ (800) 776 0188; fax (617) 926 8532; email info@earthwatch.org)

WWF
> II M85 ter Antsakarivo, BP 738, Antananarivo, Madagascar (☎ (261-2) 348 85; fax (261-2) 348 88)

SOCIETY & CONDUCT
Vintana
Thanks to early contact with Islamic traders along the Swahili coast, the Comoros and Madagascar were exposed to Islamic astrological traditions. While the Comoros remained Islamic and Madagascar became mostly Christian, many Malagasy retain some Islamic customs, and derived their own set tendencies and destinies based on the time and date of a person's birth. This 'fate', which is by no means unalterable, is known as *vintana* and is most closely observed in areas which have been exposed to Islamic influence, particularly the Antaimoro country along the south-east coast of Madagascar.

Vintana also refers to periods of high and low tendency towards good or ill fortune in a person's life, as well as the positive or negative properties of certain times of day or days of the week. These properties dictate the best times for major events: birth, circumcision, marriage, burial and so on. Therefore, certain times of day, such as sunrise, are particularly auspicious; at other times, such as the middle of the night, one should avoid tasks which may carry far-reaching consequences.

Friday is associated with nobility and considered a good day while Thursday is associated with servitude. Therefore, those born at a particularly inauspicious time must be subjected to certain rituals aimed at tempering the negative tendencies cast by their vintana.

Traditional Medicine
Western medicine is available in larger cities and towns in Madagascar and the Comoros, but the Malagasy and the Comorans are well-versed in herbal healing (known as *fanafody* in Madagascar) and many urban dwellers prefer these traditional methods, visiting market kiosks to procure the age-old remedies.

Country folk in Madagascar will often consult *ombiasy* (healers), who still hold considerable social status in traditional areas. These ombiasy not only prescribe herbal cures, they combine them with potions and rituals aimed at securing help from the ancestors. They can balance a negative vintana, or banish or communicate with a *tromba* (spirit) which has possessed an unwitting person.

In some Malagasy tribes the ombiasy also acts as an *mpanandro* (the name means The Creator of the Day, in reference to the respect placed on pre-dawn divination). The mpanandro has an intimate understanding of vintana and can predict illness or ill fortune, and sets about preventing vintana problems by balancing negative tendencies with appropriate counter-measures.

Dos & Don'ts
In the interest of minimising misunderstandings and maintaining smooth and friendly relations between foreigners and Comorans and Malagasy, visitors should consider the following guidelines:

- Don't speak too loudly and if you are upset, don't show it.
- Don't point your finger at anyone.
- Greet people when you meet them and say goodbye when parting.
- Never speak lightly of death, ancestors, or traditions pertaining to death, especially in Madagascar.
- Never scoff at local *fady* (taboos in Madagascar) and avoid attempting to discredit them using western logic.

- Never cast blame upon old people, mothers, children or rice paddies, among others.
- Remember that the Malagasy regard their country as the sacred land of their ancestors, who remain its rightful owners, and it is therefore holy soil.
- If eating at the home of a Comoran or Malagasy, wait for the eldest member of the family to invite you to eat before you start.
- Do not show your feelings, including affection for your partner, in public.
- Please try to dress appropriately. Shorts are acceptable in Madagascar, less so in the Comoros. Save your least formal gear for the beach and wear trousers or long dresses if visiting local homes, government offices and religious buildings.
- Never try to force confidences from an acquaintance; let the other person take the initiative if they wish to share their feelings.
- When speaking French, never use the *tu* form unless you're invited to do so – *tu* can be considered offensive.
- Enjoy hospitality, but know how to remain a dignified outsider.
- Never interrupt another Comoran or Malagasy while they are speaking, and never laugh at them.

RELIGION
Madagascar

During the 19th century Madagascar witnessed the comings and goings of Christian missionaries, from many denominations, who divided the country among themselves. LMS Protestantism was the first to gain a major foothold, but as French influence increased so did Catholicism. A total of 41% of the Malagasy population profess to be Christian – evenly spread between Protestantism (concentrated in the highlands) and Catholicism (mainly around the coasts). About 50% follow traditional religions, and even among devout Christians the strong respect and reverence traditionally held for the ancestors has not diminished.

There are also several Muslim communities and they comprise about 7% of the population. They are concentrated in northern towns, particularly Mahajanga (also known as Majunga), which have strong Comoran influences and Indo-Pakistani traders.

Comoros

Officially, Sunni Islam is followed by 86% of the population of the Comoros, including Mayotte, while the remaining 14% follow Catholicism (the figure is higher in Mayotte where there are more French residents).

In reality Islam is the overwhelming religion in the Comoros (excluding Mayotte), as you will see by the number of mosques (there are over 1400); the laws against alcohol (which can still be legally bought and drunk with discretion); the modest dress of Comoran women (although veils are rare); the lack of availability of pork; and the virtual absence of dogs (which Muslims deem to be unclean). The fundamentals of Islam are followed most strictly on the islands of Grande Comore and Anjouan.

However, the five daily calls to prayer from the minarets aren't as loud or dominating as in some countries, and though the *Koran* (or *Qur'an*) does govern life in the Comoros, there are still traces of animism in the form of superstitions and sorcery. The Comorans refer to their malevolent spirits or devils as djinns. Problems with these spirits require the intervention of a *wagangi* (witch doctor) who casts spells and tells fortunes in the sand.

Visitors who arrive during Ramadan will witness the grip religion has on the islands. During this holy month of fasting (set by the moon), the local people are largely subdued and edgy by day, and lively late into the night when they can eat, drink and carry on as they would at other times of the year.

Visitors to mosques must cover their heads and remove their shoes before entering, and non-Muslims should not enter a mosque on a Friday, the Muslim holy day.

History of Islam Islam is the newest and most widespread of the Asian religions. The founder was the Prophet Mohammed, but he merely transmitted the work of God to his people. Therefore, to call the religion 'Mohammedism' is wrong because it implies that the beliefs centre around Mohammed rather than around God. The proper name of the faith is Islam, derived from the word *salaam* which primarily means peace, but in a secondary sense also means surrender. The full connotation is something like 'the peace which comes by surrendering to God'. A person who follows this belief is known as a Muslim.

The founder of Islam was born around 570 AD and came to be called Mohammed, which means highly praised. His descent is traditionally traced back to Abraham. Before Mohammed there had been other true prophets, among them Adam, Moses, Abraham, Jacob and Jesus, all of whom partially received Allah's message, but Mohammed is regarded as the culmination and recipient of the final word. There will be no other prophets.

Mohammed taught that there is one all-powerful, all-pervading God, Allah. 'There is no God but Allah' is the fundamental tenet of the Islamic faith. In the early 7th century, Mohammed received the word of Allah and called on the people to turn away from pagan worship and submit to the one true God. His teachings appealed to the poorer levels of society and angered the wealthy merchant classes.

By 622 AD life had become unpleasant enough to force Mohammed and his followers to migrate to Medina, an oasis town some 300km north of Mecca. This migration, known as the *hejira*, marks the beginning of the Islamic calendar, year 1 AH or 622 AD. By 630 AD Mohammed had gained a sufficient following to return to Mecca. He died two years later, but with boundless zeal his followers spread the word, using force where necessary. By 644 the Islamic state had spread to Syria, Persia, Mesopotamia, Egypt and across North Africa.

Islam only travelled west for 100 years before it was pushed back at Poitiers in France in 732, but it continued east for centuries. It regenerated the Persian Empire, which was by then declining from its protracted struggles with Byzantium. In 711, the same year in which the Arabs landed in Spain, Muslims sailed in dhows up the Indus into India (now Pakistan). This was more a raid than a full-scale invasion, but in the 11th century all of northern India fell into Muslim hands. In the following centuries its influence spread from the Atlantic and across the Indian Ocean to the Pacific and southward across Africa.

In its early days Islam suffered a major schism; the resulting sects remain to this day and are known as the Sunnis (or Sunnites) and the Shíites. The Prophet's son-in-law, Ali, became the fourth caliph following the murder of Mohammed's third successor, and he in turn was assassinated in 661 by the governor of Syria, who set himself up as caliph. The Sunnis, who comprise the majority of Muslims today, are followers of the succession of this caliph, while the Shíites follow the descendants of Ali.

Basic Tenets of Islam After Mohammed's death Allah's word, delivered to humanity via Mohammed, was compiled in the Koran – the holy book of Islam. Much of the Koran is devoted to codes of behaviour and much emphasis is placed on God's mercy to humankind. Mohammed's teachings are heavily influenced by two other religions, Judaism and Christianity, and similarities include the belief in hell and heaven, belief in a judgement day and a similar creation theory.

Islam hangs on four pegs: God, creation, humankind and the day of judgement. Everything in Islam centres on the existence of Allah, but the distinctive feature of Islam is the appreciation of the value of the individual. In Hinduism and Buddhism, the individual is just a fleeting expression with no permanence or value, but the Islamic religion teaches that individuality, as expressed in the human soul, is eternal, because once created the soul lives forever. For the Muslim, life on earth is just a forerunner to an eternal future in heaven – or the alternative – as deemed appropriate by Allah.

Islam is a faith that demands unconditional surrender to the will and wisdom of Allah. It involves total commitment to a way of life, philosophy and law. Theoretically, it is a democratic faith in which devotion is the responsibility of the individual, unrestricted by hierarchy and petty social prerequisites, and concerned with encouraging initiative and independence in the believer. It is not bound to a particular locale – the faithful may worship in a mosque, in the bazaar or on a mountain. It is also a fatalistic faith in that everything is rationalised as the will of Allah.

The first duty of every Muslim is to submit himself or herself to Allah. This profession of faith (known as the *Shahada*) is the first of the Five Pillars of Islam, the five Koranic tenets which guide Muslims through their daily lives:

Shahada This profession of faith is the fundamental tenet of Islam. It is to Islam more or less what the Lord's Prayer is to Christianity, and is often quoted (eg to greet the newborn and bid farewell to the dead).

Salah This is the call to prayer. Five times daily – at dawn, noon, mid-afternoon, sunset and nightfall – Muslims must face Mecca and recite the prescribed prayer.

Zakat Originally, this was the act of giving alms to the poor and needy, with the amount fixed at 5% of a person's income. It has been developed by some modern states into an obligatory land tax which goes to help the poor.

Ramadan This is the ninth month of the Islamic calendar, when all Muslims must abstain from eating, drinking, smoking and sex from dawn to dusk. It commemorates the month in which the Koran was revealed to Mohammed; the purpose of the physical deprivation is to strengthen the will and forfeit the body to the spirit.

Hadj The pilgrimage to Mecca, the holiest place in Islam, is the duty of every Muslim, who is fit and can afford to make it, at least once in their life. On the pilgrimage, the *hadji* (pilgrim) wears two plain white sheets and walks around the *kabbah* (black stone in the centre of the mosque) seven times. Other related pilgrimage ceremonies include the sacrifice of an animal and the shaving of the pilgrim's head. After the journey, men are known as *hadji* and women as *hadja*.

Other Muslim customs include scrupulous attention to cleanliness, such as the ritualistic washing of hands and face. The pig is considered unclean and is not kept or eaten by strict Muslims.

LANGUAGE

French is the official language of both Madagascar and the Comoros, and is spoken by most people you are likely to meet unless you visit remote areas. Although a surprising number of people in both countries study English, to travel in either without at least a rudimentary knowledge of French (unless you speak Comoran or Malagasy) would be extremely difficult and would preclude effective communication with the people.

For information about the indigenous languages of Madagascar and the Comoros, and a list of important Malagasy and Comoran words and phrases, refer to the Facts about Madagascar and Facts about the Comoros chapters.

Pronunciation

French has a number of sounds which are notoriously difficult to produce for Anglophones.

The main causes of trouble are:

- The distinction between the 'u' sound (as in *tu*) and 'oo' sound (as in *tout*). For both sounds, the lips are rounded and projected forward, but for the 'u' the tongue is towards the front of the mouth, its tip against the lower front teeth, whereas for the 'oo' the tongue is towards the back of the mouth, its tip behind the gums of the lower front teeth.
- The nasal vowels. During the production of nasal vowels the breath escapes partly through the nose and partly through the mouth. There are no nasal vowels in English; in French there are three, as in *bon vin blanc* (good white wine). These sounds occur where a syllable ends in a single 'n' or 'm'; the 'n' or 'm' in this case is not pronounced, but indicates the nasalisation of the preceding vowel. The standard 'r' of Parisian French is produced by moving the bulk of the tongue backwards to constrict the air flow in the pharynx while the tip of the tongue rests behind the lower front teeth. It is quite similar to the noise made by some people before spitting, but with much less friction.

The following lists contain French words and phrases which may be useful to travellers.

Greetings & Civilities

Hello	*Bonjour*
Goodbye	*Au revoir*
See you soon	*A bientôt*
Yes	*Oui*
No	*Non*
Please	*S'il vous plaît*

Thank you	*Merci*
Thank you very much	*Merci beaucoup*
You're welcome	*Je vous en prie*

Excuse me (when requesting attention)
Excusez-moi
Excuse me (when apologising)
Pardon
I don't speak French
Je ne parle pas français
I don't understand
Je ne comprend pas
Can you please write that down?
Veuillez l'écrire, s'il vous plaît?

Useful Words & Phrases

How much does that cost?
Combien ça coûte?
Do you speak English/French?
Parlez-vous anglais/français?
What time does the next bus leave for ..?
À quelle heure part le prochain bus pour ..?

boat	*bateau*
train	*train*
bush taxi	*taxi-brousse*
return ticket	*billet aller-retour*
I am looking for ...	*Je cherche ...*
Where is the ...?	*Ou se trouve le/la ...?*
inexpensive	*bon marché*

Accommodation

hotel	*hôtel*
hostel	*auberge*
price, tariff	*prix, tarif*
included	*compris*
not included	*non compris*
per day	*par jour*
per week	*par semaine*
per month	*par mois*
room (usually in reference to a hotel room)	*chambre*
dormitory	*dortoir*
air-conditioned	*climatisé(e)*
single room	*chambre simple*
double room	*chambre double*
double bed	*grand lit*
extra bed	*lit supplémentaire*
twin beds	*lits jumeaux*
half board	*demi-pension*
full board	*pension complète*
meal	*repas*
breakfast	*petit déjeuner*
lunch	*déjeuner*
dinner	*dîner*
bathroom	*salle de bain*
shower	*douche*
toilet	*WC*

(pronounced 'doobl vay say' or simply 'vay say')

hot water	*eau chaude*
towel	*serviette*
wash basin	*lavabo*
deposit	*dépôt de garantie, caution*
kitchen	*cuisine*
dining room	*salle à manger*
swimming pool	*piscine*
terrace, balcony	*terrasse*
facilities	*facilités*
with	*avec*
without	*sans*
on request	*sur demande, sur commande*

Times & Dates

today	*aujourd'hui*
tomorrow	*demain*
yesterday	*hier*
in the morning	*le matin*
in the afternoon	*l'après-midi*
in the evening	*le soir*
Monday	*lundi*
Tuesday	*mardi*
Wednesday	*mercredi*
Thursday	*jeudi*
Friday	*vendredi*
Saturday	*samedi*
Sunday	*dimanche*
January	*janvier*
February	*février*
March	*mars*
April	*avril*
May	*mai*
June	*juin*
July	*juillet*

August	août
September	septembre
October	octobre
November	novembre
December	décembre

Numbers

0	zéro
1	un
2	deux
3	trois
4	quatre
5	cinq
6	six
7	sept
8	huit
9	neuf
10	dix
11	onze
12	douze
13	treize
14	quatorze
15	quinze
16	seize
17	dix-sept
18	dix-huit
19	dix-neuf
20	vingt
21	vingt-et-un
22	vingt-deux
30	trente
40	quarante
50	cinquante
60	soixante
70	soixante-dix
71	soixante-onze
80	quatre-vingts
90	quatre-vingt-dix
91	quatre-vingt-onze
100	cent
200	deux cent
1000	mille

Food

Most menus in both countries are exclusively in French. You will only see Malagasy or Comoran used in the cheapest roadside restaurants. Only about four restaurants in either country have menus with English translations, so get to know the following French words.

Seafood — *fruits de mer*

fish	poisson
trout	truite
tuna	thon
lobster	langouste, homard
sea urchins	ourites
prawns, shrimp	crevettes
squid	calmar
octopus	poulpe

Meat — *viandes*

bacon	lard
beef	boeuf
chicken	poulet
duck	canard
goat	boucan, cabri
ham	jambon
hare, rabbit	lapin
mutton	mouton
pork	porc

Vegetables — *légumes*

beans	haricots
cassava	manioc
chips	pommes frites
garlic	ail
onions	oignons
potato	patate, pomme de terre

Fruit — *fruit*

apple	pomme
banana	banane
coconut	noix de côco
custard apple	corossol
guava	goyave
lemon	citron
mango	mangue
orange	orange
passionfruit	grenadelle
pineapple	ananas
star fruit	carambol

Desserts | *desserts*

cake	*gâteau*
cheese	*fromage*
ice cream	*glace*
jam	*confiture*
pastries	*pâtisseries*
sugar	*sucre*

Drinks | *boissons*

milk	*lait*
fruit juice	*jus de fruit*
tea	*thé*
coffee	*café*
beer	*bière*
wine (red/white)	*vin (rouge/blanc)*
lemonade	*limonade*
mineral water without/with gas	*eau mineral/eau gazeuse*

Condiments

chilli	*piments*
curry	*carri*

ginger	*gingembre*
salt	*sel*
pepper	*poivre*
salad dressing	*vinaigrette*
sweet and sour	*aigre-doux*

Miscellaneous

bread	*pain*
butter	*beurre*
eggs	*oeufs*
noodles	*mines*
rice	*riz*
glass	*verre*
plate	*assiette*
cup	*tasse*
spoon	*cuiller*
knife	*couteau*
fork	*fourchette*
napkin or towel	*serviette*
bill	*addition*
receipt	*facture*
menu of the day	*plat/menu du jour*
vegetarian	*végétarien(ne)*

Wildlife of Madagascar and the Comoros

HABITATS

Each climatic region in Madagascar (and, to a lesser extent, the Comoros) is associated with a different vegetation type. These habitats include tropical rainforest along the wet east coast; heathland on the central high plateau; and savannas throughout much of the lower, drier western lowlands where the forests have been mostly destroyed.

Each of these habitats hosts a distinct set of plants and animals, most of which are found nowhere else in the world. Experts believe that Madagascar supports 3% of the world's plant species, of which over 80% are unique.

Tragically, in the 1500 to 2000 years since people first arrived on the island, over three-quarters of the forests which once spread across Madagascar have been destroyed. What is left of these forests can be categorised into three main types (though these can be divided into further types).

Sometimes called 'evergreen' or 'montane eastern forest', the true rainforest runs along almost the entire length of the eastern coast of Madagascar, and also covers much of the Comoros. Though a great deal has been destroyed, the variety of animal life continues to astound experts; about 90% is endemic. The fact that four of the five national parks – Ranomafana, Andasibe-Mantadia (also known as Périnet), Mananara Nord and Montagne d'Ambre – are prime rainforest areas indicates the importance that conservationists place on saving this habitat. As well as lemurs and a multitude of other unique and/or endangered animals, in these parks you will see a vast array of endemic palms, bamboo, ferns and orchids.

The dry, deciduous forests in the western parts of Madagascar contain shorter trees of different heights, including baobabs. Ferns and palms do not grow here because the dry season can last up to eight months a year. Though slash-and-burn farming continues to destroy much of the forest cover, you can see baobabs near Morondava and typical dry forest at the Kirindy, Ampijoroa and Tsingy de Bemaraha Reserves.

The spiny forest found in southern Madagascar is reminiscent of the deserts of Mexico, although the native Malagasy species are weird, to say the least. Naturally, cacti and other plants must be extremely hardy to survive the infrequent rains. Anywhere along the Toliara to Taolagnaro road, particularly the Beza-Mahafaly, Berenty and Andohahela Reserves, is the best place to explore the spiny forest. Typical forms include succulents such as aloes, the incredible baobabs and octopus trees.

The term habitat also applies to coastal regions and the marine world, although vegetation is not always as apparent underwater as it is on land. While not as attractive as other forests, and rarely visited by foreigners, mangroves are one of Madagascar's important marine habitats: they provide vital nurseries for fish and crustaceans; their roots slow down wave action and coastal erosion; and they supply oxygen to the mud. However, much of the mangrove cover in Madagascar has been destroyed by humans and only an estimated 350,000 hectares remain – mostly on the sparsely inhabited western coasts, including the area around Toliara. None of the common mangrove trees, such as *Avicennia marina* and *Sonneratia alba*, are endemic to Madagascar or the Comoros. For more information refer to the Southern Madagascar chapter.

Title Page: The first illustration of the indri, or babakoto: an engraving by Sonnerat in 1782 from Voyage aux Indes orientales et à la Chine.

PLANTS

Madagascar and the Comoros boast almost 12,000 species of flowering plants, which is equivalent to approximately one quarter of the flowering plants found on mainland Africa.

Medicinal Plants The World Wide Fund for Nature (WWF) recognises Madagascar as a vast source of plants which provide vital ingredients for modern medicines. Of these, 12 species are endangered. Some of the most important medicinal plants grown in Madagascar are *Catharanthus roseus*, which helps control hunger pains and tiredness; the *voatrotroka*, which is made into a tea to cure a blood disease called albuminuria and various stomach illnesses; the *famelona* or *Chrysophyllum sapotacae*, which is used to treat abdominal pains; and extracts from *Toddalia asiatica*, which are used to cure syphilis and diarrhoea.

Forests

Lalona One commonly found tree is the lalona *(Weinmannia rutenbergii)*. The Malagasy use this versatile plant as fuel for fires, to make walls and floors of houses, and for building pirogues. The Tanala or 'Forest' people, especially around the Ranomafana National Park, have a great fondness for the honey which can be made from the lalona flower.

Bamboo Madagascar and the Comoros have several endemic species of bamboo (more than mainland Africa). The golden bamboo lemur has adapted to feed almost exclusively on *Cephalostachium vigueri*, a giant bamboo which contains small amounts of cyanide. Bamboo is also used by the Malagasy to build homes and sailing boats, and to make handicrafts and household items such as shellfish containers. The young shoots are sometimes eaten by people and the pulp can be used to make paper.

Ferns A fern has roots and leaves, but no seeds, flowers or fruits. Both Madagascar and the Comoros have hundreds of species of ferns, some of which can grow over 10m high. *Cyathea* is commonly found in northern Madagascar, and the bird's nest fern *(Asplenium nidus)* and the closely related *Microsorium* are also not hard to find. Many ferns aren't spared destruction for human use: they are often used to make household items such as pots.

Palms Madagascar has over 170 species of palm trees (while Africa has only about 50). About 97% of Madagascar's palms are endemic, such as the feather palm *(Chrysalidocarpus isaloensis)* which you can see in Isalo National Park.

Palms are commonly used for building homes, as well as making baskets and pots for catching crayfish. Extracts are used as ingredients for potions used by traditional healers for exorcisms and as medicines for children's diseases. Of course, the fruits of various palms, such as the coconut, are eaten. The 20m high cycad palm lives for up to 1000 years and produces sago.

The best collections of palms you will see are at Montagne d'Ambre National Park, across the Masoala Peninsula, the Lokobe Reserve on Nosy Be and pockets of what is left of the forests on Île Sainte Marie. The definitive study of Malagasy palms is the outstanding *The Palms of Madagascar* by John Dransfield & Henk Beentje.

Raffia The raffia (or raphia) palm *(Raphia ruffia)*, which can be 12m high, is unique to Madagascar. Parts of this palm are used to make an alcoholic drink, to produce fibre, and in the construction of houses.

Ravinala Best-known of the Malagasy plants is *Ravenala madagascariensis*, called the *ravinala* in Malagasy (forest leaves), traveller's palm in English and the *palmier du voyageur* in French. The fan-shaped ravinala is found throughout the islands of the Indian Ocean and in botanic gardens worldwide. A cousin of the banana, it has been incorporated into the national seal and the Air Madagascar logo.

The ravinala is vital to nomadic and rural people because it contains a supply of pure water in the base of the leaf stalk, and is reputed to align itself along an east-west axis, providing directions for befuddled wanderers. (Take one look at a stand ravinala, however, and you'll be convinced not to rely too heavily on this method of orientation.) The palms are also used to make floors and roofs, and *falafa*, the walls of homes.

Pandanus The plants of the genus *Pandanus* are like palms, and are related to what is sometimes called a screw pine in the Pacific region. Pandanus generally have one thick stem, with twisted leaves at the end of a few branches, and roots which often appear above the ground. As you will see in some forests, like at Ranomafana National Park, many Malagasy (and Comoran) rodents, tiny reptiles and insects live among the leaves dropped from the pandanus. Local people use the leaves for strengthening the walls and roofs of their homes, and for making mats.

Orchids The world has about 30,000 species and 800 genera of Orchidaceae (curiously the name comes from the Greek word meaning 'testicle'). Madagascar, which is host to about 1000 species of the genera *Angraecum* and *Bulbophyllum*, among others, has more species of orchids than the African mainland. Many orchids are epiphytes – plants that grow attached to supports such as trees or rocks, but they are not parasitic on other plants.

The rarest species in Madagascar is probably the *Angraecum sesquipedale* – commonly known as the comet orchid – which produces gorgeous white flowers between July and September. It was made famous by the naturalist Charles Darwin who wondered how any insect could have the necessary equipment (ie a 30cm proboscis!) to pollinate the flower. *Angraecum eberneum*, a large, sweet smelling orchid found in northern Madagascar, can be up to 1m wide.

There are usually treats in store for orchid lovers: in Ranomafana you can see *Aeranthes ramosa*; in Montagne d'Ambre, there is *Bulbophyllum*

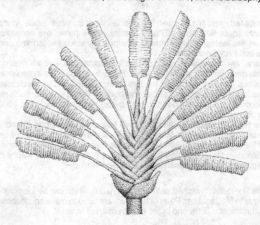

The ravinala, or travellers' palm, is a distinctive Malagasy native palm. It is now a popular plant in botanic gardens around the world.

orchidacae; on the island of Nosy Mangabe, off the north-east coast, *Cymbidiella humblotii* curiously only grows on raffia palms; and *Angraecum sororium* bears large fruit. At the Parc à Orchidées at Périnet Reserve, you can revel in lovely orchids such as *Calanthe silvatica*.

Other Forest Plants Popular with Malagasy people, lemurs and climbing plants is the large rotra *(Eugenua rotra)*, which bears edible fruit. *Euphorbia enterophora*, known locally as a *betinay*, is common in places like the Andringitra Reserve in the south, and along the south-east coast. In French the tree is called a *euphorbe parasol* because it is so wide and provides shade for animals and other plants.

In the eastern and northern forests, you may walk past, but still not notice, the huge *ramy* tree *(Canarium madagascariensis)*, which can grow up to 30m high. The sap, when dried and properly treated, is used by Malagasy to cure several ailments, including headaches.

Desert

Aloe Plants of the genus *Aloe* typically have thick spiny leaves and shallow roots. They are famous for the medicinal extract called 'aloes', used to clear the bowels. (Handy if a samosa from the local market won't do the trick.) In the dry areas of Madagascar there are 60 endemic species of aloe (one third of the world's species). Some of the most spectacular examples are at the Ampijoroa Reserve in western Madagascar, where *Aloe andringintrensis* flourishes, and in Isalo, where you will see *A. isaloensis*.

Pitcher Plant The pitcher plant's name is derived from its leaves, which are shaped like a vase or trumpet (or pitcher, we suppose) and hold liquid with which the plant traps and digests insects. The various species grow in several continents; the Malagasy representative, *Nepenthes madagascariensis*, has become a blooming tourist attraction in Amboasary, near Taolagnaro. Pitcher plants are a type of vine which either creeps along the ground or up trees. Insects, such as ants, are attracted to the lip of the 'pitcher' by special secretions. As they investigate the 'pitcher' they are trapped by downward-pointing hairs and eventually slip into the liquid below. The drowned insect thus becomes a nutritional supplement for the plant.

Baobab Another symbol of Madagascar is the baobab. Baobabs have thick trunks, large fruit shaped like gourds and remarkable branches which make the roots look like they are on top of the tree and in the air. Some baobabs are estimated to be over 1000 years old.

In Madagascar there are six distinct species (possibly up to eight); only one other is found in the whole of Africa. Like most Malagasy trees the baobab has a myriad of uses to local people, but its distinct advantage is that it is usually too solid to chop down. Among its other uses, the leaves and fruit can be boiled and eaten; rope and clothes can be made from the bark; paper can be produced from the sap; the trunks are tapped for water (they can contain tens of thousands of litres of water); and the bark is used to make houses.

Baobabs can be found in certain parts of western and southern Madagascar, on Grande Comore in the Comoros and in western Mayotte. The small *Adansonia fony*, 'only' about 5m high, can be found around Morondava. The largest, the towering but rarely seen *A. grandidieri* is most common in Madagascar near Morondava, in the Kirindy Reserve and further south in Andohahela.

Others baobabs found in Madagascar include the widespread *A.*

madagascariensis, found in the south near Faux Cap and in the far north; the rare *A. perrieri* in the north; and *A. digitata*, the only species which is also found in the rest of Africa.

Periwinkle The periwinkle, whose stems trail along the ground and produce blue flowers, was probably named after the Russian word meaning 'first' (ie the first flower of the spring). The Madagascar (or Rosy) periwinkle *(Vinca rosea)* grows wild in the south-east of the country, but is also found in many other countries in the region. Extracts from the periwinkle are used to treat leukaemia.

Elephant's Foot Madagascar has nine species of *Pachypodium*, which are often called 'elephant's foot'. (The very similar *Testudinaria elephantipes*, vital to the indigenous people of South Africa, is also called 'elephant's foot'.) Although the plants resemble mini baobabs, there is no relation between the two genera. The bulbous trunk of the pachypodium contains a moist and stringy yellow pulp which looks and smells like overcooked manioc root, and is obviously related to the yam eaten in the Pacific region. In Madagascar *P. rosulatum* can be found in Isalo National Park; others are located at Ampijoroa Reserve.

Cacti The bizarre spiny forests of southern Madagascar are home to the hideously spined Didiereaceae. The leaves grow among the spikes and are relished by some species of lemurs, which somehow don't get pierced when they embrace the plants. These species can also be tapped for water, though humans rarely enjoy the taste.

The only cacti native to Madagascar are *Rhipsalis baccifera* and *R. madagascariensis*, though there are theories that these may have been introduced centuries ago. These cacti have berries, look more like parasitic creepers and are often found in rainforests. They have no close relatives anywhere in the world, but resemble the equally unusual *boojum* and the *ocotillo* of north-western Mexico and parts of the USA.

The spiny forests near Ambovombe in the far south are full of examples of the six species of *Alluaudia*, including *A. procera*, sometimes known as the octopus tree because of its bizarre, twisting shape.

Even in the remote south cacti are threatened by roving zebu and herds of goats, which eat just about anything. The good news is that cacti are virtually ignored by humans except when they are desperate for water.

The unusual baobab is a distinctive landmark in drier parts of Madagascar and the Comoros. Despite their stout appearance, the branches are rather brittle.

Lemurs of Madagascar

One of the most widespread of the lemurs, the brown lemur is common and easily seen by visitors. Males of the six subspecies can be distinguished by their dramatically different colours; the females are considerably drabber. These are red-fronted brown lemurs; the male is on the right.

The ruffed lemur is found in the eastern rainforests and known for its loud raucous calls. There are two colour varieties; the subspecies shown here, the black-and-white ruffed lemur, is the more widespread; the red ruffed lemur is coloured rufous and black, and confined to the Masoala Peninsula. Ruffed lemurs are unusual because the female makes a nest in which she leaves her young when she is foraging.

The ring-tailed lemur perhaps epitomises everyone's notion of the lemur, although it is by no means the most widespread species. Ringtails can be readily observed at Berenty Reserve, where they spend much of their time on the ground and make ideal subjects for photos. Ring-tailed lemurs give birth in August-September, and at this time visitors can see the young clinging to the backs of their mothers.

ALL PHOTOGRAPHS BY DAVID CURL

Lemurs of Madagascar

Verreaux's sifaka is one of the most common and widespread of the lemurs. It is readily seen by visitors at Berenty, but also inhabits spiny forest where it climbs among the spikes apparently without harm. Sifakas are prodigious leapers, but also travel from tree to tree by hopping along the ground in a balletic series of upright jumps.

PAUL GREENWAY

Left: Crowned lemurs are found only in the north of Madagascar, where they may be seen at Montagne d'Ambre National Park. Males and females have different colouration, the male (shown here) has a black crown and the female a grey one.

Right: A female black lemur. Males and female black lemurs are dramatically different, with only the males being black. Nosy Be is one of the best places to see them.

DAVID CURL

PAUL SCOTT

Flora of Madagascar

The majority of Madagascar's 1000 or so species of orchids are endemic (found nowhere else). The eastern rainforests are particularly rich in orchids. Some species are epiphytes, growing on branches, tree trunks, rocks or on ferns high in the canopy. Epiphytes are not parasites, merely relying on their host for support rather than nutrition. Vanilla, one of the principal export crops of Madagascar and Comoros, is a species of orchid that was introduced from Mexico.

Some species of aloes are known the world over for their therapeutic properties. At least 38 species are native to Madagascar, where they are particularly adapted to life in the harsh spiny deserts.

ALL PHOTOGRAPHS BY DAVID CURL

The pitcher plant is so-called because of its modified leaves, which grow together in this distinctive shape. Pitcher plants grow on soils that are poor in nitrogen and have become adapted to absorb some of their nutrients from insects and other animals that fall into the pitcher and drown. Pitcher plants can be seen near Taolagnaro.

Reptiles of Madagascar

About half the world's chameleon species are found on Madagascar and among them are the world's largest and smallest. Parson's chameleon, shown here eyeing off a grasshopper at Périnet Reserve, is one of the largest and can measure 60cm. The tiny stump-tailed chameleons can be as small as 30mm when fully grown.

PAUL GREENWAY

Chameleons are superbly adapted to life in the trees, but rather slow and clumsy on the ground. When spotted in the open like this they are vulnerable to attack by birds and dogs, and to road traffic. Chameleons can be easily approached and are completely harmless.

DAVID CURL

Left: Big-headed gecko feeding on a cricket. The nine species of big-headed geckos can be easily seen by visitors to rainforest reserves and may be heard moving about at night through leaf litter.

Right: One of the colourful day geckos of the genus Phelsuma. Unique to Madagascar, the day geckos are large and spectacular, reaching a length of 30cm and beautifully adorned with colourful blotches.

DAVID CURL

DAVID CURL

ANIMALS

Madagascar (but not the Comoros) is renowned for its high percentage of endemic fauna.

Lemurs

If outsiders have heard anything at all about Madagascar they've heard about lemurs, of which 90% can only be found in Madagascar – the remainder are native to the Comoros.

Lemurs are prosimians, a suborder of primates which includes the bush-babies and pottos of Africa, and the tarsiers and loris of Asia. Nearly 30 species of lemur are currently recognised, though the numbers are liable to change as new species are found, or are discovered to be subspecies of those already known.

One innovative method of conservation is the Adopt-A-Lemur program initiated by the Duke University Primate Center, regarded as the experts in lemurs. With an annual donation starting at US$50, you can adopt a lemur for one year, and receive a photo, newsletter, adoption certificate and so on. Contact them at 3705 Erwin Rd, Durham NC 27705 (☎ (919) 489 3364); email primate@acpub.duke.edu. Alternatively, check their home-page: http://www.duke.edu/web/primate/adopt.html.

Ring-tailed Lemur *(Lemur catta)* Although it's not the most common species, the ring-tailed lemur is probably the most familiar of Madagascar's lemurs because it manages well in captivity, spends a great deal of time on the ground, is active for most of the day and exists in some numbers in the popular Berenty Reserve. It is also the most easily recognised with its long black-and-white striped tail.

Native to the dry southern areas of Madagascar, the ring-tailed lemur ranges from the spiny forest around Berenty Reserve as far north as Isalo National Park. It is the most social of lemurs, living in troops of 12 to 25 individuals, and has a complex social hierarchy.

DAVID CURL

Feeding time for ring-tailed lemurs at Tana's Tsim-bazaza zoo. The animal collection at Tsimbazaza has recently benefited from overseas assistance and provides a good opportunity to see lemurs at close range.

Brown Lemur *(Lemur fulvus)* There are several easily distinguishable subspecies of brown lemur. The most common variety is the red-fronted lemur *(L. f. rufus)*, which is present in large numbers in Berenty Reserve, Ranomafana National Park and Périnet Reserve, as well as the dry forests of western Madagascar.

They live in troops of five to 15 individuals that are normally led by a female. The male is pale grey with a black muzzle and white rings around the eyes. Females are brown with a greyish head and light orange jowls.

The race normally referred to simply as the 'brown lemur' *(L. f. fulvus)* is a nondescript grizzly brown lemur with a black face, found mainly in the northern half of Madagascar. The best places to observe it include Ampijoroa Reserve, Périnet and around Lac Alaotra.

The male white-fronted lemur *(L. f. albifrons)* is the most easily recognisable of the brown lemurs, with its white angora-like head and underbelly; the dark brown female is less descript. The only place to observe them easily is the reserve on Nosy Mangabe in north-eastern Madagascar.

The male and female Sanford's lemur *(L. f. sanfordi)* also appear quite different from each other. The male has a white ruff around his head and tufts of light fur protruding from his ears. The dark-coloured female resembles the female white-fronted lemur. Sanford's lemur inhabits the forests of northern Madagascar, particularly Montagne d'Ambre and the Ankàrana Reserve.

Another subspecies, the white-collared lemur *(L. f. albocollaris)*, is chestnut brown but takes its name from the white beard worn by the male. It is restricted to a small area of the eastern rainforest. The male of the similar collared lemur *(L. f. collaris)* sports an orange beard; this race is found only in the vicinity of Taolagnaro and is protected in Andohahela Reserve.

Crowned Lemur *(Lemur coronatus)* Both the male and female crowned lemur sport an orange crown, a dark grey cap and white underbelly. The remainder of the female is solid grey, while the male has orange cheeks and a grizzled orange-brown back and legs. The young are born between September and November. They are most frequently

The widespread brown lemur (Lemur fulvus) *is easy to see at Berenty and several other reserves in Madagascar. A race also inhabits Grande Comore on the Comoros.*

DAVID CURL

observed in the far north around Ankàrana Reserve and Montagne d'Ambre.

Mongoose Lemur *(Lemur mongoz)* One of the rarest and most endangered of the lemurs, the mongoose lemur is native to the western forests of Madagascar. With a rather dull brown body, it is most easily distinguished by its white muzzle; the female also has white cheeks. Your best chance of observing one would be on the island of Mohéli in the Comoros or in Ampijoroa Reserve, Madagascar (especially between September and December).

Red-bellied Lemur *(Lemur rubriventer)* A forest dweller, the red-bellied lemur lives in the depths of the eastern rainforest as far north as Tsaratanana and south to the Andringitra Massif, but may be most easily observed in Ranomafana. Both male and female have rust-coloured fur and a black tail. The female has a white chest and underbelly while the male has a dark underbelly and white patches around the eyes.

Black Lemur *(Lemur macaco)* Only the male black lemur is actually black; females are much lighter, with a white beard and marked white ear tufts which call to mind an eccentric English explorer. The most easily observed are those of Nosy Komba, near Nosy Be, which are well accustomed to banana-proffering tourists. They are considered sacred by the local community and are consequently protected.

Two subspecies, *L. m. macaco* and *L. m. flavifrons*, range along the north-west coast of Madagascar from Ambilobe in the north to Befotaka in the south.

Golden Bamboo Lemur *(Hapalemur aureus)* The golden bamboo lemur was first recorded in 1985 at a site now included in Ranomafana National Park. In 1986 researchers thought it was actually a new subspecies of the broad-nosed gentle lemur. Subsequent studies determined that the new lemur had more chromosomes than the broad-nosed gentle lemur and was therefore a new species.

This lemur has a dark brown back and face, a golden underbelly, and a thick, very faintly ringed brown and gold tail.

Broad-nosed Gentle Lemur *(Hapalemur simus)* The rarest of the lemurs, the broad-nosed gentle lemur was thought to be extinct until it was rediscovered in what is now Ranomafana National Park in 1972. It wasn't seen subsequently until the late 1980s. It primarily eats the pithy stems of the giant bamboo which grows in dense stands in the eastern rainforests.

Grey Bamboo Lemur *(Hapalemur griseus)* The most common of the three hapalemurs, the grey bamboo lemur is a small grey animal with four subspecies. These are found in Madagascar around Moramandia in the far north-west; near Belo-sur-Tsiribihina north of Morondava; in a tiny forested area just north of Taolagnaro; and along the east coast as far north as the Tsaratanana Massif. The last subspecies, *H. g. griseus*, is the widest ranging and is frequently observed in both Périnet and Ranomafana.

Ruffed Lemur *(Varecia variegata)* Two subspecies have been identified in Madagascar: the red ruffed lemur *(V. v. rubra)*, which is found only on the Masoala Peninsula; and the black-and-white ruffed lemur *(V. v. variegata)*, which is at home in the eastern rainforests between

Farafangana in the south and Maroantsetra in the north. One of the handsomest of lemurs, the black-and-white ruffed lemur sports a black head, vest, tail and feet, with white legs, mid-section and a prominent white ruff framing the face.

With one of the loudest voices in the lemur kingdom, the ruffed lemur communicates in short barking bellows. The best place to observe them is on Nosy Mangabe near Maroantsetra, and Maromizaha and Mantady near Périnet. It is particularly fond of wild figs.

DAVID CURL

Sportive Lemur

Sportive Lemur *(Lepilemur mustelinus)* The small greyish brown sportive or weasel lemurs, normally referred to as just lepilemurs, are exclusively nocturnal. Taxonomists are as yet uncertain whether they are a single species with six subspecies or seven individual species (in this book they're treated as one species). Typical of nocturnal lemurs, their wide staring eyes lend them a startled and timid appearance.

Lepilemurs are found in most reserves of Madagascar, but are particularly visible in Berenty and Beza-Mahafaly Reserves in the south, Périnet, and at Ankàrana Reserve in the far north.

Grey Mouse Lemur *(Microcebus murinus)* All the characteristically large-eyed mouse lemurs are nocturnal and forage for insects and fruit. Although they're difficult to observe without baiting, they are some of the most common lemurs in Madagascar and the grey mouse lemur is one of the few not threatened with extinction. Mouse lemurs are found mainly in the dry southern and western forests of Madagascar, and are frequently observed at night in Berenty.

Rufous Mouse Lemur *(Microcebus rufus)* The rufous mouse lemur inhabits the eastern rainforests of Madagascar, where it is quite abundant. Scarcely larger than a mouse, this reddish lemur is extremely agile and has been known to leap more than 3m between branches. Its very keen sense of smell is useful in sniffing out fruit and insects, which are its favourite foods.

Your best chance of seeing one is at Ranomafana, though they are also abundant at Périnet and other reserves of eastern Madagascar.

Coquerel's Mouse Lemur *(Microcebus coquereli)* This rare little lemur inhabits only scattered areas of the dry western forests of Madagascar and is extremely difficult to observe. It's normally located by finding the large round twig nests which it builds among dense foliage in the treetops.

Fork-marked Lemur *(Phaner furcifer)* A pretty, golden coloured lemur with a loud squawking voice, the fork-marked lemur is found mainly in the dry western forests of Madagascar, but has also been spotted in the eastern rainforests of the Masoala Peninsula and Montagne d'Ambre. The name is derived from the dark brown stripe which runs up its back and splits at the back of the neck into two stripes, one above each eye.

Greater Dwarf Lemur *(Cheirogaleus major)* The most remarkable thing about the dwarf lemur is that during the cool season it enters a period of hibernation lasting up to two weeks or so. It is one of only two primates to do so (the other is the similar fat-tailed dwarf lemur).

·One of the most widespread lemurs, dwarf lemurs are found throughout the eastern forest region from Montagne d'Ambre all the way to Taolagnaro in southern Madagascar, and even in the wetter areas of the north-west coast.

Fat-tailed Dwarf Lemur *(Cheirogaleus medius)* Similar to the greater dwarf lemur, this lemur also goes into a type of hibernation. Its habitat is the western forests, where food is sparse during the marked dry season, and its dormant period may last up to six months. It's thought that the hibernating lemurs live off fat reserves stored in their legs and noticeably broad tails. Your best chance of observing one will be in Ranomafana during the rainy summer months.

Woolly Lemur *(Avahi laniger)* Like all nocturnal lemurs, the woolly lemur or *avahi* has large penetrating eyes and a wide-eyed stare. Although it's not rare, it can be difficult to observe because during the day it normally huddles asleep amid dense foliage. At night, its chattering whistling is normally heard before the animal is seen.

There are two woolly lemur subspecies. The western avahi *(A. l. occidentalis)* is a very rare nocturnal lemur restricted to a few scattered forests in north-western Madagascar. Your best chance of observing one will be in Ampijoroa. More common is the eastern avahi *(A. l. laniger)* which is found throughout the eastern rainforests and is seen with relative frequency in both Périnet and Ranomafana.

Verreaux's Sifaka *(Propithecus verreauxi)* The range of the beautiful Verreaux's sifaka extends from the dry western forests around Morondava, right across the south-west and south to Berenty. These lemurs are nearly all white with a brown cap, black face and white forehead. They live in groups of three to 11 individuals, which can be either mixed groups led by a dominant female or all-bachelor troops.

Along with ring-tailed lemurs, they are among the most interesting lemurs to watch, performing incredible feats of agility which would put a monkey to shame. Most interesting are the acrobatic leaps from tree to tree, often covering up to 20m in a shot, and the incredible sifaka 'dance'. This unique method of locomotion is used in crossing open ground and involves twisting and leaping about on the hind legs in a sort of exuberant dance step. Even inactive sifakas can be entertaining, assuming some charmingly laid-back positions high in the trees.

The best place to see Verreaux's sifakas in Madagascar is in Berenty, but they may also be readily observed in Beza-Mahafaly Reserve in the south-west and in Isalo National Park. There are several subspecies: Coquerel's sifaka *(P. v. coquereli)* is most easily seen at the Ankarafantsika Reserve; Decken's sifaka *(P. v. deckeni)* is native to the Tsingy de Bemaraha Reserve in western Madagascar and up to the north of Mahajanga; the crowned sifaka *(P. v. coronatus)* is restricted to Tsingy de Namoroka in the same area. Unfortunately, in the north-west there are no local fady (taboos) against hunting sifakas so the future of the subspecies in that area is in doubt.

Diademed Sifaka *(Propithecus diadema)* The diademed sifaka is found in the eastern rainforests of Madagascar, and is frequently seen in Ranoma-fana and Périnet. It is one of the larger lemur species, weighing in at around 7kg, and also one of the most beautiful, with a relatively short tail, coal-black face, a white ruff and rich brown, grey and orange body. The rarest subspecies is Perrier's diademed sifaka *(P. d. perrieri)*, also known as the black sifaka, with a small population of 2000 individuals restricted to the Analamera Reserve in far north-eastern Madagascar. It's thought that a population may also exist in Ankàrana Reserve.

Milne-Edwards' diademed sifaka *(P. d. edwardsi)* is primarily dark brown with a cream-coloured butterfly marking across its back, and is found in the Mananara Nord National Park area of Madagascar. The silky diademed sifaka *(P. d. candidus)* is almost entirely white and exists mainly in the Marojejy Reserve in the north-east.

Golden Crowned Sifaka *(Propithecus tattersalli)* In 1974 the discovery of a new lemur near Vohémar, in northern Madagascar, was reported. Initially it was described as a subspecies of the diademed sifaka, yet it was smaller and, unlike the diademed sifaka, it bore large tufted ears and a golden patch atop its head.

When it was discovered that its very small habitat was to be clear-cut for charcoal production in 1986, several of the lemurs were captured and taken to Duke University Primate Centre in the US for study and captive breeding. There it was determined to be an entirely new species.

Its habitat is limited to a few sparse patches of rapidly diminishing forest in an environmentally degraded area. Although it's in imminent danger of extinction because of habitat loss, a local fady fortunately prohibits the hunting of these sifakas.

Indri *(Indri indri)* The black and white indri, which weighs up to 7kg, is the largest of the lemurs and is best known for its haunting early morning cry. This cry is territorial, intended to demarcate an area for a particular family group, which usually consists of two to five individuals. Its broad, round face and rounded ears lend it the endearing appearance of a cuddly teddy bear and, though it is one of the most threatened of lemur species, it is comparably easy to see because it exists in some numbers in and around Périnet.

Hairy-eared Dwarf Lemur *(Allocebus trichotis)* Until 1989, when it was rediscovered in a remote region of the north-eastern rainforests west of Mananara Nord National Park, the tiny hairy-eared dwarf lemur was thought to be extinct. Several specimens have now been captured and research is ongoing.

Aye-Aye *(Daubentonia madagascariensis)* The remarkable aye-aye is unlike any other lemur: it has large bat-like ears, a large head, a bushy tail, grizzled and tousled black fur, and a skeletal middle finger on each hand. This finger is useful in extracting the meat of the ramy nut, prising grubs from beneath tree bark, and digging into sap pustules which erupt on the bark of *Eugenia* trees – all are favoured by the aye-aye.

Several decades ago it was assumed that the aye-aye was in imminent danger of extinction. Although populations are sparse, it is in fact one of the most widely distributed lemur species and has been observed at Ankàrana, Ranomafana, Mananara Nord, Périnet and even in the dry western forests. In the mid 1960s it was introduced on Nosy Mangabe in north-eastern Madagascar.

Unfortunately, the aye-aye is considered a harbinger of evil by many Malagasy and is frequently killed by frightened villagers. Its taste for plantation coconuts endears it to few of the less superstitious. For a background of the aye-aye see *The Aye-aye & I – A Rescue Expedition in Madagascar* by Gerald Durrell.

Other Mammals

Almost 100% of native mammals in Madagascar are found nowhere else in the world.

Tenrec The 20 or so species of tenrecs form a diverse group of small, primitive insect-eating mammals that have filled the ecological niches

The tenrecs are a diverse group of small mammals unique to Madagascar. The best known are probably the spiny tenrecs, one of which is shown here. Tenrecs are regarded as among the most primitive of mammals.

DAVID CURL

occupied by shrews, moles and hedgehogs in other lands. Most species are retiring and rarely seen by visitors. The most famous are undoubtedly the spiny tenrecs, which resemble a hedgehog, but one species has evolved to live an aquatic existence like a miniature otter. The widespread common tenrec *(Tenrec ecaudatus)* is the largest species; it can attain a weight of 1.5kg and has an extraordinary reproductive rate: a female can give birth to up to 32 young at a time and may have up to 29 nipples!

Mongoose Five species of mongooses are endemic to Madagascar. The ring-tailed mongoose *(Galidia elegans)* is as elegant as the name implies, and is renowned because it is not timid when confronted by humans. With a bit of luck you can see these at Montagne d'Ambre National Park.

Bats Also prolific are the bats, of which there are 28 species. If you visit Berenty Reserve, you'll certainly see the impressive roost of flying foxes *(Pteropus rufus)*. These bats are considered quite tasty by the local populace so poaching is a problem and their numbers have been pushed to dangerously low levels.

The largest mammals native to the Comoros are fruit bats, of which there are three species. The most common is the Seychelles flying fox *(P. seychellensis comoriensis)*, which is found throughout the islands and frequently observed at dusk. The largest bat, with a wingspan of over 1m, is Livingstone's fruit bat *(P. livingstonii)*, an extremely rare species which roosts only in the highlands of Anjouan and Mohéli. Finally, there's the lost fruit bat *(Rousettus obliviosus)*, so-called because it was not observed at all during the early part of this century.

The Comoros is also host to three smaller bat species: the free-tailed bat *(Tadarida pumila)*, the lesser long-winged bat *(Miniopterus minor griveudi)* and the Anjouan bat *(Myotis goudoti anjouanensis)*.

Fosa The reddish fosa *(Cryptoprocta ferox)* (pronounced 'foosh'), the largest of Madagascar's four species of carnivore, looks more like a small and slinky puma than the mongooses or civets to which it is related. It mainly preys on lemurs but has been known to go for chickens and larger animals, including cattle, and pastoralists consider it a pest. It is found throughout Madagascar in small numbers and though its chilling cries may be heard at night in many wilder areas, it is rarely observed. According to unconfirmed reports fosas in far northern Madagascar can be up to 1.5m long.

The fosa should not be confused with another Malagasy carnivore, the striped civet *(Fossa fossana)*, locally known as a 'fossa'.

Whales & Dugongs Off the western coast of Île Sainte Marie, 500 to 700 whales swim by between July and September. Many remain to look for mates or to give birth. Seeing these is an incredible experience, and should not be missed. Some of the species include Sowerby's whale *(Mesoplodon layardi)* and Bryde's whale *(Balaenoptera brydei)*.

The dugong, or 'sea cow' *(vache de mer)* is seen infrequently, while other related cetaceans are often observed offshore as they pass through the Mozambique Channel between Madagascar and mainland Africa.

Birds

With just 250 or so species of bird, of which only 106 are endemic and 197 actually breed on Madagascar, Malagasy birdlife is not as rich as one would expect. Nonetheless, many, such as the couas, mesites, asitys and ground-rollers, are unique to Madagascar. Others are Malagasy forms of more widespread groups, such as ducks and birds of prey.

While birdwatchers won't be overwhelmed, they will be kept busy searching. Nowhere will you find the staggering variety of the African parks, but many of Madagascar's reserves hold good numbers of species; the sections on the various reserves throughout this book highlight birds where appropriate. Although all birds have a 'common' name in English, we have also included scientific names here because researchers or guides who speak only French may know them only by these names. Don't be intimidated – scientific names are a tool only. Refer to the Books section under Facts about Madagascar for details of some excellent guides to local birdlife.

Couas Most of the nine species of coua are found in the humid forest of north-western Madagascar, the spiny forests of the south and, especially, the eastern rainforests. All have a patch of bare blue skin behind the eye. The giant coua *(Coua gigas)* moves along the forest floor and is readily observed in Berenty; the unusual crested coua *(Coua cristata)*, thought by some to be the most beautiful bird in Madagascar, lives in the dry western forests.

Vangas The vangas are related to the shrikes of other continents and found all over Madagascar. It has been said that if Charles Darwin had landed on Madagascar instead of Galapagos he would have reached the same conclusions about evolution by looking at the vangas: the 14 species evolved an astonishing variety of bill shapes as they adapted to fill different ecological niches.

The distinctive sickle-billed vanga *(Falculea palliata)*, with its oversized bill, is reputed to be the herald of rain in the dry south-west; the red-tailed vanga *(Calicalius madagascariensis)* is very small but energetic when gathering food; the blue vanga *(Cyanolanius madagascariensis)* is known among local Malagasy for its plumage; and the most common, the hook-billed vanga *Vanga curvirostris*, eats small frogs and chameleons. The most extraordinary is the helmet vanga *Euryceros prevostii*.

Waterbirds Nearly half of the 75 species of waterbirds found in Madagascar are endemic. Some of the best places to look are the Tsiribihina River and Alaotra and Ihotry lakes, especially after heavy rain. Then there are the tiny but brilliant kingfishers: the red and white kingfisher *(Ipsidina madagascariensis)*; the malachite kingfisher *(Alcedo vintsioides)*; and Malagasy kingfisher *(Corythornis vintsioides)* – known locally as the *vintsy*.

There is also a variety of ducks, rails and shorebirds. Two endemic ducks, the Malagasy teal and Didier's pochard, are very scarce, and the Madagascar Flufftail is a horrendous skulker that may be seen only with much patience. The Madagascar fish-eagle *(Haliaeetus vociferoides)* is one of the most threatened birds in the world. Down to an estimated 40 individuals, its young are taken for food each year. The Madagascar coucal *(Centropus toulou)* is a large, vocal relative of the cuckoos. The coucal is widespread and has an unusual alternative name: the *tulukuckuck*.

Other Birds Some other interesting and beautiful species in Madagascar and the Comoros are the Madagascar red fody *(Foudia madagascariensis)*; the Madagascar kestrel *(Falco newtoni)*, which is occasionally seen hovering over the hauts plateaux; the Madagascar paradise flycatcher *(Terpsiphone mutata)*, with its elongated tail feathers; the magnificent Madagascar serpent eagle *(Eutriorchis astur)*; and the ubiquitous crested drongo *(Dicrurus forficatus)*.

Madagascar and the Comoros share three species of parrots. Two, the vasa parrot *(Coracopsis vasa)* and the black parrot *(C. nigra)* are common but rather dull as parrots go. The third, the grey-headed lovebird *(Agapornis cana)*, is a bright, diminutive member of this generally colourful group.

You may see the large crested ibis *(Lophotibis cristata)* along the footpaths of the Montagne d'Ambre National Park. The Madagascar turtle-dove *(Streptopelia picturata)*, known locally as a *deho*, is usually seen alone.

One of the rarest birds is the Madagascar red owl *(Tyto soumangei)*, thought to be extinct until it was rediscovered on the north-eastern coast in 1993. Madagascar and the Comoros each have a species of small Scops owl; the Comoran Scops owl is found only on the slopes of Mt Karthala on Grande Comore.

In the Comoros, also look out for the Comoros blue pigeon, drongos, sunbirds, ibis, flamingos and guinea fowl. Several species of heron are also present, though not in great numbers.

Reptiles & Amphibians

Almost 98% of Madagascar's native reptiles and amphibians are only found on Madagascar. Reptiles are not everyone's cup of tea, but, with the exception of the crocodile, the herpetofauna of Madagascar and the Comoros is diverse, often colourful and certainly unusual. If you have a specific interest, the best guide is *A Fieldguide to the Amphibians & Reptiles of Madagascar* by Frank Glaw & Miguel Vences.

Chameleons Madagascar's chameleons have come to represent the country nearly as well as its lemurs. Over half of the world's species are found in Madagascar, and there are two endemic genera, the large *Chamaeleo* and the smaller *Brookesia*.

Chameleons are among the most comical-looking of reptiles, with clamp-like feet which are used for grasping branches, a long tapering tail which rolls into a tight coil when not in use, and conical eyes which swivel independently of each other. These eyes give chameleons binocular vision and facilitate perfect aim and judgement of distance when they shoot out their long round tongue – which can zap an insect nearly a body length away in .04 of a second.

In Périnet, you can see the daddy of 'em all, the immense and dour-looking Parson's chameleon *(Chamaeleo parsonii)*. It is a contender for the title of the world's largest chameleon species and can measure up to 60cm in length. However, you are more likely to see one

An unidentified chameleon (possibly a one-horned chameleon) photographed at night at Ampijoroa Forestry Reserve.

DAVID CURL

sitting on a branch held by a child, gobbling grasshoppers by the dozen for the benefit of snap-happy tourists.

Contrary to popular belief, chameleons do not change colour to match their surroundings. Instead, the colour scheme is probably used as a defence, preventing predators from forming an image for hunting, and is tied directly to emotions and territoriality. Male chameleons intensify their colour and puff up their bodies when encountering other male chameleons in the hope of appearing intimidating to the potential rival.

Geckos In many parts of the world geckos are small, unobtrusive lizards best known for scuttling around walls at night in the tropics. However, in Madagascar they have evolved into many large, colourful and bizarre species, some of which can be readily seen by a visitor.

In the rainforests of Madagascar and the Comoros, the superbly camouflaged leaf-tailed gecko *(Uroplatus alluaudi)* blends into the nearby bark and is hard to spot. It may be easier to see the bright green geckos of the genus *Phelsuma* which, unlike their cousins, are not nocturnal. There are over 60 more gecko species in Madagascar.

Crocodiles Sadly, urban development and hunting have seriously threatened the Nile crocodile *(Crocodilus niloticus)*, which is now most common in the north-west of Madagascar. Understandably, the Malagasy who live near crocodiles, and the Malagasy people in general, regard the crocodile with reverence and fear. It is a symbol of power, and necklaces and hats decorated with crocodile teeth are often worn in traditional ceremonies.

Turtles & Tortoises The world's oldest reptiles are well-represented, but endangered because they were hunted for meat – only five of the 10 or 11 known species remain. Off the coast of the Comoran island of Mohéli, the green turtle *(Chelonia mydas)* manages to survive, thanks to local conservation efforts.

Several equally endangered species of land tortoise include the rare radiated tortoise *(Geochelone radiata)* and the world's most threatened reptile, the ploughshare tortoise *(G. yniphora)*. Called the *angonoka* in Malagasy, the ploughshare is the biggest tortoise in Madagascar, and needs at least 10 years to reach maturity. (Tragically about 70 of these rare reptiles were stolen from a breeding program in Madagascar in 1996, clearly showing that poaching is still a problem.)

White tree frog, photo-
graphed in rainforest in
eastern Madagascar.

DAVID CURL

Snakes Madagascar and the Comoros are also home to over 60 species of innocuous snakes. The most frequently observed are the Madagascar boa *(Acrantophis madagascariensis)* of the eastern forests and the giant hog-nosed snake *(Leioheterodon madagascariensis)*, which is found all around the island. *Pararhadinaea novae* is found around the Anjanaharibe-Sud Reserve.

Although there are several poisonous snakes on the island, they belong to the group known as back-fanged snakes and are harmless to humans, though not to the small rodents and frogs which are their main meal.

Frogs Madagascar is a paradise for frogophiles, with 150 species of frogs and toads (148 of these are endemic). New ones are being identified and classified all the time: about 40 have become known to science since 1970. Along with the chameleons, they are among the most colourful creatures you're likely to see in Madagascar, ranging from brilliant green, red, yellow, and orange to all shades of grey, brown, rust and black. In Périnet Reserve, you may see the golden mantella. (Unfortunately, some frogs end up as a main course in French restaurants in Madagascar.)

Fish

The thousands of kilometres of coastline around Madagascar and the Comoros support a vast array of fish and other fascinating (and some-times dangerous) creatures. These include the swordfish, sharks, stingrays, emperor fish, devilfish and lobsters. The hundreds of rivers in Madagascar are also host to an incredible number of fish: 92% of freshwater species are only found in Madagascar.

Divers in the Comoros may be lucky enough to see the flashlight fish, so called because it has a large light organ under each eye which scientists suppose is used to search for food and to communicate. By day, they stay in depths as great as 100m, but, at night, come to within 5m of the surface. Other exotic fish seen by divers include the clown-fish and cardinal fish. The rarest fish in Madagascar is the freshwater black bass.

Visiting fishing enthusiasts may be interested in the number of bream, barracudas, carangues and groupers. Comoran fishermen prefer other species: during late afternoon and sunset around Moroni harbour, and mornings at Itsandra and Planet Plage beaches, you can watch hundreds of fishing boats trying their luck at catching tiny *sim sim* (small fry). Like sardines, or the *bichiques* (a sort of small fry) of Réunion, they make good eating. Marlin, wahoo, tuna, and sharks are also relatively common in Comoran waters.

Coelacanth If the Comoros is internationally known for one thing, it is the 'prehistoric' deep-sea fish known as the coelacanth (pronounced 'SEE-la-canth'), or *Latimeria chalumnae*. Biologists and palaeontologists assumed that the 350-million year old fish, 'old four legs' as it's affectionately known, went out with the dinosaurs 70 million years ago.

Coelacanths are still caught off Grande Comore and Anjouan, but the high prices commanded by specimens and its apparently slow reproduction rate have caused concern that it may truly become extinct. See the Anjouan chapter for more information on the rediscovery of the coelacanth.

Insects & Other Invertebrates

Madagascar has the expected complement of interesting bugs, including unusual stick insects, mantids, moths, butterflies, millipedes, dragonflies and beetles. Unfortunately, there is no shortage of mosquitoes and annoying but harmless leeches, known in Malagasy as *dinta*.

Comet Moth

Moths & Butterflies The most beautiful of the invertebrates are the spectacular comet moth *(Argema mitrei)*, which can reach a length of 20cm from antennae to tail, and the brilliantly-coloured urania moth *(Chrysiridia madagascariensis)* which, though fairly common, is seldom seen by casual visitors.

About 3000 species of butterflies have been recognised, of which over 2900 are endemic. At certain spots, like the waterfalls in Montagne d'Ambre and Ranomafana National Parks, the butterflies are large, colourful and easy to spot. You may see the swallowtail butterfly *(Papilo delalandei)*, arguably the most beautiful in Madagascar.

Beetles If you look closely enough around Ranomafana you can see the red and black giraffe beetle *(Trachelophorus giraffa)*, named because of the male's long neck (though not as long as it's African namesake, you'll be glad to know!).

Spiders Madagascar also boasts a fleet of some of the world's most bizarre looking spiders, especially the thorn spider *(Gasteracantha versicolor formosa)* with its spiked orange abdomen, four times wider than it is long; and the dead leaf spider *(Augusta glyphica)*, shaped a bit like a miniature manta ray with legs. Both are seen frequently at Périnet Reserve.

Another amazing arachnid is the brown crab spider *(Phyrnarachne rugosa)*. This defends itself from predators by climbing onto a leaf and folding itself up into a blob shape like a 'T', believing that it then resembles a bird dropping and is therefore not vulnerable to attack.

Scorpions Hikers and campers must be on the lookout for scorpions, which are especially prolific in drier areas. The two brownish yellow species found in the dry western forests, are active at night and inflict an excruciatingly painful and potentially dangerous sting. Those camping in the bush should be especially careful to check their boots, shoes, tents, backpacks, sleeping bags, clothing and ground sheets.

Regional Facts for the Visitor

PLANNING
When to Go

As you'd probably imagine, Madagascar and the Comoros experience a range of climates, including every combination of hot, dry, wet and cool. Bear in mind that both countries lie in the southern hemisphere so the wet summer generally runs from November to March and the drier, cooler winter is from April to October.

For further details about the climate, refer to the Climate sections in the Facts about Madagascar and Facts about the Comoros chapters.

Madagascar The east coast is the hottest, wettest and stickiest part of the country, followed by the far north (both areas, along with the north-west coast, also suffer the odd cyclone). The driest region is the far south with the central west coast not far behind. The *hauts plateaux* (high plateaus), as the interior highlands are known, experience anything from warm and wet summers to cool, dry winters. Overnight temperatures in July and August can drop below freezing and snow is not uncommon at higher elevations.

The rainy season occurs during the summer months. It is most severe in the north and on the east coast where hot, sticky and wet conditions combine to make life miserable. Flooded roads frequently turn to quagmires and often cause public transport to grind to a halt. In fact, some areas of the country remain inaccessible from December to March. The capital, Antananarivo (known as Tana), also receives a fair bit of rain during summer. The south remains quite dry but the summer heat can be excruciating.

Far more pleasant are the dry winter months, which at least offer a chance of a dry holiday on the east coast. The north has even less rain in winter; and the hauts plateaux, west coast and south are practically bone dry with crisp nights and comfortable daytime temperatures.

Comoros The Comoros lie within the cyclone belt so foul weather is common during the summer months, with the greatest chance of violent weather in February and March. Most visitors arrive between April and October (especially during European summer holidays in July and August) to take advantage of the south-westerly trade winds which bring dry weather and cool, comfortable temperatures from the south.

Visitors may not wish to visit during the festival of Ramadan, the 30 day dawn-to-dusk fast marking the month that the Koran was revealed to the Prophet Mohammed in Mecca. It can be a difficult time for non-Muslim travellers because many restaurants are closed and tempers tend to run short. Ramadan changes each year, but is generally some time between January and March.

What Kind of Trip?

It is not difficult to travel around Madagascar and the Comoros independently. Transport by road and air is regular (less so by sea), and just about everywhere you will want to go has a good range of accommodation and restaurants. At most major towns and tourist attractions you can easily arrange short organised tours, such as treks and trips by pirogue, if you wish.

The major disadvantages for some travellers (which is why some may prefer to join an organised tour) are that you may not speak French, which is overwhelmingly the major language of tourism; the roads are often bad; and overland transport is always uncomfortable, and prone to delays and breakdowns.

Maps

You can pick up good maps of Madagascar and the Comoros in these countries, but they won't be much cheaper than in your own country and the choice is limited. If you are including Madagascar and/or the Comoros on a trip around Africa or the Indian Ocean, get your larger scale maps at home.

Serious trekkers may want to pick up the very detailed 1:500,000 TPC or 1:1,000,000 ONC maps published by the US Defense Mapping Agency Aerospace Center. However, most of these maps cover the ocean and are not good value. You can pick up detailed maps at the FTM office in Tana (refer to the Madagascar Facts for the Visitor chapter for details).

What to Bring

What to bring will depend on your intended budget, itinerary, mode of travel, time of visit and length of stay.

While travelling as light as possible is always a good idea if you want to enjoy yourself, some items will be required if you can't splash out on top-end hotel accommodation. Bring a sleeping bag if you're slumming it (to avoid sleeping on vermin-infested bed sheets). If you are doing any trekking or visiting more remote reserves, especially in Madagascar, a tent and sleeping bag will be required; otherwise it is not necessary and will only be an inconvenience.

Luggage Backpacks are usually recommended as the most practical and useful carry-all; internal-frame packs don't get battered around or broken quite as easily as those with external frames, but a few travellers maintain that framed packs are more comfortable for long-distance trekking because they're cooler and better balanced. Buy the most sturdy and well-made pack you can afford, paying special attention to the strength of zippers, straps and tabs.

A small padlock to secure the bag's contents from opportunistic thieves is a good idea, though some people say that it may encourage people to take the whole bag. Also, take a few plastic bags to protect against dust and rain when your luggage is attached to the top of a *taxi-brousse* (bush taxi).

Clothing The areas covered in this book lie mainly in the tropics. However, there is a broad range of climatic conditions, varying from Madagascar's cool highlands to the hot and dusty southern deserts, the humid tropical far north and the sticky east coast where the year is divided into two seasons: wet and wetter.

If you're travelling in the dry period between May and August, bring a range of clothing. You can expect T-shirt weather during the day across most of the region, but mornings and evenings can be quite chilly and overnight temperatures can dip to freezing in the highlands. You won't need thermal underwear but you'll appreciate a light jacket, a long-sleeved jumper and some warm socks.

If you'll be spending most of your time in humid regions much of your wardrobe should consist of light cotton. A bathing costume will also be requisite if you want to get the most out of the hot springs and glorious beaches of Madagascar and the Comoros. During the rainy season you'll need waterproofs and sturdy footwear; a light wrap-up plastic cape or raincoat will minimise the effects of a sudden downpour. If trekking you'll need good boots and lightweight long trousers to discourage leeches (which are abundant after rain).

Although you won't need formal wear in Madagascar or the Comoros, it may be useful to have a smart pair of trousers and shirt, or a dress or skirt, for dinners out, as well as a decent pair of shoes. This outfit may also expedite Customs and Immigration procedures and help you appear more respectable in the eyes of officials.

Other Items Additional items which will come in handy include a small travel alarm clock, torch (flashlight), sunscreen with a rating of at least 10 (this item is either unavailable or prohibitively expensive in Madagascar and the Comoros), Swiss Army-style knife, clothes line, basic first-aid kit (see the Health chapter at the end of this book), water bottle and water purification tablets, plastic ground sheet (if camping or staying in bottom range hotels), towel, sewing kit, photographic equipment and all the film you think you'll need (though beware of duty-free restrictions – see under Customs in the Facts for the Visitor chapters. You can stock up on print film in most major towns). Don't forget to bring enough batteries to power all the gadgetry for the duration of your stay. Local batteries – which may or may not be new when purchased – have been known to expire after just a minute or two in a torch and in less than 10 seconds in a Walkman.

If you'll be travelling rough, you may also want to bring along some emergency rations, such as a jar of peanut butter, Marmite or Vegemite. The last two will hold their own against anything Madagascar can serve up! Earplugs are essential if you are a light sleeper – this is a noisy part of the world.

SUGGESTED ITINERARIES

Your itinerary will depend on several obvious factors: the amount of time and money you have, what your interests are (beaches, wildlife, culture and so on), your ability to withstand discomfort and tedium when using overland transport, and, to a lesser extent, when you go.

Unless you have far more time than money, you will probably want to save time and damage to your back by flying one way and returning overland (or vice versa). Most travellers with limited time and money will probably bypass the Comoros because it involves a long boat ride or a pricey airfare, and the cost of travel there, especially on Mayotte, is about three times higher than in Madagascar.

One week
Base yourself in and around Tana because you won't have time to see much. See what Tana has to offer; visit Lac Itasy and/or Lac Mantasoa; go to Ambohimanga; quickly explore Parc National d'Andasibe-Mantadia (aka Périnet Réserve); or take a side trip by train to Antsirabe.

In one week you will only have time to explore one island of the Comoros; it should be Grande Comore, where the transport to and around the island is best.

Two weeks
(a) Concentrate on seeing the attractions along the main highway (and the best road) between Tana and Toliara. After visiting Tana, take the train to Antsirabe to visit nearby villages, lakes and thermal baths; maybe stop over at Ambositra before going to Fianarantsoa for a few days to explore vineyards, tea plantations and Ambalavao; make a slight detour for a day or two to Parc National de Ranomafana – a worthy alternative to Périnet; maybe stop off at Ihosy before spending two days exploring Parc National de Isalo, staying at Ranohira; continue to Toliara, and head immediately to Ifaty to relax and enjoy world-class diving.
(b) To avoid a lot of travelling, explore Tana, Périnet, Toamasina (aka Tamatave), a beach resort such as Mahavelona on the way to Île Sainte Marie, and then spend a few days relaxing and swimming at this magnificent island.

Two weeks is enough to quickly see the Comoros, including Mayotte, if you fly between each island, but there will be no time to combine it with a trip to Madagascar.

One month
Spend two weeks doing the route suggested earlier but more slowly, and, depending on your interests, add some of the following: (a) the fantastic train ride between Fianarantsoa and Manakara (if it's running). Explore Manakara and return to Fianarantsoa, stopping at Ranomafana; (b) detour from Antsirabe to Miandrivazo and take a pirogue trip for several days to Belo-sur-Tsiribihina and explore nearby parks; (c) for the adventurous, travel overland from Toliara to Taolagnaro (Fort Dauphin); (d) see the attractions around Tana mentioned earlier; (e) take a flight from Tana to Mayotte or Moroni and spend a week exploring Grande Comore and/or Anjouan; or (f) take a week or 10 days travelling to Île Sainte Marie, via Périnet and Toamasina.

Two months
In two months you will probably see most of what you want. Spend about half the time slowly travelling along the road between Tana and Toliara, combined with a few of the side trips listed earlier.

In the second month you will have time to explore northern Madagascar: fly to Nosy Be for a few days; catch a ferry and taxi-brousse to Antsiranana (Diego Suarez); explore Parc National de Montagne d'Ambre; fly to Sambava and visit Andapa and Antalaha; take a boat or flight (if available) to Île Sainte Marie and back to Tana via Toamasina, Mahavelona and Périnet. You may also have time to take a short trip to the Comoros and Mayotte, which are connected by air to Nosy Be and Mahajanga (Majunga).

HIGHLIGHTS OF MADAGASCAR & THE COMOROS

National Parks

Nioumachoua Marine Reserve (Mohéli) A reserve to protect green turtles on several tiny islands. Camping is allowed and is a magical experience if you see turtles laying their eggs.

Parc National d'Andasibe-Mantadia (Eastern Madagascar) Commonly known as the Périnet Reserve, this is the best place to see and hear the indri, among many other unique animals. Easy to reach from Toamasina or Tana; there are several places to stay near the park.

Réserve Privée de Berenty (Southern Madagascar) An excellent private reserve with spiny forest and lemurs. Although it mainly caters for organised groups and is expensive to visit, it is well worth the effort.

Parc National de Ranomafana (Central Madagascar) A well set up park in which to see lemurs and lovely landscapes. Easy to get to from Fianarantsoa and there are several good places to stay in Ranomafana village, which has thermal baths.

Parc National de Montagne d'Ambre (Northern Madagascar) A pretty national park with waterfalls and lemurs. Easy access from Antsiranana; horses and cars are allowed in the park. You can hike for several days south to Ankàrana Reserve.

Natural Landscapes

Parc National de Isalo (Southern Madagascar) Renowned less for wildlife than canyons, caves and natural swimming pools – and plenty of good hikes. On the main road between Tana and Toliara; well set up.

Lac Mantasoa (Antananarivo) A large artificial lake, great for short hikes, water sports and camping. Easy to get there on a day trip. You can camp, but ask locals first; there are also two pricey lodges to stay on the lake.

Tsingy de Bemaraha (Western Madagascar) Incredible examples of limestone *karst* pinnacles in an eerie landscape. Part of a designated reserve; access is very difficult and only by 4WD, trekking or zebu-cart.

Lac Kinkony (Western Madagascar) A wonderful secluded lake with unique birds and lemurs. It is not easy to get to and camping is the only option.

Avenue du Baobab (Western Madagascar) The best examples of unique baobabs; one of the most photogenic places. Easy to get to from Morondava; try to get there at sunset or dawn for photos.

Lac Salé (Grande Comore) The most accessible volcanic crater lake in the Comoros. Easy to get to from Moroni and to walk around; great views of the island.

Activities

Mt Karthala (Grande Comore) For the hardy, a trek up the omnipotent volcano is popular and easy to organise. It can be done in one day, but allow two.

Mohéli (Comoros) Plenty of day hikes to choose from along beaches or through the forests. You can take day hikes, or camp if you want to, but you must be self-sufficient.

Whale-watching (Eastern Madagascar) A boat trip to watch whales off the west coast of Île Sainte Marie is an incredible experience. Plenty of whales swim by between July and September.

Masoala Peninsula (Eastern Madagascar) The only way from the east coast to Maroantsetra is this four or five day trek through spectacular rainforest. This is a very tough trek; you must be fully equipped and have a guide.

Ifaty (Southern Madagascar) World-class diving, comparable to the Red Sea and the Maldives. Reached along a very rough road from

Three months

This is as long as your visa will normally allow, and is probably long enough to see it all anyway. Spend two months seeing as much as you can, as described above, allowing for inevitable delays. Three months will give you time to detour to the

Comoros and see it all in two to three weeks. If you have the energy you could also do a trek across the Masoala Peninsula, or between the east coast and Lac Alaotra; and you'd have time to visit remote areas around Sambava and organise a trip down the Canal des Pangalanes.

Toliara; there are numerous bungalow complexes on the beach, and diving centres are well set up for trips and equipment.

Nosy Komba & Tanikely (Northern Madagascar) Just off the coast of Nosy Be, these islands offer excellent diving and snorkelling. Hire a dhow or go on an organised tour; bring your own snorkelling gear; also visited by diving centres.

Sights & Villages

Zoma (Antananarivo) This incredibly large and colourful market is held every day, but reaches its climax on Friday.

Mahafaly Tombs (Southern Madagascar) In remote desert areas, the large and colourful tombs of the Mahafaly people are renowned for their intricate carvings. There are many *fady* (taboos) about these tombs; do not stand too close unless invited by a local.

Itsandra (Grande Comore) An ancient village full of crumbling Islamic forts, homes and mosques. Close enough to walk to from Moroni, with a lovely public beach adjacent; a guide is needed to show you around the village.

Museums

Mosea Akiba (Western Madagascar) The best museum in Madagascar, it contains excellent displays in French and English. Just up from the beach at Mahajanga.

Musée Regional de L'Université de Toamasina (Eastern Madagascar) A well organised cultural museum of traditional implements and household items. In the middle of Toamasina; detailed tours are available (in French).

Journeys

Fianarantsoa-Manakara Train (Central & Eastern Madagascar) The best train ride in the country; the trip takes nine hours or more through the rainforest, but is often delayed or

cancelled; food can be bought at villages along the way.

Canal des Pangalanes (Eastern Madagascar) Travel by boat independently, or on an organised tour, down the 600km chain of artificial and natural canals and lakes from Toamasina to Farafangana. You'll need lots of time and/or money; this trip is yet to be developed for tourists, but it will be.

Tsiribihina River (Western Madagascar) A three to five day trip by pirogue or any type of boat through magnificent forests. Not difficult to organise for the hardy independent traveller; expensive tours are also available.

Beaches & Islands

Île Sainte Marie (Eastern Madagascar) A wonderful range of lovely beaches; also diving and whale-watching. Easy to reach by plane or boat; there is a surprisingly large range of good-value bungalows to stay at.

Grande Comore (Comoros) Several great public beaches, eg Itsandra village and Bouni, and two other private beaches for hotel guests. Camping is possible near secluded public beaches; transport to remote places is not regular.

Nosy Be (Northern Madagascar) A few glorious beaches, such as Andilana and Ambatoloaka; diving and trekking available. Prices on Nosy Be are high; access is easiest by plane.

Ramena (Northern Madagascar) The best beach north of Sambava and a great place to relax for a few days. Close to Antsiranana, there are two very nice and cheap bungalow complexes to stay at.

Mahavelona (Eastern Madagascar) One of a few great beaches to stay along the eastern coast. Access is easy from Toamasina and Tana and there are many nice bungalow complexes right on the beach. ■

VISAS & DOCUMENTS
Passport

Naturally a passport is essential; it's the most basic travel document. To avoid theft in danger areas like the markets in Tana, or

damage while trekking, it may be an idea to leave your passport at the hotel (if it is secure) and take a photocopy with you.

Before planning your trip, ensure that your passport is valid for the entire period you will be away, and that it has several empty pages for stamp-happy Immigration officials.

Visas

All visitors to Madagascar must have a visa *before* arriving in the country. For the Comoros, all foreigners can obtain a visa on arrival by air or sea. The visa requirements for Mayotte are the same as for France. Refer to the individual Facts for the Visitor chapters for more information.

Visas for Nearby Countries

If you would need a visa for France, then you will also need one for Réunion and Mayotte. Visas are available at the French Embassy in Moroni, or at the Consulate in Tana. The French Consulate (☎ (261-2) 214 88), at the back of the embassy in Tana, is open from 7.30 to 11.30 am on weekdays. You must fill out three identical forms, provide one photo, and pay a hefty fee of up to FMg 160,000 (depending on where you are from). The visa can be collected later that afternoon.

For the Seychelles, everyone gets a visa on arrival; and for Mauritius, most foreigners can obtain a visa at the international airport. Visa requirements for South Africa and Kenya often change, so check before you leave home.

Travel Permits

The only permit you need for any travel is the official entrance permit for all national parks and reserves in Madagascar. There is also a not-so-official permit required to visit the marine reserve south of Mohéli in the Comoros. Refer to the individual chapters for more details.

Travel Insurance

A travel insurance policy to cover theft, loss and medical problems is a good idea. The policies handled by STA Travel and other student travel organisations are usually good value. Some policies offer lower and higher medical-expense options; the higher ones are chiefly for countries such as the USA which have extremely high medical costs. There is a wide variety of policies available; check the small print:

Some policies specifically exclude 'dangerous activities' which can include scuba diving, motorcycling, or even trekking. A locally acquired motorcycle licence is not valid under some policies.

You may prefer a policy which pays doctors or hospitals direct rather than one where you must pay on the spot and claim later. If you have to claim later make sure you keep all documentation. Some policies ask you to call back (reverse charges) to a centre in your home country where an immediate assessment of your problem is made.

Check that the policy covers ambulances or an emergency flight home, and not just back to the place where you purchased the policy.

Driving Licence & Permits

To hire a car in Madagascar you will need an international driving licence – but rarely is any form of documentation needed to rent a motorcycle. In the Comoros and Mayotte a French driving licence will do; otherwise, you will also need an international licence.

EMBASSIES

If you have an embassy or consulate in Madagascar or the Comoros (there is only a French Embassy in the latter), it's a good idea to register if you are planning to stay long. If going to remote areas you may want to provide them with a rough itinerary. Registering will make things easier should you lose your passport, have an accident or get lost. Refer to the Madagascar Facts for the Visitor and the Grande Comore chapters for lists of foreign embassies and consulates.

CUSTOMS

There is nothing particularly difficult or unusual about local Customs regulations; no Customs declaration forms are filled in when you arrive or leave. There are, however, strict laws about taking out any product which is antique, or made from an endangered species, such as coral, shells, furs etc.

Refer to the individual Facts for the Visitor

chapters for more information about what duty-free items you can bring into the countries.

MONEY
Costs

Madagascar is cheap and the Comoros aren't, which is why so many more people ignore the latter. Even if you have to pay for some items in foreign currencies and pay more for some things than locals, Madagascar is still good value. Decent low to middle-range accommodation in Tana and Nosy Be is comparatively pricey at about US$15 for a single or double, but if you can avoid these places good accommodation, including bungalows on the beach at Île Sainte Marie, cost from US$6 to US$10 per room. Malagasy meals cost about US$1; filling, tasty western meals are about US$3 each. Large bottles of beer cost from US$1 to US$1.50.

The bad news is that the overvalued Comoran franc, which is linked to the French franc, makes the Comoros pricey – about two to three times more expensive than Madagascar. Ordinary middle-range accommodation (there is very little in the bottom-end range) costs about US$30 for a double; sometimes slightly less for a single. Meals are pricey at about US$6 for decent western food.

Worse news is that Mayotte is even *more* expensive. The cheapest hotel room is US$30, and most places cost more. Western meals are around US$8 each, and there is very little Mahorais food to buy.

To save some money around the Comoros, travel in a group of three and share a room; buy your food at the markets; and try hitching rides on boats around the islands.

Multiple Pricing

In Madagascar airfares, mid to top-range hotels and entrance fees to museums have three levels of pricing: one for local Malagasy, another for foreign residents (ie diplomats, aid workers etc) and a third for foreign non-residents (ie you and me). There is almost nothing you can do about this.

Before you get angry, as some travellers do, remember that the average wage for the Malagasy is appallingly low and that you get a *lot* of Malagasy francs for your own currency.

Importantly, the cost of all local transport in Madagascar, including *taxis-brousse* and trains, as well as restaurants, bottom-end hotels and other low-level items, is the same for everyone.

Currency Exchange

French francs are easily the most convertible currency in the region, especially in the Comoros (where the Comoran franc and French franc are interchangeable), and on Mayotte, where only the French franc is used. Other major currencies, such as US dollars, UK pounds, Deutschmarks and Swiss francs, are also easy to change. Australian, New Zealand and Canadian dollars, South African rand and Mauritian or Seychelles rupees are less widely accepted and may cause you inconvenience.

Changing these major currencies (in cash or travellers' cheques) to local francs is easy in all major towns in both countries. See the Money sections in the individual Facts for the Visitor chapters for exchange rates and other details.

Credit cards are of limited use in Madagascar and the Comoros, except to pay for airline tickets and top-end hotels. On Mayotte, they are useful if you're staying at an up-market hotel or taking an organised tour. In Madagascar and Mayotte you can get cash advances in local currency on your Visa or MasterCard.

Tipping

Tipping is not the norm, except in up-market hotels in Tana, resorts on Grande Comore and Nosy Be (Madagascar), and generally in the French-influenced Mayotte. Tipping is generally not encouraged by local tourist authorities, but rounding up a restaurant bill to avoid carrying loose change or tipping for particularly good service is always appreciated by poorly paid staff.

Bargaining

In Madagascar and the Comoros (though not so much on Mayotte) bargaining for goods and services is a way of life, except in up-market hotels and when organising some transport or buying food. It particularly holds true for all market items and handicrafts – such commodities are considered to be worth whatever their owners can get for them. In either country the concept of a fixed price is virtually unknown except in mid to top-range hotels, restaurants and shops.

In smaller shops and markets, don't pay the first price asked. If you do, out of ignorance or guilt about how much cash you have on hand relative to the local economy, you'll not only be considered a half-wit but you'll be doing your fellow travellers a disservice. Such actions will create the impression that all foreigners are equally stupid and are willing to pay any outrageous price named!

Furthermore, tourists in well-visited areas who voluntarily pay higher than market value actually cause price increases. They thereby put some items and services out of reach of locals who generally have less disposable cash. And who can blame them? Why sell an item to a local when foreigners will pay twice as much? (This is a serious problem in any place visited by overland travel companies.)

Still, no matter how adept your bargaining skills you won't be able to get things as cheaply as the locals can – so don't get angry. To traders and owners of transport, hotels and cafes, foreigners represent wealth and it's of little consequence whether it's a valid assessment or not in your case. And remember there is no such thing as a 'right price'; when the buyer and seller are both happy about the price, it is then 'right'.

Bargaining is normally conducted in a friendly and spirited manner, though there are occasions when it degenerates into a bleak exchange of numbers (particularly if your command of French, Comoran or Malagasy is limited). Some vendors will actually start off at a price four (or more!) times higher than what they are prepared to accept, though it's usually lower than this. Decide what you want to pay or what others have told you they have paid; your first offer should be about half of this. At this stage the vendor will often laugh or feign outrage, but the price will quickly drop from his or her original quote to a more realistic level, especially if you make moves to leave. When the price drops for the first time, begin making better offers until you arrive at a mutually agreeable price.

There may be times when you cannot get a shopkeeper to lower the price to anywhere near what you know the product should cost. This probably means that many tourists have passed through and if you refuse to pay the outrageous prices, some other fool will.

There's no reason to lose your temper when bargaining. If you become fed up with an obstinate vendor or the effort seems a waste of time, politely take your leave. Sometimes vendors will change tack and call you back if they think their stubbornness may be losing a sale. If not, you can always look for another vendor or try again the following day.

POST & COMMUNICATIONS

Post

Every major town in both countries has a post office which works reasonably well, though the smaller ones may run out of stamps and service may be slow. Post to and from Madagascar and Mayotte is usually fine, but is less reliable in the Comoros (at the time of writing we have been waiting three months for postcards from the Comoros to reach Australia). To send and receive mail, especially at a poste restante, do it at Mayotte, Moroni or Tana.

In many addresses, you will see the letters BP, meaning *boîte postale*, the French words for post office box. These are regularly used for sending mail because normal addresses are complicated and unreliable.

Telephone

Telephone services in the region have improved markedly over the past few years, but making international calls is still not cheap. The quickest and least painful way to make a local, domestic or international call is to buy a *telecarte* (telephone card) for Madagascar, the Comoros or Mayotte; these can be used at most public telephones in the respective countries. Placing long-distance calls at the main telephone office in town is easier than it used to be, and only takes a few minutes in Tana. It will take longer elsewhere, so it's often best to wait until you are in a major city where communication facilities are better.

The telephone area codes for each major town and area are mentioned throughout the book and, for Madagascar, also listed in the Facts for the Visitor chapter. If it is not listed, for instance in a remote region, you will have to go through an operator to place the call. When dialling Mayotte from France, remember to add 0269 to the start of the number. (269 is still the normal code for calls to Mayotte from outside France.)

Fax & Email
From some buildings near the main post offices in Madagascar you can send and receive faxes, but try to wait until you are in Tana or somewhere more developed or used to dealing with foreigners. Like international telephone calls, prices for long-distance faxes are not cheap.

From a place at the back of the main post office in Moroni, one faxed page costs CF2000 to anywhere in the world. Faxes cost more from the main post office on Mayotte.

Email is slowly catching on in Madagascar, Mayotte and on Grande Comore, but we were unable to find any place where visitors can send or receive it. If you find one please send us an email and let us know!

BOOKS
Most books are published in different editions by different publishers in different countries. As a result, a book might be a hardcover rarity in one country while it's readily available in paperback in another. Fortunately, bookshops and libraries search by title or author, so your local bookshop or library can best advise you on the availability of the titles recommended here, and those listed in the Books section in the individual Facts for the Visitor chapters.

Books in English are extremely rare in Comoran and Malagasy bookshops so you're advised to bring reading material from home. Naturally paperbacks are best, and when you've finished with them you may be able to swap them with other travellers.

In preparation for shoestring travelling, you may want to take a look at a general work called *The Tropical Traveller* by John Hart.

Lonely Planet
If you're travelling further afield in the Indian Ocean or around southern or eastern Africa, Lonely Planet also publishes guides to *Mauritius, Réunion & Seychelles*; *Kenya; East Africa; South Africa, Lesotho & Swaziland*; *Zimbabwe, Botswana & Namibia*; *Malawi, Mozambique & Zambia*; and *Africa – the South*. For an extended journey through the African continent, there's *Africa on a shoestring*.

Lonely Planet travel atlases are available for *South Africa, Lesotho & Swaziland; Zimbabwe, Botswana & Namibia;* and for *Kenya*. Travellers will find the Lonely Planet *French phrasebook* useful in Madagascar and the Comoros.

ONLINE SERVICES
If you have access to the Internet it is definitely worthwhile checking out what is available on the World Wide Web about Madagascar and the Comoros. There are many sites dedicated to Malagasy and Comoran environmental issues, lemurs, music, birds and palms, to name just a few, but the sites tend to come and go so they aren't listed here.

The online services below contain more general information, but the list is by no means complete.

CARE
(http://www.care.org/world/profiles/comoros/html); background information about the Comoros from the aid agency

CIA
(http://www.odci.gov/cia/publications/95fact/ma.html – add cn.html for the Comoros or mf.html for Mayotte); excellent background information on Madagascar

Duke University
(http://www.duke.edu/web/primates.html); very interesting information on ecological issues, especially lemurs

Lonely Planet
(http://www.lonelyplanet.com); information provided by other travellers and updates

Madagascar Embassy
(http://www.embassy.org/madagascar); sometimes dated, but good general information for travellers

Madagascar On Line
(http://dts.dts.mg/creapro/madon); current politics and other general information in English and French

Madagascar Tribune
(http://www.jstechno.ch/creapo.mg/tribune); stories from the French-language daily newspaper in Madagascar

Midi Madagasikara
(http://dts.dts.mg/midi/midi.html); stories from the French-language daily newspaper in Madagascar

US State Dept
(http://travel.state.gov/comoros.html); travel information about the Comoros

NEWSPAPERS & MAGAZINES

Besides locally produced newspapers and magazines, which are printed mainly in French, French speakers can pick up recent copies of French newspapers, such as *Le Monde*, and various magazines. You are more likely to find these in major cities in Madagascar, and on Mayotte, though not in the remote islands of the Comoros.

English speakers may be able to pick up a copy of *Time* or *Newsweek* in Tana, Moroni or Mayotte, but don't be disappointed if the only thing you can read in English in Madagascar is the label on a bottle of Three Horses Beer.

RADIO & TV

In Tana, French speakers will want to tune to Alliance FM92, run by the local Alliance Française. You can pick up a leaflet from its office which details weekly programs, or just tune in for current affairs, talk shows and music. Most major cities in Madagascar, Mayotte and, sometimes, the Comoros, have programs in the French language. There is nothing in English or any other European language.

If you have a short-wave radio, you can easily pick up BBC Radio, Voice of America and other major stations from Europe (but not Radio Australia).

Most of the stuff on local TV is French, or dubbed into French. There is no English-language TV, but up-market hotels in Tana and on Grande Comore have satellite TV which broadcasts CNN news from the USA.

PHOTOGRAPHY & VIDEO
Film & Equipment

Film is normally more expensive in Madagascar and the Comoros than it is at home so stock up before you set off (see the Customs section in the relevant Facts for the Visitor chapters for duty-free allowances). There are photographic and processing shops in major towns, but take spare batteries for cameras and flash units since they're very expensive in Tana, Moroni and Mayotte, and normally not available elsewhere.

Other useful accessories to bring include a small flash, cable release, polarising (UV) filter, lens cleaning kit (fluid, tissue, aerosol), and silica-gel packs to protect against humidity. Also, make sure your equipment is insured.

Fujicolor or Kodacolor 100 are the most popular and readily available print films in Madagascar, the Comoros and Mayotte. If you're shooting slides you'll probably get the best results with Fujichrome 100, Velvia or Kodachrome 64; these will be almost impossible to find in Madagascar or the Comoros but are available on Mayotte. Polaroid film is only available on Mayotte.

Photography

The best times to take photographs on sunny days are the first two to three hours after sunrise, and the last two to three before sunset. This brings out the best colours and takes advantage of the colour-enhancing, long red rays cast by a low sun. At other times, colours will be washed out by harsh sunlight and glare, though it's possible to counter this by using a polarising (UV) filter. If you're shooting on beaches, remember to adjust for glare from water or sand. Remember to keep your photographic equipment well away from sand and salt water. Don't leave your camera for long in direct sunlight and don't store used film for long in the humid conditions because it will fade.

When photographing outdoors, take light readings on the subject and not the brilliant background or your subject will turn out underexposed. Likewise for people shots, dark faces will appear featureless if you set the exposure for the background light.

Video

Properly used, a video camera can give a fascinating record of your holiday. As well as videoing the obvious things – sunsets and spectacular views – remember to record some of the ordinary everyday details of life in the country. Often the most interesting things occur when you're actually intent on filming something else. Remember too that, unlike still photography, video 'flows'... so, for example, you can shoot scenes of countryside rolling past the train window to give an overall impression that isn't possible with ordinary photos.

Video cameras these days have amazingly sensitive microphones and you might be surprised how much sound will be picked up. This can also be a problem if there is a lot of ambient noise – filming by the side of a busy road might seem OK when you do it, but viewing it back home might simply give you a deafening cacophony of traffic noise. Two good rules for beginners are to try to film in long takes, and don't move the camera around too much. Otherwise, your video could well make your viewers seasick! If your camera has a stabiliser you can use it to obtain good footage while travelling on various means of transport, even on bumpy roads. And remember, you're on holiday – don't let the video take over your life and turn your trip into a Cecil B De Mille production.

Make sure you keep the batteries charged, and have the necessary charger, plugs and transformer for the country you are visiting. It is usually worth buying at least a few cartridges duty-free to start off your trip. Don't expect to be able to buy any spare parts or film in this part of the world. Finally, remember to follow the same rules regarding people's sensitivities as for still photography – having a video camera shoved in their face is probably even more annoying and offensive for locals than a still camera. Always ask permission first.

Restrictions

Don't take photographs of airports or anything that appears strategic or looks remotely like police or military property. In the Comoros, take care to avoid such subjects as the President's residence on the coast road between Moroni and Itsandra. The same applies around the Foreign Legion and defence establishments on Mayotte.

Photographing People

As in most places, the quest for the perfect 'people shot' will prove a photographer's greatest challenge. Photographing people, particularly dark-skinned people, requires more skill than snapping landscapes. Make sure you take the light reading from the subject's face, not the background. It also requires more patience and politeness.

While many Malagasy and Comorans will enjoy being photographed, others will be put off. Some Muslim Comorans consider photos to be graven images which are prohibited by the Koran. Other people may be superstitious about your camera, suspicious of your motives or simply interested in whatever economic advantage they can gain from your desire to photograph them.

The main point is that you must respect the wishes of the locals, however photogenic or colourful, who may be camera shy for whatever reason. Ask permission to photograph if a candid shot can't be made and don't insist or snap a picture anyway if permission is denied.

Often, people will allow you to photograph them provided you give them a copy of the photo for themselves, a real treasure in these countries. Understandably, people are sometimes disappointed not to see the photograph materialise immediately. If you don't carry a Polaroid camera make it clear that you'll have to take their address, and *please* send them a copy of the photo if you have promised to do so.

Photographing Wildlife

If you want to score some excellent wildlife shots effortlessly, a good lightweight 35mm single-lens reflex (SLR) camera, a UV filter, and a 70mm to 200mm zoom or telephoto lens should do the trick. If your subject is nothing but a speck in the distance or is up a tree, try to resist wasting film on it (unless you have a powerful lens) but keep the camera ready. Anything can happen at any time.

TIME

Madagascar, the Comoros and Mayotte are three hours ahead of UTC (Universal Time Coordinated) or GMT (Greenwich Mean Time). This means in the northern winter they are 11 hours ahead of Los Angeles, San Francisco and Vancouver; eight hours ahead of New York and Toronto; and three hours ahead of London (or two hours ahead from April to October). The region is one hour ahead of Johannesburg year-round and five hours behind Perth (Australia). There is no summer time in the region because the tropical days and nights are about the same length day in day out.

ELECTRICITY

Voltage for just about everywhere in Madagascar and the Comoros varies from 110V to 220V, depending on the area; to be on the safe side assume 220V when in doubt. All outlets in Madagascar, the Comoros and Mayotte take European-style two-pin round plugs.

All major towns have electricity 24 hours a day. Remote areas may not have electricity – for example Ranohira, in southern Madagascar, which is on the main travellers' route. Outside the main towns, on the more remote islands of the Comoros, and even sometimes on Mayotte, blackouts are not uncommon, so carry a torch (flashlight) and candles with you.

WEIGHTS & MEASURES

Madagascar, the Comoros and Mayotte use the metric system. For help converting between imperial and metric measures, refer to the table on the inside back cover of this book.

An odd unit of measure in use in Madagascar is known as the *kapoka*. Although it varies in size, it's normally defined as the amount of rice or other dry goods that will fit into an empty tin of Nestlé *lait sucre concentré* (condensed milk).

LAUNDRY

There are no laundry or dry-cleaning services in Madagascar or the Comoros, but there are on Mayotte. Detergents are widely available, but if you don't want to do your own washing your hotel can arrange for someone – usually a member of staff – to do it.

In a mid-range hotel in Tana, expect to pay about FMg 5000 to wash a pair of jeans, FMg 4500 for a shirt or blouse and FMg 1500 for underwear. In the Comoros the costs are higher – about CF750 for jeans, CF450 for a shirt/blouse and CF225 for underwear; on Mayotte everything is far more expensive, and you will pay as much as F25 (jeans), F20 (shirt/blouse) and F5 (underwear).

HEALTH

See the separate chapter at the end of this book for details of predeparture planning, precautions and remedies for visitors to Madagascar and the Comoros.

TOILETS

Virtually every hotel and bungalow complex in Madagascar and Mayotte has a private or communal European-style sit down toilet. They may not always be clean or have toilet paper, so you may want to bring your own.

(Toilet paper is easy to buy in Madagascar and Mayotte; less so in the Comoros.) Next to the toilet there will be an overflowing bucket which is where you put your used paper – not in the toilet because it will block the drain. In some places with an Islamic influence, like Mahajanga, and most bottom-(oops)-end hotels in the Comoros (but not Mayotte), most toilets are the squat-style hole in the ground.

There are virtually no public toilets anywhere. So if you are camping, or *really* have to go, you may be forced to stand or squat to relieve yourself in public like many locals do – whether it's a main street in Tana, or a tourist beach on Grande Comore.

WOMEN TRAVELLERS

Women travellers will have few problems in this region. If you travel long enough you may come across the very occasional macho idiot, but he is more often an expat or fellow traveller than a local man. Malagasy men are relatively easy to dissuade or ignore, and they invariably respond appropriately to a stern *non!* At Malagasy beaches and tourist hot spots, where women may dress more informally, men tend to become a little more annoying because they are under the impression that foreign women there are 'easier prey'.

Women travellers have generally found Comoran men to be charming and well-mannered. If a Comoran man is interested, his intentions are obvious from the start but not intrusive, and they also understand the word *non*! Dressing appropriately will also help Comoran men understand that a lone women is not 'free and easy'. Outside of the resort beaches in the Comoros never wear shorts, sleeveless shirts or bathing costumes; pack skirts and sleeved shirts as well as a couple of scarves which will cover your hair if visiting mosques or Comoran homes.

Mayotte is far more relaxed and has a permanent 'resort' atmosphere, so shorts for locals and visitors are almost mandatory.

GAY & LESBIAN TRAVELLERS

Homosexuality in Madagascar and the Comoros, including Mayotte, is not illegal – but it is in Madagascar if a male or female is under 21 years old. Homosexuality is not practised openly and no places or organisations cater for gay and lesbian travellers. As with relations between heterosexual western couples travelling in the region – both married and unmarried – gay and lesbian travellers should exercise discretion and refrain from displaying overt affection towards each other in public.

DISABLED TRAVELLERS

Madagascar and the Comoros cater entirely for able-bodied foreigners, so disabled travellers will find it very difficult to see much of the island without problems. Overland travel is only possible for the fit, and for people who can meld into a sardine can-like taxi-brousse. Also, there are no wheelchair facilities anywhere; hospitals are poor, at best, and rarely cater for special needs; and footpaths overflow with people.

Having said that, if you stick to flying to developed places like Île Sainte Marie, Taolagnaro (Fort Dauphin), Antsiranana (Diego Suarez) and Nosy Be; use chartered taxis or hire a vehicle; and stay in up-market hotels, problems will be minimised. Always bring whatever equipment and medications you may need, and consider bringing an able-bodied companion.

SENIOR TRAVELLERS

While most visitors are young, there is no reason why senior travellers cannot enjoy a visit to the region as long as your vision is good, you are not incapacitated, and are in reasonable health.

You may want to select a few slower-paced and developed destinations, fly rather than take uncomfortable and tedious overland transport, and stay in better hotels. Alternatively, go on an organised tour (although none of the local or foreign travel companies cater especially for senior travellers). Take all medication and special equipment you need with you, and don't expect any special care from the hospitals in the region.

TRAVEL WITH CHILDREN

With their marvellous beaches and national parks, Madagascar and the Comoros are great places to take the kids. An increasing number of French people take theirs to the islands as independent travellers, or on packaged tours. Children can often enhance your encounters with local people because they are great conversation openers, and often possess little of the self-consciousness and sense of cultural differences which can inhibit interaction between adults.

Nevertheless, travelling with children can be hard work; keeping them entertained and making sure they don't fall under a taxi-brousse can be tiresome. Ideally the burden needs to be shared between two adults. There are no general safety or health problems about travelling with children in the region, but you may need to take extra care about food hygiene because children can be more susceptible to stomach bugs. You should take most of their basic needs like toys, nappies (diapers), powders etc, though some of these things may be available in Tana, Mayotte and Moroni.

For more information about the various joys and hassles of travelling with children, refer to the excellent *Travel with Children* by Lonely Planet's own Maureen Wheeler; she has managed to take her children to many places around the world – and survived.

DANGERS & ANNOYANCES

Travelling around Madagascar is not dangerous and you should never be paranoid about safety – but it pays to be prepared and pre-warned.

The good news is that the Comoros, as yet uncorrupted by tourism, must be one of the world's safest countries for travellers. That doesn't mean there's no crime, only that it's negligible. The Muslim Comorans resign themselves to their fate, ascribing their economic standing, whatever it may be, to the will of Allah. To resort to crime, they believe, would cast both social and divine shame upon the perpetrator's entire family. Even the most ruthless character would think twice before doing such a thing.

Security

Parts of Madagascar do present some potential security problems for visitors. Although rural areas are relatively safe, provincial cities are experiencing growing crime rates and Tana is becoming increasingly risky for foreign travellers. It's often quoted that Tana is statistically safer than London or New York, but the figures don't take into account that most crime in Tana is directed at foreigners and others who appear to have something to lose. National origin and skin colour are irrelevant; obvious foreigners or those who appear to have something of value (this extends to foreign-made trainers and T-shirts bearing catchy slogans) are at risk.

Remember: there's no call for paranoia and certain basic precautions will help minimise risks while still allowing you to enjoy the best of what Madagascar – and Tana – have to offer.

Pre-Departure Precautions Travel insurance is essential for the replacement of valuables. The cost of a good policy is a worthwhile price to pay for peace of mind, minimum disturbance or even abrupt termination of your travel plans.

Loss through violence or petty theft is an emotional and stressful experience which can be reduced if you think ahead. The less you carry with you, the less you have to lose. Don't bring jewellery, chains or expensive watches; if you do wear a watch, use a cheapie worth a few dollars. Even better, buy a cheap watch in a local market and keep it hidden in your pocket. (The author had his cheap watch ripped right off his wrist at 6 pm on the main street of Tana and a colleague had his watch pinched from inside his pocket!) It may also be considered an insensitive affront to the less fortunate if tourists stroll around flaunting expensive jewellery, watches and cameras.

Be prepared for the worst – make three copies of your important records: a photocopy of your passport (page with passport number, name, photograph, location where issued and expiration date and all valid visas); travellers' cheque numbers; credit card numbers; airline tickets; contact addresses, etc. Keep one copy with you, one with your belongings and the other with a travelling companion if possible – if not, leave it with someone at home whom you can ring if required.

Accessories Backpacks should be fitted with double zippers which can be secured using small combination locks. Padlocks are also good, but are easier to pick. A thick backpack cover or modified canvas sack improves protection against pilfering and general wear and tear. Double zippers on your daypack can be secured with safety pins to reduce the risk of petty thieving. A bicycle combination lock or padlock (steel or chain) is recommended for chaining luggage to hotel fixtures, like sinks, when you're away from your room.

In dodgy hotels, a padlock or combination lock of medium size is useful to replace the padlock you find on your hotel door. Rubber wedges are also handy to prevent access to doors or windows.

Don't keep all your valuables together: distribute them about your person and baggage to avoid the risk of losing everything in one fell swoop.

Various types of money belts are available which can be worn around the waist, neck or shoulder. Those made of leather or cotton material are more comfortable than the synthetic variety. Money belts are only useful if worn *under* clothing – pouches or 'bum bags' worn outside clothing are easy prey and should never be used.

The recognised danger area in Tana is the Zoma, the market in the Analakely district, where thousands of umbrella-crowned stalls turn the streets into often impenetrable mazes of vendors, shoppers and shady characters. Although Friday is the main market day there are permanent stalls every day (fewer on Sundays), so always take care when browsing and shopping.

The open market harbours bag and camera snatchers and skilful pickpockets. The extra pair of eyes provided by a travelling companion is an obvious asset, but the best advice is to carry nothing but enough small change for your intended purchases. Some women have even had expensive-looking earrings ripped from their ears – so always be careful.

Precautions There are certain key things you can do to reduce attention from criminals. Your style of dress should be casual and inexpensive. Never carry a daypack in Tana unless it's absolutely necessary; if you must, then wear it local fashion: strapped in front like a kangaroo's pouch. In public transport, taxi-brousse stations, restaurants, shops or elsewhere, whenever you have to put your pack down, keep your foot or a chair leg through the strap. Both of these precautions will make things more difficult for furtive fingers or bag-slashers.

If you have a camera, don't wander around with it dangling over your shoulder or around your neck – keep it out of sight. It's also unwise to keep it in a swanky camera bag which would be an obvious target. If you want to carry a camera in Tana keep it in your daypack or use an opaque plastic bag from a local shop.

Get used to keeping small change and a few banknotes in a shirt pocket to pay for small purchases and taxi or bus fares, so you don't have to extract large amounts of money which could quickly attract attention. This will also be useful if you are assailed by a mugger. If you carry a wallet keep it in a zippered or buttoned inside pocket; don't carry it in your back pocket, and don't use it on public transport or in crowded places where it might attract unwelcome attention.

Before arriving in a city (especially Tana), have a map or at least a rough idea about orientation and try to plan your schedule so you don't arrive at night. Be observant and learn to move purposefully like a street-smart local. The extra pair of eyes of a travelling companion is also useful, as solo travellers are more easily distracted.

The Streets Thieves watch for travellers and tourists leaving hotels, bus terminals, railway stations, banks, tourist sights –

places with lots of foreigners – then follow their targets.

If you notice you're being followed or closely observed, it helps to pause and look straight at the person(s) involved, or, if you're not alone, simply point out the person(s) to your companion. This makes it clear that the element of surprise favoured by petty criminals has been lost.

In Tana – *especially* in Tana – foreigners should never venture too far from their hotel on foot after dark, walk to the railway station early in the morning or use stairways at night. If you ignore this warning, your chances of being eventually mugged are high and there have been some nasty incidents.

For more tips on how best to avoid any problems in Tana, refer to the Dangers & Annoyances section in the Antananarivo chapter.

Public Transport Taxi drivers worldwide are known for their less than straightforward dealings, and those in Madagascar and the Comoros are no exception. However, while they'll do anything they can to overcharge you, you're at very little risk of robbery or other shady dealings from taxi drivers in either country.

When entering or leaving a taxi, it's advisable (particularly for solo travellers) to keep a passenger door open while loading or unloading luggage – particularly if this is being done by someone other than the driver. This reduces the ease with which a taxi can drive off with the luggage, leaving you behind. If you are concerned about your driver make a note of the car's registration number and report it to the police if necessary.

A neater solution for those who travel light is to fit luggage inside the taxi rather than in the boot. However, never leave anything lying loose on the seat. In Tana there have been incidents of bag snatching through open windows of taxis. Before starting, question the presence of any characters accompanying the driver and don't hesitate to take another taxi if you feel uneasy.

When getting in a taxi-brousse, the driver or tout will almost always offer to take your luggage and put it in the vehicle. Some travellers go berserk when this happens. Don't panic, he is only helping you to claim a spot on that particular vehicle, but stay close to your bag. It is not unusual for a taxi-brousse, with your luggage inside or on top, to suddenly speed off without you to look for other passengers. Again, don't panic (too much). If you are concerned, always stay in the taxi-brousse. But remember that taxi and taxi-brousse drivers have a lot to lose (ie their licence and therefore livelihood) by stealing foreigners' luggage, and if there are plenty of other locals around it will be almost impossible for someone to secretly steal your huge backpack even if they want to.

Try to avoid travelling overland on public transport after dark because it often gets cold and your gear will be less secure at night. Also, main roads have no street lights, and taxis-brousse have inadequate headlights, so drivers won't see the numerous potholes, stray zebus and wide ox-carts.

Hotels If you consider your hotel to be reliable, place valuables in its safe and get a receipt. Make sure you package your valuables in a small, double-zippered bag which can be padlocked, or use a signed seal which will easily reveal any tampering. Count money and travellers' cheques before and after retrieving them from the safe – this should quickly identify any attempts to extract single bills or cheques which might otherwise go unnoticed.

If possible, use your own padlock or combination lock on the room door. Although it's not recommended that you leave valuables in your room, some travellers use a bicycle chain to fix baggage to immovable fixtures like a sink; thieves will then have to slash your bag open or remove the sink to steal it.

The Beach Don't take any valuables to the beach and never tempt a passing thief by leaving your belongings unattended. Just take the minimum: swimsuit, towel, hat, T-shirt, sunscreen and enough money for a meal and drinks.

Officials

Malagasy and Comoran government officials are, for the most part, courteous and helpful, but the administration of important jobs is believed to require lots of time so lots of time is normally allotted. When you're told to 'come back tomorrow afternoon' (or next Monday, or in three weeks time...), or you're faced with what you consider an unreasonable wait for a particular service, becoming agitated or impatient will get you nowhere. Officials like nothing more than teaching foreigners a lesson in legendary Malagasy and Comoran patience.

A better ploy is to smile, make a bit of pleasant conversation, maybe explain that you have a plane to catch later that afternoon (or whatever), and ask if perhaps there might be some way the process could be expedited, just this once. If that doesn't work, you're probably stuck with the wait unless you're willing to risk offering some sort of a *pourboire* (tip) for speedy service. However, setting such a precedent is not advised and may cause inconvenience to future travellers.

On the island of Mohéli, in the Comoros, we were stopped by bored officials from the Immigration, police and Customs offices three times within two days (but only one other time during three months' research in Madagascar and the Comoros). Passports were checked and a few standard questions were asked but there were no hassles. If you get stopped, just smile, answer succinctly and move on quietly.

Riots

While Madagascar is comparatively peaceful for a country plagued by so many problems, rioting is not an uncommon form of protest. Some are racially motivated; for instance, during the Mahajanga riots in 1977 the large Comoran community was set upon. Hundreds were killed and the rest were airlifted to the Comoros.

Violence in Toliara and other cities has been directed at Indo-Pakistani traders, who are resented for their business acumen and have become the scapegoats for the system.

The French expatriate population has suffered to a lesser extent, but other foreigners of European origin have never been a target for anything but very occasional robbery and petty crime.

Then there were the 'kung fu' riots in 1985 which left 31 dead. Kung fu had become a craze after Bruce Lee films reached the country in the 1970s, spawning numerous clubs with predominantly right wing memberships. When the president outlawed the clubs, kung fu brigades took to the street and vented their wrath upon the bully boys in the presidential youth movement (Tanora Tonga). The kicking, screaming and chopping rebels were eventually subdued and 'pacified' by Government tanks.

During the time of research, peaceful protests were held in the Comoros by unpaid public servants. At any time around an election (which seems to be often), marches and gatherings in Madagascar have the potential to be volatile.

Police & the Army

The police and army may not be entirely effective, but neither are they very bothersome or intrusive, and are mostly disciplined enough not to throw their weight around. In all three countries civil liberties are generally respected. In the Comoros, the presidential guard on Grande Comore should be kept at a respectful distance.

In Madagascar, it's often difficult to distinguish army from police and vice versa because they wear a mix 'n match variety of camouflage and khaki uniforms. The youths in green uniforms are doing their two years' compulsory national service.

If there is trouble, contact your embassy for advice (or the nearest French consulate if you're in the provinces). If you have any trouble with rip-off merchants, threaten to report them to the relevant tourist department or *direction du tourisme*.

Whether local or foreign, drivers of any vehicle may be stopped for a vehicle or licence check. They are normally looking for defects on taxis-brousse (not hard to find!) and usually leave foreigners alone. But if your vehicle or papers are not up to scratch, a small on-the-spot 'fee' may be requested (this is an unofficial fee, but it is normal practice).

In Tana, we were stopped by some plain clothes policemen in the Place de l'Indépendance. They showed us an unimpressive identity card and politely demanded to see our passports (ostensibly to check the validity of the Malagasy visa). This was unnecessary and annoying (especially because we were robbed a few hours later in Zoma market – and there wasn't a policeman in sight!). Before handing over your passport to anyone on the street, always be entirely sure about their motives and identity; perhaps check with a uniformed policemen first.

Begging

There is almost no open begging in the Comoros. In fact, what little begging one encounters is nearly always of the *m'zungu, donnez-moi un cadeau* ('foreigner, give me a present') variety – opportunistic begging started and encouraged by altruistic foreigners who indiscriminately bestow gifts on strangers. For further comments, see under Gift Giving later in this section.

In Madagascar, however, it's another story. One of the most distressing aspects of travel there is the constant presence of beggars. Foreigners are mobbed with requests of all sorts and overloaded consciences must constantly sort out who receives and who doesn't.

Since giving even a pittance to every beggar encountered will be financially impossible for most visitors, each traveller must judge for themselves what constitutes an appropriately humanitarian response. Some travellers choose to give only to the most pathetic cases or to those enterprising individuals who provide some value for money, such as by singing or playing a musical instrument.

Many beggars, especially the throngs on the streets of Tana, are desperately poor, uneducated, homeless people. Many are immigrants from rural areas who are in genuine need, and most of these are women and children with no chance of employment, no help from the government and no hope of ever changing their situation. Then there are the elderly and physically or mentally impaired who have no other possible means of support. Any of these people may be especially good candidates for a small donation. For those who go begging for bones, scraps and leftovers, or others who are struggling to change their situations, a bowl of soup or a nutritious hot meal will go a long way.

It's best not to give money to the numerous children who beg since it will lead to their exploitation by unscrupulous adults; give the impression that something can be had for nothing; and encourage the children or the parents or minders to forego any possible schooling. For a child who appears hungry, a piece of fruit, bread or any other healthy snack will be appreciated; if such gifts are refused and money is demanded, it should be fairly obvious what's going on.

If beggars (or hawkers) become too persistent, the Malagasy term for 'no' *(tsy misy)* is far more effective than the French *non*, regardless of how loudly you scream the latter.

Gift Giving

Away from the capital, most begging is opportunistic and for many visitors is the least appealing aspect of Madagascar. At first, it may seem charming to be surrounded by eager children (and often adults), hands extended, demanding *cadeaux, stylos, bonbons, monnaies* (gifts, pens, sweets, coins) and so on, but it soon becomes a damned nuisance and renders impossible any real communication between foreigners and otherwise charming locals.

This is a growing problem worldwide, but it's particularly severe in Madagascar and is perhaps caused by the nature of the easily disrupted traditional society. Western visitors from high-tech, fast-paced countries are rarely able to remain long enough to appreciate the uniqueness of the country and its long-established culture, traditions governing ethics and social interaction.

Many visitors to rural areas are shocked by the apparently 'backward' or 'primitive' conditions they encounter. Moved to compare the locals' lot with their own, they suffer pangs of conscience or feel outrage at inequalities. Hoping to salve feelings of guilt or inspire goodwill, they dole out such western goodies as sweets, pens, cigarettes, money, etc. In fact, some foreign tour agencies actually advise their clients to carry along 'sweets and pens as gifts for local children'.

While this generosity is undoubtedly well-intentioned, the long-term consequences of indiscriminate gift giving are undeniable. What at first appears to be a magnanimous gesture and a salve for the conscience is actually one of tourism's most destructive and disruptive forces.

With the political, economic and environmental problems that plague Madagascar, the effects are magnified. Gifts of sweets and cigarettes cause dental and health problems which the Malagasy have no means to remedy. Gifts of money impose a foreign system of values and strain established systems of barter and mutual help. Begging for pens from foreigners becomes little more than a game for children who have no schools or paper.

The damage isn't confined to any one facet of the population. In areas where there's a lot of tourism, outside influences can erode pride, identity and self-sufficiency as people come to expect (and in extreme cases, depend upon) the handouts. In more traditional areas, people may even be innocently inspired to migrate to Tana in search of the easy goodies doled out by outsiders; their chances of success could not be worse.

So, please don't play Father Christmas or Uncle Sam and create beggars of a traditionally proud and independent people. If you wish to be accepted as a friend and fellow human being, the encounters will be more pleasant for everyone if you perhaps share a conversation, teach a game or show a photograph of your friends or family.

In remote villages, when a gift becomes appropriate (for example, after you've shared a meal with a family or enjoyed a long and pleasant discussion) share something that won't disrupt the local culture or lifestyle, such as fruit, vegetables, rice or a useful item purchased at the local market.

Community Help Those who are serious about making a positive impact in Madagascar or the Comoros should look for opportunities to help at the community level. The greatest challenges at the moment include the improvement of health and educational standards in both rural and urban areas, promotion of environmental conservation, wise use of agricultural land and looking after street children.

Individuals will be able to help most effectively by donating materials to local schools or hospitals; contributing to locally active charities with proven track records; and volunteering their time and expertise on worthwhile aid, agricultural or conservation projects. Some organisations involved in local human development which would certainly welcome donations are listed under Volunteer Organisations later in this chapter.

Marine Dangers

Unless you're a marine biologist, don't touch coral, shells or fish – some of them sting, cut and occasionally kill. In particular, watch out for sea urchins; the gaudy and easily recognisable lionfish with its poisonous spined fins; and the cleverly camouflaged and extremely poisonous stonefish. Also, learn to recognise cone shells and never disturb one; their sting can be deadly.

When diving or snorkelling, wear full-shoe fins. Wear plastic reef shoes or other suitably tough footwear when windsurfing, sailing or participating in other water sports.

Currents can be tricky so don't swim or allow yourself to drift too far from the boat or shore. Keep away from the surf breaking on the reef edge or anywhere else for that matter; one hefty wave can turn a human being into fish fodder!

The Mozambique Channel and the east coast of Madagascar are some of the most shark-infested waters in the world. To keep

Coral

Many of the coastlines in Madagascar and the Comoros are fringed by coral reefs – fragile environments of calcareous deposits secreted by tiny marine animals known as polyps. The glorious white sand beaches of the Indian Ocean are composed of dead coral, shells and marine diatoms ground up by millennia of wave action. Without the reefs, many of these beaches would eventually erode and disappear. The reefs also provide shelter and habitat for numerous fish, shells, crustaceans, sea urchins and other marine life, which in turn provide a food source for larger fish as well as humans, both directly and indirectly.

Coral is usually stationary and often looks decidedly flowery, but in fact it's an animal – and a hungry carnivorous one at that. Although a 3rd century AD Greek philosopher surmised its faunal nature, coral was generally considered to be a plant until about 250 years ago.

Corals are Coelenterates, a class of animals which also includes sea anemones and jellyfish. The true reef-building corals, or Scleractinia, are distinguished by their lime skeletons. These almost indestructible skeletons actually form the reef, which gradually builds up as new coral continually builds on dead coral.

Coral takes a number of forms, but all are distinguished by polyps – tiny, tube-like fleshy creatures which resemble their close relations, the anemones. The top of the 'tube' is open and ringed by waving tentacles which sting and draw passing prey into the polyp's stomach (the open space inside the tube). Each polyp is an individual creature which can reproduce by splitting to form a coral colony of separate but closely related polyps. Although each polyp catches and digests its own food the nutrition passes between the polyps to the whole colony. Most coral polyps only feed at night; during the day they withdraw into their hard limestone skeleton and it is only after dark that a coral reef can be seen in its full, colourful glory.

Hard corals come in many forms. One of the most common and easiest to recognise is the staghorn coral, which grows by budding off new branches from the tips. Brain corals are huge and round with a surface looking very much like a human brain. They grow by adding new base levels of skeletal matter and expanding outwards. Flat or sheet corals, like plate coral, expand at their outer edges. Many corals can take different shapes depending on their environment. Staghorn coral can branch out in all directions in deeper water or form flat tables when they grow in shallow water.

Like their reef-building relatives soft corals are made up of individual polyps, but they do not form a hard limestone skeleton. Without the skeleton which protects hard coral it would seem likely that soft coral would fall prey to fish. But they seem to remain relatively immune, either because of toxic substances in their tissues or because of the presence of sharp limestone needles which protect the polyps. Soft corals can move around and will sometimes engulf and kill off a hard coral.

Coral catch their prey by means of stinging nematocysts. Some corals can give humans a painful sting and the fern-like stinging hydroid should be given a wide berth.

Coral Reef Symbiosis

A number of reef species engage in interesting symbiotic relationships, where two unrelated species get together in some activity for their mutual good.

The best recorded and, to the casual onlooker, most visible of these relationships is probably that of the anemone fish and the anemone. The brightly coloured anemone fish is a type of damselfish which lives among the stinging tentacles of sea anemones. The bright orange clown anemone fish has white vertical stripes edged with black, and is one of the most instantly recognisable fishes on the reef. A typical group of anemone fish will consist of several males and one larger female. They spend their entire life around the anemone, emerging briefly to feed then diving back into the protective tentacles at the first sign of danger. Anemone fish are not naturally immune to the anemone's sting; it is thought they gradually acquire immunity by repeatedly brushing themselves against the tentacles. Possibly they coat themselves with a layer of the anemone's mucus and the anemone does not sting the fish, just as its tentacles avoid stinging one another.

The relationship is probably somewhat one-sided: the anemone fish may attract other fish within the anemone's grasp, but an anemone can live without them and anemone fish are never seen without a protective anemone nearby.

Another interesting reef relationship involves the cleaner wrasse, which performs a service for larger fish. The little wrasse set themselves up at 'cleaner stations', perform a small 'dance' to indicate they're ready for action, then wait for customers. Larger fish are attracted to the dance and the cleaner wrasse zips around nibbling off fungal growth, dead scales, parasites and the like. They will actually swim right into the mouth of larger fish to clean their teeth! Obviously this must be a tempting opportunity for the larger fish to get a quick free meal, but cleaner-fish are not threatened while they're at work.

The cleaner stations are an important part of reef life; some fish regularly travel considerable distances for a clean and brush up, and experimental removal of the cleaner-fish from a section of reef has resulted in an increase in diseased and unhealthy fish, and a fall in the general fish population. Certain varieties of shrimps also act as fish-cleaners, but in nature every situation presents an opportunity for some other creature and the reef also has false cleaners. These tiny fish masquerade as cleaners and then quickly take a bite out of the deceived larger fish. They've been known to take a nip at swimmers!

Even coral itself takes part in a symbiotic relationship. Within the cells of coral polyps are tiny single cell plants known as zoocanthellae. Like other plants they utilise sunlight to create energy and they also consume carbon dioxide produced by the coral. Their presence enables coral to grow much faster.

Sex & Coral

For the coral, sex may be infrequent (it only happens once a year) but when the time comes, it's certainly spectacular. Some colonies of coral polyps are all male or all female; polyps of other colonies are hermaphrodite, ie both male and female. In a few types of coral, hermaphrodite polyps can produce their own young which are released at various times over the year. In most cases, however, the sperm of these polyps cannot fertilise their own eggs or other eggs from the same colony.

Although the mass spawning which creates new coral only takes place once a year, the build up to the big night lasts for six months or more. During that time the eggs, which are initially white, turn pink, red, orange and other bright colours as they ripen. At the same time, male polyps develop testes and produce sperm.

The big event comes in late spring or early summer, beginning a night or two after a full moon and building to a crescendo on the fourth, fifth and sixth nights. At this time water temperatures are ideal and there's a minimum of tidal variation. The eggs and sperm from the hermaphrodites are bundled together and a half-hour before spawning time the bundles are 'set': they are held ready at the mouth of the polyp and are clearly visible through the thin tissue. Suddenly, all across the reef, these tiny bundles are released and are allowed to float upward towards the surface.

Remarkably, all over the reef this spawning takes place simultaneously. Different colonies release their egg and sperm bundles, single sex polyps eject their sperm or their eggs and everything floats upward. The egg and sperm bundles are large enough to be seen with the naked eye and are spectacular when released en masse. The release has been described as a fireworks display or an inverted snowstorm. Since the event can be so accurately predicted divers are often able to witness it.

Once at the surface the bundles break up and the sperm swim off in search of eggs of the same coral species. Obviously corals of the same species must spawn at the same time in order to unite sperm and eggs of different colonies. It's not easy for an individual sperm to find the right egg amid the swarm, but biologists believe that by spawning all at once they reduce the risk of being consumed by the numerous marine creatures which would prey on them. By spawning soon after the full moon the small tidal variation means there is more time for fertilisation to take place before waves and currents sweep them away.

Once fertilisation has occurred, the egg cells begin to divide and within a day have become swimming coral larvae known as planulae. These are swept along by the current, but sink to the bottom after several days and, if the right spot is found, the tiny larvae become coral polyps and a new coral colony is begun.

Coral Reef Conservation

In the interest of preserving this complex and vital environment, visitors may want to consider the following recommendations:

* Avoid touching or breaking coral branches, whether or not they appear to be dead.
* Don't practice sailboarding or boating in shallow lagoons where coral is present.
* Leave shells, starfish, sea urchins and other creatures where you find them.
* If at all possible, avoid walking on coral beds; swim or stick to the sandy bottoms.
* Don't fish in reef areas; anchors, hooks, harpoons, nets and other fishing apparatus are deadly to coral.
* Don't throw rubbish into the sea from the shore or from boats. It winds up fouling reefs and beaches.
* Resist buying shells, coral jewellery and other marine products, regardless of their origin. By avoiding this largely illegal trade, you're preserving the reefs in other parts of the world. ■

risks to a minimum, seek local advice in unfamiliar areas, don't swim too far from shore (not a good idea, anyway), avoid swimming during the late afternoon, and keep away from the mouths of rivers and ravines.

Unfortunately, locals often use the ocean and beaches in lieu of toilets and a proper sewerage system. While this is far less common in places where tourists are likely to congregate, never swim in the ocean near a main town, and look out for nasty bits and pieces floating in the water and lying on the sand (and, often, on the streets).

LEGAL MATTERS

Almost without exception, foreigners are subject to the laws of the country they are in. If you break the law in Madagascar and the Comoros you will subject to their penalties, and on Mayotte, French law.

Of course, growing, possessing, using and selling any normally illegal drug will result in long gaol sentences. Madagascar, the Comoros and Mayotte don't have any peculiar laws. If you do get arrested, immediately ask to see a representative of your country, and if you don't speak French, find someone who speaks your language.

ACTIVITIES

For information about diving, snorkelling, water sports, whale-watching and cycling in Madagascar, the Comoros and Mayotte, refer to the Activities section in the individual Facts for the Visitor chapters.

The following section provides an overview of, as well as some suggestions about, trekking and hiking around Madagascar and the Comoros. For details about specific treks and hikes in the Comoros, refer to the special Trekking in the Comoros section later in the book, and the individual chapters for each region of Madagascar. Information about camping can be found under Accommodation later in this section.

Hiking

Madagascar, and especially the Comoros, are perfect for exploring on foot: some roads are so bad that taking public transport is always uncomfortable and sometimes impossible. You will certainly get off the 'beaten track' and visit places where very few travellers ever go. And you will be able to soak up the scenery far more than if you are squashed into the back of a taxi-brousse.

Long-distance hiking in the Comoros is not possible because the islands are so small, but camping is fine. However, overnight hiking and camping are not actively encouraged by authorities on Mayotte. It is best to ask about current regulations and any official campgrounds on the island at the tourist office on Mayotte.

Naturally, there are a few things to know about hiking in Madagascar and the Comoros. The first thing to do is find the best and most detailed map available. The best source in Madagascar is the FTM office in Tana, which has very detailed 1:100,000 maps that are ideal for hikers (see under Maps in the Madagascar Facts for the Visitor chapter). You can only buy maps (which are suitable for hiking) of each island in the Comoros in Moroni and Mayotte – or get them at home.

In many areas of Madagascar, the landscape changes little and it's easy to get lost – so bring a reliable compass. Be aware that many people in rural areas have little, if any, literacy skills, and if they can read they may not understand a map. On the other hand, if you get lost, they'll be happy to help, and will walk with you and show you the way, even if it's several kilometres – but only if they understand where you wish to go.

Few rural Malagasy or Comorans speak French (none speak English), so buying a Malagasy or Comoran dictionary is very useful. A very handy phrase in Malagasy is *Ity ny lalana mahankany ...'* which means 'Is this the way to ...?' Be prepared for constant staring and frequent demands for medical provisions – a difficult thing to cope with.

Be careful where you pitch your tent; locals may scare you with tales of nasty zebu rustlers, but we have never heard of any foreigner having problems. In villages, people are happy to help, and you can usually sleep in a school or local home. You will be expected to pay for this: about FMg 10,000 (in Madagascar) and CF1000 (in the Comoros) per night per person for accommodation and two meals is reasonable.

And finally, as obvious as it sounds, don't forget to carry water containers. Very little drinkable water is normally available except in villages. You should always boil or purify drinking water in rural areas. The best idea is to carry a pocket-sized water filter if you can. There may not be enough water to wash thoroughly, and lakes or rivers can often be the source of bilharzia.

Hiring a Guide When walking around the national parks in Madagascar, guides are compulsory and you will have little choice about which guide you have. For other treks, such as crossing the Masoala Peninsula in north-eastern Madagascar, as well as arranging a pirogue trip down the Tsiribihina River (western Madagascar), a guide is really necessary, but not compulsory. They will help organise the trip, find porters, locate trails, introduce you to locals, cook food, make shelters and so on. A guide will also enhance your ability to communicate with local people and help you to understand local *fady* (Malagasy taboos) and traditions.

However, before hiring a guide, there are a few things to consider:

- Although more and more guides are learning a bit of English (and a few are working on German or Italian), for the most effective communication with guides you will need some knowledge of French.

- Few guides are formally trained and many so-called 'guides' (and especially porters) are simply taking advantage of a money-making opportunity during the agricultural off-season.

- If you merely want someone who has been reared in the area, knows about local customs and won't get you too lost, you should have no problem finding a guide. If you have a special interest or want someone who's knowledgeable about a certain subject, you may have to spend some time searching.

- Seek recommendations from other travellers or from local businesspeople who regularly deal with tourists.

- Establish in advance who will carry what. Some guides won't mind carrying their own supplies as well as some of the food and other community goods, but others will require that the client either carry everything or hire a porter to carry it.

- Be particularly wary when hiring porters. Nearly anyone can work as a porter and, occasionally, access to mystery laden foreign backpacks or high-tech gear inspires greater temptation than some can handle. To avoid problems, try to hire people who are experienced and are well-known (for all the right reasons) in the community.

- For longer trips, the guide will normally provide cooking pots and utensils while the client is expected to provide food for the entire entourage for the length of the trip.

- When purchasing supplies, guides will often encourage you to buy far more than you could use in a hope that you'll bestow any leftovers upon them after the trip. Whether or not this bothers you, you'll still have to carry all the extra stuff on the trip – or pay someone to carry it.

- Be wary of an old trick. Your guide tells you that there are other people accompanying you on the trek, thereby sharing the overall cost. Lo and behold, the morning of your departure, these unknown, fellow travellers can't come because they are 'sick' (food poisoning is always a good 'un). You will then have to quickly decide whether to go on the trek anyway – and therefore pay far more than originally quoted – or cancel it.

- Although groups of clients normally hire one guide between them, if you have more than five people in a group, your chances of getting close to wildlife will be slim and the guide will exhaust himself trying to cater for everyone. You'll have better luck splitting into smaller groups and hiring more than one guide.

- Many guides like to invite friends or relatives along as helpers. While helpers can be useful in locating wildlife (and the extra company can greatly enhance enjoyment of the trip), at the end they will often demand the same fee as the original guide. If this is a problem for you, ascertain in advance how much extra you'll be expected to pay for their services.

- Deciding whether to tip a guide or porter – and if so, how much – can be difficult. The outrageous amounts and other gifts demanded by some guides and porters are the result of overtipping by well-meaning big spenders.

- Tip for good or skilful service, but keep the amount relative to local standards. For example, 10% on a short hike and for a trip of three days around 5% would be appropriate.

• For longer treks, always make a written agreement. This should include details regarding payment, deposits paid, number of assistants, arrangements for food and water, what should be carried by who and transport, if any, to or from the start or finish of the trip.

COURSES

Unfortunately, very few courses are available for foreigners to learn more about Malagasy and Comoran art, culture, people, environment, language, traditional beliefs and so on.

Nothing is regularly and readily available, but the best places to start making inquiries are the cultural centres in Tana or Moroni, depending on which language you speak. In Tana, contact the American Cultural Centre, Cercle Germano-Malagasy, and, especially, the Alliance Française, which also has branches in most cities in Madagascar. In Moroni, contact the Alliance Franco-Comorienne. While the courses are mainly for locals and resident expats, foreigners are often welcome – though it is prudent and courteous to make polite inquiries first.

WORK

Finding work teaching English is fairly easy in Madagascar (but less so in the Comoros), because many locals want to learn it. Most educated Malagasy can speak fluent French by the time they leave school, and the Alliance Française has the market cornered anyway, so there is little call for teaching French.

The best places to start asking around about teaching a foreign language are the French, German and English cultural centres in Tana; the French cultural centre in Moroni; and the English Language Institute in Tana (☎ (2) 358 83) or Antsirabe (☎ (4) 481 80).

There are precious few other opportunities for paid work in either country. Remember that you will probably be paid local wages – certainly not at western rates, unless you are highly qualified – and you will incur the wrath of the Immigration department if you overstay your visa or work without permission.

Volunteer Organisations

There is scope for working as a volunteer for an aid or development agency, particularly if you have any expertise in health, environment or education. Normally, agencies want you to apply in your own country before coming to Madagascar; issues like transport, accommodation, visas and so on have to be sorted out first.

Besides the CARE office in the Place de Badjanani (Moroni), and Zaza Faly (see the following list), all agencies listed below are in Antananarivo, Madagascar (the international telephone access code is 261-2). Refer to the Flora & Fauna section in the Facts about the Region chapter for details of environmental agencies which may be seeking volunteers.

Assocation Française des Volontaires du Progres (☎ 239 73)
CARE International, 11 Rue Radama 1er, Tsaralanana (☎ 435 26; fax 423 90)
Croix Rouge Malagasy, 11 Rue Patrice Lumumba, Tsalalana (☎ 221 11) – the Malagasy Red Cross
GTZ, BP 869, Nanisana (☎ 404 95; fax 414 07) – a German-run and funded agency
Peace Corps, II Y 14 bis Ambaranjana (☎ 313 30)
UNESCO, 11 Rue Naka Rabemanantsoa, Behoririka (☎ 217 61)
UNICEF, Rue Robert Ducrocq, Behoririka (☎ 280 83; fax 304 01)
US-AID, Immeuble Vonisoa, Ambohijanahary-Andrefana (☎ 254 89; fax 348 83)
Zaza Faly, Oberonstr. 8a, 13129, Berlin (☎/fax (030) 474 4018) & Lot 07-Q-80, Route de Betafo, 110 Antsirabe, Madagascar (☎ (4) 489 28) – a German organisation which helps street children in Antsirabe and Antananarivo

ACCOMMODATION

The busiest times in Madagascar are during holiday periods – around Easter, Christmas/New Year (15 December to 15 January are generally regarded as the 'peak season' by hotels during the Christmas/New Year break) and during European holidays from late July to late August – though you'll normally be able to find an empty room at any time of the year. However, decent hotels in Tana are always busy and some bungalow complexes at popular places like Nosy Be regularly fill up, so it's worth a quick telephone call to book a room ahead.

In the Comoros the range of accommodation is not good, places to stay are sometimes hard to find and most places are poor value. They are also expensive, especially when compared to Madagascar. Outside of Mayotte (where accommodation is very expensive), not even the tourism authorities have a clue what visitors are looking for, so this aspect of travel in the Comoros can be disappointing. This is reason enough to bring a tent and go camping (except on Mayotte).

Camping

It's possible to camp anywhere in Madagascar and the Comoros without restrictions (except on Mayotte), but thanks to the hospitality of villagers and potential security problems (see the Hiking section earlier in this chapter), most hikers can stay in local schools or homes, for which you will be charged a small fee. If you do camp, be discreet (unless you want scores of inquisitive onlookers) and please be careful of the local environment.

Some national parks and reserves in Madagascar have designated campgrounds, which allow you to be that much closer to the forests, and to enjoy early morning and nocturnal walks to spot lemurs and indri. However, camping on Mayotte is not actively encouraged, so you may have to pay the exorbitant hotel prices or bypass the island completely if you are on a budget.

The nicest camping spots on the Comoros are on the islets south of Mohéli where, in the right season, you can watch turtles struggling ashore to lay their eggs. The beaches on Grande Comore are also excellent spots to pitch a tent if you can find somewhere secluded (this is not always easy on a crowded island).

Minimum Impact Camping Anyone camping in the wilderness, national parks or other fragile areas should take note of the following guidelines:

Select a well-drained site and, especially if it's raining, use a plastic or other waterproof groundsheet to avoid having to dig trenches.

Along popular routes, camp only in established sites.

Biodegradable items such as fruit peels may be buried, but food residue and cigarette butts should be carried out, lest they be dug up and scattered by animals.

Use established toilet facilities if they are available. Otherwise, select a site at least 50m from water sources, and bury waste in a hole at least several cm deep. If possible, burn the used toilet paper or bury it well.

Use only biodegradable soap products (you'll probably have to carry them from home). To avoid thermal pollution (the creation of non-natural temperatures in a natural environment) and damage to fish or amphibian eggs or other organisms, do not pour hot water into cool streams.

When washing up with hot water, either let it cool to outdoor temperature before pouring it out or dump it in a gravelly, non-vegetated place away from natural water sources.

Wash dishes and brush your teeth well away from watercourses.

In the interests of protecting forest resources use a self-contained stove, such as a multi-fuel stove (like 'MSR' brand) or a methylated spirits burner. If you must build a fire, try to select an established site and keep the flame as small as possible. Use only fallen, dead wood and when you're finished make sure ashes are cool and buried before leaving.

In many rural areas food and water are in short supply, so carry along all you'll be needing and don't rely on local hospitality – but enjoy it when it is offered and give something back in return.

Military Messes

If all the hotels are full or too expensive, military messes in Madagascar offer a cheap alternative. They are run more like hostels than hotels, but are clean, well-kept and generally safe (look after your gear like you would in a hostel). There's one in each of the major towns, but the best and most accessible for foreigners is in Antsirabe.

Bungalows

The word 'bungalow' has an amazing range of definitions. On Grande Comore, it may be a thatched construction right on the beach and likely to fall down after the next decent wind; in Toliara, in southern Madagascar, a bungalow is any free-standing building, none of which are even remotely close to any beach; on the islands and coast of eastern Madagascar, they are lovely thatched huts, with concrete bases, often with private bathroom; and on Nosy Be, they can be modern, luxurious, made of concrete and very expensive. In short, a bungalow can vary enormously in facilities and price.

The best place to really enjoy what a bungalow has to offer – a sea view and seclusion – is, naturally, on the beach. The cheaper places are invariably run by Malagasy, ie not a foreign expat, and not right on (but still close to) the beach. The cheaper bungalows rarely have hot water, and the rooms are often spartan, but the fact that you can have the beach at your doorstep, and enjoy endless meals of fresh fish, for as little as about US$9 per double (not including meals) is good enough for most people.

Hotels

The Malagasy tourist authorities have a star and *ravinala* (travellers' palm) rating system for hotel accommodation and restaurants. These ratings aren't strictly reliable and the number of stars assigned is more often a reflection of the price than the standards. Still, a one-star hotel or a one-ravinala restaurant is probably nicer than one without any stamp of approval. The top hotel rating is five stars while top restaurants merit a maximum of three ravinalas.

Most major towns and resorts in Madagascar and Mayotte (but not outside of Grande Comore in the Comoros) have top-range places that cater mainly for package tourists and businesspeople. Rooms in these places cost about the same as top-range places in your own country, and while they include luxuries such as air-con and TV they are rarely good value. Non-resident foreigners normally have to pay in foreign currency, ie French francs or US dollars.

If you are travelling as a double (and particularly if a triple) and want a bit of luxury, try some of the places in the middle price bracket. These range from abominable overpriced pits to friendly, shabby and dilapi-

dated gems, cosy family-run hotels and beach resorts. Rooms are normally equipped with a wash basin and bidet; most have rooms with hot water. Most middle-range hotels in Madagascar, and especially in the Comoros, allow foreigners to pay in local currency, or you can usually pay in French francs.

Finally, there are the basic local establishments which in many cases offer perfectly acceptable accommodation. As a general rule, the lower the standards, the more negotiable the prices. Although you will run across some real dives, some of which are brothels, Malagasy or Indo-Pakistani run hotels are generally quite good value. However, there are very few bottom-end places in the Comoros and none on Mayotte; accommodation prices in these two places are about three times higher than Madagascar.

Inevitably, you will be hit for a tourist tax in Madagascar and the Comoros (not Mayotte). In Madagascar, this costs FMg 1000 to FMg 3000 per room per night, depending on the level of accommodation, and is usually added to your bill as an extra. In some places there may even be an additional local tax per visit (ie for each stay at each hotel in the region). In the Comoros, the tourist tax of CF500 to CF750 per room per night is included in the hotel price.

When checking into a hotel or other formal accommodation, guests usually have to complete a registration form detailing all the usual questions, including your parents' names.

To make the most of your trip, here are a few tips:

- If you frequently stay in bottom-end hotels, you'll probably want to carry a sheet sack or sleeping bag (otherwise it is not necessary).

- In all hotels you should have a torch (flashlight); a small padlock for dodgy doors; a bicycle chain for fixing your bags to room furniture; and mosquito coils (available locally and very cheap).

- In northern Madagascar, and other particularly hot places (but not in Tana), a ceiling or portable fan is essential and should always be provided (if you haven't paid for air-conditioning).

- Mosquito nets are needed in particularly bad areas, like Nosy Be (but not Tana) – make sure they don't have gaping holes.

- Prices are normally quoted for the room, regardless of whether there is one or two people, so single travellers can save money by travelling in pairs. Many places have double beds, rather than two single beds, so make it clear what you want. Most hotels will provide a bed for a third person for a small additional charge.

FOOD
Malagasy Food

In Malagasy, food is *sakafo*. For the locals, the dominant element in any meal is *vary* (rice), which is an ironic name, because the quality and choices rarely vary. Malagasy food doesn't accompany anything; everything accompanies the rice.

In a local *hotely* (cheap roadside canteen), the chalked menu (usually in Malagasy) will normally offer a big plate of rice, with perhaps a few tidbits of stewed or boiled *hen'omby* (zebu), *hen'andrano* (fish), *hen'akoho* (chicken and duck, which is invariably tough and stringy) or simply *ro* (a leaf-based broth). These stodgy and relatively tasteless dishes are cheap but rarely filling.

Along with the main course, you'll often get a small bowl of *rano vola* (also called *ranon'apango*, the result of adding boiling water to the residue left in the pot used to cook rice), or *brêdes* (boiled greens) in water. These are used to wash down the rest of the rice.

Other than rice, favourite dishes include *romazava* (beef and vegetable stew) and *ravitoto* (pork stew with manioc greens). These dishes, as well as various fish recipes, are frequently accompanied by *achards* (a hot pickled vegetable curry); a fiery sauce made from the *pilipili* or *tsiperifery* pepper; or by *rougaille*, a sauce made from peeled tomatoes, ginger, onions, lemon and hot peppers.

The Vietnamese-derived *mi sao* (vegetables with noodles) is also popular. An unexpected delight is the Malagasy version of *soupe chinoise* (Chinese soup): noodles, vegetables and, in nicer restaurants, a blend of meat or seafood in a delicious broth heavily spiced with coriander. Ordinary soup is known as *lasopy*.

In many villages, the starchy cassava or manioc root, which resembles a yam but tastes entirely different, constitutes a major part of the diet and is used as a bread substitute. It's not exactly bursting with flavour, but when well-cooked it's quite edible. Normal bread is called *mofo* and is mostly baked in baguettes. A pleasant legacy of French colonialism is the quality and availability of tasty bread rolls and pastries throughout the country.

On the coast, you can enjoy a large range of cheap seafood, including crab, crayfish, shrimp, prawns and oysters for far less than you would probably pay at home.

In addition to coconuts, there is a variety

A *Vary* Important Crop

Rice (*vary*) is an integral part of Madagascar's agriculture, cuisine and culture. However, the Malagasy love affair with rice did not come with the original settlers from Asia, as you would probably expect, but much later. It was a king of the Merinas, the unpronounceable Andrianampoinimerina (that's the shortened version – if you think that's long you should see his full name) who realised the importance of rice to the survival of the Merina and Malagasy people. The great king has often been quoted as saying things like 'the seas are the limits of my rice fields'. Like other countries in the region, the seasons, language, measure of time and general way of life in Madagascar, especially in rural areas, continue to revolve around this vital grain. While rice manages to feed most Malagasy people (although these days a lot has to be imported), its cultivation requires large paddies. These are often created by tavy, the slash-and-burn method of destroying forests. As the population continues to increase dramatically, and more and more rice is needed, the pressure on the land remains intense. ∎

of *voankazo* (tropical fruits). The most popular are *voasary* (oranges) and *akondro* (bananas), as well as *tapia*, small red berries which taste similar to dates and are often available in markets. From October to December, especially in the far north, it's the season for pineapples, lychees, mangoes and bananas. They often just drop out of the trees along the streets and in the villages, so help yourself – but ask first if there is a house nearby. In the markets around Tana, you'll also find peaches, pears, apricots and apples, which grow well in the cool highlands.

Of the hundreds of things one can do with a banana, the Malagasy have found a very appealing one: pour rum over it and set it on fire. The result, *banane flambée*, is unofficially the national dessert. Every dessert menu has bananes flambées (and often *only* bananes flambées!) so if you have a sweet tooth, you'd better get used to them. (The Malagasy also refer to a stud or Romeo as a banane flambé.)

The Malagasy also love yoghurt, which is delicious and safe and available at most stalls. Other stalls offer a variety of cheap

sweet and savoury tidbits, ice creams and soups. Try peanut brittle, coconut sweets, banana fritters and *parique*, a concoction made from peanuts, rice and sugar, wrapped tightly in banana leaves, baked and sold in slices.

Malagasy cheeses, which are made almost exclusively in the south central highlands, come in several varieties. Look for an especially delicious pepper cheese. Cheese production elsewhere in Madagascar is limited by the zebus' generally low milk output.

Comoran Food

Comoran cuisine is based on a blend of Indian, Arabic, French and African cooking, and while it isn't exactly world class, it's certainly tasty. Most of the standard meals include some combination of rice and meat, or fish flavoured with a combination of such locally produced spices as vanilla, cardamom, coriander, black pepper, cloves, nutmeg and cinnamon.

Favourite fish include tuna, grouper and

Delicious Fish Dishes from Madagascar & the Comoros

Parrotfish in Marinade Like all migrants, Madagascar's first settlers brought their own language, culture and eating habits. Along much of the coast people prepare parrotfish, a multi-coloured fish, in a style that originated in Tahiti. This is a traditional recipe that has been transmitted by word of mouth from time immemorial.

First, raw fish is marinated for a few hours in green lemon juice, green pepper and small pieces of ginger. The marinade enhances the flavour of the fish, which is covered in coconut milk just before serving. This coconut milk should not be confused with the liquid found inside coconuts, which is also called milk; in this context it means grated coconut flesh that has been pressed in a piece of cloth. Parrotfish in marinade is served with rice and *rougaille*, a sauce made from raw, peeled and crushed tomatoes flavoured with lemon, ginger, baby onions and chilli.

La ntouzi fi wanazi Fish are abundant in the tropical waters surrounding the Comoros. The most famous of these is unbdoubtedly the coelacanth, whose flesh (according to the few folk who have tasted it) is meant to be as refined as lobster although we advise you not to sample this rare fish. The daily diet of Comorans includes plenty of other species – and coconut fish is the national dish. It is traditionally made by the women from firm slices of tuna or grouper. The fish is first cooked in a *court-bouillon* of fresh tomatoes, onions and green pepper. Halfway through the cooking, the sauce is flavoured with the soft flesh of a green coconut.

This dish is served with rice and *mataba* (young cassava leaves prepared like spinach), to which some coconut milk is added towards the end of cooking. ■

parrotfish, and octopus is very popular. Meats include chicken, goat, mutton and zebu; occasionally, lobster and shellfish are available as well. Commonly used local vegetables are yam, aubergine (eggplant), onion, taro, manioc and a local type of pea known as *ambrevade*.

Most typical Comoran recipes call for coconut cream, the liquid derived by pressing the meat of green coconuts, which lends a delicious flavour to just about anything. It's frequently added to rice to give it a bit of zest. The result is known as *riz coco* (in Comoran: *myale ya hanazi*), a component of the favourite recipes, *poulet au coco (ntouzi wankuhu wanazi)* and *poisson au coco (ntouzi mfi wanazi)* – chicken or fish cooked in coconut cream and ladled over coconut rice. Other items which are frequently altered and improved by cooking with coconut cream include manioc leaves, aubergines, peas, octopus, beef and papaya.

If you're not on a tight budget, splash out at least once on a meal of *langouste à la vanille* (lobster in vanilla sauce).

Curry in various forms is also popular on Grande Comore and Mayotte where some Indo-Pakistanis have settled. The most popular savoury snacks seem to be the *brochette* (a skewer with small pieces of meat) and *samosa* (or *sambo*), which, like samosas everywhere, is a triangle of pastry filled with spicy meat and vegetables then deep-fried. Favourite sweets include various types of cakes and sorbets.

Restaurants

While you should try some Malagasy or Comoran food at some stage, if you avoid remote areas and go to places where there are tourists (local and foreign) and plenty of people (which is most places in Madagascar) you will always be able to find good, tasty western foods. These include dishes with fish, chicken, duck, and steak (normally zebu), as well as Indian, Chinese, French and Italian cuisine. Where there are tourists, there are usually pizzas – though one traveller remarked: 'you would never expect that such a large variety of foods in Madagascar could be lumped under the name 'pizza'.

Vegetarians will not suffer much. They will be able to choose a few simple non-meat dishes – such as fried rice or soup – in restaurants just about everywhere.

Every city and town has rows of street stalls where you'll find a variety of inexpensive Malagasy or Comoran snacks and quick meals. The sambos are usually good, but things do tend to sit around awhile before being sold. Try to buy only items which are still hot or are cooked before your eyes.

One step up from the street stalls is the *salon de thé*, a tea room which offers a variety of pastries, cakes, ice cream and other sweet snacks and drinks. Many do sandwiches, sausage rolls, sambos and other savoury snacks, but incredibly they are often closed during the lunch hour and also shut during the evening. They are great for breakfasts if you can wait until about 8 am (when they normally open).

Most restaurants offer a *menu du jour* (three-course set menu), or a *plat du jour* (daily special) which are often good value. To make the most of your trip, here are a few tips:

Some restaurants will only show you a food menu, so you may end up ordering expensive drinks without knowing it. Ask to see the drinks list.

The *petit dejeuner complet* (complete breakfast) is very rarely more than a roll with butter and jam and a cup of tea or coffee, for which you will be grossly overcharged. It is usually cheaper to order an omelette or fried eggs (which come with bread; if not, ask for it), and a tea or coffee. Alternatively, buy bread and tea from a market or hotely for far less.

Many Chinese restaurants include rice in the price of a main course, so ask before ordering another huge plate. Plain, boiled rice is called *riz blanc* (white rice), *riz nature* (plain rice) or *riz vapeur* (steamed rice).

For ecological reasons please refuse offers or opportunities to sample coelacanth (a rare fish), or the meat of sea turtles or fruit bats. ■

The French addition of *au salade* to the name of a meal usually just means that the main ingredient comes with a droopy piece of lettuce. If you want a salad, order it separately.

Self-Catering

You can easily buy enough fruit, bread, snacks and tinned foods to create your own meal, but unless you are in Tana (where it is often unsafe to visit a restaurant at night), or Mayotte and Nosy Be (where meals are expensive), you won't save a lot of money by self-catering.

The markets will naturally be your best bet for fresh produce, such as fruit, vegetables and bread, but in areas frequented by tourists you'll still have to bargain hard to get a fair price. When *vazahas* and *mzungus* (tourists) go shopping in the markets, some traders think all their Christmases (or the Muslim equivalent) have come at once. If you think a price has been unfairly increased ask another vendor, or watch to see what the locals are paying.

Nearly every town and village of any size has at least one family-operated grocery store selling essentials such as tinned fish, corned beef, packaged biscuits and powdered soup, and the ubiquitous Coke. However, all of these items will be relatively expensive.

In Tana there are a couple of well-stocked supermarkets, but they tend to cater for wealthy locals and expats. In Moroni and Mayotte there are several relatively well-stocked food shops, but as most things are imported, prices are high.

DRINKS

Non-Alcoholic

Most Malagasy soft drinks are produced by Star Breweries; they include Caprice Orange and Bon Bon Anglais (which the previous author of this book described as 'disgusting', but the current author thought was OK). Coca-Cola is available in just about every village and town in Madagascar and the Comoros, but prices will be considerably higher than locally made bottled soft drinks.

The French company Eau Vive has become a generic term for bottled water and has a virtual monopoly in Madagascar; other brands are available in the Comoros. Rather than spend your hard-earned money on expensive imported water in non-biodegradable plastic bottles, please consider continually refilling one bottle with safe tap water and using a purification tablet.

Milk seems to be available only in the central plateau area around Tana and Fianarantsoa. Elsewhere you'll get only condensed milk, the Nestlé *lait sucré concentré,* or the powdered stuff.

French influence ensures that coffee is more popular than tea. If you like strong tea, try the excellent *thé artisan* in the tiny cafes in the *medinas* of the Comoros. On Mayotte, drinks are expensive, but there's more variety. Here you can buy a real *café noir* or cappuccino.

Alcoholic

Rotgut If you're visiting Malagasy family or friends and are offered a *toaka gasy, betsabetsa, trembo* or *litchel,* you'll have to tread that fine line between being polite and being careful. The toaka gasy is a crude rum made from distilled rice and sugar cane; betsabetsa is fermented sugar cane juice; trembo is a coconut toddy; and litchel an alcoholic fruit drink made from lychees.

Up the scale a bit is the commercially distilled rum called *roma;* try Saint-Claude, which is distilled in Vohibinany (Brickaville) near the east coast of Madagascar; or Djamandjary, which is produced on Nosy Be. The rum is often enhanced by the addition of such items as vanilla beans, sugar, honey or even lemon grass. The result is known as *rhum arrangé.*

As you probably know, Islamic law prohibits the consumption of alcohol and most Comorans profess not to partake of it. In reality, however, it seems only the most traditional people are complete teetotallers. A popular drink is the local version of the coconut trembo. A non-alcoholic version of trembo is also available.

Some restaurants in Madagascar produce their own rum and coconut milk punch called *punch aux cocos* (often just 'punch coco'). When it's well-produced, it can be reminiscent of Bailey's Irish Cream. You'll get a particularly nice drop of it on Île Sainte Marie and Nosy Be.

Beer The Malagasy national brew, THB or Three Horses Beer (just about the only three words of English you may see in the whole country) is brewed by Star Breweries at Antsirabe and Tana. When cold, it's perfectly acceptable by any standards. Star has also launched two stronger lagers known as Gold and Queen's which are slightly better, and more expensive, than THB. Star also produces a refreshing light beer and lemon concoction called Fresh (which we thought was barely drinkable). In the Comoros and Mayotte, Castle beer from South Africa is

about all you can buy – and it's expensive in both places.

Wine One of Madagascar's surprises is the wine produced around Ambalavao and Fianarantsoa, at elevations of 800m and 1000m. These fruity, almost sweet, wines were introduced by the Swiss in the 1960s. The ones to try are Lazan'i Betsileo in white, red and rosé; Côteaux d'Ambalavao in rosé; Soivet Farfadet in white; Chateau Verget in red; and Côtes de Fianar, also in red. Lazan'i Betsileo also produces an interesting greyish wine, appropriately known as *gris*. There's also a sparkling wine known as Vatoraraka.

For those with more refined tastes, imported French wines are available in Tana and Mayotte, but are, of course, expensive.

Getting There & Away

However you're travelling, it's worth taking out travel insurance. Work out what you need. You may not want to insure that grotty old army surplus backpack – but everyone should be covered for the worst possible case: an accident, for example, that will require hospital treatment and a flight home. It's a good idea to make a copy of your policy in case the original is lost. If you are planning to travel for a long time the insurance may seem very expensive – but if you can't afford it, you certainly won't be able to afford to deal with a medical emergency overseas.

AIR

This general discussion is designed to give you:

* some basic ideas on how to reach eastern and southern Africa and islands in the Indian Ocean from major parts of the world which do not have direct flights to Madagascar and the Comoros. These include the USA, Canada, some European countries and Australia.
* some advice on buying tickets and finding discounts.

More information about direct flights to Madagascar, the Comoros and Mayotte is provided in the relevant Getting There & Away chapters.

Buying Tickets

Your plane ticket will probably be the single most expensive item in your budget, and buying it can be an intimidating business. There is likely to be a multitude of airlines and travel agents hoping to separate you from your money, and it is always worth putting aside a few hours to research the current state of the market.

Buying an ordinary economy-class ticket is not the most economical way to go, but it will give you maximum flexibility and the ticket is valid for 12 months.

Students and those under 26 (under 29 in the USA) can often get discounted tickets, so it's worth checking first with a student travel bureau to see if there is anything on offer (some are listed later in this chapter). Another option is an advance purchase (Apex) ticket; these have restrictions, but are usually between 30% and 40% cheaper than the full economy fare. You must purchase your ticket at least 21 days in advance (sometimes more) and you must stay away for a minimum period (usually 14 days) and return within 180 days (sometimes less). The main disadvantages are that stopovers are not allowed and any change to dates of travel or destination incur extra charges. Stand-by fares are yet another possibility. Some airlines will let you travel at the last minute if there are seats available just before departure. These tickets cost less than the economy fare but are usually not as cheap as the advance-purchase fares.

Of all the options, however, the cheapest way to go is via the so-called 'bucket shops': travel agencies which sell discounted tickets. Airlines only sell a certain percentage of their tickets through bucket shops so the availability of seats can vary widely, particularly in the high season. You have to be flexible with these tickets, although if the agents are sold out for one flight they can generally offer you something similar in the near future.

Shopping Around Start early: some of the cheapest tickets have to be bought months in advance and some popular flights sell out early. Talk to other recent travellers – they may help you to avoid some of the common mistakes. Look at advertisements in newspapers and magazines (not forgetting the press of the ethnic group whose country you plan to visit), consult reference books and watch for special offers. Bucket shops generally advertise in newspapers and magazines; there's a lot of competition and different routes available so it's best to telephone first and then rush round if they have what you want.

An increasingly popular and useful way of getting information about current flights and fares, and even booking tickets directly with the airlines or travel agencies, is to look at relevant world wide web sites. As well as the award-winning site run by Lonely Planet (http://www.lonelyplanet.com), the site run by the Madagascar embassy (http://www. embassy.org/madagascar; email malagasy@embassy.org) in Washington is a good place to start getting recent information and ideas. Refer to the Online Services section in the Regional Facts for the Visitor chapter for some ideas about where to start surfing the Net.

Once you have done this, phone around (or email) travel agents for bargains. (Airlines can supply information on routes and timetables, but, except at times of interairline warfare, they do not supply the cheapest tickets.) Find out the fare, the route, the duration of the journey and any restrictions on the ticket. Then sit back and decide which is best for you.

You may discover that those impossibly cheap flights are 'fully booked, but we have another one that costs a bit more ...' Or the flight is on an airline notorious for its poor safety standards and leaves you in the world's least favourite airport in midjourney for 14 hours. Or they claim to have only two seats left for that country for the whole of July, which 'we will hold for you for a maximum of two hours ...' Don't panic – keep ringing around.

Use the fares quoted in this book as a guide only. They are approximate and based on the rates advertised by travel agents at the time of research. Quoted airfares do not necessarily constitute a recommendation for the carrier.

Bucket Shops If you are travelling from the UK or the USA, you will probably find that the cheapest flights are being advertised by obscure bucket shops whose names haven't yet reached the telephone directory. Many such firms are honest and solvent, but there are a few rogues who will take your money and disappear only to reopen elsewhere a month or two later under a new name.

If you are suspicious about a firm don't give them all the money at once – leave a deposit of 20% or so and pay the balance when you get the ticket. If they insist on cash in advance go somewhere else. And once you have the ticket, ring the airline to confirm that you are actually booked on the flight.

Travel Agencies You may decide to pay more than the rock-bottom fare by opting for the safety of a better-known travel agent. Firms such as STA Travel (which has offices worldwide), Council Travel in the USA, or Travel CUTS in Canada are not going to disappear overnight, leaving you clutching a receipt for a non-existent ticket. All offer good prices to most destinations.

For ideas about where to start asking about fares to Madagascar and the Comoros, also refer to the travel agencies and tour companies listed in the respective Getting There & Away chapters. Many of these companies specialise in trips to this part of the world; they have information about flights and should be able to offer competitive fares whether you are taking a tour with them or not.

Precautions Once you have your ticket write its number down, together with the flight number and other details, and keep the information somewhere separate. If the ticket is lost or stolen this will help you to obtain a replacement.

It's sensible to buy travel insurance as early as possible. If you buy it the week before you fly you may find, for example, that you're not covered for delays to your flight caused by industrial action, or cancellation costs should you unexpectedly become sick.

Air Madagascar One factor worth considering when you decide to fly to Madagascar is that the national carrier, Air Madagascar

>O<O<O<O<O<O<O<O<O<O<O<O<O<O<O<O<O<O<O<O<O<O<O<O<O<

Air Travel Glossary

Apex Apex, or 'advance purchase excursion' is a discounted ticket which must be paid for in advance. There are penalties if you wish to change it.

Baggage Allowance This will be written on your ticket and usually includes one 20kg item to go in the hold, plus one item of hand luggage.

Bucket Shop This is an unbonded travel agency specialising in discounted airline tickets.

Budget Fare These can be booked at least three weeks in advance, but the travel date is not confirmed until seven days before travel.

Bumped Just because you have a confirmed seat doesn't mean you're going to get on the plane – see Overbooking.

Cancellation Penalties If you have to cancel or change an Apex ticket there are often heavy penalties involved; insurance can sometimes be taken out against these penalties. Some airlines impose penalties on regular tickets as well, particularly against 'no-show' passengers.

Check-In Airlines ask you to check in a certain time ahead of the flight departure (usually one to two hours on international flights). If you fail to check in on time and the flight is overbooked, the airline can cancel your booking and give your seat to somebody else.

Confirmation Having a ticket written out with the flight and date you want doesn't mean you have a seat until the agent has checked with the airline that your status is 'OK' or confirmed. Meanwhile you could just be 'on request'.

Discounted Tickets There are two types of discounted fares – officially discounted (see Promotional Fares) and unofficially discounted. The lowest prices often impose drawbacks like flying with unpopular airlines, inconvenient schedules or unpleasant routes and connections. A discounted ticket can save you other things than money – you may be able to pay Apex prices without the associated Apex advance booking and other requirements. Discounted tickets only exist where there is fierce competition.

Full Fares Airlines traditionally offer first class (coded F), business class (coded J) and economy class (coded Y) tickets. These days there are so many promotional and discounted fares available from the regular economy class that few passengers pay full economy fare.

ITX An 'independent inclusive tour excursion' (ITX) is often available on tickets to popular holiday destinations. Officially it's a package deal combined with hotel accommodation, but many agents will sell you one of these for the flight only. They'll give you phoney hotel vouchers in the unlikely event that you're challenged at the airport.

Lost Tickets If you lose your airline ticket an airline will usually treat it like a travellers cheque and, after inquires, issue you with another one. Legally, however, an airline is entitled to treat it like cash and if you lose it then it's gone forever. Take good care of your tickets.

MCO A 'miscellaneous charge order' (MCO) is a voucher that looks like an airline ticket, but carries no destination or date. It is exchangeable with any IATA (International Association of Travel Agents) airline for a ticket on a specific flight. Its principal use for travellers is as an alternative to an onward ticket in those countries that demand one, and it's more flexible than an ordinary ticket if you're not sure of your route.

No-Shows No-shows are passengers who fail to show up for their flight. Full-fare passengers who fail to turn up are sometimes entitled to travel on a later flight. The rest of us are penalised (see Cancellation Penalties).

>O<O<O<O<O<O<O<O<O<O<O<O<O<O<O<O<O<O<O<O<O<O<O<O<O<

(affectionately known as Air Mad to anyone who has flown with them), currently offers a 50% discount on flights around Madagascar if you book a flight to Madagascar with them. If you intend to do some serious travelling around Madagascar, and don't enjoy long, uncomfortable rides on crowded public transport along rough roads, you will probably do some flying. Getting tickets for internal flights at half price is certainly worthwhile.

The type of discounts and specials offered

On Request This is an unconfirmed booking for a flight (see Confirmation).

Open Jaws This is a return ticket where you fly out to one place but return from another. If available, this can save you backtracking to your arrival point.

Overbooking Airlines hate to fly empty seats and since every flight has some passengers who fail to show up (see No-Shows), airlines often book more passengers than they have seats. Usually the excess passengers make up for those who fail to show up, but occasionally somebody gets bumped. If this happens, guess who it is most likely to be? The passengers who check in late.

Point-to-Point This is a discount ticket that can be bought on some routes in return for passengers waiving their rights to a stopover.

Promotional Fares These are officially discounted fares like Apex fares, available from travel agents or direct from the airline.

Reconfirmation At least 72 hours before departure time of an onward or return flight, you must contact the airline and 'reconfirm' that you intend to be on the flight. If you don't do this the airline can delete your name from the passenger list and you could lose your seat. You don't have to reconfirm the first flight on your itinerary or if your stopover is less than 72 hours. However, it doesn't hurt to reconfirm more than once.

Restrictions Discounted tickets often have various restrictions on them – advance purchase is the most usual one (see Apex). Others are restrictions on the minimum and maximum period you must be away, such as a minimum of 14 days or a maximum of one year. See Cancellation Penalties.

Round-the-World An RTW ticket is just that. You have a limited period in which to circumnavigate the globe and you can go anywhere the carrying airlines go, as long as you don't backtrack. These tickets are usually valid for one year, the number of stopovers or total number of separate flights is worked out before you set off and they often don't cost much more than a basic return flight.

Stand-By A discounted ticket where you only fly if there is a seat free at the last moment. Stand-by fares are usually only available on domestic routes.

Tickets Out An entry requirement for many countries is that you have an onward or return ticket, in other words, a ticket out of the country. If you're not sure what you intend to do next, the easiest solution is to buy the cheapest onward ticket to a neighbouring country or a ticket from a reliable airline which can later be refunded if you do not use it. (See also MCO.)

Transferred Tickets Airline tickets cannot be transferred from one person to another. Travellers sometimes try to sell the return half of their ticket, but officials can ask you to prove that you are the person named on the ticket. This is unlikely to happen on domestic flights, but on an international flight tickets may be compared with passports.

Travel Agencies Travel agencies vary widely and you should choose one that suits your needs. Some simply handle tours, while full-service agencies handle everything from tours and tickets to car rental and hotel bookings. A good one will do all these things and can save you a lot of money, but if all you want is a ticket at the lowest possible price, then you really need an agency specialising in discounted tickets. A discounted ticket agency, however, may not be useful for other things, like hotel bookings.

Travel Periods Some officially discounted fares, Apex fares in particular, vary with the time of year. There is often a low (off-peak) season and a high (peak) season. Sometimes there's an intermediate or shoulder season as well. At peak times, when everyone wants to fly, not only will the officially discounted fares be higher, but so will unofficially discounted fares and there may simply be no discounted tickets available. Usually the fare depends on your outward flight - if you depart in the high season and return in the low season, you pay the high-season fare. ■

by Air Mad tend to change from time to time, so check with them or your travel agent (though the latter may not know everything there is to know about Air Mad special fares). For more information refer to the Madagascar Getting There & Away chapter, which also lists the major international offices and representatives for Air Madagascar.

Air Travellers with Special Needs

If you have special needs of any sort – you've

broken a leg, you're vegetarian, travelling in a wheelchair, taking the baby, terrified of flying – you should let the airline know as soon as possible so that they can make arrangements accordingly. You should remind them when you reconfirm your booking (at least 72 hours before departure) and again when you check in at the airport. It may also be worth ringing round the airlines before you make your booking to find out how they can handle your particular needs.

Airports and airlines can be surprisingly helpful, but they need advance warning. Most international airports will provide escorts from check-in desk to plane where needed, and there should be ramps, lifts, accessible toilets and reachable phones. Aircraft toilets, on the other hand, are likely to present a problem; travellers should discuss this with the airline at an early stage and, if necessary, with their doctor.

Guide dogs for the blind will often have to travel in a specially pressurised baggage compartment with other animals, away from their owner; though smaller guide dogs may be admitted to the cabin. All guide dogs will be subject to the same quarantine laws (six months in isolation etc) as any other animal when entering or returning to countries currently free of rabies, such as Britain or Australia.

Deaf travellers can ask for airport and in-flight announcements to be written down for them.

Children under two travel for 10% of the standard fare (or free, on some airlines), as long as they don't occupy a seat. They don't get a baggage allowance either. 'Skycots' should be provided by the airline if requested in advance; these will take a child weighing up to about 10kg. Children between two and 12 can usually occupy a seat for half to two-thirds of the full fare, and get a baggage allowance. Push chairs can often be taken as hand luggage.

Student Travel

Worldwide, there are a number of student travel organisations which offer bargain-basement airfares to out-of-the-way destinations the world over, including to the Indian Ocean and east and southern Africa. Organisations which offer student services include:

Australia
STA Travel, 224 Faraday St, Carlton, Victoria 3056 (☎ (03) 9347 6911)
STA Travel, 1A Lee St, Railway Square, Sydney, NSW 2000 (☎ (02) 9212 1255)

Canada
CHA, 333 River Rd, Vanier, Ottawa, Ontario KIL 8H9
Canadian International Student Services, 80 Richmond St W #1202 Toronto, Ontario M5H 2A4 (☎ (416) 364 2738)

New Zealand
STA Travel, 10 High St, Auckland (☎ (09) 309 9995)

UK
Campus Travel, 52 Grosvenor Gardens, London SW1 OAG (☎ (0171) 730 8111)
CTS, 220 High St, Kensington W14 4NL (☎ (0171) 937 3366)
STA Travel, 86 Old Brompton Rd, London SW7 3LQ (☎ (0171) 581 4132)

USA
Whole World Travel, Suite 400, 17 East 45th St, New York, NY 10017 (☎ (212) 986 9470)
STA Travel, 166 Geary St, San Francisco, CA 94108 (☎ (415) 391 8407)
STA Travel, Suite 507, 2500 Wilshire Blvd, Los Angeles, CA 90057 (☎ (213) 380 2184)

The USA

The *New York Times*, the *LA Times*, the *Chicago Tribune* and the *San Francisco Examiner-Chronicle* all produce weekly travel sections in which you'll find any number of travel agents' ads. Council Travel and STA Travel have offices in major cities nationwide. The magazine *Travel Unlimited* (PO Box 1058, Allston, Mass 02134) publishes details of the cheapest air fares and courier possibilities (these offer a chance for a free/heavily subsidised fare if you carry documents or parcels for a reputable courier or delivery company) for destinations all over the world from the USA.

North America is a relative newcomer to the bucket shop traditions of Europe and Asia, so ticket availability and the restrictions attached to them need to be weighed against what is offered on the standard Apex or full economy (coach) tickets. Do some homework before setting off.

The magazines specialising in bucket shop advertisements in London (see the UK section later in this chapter) will post copies so you can study current pricing before you decide on a course of action.

One of the recognised experts in tours to Madagascar is Cortez Travel, 124 Lomas Santa Fe Drive, Solana Beach, CA 92075 (☎ (619) 755 5136 or (800) 854 1029; fax (619) 481 7474; email cortez-usa@mcimail.com). They mainly run tours, but will have information on direct and good-value airfares.

Tickets Owing to excessive competition between carriers and a lot of governmental red tape in determining fare structures, flights originating in the USA are subject to numerous restrictions and regulations. This is especially true of bargain tickets; anything cheaper than the standard tourist or economy fare must be purchased at least 14 days, and sometimes as much as 30 days, before departure.

In addition, you'll have to book departure and return dates in advance and these tickets will be subject to minimum and maximum stay requirements: usually seven days to six months, respectively. It's often cheaper to purchase a return ticket and throw away the return portion than to pay the one-way fare.

Economy fares must often be purchased two weeks in advance and restrict you to a minimum stay of two weeks and a maximum stay of three months. From the USA, open tickets which allow an open return date within a 12-month period are generally not available, and penalties of up to 50% are imposed if you make changes to the return booking.

Flights Most travellers flying from the east coast of the US to the Indian Ocean region will probably have to think about flying via Paris (France), Moscow (Russia), Frankfurt or Munich (Germany), or Zurich (Switzerland) directly to Madagascar, the Comoros

or Mayotte – or, perhaps, combine it with a stopover in southern or eastern Africa, Mauritius or Réunion. The most direct, but not the cheapest, way to the region from the east coast is to fly from New York or Washington to Paris, from where there are direct connections to Madagascar and Mayotte on Air France, and to Moroni, on Grande Comore, with Nouvelles Frontières.

If you have time to shop around, it may well be cheaper in the long run to fly first to London from the east coast of the USA using Virgin Atlantic (from around US$500 one way), or standby on other airlines for a little more, and then to buy a bucket shop ticket from there. But you must do your homework to be sure of this. The cheapest fare we heard about from the east coast was to take any cheap flight to London, then an Aeroflot flight to Antananarivo, through Moscow, for about US$750 return.

From the west coast of the USA you may also have to go via Europe, or fly to South-East Asia and get onward connections from Singapore, Kuala Lumpur or Mumbai (Bombay) on Air Mauritius.

Canada

As with US-based travellers, Canadians on the east coast will probably find the best deals travelling via France, Germany, Switzerland or Russia. The quickest, though not necessarily the cheapest, way from Montreal is an Air France flight to Paris, from where there are direct connections to Madagascar, Mayotte and Moroni. From the west coast of Canada, connections through Singapore, Kuala Lumpur or Mumbai (Bombay), or backtracking to Europe, are the only options.

Travel CUTS has offices in all major cities. The *Toronto Globe & Mail* and the *Vancouver Sun* carry travel agents' ads. The magazine *Great Expeditions* (PO Box 8000-411, Abbotsford BC V2S 6H1) is also useful.

Australia & NZ

Getting to Madagascar or the Comoros from Australia will probably mean getting to Mauritius or South Africa first. The quickest and best way is on the Air Mauritius flight which travels overnight from Melbourne on Saturday, stops in Perth, and continues to travel overnight to Mauritius. You may then be lucky enough to get a direct connection a few hours later to Tana or Moroni. On the way back, the flight leaves Mauritius on Friday. The return fare from Melbourne/ Sydney to Mauritius is about A$1600, but can be discounted by travel agents to A$1350.

Alternatively, go to Singapore on Singapore Airlines then get a connection to the Seychelles, or to Mauritius with Air Mauritius or South African Airways (about A$1320 return). Other airlines which link Australia and Africa are Qantas, which flies to Johannesburg and Nairobi from Melbourne and Sydney, Air Zimbabwe and South African Airways. Another option is to go to Kuala Lumpur or Mumbai (Bombay) and then catch a connecting Air Mauritius flight to Mauritius or Johannesburg – but this is a roundabout way of getting there.

Kiwis will have to get to Australia first and then catch a direct flight to Mauritius or South Africa. Alternatively, catch a flight to Singapore or Kuala Lumpur and a connection to Mauritius and South Africa, and then another one to Madagascar or the Comoros.

Australasians can also purchase a Round-the-World (RTW) ticket via Africa, visiting the Indian Ocean as an add-on from either Harare (Zimbabwe) or Nairobi (Kenya). However, these often only include stopovers in the northern hemisphere and a surcharge is levied if the traveller wants to include Africa.

The best publications for finding good deals are the Saturday editions of daily papers such as the *Sydney Morning Herald*, Melbourne *Age* and the relevant papers in other states, and sometimes the *Australian*. STA and Flight Centres International are major dealers in cheap air fares. Check the travel agents' ads in the Yellow Pages and ring around.

The UK

Discounted Tickets There are bucket shops by the dozen in London. Several London magazines carry bucket shop advertising and may help put you onto discounted fares to Johannesburg, Nairobi, Mauritius or Réunion.

A word of warning, however: don't take the advertised fares as gospel. To comply with advertising laws in the UK, companies must be able to offer *some* tickets at their cheapest quoted price, but they may only have one or two available each week. If you're not one of the lucky few you'll be looking at higher priced tickets.

Most British travel agents are registered with ABTA (Association of British Travel Agents). If you have paid for your flight to an ABTA-registered agent who then goes out of business, ABTA will guarantee a refund or an alternative. Unregistered bucket shops are riskier but also sometimes cheaper.

The best thing to do is begin looking for deals well in advance of your intended departure so you can get a fair idea of what's available. Following is a list of publications and organisations in the UK which have travel information for budget travellers:

Africa Travel Now
> This is a quarterly newspaper put out by the Africa Travel Centre (☎ (0171) 387 1211), 21 Leigh St, London WC1H 9QX. It's free and, as its name indicates, it specialises entirely in travel to and around Africa. It contains an excellent rundown of discount flights to most major cities in Africa.

Globe
> A newsletter published by The Globetrotters Club which covers obscure destinations and can help in finding travelling companions; BCM Roving, London WC1N 3XX.

Time Out
> Universal House, 251 Tottenham Court Rd, London W1P 0AB (☎ (0171) 813 3000). This is London's weekly entertainment guide and contains travel information and advertising. It's available at bookshops, newsagents and newsstands.

Trailfinder
> This magazine is put out quarterly by Trailfinders (☎ (0171) 938 3366; fax (0171) 938 3305), 42-50 Earls Court Rd, London W8 6EJ. They can fix you up with all your ticketing requirements as well. They've been in business for years and their staff are friendly.

TNT Magazine
> This magazine is based at 52 Earls Court Rd, London W8 (☎ (0171) 937 3985). Free copies can be picked up at most London underground stations and on street corners around Earls Court and Kensington. It caters to Aussies and Kiwis working in the UK and is therefore full of travel advertising.

In these magazines you'll find discounted fares to destinations such as Nairobi (Kenya), Dar es Salaam (Tanzania), Harare (Zimbabwe) and Johannesburg (South Africa), but usually not to the French-speaking countries. Most of them tend to use Eastern European and Middle Eastern airlines.

Typical one-way/return fares to Africa from London include the following: Dar es Salaam (UK£320/640); Johannesburg (UK£270/450); Nairobi (UK£230/359); and the Seychelles (UK£385/770).

Also look for travel agents' advertisements in the Sunday papers, travel magazines and listings magazines.

To initiate your price comparisons, you could contact travel agents such as Trailfinders or STA Travel (☎ (0171) 937 9971) in London; or the helpful Travel Bug (☎ (0161) 721 4000) in Manchester. For courier flight details, contact Polo Express (☎ (0181) 759 5383) or Courier Travel Service (☎ (0171) 351 0300).

Continental Europe

European travellers who want to fly directly to Madagascar, the Comoros or Mayotte can do so from Paris, Munich, Frankfurt, Zurich or Moscow. Each of these cities has regular connections to every other major city in Europe. The newsletter *Farang* (La Rue 8, 4261 Braives, Belgium) deals with exotic destinations, as does the magazine *Aventure au Bout du Monde* (116 Rue de Javel, 75015 Paris).

For more details about direct flights to Madagascar, the Comoros and Mayotte, refer to the Madagascar Getting There & Away and the Comoros Getting There & Away chapters.

If you want to start your trip in a European capital without direct flights, or you want to tie in a trip to Africa or the nearby islands in the Indian Ocean, the major transport hubs to head for are Johannesburg (South Africa), Nairobi (Kenya), Mauritius and Réunion. There are many flights from Europe to other places in Africa, but you will be limited by the surprisingly few connections from mainland Africa and the Indian Ocean region to Madagascar and the Comoros.

Most major European airlines fly to Africa. For example, Alitalia fly from Rome to Nairobi twice a week, with connections to Johannesburg. (Lufthansa are in the process of increasing and rearranging their schedules to southern Africa.) It is usually cheaper to take a connection between Africa and Europe on a regional African airline like Air Kenya, Air Zimbabwe and, especially, Air Mauritius. The latter flies from Mauritius to Rome, Munich, Zurich, Geneva, Frankfurt, Vienna and Brussels once a week; to London twice a week; and to Paris five times a week.

Réunion is another very popular place to start your exploration of the Indian Ocean region. Air France flies from Paris at least every day to the capital, Saint-Denis. From Réunion there are daily connections to Moroni and Mayotte on Air Austral; and to major cities on Madagascar, such as Antananarivo, Nosy Be, Taolagnaro (Fort Dauphin) and Île Sainte Marie, on the tiny TAM airlines (sometimes written as TTAM).

Air France is also worth checking out for flights from Paris to other African destinations, since it offers student discounts for those under the age of 26.

A charter-flight company popular with travellers in Europe is Nouvelles Frontières. They charter flights from Paris to various African destinations and they have offices in several European countries. Their main contact addresses are:

France
> 87 Rue de Grenelle, 75013 Paris (☎ (0803) 33 33 33)
> 11 Rue d'Maxo, 13001 Marseilles (☎ 91 54 18 48)

Belgium
> 2 Blvd March, Lemonnier, 1000 Brussels (☎ (02) 547 4444)

Switzerland
    10 Rue Chantepoulet, 1201 Geneva (☎ (022) 732 0403)

Africa

The two major transport hubs in Africa for flights to Madagascar and the Comoros are Nairobi and Johannesburg. Refer to the sections in the rest of this chapter about how to reach these two cities from other parts of the world. Until recently, Sudan Airways flew from Khartoum to Moroni, so look out for other fascinating connections between Africa and Madagascar or the Comoros.

Interair, based in Johannesburg, offers some interesting possibilities. For example, it flies from Johannesburg to Kampala (Uganda) for US$320 one-way, and to Ndola (Zambia) for US$335 one-way, and has regular connections from Johannesburg to Tana and Moroni.

Refer to the respective Getting There & Away chapters for more information about flights between mainland Africa and Madagascar and the Comoros.

Asia

The major carrier around this part of the Indian Ocean, Air Mauritius, has regular connections from Mauritius to Madagascar and the Comoros, as well as flights from Mauritius to Kuala Lumpur (US$484/599 one-way/return) once a week; to Hong Kong (US$388/652) and Singapore (same fare as Kuala Lumpur) twice a week; and to Mumbai (Bombay) (US$496/668) three times a week.

There are bucket shops (of a sort) in New Delhi, Bombay and Calcutta. In New Delhi, Tripsout Travel, 72/7 Tolstoy Lane (behind the Government of India tourist office on Janpath), can be recommended. It's popular with travellers and has been in business for many years.

Pakistan International Airlines (PIA) and Air India fly from Karachi to Nairobi, and from Delhi and Bombay to Nairobi, respectively. From Karachi the standard economy fare is around US$296/430 one way/return. From Delhi it's around US$535/775.

The only airline with direct links to the Middle East is Emirates Airlines, of the United Arab Emirates, which flies between Dubai and Moroni. Air France also flies to Jeddah (Saudi Arabia) and Djibouti from Paris.

Other Indian Ocean Countries

Once you reach the Indian Ocean region, island-hopping becomes easier and cheaper. The best way of covering the area is with a return air ticket using several airlines. The only requirement is that you continue the route in a circle, ie without doubling back. This means you can probably take in Madagascar, the Comoros, Kenya, Mauritius, Réunion and/or the Seychelles using one circular ticket.

One excellent fare is a ticket valid for three weeks with Air Mauritius. For US$604, you can fly between Nairobi, Tana, Mauritius and Réunion and back; whereas the 'regular' return flight between Nairobi and Tana costs about US$400.

Airpass For good value and convenience, the Indian Ocean Airpass issued by Air Austral is worth considering. Starting in either Réunion or Mauritius, you can stop at between five and eight places – Nairobi, one of four cities (including Tana) in Madagascar, Mauritius, Réunion, Mayotte, Moroni and the Seychelles – for US$650 (for five stops) and US$1078 (eight stops).

South America

Just about the only convenient flights between South America and Africa are those operated by Varig and South African Airways (SAA). Varig flies between Rio, via Sao Paulo, and Johannesburg on Tuesday and Friday from US$1079/1096 one-way/ return.

OVERLAND TO AFRICA

It's possible to travel overland from Europe

to Africa via the Middle East or north Africa. Routes depend on current political problems in Africa; because of current upheavals in Algeria, the only safe way to southern Africa is the 'Nile Route' from Egypt to Sudan, Eritrea, Ethiopia and Kenya. From Kenya you can fly to the Comoros or Madagascar, go to Tanzania and look for a boat or flight, or continue overland to Johannesburg and fly from there.

You can travel overland through Africa independently, using a combination of just about every imaginable form of transport, or take an organised tour through an overland bus company.

SEA

Opportunities for travelling long-distance by sea to Madagascar or the Comoros are limited to cruise liners, yachts and the very, very occasional cargo ship. There is virtually nothing available from Europe or Australia, and certainly nothing, other than cruise ships, from North America.

Cargo Boats

With some patience and a willingness to rough it, you can pick up a lift on a local cargo boat to Madagascar from Mauritius, Réunion or the Comoros. To the Comoros, start looking for a lift in western Madagascar or mainland Africa, particularly Zanzibar, the island off the coast of Tanzania, or Mombasa in Kenya.

For more details about getting to Madagascar or the Comoros by boat from places in the Indian Ocean region, refer to the individual Getting There & Away chapters.

Cruises

The following cruise companies sometimes sail through this part of the world from the USA, but they only want your custom if you have heaps of money: Royal Viking Lines, 750 Battery St, San Francisco, CA 94111 (☎ (415) 398 8000); and Salen-Lindblad,

133 East 55th St, New York, NY 10022 (☎ (800) 223 5688).

Yachts

You may also be able to hitch a lift on a private yacht. These mainly sail from South Africa or France to Grande Comore, the French 'resort' island of Mayotte, and Nosy Be on Madagascar. The objective of the yacht owners is often the art of sailing rather than the ports of call so you may not go to places you particularly want, nor in any hurry.

If you want to try crewing on a yacht, your best chances of finding something will be in Nosy Be, Moroni and Mayotte. Yacht owners are often quite fussy about whom they'll take and experienced sailors will naturally have a better chance of being selected. Skippers normally look for someone with at least some cash reserves as well as sailing experience. There is rarely any such thing as a free ride, even if you are working as crew. Plan on paying at least US$20 per day for expenses. You must also have the right temperament, as conditions are difficult aboard a yacht. There's no privacy, nowhere to escape if tension breaks and at sea the skipper's word is law.

Naturally, sailing time depends on the weather conditions and wind direction. About 160km in 24 hours is a rough rule of thumb. There is no long-distance sailing between or around Madagascar and the Comoros during the cyclone season (December to April).

WARNING

The information in this chapter is particularly vulnerable to change: prices for international travel are volatile, routes are introduced and cancelled, schedules change, special deals come and go, and rules and visa requirements are amended. Airlines and governments seem to take a perverse pleasure in making price structures and regulations as complicated as possible. You should check directly with the airline or a travel agent to make sure you understand how a fare (and ticket you may buy) works. In addition, the travel industry is highly competitive and there are many lurks and perks.

The upshot of this is that you should get opinions, quotes and advice from as many airlines and travel agents as possible before you part with your hard-earned cash. The details given in this chapter should be regarded as pointers and are not a substitute for your own careful, up-to-date research.

Madagascar

Facts about Madagascar

Madagascar is so distinct from the African mainland, the islands of the Indian Ocean and just about anywhere else that it's hard to avoid becoming overly effusive with adjectives to describe it. To begin with, most of the island's flora and fauna are found nowhere else in the world. Even the offshore waters are home to such creatures as the coelacanth, a deep-sea fish long presumed extinct and the 'missing link' between sea creatures and land animals.

The most quoted passage about Madagascar is attributed to doctor and naturalist Joseph Commerson, who spent several months there in 1770:

I can declare that Madagascar is truly the naturalist's promised land. There, nature appears to have isolated itself within a unique sanctuary to work on models other than those to which she is subjugated elsewhere. One encounters the most bizarre and marvellous forms at every footstep.

Despite the island's long isolation the Malagasy people, united by a common language and culture, are racially mixed and their history on the island extends back only 1500 to 2000 years. The first inhabitants of the island were Malay-Polynesians who crossed the Indian Ocean from Indonesia and South-East Asia. Later these early settlers mixed with new arrivals – African slaves, Arab, Indian and Portuguese traders, and French colonials – to form the 18 official 'tribes' (actually more like clans) which inhabit the island today.

Some towns, such as Toamasina (also known as Tamatave), Toliara (Tuléar) and Antsirabe, are crowded with rickshaws (called *pousse-pousses*) – a legacy of past Chinese influences – and the countryside is cultivated with terraced rice fields. On the other hand, in the central highlands during winter the people wearing hats and swaddled in large blankets may conjure up images of Ethiopia or even the Andes.

MADAGASCAR FACTS

Official Name: Republic of Madagascar
Capital: Antananarivo
Head of State: President Didier Ratsiraka
Official Languages: Malagasy and French
Official Religions: Christianity and Islam
Currency: Franc Malagasy (FMg)
Exchange Rate: approx. FMg 4300 = US$1
Area: 594,180 sq km
Population: approx. 14 million
Population Growth Rate: 3.18%
Time: GMT/UTC +3
Per Capita GNP: US$790
Inflation rate: 35%

The cultural element isn't the only factor distinguishing Madagascar from the African mainland. None of Africa's carnivores, apes, antelope, elephants or poisonous snakes have found their way across the Mozambique Channel, and Madagascar's native wildlife has developed in its own way.

And the landscape itself is unique, ranging from lush tropical rainforest along the east coast (though much of the forest has been destroyed) to mountain heath and grassland in the highlands and arid, thorny scrub in the south. Unfortunately, Madagascar has also provided the world with a new geological term, *lavaka*, which means 'holes' in Malagasy and refers to the gaping 'amphitheatres' caused by deforestation and erosion that now pock much of the highland landscape.

Madagascar is now accessible to just about anyone – from package tourists heading for Nosy Be's sunny beaches to down-to-earth travellers prepared to experience the potholes (literally) in Madagascar's infrastructure. One of the country's greatest appeals is that it hasn't yet attracted the hordes of tourists that nearby countries have. This is a debt owed primarily to its poor transport system and lack of services in many areas. However, things are changing fast and lots of adventurous travellers, and quite a few package tourists, are rapidly getting wise to Madagascar (and vice versa).

Still, the Malagasy haven't yet become blasé about foreign tourists. Away from frequently visited areas, outsiders are likely to be treated to traditional Malagasy hospitality as long as they have some knowledge and appreciation of local ways and etiquette. Foreigners and outsiders will also be accorded a great deal of attention, but if you are of European origin the word *vazaha*, the name used for light-skinned foreigners, will seem to hover in clouds around you. The Malagasy in the countryside will be as interested in you and your ways as you are in them and theirs.

HISTORY

For an overview of the history of Madagascar before colonisation by the French refer to the History section in the Facts about the Region chapter.

French Rule

Late in the 19th century the Merina rulers actually sided with the British, despite the fact that on the political and strategic fronts the British were becoming less interested in Madagascar as a colony – especially after the opening of the Suez Canal in 1869.

In 1890 France and Britain signed a treaty which outlined their respective spheres of influence. It stated that Britain would recognise French control over Madagascar in return for French recognition of British sovereignty in Zanzibar.

In 1894 from their east coast stronghold at Toamasina, the French demanded the capitulation of Queen Ranavalona III and her government. When it wasn't forthcoming, the French Army, under General Duchesne, marched on Antananarivo. To the surprise of the Merina the French didn't launch their attack from the port of Toamasina, but from Mahajanga on the west coast.

When they arrived in the capital on 30 September 1895, 11,000 French soldiers had perished of various diseases. Although only 4000 remained fit enough to fight they easily overcame the Merina defences, which had also been decimated by sickness and starvation. Ironically, the remaining Merina defenders were commanded by a former British artillery officer, Major John Graves.

Colonial Administration After the invasion the French set up a colonial administration with General Joseph Galliéni as the first governor general. Galliéni attempted to destroy the power of the Merina aristocracy by suppressing the Malagasy language and all British influence. French became the official language and in 1897 Galliéni managed to abolish the monarchy by sending Queen Ranavalona III into exile in Algeria.

Although the governor general abolished slavery on the island, he replaced it with an almost equally exploitative system of taxes. In essence this resulted in forced labour for anyone who couldn't pay. Land was expropriated by foreign settlers and companies, and a coffee-based import and export economy developed.

In the years that followed the French forged ahead with their development plan, pouring their efforts into transport systems, construction projects, education and economic developments.

After being trained and educated to French standards, a new Malagasy elite emerged and resentment grew in all levels of society. Not surprisingly, several nationalist movements evolved among the Merina and Betsileo tribes (the most revered leader, Jean Ralaimongo, was a Betsileo). Strikes and demonstrations resulted.

WWII & Post-War Nationalism During WWII the French in Madagascar came under the authority of the Vichy Government of Marshal Pétain. Occupying British forces captured Antsiranana (Diego Suarez), ostensibly to prevent the Japanese using it as a base. Antananarivo and the other major towns also fell to the British, but were handed back to the Free French of General de Gaulle in 1943.

Post-war Madagascar experienced a nationalist backlash; the resentment culminated in the insurrection of March 1947, led by Joseph Raseta and Joseph Ravoahangy, which was crushed by the French at the cost of several thousand Malagasy lives (estimates range as high as 80,000). When the revolt was eventually put down its leaders were exiled.

In the 1950s political parties were formed; the most notable was the Parti Social Démocrate (PSD – pronounced 'pish dee') of the French National Assembly member, Philibert Tsiranana. When de Gaulle returned to power in France in 1958, the Malagasy voted in a referendum to become an autonomous republic within the French 'community' of overseas nations. Madagascar made a peaceful transition to independence and in 1960 Tsiranana was elected as the first president.

Independence
Philibert Tsiranana Under Tsiranana the French were permitted to retain control over trade and financial institutions and maintain military bases on the island. In effect the *colons*, as the French were known (Tsiranana referred to them as 'The 19th Tribe'), still ran the shop.

Although the Merina were the most Gallicised of the Malagasy tribes, they were also the most opposed to the French, and their brand of republicanism leaned towards the Soviet camp. Tsiranana, who was a *côtier* (person from the coast) and not a Merina, maintained 'dialogue' with South Africa and refused to establish diplomatic contact with communist countries.

As the already unpopular leader sunk ever lower in public opinion and esteem, the Malagasy economy also slumped. Until 1970 the country had been a major exporter of rice, but in that year Madagascar had begun to import rice for the first time. Tsiranana's propensity for rigging elections and his brutal repression of an uprising in the south in 1972 proved to be his undoing.

Although 85% of the nation's industry remained under French control the former colonial power did not interfere in September 1972 when, after massive anti-government demonstrations, Tsiranana resigned and reluctantly handed power over

to his army commander, General Gabriel Ramantsoa.

Military Control Ramantsoa took over and initiated a fundamental change in Malagasy policy. Aid agreements with France were renegotiated, French military bases were closed down and there was a return to the collectivisation of agriculture, land and crops that had been practised in rural areas before the colonial era. The new government also severed diplomatic relations with South Africa, Israel and Taiwan, and formed links with China and the former USSR.

The closure of the French military bases and Madagascar's withdrawal from the Communauté Financière Africaine (CFA) zone, following abortive aid negotiations, led to a wholesale departure of the French farming community. The exodus was a painful reminder of how dependent the Malagasy people remained on French capital, skills and technology. Major differences in opinion began to surface over the direction of the government's economic policies.

In February 1975, after several coup attempts, the general was forced to step down and was replaced by Colonel Richard Ratsimandrava. He promised to follow the progressive line of his predecessor but with more vigour. Ratsimandrava was shot dead in his car within a week of taking office and a rebel group of army officers promptly announced a military takeover. The Merina blamed the murder on rebels of a dissident paramilitary group made up of coastal tribes.

The military officers who had usurped power were quickly routed by officers loyal to the ex-president and a new government headed by the former foreign minister, Admiral Didier Ratsiraka, came to power.

The Second Republic
In the meantime production of the country's principal exports – vanilla, coffee, cloves and meat – had stagnated. The education system had also collapsed and there had been little, if any, economic development. Banks, insurance companies and other major businesses were nationalised without com-

pensation and most of the remaining French residents bailed out, taking with them most of the country's badly needed technical skills.

Ratsiraka attempted radical political and social reforms in the late 1970s, abandoning all of Tsiranana's pro-western policies. He severed all ties with France and continued courting favour with communist nations. In imitation of the Chinese leader Mao Zedong, Ratsiraka even compiled a 'red book' of government policies and theories.

But he was more pragmatic when it came to economics. Initially, all the banks were nationalised and a network of public corporations was set up to deal with the agricultural and marketing sectors of the economy. French nationals were also barred from the import-export sector and the government turned to the USSR to supply its armed forces with military hardware. In 1981-82, a debt crisis forced Ratsiraka to rethink his position and suspend the reforms, despite heated debate in the national assembly. Unpopular austerity measures designed to attract International Monetary Fund (IMF) and World Bank loans were adopted. Thereafter, the Malagasy economy recovered slightly but any gains were short-lived.

In March 1989, Ratsiraka was dubiously 'elected' to his third seven-year term, sparking off a series of riots which left six dead and at least 70 injured. Early 1991 saw months of demonstrations in which hundreds of thousands of citizens demanded the president's resignation. From May 1991 to January 1992 the government, economy and transportation systems ground to a halt when general strikes were called by Forces Vives (Living Forces) candidates seeking to bring a quick end to Ratsiraka's rule.

Almost at the end of his rope, the president agreed to forge a revised constitution to be voted upon in a public referendum sometime in the hazy future. On 8 August 1991, he appointed Antananarivo mayor Guy Razanamasy as head of the interim government.

No-one bought the window-dressing and on 10 August 1991, 31 peaceful demonstra-

tors were killed by the North Korean-trained presidential guard in front of Ratsiraka's opulent new palace (designed and built with North Korean aid). In protest, some senior army officers defected to the opposition. The showdown had begun and nine days later, Ratsiraka declared Madagascar a federation of six states with himself as president. At this stage the French stepped in, calling for a 'rapid and controlled popular consultation' on Madagascar's future.

In late October 1991 an agreement was signed by Ratsiraka, prime minister Razanamasy and representatives of the Forces Vives opposition party; this established a transitional state under Razanamasy in preparation for popular elections and the birth of the so-called 'Third Republic'. Still Ratsiraka refused to step down; on 29 July 1992 there was an attempted civilian coup, but the rebels failed to gain popular support and were forced to surrender.

The 'Third Republic'

Just three weeks after the failed coup attempt a referendum was held, resulting in 70% approval of the new draught constitution which limited presidential powers and established Madagascar as a unitary republic rather than a federation of six states. Unfortunately, the vote was effectively nullified by the violence which surrounded the election; nearly 25% of the electorate was prevented from voting by protesters demanding a federal state. Nonetheless, the referendum was declared legal and elections were scheduled for later in the year.

Leading up to the first round of elections (which, after much shuffling, took place on 25 November 1992), civil unrest culminated in the blockading of the capital and the bombing of a railway bridge between Toamasina and Antananarivo by forces demanding a federal state. For weeks the capital was without petrol and transportation services were disrupted.

The first round of elections, which remained remarkably peaceful, resulted in opposition candidate Professor Albert Zafy, a surgeon, coming in with 45.8% of the vote compared with Ratsiraka's 29%. The remainder was shared between six other candidates. Naturally, Ratsiraka's support was strongest in his native Toamasina; Antananarivo and Antsiranana came in strongly for Zafy.

The final race between the two leading candidates took place in February 1993 and Zafy came out ahead with 70% of the vote, thus ending 17 years of Ratsiraka's dictatorship.

Ratsiraka Returns!

Years of communist-style dictatorship and mismanagement made it extremely difficult for Zafy's new government to ignite the economy and gain the trust of the people. International debt skyrocketed, and the country could not even pay the crippling interest. Zafy refused strict conditions imposed by the IMF and other loan institutions, and sought outside help to obtain money. This lead to allegations of money-laundering and dealings with known drug-traffickers.

The 70-year-old Zafy was unexpectedly impeached by his parliament in July 1996 for 'abuse of authority', and 'exceeding his constitutional powers', which included trying to sack his prime minister. The matter was taken to the high court, which upheld the parliament's action. The first round of new presidential elections was called in November 1996; among the 15 candidates was the former dictator, Ratsiraka, who had been in exile in France for the previous 19 months.

To the surprise of everyone, including international monitors, Ratsiraka finally won the presidential elections with 50.7% of the vote. Zafy, who came a very close second with 49.3%, predictably complained about vote-rigging. Appealing for Madagascar to become something called a 'Humanist and Ecological Republic', Ratsiraka took office again in February 1997. The fact that only 25% of the 6.5 million registered voters bothered to cast a ballot indicates an overwhelming lack of interest and trust in whoever is running the country.

GEOGRAPHY

The island of Madagascar lies in the Indian Ocean, separated from Mozambique on the African continent by the 400km-wide Canal de Mozambique (Mozambique Channel). The Tropic of Capricorn crosses at the latitude of Toliara so all but the island's southern tip lies within the tropics. The main island sits amid a number of smaller islands and coral atolls, including Nosy Be and Île Sainte Marie.

Madagascar is the world's fourth largest island, after Greenland, New Guinea and Borneo (Australia is regarded as a continent). It is about 1580km long from northeast to south-west, and 571km wide at its widest point. With a surface area of 594,180 sq km and a coastline of over 5000km, it is well over twice the size of the UK.

The island can be divided geographically into three parallel north-south zones: the low plateaus and plains in the west; the high central plateau; and the narrow coastal strip in the east. Politically, Madagascar is divided into six states: Antananarivo, Toliara, Fianarantsoa, Mahajanga, Toamasina and Antsiranana. The national capital is Antananarivo, more commonly known as Tana.

There are no really high mountains, but the *hauts plateaux*, which run nearly the length of Madagascar from north to south, form the backbone of the island. These range from 750m to 1350m above sea level. The three principal massifs (rocky mountain ranges) are the Tsaratanana in the northwest; the Ankaratra, south of Antananarivo; and the Andringitra, not far from Fianarantsoa. At 2876m the volcanic peak of Tsaratanana is the country's highest point.

The eastern edge of the hauts plateaux abuts the abrupt escarpments which plunge down through rainforested hills to a narrow coastal plain. Along the virtually linear eastern coast a chain of artificial and natural lakes and canals, more than 600km long, forms an inland waterway known as the Canal des Pangalanes.

West of the hauts plateaux is a distinct but less dramatic escarpment which drops away gently in a succession of hills to the broad lowland strip along the coast. Like most of the island the western zone was once extensively forested; it is now principally a vast savanna with sparse stands of deciduous trees. This region supports Madagascar's most intensive cultivation. The western coastline is marked by alternating mangrove swamps and long, sweeping sandy beaches, and offshore one finds some of the world's finest coral reefs.

GEOLOGY

Unlike the neighbouring islands of Mauritius, Réunion, Rodrigues and the Comoros, Madagascar is not the product of volcanic activity, though volcanoes did form such attractions as the Montagne d'Ambre mountain, Ankaratra Massif and Lac Itasy. Rather, Madagascar is considered a continental island and owes its formation to the process of plate tectonics, or continental drift.

Around 250 million years ago Pangaea, the earth's original landmass, broke up into the two supercontinents called Gondwana and Laurasia. Over the next 65 million years the huge southern portion, Gondwana, began drifting north, losing large sections along the way. Australia and Antarctica, then a single landmass, were left behind. Sometime later the chunk that was to become India freed itself and headed north towards Laurasia.

Around 165 million years ago South America separated from Africa and headed north-west. Madagascar, which had been attached to the African continent (somewhere around present-day Somalia), also broke free and eventually took its present shape.

Geologically, most of Madagascar (except the west coast) consists of a crystalline bedrock base. Much of the west coast consists of sedimentary material overlain by red lateritic sandstone. Deposits of minerals and semiprecious stones occur, particularly throughout the highlands, and include jasper and agate, zircon, rose and smoky quartz, moonstone, tourmaline, morganite beryl and amethyst. Unfortunately, they are not in large or commercially viable quantities, though they are sufficient to supply the tourist demand for colourful souvenirs.

One spectacular type of landscape which you can see in northern and western Madagascar is karst, a rocky countryside of caves, potholes and underground rivers formed by limestone. Known locally as *tsingy*, this geological formation is outstanding and unique, and is protected as part of the Tsingy des Bemaraha and Ankàrana Reserves.

Flying over Madagascar, it will become obvious where the once lush green island received the sobriquet, 'Great Red Island'. Centuries of deforestation have subjected the red lateritic soil to erosion; in the most dramatic cases the ground has slumped, leaving hideous gaping pockmarks – lavaka – over much of the highland landscape. The scoured soil eventually finds its way to vast rivers, staining them the colour of blood. At river mouths along the west coast, where loads of precious topsoil haemorrhage into the ocean, the seawater is coloured a lurid red far beyond the coast.

CLIMATE

Owing to its altitudinal variation and north-south orientation, Madagascar experiences a variety of climatic conditions. Trade winds prevail from the east and the monsoons from the north-west, so most of the precipitation is dumped on the east coast, the eastern slopes and in the far north. As a consequence, areas south-west of the highlands remain almost perpetually parched.

Most of the country is characterised by distinct wet and dry seasons, the lengths of which depend mainly on altitude and latitude. Officially, the wet season lasts from November to March, though it can start as late as Christmas, and the dry season is from April to October.

Rainfall ranges from about 300mm annually in the arid south-west to 300cm at Nosy Be, and over 360cm on the eastern escarpments. In these areas the 'dry' season lasts only a few weeks. From January to March, the east coast, the far north and sometimes the far south are subject to cyclones. Don't underestimate the risk of travelling at this time: in February 1994 Cyclone Geralda caused extensive damage and several hundred deaths along the east coast around Toamasina, and in early 1997 Cyclone Gredelle wreaked havoc (reports claimed up to 100 deaths) around southern Madagascar.

Average dry season (winter) temperatures vary from a maximum of 30°C in coastal areas (though the mercury has climbed as high as 44°C on occasion) to around 25°C on the hauts plateaux. At the highest elevations, temperatures can drop to -15°C during the winter months and snow is not uncommon. The night-time temperature in Tana and surrounding areas can fall to about 0°C in July and August.

In arid areas of the south the dry season is long and very hot: what little rain there is may fall within a few weeks over December and January. Along the western coast the wet season is short, lasting from about November to February, and the dry and wet seasons are always hot.

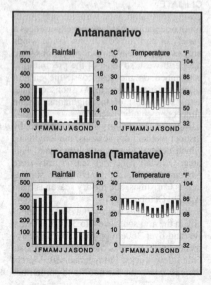

ECOLOGY & ENVIRONMENT

Most of Madagascar's flora and fauna was already there when humans reached the island about 1500 to 2000 years ago. The colonists brought with them rice and zebu cattle, the dietary and cultural staples which had sustained them in their former homelands.

When the landscape was radically altered to accommodate the foreign crops and herds vital to human settlement, native animals were the first casualties. By the time the first Europeans arrived, countless species had already disappeared forever, including pygmy hippos; gorilla-sized, ground-dwelling lemurs; and the *Aepyornis* (elephant bird), thought to be the largest bird that ever lived, whose eggs and egg shells are found littered around the island's southern tip. (It is illegal to remove or collect the fragments of eggs.) Tragically, deforestation has continued to the present day; the country has already lost over 85% of its natural forest cover and most of Madagascar's unique species are at extreme risk of extinction.

Although hunting has taken its toll of animal populations, the greatest danger to Malagasy wildlife is loss of habitat. In the eastern forests, slash-and-burn methods, known as *tavy*, have opened previously inhospitable regions to agriculture. Unfortunately, without careful tending, weeding and fertilisation the plots are rendered infertile in as little as a year in some places, and the farmers must find another plot to start the process over again.

In the drier western regions immense areas of natural scrub are burned to provide pasture for cattle and other domestic herds. In poorer areas goats are raised and the lands are rendered barren when the animals eat even the roots of covering vegetation. It's estimated that a staggering 30% of Madagascar's surface area is burned or re-burned each year.

This environmental destruction has not only decimated wildlife habitat, it threatens to turn much of the country into an eroded and uninhabitable wasteland. While Madagascar requires more and more agricultural land to support its burgeoning population, large swathes of the interior have already become infertile and unusable. Although the government has introduced measures to halt new burning and encourage maintenance of lands already cleared, they are not enforced.

The World Wide Fund for Nature (WWF) makes the following assessment:

During the past decade, the international conservation community singled out Madagascar as one of the ecologically richest countries on this planet. Despite such bountiful riches, Madagascar is one of the economically poorest countries in the world and, sadly, one in which its natural heritage of biological diversity is the most at risk. In recent years, this dichotomy – more evident in Madagascar than many other countries – has created a tension between the proponents of preservation (which is frequently confused with conservation) and those of development.

In Madagascar, as elsewhere, environmental issues cannot be addressed in isolation of the demographic pressures or typical rural agricultural practice which, unfortunately, often lead to the unsustainable exploitation of available resources.

Poverty, isolation and poor education are often the greatest obstacles to success in conservation, and Madagascar is no exception. In fact, the frequent reference to the 'spiral of environmental degradation and poverty to which Madagascar appears to be confined' is justified in terms of reverse economic growth and increased demand for natural resources at

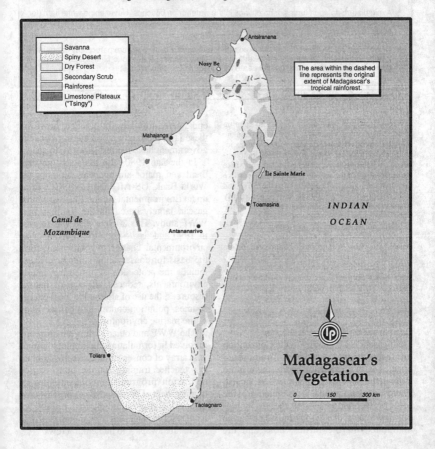

Savanna
Spiny Desert
Dry Forest
Secondary Scrub
Rainforest
Limestone Plateaux ("Tsingy")

The area within the dashed line represents the original extent of Madagascar's tropical rainforest.

Antsiranana
Nosy Be
Mahajanga
Ile Sainte Marie
Toamasina
Canal de Mozambique
Antananarivo
INDIAN OCEAN
Toliara
Taolagnaro

Madagascar's Vegetation

0   150   300 km

Marine Turtle Conservation

Although marine turtle numbers are dwindling rapidly, the Indian Ocean is still home to four species: the loggerhead *(Caretta caretta)*, green turtle *(Chelonia mydas)*, hawksbill *(Eretmochelys imbricata)* and leatherback *(Dermochelys coriacea)*.

Their decline has largely been caused by demand for their edible flesh and eggs, which are highly prized by local fisherfolk, and their carapace, which humans turn into fashionable ornaments (tortoiseshell). Pollution also takes a toll, and according to the Convention on International Trade & Endangered Species (CITES), marine turtles now rate among the world's most threatened species.

Visitors can help ensure that marine turtles have a future. When visiting Madagascar and the Comoros – or any other country where sea turtles nest or turtle products are available – please consider the following suggestions:

- Avoid eating turtle meat or soup.

- Don't buy sea turtle product souvenirs, such as tortoiseshell (also known as hawksbill shell) jewellery, ornaments, or stuffed turtles.

- Avoid disturbing adult turtles or hatchlings in the water or on beaches. Never shine white light (for example, car headlights or torches), which can frighten nesting females and attract hatchlings away from the safety of the sea.

- Don't throw plastic litter into the sea or coastal waterways. Plastic bags are particularly dangerous to sea turtles who frequently mistake them for tasty jellyfish; the plastic blocks their digestive system, causing a slow and painful death by suffocation or starvation. ■

---

any cost. New proposals in the country to open up protected areas to exploitation, to try and reverse the economic trend are unwise in the current eco-socio-political environment where governments are transitional, cooperation at local level is limited, and where the biodiversity of the country is particularly sensitive to even minor change. This means that the WWF and other conservation organisations must be particularly sensitive to traditional values and systems and particularly creative in developing new initiatives.

Madagascar has already lost about 85% of its natural forest systems; fertile soils pour out into the oceans; countless species have disappeared before becoming known to science; and most Malagasy people seek a living on overused, and often marginal, lands which can no longer support existing populations.

Conservation Policies & Efforts

Madagascar is a signatory to the Convention on International Trade in Endangered Species (CITES) so, in theory, there is no trade in the wide range of animals on the list. There are also national laws which provide some protection for selected species, including all primates, the dugong and other marine mammals, marine turtles, boas and the endangered tortoises. In practice, however, these laws are rarely enforced, nor does the government have the resources to do so.

In the late 1980s the Malagasy government and major aid agencies, notably the World Bank, US-AID and UNESCO, drew up an Environmental Action Plan for Madagascar, largely based on the findings of a WWF study. This 20 year plan was ratified in 1990 and led to the development of an environmental charter; together they form the basis for conservation strategies. These include the protection of remaining natural environments, reduced wastage of natural resources, the use of alternative local energy sources, pollution control and conservation of the marine environment.

The WWF and other groups are currently involved in formulating and implementing a vast array of conservation measures, including teacher training, public conservation education programs, media campaigns, management of protected areas, organisation of local conservation groups, training of local reserve managers and rangers, and debt for nature swaps – to name but a few.

▷◁▷◁▷◁▷◁▷◁▷◁▷◁▷◁▷◁▷◁▷◁▷◁▷◁▷◁▷◁▷◁▷◁▷◁▷◁

World Wide Fund for Nature (WWF)

The WWF recognises Madagascar as one of the highest conservation priorities in the world, and consequently allocates vast resources to protecting endangered and unique animals, plants and ecosystems throughout the country. Working closely with Malagasy, and many other international environmental and aid agencies, the WWF has been able to help establish and run national parks and reserves, such as the Parc National de Montagne d'Ambre; educate local people about conservation, such as publishing the excellent magazine for local children called *Vintsy*; and help develop local communities, mainly in the area of health and education.

In Madagascar, the main aims of the WWF continue to be:

* the 'conservation and rehabilitation of forests and woodlands' – these are vital habitats for flora and fauna but are being devastated by overgrazing, slash-and-burn farming, logging for fuel and building materials, and urban sprawl

* the 'conservation and revitalisation of wetlands and coasts' – these are the habitats for fish and other vital foods, as well as water, for local communities

* the 'conservation of global diversity of forms of life' – saving plants which provide essential ingredients for medicines is a priority

For more information about the WWF and its work you can contact its head office is Switzerland, or one of its major offices:

Australia
    Level 17, St Martin's Tower, 31 Market St, GPO Box 528, Sydney, NSW 2001 (☎ (02) 9261 5572)
Canada
    60 St Clair Ave East, Suite 201, Toronto (☎ (416) 923 8173)
France
    151 Blvd de la Reine, F-78000 Versailles (☎ 02 39 50 75 14)
Germany
    Hedderichstr. 110, PO Box 70, 11 27, D-6000 Frankfurt a/M 70 (☎ (069) 60 50 030)
Madagascar
    Lot Près II M85 ter Antsakaviro, BP 738, Antananarivo 101 (☎ (2) 348 85)
Switzerland
    Avenue du Mont Blanc CH-1196, Gland (☎ (022) 64 91 11)
UK
    Panda House, Weyside Park, Godalming, Surrey GU17 1XR (☎ (0483) 426 444)
USA
    1250 24th St NW, Washington DC 20037 (☎ (202) 293 4800) ■

▷◁▷◁▷◁▷◁▷◁▷◁▷◁▷◁▷◁▷◁▷◁▷◁▷◁▷◁▷◁▷◁▷◁▷◁▷◁

Ecotourism

For their part, all visitors can contribute to preserving Madagascar's unique creatures and environment. Although the word has been thrown around for several years by various and sundry travel companies, 'ecotourism' means more than simply spending a holiday in a natural area. It also involves adopting a code of behaviour and practice which will result in the least possible effect on the environment of the area being visited. The following are a few suggestions:

Don't buy anything which will encourage or create a market for products from endangered species, or wildlife which may become endangered. It is illegal in Madagascar to buy and take out live animals, shells, tortoiseshell products, coral etc. In the interests of archaeology and heritage preservation, don't purchase or remove anything represented as a historical relic or antique.

Spend money wisely; encourage vendors, businesses and agencies (especially Malagasy ones) which may be using environmentally sensitive practises, even if these are inadvertent. For example, oil lamps and toy Citroëns made from recycled tins make unique souvenirs.

Especially when travelling in national parks or remote areas, don't demand standards which would place undue strain on local resources. Where possible, stay in local accommodation and eat local foods. Tourist class hotels often sap power, water and labour resources at the expense of local communities; for example, exotic goods and food items must be trucked in from elsewhere, and require both energy and infrastructure to manage; and hot showers are often heated with scarce firewood in areas which have problems with deforestation.

Pay national park and reserve fees to the proper authorities and avoid the temptation to take advantage of unofficial channels. These fees help maintain the parks, protect the park environment, develop the local economy and – importantly – show the local people that more money can be made from looking after the flora and fauna than from chopping down the forest.

Try to foster local interest in nature and the environment by communicating your enthusiasm, especially to guides and other tourism-oriented people. Encourage guides to learn as much as they can about the plants, animals, local cultures and geology. Also, set an example by respecting nature – and carry out your rubbish.

Consider the section on Minimum Impact Camping under Accommodation in the Regional Facts for the Visitor chapter.

Finally, don't always assume outsiders know more than local people when it comes to the environment and co-existing with nature. They've been doing it for years and may have some useful tips of their own!

NATIONAL PARKS

In a desperate effort to halt deforestation, to protect endangered animals and precious landscapes, and to save water sources for vital rivers, national parks and reserves were first established under the French colonial government as early as 1927. In 1985 there were 36 protected reserves and now there are over 50 national parks and reserves, covering about 12% of the uninhabited land. This percentage may look impressive, but only a few of these reserves are actively protected, and even fewer are accessible to tourists.

Management Ownership and management of the various parks and reserves can be a bit confusing. They are either privately owned (eg the Réserves Privée de Kaleta and de

Berenty in the far south); co-run by a development agency, such as the German GTZ agency at the Station Forestière et Piscicole de Manjakatompo, near Tana; run, paradoxically, by a logging company (eg Réserve Forestière de Kirindy); or by one of three organisations:

ANGAP
Established in 1991, the Association Nationale pour le Gestion des Aires Protegées (National Association for the Management of Protected Areas) is an impressive, non-government Malagasy organisation. ANGAP runs most national parks in cooperation with other agencies such as CARE, Conservation International and UNESCO. The ANGAP head office is at 1 Rue Naka Rabemanantsoa, Antanimena, Antananarivo; BP 1424 (☎ (2) 305 18; télécel (mobile telephone) ☎ (2) 813 74; fax (2) 319 94; email ANGAP@bow.dts.mg).

Département Eaux et Fôrets
Part of the Ministry of Agriculture, the Malagasy Department of Water & Forests is located in Nanisana, Antananarivo (☎ (2) 406 10). It has offices in most major towns and near national parks.

World Wide Fund for Nature (WWF)
Lot Près II M85 ter Antsakarivo, BP 738, Antananarivo 101 (☎ (2) 348 85; fax (2) 348 88). This well-known Swiss-based organisation has offices in major towns which are near important projects, including Antsiranana (Diego Suarez) and Taolagnaro (Fort Dauphin).

Categories ANGAP places their many parks and reserves into three main categories:

Parc National
In the five national parks, all farming, hunting and logging by local farmers, as well as living in the park, is prohibited. Guided visits by foreigners are permitted.

Réserve Spéciale
The 23 special reserves protect less important areas of flora and fauna. They can be visited by foreigners, and locals can live in the reserve, but farming, hunting and logging is prohibited.

Réserve Naturelle Intégral
In the 11 completely natural reserves access is strictly forbidden for locals and foreigners, except authorised researchers.

To add to the confusion, a few places have been designated as places of biological interest (Site d'Intérêt Biologique) and there are also a few forestry reserves (Réserve Forestière). Foreigners can visit these areas and locals can live in them, but little research is done and very few funds are allocated for development.

Popular Parks The following is a rundown of the most popular parks and reserves (in alphabetical order); it is by no means a complete listing:

Parc National d'Andasibe-Mantadia (aka Périnet Reserve)
An extremely popular reserve; this is the best place to see and hear the unique indri, the largest of the lemurs, as well as several other lemur species, chameleons and other fauna.

Parc National de Isalo
The wild and spectacular landscapes of Isalo offer fabulous trekking and are home to unusual vegetation and several species of lemur.

Parc National de Mananara Nord
This remote national park and UNESCO Biosphere Reserve includes large areas of primary rainforest, coastal vegetation and coral reef. It protects several species of lemur, including the aye-aye and the hairy-eared dwarf lemur.

Parc National de Montagne d'Ambre
Just south of Antsiranana, this national park is the best place to see the crowned lemur. The landscape is also wonderful, with pleasant rainforest and waterfalls.

Parc National de Ranomafana
This park preserves a large area of eastern rainforest and is home to a vast array of species, including many species of lemur. It is the only known habitat of the golden bamboo lemur and the extremely rare broad-nosed gentle lemur.

Réserve d'Analamera
A remote and beautiful reserve that lies on the Analamera Plateau in the far north-east. Of major interest is Perrier's diademed sifaka, which is found only here and in the nearby Ankàrana Reserve. The Analamera Reserve is currently under the administration of the WWF, which plans to develop it for tourism and to improve access.

Réserve d'Ankarafantsika & Réserve Forestière d'Ampijoroa
This lonely reserve and forestry station near Mahajanga is a good place to see sifakas, brown lemurs and even mongoose lemurs.

Réserve de Nosy Mangabe
Nosy Mangabe in eastern Madagascar is a remote, beautiful island with a variety of wildlife. It is probably the best place to see aye-ayes in the wild.

Réserve des Tsingy de Bemaraha
This reserve protects the other-worldly karst (tsingy) landscapes of the remote Tsingy de Bemaraha in western Madagascar.

Réserve Privée de Berenty
This private reserve is one of the most popular and worthwhile attractions in Madagascar, offering the opportunity to see ring-tailed and brown lemurs and sifakas, as well as nocturnal lemurs and other wildlife. It also contains one of the country's last stands of gallery forest.

Réserve Spéciale de l'Ankàrana
This beautiful massif has been bizarrely eroded into karst pinnacles and caverns, creating sheltered habitats for large populations of lemurs and cave-dwelling crocodiles. Many of the caves are held sacred by the local Malagasy.

Réserve Spéciale de Beza-Mahafaly
This rather difficult-to-reach reserve lies near Toliara. It protects significant areas of spiny forest and gallery forest, providing the habitat for ring-tailed lemurs and sifakas.

Station Forestière et Piscicole de Manjakatompo
This is a newly established reserve near Tana which was created with the help of the GTZ. It is well set up and accessible, and makes an enjoyable and easy day trip from the capital.

Permits All foreigners wishing to visit any park or reserve in Madagascar, regardless of which company or agency runs them, require a permit. This is simply a means of obtaining funds for maintenance and development, and to keep an eye on visitors. Always keep your ticket: you may need to show it to an official during your visit or when you leave. On the back of the ticket provided by ANGAP is another gentle reminder in French and English about the regulations of visiting parks.

You can obtain a permit at the entrance to all the major parks and reserves, which includes just about all those listed in this book, or from an office run by ANGAP, WWF or the Water & Forest Department in the nearest major town. If you go to a remote park which does not have an office, or you wish to buy your permit(s) in Tana, you can buy them at the WWF or ANGAP head

>0>0>0>0>0>0>0>0>0>0>0>0>0<

Visiting National Parks
Agencies involved in the national parks of Madagascar ask that you consider the following guidelines:

* Keep to existing paths
* Do not litter, and take out all rubbish
* Do not camp in unofficial areas
* Bury your waste and toilet paper
* Do not touch or remove plants Take all necessary equipment, and don't rely on local villagers for food, drink or shelter
* Only light fires in designated areas
* Respect local customs and ask about *fady* (taboos)
* Use an official guide
* Do not feed animals
* Do not enter a park without a ticket
* Keep noise to a minimum ■

>0>0>0>0>0>0>0>0>0>0>0>0>0<

offices; their addresses are listed earlier in this section.

In September 1997 the fee for non-resident foreign adults (ie most tourists) to each ANGAP park and reserve increased to a hefty FMg 50,000 (FMg 2500 for any non-resident foreign child under 14 years). This permit allows you to stay in one park or reserve for three continuous days. For foreign residents the fee is FMg 35,000 for three days; and for Malagasy FMg 2500 for three days. If you are a consultant or researcher you pay FMg 125,000 for three continuous months for each park or reserve, and film-makers get a permit for 15 continuous days for a whopping FMg 500,000. At the time of research, it was unclear whether the permits for parks run by the WWF and other agencies will also increase in line with ANGAP – but it seems likely they will.

While the ANGAP fees seem high, it is reassuring to know that 50% of monies raised from all permits is handed back to the local people for development purposes. The remaining 50% goes to ANGAP to fund their excellent organisation, and to build roads, run local education programs, provide displays and so on.

The ANGAP office in Tana (open from 8 am to midday, and from 1 to 4 pm on week-days) is worth visiting if you are going to spend much time in the parks or reserves. You can buy wonderful calendars, handy brochures with maps (FMg 7500), videos, posters, magazines, T-shirts and books on Malagasy flora and fauna at the shop on the ground floor. Some staff speak English; they all speak fluent French.

Guides All parks and reserves run by ANGAP, and most of the parks run by the other agencies, state that you must hire a guide during your visit. This ensures that foreigners behave themselves in the park, and it creates employment and promotes a local economy based around conservation. Guides will also enhance your appreciation of local flora and fauna by, for example, explaining the various plants and spotting lemurs. If you ask, most major parks can find a guide who speaks French, English, Spanish, Italian, German or Japanese – and some are 'specialists' in flora and birds.

The new ANGAP regulations established in September 1997 state that guides will be paid FMg 2500 per visitor. As guides currently earn from FMg 20,000 for a few hours' walk to FMg 40,000 for a full day, we are unsure how ANGAP will regulate the new price schedule. The charge for hiring guides is always listed somewhere in the entrance offices, and the fees are non-negotiable anyway.

For more information about hiring guides, refer to the Activities section of the Regional Facts for the Visitor chapter.

Literature You can pick up a copy of the ANGAP quarterly magazine, *Hanitriniala*, from the ANGAP and WWF offices and major bookshops in Tana. Among other things, it contains current information on the various parks and discussions about ecological issues. At FMg 1500, this excellent, French-language publication is sensibly affordable for Malagasy people. It is well worth buying.

Also priced for the benefit of local Malagasy, and available at ANGAP, WWF and bookshops in Tana, is the impressive quarterly published by the WWF called *Vintsy* (FMg 300). It is more oriented towards children as a way of encouraging an interest in local ecology, and is printed in French and Malagasy.

GOVERNMENT & POLITICS

From 1975 to 1993 the Repoblikan'i Madagasikara or Republic of Madagascar was ruled by President Didier Ratsiraka as Le Deuxième République (The Second Republic) under a totalitarian and nominally Marxist ideology. In the lead up to the 1989 elections party pluralism was introduced and a market economy began to emerge, but among widespread accusations of ballot rigging Ratsiraka was somehow elected to a further seven year term.

The elections in February 1993 ended Ratsiraka's 17 years of dictatorship in favour of Albert Zafy and his Forces Vives (CFV) party, a vast coalition comprising representatives from numerous parties with lively names, such as Measures and Weights, Torch and Progress.

Following the impeachment of Zafy in mid-1996, new presidential elections were held. All seemed to be forgiven when, in a surprise result, Ratsiraka was elected again for a five year term. The current Prime Minister is Norbert Ratsirahonana.

Madagascar is ruled by a bicameral (two chamber) parliament. Two-thirds of the upper house or *senat* is elected by an electoral college and the remainder is appointed by the president. The *assemblée nationale* (national assembly) has 138 members elected for a four-year term from 57 constituencies throughout the country.

The country is politically divided into six divisions: Antananarivo, Antsiranana, Fianarantsoa, Mahajanga, Toamasina and Toliara. Local government organs include the *faritany* (provinces), *fivondronampokotany* (préfectures), *firaisampokotany* (counties), *fokontany* (individual communities) and *fokonolona* (village social committees).

Some Economic Statistics
- GDP per capita: US$790 per annum
- GDP growth rate: 2.8% per annum
- Inflation rate: 35% per annum
- Major exports: coffee, vanilla, cloves
- Major imports: manufacturing goods, food, petrol
- External debt: more than US$4.5 billion ■

ECONOMY

Although Madagascar is potentially a rich country, any economic gains have been quickly swallowed by a number of setbacks, including droughts, governmental corruption, widespread environmental destruction (followed by erosion), lack of wise and experienced management, low foreign reserves, continuing high inflation and unrestrained population growth.

The national economy is still based on agriculture and fishing, which employ about 85% of the people, provide up to 70% of export earnings (mainly coffee, vanilla and cloves) and 30% of the Gross Domestic Product (GDP). Industry – mainly textiles, car manufacturing and glassware – account for only 13% of the annual GDP, which at US$790 per capita is one the lowest in the world.

Rice is the most important commodity and the primary indicator of economic well-being. Until 1971 the country produced enough to feed itself and have some left over for export. In 1976 the government nationalised rice paddies; predictably, the move failed miserably and the crops were denationalised in 1984. Madagascar now exports only its finest quality rice, importing lesser quality rice to meet its growing demand.

In the arid deep south, where agriculture is tenuous at best, famine is a reality. In recent years an estimated 40,000 people have perished in an enduring famine in the south and south-west regions. Some international aid organisations predict that in the south the drought, compounded by widespread environmental destruction, may result in a tragedy on the scale of Somalia in the early 1990s.

Exports crops such as vanilla, sisal, coffee and cloves have also suffered badly from plummeting international prices, bad management and unfavourable climatic conditions. The immense herds of zebu kept by the Antandroy and Mahafaly tribes of the arid south, as well as the Sakalava in the west, are also in decline, primarily because of drought. In fact, Madagascar's zebu population has only now been surpassed by the human population.

In recent years the government has attempted to attract foreign investment, but strict conditions and excessive state control offer few incentives to many potential firms. Nonetheless, several big companies have considered the possibility of exploiting some of the country's untapped mineral and oil resources. Tourism is being promoted as a major earner of foreign exchange.

Madagascar still depends heavily on France for most of its trade: 33% of Madagascar's exports go to France, which provides 31% of Madagascar's imported goods. France, the USA (Madagascar's second largest trading partner), Japan, South Africa and Germany provide the bulk of foreign aid. In 1996, the European Union authorised a five year loan of FMg 9 billion for redevelopment, and the World Bank (after Zafy was dismissed) came in with US$250 million worth of development projects.

POPULATION & PEOPLE

The Malagasy people are descended primarily from Malay-Polynesians who arrived around 1500 to 2000 years ago. Evidence of the use of stone tools over 2000 years ago may indicate that the island was settled earlier.

The country's rapidly growing population of approximately 14 million is double what it was at the time of Independence in 1960, and is expected to double again by 2015. Nearly half of Madagascar's population is

Some Population Statistics
- Population: approx. 14 million
- Density: 23.8 persons per sq km
- Population aged 0-14 years: 47%
- Population growth: 3.18% per annum
- Birth rate: 4.48% per annum
- Death rate: 1.99% per annum
- Infant mortality: 12%
- Doctor ratio: one per 9939 people
- Life expectancy: male 52 years; female 55 years
- Fertility rate: 6.62 children per woman
- Literacy: male 88%; female 73% ■

under 14 years of age. While this may seem alarming there are only 24 people per sq km in Madagascar, compared with 236 in the UK and 101 in France.

Apart from the 18 Malagasy tribes, the population of Madagascar includes Europeans (mainly French), Comorans, Indo-Pakistanis and Chinese. On the surface many of these seem to be well integrated into the Malagasy community and race relations are generally good. However, there is a great deal of resentment toward the merchant classes, who are primarily comprised of Indians and Pakistanis. In early 1987 riots against Indo-Pakistani merchants, mainly in the west and south-west, forced many people to migrate to Réunion or farther afield. Such outbreaks are rare, but those who spend some time in the country may become aware of subtle undercurrents of unease or inequality between the relatively wealthy and educated Malagasy of the hauts plateaux and those of the poorer and more provincial coastal regions. Even within Merina society itself a subtle caste system based on skin tone is in evidence.

The inhabitants of Madagascar are known in English as Malagasy and in French as Malgache; either of these spellings renders the pronunciation 'mal-*GASH*'. Despite their geographic proximity to Africa and their mixed ancestry (especially around the coasts), the Malagasy do not like to be referred to as African.

The genuine warmth of the reception most foreigners receive is surprising given the island's recent history; the Malagasy are undoubtedly some of the most free and easy, friendly folk around. Providing their traditions are treated with respect, their hospitality can be hard to match. In very remote areas, some young children may have been told frightening tales about white folk, seen violent videos full of violent white people, or may never have seen a European face before, but as independent travellers and tour groups fan out across the country in search of the new and exotic, this is becoming increasingly rare. Sadly, foreigners are now more likely to be accosted for gifts rather than to be regarded with fear.

The 18 Tribes

Although the country officially shares one basic culture and language, the Malagasy people are divided into 18 tribes whose boundaries are based on old kingdoms rather than ethnic characteristics.

While some groups, such as the Merina of the Antananarivo area, are predominantly Indonesian in appearance and others, such as the Vezo of the south-west coast, clearly have close affinities with black tribes of East Africa, most Malagasy people are of mixed ancestry.

Antaifasy

The name of this small tribe means 'Those Who Live in the Sand'. They inhabit the east coast region around Farafangana.

Antaimoro

The name means 'Those From the Coast'. The Antaimoro, who live on the east coast near Manakara, are among the most recently arrived Malagasy and have relatively close ties with the Arab world. They use a form of Arabic script called *sorabe*, with which they have preserved old Islamic traditions, and practise *sikidy*, a form of divination using seeds.

Antaisaka

The name of this highly traditional tribe means 'Those From Sakalava Country'. This small tribe is an offshoot of the Sakalava and primarily occupies a region on the south-east coast. Historically, the Antaisaka had a reputation for producing great warriors.

Antakàrana

The name of this very small tribe, which inhabits the Ankàrana area of the far north, means 'Those From the Cliffs', in reference to the main Ankàrana massif. Primarily fisherfolk and pastoralists, they retain strong Islamic influences.

Antambohoaka

The name of this tribe in the south-east near Mananjary means 'Those of the Community'. They still cling to some Islamic traditions, including their refusal to eat meat unless all the animal's blood has been removed.

Antandroy

The semi-nomadic Antandroy, 'Those of the Thorns', are one of the poorest tribal groups and live in the dry and desolate spiny forest of the far south. Because their region lacks water, they eat very little rice, instead growing cassava and maize. They are mainly occupied with making and selling charcoal. Many people leave the land to find work elsewhere.

Antanosy

The name of this far southern tribe means 'Those of the Island', after a small island in the Fanjahira near Taolagnaro. After fleeing Merina domination, they settled in a large area of the far south-east. Their lives are controlled by numerous *fady* (taboos).

Bara

The name of this south central tribe is thought to be of mixed Bantu origin but its meaning is unknown. Tall, slender, dark and graceful, the Bara have the most markedly African features of any Malagasy tribe.

They are primarily pastoralists with a historical reputation for fierce warlike behaviour and are well known for cattle rustling *(dahalo)* as a test of manhood and proof of worthiness for marriage.

Betsileo

The name of this tribe means 'The Invincibles'. They live around the Fianarantsoa region and are known for their wood carving and agricultural skills, especially rice terracing and cultivation.

A well-known subgroup, the **Zafimaniry**, occupies the territory east of Ambositra; the artistry of these celebrated wood carvers is renowned throughout the country.

Betsimisaraka

This tribe, which inhabits most of the central and north-east coastal region, is called 'Those Who are Inseparable' after their confederation was forged from several smaller tribes in the early 18th century. They are primarily agriculturalists, planting and tending coffee, sugar cane and cloves.

The Betsimisaraka are the second most numerous tribe in Madagascar. The people of Île Sainte Marie, which is part of Betsimisaraka territory, are often considered the 19th tribe of

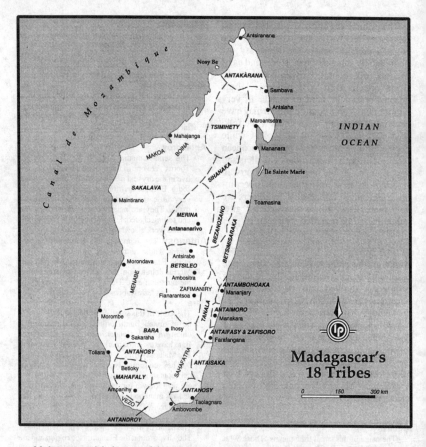

Madagascar's
18 Tribes

0   150   300 km

Madagascar, mainly because of their historical ties with the French and other foreigners.

Bezanozano

The name of this small tribe means 'Those With Many Little Plaits', in reference to their African style coiffures. Their mountainous rainforested territory lies along a thin north-south strip between Antananarivo and the coast.

Mahafaly

The name of this agricultural tribe means 'Makers of Taboos'. They inhabit the southern and south-western areas of Madagascar, overlapping in places with the Antandroy and Antanosy territories.

Relative latecomers to the island (they are thought to have arrived less than 900 years ago), the Mahafaly stubbornly resisted Andrianam-poinimerina's unification efforts and remained more or less independent until the French colonisation.

The Mahafaly tombs are reputed to be the most colourful and skilfully conceived on the island and they are also known for their fanciful *aloalo* (elaborate wood carvings, normally over one metre high) and stelae which are used on tombs to illustrate scenes from the ancestors' life. Among other tribes, the Mahafaly have a reputation for wisdom.

Merina

The name of this ruling tribe means 'Those From the Highlands', and they bear the lightest skin and most Asiatic features of any Malagasy tribe. It was the Merina kings who succeeded in unifying Madagascar under a single government and for that reason, the Merina capital, Antananarivo, now serves as the national capital.

The Merina utilise a unique three-caste system largely based on skin tone: *andriana*, the nobles; *hova*, the commoners; and *andevo*, the workers.

Sakalava

The name Sakalava means 'Those of the Long Valleys' and refers to those occupying a vast area of western Madagascar which extends from Toliara in the south to north of the Betsiboka river in the north-west.

This primarily dark-skinned tribe started as a confederation of several earlier groups. The far-flung nature of their territory has never promoted a great deal of unity and they split early on into two great kingdoms: the Menabe in the south and the Boina in the north.

Within their territory live two other prominent subgroups: the **Makoa**, descendants of African slaves who have settled around the mouth of the Onilahy river near Mahajanga; and the **Vezo**, fisherfolk who inhabit the far south-western coasts around Toliara. The latter are known for the large outrigger canoes used for fishing expeditions on the high seas.

Sihanaka

The name Sihanaka means 'Those Who Wander in the Marshes'. These fisherfolk and rice-growing agriculturalists primarily inhabit the swampy lowlands surrounding Lac Alaotra. They are responsible for draining the lake area, which is now known as the 'granary of Madagascar', for the cultivation of rice.

Tanala

The name means 'Those of the Forest'. These people inhabit the mountainous area of the eastern rainforests around Ranomafana. Primarily agriculturalists, they clear forested land by burning to make way for the growing of coffee and rice. They are renowned for harvesting and eating local honey.

Tsimihety

The name of this north-western tribe, which means 'Those Who Don't Cut Their Hair', stems from their refusal to cut their hair – a symbolic act which was traditionally a sign of respect and mourning – upon the death of a Sakalava king. Pastoralists and rice farmers, the Tsimihety have a reputation for being passive.

Zafisoro

The origin of the name Zafisoro is unknown. This small tribe inhabits the same region as the rival Antaifasy.

EDUCATION

In 1972, in the hope of making education more accessible to the masses, Madagascar replaced French with Malagasy as the official language of instruction. However, in 1986 French was reintroduced in secondary schools in order to facilitate international communication.

Officially, 87% of school-aged children attend primary school at one time or other, but in reality only about one-third of children complete a primary education and perhaps less than 10% finish secondary school. Figures are usually lower, but unknown, in rural areas.

The literacy rate in Madagascar is around 40%, but most literacy is concentrated in cities and larger towns. Sadly, things are getting worse. A growing number of children in Tana are being withdrawn from school by their parents, who can't afford the school fees or need the extra income their children can bring in by begging or hawking on the streets. Also, partly because of austerity measures imposed on the country by the World Bank, hundreds of schools have been closed over the past few years, spending on education has been severely slashed and salaries of teachers are irregularly paid.

ARTS

Dance & Hira Gasy

If you're lucky, or persistent, you may be able to attend a *hira gasy*. These popular music, dancing and storytelling spectacles are held in the highlands. (In fact, a hira gasy is held in Tana on most Sunday afternoons – refer to the Antananarivo chapter for details).

A hira gasy is performed by a number of wildly clad troupes, known as *mpihira gasy* or *mpilalao*, which consist of 25 performers each (18 men and seven women). These troupes hold competitions for the best costume and the most original, moving or exciting performance.

The performance begins with a complicated and eloquent *kabary* (a discourse performed by an orator). The skill of these speakers, who are normally respected elders, would shame western politicians. After the rhetoric, other members of the troupe illustrate the message set forth by their speaker in wonderfully exuberant song and acrobatic dances accompanied by tinny trumpet and clarinet music. Each dancer is dressed in a long gown, called a *malabary*, while ladies also wear the traditional scarf, called a *lamba*.

The themes are always upbeat, extolling the virtues of honesty, upholding traditions, and encouraging young people to respect their parents. The competition winner is selected by the audience's response to the performances.

If you can't make it to a hira gasy, two of the best places to see some traditional Malagasy dancing are at the Rova (King Andrianampoinimerina's palace) in Ambohimanga, about 20km north of Antananarivo; and at the Grill du Rova restaurant in Tana. Otherwise, contact the tourist office or the various cultural centres in Tana for details about possible performances.

Music

Most contemporary and traditional Malagasy music revolves around favourite dance rhythms: the Indonesian and Kenyan influenced *salegy* of the Sakalava tribe; the African *watsa watsa*; the *tsapika*, which originated in the south; the *basese* from the north; the *sigaoma*, similar to black South African popular music; and the Creole *sega* of Mauritius, Réunion and the Seychelles.

Traditional These dance rhythms are accompanied by instruments such as the flute, whistle and *valiha*. The latter is a unique stringed instrument, with 28 strings of varying lengths stretched around a tubular wooden sound box – it resembles a bassoon but is played more like a harp. It is also still played in Malaysia and Indonesia, the ancestral homeland of the Malagasy – evidence that it was bought to Madagascar by the earliest settlers of the island. The recognised expert on the valiha is Rakotozafy, who played and recorded valiha music for a couple of decades.

The *lokanga voatavo* (cordophone), which has a gourd as a resonator, is also popular, and the Malagasy also play a variety

of guitars, including the *kabosy*, a small ukelele-type guitar. A single-stringed instrument, the *jejolava*, is played with a bow and has a coconut-shell sound box. The continued use of accordions reflects the French influence and a variety of percussion instruments is also used. The most widely used traditional wind instrument is the *kiloloka*, a whistle-like length of bamboo capable of only one note. Melodies are played by a group of musicians, each producing their note as necessary, much like a bell ensemble. The traditional Malagasy flute is known as a *sodina*.

Perhaps the most renowned Malagasy musician is Paul Bert Rahasimanana, better known as Rossy, who began his career performing *vaky soava*, a rhythmic, choral music accompanied only by hand-clapping. He further developed his individual style by adding instrumental accompaniment and, through local concerts and radio performances, he and his band achieved popularity in Madagascar. Rossy's most popular recording, *Island of Ghosts*, was composed to accompany the film *Mbola Tsara*, and in 1995 he released *Bal Kabosy*. The music combines instrumental styles, drawn from traditional sources throughout Madagascar, with highly allegorical lyrics which weave together themes of poverty, love, loss and hope.

Modern Madagascar boasts numerous excellent folk and pop musicians. The best known of the contemporary Malagasy pop groups and singers is Dama, who was popular enough to get elected to parliament in 1993, Rebika, Tearano, Tiana and the perennial favourites Mahaleo. Malagasy groups who have toured internationally, mainly in France and the UK, include Njava and Tarika (which means 'The Group'). Members of Tarika play the valiha and kabosy; their most recent album, *Son Egal*, was released in 1997.

You can easily buy official (and pirated) tapes and compact discs of traditional and modern Malagasy music in the markets, in specialised music shops and bookshops in the major towns throughout Madagascar; and at import record stores overseas, particularly in France. One of the best places to watch and hear music from Madagascar, as well as from nearby islands like Mauritius and Réunion, is the annual music festival held on the island of Nosy Be in late May.

Literature

The first literature didn't appear until the 1850s when the first Malagasy historian, Raombana, faithfully recorded 8000 pages about the reign of Ranavalona I. Modern Malagasy poetry and literature didn't really flower until the 1930s and 1940s. The best known figure was the poet Jean-Joseph Rabearivelo, whose themes revolved around human connections with the earth as the land of one's ancestors. He committed suicide in 1947 at the age of 36.

In recent years, Fianarantsoa has developed into a literary capital of sorts and a number of Malagasy writers and novelists, including Jean Ndema, Rakotonaivo, Rainifihina Jessé and, especially, Emilson D Andriamalala, are kept busy pouring out the country's literary heart.

Highly prized traditional oratory, called *kabary*, takes several forms including speech-making and storytelling. Competitions are often held between several kabary experts and it is an integral part of the hira gasy. Kabary originated in early political assemblies in which each councillor spoke in turn, offering advice and opinions. It was eventually popularised and extended to the general public as a form of entertainment, growing more and more imaginative until it became the art form that it is today.

A kabary competition begins with the orator delivering a series of proverbs and introductions, using allegory, double entendre, metaphor and simile. They continue speaking for as long as possible while avoiding direct contact with the subject at hand. Only those with a fluent knowledge of Malagasy will be able to fully appreciate the incredible palaver and the skill involved.

The Malagasy also love another oral tradition, the *ohabolana* (proverb), which imaginatively (and compulsively) use wise and witty sayings to express thoughts and opinions on a variety of subjects – some of which don't always translate so well.

He who refuses to buy a lid for the pot will eat badly cooked rice.

Invite a big eater and he will finish the meal; advise a fool and he will waste your time.

You can trap an ox by its horns and a man by his words.

While listening to a kabary well spoken, one fails to notice the fleas that bite him.

Football in the rice paddies has neither rules nor techniques, and isn't known to be an entertaining spectacle.

For those who read French, there are still a few copies of the book *Ohabolana ou Proverbes Malgaches*, by Réverand JA Houlder, floating around in Tana bookshops. This 216-page treatise is the standard work on the subject.

Architecture

Each region of the country has its own architectural style and building materials. On the hauts plateaux, brick is the preferred construction material because few trees remain in the region and brick conserves heat better on cold winter nights.

Coastal homes, on the other hand, are constructed of lighter local materials, including the *Alluaudia* cactus in the Antandroy region of the south, the fronds of the *Raffia* palm in the far north and the *Ravenala* (or travellers' palm) on the east coast. You can see an excellent example of the latter at the museum in Toliara.

Unlike African homes, Malagasy structures are normally quadrangular. In Imerina, the Merina country of the hauts plateaux, the typical home is tall and narrow with multiple storeys, and constructed mostly of red brick with small windows. The homes normally open to the west, with brick pillars in the front supporting open verandahs. Further south, around Fianarantsoa, the houses are similar to those of Imerina, but are trimmed in amusingly and elaborately carved wood.

PAUL GREENWAY

An example of typical Betsileo architecture in central Madagascar; note the wooden balcony. In parts of the island it is considered simpler to build a new dwelling than to renovate an old one.

SOCIETY & CONDUCT

Most aspects of Malagasy culture have been transplanted on the island from other continents. Belief in *vintana* (or destiny) may have its roots in Islamic cosmology, while the religious significance and status of cattle are clearly linked to the Malagasy's African roots.

Beyond the cities and accessible towns, traditional values have more influence over people's lives than introduced religions. In fact, the most pervasive aspect of traditional Malagasy culture is *razana* (ancestors, and the reverence and respect accorded them), but it's impossible to generalise these practises because each tribe handles funeral and burial rites in its own way. Among most tribes, reverence for the ancestors is manifest in a complex system of fady (see next section) and burial rites. For the Merina and several other tribes, this veneration even extends to periodic *famadihana* (exhumation and reburial).

If you're interested in learning more about traditional Malagasy culture, the best and most accessible work is *Madagascar – Island of the Ancestors* by John Mack. The new US-based Madagascar Museum Society is also worth contacting; its web site is http://squash.la.psu.edu/plarson/mms/homepage.html. For more general information about traditions, refer to the Society & Conduct section in the Facts about the Region chapter.

Fady

In simple terms, fady is a system of local taboos attributed to the ancestors and aimed at keeping them as content as possible. For example, it may be fady to whistle on a particular stretch of beach near one village or to walk past a sacred tree in another. It may be fady to eat pork in one village, while a neighbouring village is squealing with pigs. There are thousands of these superstitions and they have great influence over the country people.

Although foreigners and other outsiders are normally exempted from fady (or are excused for breaking it), it shouldn't be taken lightly. Because it's almost impossible to anticipate the fady that applies to any specific place, there's not very much travellers can do but ask and be especially careful in the vicinity of tombs or burial sites. For some information about visiting highly traditional areas, see Visiting Villages later in this section.

Famadihana

The famadihana (turning of the bones), also known as 'second burial', is primarily a Merina custom, but it has also been adopted by some other tribes. The Merina hold their dead dear – but not departed. Their ancestors, the razana, remain with the family after death and play as great a part in the family as when they were alive. The source of most fady, the ancestors are revered, consulted, placated and petitioned to bestow good fortune on the family.

Whenever a family feels the necessity to visit an ancestor; or wishes to bring home the body of a family member who has died elsewhere; or if the family tomb is full and the bodies must be buried somewhere else; or if another family tomb has been built, the family will throw a party in honour of the ancestor – and invite them along.

Although it can be a sombre occasion, the famadihana is more like an Irish wake than a funeral and isn't normally a time for mourning. The costs of the celebration, which can last up to two days, are enormous and include catering for all the guests, employing a band, hiring an *ombiasy* and sacrificing the appropriate number of zebu.

The ritual itself begins with the exhumation of the body, which is then washed and rewrapped in new shrouds. Family members visit with the guest of honour, hugging them, chatting or singing to them, and even dancing with them. In the end the honoured ancestor is returned to his or her resting place, often accompanied by gifts. Even devout Christians, including ministers and priests, have been known to attend famadihana and the families concerned are frequently practising Christians.

Most famadihana occur during the winter months of August and September. The presence of strangers is often considered a positive omen and visitors may well be asked to honour the family and the razana with their presence. Although some travellers may catch a glimpse of a famadihana procession, few are privileged enough to actually attend one, so if you are invited, count yourself extremely fortunate. Please *always* ask permission before even contemplating taking photographs.

Dress

Among the Merina of the highlands, the most distinctive element of female dress is the lamba, a white silk, cotton or synthetic scarf which is worn around the shoulders and often draped over the head, with one tail hanging behind. When this tail falls on the right side of the body, it signifies that the wearer is in mourning and is known as a *lamba maitso* ('green cloth'), even though it isn't necessarily green.

On special occasions, certain people wear red lambas, signifying authority. The *lamba mena* (literally, 'red cloth'), which is rarely actually red, is a burial shroud. The name probably just reflects the authority of the ancestors.

Women of other tribes, particularly the Sakalava and the Antakàrana, normally wear colourful dyed cotton lambas which they also use for carrying babies and young children while shopping, walking through town or working in the fields. The weavers of Ambalavao are especially adept at creating colourful lambas in complex geometric patterns.

Malagasy men also wear lambas, either tied around the waist or around the shoulders, but another outstanding feature of male dress is the omnipresent hat. The Betsileo generally wear four-cornered hats, the Merina wear rice straw hats and the Bara of the south-west favour cone-shaped hats.

Malagasy creativity also extends to some pretty interesting headgear – just take a walk around Tana!

Visiting Villages

Those who visit a remote village or small town without a guide should carefully consider the impact of their visit and all the responsibilities and implications it carries – and also keep in mind that fady are a very real aspect of everyday life.

While it will be impossible for foreigners to know the intricacies of local fady without being told, some general guidelines will hold true throughout most of the country. In general people, property, family relationships and ancestors must be respected. Visitors, especially male, should not touch women, babies or elders (though a handshake is normally OK), or their belongings, or make comments about women or children unless invited to do so by a local man. Also, don't touch or make light of anything which in any way relates to the ancestors and take special care in the vicinity of tombs; don't photograph them or even touch them unless you're told it's all right to do so. It's OK to ask, but if they say no, don't do it! If there's no-one to ask, don't do it anyway.

Before outsiders will be accepted, they must satisfy the villagers' curiosity and allay any misgivings they may have. Seek out the local *raiamandreny* (head of the *fokontony*, the people's executive committee) and introduce yourself.

At this stage, you'll probably be offered food and a bed or house reserved for travellers. However, don't descend upon a village expecting hospitality from the locals; carry sufficient food for your proposed stay and please share what you have with your hosts.

If you are invited for meals or to share someone's home, you should expect to pay for your food and accommodation, though villagers may refuse money as payment or thanks, preferring instead condensed milk, chocolate, cigarettes or other items not available from the village shop. However, don't play Father Christmas and hand out gifts indiscriminately, lest you introduce foreign values or give the Malagasy misleading ideas about foreigners and/or western culture in general.

In the past, foreign travellers have managed to avail themselves of all sorts of courtesies and considerations by presenting a letter of introduction explaining their origins and interests. It is preferably in Malagasy, on official-looking notepaper and written by someone who at least sounds important. Whether or not this letter is appropriate is debatable. Nowadays, travellers are wandering further and further into rural areas and some frequently visited villagers are getting wise to the method. Nevertheless, in some places it will still be considered a gesture of respect; if you prefer to carry one as a courtesy organise it through a Malagasy consul, another official contact in your own country or through Malagasy friends in larger towns.

Malagasy hospitality is legendary but it does have its limits. Generally, the Malagasy are a patient, reserved and insular people, especially when it comes to innermost feelings and problems. These are rarely discussed between family members – let alone with new friends – and their sense of privacy should be respected. Similarly, foreigners discussing their own sentiments and private affairs in too much depth may be met with surprise or suspicion.

The Malagasy are also quite private and possessive about their culture and its deeper implications. Foreigners should always remain aware of their place as outsiders and not feign immediate intimacy with individuals, attempt to adopt the Malagasy culture or 'become' Malagasy, even in the superficial sense.

LANGUAGE

Madagascar has two official languages: Malagasy and French. Malagasy is the everyday spoken language while French is often used for business and administrative purposes. But don't expect French to be spoken or understood outside of major towns.

Although many Malagasy students are enthusiastically learning English, relatively few people speak it, and it's largely confined to tourism-oriented facilities and their services. Having said that, one can usually find someone willing to try out whatever words they might have picked up at school or elsewhere.

French

Unless you're travelling on an organised tour, it will be essential to speak at least basic French if you are to get by comfortably in cities and towns. In rural areas, where knowledge of French is much less widespread, you'll almost always find someone who speaks enough to permit communication.

For a run down of useful French words and phrases, refer to the language section of the general Facts for the Visitor chapter at the beginning of this book.

Malagasy

Even if you speak French, there's a good case for learning a few words of Malagasy as well. For example, most market stall holders, even at the Zoma in Antananarivo, know only enough French to be able to sell their products. Beyond the major towns, a little Malagasy will go a long way toward fostering goodwill and understanding. As there are only minimal regional variations in the language, a basic set of words will be of help throughout the island.

Malagasy belongs to the Austronesian family of languages, which also includes Indonesian and Polynesian. Scholars have traced Malagasy's closest linguistic cousin to southern Borneo. But just as Malagasy culture has absorbed aspects of several other cultures, the language too has adopted and adapted many words from Arabic, French, English and others.

Grammar The grammar of Malagasy is markedly different from that of English or other Indo-european languages, reflecting a very different world view. Native speakers, for instance, tend to avoid beginnning a phrase with the word 'I'. Verbs and adverbs of place (there are over sixteen ways to say

'here' and 'there') are also notoriously tricky for beginners.

If you're serious about learning Malagasy, it will be worth investing in one of the dictionaries or instructional textbooks available in Tana bookshops (see the Books section in the Madagascar Facts for the Visitor chapter).

Pronunciation In response to King Radama I's request to the LMS for help with education and the development of Madagascar, a mission was sent which included two Welshmen, David Jones and David Griffiths. Together with the king himself, they set about romanising and transliterating the Malagasy language. Based on the Merina dialect, this 'standard Malagasy' has since then served as the national language for education, mass communication, evangelisation and administration.

The Malagasy alphabet has 21 letters; the letters 'c','q','u', 'w' and 'x' do not exist. In words borrowed from English, French or other languages, the 'c' is replaced by an 's' or 'k', the 'q' is replaced with 'k' and 'x' with 'ks'.

All the individual sounds of Malagasy are common to English and are therefore easily pronounced. The conventions for vowel orthography might at first seem strange, but otherwise, unless noted, sounds follow anticipated pronunciation.

a	'a' as in 'father'. At the end of a word, it is often barely audible.
i, y	'ee' as in 'feet'. Note: As in English, at the ends of words 'i' is spelt 'y' (biby 'bee-bee').
o	'oo' as in 'food'
e	'ey' as in French é
ai	'y' as in 'my'
ao	'ow' as in 'cow'; sometimes closer to 'o' as in 'toe'.
oa	pronounced 'oo-ah'
eo	pronounced 'é-oo'
j	is pronounced 'dz' (rojo 'roo-dzoo')
r	is rolled
g	is always hard as in 'good'

h is practically silent in most words

gn, n as the 'ng' in 'song'. This velar, or nasal, n occurs only in certain coastal regions.

Accents As in English, certain syllables in Malagasy are heavily stressed, whereas others are scarcely pronounced. Good-bye, 'veloma', for example, emerges as *ve-LOO-m*. Also, an incorrect accent can change the meaning of a word: *ta-NA-na* 'town'; *TA-na-na* 'hand'. To aid pronunciation, in the glossary that follows, stressed syllables are marked by an accent (eg *làfo*).

Practice makes perfect. The following list of useful words and phrases will help to get you started:

Greetings & Civilities

yes	*èny/èka*
no	*tsìa*
('No' is also expressed as *UH-uh-UH*)	
Good day. (any time)	*Salàma*
Hello./How do you do?	*Manào ahòana ianào.*
Sir/Madam	*Tòmpoko*
Excuse me/Please.	*Azafàdy.*
Thank you (very much).	*Misàotra (Indrìndra).*
You're welcome.	*Tsy mìsy fisàorana.*
good/bad	*tsàra/ràtsy*
I'm fine.	*Salàma tsàra àho.*
Very well, thank you.	*Tsàra fà misàotra.*
Welcome.	*Tònga sòa.*
Goodbye.	*Velòma/Màndra-pihàona.*

Language Difficulties

I understand.	*Àzoko.*
I don't understand.	*Tsy àzoko.*
Do you speak English?	*Mahày mitèny englìsy vè ianào?*
Please repeat that.	*Mbà averèno azafàdy.*
Is there someone who speaks French/English?	*Mìsy òlona ve mahày mitèny frantsày/anglìsy?*

Useful Phrases

My name is ...	*... nò anàrako.*
OK/Alright.	*Ekèna*
How much?	*Ohatrìnona?*
too expensive	*làfo lòatra/làfo bè*
very cheap	*tèna mòra bè*
I'm in a hurry.	*Màika àho.*

Getting Around

I want to go to (Analakely/ the bank).	*Tè handèha hò (àny Analakely/any amin'ny labanky) àho.*
What time does the ... leave/arrive?	*Amin'ny fìry ny fandehànan'ny/ fahatongàvan'ny ...?*
bus	*fiàrabe/aotôbìsy*
train	*fiàran dalamby*
aeroplane	*fiaramanìdina*
taxi	*fiàra-karètsaka/ takìsy*
rickshaw	*posipòsy*
canoe	*làkana*
Where is the ...?	*Aìza ny ...?*
bus stop	*fijanònan'ny aotobìsy*
train station	*gàra*
taxi-brousse	*fiàran'ny tantsàha/ takìsy boròsy*
Where does this bus go?	*Ho aìza ity aôtobìsy ity?*
Does the bus go to ...?	*Mankàny ... ve ny aôtobisy?*
Where is the ticket office?	*Aìza ny fivaròtan-kàratra?*
I'd like a ...	*Mìla ... àho.*
one-way ticket	*kàratra mandròso*
return ticket	*kàratra mivèrina*
first-class	*kilêsy voalÿhany*
second class	*kilàsy faharòa*
left-luggage locker	*fametràhan'èntana*
I'd like to hire a ...	*Tèhanòfa ... àho.*
bicycle/motorcycle	*bisikilèta/môtô*
car	*fiarakodìa/ aôtomôbìlina*

Directions

How do I get to ...?	*Aìza ny làlana mankàny ...*
Is it near/far?	*Akàiky/Làvitra vè?*
(Go) straight ahead.	*(Mandehàna) mahìtsy.*
(turn) left	*(mihodìna) havìa/ankavìa*
(turn) right	*(mihodìna) havànana/ankavànana*
north	*avàratra*
south	*atsìmo*
east	*atsinànana*
west	*andrèfana*

Around Town

Where is the/a ...?	*Aìza mòa ny ...?*
bank	*bànky*
city centre	*tàmpon-tanàna*
embassy	*màso ivòho/ ambasàdy*
police	*pôlìsy*
post office	*pàositra*
telephone centre	*tràno fandefàsana telefàonina*

What time does it open/close?	*Amin'ny fìry no mivòha/mihìdy?*
I'd like to make a telephone call.	*Te hiàntso àmin'ny telefàonina àho.*
I'd like to change some money/ travellers' cheques.	*Te hanakàlo vòla/taratàsim-bòla àho.*

Accommodation

I'm looking for a ...	*Mitàdy ... àho.*
youth hostel	*tràno fandràisana tanòra*
camping ground	*toèrana fanàovan-dàsy*
hotel	*hôtèly mìsy fandrìana*

I'd like a to book a ...?	*Mìla ... àho.*
bed	*fandrìana*
single room	*èfitra ho an'òlona tòkana*

double room	*èfitra ho an'òlon-dròa*
shower	*èfitra fandròana*
for one/two night/s	*àlina rày/ròa*
How much is it per night/per person?	*Ohatrìnona isan'àlina/ isan'òlona?*
Can I see the room?	*Azoko jerèna ve ny èfi-tràno?*
Where is the toilet?	*Aiza ny gabinè?*
It is very dirty/noisy/ expensive.	*Tèna malòto/ mitabatàba/làfo ilày ìzy.*

Food

breakfast	*sakàfo maràina*
lunch	*sakàfo antoàndro*
dinner	*sakàfo harìva*
grocery store	*tsenakèly/episery*
market	*tsèna*
restaurant	*hôtèly fisakafoànana*
water	*ràno*
bread	*mòfo*
beef	*òmby*
chicken	*akòho*
pork	*kisòa*
coffee	*kafè*
tea	*ditè*
fruit	*voankàzo*
I am a vegetarian.	*Fàdy hèna àho.*

Time & Dates

What time is it?	*Amin'ny fìry zào?*
When?	*Rahovìana? (future) Ovìana? (past)*
today	*androàny (past part of day) anìo (part of day to come)*
tonight	*rahàlina*
tomorrow	*rahampìtso*
yesterday	*omàly*
Monday	*alatsinàiny*
Tuesday	*talàta*
Wednesday	*alarobìa*
Thursday	*alakamìsy*
Friday	*zomà*

Saturday	*asabòtsy*	to have diarrhoea	*mivàlana*
Sunday	*alahàdy*	to be dizzy	*fànina*
		to be vomiting	*mandòa*
Numbers		to be nauseous	*maloilòy*
1	rày (ìsa for counting)	malaria	*tàzo*
2	ròa	medicine	*fanafòdy*
3	tèlo	antiseptic	*antiseptìka*
4	èfatra	aspirin	*aspirìnina*
5	dìmy	condoms	*sàtro-bòto* or *kapôty*
6	ènina	contraceptive	*fòmba tsìmampitèraka*
7	fito	sanitary napkins	*serviètam-behivàvy*
8	vàlo	sunblock cream	*mènaka àro-*
9	sìvy		*masoàndro*
10	fòlo	tampons	*tsèntsin'ìsy*
100	zàto		
1000	arìvo		
10,000	ray àlina	**Emergencies**	
one million	ray tapitrìsa	Help!	*Vonjèo!*
		Police!	*Pôlìsy!*

Health

		danger	*lòza*
I need a doctor.	*Mìla dokotèra àho.*	Call a doctor/	*Antsòy ny dokotèra/*
Where is a hospital?	*Aiza no mìsy ny hôpitàly?*	ambulance!	*ambulance!*
		Go away!	*Mandehàna/*
I'm diabetic/epilep-tic/asthmatic.	*Vòan'ny diabèta/ àndro be/ sohìka aho.*		*Mialà tèo!*
		I've been robbed.	*Vòan'ny mpang- àlatra àho.*
I'm allergic to anti-biotics/penicillin.	*Tsy mahazàka antibiotìka/penisil ìnina àho.*	I've been raped.	*Nolotòin'òlona àho/ Novetavetàin'olon a aho.*
I'm pregnant.	*Bevòhoka àho.*	I'm lost.	*Vèry àho.*

Dialects
Despite the linguistic unity of Malagasy, regional differences do exist, and in some coastal areas, standard Malagasy is shunned. The three broad language groups are those of the highland plateaus, the North and East, and the South and West. And even these have regional variations. The following table indicates a few of the lexical and phonetic differences between standard Malagasy and some other dialects.

English	Highlands	East	Southwest
Greetings	*Manao ahoana.*	*Mbola tsara anarô?*	*Akore aby nareo?*
reply	*Tsara.*	*Mbola tsara.*	*Tsara/Soa.*
What's new?	*Inona no vaovao?*	*Ino vaovaonao?*	*Taliliol*
reply	*Tsy misy.*	*Ehe, tsisy fô manginginy.*	*Mbe soa.*
Where?	*Aiza?*	*Aia?*	*Aia?*
Who?	*Iza?*	*Ia?*	*Ia?*
white	*fotsy*	*fotsy*	*foty*
spouse	*vady*	*vady*	*valy*
ancestor	*razana*	*raza*	*raza* ∎

Facts for the Visitor

Maps

Many locally produced maps are based on the work of French colonial cartographers and are becoming outdated. They vary in format and quality, depending on the degree of alteration by successive governments, but they are generally quite accurate. All official maps are produced by the Foiben Taosarintanin'i Madagasikara (FTM) – known in French as the Institut Géographique et Hydrographique – at Làlana Radama Ntsoa RJB, Ambanidia, Antananarivo; BP 323 (☎ (2) 229 35).

The country is generally covered by 11 sheets of FTM maps at a scale of 1:500,000: *Antsiranana*, *Mahajanga*, *Antalaha*, *Maintirano*, *Toamasina*, *Morondava*, *Antananarivo*, *Toliara*, *Fianarantsoa*, *Ampanihy* and *Tôlañaro (Taolagnaro)*. These maps are available in most bookshops in Antananarivo (Tana) and, usually, in major towns throughout Madagascar. In less detail, Madagascar is also covered at 1:1,000,000 in four FTM sheets: *Antsiranana*, *Antananarivo*, *Fianarantsoa* and *Taolagnaro*.

If you are trekking or cycling, you should try to get the more detailed 1:100,000 series of maps; these are only available at the FTM office. FTM also produces town plans for Antananarivo, Fianarantsoa, Toamasina (also known as Tamatave), Antsiranana (aka Diego Suarez) and Toliara (Tuléar); a 1:10,000 series of eight sheets covering Antananarivo and environs; and tourist maps of the islands of Nosy Be and Île Sainte Marie which include the main town on each. There are no town plans for Mahajanga or Taolagnaro. However, there is little point buying these town or island maps as the maps in this book are more than adequate.

FTM also has a very good and readily available, but expensive, general 1:2,000,000 map of the country (with a brown and blue cover) entitled simply *Madagasikara Carte Routiere* (FMg 24,000). It is

overall the best locally produced map showing roads and villages, and is good enough for general travelling unless you are trekking or cycling into remote areas.

The best foreign map of Madagascar is the 1:2,000,000 sheet published by both Altäir in Spain and Kartográfiai Vállalat in Hungary.

TOURIST OFFICES
Local Tourist Offices

At last Madagascar has its own tourist office – a belated indication of how important the tourist industry is to the country. The Maison du Tourisme de Madagascar is well located at the Kianja ny Fahaleovantena (aka Place de L'Indépendance) in Haute-Ville, Antananarivo; BP 3224, directly opposite Le Buffet du Jardin restaurant – (☎ (2) 325 29; fax 325 37). Don't be fooled by another person or agency which purports to be from a 'Madagascar Tourism Office' or such like.

The tourist office can provide some free and useful brochures and booklets, such as *Madagascar, Island of Nature*, printed in French and English; the glossy eight-page *Bienvenue à Madagascar* written in French and German; and handy pamphlets, in French, about each major town and resort island – but don't get annoyed if the office runs out of these. Staff speak English and French, and some German.

You may as well visit the office anyway because you are subsidising its existence to the tune of FMg 1000 to FMg 3000 per room per night through the compulsory tourist tax. If you need any more information, or want to complain to someone higher than the tourist office, you can try contacting the Ministère de Tourisme, Rue Fernand Kassanga, Tsimbazaza, Antananarivo; BP 610 (☎ (2) 262 98).

Every major town and resort island also has a non-government tourism association made up of owners of local hotels and restaurants. On Nosy Be, the local association has its own tourist office, but one is yet to appear in any other place. Still, if you want any specific information or want to make a complaint they are worth contacting. The main associations are: Toamasina (☎ (5) 322 26); Antsiranana (☎ (8) 229 25); Nosy Be (☎ (8) 228 54); Taolagnaro (☎ (9) 212 38); Fianarantsoa (☎ (7) 514 86); Toliara (☎ (9) 419 00); and Mahajanga (☎ (6) 237 81).

Tourist Offices Abroad

The Madagascar tourist ministry has yet to set up any tourist offices overseas, relying on Air Madagascar (refer to the Madagascar Getting There & Away chapter for a full listing of airline offices overseas) and Malagasy consulates and embassies (refer to the Embassies section following) to act as de facto tourist offices. Air Madagascar and the Malagasy diplomatic missions can provide some basic maps and information, but you will probably have to wait until you visit the tourist office in Tana for anything specific.

Another alternative is to contact the Indian Ocean Regional Tourist Commission (refer to the Comoros Facts for the Visitor chapter for details).

VISAS & DOCUMENTS
Visas

All visitors except citizens of several African countries must have a visa issued by a Malagasy embassy or consulate. Currently, visas are valid for up to three months from the date of entry; usually you must be in and out of Madagascar within six months of the date of visa issue. Ask your embassy or consulate to give you a three month visa, if you need that long, because they are difficult and expensive to extend.

Most Malagasy consulates and embassies follow similar procedures, and visas take two to three days to issue. They usually cost the equivalent in the local currency of about US$33/39 for a single/double entry – though some consulates will charge the equivalent of US$33 for each entry, and others, such as the consulate in Denmark, charge the equivalent of US$70 for a single-entry visa.

You will need to fill out four forms, send four photographs and provide a copy of your ticket or itinerary from your travel agent – normally you must have a ticket out of the country before you are allowed in. Your passport should have a few spare pages, and should not be due to expire during your visit.

Transit visas (valid for 24 hours) and other visas, valid for a few days, are available at the international airport in Tana. However, this can only be obtained if you have arrived on a flight from a country which does not have a Malagasy embassy or consulate. (Currently, all of the handful of flights to Madagascar come from countries with a Malagasy diplomatic mission.) It is important to understand that if you come, for example, from the Netherlands, which does not have an embassy or consulate, but you have arrived on a flight from Paris, where there is an embassy, you will still need a visa before you arrive. Normally, you won't be allowed on the plane unless you have a visa for Madagascar.

If you are arriving or departing by sea from the Comoros, Mauritius or mainland Africa, getting a visa for Madagascar is harder but not impossible. You will have to prove to the immigration official where and when you intend to arrive, and have some proof of departure (which can be impossible if leaving Madagascar by sea) before getting a visa.

Visa Extensions

Recent immigration regulations state that three-month visas (which are enough for most travellers anyway) cannot be extended; you must return to your own country, or another country with a Malagasy embassy or consulate, and get another visa.

A *prolongation* (visa extension) probably won't be provided unless you have a very good reason, such as being an official researcher. If you weren't given a three month visa in the first place they may be more sympathetic, but you will still have to beg and grovel.

If you want to try for a visa extension, contact the Ministère de l'Intérieur, Anosy,

Antananarivo, near the Hilton Hotel; or the commissariat of the Polisy Nasionaly (National Police) in the provincial capitals of Toliara, Antsiranana, Fianarantsoa, Toamasina and Mahajanga.

Applications for extensions must be accompanied by two application forms detailing your life history (there are questions about your family, work history, education and bank accounts); three passport photos; a typed letter in French explaining why you want to stay longer (including how much longer – prepare this before you leave home); and a FMg 140,000 fee and FMg 400 stamp. You may also be asked to produce airline tickets out of the country and/or proof of funds, and a letter from your hotel proving that you are of 'good character'. If successful, you should be able to pick up your passport about 48 hours later.

Failing that, you can always go to a nearby country, such as the Comoros or Mauritius, secure a new visa then return.

Travel Permits
The only permit required when travelling around Madagascar is the compulsory entrance fee for visiting designated national parks and reserves. Refer to the National Parks section in the Facts about Madagascar chapter for details.

EMBASSIES
Madagascar Embassies & Consulates Abroad
In addition to the following, Madagascar has embassies in Beijing, Belgium, Moscow, Tokyo and Vienna (Austria).

Australia
7th floor, 19-31 Pitt St, Sydney, NSW 2000 (☎ (02) 9252 3770; fax (02) 9247 8406)
Canada
282 Somerset St West K2P OJ6, Ottawa (☎ (613) 563 2506; fax (613) 231 3261)
Comoros
Air Madagascar office, Volovolo (☎ 73 22 90) (note: there is no Madagascar consulate in Mayotte)
Denmark
c/o DZ Holding, Skodsborgvej 242, Naerum

France
Embassy – 4 Ave Raphaël, 75016 Paris (☎ 05.45.04.62.11)
Consulate – 234 Boulevarde Périer, 13008 Marseille (☎ 04.91.53.47.61; fax 04.91.53.79.58)
Germany
Embassy – Rolandstrasse 48, 53179 Bonn Bad; Godesberg Post-fach 188 (☎ (228) 953 590; fax (228) 334 628)
Consulate – Holstenplatz 18, 22765, Hamburg (☎ (40) 38 101 984; fax (40) 38 101 677)
Consulate – Wilhelm Buschstrasse 5, 40474, Düsseldorf (☎ (211) 432 643)
Italy
84/A Rome, via Richard Zandonai (☎ (6) 30 77 97; fax (6) 329 4306)
Kenya
Air Madagascar, 2nd floor, Hilton Hotel, PO Box 41723, Nairobi (☎ 225 286)
Mauritius
Rue Guiot Pasceau Ave, Queen Mary, Floréal, Port Louis (☎ 686 5015; fax 686 7040)
Réunion
51 Rue Juliette Dodu, 97461 St-Denis (☎ 02.62.21.05.21)
Switzerland
Birkenstrasse 5, 6000, Lucerne (☎ (41) 211 27 21)
Consulate – Kappelergrasse 14, 8001, Zurich (☎ (1) 212 85 66)
Tanzania
Magoret St 135, Dar es Salaam; PO Box 5254 (☎ 294 42)
UK
16 Lanark Mansions, Pennard Rd, London, W12 8DT (☎ (0181) 746 0133; fax (0181) 746 0134)
USA
Embassy – 2374 Massachusetts Ave NW, Washington, DC 20008 (☎ (202) 265 5525; fax (202) 483 7603)
Honorary Consulate – University of California, 2299 Piedmont Ave, Berkeley, CA 9470 (☎ (510) 643 8301)
UN Mission – Room 404, 801 Second St, New York, 10017 NY (☎ (212) 744 3816)
Honorary Consulate – 410 East St NE, Vienna, VA 22180 (☎ (703) 319 0931)

Foreign Embassies in Madagascar
All foreign diplomatic embassies and consulates are based in Antananarivo, although French consulates are located in several major towns (refer to the individual chapters for contact details). The nearest embassy or consulate for some countries, especially those from the British Commonwealth such

as Australia, is in Mauritius or Pretoria (South Africa).

Canada
    Villa Paule II M62C, Androhibe, Antananarivo; BP 4003 (☎ 425 59)
Comoros
    Lot VK63 AC, Ambohitsoa, Antananarivo (☎ 296 37)
Denmark, Norway & Sweden
    1 Bis Rue Patrice Lumumba, Tsaralalana, Antananarivo (☎ 223 56)
France
    Embassy – 3 Rue Jean Jaurès, Ambatomena, Antananarivo; BP 204 (☎ 237 00; fax 294 30)
    Consulate – Làlana Refotaka, Ambatomena, Antananarivo (at the back of the Embassy) (☎ 214 88)
Germany
    101 Rue Pasteur Hans Rabeony, Ambodirotra, Antananarivo; BP 516 (☎ 238 02; fax 266 27)
Italy
    22 Rue Pasteur Rabary, Ankadivato, Antananarivo; BP 16 (☎ 215 74; fax 238 14)
Mauritius
    Route Circulaire Anjahana, Antananarivo; BP 6040 (☎ 321 57; fax 219 39)
Netherlands
    88 Lotissement Ivandry, Antananarivo (☎ 422 22; fax 431 84)
Seychelles
    BP 1071, Antananarivo (☎ 209 49)
South Africa
    II J169, Ivandry, Antananarivo (☎ 424 94; fax 435 04)
Switzerland
    Imm. ARO, Antsahavola, Antananarivo (☎ 629 97; fax 289 40)
UK
    Imm. Ny Havana, 67 Ha, Antananarivo; BP 167 (☎ 277 49; fax 255 90)
USA
    14 Rue Rainitovo, Antsahavola, Antananarivo (☎ 212 57; fax 345 39)

There are also embassies or consulates for Austria, Belgium, China, Indonesia, Japan and Spain in Tana.

CUSTOMS

Officially, visitors to Madagascar may import 500 cigarettes or 25 cigars, one litre bottle of alcohol, two still cameras, one video camera, 10 rolls of film and one typewriter (woe unto those who normally travel with two!) duty-free.

If you have any problems, or queries, contact Customs at Ivato airport (☎ 440 32).

MONEY

In 1973 Madagascar abandoned the Communauté Financière Africaine (CFA) currency zone and created its own medium of exchange, the franc Malagasy, written as FMg.

Despite two major devaluations in recent years, the artificial economy and currency controls instituted by the former Marxist government, the Malagasy franc is overvalued and the country is experiencing a shortage of foreign exchange.

Costs

Happily, Madagascar remains a cheap place to travel. Real dives, often doubling as brothels, can be found for as little as FMg 10,000 per room, but if you want some basic security, comfort and cleanliness, bottom-end rooms will cost about FMg 20,000 to FMg 30,000. Prices will be a fair bit higher – up to double – in Tana, the expensive resort of Nosy Be (but not on Île Sainte Marie) and in some regional cities, such as Mahajanga (which for some reason is expensive).

A meal of Malagasy food will cost about FMg 2000 to FMg 3000 in a street stall and FMg 4500 in the cheapest *hotely* (a small informal canteen serving basic meals). A decent western meal in a good restaurant will cost around FMg 10,000 to FMg 12,000. Naturally, extra courses, and delicacies like lobster and drinks will add to the bill considerably – and prices in Tana and Nosy Be are a little higher than in the rest of the country.

Travelling around the countryside on local transport is very cheap (you can pay local prices in local currency) but usually uncomfortable. Non-resident foreigners, which covers most tourists, have to pay for airfares in foreign currency. Prices for airfares are expensive compared to overland travel, but still reasonable in comparison with other countries.

Currency

For ease of exchange, the best currencies to

carry in cash and/or travellers' cheques are French francs, followed by US dollars, UK pounds and Deutschmarks. Swiss francs, Japanese yen, Italian lira and, sometimes, South African rand are also acceptable, but possibly only in Tana.

The Malagasy franc is worth 100 centimes (but you certainly won't see any of these worthless coins). Malagasy bank notes come in denominations of 25,000, 10,000, 5000, 2500, 1000 and 500, and coins in common use come in denominations of FMg 5, 10, 20 and 250, as well as 5, 10 and 20 *ariary*.

The coins can be a little confusing: the ariary is worth FMg 5, so the 5 ariary coin is equivalent to FMg 25 and the 20 ariary coin is worth FMg 100. (To make it more complicated, the ariary is also occasionally referred to as a *piastre*, *drala* or *parata*.) In any event, coins are basically worthless and not worth carrying around – get rid of them as soon as you can.

As the highest note is FMg 25,000 changing US$500, for example, will give you a thick wad of large notes. Try to change a FMg 25,000 as often as you can in larger restaurants and hotels: you will get a look of horror or disgust if you give FMg 25,000 to a Malagasy hotely owner, taxi-brousse driver or local market trader.

Currency Exchange

The exchange rate fluctuates every day in accordance with any minor change in Malagasy government policy and spending, and any general political confusion – for instance, purchase of another Air Madagascar aircraft, announcement of another World Bank loan or impeachment of another president.

During our three months of research, the exchange rate increased by about 10%, so don't change too much money too soon; you will almost certainly get a better exchange rate next week. By the time you read this, the exchange rates will have changed considerably. For an idea about the current exchange rate, try to get some information from the Internet pages – refer to Online Services in the Regional Facts for the Visitor chapter.

Country	Unit		FMg
Australia	A$1	=	3236.29
Canada	C$1	=	3191.43
France	FFr1	=	810.46
Germany	DM1	=	2737.98
Italy	ItLir1	=	2.7957
Switzerland	SwFr1	=	3158.44
UK	UK£1	=	7304.27
USA	US$1	=	4315.05

Changing Money

Four main banks have branches throughout Madagascar: Bankin'ny Tantsaha Mpamokatra (BTM), Banky Fampandrosoana'ny Varotra (BFV), Banque Malgache de l'Océan Indien (BMOI) and the Bankin'ny Indostria-Crédit Lyonnais (BNI-CL). At least one of these banks – and often all four – will be in every major town. They change recognised brands of travellers' cheques and cash in major currencies, though in smaller towns you may have more difficulty changing money. In Tana the one and only branch of the Union Commercial Bank (UCB) will also change money.

These banks are open from about 8 to 11 am and 2 to 4.30 pm, Monday to Friday – but opening times vary between banks. They all close on the afternoon before a public holiday. When changing money outside Tana carefully check the weekly exchange rates in the French language newspapers from Tana; the rates telexed from the head offices often contain errors. And always check to see if the banks charge any commission: the BFV and BNI-CL banks don't charge anything extra, but the BTM bank did at the time of research.

It is important to note that most banks and companies such as Air Madagascar will not accept US$100 bills because a number of forgeries are doing the rounds.

A new innovation are the internal travellers' cheque or *chèques de voyage* issued by the BTM and BNI-CL banks. They are no safer than carrying your own foreign travellers' cheques (which can be readily exchanged), but are useful if you're going to remote areas where the BTM and BNI-CL banks will change their own, but not foreign, travellers' cheques. The BTM bank issues their 'Ravinala' cheques in denominations of FMg 50,000 to FMg 2,000,000, and the BNI-CL bank has an identical system called 'Le Chèque Bleu'.

Most up-market hotels in Tana and major towns will change US dollars and French francs in travellers' cheques and cash for guests (and occasionally the public), but not surprisingly the exchange rate is usually about 10% lower than the banks'.

Airport Currency exchange facilities at Ivato international airport in Tana are limited to a couple of exchange counters on the main level; they are normally open for international arrivals. However, if you arrive from another country at a small regional airport, such as Île Sainte Marie or Mahajanga, there will almost certainly be no exchange facilities. Make sure you have enough Malagasy or French francs to last until you get to a bank.

It is also very important to note that you cannot change Malagasy francs into any foreign currency at the bank counters at the airport at Tana, and there are usually no money-changing facilities at other airports in the country. Change all your money back at a major bank in Tana. Some travellers have reported difficulties in doing this, so it's best not to change too much money close to your departure date.

Currency Declaration
Thankfully, Malagasy tourist and financial authorities have recently abolished regulations which entailed painstakingly completing a currency declaration when you arrived and when you changed money. On arrival you may be casually asked how much money you have by an immigration officer, but there is no need to prove anything unless you admit to having more than 50,000 French francs in cash or travellers' cheques (which is a *lot* of money if you're travelling around Madagascar).

Some departing travellers have been asked by immigration officials to show a few bank receipts to prove they changed some money legally. There is no black market, and

you will be given a receipt whenever you change money at a bank, so it's a good idea to keep receipts anyway. It is officially illegal to export more than FMg 25,000.

Credit Cards
Credit cards are of limited use in Madagascar, but they can be used at up-market hotels in major cities and resorts, offices of TAM airlines, Air Madagascar offices (mainly in Tana) and at larger travel companies.

Cash advances up to the Malagasy franc equivalent of 2000 French francs are available with a Visa card through the BFV bank, or with a MasterCard at a BTM bank. Credit card advances are quicker and more reliable at major bank branches in Tana.

American Express is represented by Madagascar Airtours (☎ 241 92), which has two offices in Tana – next to Air Madagascar and in the Hilton Hotel arcade – and in Nosy Be, Antsiranana, Toliara, Fianarantsoa and Toamasina.

POST & COMMUNICATIONS
There are post offices in every main town throughout the country. They are normally open Monday to Friday from about 8 am to noon and from 2 to 6 pm, and on Saturday morning from 8 am until noon, but post offices have different opening times in Tana (refer to the Antananarivo chapter). The countrywide postal service is generally reliable and few things go astray. However, don't post envelopes or parcels containing anything of value. To foil the stamp-steaming fringe, you may wish to have stamps franked before placing letters or postcards in the mailing box.

If you're sending post to a private address in Madagascar, be sure to indicate the neighbourhood or suburb in the address as well as the city or town name.

Postal Rates
Postal rates are low, but they increase regularly. Currently, postcards cost FMg 550 to Asia, the USA, Canada, Australia and New Zealand; and FMg 750 to Europe (but a little less to France). Normal-sized letters cost

FMg 2000 to Asia, the US, Canada, Australia and New Zealand; and FMg 1000 to Europe, including France.

These days you are rarely given any of the large, colourful stamps for your letters or postcards; these lovely stamps are normally sold to collectors and souvenir hunters. But if you do get some large stamps, one reader suggested that you 'bring a sponge and dunk it in the nearest puddle'. Don't be surprised if smaller post offices run out of stamps completely.

Poste Restante
In Tana, the poste restante is at the main post office on Làlana Ratsimilaho, near the Hôtel Colbert in Haute-Ville. The staff are friendly and efficient, but check under both given and family names as a matter of course. To ensure proper filing it would still be wise to have correspondents capitalise and underline the surname. Poste restante is unreliable in country towns and your mail may even be sent to the poste restante in Tana anyway.

Telephone
Thanks to satellite technology international telephone lines are good, but internal telephone services won't win any awards. From Tana you can phone Paris or Sydney just about anytime, but getting through to Toliara or Antsiranana can be another story.

International calls can be made from private telephones; at your hotel (but often at double the normal rates); from a Telecom office next to or in main post offices throughout the country; or from the occasional Agence d'Accueil Telecom office (also known as AGATE). At a Telecom office overseas calls must be made through an operator, but you'll normally get through in a few minutes at a major town. In Taolagnaro (Fort Dauphin) the whole telephone system runs on solar power, so if the sun ain't shining you may not be able to make any calls for a while!

Your best chance of making a direct and clear call is to buy a *telecarte*, which can be used at most public telephones (if you can find one that is working and without a long line of impatient callers) for local, domestic and international calls. These cards come in multiples of 25 units (FMg 10,000) for local calls – they don't last long on an international call – and up to 150 units (FMg 60,000).

International calls are charged for a minimum of three minutes; you are then charged for each part of every additional minute. Rates are very high: to France and French-speaking Africa, the current rate from the main post office in Tana is FMg 40,665 for the first three minutes; FMg 94,569 to the USA and Canada; and FMg 70,848 to Australia and New Zealand. Local calls start from about FMg 1000 for three minutes in Tana; double that if you use a hotel telephone. Calls around the countryside are cheap, and naturally vary depending on the distance.

When you're phoning Madagascar from overseas, dial your country's international access code followed by Madagascar's country code (261), the local area code then the number. When phoning from Madagascar, dial 16 to get an international line, then the country code of the country you're calling and the desired area code and number.

The district telephone area codes which you can use for automatic direct dialling for each main town are listed in the following table and throughout the book. For more remote areas without automatic direct dialling facilities, you will need to go through a local operator first.

Telephone Area Codes

Ambalavao	763
Ambanja	850
Ambatondrazaka	4
Ambositra	7
Andasibe	461
Antalaka	8
Antananarivo (Tana)	2
Antsirabe	4
Antsiranana (Diego Suarez)	8
Belo-sur-Tsiribihina	454
Farafangana	7
Fianarantsoa (Fianar)	7
Iharana (Vohémar)	840
Ihosy	740
Île Sainte Marie	567
Ivato	2

Mahajanga (Majunga)	6
Mahambo	5710
Mahavelona (Foulpointe)	5710
Manakara	7
Mananjary	7
Miandrivazo	458
Moramanga	4
Morombe	980
Morondava	4
Ranohira	742
Ranomafana	7610
Sambava	885
Taolagnaro (Fort Dauphin)	9
Toamasina (Tamatave)	5
Toliara (Tuléar)	9

Fax & Email

Faxes can often be made from an AGATE office or an up-market hotel. Prices are high; you are charged a minimum of three minutes even if you send one page of fax. Email is used by businesses, but we do not know of any place where visitors can send or receive an email message.

BOOKS

Few English-language are books available, so English speakers will need to bring their own reading material to fill in the long waits at taxi-brousse and train stations, and for the evenings. French speakers are well catered for, not surprisingly: a large range of pulp novels and serious literature, as well as local and French newspapers and magazines, is available in major towns.

A few years ago it was difficult to find anything written about Madagascar, but a recent resurgence of interest in this unique island has spawned a growing number of works and studies, especially about culture and natural history. The major bookshops in Tana – particularly the Librairie de Madagascar – are good places to pick up some books about Madagascar in French and, occasionally, in English, German and Italian.

People & History

If you're looking for a good overview of Malagasy culture, get hold of the superb ethnographic study *Madagascar, Island of the Ancestors* by John Mack. By the same author, there's also *Malagasy Textiles* – an introduction to Malagasy textile design as well as dyeing and weaving methods.

Comprehensive histories can be found in *The Great Red Island* by Arthur Stratton; and *Madagascar Rediscovered – a History from Early Times to Independence* and the shorter *A History of Madagascar*, both by Mervyn Brown – the latter is available in Tana and worth picking up for a readable history of the island. The Mauritian historian, Auguste Toussaint, deals with Malagasy history in his *History of the Indian Ocean*.

Natural History & Field Guides

Recognised as the best book dealing with Madagascar's natural history is the (unimaginatively-titled) *Madagascar – A Natural History* by Ken Preston-Mafham. This large, glossy book is crammed full of colour photos and enlightening text about everything from the rocks to baobabs, and insects to lemurs. A more technical treatment is *The Primates of Madagascar* by Dr Ian Tattersall, and reptile lovers will want *A Fieldguide to the Amphibians & Reptiles of Madagascar* by Frank Glaw & Miguel Vences.

For a bit of information about all wildlife written in layman's language, the best book to buy is *Madagascar Wildlife: A Visitor's Guide* by Hilary Bradt, Derek Schuurman & Nick Garbutt. It contains excellent photos and guides to the main national parks, and is available in Tana bookshops for FMg 82,000.

If you're specifically interested in lemurs, look for the hefty *Lemurs of Madagascar & the Comoros* by C Harcourt; it helps with identification, and provides a concise history of their discovery and conservation. A more portable choice with lots of colour plates is the *Field Guide to Mammals of Africa including Madagascar* by T Haltenorth & H Diller.

Birdwatchers will probably want a copy of the pamphlet *A Birder's Guide to Travel in Madagascar* by Gardner; or the more comprehensive, expensive and chunky *Field*

Guide to the Birds of Madagascar by Olivier Langrand & Bretagnolle. A more portable option would be the standard work *Robert's Birds of Southern Africa* by MacLean. The World Wide Fund for Nature (WWF) office in Antsiranana sells an excellent booklet about the birds of the Parc National de Montagne d'Ambre.

Divers and other a-fish-ionados should look for a copy of *A Field Guide to the Coral Reef Fish of the Indian and West Pacific Oceans* by RH Carcasson; *Underwater Guide to Coral Fishes of the Indian Ocean* by Addison & Tindall; or *A Guide to Common Reef Fish of the Western Indian Ocean* by KR Bock. More specialised is the *Field Guide to the Sharks & Rays of Southern Africa* by Campagno & Ebert.

For the authoritative word on the island's 1000 or so species of orchid, see *An Introduction to the Cultivated Angraecoid Orchids of Madagascar* by AW Holst and FE Hillerman. One of the most impressively detailed and presented books about Madagascar is the huge and expensive *The Palms of Madagascar* by John Dransfield & Henk Beentje.

The most complete coverage of Madagascar's national parks and protected areas is the French-language *Madagascar: Revue de la Conservation et des Aires Protégées* by ME Nicholl & Olivier Langrand. It gets a bit technical, but offers good overviews of all the parks and reserves; the maps are useful for locating the lesser-known parks and reserves.

Another French-language environmental study of Madagascar, *Madagascar: Profil de l'Environnement*, edited by MD Jenkins, focuses on the country's environmental problems. It includes an extensive appendix in English, detailing all the species found in the country. From the same publisher is the conservation proposal in English: *Lemurs of Madagascar: An Action Plan for their Conservation 1993-1999* by Mittermeir, Konstant, Nicholl & Langrand. It's a technical but worthwhile read for anyone looking for positive projections for the future of Madagascar's lemurs.

Travel

The earliest detailed personal narrative of Madagascar is *Robert Drury's Journal*. It's the record kept by an English sailor who was shipwrecked off southern Madagascar in 1701 and subsequently became a slave to the Antandroy royal family. He eventually escaped to the west coast where he was again captured, this time by the Sakalava, and enslaved until his rescue in 1717. This amazing tale provides proof that truth can be far more incredible than fiction.

One of the most entertaining works about Madagascar is the one that started all the popular interest in the island's natural history, *Zoo Quest to Madagascar*, by nature commentator Sir David Attenborough. Attenborough tells of a visit to the country, shortly after Independence, when he went in search of lemurs, chameleons and the eggs of extinct birds, among other things. His trip took him to Périnet reserve, Lac Ihotry and Ampanihy in the south-west. A synopsis of this book found in *Journeys to the Past*, by the same author, is more widely available.

The Aye-aye and I by Gerald Durrell focuses on the aye-aye, once thought to be extinct, and Durrell's efforts to set up a captive breeding program in Jersey in the Channel Islands. It also deals with a number of other creatures endemic to Madagascar. *Ark on the Move*, by the same author, includes zoological rambles in Madagascar and other islands of the Indian Ocean.

The first modern narrative about travel in Madagascar, and the first of several written by intrepid women, is Dervla Murphy's *Muddling Through in Madagascar*. Murphy and her teenage daughter spent several months in 1983 haphazardly backpacking around the southern part of the country having a variety of experiences. It's a humorous and entertaining read, but much of it should be taken as anecdotal rather than fact.

A highly recommended publication is *Lemurs of the Lost World* by Dr Jane Wilson, which mainly describes a 1986 study expedition to the crocodile caves of Ankàrana in far northern Madagascar. Wilson is a medical doctor (as well as a very competent writer) who focuses primarily on her lemur studies, but also offers refreshingly humble and interesting insights into the people and wildlife she encounters.

Another is *Distant Shores* by Sally Crook. The author was the cook on the Sarimanok Expedition, a journey by traditional sailing craft from Indonesia to Madagascar, intending to prove that the first Malagasy could have made the journey directly.

Dancing with the Dead: A Journey through Zanzibar and Madagascar by Helena Drysdale traces the author's journey around Madagascar searching for evidence of her pirate uncle. And finally English author Christina Dodwell traipses through remote parts of the country in *Madagascar Travels*, though her 'adventures' in this thin volume seem a little contrived.

General

The nicest coffee-table photo collection is *Madagascar – a World out of Time* by F Lanting. The ethereal photos capture well the evocative nature of Madagascar's land and people. Other large French-language books worth getting if you can afford them (and which may be available in Madagascar) are *Île des Esprits* by Jacques-Yves Cousteau and François Sarano, and *Sourires de Madagascar* by Viviane Bournique et al. Available in Tana, *La Cuisine de Madagascar* obviously contains a collection of Malagasy recipes in French.

Dictionaries

If you cannot find anything suitable at home, you can buy Malagasy-English and English-Malagasy, as well as Malgache-Français and Français-Malgache, dictionaries at major bookshops in Tana. You may also find a dictionary for Malagasy and Italian or German. As mentioned before, a basic knowledge of French is enough to get by with, unless you are going to remote areas or want to converse in the indigenous language.

Two particularly useful dictionaries for English-speakers are the blue *An Elementary English-Malagasy Dictionary* and the pink

Malagasy to English *Diksionaera Malagasy-Englisy*. Kauderwelsch Verlag print a very useful German-Malagasy dictionary, which is only available in Germany.

The *Dictionnaire Malgache Dialectal-Français: Dialecte Tandroy* by Narivelo Rajaonarimanana & Sarah Fee will serve you well in the remote regions of the south, where some Malagasy speak little or no French, or resent speaking the Merina-dominated Malagasy language. This is not yet available in Madagascar.

FILMS

Madagascar's film industry is virtually non-existent. In 1988 Raymond Rajaonarivelo, a Malagasy director who studied cinema in France, made the feature-length *Tabataba* (which means The Spreading of Rumours) on the south-east coast of the island. The film is set during the bloody 1947 rebellion against French rule in the small village of Maromena, near Manakara.

The Madagascar government's perpetual lack of funds ensures that little or no money is allocated to supporting the local film industry. Very few cinemas have survived in Madagascar. They have been replaced by cheap and nasty video clubs which show action or martial arts films, often from China, dubbed into French and/or Malagasy.

NEWSPAPERS & MAGAZINES

Three national newspapers (FMg 1000 each) – the *Midi Madagasikara* (which is annoying because you have to slice open the tops of the pages to separate them), the *Madagascar Tribune* and the *L'Express de Madagascar* – are printed every day in Tana (and are sometimes available a little later in major towns throughout the country). Written in Malagasy and French, they are a good source of information about politics and entertainment in Tana. They also provide important contact details for available doctors, emergency numbers and so on, and vital horoscopes and racing tips, but they are no good for international news.

Other regular newspapers include *Langoro* (FMg 1500), a political monthly written in French and Malagasy; and the economic *Mada Economie* (FMg 1500), which is printed twice a month.

A few tourist magazines are worth picking up, particularly if you can read French. Available from major bookshops in Tana, and sometimes around the countryside, they contain some reasonably interesting articles about Madagascar; information about current and future festivals and concerts; details about opening hours of museums; emergency telephone numbers; and ads for new travel companies, hotels and so on.

These magazines are: *Madactualities Tourism & Loisirs* (FMg 8000), published bimonthly in English and French; the widely available monthly, *Revue de l'Océan Indien Madagascar* (FMg 10,000), which is written in French and includes profiles on tourist destinations; *Tana 7 Jours* (FMg 5000), a weekly magazine mainly for residents, listing what's on in Tana, TV programs, horoscopes etc; and the free *Le Petit Guide de Poche Antananarivo*, which is a pocket guide of useful contact details, and lists of hotels and restaurants for tourists.

Foreign magazines and newspapers, such as *Le Monde*, *Time* and *Der Spiegel*, are sometimes available in major Tana bookshops or the Hilton hotel arcade for loads of FMg, but nowhere else in the country. If you just want to catch up on foreign news go to the reading room at the American, French or German cultural centres in Tana.

RADIO & TV

The main Malagasy-language radio stations in Tana are Radio RNM 1 and 2 (FM 99.3 and FM101) and Radio Lazan'Iarivo (FM 106). In French there's Radio Antsiva (FM 97.7), Korail (FM 90), and Alliance Française (FM 92). Every major town around the country has its own FM radio station playing a mixture of Malagasy and western pop with Malagasy and French-speaking DJs.

The TV stations based in Tana (and available with appropriate antennae around the country) are predominantly in the Malagasy language and called MA-TV, RTA and the government-run TVM. Canal and Horizons broadcast programs in French.

To find out what radio and television programs are on in Tana, buy the weekly *Tana 7 Jours*.

PHOTOGRAPHY & VIDEO

Film is reasonably expensive in Madagascar and outside the larger towns it can be difficult to come by. It's always a good idea to carry an adequate supply of your preferred film from home (see the Customs section for duty-free limitations). In Tana expect to pay about FMg 16,000 for a roll of 24 prints; FMg 19,500 for 36. Slide film is also available but very expensive.

Processing isn't generally of high quality and you'd do well to wait until you get home. For general photography hints, see Photography & Video in the Regional Facts for the Visitor chapter.

HEALTH

The following brief section refers specifically to Madagascar. For a rundown of general travellers' health concerns and tips in this part of the world, see the Health chapter at the end of the book.

Water

'Water' in Malagasy is *rano* and 'sea' is *ranomasina*, which means 'sacred water'. Tap water in Tana and all major towns (except Manakara and Andoany on Nosy Be) is generally safe, but you're still advised to use purification tablets. However, avoid drinking tap water after it has rained – look for the tell-tale muddy gunk coming out of the tap.

Eau Vive bottled water is widely available but expensive. We urge you to consider not spending your hard-earned money on imported mineral water in non-biodegradable bottles when the local water, especially when purified, is OK to drink.

Malaria & Other Diseases

Coastal regions are the riskiest places for malaria; Taolagnaro is one of the worst areas in the country. The mosquitoes and sand ticks are also murderous on Nosy Be, Île Sainte Marie and in the forests around Parc National de Montagne d'Ambre – but there are surprisingly few at Antsiranana or Tana.

Leeches can be annoying in the eastern forests, especially after rain, but they aren't a health threat. Avoid them by wearing long trousers and decent shoes, and by spraying Baygon (available in supermarkets and large grocery shops in major cities) on to your boots and legs before venturing into the rainforest. Always avoid walking barefoot (except on tourist-oriented beaches) lest you invite 'chigger' mites to burrow into your feet and lay eggs.

If you're coming from certain high-risk African countries, or other suspect areas, you will need to have proof of vaccination against cholera and yellow fever. Other diseases associated with African travel, like bilharzia and hepatitis, are also a threat in Madagascar. Hepatitis is spread through contaminated food or water, so watch what you eat and drink. The parasite which carries bilharzia is found in freshwater streams, lakes and often dams (but not in the ocean), so be careful where you swim or wash. (Local people won't know where bilharzia may be a problem.)

The bubonic plague is not uncommon in some parts of the country; it has been found around Tana and Mahajanga in years gone past. Make a lengthy detour around any dead animal you see.

An estimated 18% of the people carry worms, often contracted by eating produce grown in the ground and fertilised with infected pig or sheep poop. Try to avoid eating raw lettuce, spinach, parsley, cauliflower, broccoli, mushrooms and strawberries, regardless of how delicious they look.

Hygiene

Many Malagasy throw coyness and refinement to the wind when nature calls and any area of open ground in a city or town, and any stretch of beach and water (but less so in tourist-oriented beaches), is liable to be used as a public convenience. Be vigilant when walking on the grass, especially in Tana.

Although most hotel and restaurant toilets function well, the zero absorbency Malagasy toilet paper refuses to be flushed and is therefore normally deposited in an overflowing basket beside the toilet.

In cheaper hotels, there is sometimes a risk of bed bugs and lice; use a sleeping sheet or plastic ground sheet.

Hospitals

Malagasy hospitals are poor by western standards, primarily because medical supplies and equipment are in short supply. For difficult, non-emergency surgery or treatment of long-term serious medical problems, the best idea is to go home, or catch a flight to Mauritius, Réunion, Kenya or South Africa.

If you become ill enough to require medical attention, contact your embassy or consulate (if you have one) for advice and referrals. As a last resort, talk to someone at the tourist office or your hotel. If your condition isn't too serious, you may be sent to a private hospital which will cost around FMg 100,000 to FMg150,000 per day, including room, meals, tests and treatment.

There is no ambulance service outside Tana and the hospitals or clinics in other cities are much worse off for staff, medicines and equipment. If you become ill or suffer an accident outside Tana, try to arrange a flight back to the capital (getting a taxi-brousse will only make it worse).

Refer to the Medical Services section in the Antananarivo chapter for details about hospitals in the capital. If you are unfortunate enough to need a hospital outside Tana, the hospitals listed below are adequate for emergencies; otherwise return to Tana, or get out of Madagascar. Some of the best regional hospitals, such as the one at Toamasina, have new equipment donated by Japan while others, such as the one at Nosy Be, are, according to expert expats, woeful.

Town	Hospital Name	Telephone
Antsiranana	Centre Hospitalier Régional	(8) 210 61
Fianarantsoa	Centre Hospitalier Régional	(7) 510 16
Mahajanga	Centre Hospitalier Universitaire	(6) 229 15
Toamasina	Centre Hospitalier Régional	(5) 320 18
Toliara	Centre Hospitalier Régional	(9) 427 24

BUSINESS HOURS

Government offices are normally open from 8.30 am to noon and 2 to 3.30 or 4 pm, Monday to Friday. On the *hauts plateaux* shopping hours are from 8 am to noon and 2 to 5.30 pm, Monday to Friday, with most shops closed on Saturday afternoon and Sunday.

Between November and April in the hot and sticky coastal towns and villages, shops are open from 7 to 11.30 am and 3 to 6 pm. In the middle of the day, locals have a welcome siesta (which is recommended for visitors too).

Salons de thé often close for two hours at lunchtime; most other restaurants remain open until late in the evening, though some are exclusively lunchtime venues.

PUBLIC HOLIDAYS & SPECIAL EVENTS

Public holidays, when government offices and major private companies close, are:

New Year's Day – 1 January
Insurrection Day – 29 March (celebrates the rebellion against the French in 1947)
Easter Monday – March/April
Labour Day – 1 May
Anniversary Day – 8 May
Organisation of African Unity Day – 25 May
National Day – 26 June
Christmas Day – 25 December
Republic Day – 30 December

Festivals

Other important dates which are celebrated (though not with a public holiday) throughout the country are listed below. Many of these dates change every year, so to find out the exact dates for some festivals and ceremonies you will have to make local inquiries. For further information about some of these festivals, refer to the Society and Conduct section in the Facts about Madagascar chapter.

March
    Alahamady Be (the low-key Malagasy New Year)
April/May
    Santabary (the first rice harvest)
    Ascension Day (40th day after Easter)
May
    Pentecost Monday
May/June
    Donia (a traditional music festival held on Nosy Be)
June
    Fisemana (a ritual purification ceremony undertaken by the Antakàrana people)
June to September
    Famadihana ('turning of the bones' burial ceremony)
June to December
    Sambatra (circumcision festivals are held by most tribes between June and September, though in the south-west they are in November and December)
15 August
    Assumption
1 November
    All Saints' Day
November/December
    Gasytsara (a contemporary music festival)

ACTIVITIES

Diving & Snorkelling

Although the coral reefs and marine life are suffering from environmental pressures similar to those affecting terrestrial wildlife, Madagascar still has some outstanding diving locations – and no doubt others await discovery. Currently, the best diving is at the tropical islands and islets around Nosy Be; along the west coast, particularly around Ifaty in the south-west; and the southern end of Masoala Peninsula, although access is very difficult.

An increasing number of well-run companies offer internationally recognised diving courses and trips for qualified divers at Île Sainte Marie, Nosy Be, Ifaty, Morondava

>=()<

Considerations for Responsible Diving

The popularity of diving is placing immense pressure on many sites around the world. Please consider the following tips when diving and help preserve the ecology and beauty of reefs:

- Do not use anchors on the reef and take care not to ground boats on coral. Encourage dive operators and regulatory bodies to establish permanent moorings at popular dive sites.
- Avoid touching living marine organisms with your body. Polyps can be damaged by even the gentlest contact. Never stand on corals, even if they look solid and robust. If you must secure yourself to the reef, hold fast only to exposed rock or dead coral.
- Be conscious of your fins. Even without contact the surge from heavy fin strokes near the reef can damage delicate organisms. When treading water in shallow reef areas, take care not to kick up clouds of sand. Settling sand can easily smother the delicate organisms of the reef.
- Practise and maintain proper buoyancy control. Major damage can be done by divers descending too fast and colliding with the reef. Make sure you are correctly weighted and that your weight belt is positioned so that you stay horizontal.
- If you have not dived for a while, have a practice dive in a pool before taking to the reef. Buoyancy can change over an extended trip: initially you may breathe harder and need more weighting; a few days later you may breathe more easily and need less weight.
- Take great care when inspecting underwater caves. Spend as little time in them as possible because your air bubbles may be caught within the roof and thereby leave previously submerged organisms high and dry. Taking turns to inspect the interior of a small cave will lessen the chances of damaging contact.
- Resist the temptation to buy corals or shells. Aside from the ecological damage, taking home marine souvenirs depletes the beauty of the site and spoils the enjoyment of others.
- Respect the integrity of marine archaeological sites, such as shipwrecks. They may be protected from looting by law.
- Take home all your rubbish – and any litter you may find as well. Plastics in particular are a serious threat to marine life. Sea turtles may mistake plastic for jellyfish and eat it.
- Resist the temptation to feed fish. You may disturb their normal eating habits, encourage aggressive behaviour or feed them food that is detrimental to their health.
- Minimise your disturbance of marine animals. In particular, do not ride on the backs of turtles as this causes them great anxiety. ∎

>=()<

and Mahavelona (Foulpointe). Before you can enrol in a diving certificate course, known locally as *un baptême* (literally, 'a baptism!') your general ability, health and qualifications must be checked by the operator. All beginners must be able to swim at least 200m before proceeding. Often, operators will also require a health certificate stating that you're a suitable diving candidate.

Many tourist hotels in Madagascar also offer diving 'instruction' and hire out equipment, but unless they're licensed to teach recognised diving certification courses, there's a risk of ending up with dodgy equipment and inexperienced teachers.

Cycling

The appalling roads are perfect for masochists and adventurous mountain-bike riders. You can hire mountain bikes in Tana and Antsiranana, and on the islands of Nosy Be and Île Sainte Marie, but for long-distance trips you will have to bring your own bike. Refer to the Madagascar Getting Around chapter for information about places to take your mountain bike.

Whale-watching

Two places to watch these magnificent creatures in the right season are around Taolagnaro and off the west coast of Île Sainte Marie (see the Eastern Madagascar chapter for more details). If you are lucky enough to be there when some whales come by forget any apprehension and fork out the high cost of a boat trip because whale-watching is a truly wonderful experience.

Hiking & Trekking

Hikers and trekkers will find a number of great hikes of varying difficulty in Madagascar. Though there are some relatively well-known options (some of which are easy to organise with local travel agencies and guides) the adventurous will still find scope for trailblazing, for instance across the Masoala Peninsula, the Ankaratra and Andringitra massifs, and east of Lac Alaotra.

However, you should be aware that trekking in Madagascar is often *not* a 'wilderness experience'. There are so many populated areas in the country that almost all hiking trails are actually used regularly by local villagers and farmers as thoroughfares, so it is very hard 'to get away from it all'.

Guided walks lasting from several hours to several days are easy to arrange in Madagascar's many national parks, but most of the interesting destinations will require guides and overnight camping. For more information on hiking and trekking, refer to the Activities section of the Regional Facts for the Visitor chapter, and for guidelines on minimum impact camping, see under Accommodation in the same chapter.

ENTERTAINMENT

The best way of finding out what is going on in Tana is to contact the various cultural centres, read the local newspapers and magazines (which are mainly written in French, but occasionally in English) or visit the tourist office. In the countryside it's just a matter of asking and asking – or being in the right place at the right time.

Cinema

Almost no town in the country, including Tana, has a functioning cinema. For quality films, try the American, German and French-run cultural centres in Tana, particularly the Centre Culturel Albert Camus (CCAC)

which shows quality new and old French-language flicks on most days.

Just about every village, and suburb of major towns, has a video club which normally shows violent martial arts films dubbed in French and/or Malagasy. These are often worth going to just for the experience:

The show in Ranohira started with some people carrying a TV, a video and a power generator to the school room. After everything was installed, the crowd of about 200 (maybe one-tenth of the village) invaded the room. The furthest away from the screen anybody was, was 10m. The film was an action film in French, which 80% of the spectators did not understand. The quality of sound combined with the tiny screen made it very difficult to follow the plot. But people were chatting, smoking and obviously having fun.

Sanne Friedrich, Switzerland

Theatre

The CCAC also offers excellent theatre programs, including performances by professional Malagasy troupes as well as visiting French companies, artists and directors. In addition, it hosts jazz, rock and classical music programs, and art exhibitions. The various Alliance Française centres around the country also offer some theatre shows.

Traditional Music & Dance

At the Théâtre Municipal in the Isotry district of Tana you may be lucky enough to catch a rehearsal or performance of Malagasy theatre, or a musical show or contest. Traditional performances, such as the *hira gasy*, take place in community centres known as *tranompokonolona* – there's one near the Alliance Française building in Tana.

Another excellent place for regular performances of traditional music and dance, with great food, is the Grill du Rova restaurant in Tana. Sadly, there are no regular tourist-oriented traditional shows outside Tana.

SPECTATOR SPORTS

Athleticism is a necessity for survival throughout most of Madagascar and football (soccer) is the favourite means of channelling athletic ability into fun. In the cities and towns, boys play in the streets with tightly rolled bundles of newspaper tied and shaped by string. Most major towns have a local competition and games are usually held on Sunday afternoons. Entry costs about FMg 5000 and the games are great fun if only to watch the spectators enjoying their day off. Out in the countryside the rice paddies become impromptu football pitches (in the dry season, of course). Basketball and volleyball are also popular spectator sports.

The French had little influence on local recreation and *pétanque* (a type of lawn bowls) has only recently caught on among the Malagasy elite. Tana has tennis and golf clubs. These are legacies of the colonial power and are enjoying some popularity with the rich Malagasy as well as expats, for whom they were historically reserved.

With the younger set, the main game seems to be *foosball*, a table version of football played by rows of little players hanging on metal rods. The national game, and a favourite local pastime, is the board game *fanorona*, a complicated Malagasy version of draughts. It is most often played by men in town squares on lazy afternoons (which is most days). Games of dominoes, where the men loudly thwack the domino pieces on the table, are popular.

Another popular board game – and one which is easier to learn than fanorona – is *katra*, which involves shifting piles of stones around the board until one player has collected all the stones on his or her side. It's a great pastime for slow periods and the Malagasy are enthusiastic teachers, so ask someone to show you how it works.

One unpleasant spectator sport which we saw in Antsiranana is cock-fighting; the claws of drugged cocks are tied with deadly spikes while a crowd of mostly drunk men scream and bet money on which animal will survive.

THINGS TO BUY

Madagascar offers a wonderful selection of handicrafts and souvenirs. Just about anything that's available elsewhere in the country can be found in Tana at the Zoma market and the umbrella-covered stalls lining Araben'ny Fahaleovantena. Bargaining is the norm and any initial price asked for an item will be at least twice what the seller is prepared to take (just hope you don't follow a group of well-off package tourists). Prices in less touristed parts of the country will always be lower.

Among the items to look out for are those featuring semiprecious stones (but beware of export regulations), such as the beautiful and colourful solitaire and chess sets; Malagasy musical instruments, particularly the *valiha* (as low as FMg 12,000 for a miniature version); leather goods, especially bags, sandals and belts; basketry; wood carvings and beautiful wood inlay boxes (FMg 12,000 to FMg 20,000); crocheted and embroidered tablecloths; Antaimoro paper; dried flowers pressed between translucent sheets of paper; zebu horn bracelets (FMg 10,000 or so each); and handmade model Citroëns and pousse-pousse drivers (guaranteed to give you nightmares if you have been to Antsirabe).

Straw or raffia hats come in all shapes and sizes, including top hats, boaters, sombreros and pillboxes; some are quite elegant. To achieve the real Betsileo or Merina look, you'll need a *lamba* (scarf) or a *malabary* (a men's garment which resembles a nightshirt) to keep out the chill on the hauts plateaux.

Locally grown processed and powdered spices make especially nice gifts: white or black peppercorns, cinnamon, cloves, saffron and vanilla. Other cheap souvenirs worth picking up are the large, bright stamps (mainly available in the post offices in Tana) which highlight, among other things, the wonderful flora and fauna of the country.

Of the other main towns, Ambositra is particularly noted for wood carving, as well as raffia work and silk (though you'll find precious little of it these days); Ambalavao is known for its silk, wrought iron and Antaimoro paper; Ampanihy specialises in mohair carpets; Nosy Be is known for its spices; Fianarantsoa is known for the production of wine and tea; and Antsirabe is the centre for buying semiprecious stones (check the Customs regulations before buying).

Export Permits

Officially, you should ask for a *certificat de ventre* (certificate of sale) for anything you buy which costs more than about FMg 20,000 (that covers many souvenirs) to prove to any inquiring Customs officer that the item is not antique. This is rarely enforced, or enforceable, however, and only necessary if you buy something which is, or looks, really expensive or old.

However, Customs laws are enforced when it comes to live endemic plants (such as vanilla, though not processed vanilla powder or other powdered spices), mounted insects (particularly butterflies, although it may be possible to export specimens that have been specially bred for the purpose – check with the Ministière de l'Agriculture); tortoiseshell products, precious or semiprecious stones, jewellery, antique coins, crocodile skin products, stuffed animals (especially lemurs), fossils (including Aepyornis egg shells), and funerary art, antiquities and other sensitive cultural items. Furthermore, in the interest of happy and

alive butterflies, crocodiles and tortoises everywhere, we'd ask you to abstain from purchasing such items in the first place.

Officially, to take out these items you should obtain a receipt showing purchase and then a permit from the relevant ministry (which seems to change more often than the exchange rate). If you do have a very good reason (such as collecting specimens for a foreign museum), permit applications for plant and animal products should be made to the Ministère de l'Agriculture, de l'Elevage et des Eaux et Forêts, Antsahavola, Antananarivo (☎ (2) 406 10); for cultural items and antiquities, apply to the Ministère de la Culture et de la Communication, Antananarivo (☎ (2) 205 11); and for precious and semiprecious stones, contact the Ministère de l'Industrie, des Mines et de l'Energie in Ambohidahy, Antananarivo.

You should take the item or items in question to the ministry office or, if they're too large, simply take a list (in French) describing each item. You must also bring your Malagasy visa and receipts of purchase, and buy an appropriate number of stamps from the treasury office near the Hilton Hotel. The ministries will advise you of the amount of tax required for each item.

Getting There & Away

This chapter deals with travelling to Madagascar *directly* from Europe, Africa and the Indian Ocean region. For general information on getting to the region from other parts of the world – such as Australia, New Zealand, the USA, Canada and other parts of Asia – and finding a good ticket deal, refer to the regional Getting There & Away chapter at the beginning of the book.

AIR

As in all Indian Ocean islands, most visitors arrive by plane to the capital, Antananarivo (commonly called Tana), though some flights from the Comoros, Mayotte and Réunion fly into and out of other large cities in Madagascar.

When flying to Madagascar there are a few matters to be aware of:

- As soon as you arrive, confirm your departure, and reconfirm it at least three days before you leave; and confirm all internal flights you have booked overseas.
- Foreign non-residents (which means you and me) must pay for all domestic, and international fares from Madagascar, in foreign currency.
- The frequency of flights between Madagascar and Europe and Africa varies according to demand and the particular season.
- The low season is generally from about 16 September to 14 July; the high season (when flights are more expensive and the country is more crowded with tourists) is from about 15 July to 15 September.
- All airlines have a depressing knack of regularly changing schedules, so use the information in this section only as a guide and check everything with your travel agent.

Air Madagascar

If you fly into Madagascar on Air Madagascar (commonly referred to as Air Mad) you are currently entitled to a 50% reduction on the cost of their internal flights. These entitlements do change regularly, however: sometimes the discount is only 30%; you may have to buy an 'airpass'; you may

receive four free internal flights instead (as some Germans reported); or you may have to buy your Air Mad ticket in Europe rather than somewhere in the Indian Ocean region.

Whatever the discount or extra entitlements, always check out what Air Mad has to offer (refer to the list of Air Mad offices following). If you plan to see a lot of the country you will need to fly to avoid some excruciating overland travel. If you are entitled to an internal discount or free flights make all your bookings in Tana, and be firm with Air Mad staff who may not have heard of these discounts/specials.

Special Fares

If you intend to visit a few other countries in eastern Africa or the Indian Ocean region, ask your travel agent or the relevant airlines about any special deals they have. One reader was able to buy a special Air Mauritius/Air Mad ticket (valid for three weeks) in Nairobi. This took him from Nairobi-Tana-Mauritius-Réunion-Mauritius -Nairobi for US$604, which is only about US$200 dearer than the ordinary Nairobi-Tana return flight.

Europe

Direct travel (with a stopover) between Europe and Madagascar is currently limited to three airlines, which depart from only three countries. Check for any future changes: at the time of research there were rumours of flights to Tana on Lufthansa and Alitalia from Germany and Italy. Rather than fly directly to Madagascar, you can fly to, and stop off, at Réunion, Mauritius, East Africa or the Comoros (refer to the regional Getting There & Away chapter for details).

Air Mad flies from Paris to Tana, via Nairobi, on Wednesday and Friday, and from Tana to Paris, via Nairobi, on Sunday and Thursday. Tickets cost US$1134 return. These Paris-Nairobi-Tana flights often go via Munich, Frankfurt or Zurich. If you wish to visit the Comoros ask Air Mad because it occasionally stops off at Moroni on the way to Tana.

Air France flies from Paris to Tana, via Nairobi, on Monday and Thursday, and from Tana to Paris, via Nairobi, on Tuesday and Friday for the same price as Air Mad. For some reason passengers are not allowed to get on or off at Nairobi. The stop is just for refuelling so this is no good as a connection between Madagascar and mainland Africa.

Lastly, Aeroflot flies from Moscow to Tana via Zurich on alternate Thursdays (possibly more often when there is enough demand). It charges US$1200 for a return ticket valid for a year, or US$1000 return for a ticket valid for three months. One traveller wrote to us about a good deal: a return ticket from London to Tana via Moscow on Aeroflot for as little as US$750. While Aeroflot is cheap, it doesn't enjoy a great reputation for reliability or safety, and your flight may go via places like Cyprus and Aden whether you want to or not.

Africa

In addition to its stopover on the Paris-Tana flights, Air Mad also flies between Tana and Nairobi on Monday in high season for US$306/404 one-way/return. Air Mad also goes to Johannesburg on Saturday (and sometimes Wednesday), and back on Sunday (and sometimes Tuesday) for US$446/612.

The best link between Madagascar and mainland Africa is the South African airline, Interair. It flies from Johannesburg to Tana on Tuesday (and returns on Wednesday) for US$871 return, but you can get special fares for US$612 return. Interair also flies from Jo'burg to Réunion, the Comoros, the Seychelles and other interesting points within Africa. Its main office is Jan Smuts Office Park, Unit 12, Johannesburg (☎ (11) 397 1445; fax (11) 397 1468).

Indian Ocean

Madagascar is well serviced with regular direct flights from all nearby islands. Air Mad flies from Tana to the Seychelles on Tuesday (back on Wednesday) for US$714 return; to Moroni, in the Comoros, on Friday for US$148/297 one-way/return (from Mahajanga (Majunga): US$127/254); to Mayotte on Thursday and Saturday, for US$144/272 (from Mahajanga: US$107/213); to Mauritius on Sunday and Friday for US$245/322; and to Réunion every day but Wednesday for US$336 return (one-way tickets are not allowed), often via Toamasina (US$149/298).

Air Austral has a complicated range of flights linking Réunion with Tana, Toamasina and Nosy Be, as well as Mauritius, the Seychelles, the Comoros and mainland Africa. It also links Mayotte with Mahajanga as part of a combined Air Austral-Air Mad flight between Tana and Mayotte. The prices for these Air Austral flights are virtually the same as Air Mad's. The Air Austral head office in Réunion is 4 Rue de Nice, 97400, Saint-Denis (☎ 90 90 90; fax 90 90 91).

The other Réunion-based airline is Transports et Travaux Aeriens de Madagascar, conveniently known as TAM (but sometimes written as TTAM). TAM flies from Réunion to Tana for the same price as Air Mad. It also has direct flights, or connections through Tana, from Réunion to Antsiranana (Diego Suarez), Nosy Be, Île Sainte Marie, Taolagnaro (Fort Dauphin), Toliara (Tuléar), Mahajanga and Toamasina (Tamatave). For more information about the cost and frequency of these flights refer to the individual Getting There & Away sections in this book. TAM's head office is 3 Rue de Nice 97 400, Saint-Denis (☎ 94 38 48; fax 94 39 49).

Air Mauritius has a range of flights from Port-Louis (the capital of Mauritius) to Tana for the same price as Air Mad, and also to Johannesburg, Nairobi, the Comoros (Moroni) and Réunion. The head office is at Air Mauritius Centre, Rue Président JF Kennedy, Port-Louis (☎ 208 7700; fax 208 8331).

Finally, the quirky Comoros-based Amicale Comores Air (refer to the Comoros section later for details) flies between Moroni and Mahajanga on Monday for US$310 return.

Airpass

Air Austral offers an Indian Ocean airpass which is convenient and reasonably good value. Refer to the regional Getting There & Away chapter for details.

Air Madagascar Offices

Air Mad's head office is at 31 Araben ny Fahaleovantena, BP 437, Antananarivo (☎ 222 22). The following is a list of Air Mad offices and representatives overseas. For a list of offices for airlines in Tana which serve Madagascar, refer to the Getting There & Away section of the Antananarivo chapter.

Australia
    7th floor, 19-31 Pitt St, Sydney, NSW 2000 (☎ (02) 9252 3770; fax (02) 9247 8406)
Austria
    Landstrasser Hauptstr. 2, Hilton Center Top 1618, A-1030, Vienna (☎ (0222) 713 9060; fax (0222) 713 9052)
Comoros
    Madagascar consulate, Volovolo (☎ 732 290)
France
    29-31 Rue des Boulets, 75011 Paris (☎ 05 53 27 31 19; fax 02 43 79 30 33)
Germany
    Frankfurter Airport Center, Hugo-Eckener-Ring, Hbk 11, D-60549, Frankfurt (☎ (069) 6907 2700; fax (069) 6905 9206)
    Herzog-Rudolfstrasse 3, D-80539 Munich 22 (☎ (089) 2900 3940; fax (089) 2900 3946)
Italy
    International Tourist Representative, via Bissolati 76, Rome (☎ (06) 487 1432; fax (06) 488 3342)
Kenya
    Hilton Hotel Arcade, PO Box 41, 723 Nairobi (☎ (02) 218 393)
Mauritius
    Rogers & Co Ltd, Rogers House, 5 Rue Président JF Kennedy, Port-Louis (☎ 208 6801; fax 212 0218)
Réunion
    9 Rue MacAuliffe, 97 641, Saint Denis (☎ 41 63 41; fax 21 10 08)
South Africa
    Aviation GSA International, 6th floor, Sandton City Office Tower, Sandton City Shopping Centre, Johannesburg (☎ (11) 784 7724; fax (11) 784 7730)
Switzerland
    Atash/Geneve, 1-3 Rue Chantepoulet, 1201 Geneva (☎ (22) 732 4230; fax (22) 731 1690)
    Flug Hofstrase 61, 8152 Glattbrugg, 8035, Zurich (☎ (01) 810 8584; fax (01) 810 9119)

UK
    Aviareps Airline Management, Premiere House, Betts Way, Crawley, West Sussex, RH 10 2GB (☎ (01293) 526 426; fax (01293) 512 229)
USA
    Cortez Travel, 124 Lomas Santa Fe Drive, Solana Beach, CA 92075 (☎ (800) 854 1029; fax (619) 481 7474; email cortez-usa@mcimail.com)

Arrival

Ivato International Airport at Tana was once one of the most disorganised airports in the world, but the arrival procedure has been commendably streamlined and is now very easy. After entering the terminal you are handed a brief disembarkation form to fill in (have a pen ready as there are none available for the public). Immigration is a breeze unless you had to get a visa; if so, your visa will be inspected for a moment. Then wait for your luggage. At the perfunctory customs inspection you may be asked how much money you have, but (unlike previously) you do not have to show any of it or fill out a currency declaration. Then comes the hard work: squeezing through the throng of taxi drivers, and bargaining for a ride to the city.

Air Mad and the tourist office have counters at the international airport (which should be staffed when international flights arrive). The counters are worth visiting if you need to immediately confirm another flight or want some other information quickly, such as the current taxi fare from the airport to the city.

In contrast, arriving at the small international airports at Antsiranana, Nosy Be, Mahajanga, Toamasina, Île Sainte Marie, Toliara and Taolagnaro on a regional airline can often be chaotic, especially at peak season. Facilities are woefully inadequate, and loads of tired passengers are forced to stand around for what seems like an eternity to check-in, clear customs, immigration and so on.

Money It is very important to note that the only international airport in Madagascar with guaranteed money-changing facilities is at Tana, where several bank counters are open every day at the time of an international arrival. All other minor, regional airports where international flights occasionally land will probably have nowhere to change money. So you must have enough Malagasy francs, French francs or, at a pinch, US dollars to last until you find a bank in the city.

You cannot change Malagasy francs back into foreign currency at the Tana airport (or any other airport) – you must do this at a bank in the city.

Departure

While entering Madagascar is a lot easier than it was, unfortunately leaving the country isn't always quite as hassle free. Hopefully, things will improve. Usually, it goes something like this:

Step 1
Scramble to pay your departure tax (see Departure Taxes following for details) at a counter where you must also obtain an embarkation form. You can save some time and effort by getting the form and paying the tax at another counter just before the immigration booths, after checking-in.

Step 2
Wait to be allowed into the departure terminal while your passport is checked twice.

Step 3
Wait while your luggage goes through the x-ray machine. If you are unlucky your bags may also be subjected to a laborious manual search.

Step 4
Scramble to, and then wait in line at, the disorganised check-in counter. You will be allocated a seat number when you check in.

Step 5
Proceed through immigration; this is fairly painless.

Step 6
Undergo another check of your passport and cabin luggage.

Step 7
Wait in the transit lounge where the overpriced snack bar and shops may be closed.

SEA

Travelling to and from Madagascar by boat is certainly not impossible, and is a great way to visit nearby islands and the mainland of Africa. But you will need plenty of time and plenty of determination. And you must be aware that travel will be mostly on cargo ships (unless you hitch a ride on a yacht as a crew member), so sleeping and eating conditions will be rough. Also seas will be turbulent at times, and organising visas and dealing with immigration officials who are not used to foreigners travelling by boat can be almost as frustrating as finding a boat.

If these factors don't put you off, remember that sailing may not save you a lot of money and it will certainly be more hassle than flying, especially if you factor in the number of days it takes to find a boat, wait for it to leave and then sail.

Comoros

Between the Comoros islands (mainly Grande Comore and Anjouan) and Madagascar, there are boats every week or two, often via Mayotte. For more details refer to the Getting There & Away sections in the Mahajanga (Western Madagascar) and Comoros chapters. As a foreigner on a cargo boat from Moroni (on Grande Comore) to Mahajanga you will probably be charged about US$200 one-way. Try to bargain for far less because this is more than the Moroni-Mahajanga flight.

Africa

As far as cargo ships are concerned there's only one port in the Indian Ocean: Mombasa (Kenya). Knock on the door of all shipping agencies to find out what is going on. Dar es Salaam (Tanzania) has no traffic with its eastern neighbours, and Mozambique, though much closer, is an absolute dead end for sailing boats and cargo ships.

Yves Périsse, France

Besides Mombasa, the best place to wait around for a lift on a cargo boat is the island of Zanzibar, off the coast of Tanzania, which is linked religiously and culturally with the Comoros islands. A boat from Zanzibar to Grande Comore, and then on to Mahajanga (or reverse) should leave every week or two, but it is a matter of asking and asking. And then waiting.

From South Africa one intrepid traveller was able to travel by boat from Durban to Madagascar. This was not an organised passenger boat, but he suggested that anyone interested should make inquiries with the

South African tourism department. The other place to ask about a lift on a cargo boat is Cape Town.

Indian Ocean

Between Madagascar and Mauritius and Réunion, it is easier to pick up a ride on a cargo boat. All boats to these islands leave from Toamasina (commonly known as Tamatave), on the east coast of Madagascar. The best agencies to check out are SEAL and the Mediterranean Shipping Agency (MSC), both in the port area at Toamasina.

MSC has a weekly cargo/passenger boat, with excellent cabins and food for passengers, between Toamasina and Mauritius and/or Réunion. However, MSC must telex its office in Europe for permission to take a foreigner as a passenger, which all takes time. Expect to pay about US$150 from Toamasina to Mauritius (or vice versa), which is a lot cheaper than the airfare.

Other Countries

Madagascar is an increasingly popular stopover for cruising yachts, mainly from France and South Africa, so if you have the contacts, patience and/or money you may be able to hitch a ride. Finding work as a crew member between Madagascar and South Africa, Mayotte, Réunion or Mauritius is more likely, but you will probably still have to pay for the trip. The yachting season runs from April to November, and your best chances of finding a lift will be at the harbour in Nosy Be, Toamasina, Mahajanga and Île Sainte Marie.

Arrival & Departure

So few foreigners travel by sea to or from Madagascar that the customs and immigration procedures are fairly haphazard and often non-existent. There may not be anyone official at the port in Madagascar (or anywhere else, such as the Comoros, for that matter) to meet the boat, so you may have to go to the immigration office to get an entrance or exit stamp yourself. If you don't you may get into real strife. In any case, always ask the boat owner about customs and immigration procedures – he may organise everything for you anyway.

ORGANISED TOURS

Just 10 years ago Madagascar was a virtually unknown destination, largely undiscovered by travellers and ignored entirely by package tour operators. That's all changed, and an increasing number of companies are making Madagascar accessible and acceptable to just about everyone.

If you're interested in an organised tour as an easy way of seeing the country – but are willing to sacrifice a fair bit of money and flexibility – numerous international operators offer a wide variety of options. For a list of reputable travel companies within Madagascar which operate organised tours, see Travel Agencies in the Antananarivo chapter.

The following are a few of the international companies operating tours to, and around, Madagascar:

Australia
  Adventure Associates, 197 Oxford St, PO Box 612, Bondi Junction, Sydney, NSW 2022 (☎ (03) 9389 7466; fax (03) 9369 1853)
  Far Horizons, George St, PO Box 96, Truro, SA 5356 (☎ (085) 8640 255; fax (085) 8640 065) – it offers very up-market tours around the Indian Ocean region
Austria
  AKL Travel GmbH, Flötzerweg 28, A-4030 Linz (☎ (0732) 313 575; fax (0732) 313 576)
France
  Comptoir des Déserts, 23 Rue du Pont-Neuf, Paris 75001 (☎ 02 40 26 19 40; fax 04 42 21 47 07)
  MVM, 70 Rue Pernety, Paris 75014 (☎ 03 44 70 80 81; fax 02 43 27 78 84)
  Ylang-Ylang Tours, 133 Rue de Vaugirard, Paris 75015 (☎ 02 40 61 03 03; fax 02 40 61 07 05) – an impressive Malagasy-run outfit
Germany
  Madagascar Adventures, Knesebeckstr. 30, D-10623, Berlin (☎ (030) 881 1190)
  Trauminsel Reisen, Summerstr. 8, D-82211 Herrsching (☎/fax (08152) 931 920)
  TUI, Karl-Wiechert-Allee 23, D-30620, Hannover (☎ (0511) 567 2546)

Italy

Adventure del Mondo, Circonv, Gianicolense 41, 00152, Rome (☎ (06) 588 0661; fax (06) 580 9540)

Vacanze, SRL 20122, Milano, via Paoloda Cannobio 33 (☎ (02) 85 391; fax (02) 853 9295)

Netherlands

African Holidays, Emrikweg 31 2031, BT Haarlem (☎ (23) 421 334; fax (31) 2342 1574)

Baobab Travel, Haarlemmerstraat 24-26, 1013ER, Amsterdam (☎ (20) 627 5129; fax (20) 624 5401

Switzerland

Kuoni Travel, Nove Hard 7, CH-8037, Zurich (☎ (01) 277 4444; fax (01) 272 4567)

Lets Go Tours, Vorstadt 14, Postfach 321 8201, Schaffhausen (☎ (53) 24 10 77; fax (53) 24 60 77)

UK

Hann Overland, 100B High St, Godstone, Surrey RH9 8DR (☎ (0883) 754 4705; fax (0883) 744 706) – offers rough month-long overland trips from top to bottom

Reef & Rainforest Tours, 205 North End Rd, London W14 9NP (☎/fax (0171) 381 2204) – has a strong focus on wildlife viewing

Silk Cut Travel, Monn House, College St, Peterfield, Hampshire GU32 3JN (☎ (01730) 265 211; fax (01730) 268 482)

USA

Above the Clouds, PO Box 398, Worchester MA 01602-0398 (☎ (508) 799 4499; fax (508) 797 4779; email sconlon@world.std.com) – trekking and diving to remote areas

Earthwatch, 680 Mt Auburn St, PO Box 9104, Watertown, Massachusetts (☎ (800) 776 0188; fax (617) 926 8532; email info@earthwatch.org) – it runs 'volunteer' ecotourism trips

Green Tracks, 4324 Stadium Dr, Fort Worth, TX 76133 (☎ (800) 9-MONKEY; fax (817) 921 6769; email gnzg54a@prodigy.com) – great for ecotourist trips

Lemur Tours, 2562 Noriega St 203, San Francisco, CA 94122 (☎ (415) 681 8222) – obviously specialises in lemur tours

Wings Inc, 1643 N Alvernon Way, Suite 105, Tucson, Arizona, 85712 3350 (☎ (520) 320 9868; fax (520) 320 9373) – specialises in birdwatching tours

Cortez Travel, 124 Lomas Santa Fe Drive, Solana Beach, CA 92075 (☎ (800) 854 1029; fax (619) 481 7474; email cortez-usa@mcimail. com) – an excellent company which arranges individual packages as well as custom tours for organisations

DEPARTURE TAXES

Predictably, all travellers (Malagasy and foreigners) are slugged for a departure tax every time they board a plane. For internal flights, the tax is FMg 8000 (payable in Malagasy francs only). For international flights to what are regarded as 'regional centres' (ie the Comoros, Mayotte, the Seychelles, Mauritius and Réunion), the departure tax is FMg 60,000 or F80; to all other international destinations, you have to pay FMg 80,000 or F100.

You can pay the international departure tax in Malagasy francs, French francs cash or travellers' cheques, or in US dollars cash. You can get change in French francs (or Malagasy francs if you want to buy a last minute drink or souvenir), but try to avoid getting coins which are sometimes hard to exchange in other countries. In all cases, you pay your departure tax at a counter at the domestic or international airport (depending on the type of flight).

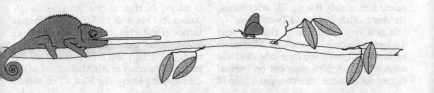

Getting Around

However you look at it, getting around Madagascar is always an adventure. It's travelling in its purest form – testing, trying and terrific. Anything can happen and anything does. Even air travel offers its share of thrills: although Air Mad (despite its name) is safe, comparatively cheap and relatively efficient, hitches are not uncommon.

If you're on a tight budget or have only limited time, it's a good idea to make an itinerary – but don't be reluctant to abandon it if things go awry. Travelling by road, rail or sea one-way and returning by air (or vice versa) is worthwhile to avoid covering the same ground twice. Those planning on using the ubiquitous *taxis-brousse* should allow plenty of time and take climatic factors into account.

AIR
Air Mad

Air Madagascar (once known officially as Madair, but now known affectionately as Air Mad) has a surprisingly wide and busy network of flights to over 60 destinations throughout the country. If you intend to travel a lot it's worth picking up a free timetable from the Air Mad head office in Tana: it lists all flights (but not fares). And remember that schedules often change during the peak season (14 July to 15 September).

Some flights, especially smaller planes to more remote destinations, can be delayed and cancelled. (Having said that, all but one of the dozen flights we took left on time.) On long-haul international routes Air Mad operates its Boeing 747, which has accurately been described as 'Madagascar's National Debt'. On popular domestic routes Air Madagascar runs mainly Boeing 737 workhorses, Hawker Siddeley 748s and Twin-Otters.

It is a very good idea to find out what discounts, specials or extras Air Mad offers for internal flights if you fly into Madagascar on Air Mad. A 50% discount on internal flights, for instance, can save you a heap of

money, and make flying a cheap alternative to long-distance overland travel. (Refer to the Madagascar Getting There & Away chapter for details about this.)

TAM Airlines

The skies were recently opened up to foreign competition in an effort to keep prices low and standards high. This seems to have worked because Air Mad has vastly improved from several years ago and there is a new internal airline, Transports et Travaux Aeriens de Madagascar (TAM). Sometimes written as TTAM, this Réunion-based company flies between Taolagnaro (also known as Fort Dauphin), Toliara and Antananarivo (Tana); between Tana and Île Sainte Marie via Toamasina (Tamatave); and between Tana and Mahajanga (Majunga), and then on to Nosy Be and Antsiranana (Diego Suarez). The prices for internal TAM flights are exactly the same as Air Mad, but TAM is often more comfortable and usually more reliable than Air Mad.

Fares & Tickets

The fares for Air Mad and TAM flights are probably cheap compared to your own country, but not great value compared to some African or Asian countries. The reason is that non-residents – ie tourists – have to pay for all internal and international flights in foreign currency. Air Mad and the government which owns it need as much of the hard stuff as they can get. For information about the cost of fares around the country, refer to the Domestic Air Routes map and the relevant sections throughout the book.

You can pay for Air Mad and TAM tickets in major foreign currencies (cash): US dollars (but not with US$100 bills), French francs, Deutschmarks, pounds sterling, Swiss francs and, maybe, South African rand. (US dollars and French francs are the preferred currency in Air Mad offices in the countryside.) Every Air Mad office should

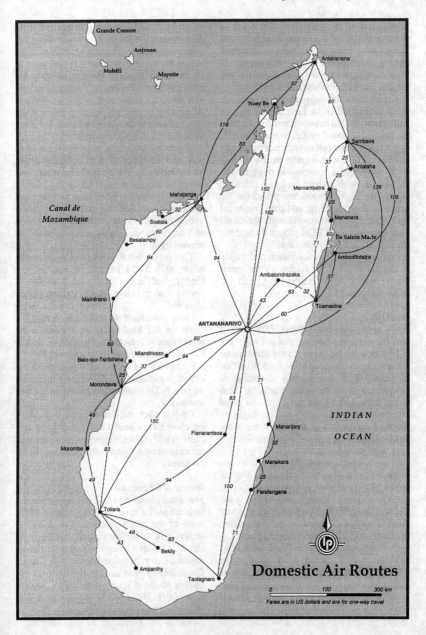

Canal de
Mozambique

INDIAN
OCEAN

Domestic Air Routes

0   150   300 km

Fares are in US dollars and are for one-way travel

have a list of all fares from that point of departure. You can ask to check the list if you think you're being deliberately overcharged (which can happen). This won't happen in TAM offices, which are more organised and usually list fares in their office windows.

Credit cards are only readily accepted at the Air Mad office in Tana. Don't rely on using a credit card to buy tickets for Air Mad flights at a regional office. You can usually buy a ticket at a travel agency in a major city outside of Tana with a credit card – but you may be charged a commission of up to 6%. (If you pay with a credit card you still have to pay the high non-resident price, but the fare is charged in FMg, and then converted into your own currency through the credit card company.) All TAM offices throughout the country accept credit cards.

The baggage allowance for internal flights is normally 20kg; for flights on the small Twin-Otters it may be a strict 10kg – and you may be charged for any extra weight.

Booking

Air Mad likes to have its flights fully booked and they'll often appear that way on the computer whether or not it's the true state of affairs. This can happen at the Air Mad office in Tana, which has a small allocation of tickets, say, from Île Sainte Marie to Tana. Once these tickets are sold, the Air Mad computer in Tana will say the flight is 'booked out' when in fact there are seats available from the point of departure – in this case, Île Sainte Marie.

If Air Mad claims a flight (which does not originate in Tana) is 'booked out', it is often worth taking a chance, and waiting until you get to the point of departure to buy your ticket. If in doubt ring the particular regional Air Mad office to determine the availability of tickets and, if possible, reserve a seat.

If you book a flight in Tana from, say, Mahajanga to Tana, the Air Mad office in Mahajanga will almost certainly not know of your reservation, so you must confirm your ticket as soon as you arrive (or ring the Air Mad office in Mahajanga beforehand) – and hope they have a seat. In the peak season, and

to popular and remote destinations like Antsiranana, Île Sainte Marie and Nosy Be, you may meet frustrated travellers with tickets but no reserved seats. If you want to fly from one regional town to another, for example from Toliara to Taolagnaro, you will have to book your flight in Toliara. Always try to visit any Air Mad office at the time of opening (or queue up before it opens) to beat the ticket-waving throng.

If you are travelling to somewhere one-way, and returning overland, you can avoid a lot of hassle by flying *from* Tana, where you can get a definite reservation on Air Mad. If you travel overland from Tana to a regional town, you may find that you have no reservation (despite what your ticket may say) and no seats or flights are available for several days.

The problems mentioned above rarely occur with TAM because it has so few flights, and is computerised – which is reason enough to use TAM to the few places it covers.

Once you have successfully booked a flight on Air Mad or TAM, confirm your reservation at least three days before departure. You can do this by telephone, but it's safer to visit the office once you are in the city of departure – an official looking stamp on your ticket from the airline office is more reassuring.

On Air Mad and TAM flights you rarely get more than a boiled lolly to suck on, and a tiny cup of tea/coffee to drink (or spill), and the only thing to read is the sick bag, so be prepared.

Arrival & Departure

The domestic airport in Tana is next to the international airport at Ivato, about 14km north of the centre of Tana. The domestic airport is fairly well organised, but get to the check-in counter at least 90 minutes before departure for popular flights and for all flights during peak season. For regional airports, about 45 to 60 minutes before departure is OK if you have a reserved seat. If you are on a waiting list get to the particular airport a little earlier than normal.

At regional airports the checking-in procedure is a little disorganised. Arrive before the official check-in time; place your ticket in a line on the counter (and keep your eye on it); wait for your ticket to be looked at and your name to be yelled out; place your luggage on the scales; and then pay your departure tax. You never get an allocated seat on any internal Air Mad or TAM flight, so if you want a decent seat line up early at the terminal door.

At regional airports the *livraison des baggages* (luggage collection) is often a real log-jam. Amid much shoving and jostling of passengers, and hovering hotel touts and drooling taxi drivers, you often have to point out your luggage and get the tag on your luggage checked against your receipt (which you should *always* hang on to). A taxi driver you have chosen will usually get your bag for you at no extra cost; a porter relies on a tip.

When checking in your bags make absolutely certain that the tag slapped onto your luggage matches your destination – otherwise you may be in Île Sainte Marie while your bags may be in Morondava.

Rental

If you are flush with cash, and need to go somewhere remote, you can arrange the (ultra-expensive) hire of a light aircraft, with pilot, from several agencies in Tana. These include TAM (☎ 315 05), Aero-Club de Tananarive (☎ 332 19) and Madagascar Flying Service (☎ 313 27).

BUS & MINIBUS

Between Tana and other nearby towns, such as Toamasina, Antsirabe, Mananjary, Manakara and Fianarantsoa – but not between each town – a range of decrepit buses and newish minibuses are an alternative to the general taxi-brousse. Throughout the country, including Tana, all buses and minibuses leave from the general all-purpose taxi-brousse stations.

Buses are usually cheaper than the nine-seater *taxi-be*, but dearer than the sardine-can-on-wheels utilities known as a baché. Buses go slowly and carry more passengers, so they take a long time to fill up and are constantly stopping for people to get on or off. They are not always comfortable either:

We booked our seats three days in advance for the bus from Fianarantsoa to Ranohira. Upon arriving at the station, the company had sold far more seats than initially promised, and forced six people, and other kids, per row. It finally stowed 47 persons in a bus for officially 25. The bus left two hours late and after a nine hour trip, the driver stopped along the road to say hello to a friend...

Frederic Vereecken & Colette Storme, Belgium

Minibuses are more comfortable, quicker, stop less often and fill up faster than buses. They are slightly more expensive than a bus, but usually cheaper than the taxi-be.

One new tourist-oriented bus does the long haul down the main highway between Tana and Toliara. The *Confo Express* leaves Tana on Tuesday and Toliara on Thursday. You pay twice as much as the local bus, but this private bus is considerably more secure and comfortable. Other less frequent but comfortable tourist buses link Tana with Toamasina, and Toamasina with Soanierana-Ivongo for the ferry across to Île Sainte Marie. Refer to the relevant chapters for more details.

TAXI-BROUSSE

The most popular and least expensive form of road transport in Madagascar is the taxi-brousse, a generic word used by travellers (and throughout this book) to describe any form of public transport which is not a minibus or bus. These taxis-brousse are always slow and unreliable but often great fun. However, if you are on a tight schedule avoid using taxis-brousse on long hauls, otherwise you may spend most of your trip at the side of a road waiting for repairs.

The term taxi-brousse (bush taxi) covers a variety of vehicles. One type, also called a baché, is a Peugeot open-air wagon with a canvas-covered canopy frame arching over the cargo area. A comfortable human load is

---

The Annual Taxi-Brousse Check

It may be hard to believe, but there are actually some regulations concerning the safety of taxis-brousse in Madagascar! However, with public transport stretched to the limit, negligible resources to repair or replace vehicles and an ever-growing population, these rules are understandably (but unfortunately for the traveller) ignored. The police carry out occasional checks of taxis-brousse at roadblocks, but while the vehicle will have bald tyres, broken brake lights, a door attached to the car by wire and about 15 passengers over the limit, the police will probably only check to see if the first aid box is complete! There is also an annual taxi-brousse check, as two readers were able to witness first hand:

To get through the annual check the driver of a non-roadworthy vehicle (which includes *all* taxis-brousse in Madagascar) has to pay a bribe. It is cheaper to use the innovative Malagasy system of sharing working parts between vehicles, for a small fee. For example, at the time of the check a satisfactory brake system from among the taxis-brousse is removed and placed in the vehicle going for a check. The same goes for the rest for the engine and tyres.

Heike Alber & Andreas Letto

---

six along each side bench and one in the middle at the back, but about 20 is a normal minimum load. Our record was 27 people, plus cargo, in the back of a baché – and six, plus driver, in the front.

Other vehicles generally lumped under the term taxi-brousse are *cars-brousse* and *auto-cars*, which are the large Renaults, Mercedes or Peugeots that link nearly every town and city in the country that are accessible by road – weather and road conditions permitting.

The taxi-be, also called a *taxi-familial*, is literally a 'big taxi'. These Peugeot 404 and 504 estate/station wagons are slightly more expensive, but are in theory more comfortable and faster than travelling by any other vehicle, including buses and minibuses. The taxi-be is designed to carry nine passengers, including driver (ie, three along each of the three rows of seats), but it isn't rare to stuff in at least 12 people. Try to book the front seat beside the window; the rear seats can be very cramped, uncomfortable and airless.

Almost without exception, all of these vehicles are in a dilapidated state. The only windscreen wipers, petrol gauges or speedometers you're likely to see working are in Japanese 4WD vehicles driven by aid agencies and up-market tour groups. One taxi-brousse we took between Manakara and Fianarantsoa broke down 27 times during what should have been a five-hour journey.

All independent travellers in Madagascar can relate a favourite horror story (or three) about their trips on taxis-brousse, but some are a little more unusual:

In the taxi-brousse from Mahajanga to Tana I was exposed to Christian Hallelujah music from the car hi-fi for the whole nine hours of the drive. But the greatest torture came when the driver and his wife began mercilessly to sing the Lord's praises too. My tip: when you want to travel like the locals, don't forget the earplugs!

Daniel F Mueller, Germany

The most creative use of a FMg 25,000 bill we came across was using it as a funnel to pour petrol from a mineral water bottle into the tank of a taxi-brousse, then drying it by letting it hang from the window.

Heike Alber & Andreas Letto, Germany

The fact that the taxis-brousse continue to operate long after any self-respecting vehicle would have been consigned to a scrap heap is a tribute to French technology and the ingenuity of Malagasy popular mechanics. Some of these vehicles seem to be held together by wire or the crudest of welding, and there are frequent periods *en panne* (broken down). They are usually repaired within an hour or two, often with the assistance of another passing taxi-brousse or truck.

Booking a Ticket

It comes as no surprise that most taxi-brousse stations are chaotic. At every station in any major town you will be accosted by taxi-brousse touts who will steer you to their particular ticket office, depending on your destination. Although annoying, these touts are very useful as a way of finding where you can buy a ticket – ticket booths are often lumped together according to their destinations.

Only when you give a tout or driver your luggage, or buy a ticket, are you generally committed to that vehicle. Some travellers scream when a tout or driver takes their luggage. Don't panic: they are honest (though not necessarily so when quoting a fare) and just want to ensure that you are committed to their vehicle.

For any distance over about six hours (for instance, from Tana to Mahajanga) or more infrequent departures, such as Manakara to Fianarantsoa, it is worth booking a seat at least the day before you want to go. You will get a ticket with the fare, destination and 'time' of departure (which is when you should get to the departure point, but is almost certainly not when the taxi-brousse will leave). Buying a ticket in advance will guarantee you a place on the vehicle, but not any particular seat unless you have pre-arranged something. However, pre-booking a seat does tie you to one vehicle, which may remain stationary and wait for other passengers while other full vehicles leave. This can be very frustrating.

For popular, regular and shorter trips, it is easy enough to just turn up at the taxi-brousse station when you want to leave and buy your ticket. Always check out the range of vehicles on offer, and consider the mechanical reliability of the taxi-brousse, the comfort of seats, which seats are available, and, importantly, which vehicle is leaving sooner. Don't always believe what the taxi-brousse touts tell you if you ask them which vehicle is leaving soonest.

Fares

The fares for all trips are set by the govern-ment. So all taxis-brousse of the same type going from Manakara to Mananjary, for example, will cost the same, but the fare will be slightly higher for a comfortable taxi-be or a quicker minibus. A higher price for something quicker, safer and comfortable may be substantial for a local, but for a foreigner it is negligible and always worth considering. You may be quoted or charged a little extra for a front seat; this is worth paying for on a long ride.

Foreigners are occasionally overcharged by dishonest taxi-brousse touts or ticket sellers but this is fairly rare. If you are in any doubt, and think you are being overcharged, ask a local what they are paying (there is no dual-pricing for foreigners on public road transport), or ask to see the list of official fares which should be posted in the ticket office or in the vehicle.

Roads

Of the 40,000km of road in Madagascar only 4694km is sealed, and most of this is often little more than a series of potholes rimmed by thin strips of tar. The rest of the country's roads are made of mud, sand, rocks and air (ie potholes).

The only main mostly paved roads or *routes nationales* are: RN1b from Tana to Tsiroanomandidy; RN2 from Tana to Toamasina and RN5 continuing north to Soanierana-Ivongo; RN4 to Mahajanga from Tana (often difficult when it rains); RN6 from Ambanja to Antsiranana; RN7, the main highway from Tana to Toliara (about 95% paved); and RN31, RN34 & RN35 from Antsirabe to Morondava. There are some appalling stretches of 'highway' which must be seen to be believed; for example, RN13 from Ihosy to Ambovombe in the south-east, or RN6 between Ambanja and Antsohihy in the north-west.

During the rainy season, from November to March, several main roads (in particular the routes between Toliara and Taolagnaro, Ihosy and Ambovombe, and Mahajanga and Antsiranana) are often rendered impassable. Nonetheless, most accidents are caused by human failing, especially drunkenness, rather than dangerous vehicles and roads.

If you are working out an itinerary, you should not rely on any form of overland public transport to travel more than 40km/h on a decent road; or more than 20km/h on a bad road. This will factor in minor breakdowns but not major ones; and you should always allow an hour or two for a vehicle to fill up before it even leaves.

Some roads, particularly in the far northeast from Soanierana-Ivongo to Antsiranana, are prone to flooding throughout the year and have several broken bridges, a legacy of heavy truck traffic. You'll sometimes come across a bevy of truckies effecting temporary repairs to a previous temporary repair on a floorless iron bridge, with planks and by rearranging loose steel girders and plates.

The Journey

Any *Guinness Book of World Records* attempt at cramming people into a Mini would be put to shame by the Malagasy use of vehicle space, and it's a good way to get very close to the local people. Few journeys pass without incident and, as a result, a sense of camaraderie is normally fostered between passengers.

On top of, and interspersed with, the seething human mass is luggage of various sizes and shapes: animals, vegetables, minerals, bags, crates, rice, chickens, bundles of hats and mats, charcoal, mail and fuel. Your major item of luggage will probably have to be roped on to the roof as well. Make sure there is nothing valuable or breakable inside and keep checking on it to make sure it is properly protected from the dust or rain. Have a sturdy plastic bag inside or outside your backpack to protect its contents.

Allow plenty of time in your plans for taxi-brousse trips. Journeys which should take two hours can take four or five, and a five hour journey can take all day. It all depends on the length of the wait before you actually get going, the number of breakdowns en route, the motivation of the driver and the state of the roads.

The ideal place to sit is beside the driver,

but this coveted spot is occasionally shared by up to six people. It's usually assigned on a first come first served basis. Tourists will have the best chances of securing this prize if they:

* appear interested in seeing the Malagasy countryside;
* act the poor, beleaguered traveller with the bad back, sore feet and travel sickness; or
* offer to pay a bit more or bring a pack of cigarettes for the driver. Sometimes the front seat is kindly offered to the foreigner without all the rigmarole.

Taxis-brousse rarely leave on schedule, not even when they're full. In most cases they wait until they are overflowing and packed like sardines. In fact, they'll often wait an hour for just *one* more passenger. Before hitting the road, they may spend an hour circling in the hope that someone will suddenly decide to drop everything and climb aboard. One way to speed up a departure, and make yourself very popular with other impatient passengers, is to pay for the empty seat(s) for the length of the journey (thereby providing more comfort), or on the understanding that you will pay the difference between the full fare and the partial fare of any passenger(s) picked up along the way.

If at all possible, never travel on a taxi-brousse after dark because your luggage is less secure at night. While you are asleep drivers will get tired and there are no streetlights along the main roads, so if a large pothole doesn't create havoc, a large stray zebu may. Also, you miss the scenery by travelling at night.

If going on a long haul, simply break up the journey by staying somewhere overnight and travel during the day. Drivers on long-distance trips may stop for the night anyway, leaving passengers to sleep in the vehicle or out on the ground, or to seek accommodation in a local hotel or private home. If you are planning to take a taxi-brousse after dark, have a jacket or jumper (sweater) handy as the evenings can often be surprisingly chilly.

SHARE-TAXI

For short hauls in some parts of the country,

particularly in the northern regions, you will have to squeeze – and we mean *squeeze* – into a share-taxi. The worst example we experienced was in a miniscule Renault T4L into which nine people, plus driver, were crammed. From places like Antsiranana to nearby villages, more spacious share-taxis roam the streets looking for passengers.

TRAIN

You will travel in a traditional atmosphere indeed, you will enjoy spectacular tunnels of vegetation. But trains are rarely on time: some of them are cancelled without notice. You can never be sure to reach your destination before you really made it...

We are not sure what the final sentence means, but the rest of this advice from a locally produced government tourist publication is refreshingly honest. Train travel *is* great fun, but slow and prone to delays and cancellations.

The 1020km of track in the Malagasy rail system, known as the Réseau National des Chemins de Fer Malgaches (RNCFM), were built during the colonial period. There are four main lines in the country, though at any one time at least one track will probably be damaged and under repair. (At the time of research the Tana-Toamasina track was damaged but due to reopen later.)

The train between Tana and Antsirabe travels in both directions on most days, and takes about four hours. The Tana-Toamasina train leaves from both places once or twice a week and takes about 10 hours. This is a great rail line because you can break up the journey at Moramanga and head up to Lac Alaotra or visit the Parc National d'Andasibe-Mantadia (commonly known as the Périnet Reserve), or use it to get to the Canal des Pangalanes. The train along the branch line between Tana and Ambatondrazaka, via Moramanga, travels a couple of times a week in both directions and takes about seven hours.

If you want to go on one train trip (and it's working, and you have plenty of time) take the train between Fianarantsoa and Manakara. It travels twice a week in either direction and takes about nine hours, although things don't always go to plan:

Everything went more or less smoothly until the slope went up. The train glided backwards down the hill, though the motorman desperately tried to accelerate. Ten times the train crept up the hill some 20m, but each time it slid down. Suddenly some helpers jumped down from the locomotive, took palm tree leaves from the side of the track and cleared the tracks. Then they poured sand and small stones so as to augment friction between the wheels and the tracks.

What caused all this was a caterpillar plague. Thousands of them were on the plants and on the tracks and because of the pressure of the wheels, they formed a liquid on the tracks like brown soap. At a certain point later, the wheels were overheated and smoke and fire came from under the locomotive. Eventually we arrived at Fianarantsoa, having done 165km in 12 hours.

Frederic Vereecken & Colette Storme, Belgium

Classes & Fares

Every train has a choice of 1st or 2nd class travel with a 30% to 45% difference in price. First class travel is comfortable but not plush. Locals normally travel 2nd class, so it's more crowded but offers more contact with Malagasy travellers. Foreigners pay the normal price in FMg.

There are no buffet cars on the trains, but at major stops you'll normally find swarms of platform hawkers. The trips, though scenic, can be as rough as the roads in some places and occasionally trains rattle off the rails. To find out what is currently going where and when, just go to the station and ask someone. For more information about ticket prices and times of departures refer to the relevant chapters throughout the book.

La Micheline

The Micheline is a special single-car 'train' which runs on rubber tyres between Tana and Toamasina. Groups of up to 19 people can hire a Micheline for any rail journey, but it often runs anyway so you don't have to be in a group to get a ticket. They often have a bar and music, and thanks to the rubber tyres provide a much smoother ride than the conventional trains. Refer to the Toamasina section in the Eastern Madagascar chapter for more details.

CAR & MOTORCYCLE

The Malagasy drive their primarily French vehicles on the right-hand side of the road. Compared to European drivers they are generally cautious and conservative, both in the city and on the open road. It may have something to do with their temperament, but it is more likely caused by the state of the roads.

When driving on wet roads be especially wary of potholes which fill with water and offer no clues as to their depth. Most taxi-brousse drivers can tell tales of wheels buckling, axles and chassis snapping, and, on rare occasions, even entire vehicles disappearing into deep holes in the road (or so they say). If you intend to drive, the best information about road conditions will be available at taxi-brousse stations.

The police occasionally stop vehicles and carry out random checks, perhaps in the hope of detecting any of the 1001 possible (and probable) infractions of the vehicle code. These could include 'overcrowding' or 'vehicle held together with string', but it all seems to be quite friendly and few drivers are ever 'fined' more than a few hundred FMg.

It may be stating the obvious, but the roads, traffic and regulations in Madagascar are unique. Be aware of herds of zebu blocking the roads; very slow and wide ox-carts; diabolical traffic in the cities; markets and stalls spread out onto the footpath and road; and broken down vehicles dotting the highways. Roads are sometimes little more than solidified mud, and bridges occasionally collapse. Don't even contemplate driving around Tana – it is quicker to walk, and damage to the vehicle through minor accidents and vandalism is quite possible. And finally, as one tourist brochure poignantly reminds drivers: 'be aware that the basic axiom of the highway code is that the bigger you are, the more you have the right of way'.

Rental

Car To rent a car drivers must be at least 23 years old and have held a driving licence for one year. Rental costs are horrendously expensive. For the smallest Peugeot or Subaru car expect to pay at the very least FMg 65,000 per day (for a minimum of two days). The FMg 600 or more per km will add to your bill considerably – Madagascar is a big country. If you want a larger car, you will pay at least FMg 100,000 per day and FMg 800 per km; for a 4WD it is FMg 140,000 per day and FMg 1000 per km.

And that is not all. You will need to take out compulsory insurance of FMg 30,000 per day; you pay for petrol (gasoline); and a sales tax of 20% is slugged onto the bill. If you want a driver (a good idea, because insurance and liability for accidents will be far less) it will cost an extra FMg 20,000 per day. Most agencies will insist that you pay for a driver anyway, but you don't have to. You can get other deals for longer rentals – but always check out the hidden extras.

In Tana, the following agencies are reliable and well established:

AKL Travel, Lot II i34, Ampandrana – Bel'Air (☎ 262 05; fax 355 05)
Avis, 3 Rue Patrice Lumumba, Tsaralalana (☎ 204 35; fax 216 57) – it is very expensive
Eurorent, 2 Bis rue Rahamefy (☎ 297 66; fax 297 49)
Locauto, 52 Ave du Juin 1960 (☎ 219 81; fax 248 01)
Somalotra, 16 Rue Karija, Tsaralalana (☎ 303 63; fax 353 19) – the best prices in town

Taxi & Taxi-brousse You can also hire any type of taxi-brousse waiting at a station, or a taxi roaming the street. The fare should be one fare multiplied by the number of passengers the driver hoped to pick up. But still bargain hard. If possible, make sure the driver is sober and has adequate spare parts for any long-distance trip, and write the agreed fare on paper after asking about 'extras' like petrol and waiting time.

Motorcycle None of the agencies mentioned above rent motorcycles. You can only hire them by the hour or day on the resort islands of Nosy Be and Île Sainte Marie (but you can't take them off the island). Motorcycles range from a Honda or Yamaha 125cc to a tiny Peugeot *mobylette* – a glorified bicycle but great fun nevertheless.

If you are concerned about protecting your skull, you may want to bring a helmet – none are available in Madagascar. Rarely do you need to show a licence or proof that you know how to ride a motorcycle when you rent.

Petrol

Malagasy petrol stations belong to the state oil company, Solima. They're increasingly common in towns and cities, but virtually non-existent in remote parts of the countryside. Currently, petrol costs FMg 1850 per litre, which is prohibitive for most Malagasy people.

BICYCLE

In the words of one enthusiastic cyclist who travelled 4000km by mountain bike in three months, 'Madagascar is made for mountain bikes and vice versa' – and it's true.

If you go to remote areas, you can usually stop for the night in villages along the way, after asking the teacher or a local dignitary for permission to pitch your tent and light a fire. You would have to be self-sufficient with food and water.

However, if you plan your trip thoroughly and stick to the main roads and towns, you can stay at hotels and eat at restaurants along the way, relieving you of heavy luggage. You and your bike can also often hitch a ride on regular public transport (particularly easy on trains) if you get tired or fed up with the roads.

The only drawbacks to any type of mountain bike riding are a lack of spare parts (so bring your own), though many Malagasy are masters at fixing *anything*; and the fact that you will constantly be the centre of attention, which can be disconcerting at times. The advantage, of course, is visiting areas that no other foreigner relying on public transport or a private vehicle can reach – but watch out for snakes and tortoises lying in the middle of the road.

You can hire mountain bikes in Taolagnaro, Antsirabe, Île Sainte Marie,

Morondava and Nosy Be, but they are normally just for local use. Don't even consider riding a bike in Tana, but the Grill du Rova restaurant (refer to the Places to Eat section in the Antananarivo chapter) organises weekend mountain bike trips, with bike hire, tents and food (BYO sleeping bag), to local spots such as Lac Mantasoa for about F300 per person for the weekend.

Here are a few comments about travelling on a mountain bike in some parts of the countryside:

Eastern Madagascar
  Tana to Andasibe (for Périnet Reserve) and then to the coast at Ambila-Lemaitso is a good trip. From there to Toamasina the scenery is boring and there are some hills, so a taxi-brousse is not a bad idea. From Toamasina to Mahavelona the road is pleasant and flat; and the scenery north to Soanierana-Ivongo is fantastic. Further north, the road is loose sand and a real struggle. It gets even worse further on.

Northern Madagascar
  Antalaha to Iharana (Vohémar) is excellent for mountain bikes (not so great for other vehicles). Though this road is not tarred all the way the scenery and villages are marvellous. From Iharana to Ambilobe, however, the road is appalling. It is bad enough by bus and there are hardly any facilities along the way. From Antsiranana to Tana the route is partially paved but sparsely populated, and you will have to take your own supplies of water and food, as well as camping equipment.

Southern Madagascar
  Travelling south of Tana along the main RN7 highway is busy and hilly to start with, but there are good places to stop and eat along the way. This is the most interesting part of the country (refer to Suggested Itineraries in the Regional Facts for the Visitor chapter for some ideas).

HITCHING

Hitching is never entirely safe in any country in the world and we don't recommend it. Travellers who decide to hitch should understand that they are risking a small but potentially serious risk. Nonetheless, many people choose to hitch and the advice that follows should help to make their journey as fast and safe as possible.

Hitching isn't really a viable alternative in Madagascar, despite the people's generosity.

Traffic outside and between the towns and cities is thin, and you are only likely to flag down a taxi-brousse, taxi-be or truck – most of which will be full. In any case you'll almost certainly have to pay for the ride.

One reader was lucky enough to score a free trip in an air-conditioned 4WD all the way to Toliara from Ranohira with a tourist, but hitching rides is usually tough work:

The trip from Toliara to Amboasary (568km) took me five days. On the first day, I arrived at 6 am at the taxi-brousse station for the only truck that day. At the office, they told me that the driver was sick: come back tomorrow. Day two: the truck was being repaired. When it was finished, the goods, 5000 people and their luggage were loaded into the truck – nine hours later. A terrible eight hour ride to Betioky completed this horror day. On day three I waited three hours for onward transport. Day four, after five hours of waiting, a truck loaded with maize bags brought me to Beloha. Day five, I arrived in Amboasary.

Pieter Janssen, The Netherlands

Truck drivers normally charge a similar rate to the taxis-brousse and can handle road conditions which thwart lesser vehicles, but they are painfully slow and can be even more uncomfortable than a taxi-brousse if you have to share with 30 passengers, 50 bags of rice and a smelly zebu.

Although it's unwise for women to hitch alone or in all-female groups, women can feel relatively secure accepting lifts from truck drivers if there are other passengers aboard.

WALKING

Getting around on one's own feet is the Malagasy way and in this country of great distances and largely impassable roads a whole new world of possibilities opens up for the traveller willing to walk.

For some suggestions and tips about hiking and trekking, see the Activities sections in the Regional and Madagascar Facts for the Visitor chapters. Related topics may be found under Visiting Villages (Society & Conduct section) in the Facts about the Region chapter and Camping (Accommodation section) in the Regional Facts for the Visitor chapter.

BOAT

Pirogues or *lakana* (dugout canoes) are the primary means of transport for locals between remote coastal villages, but travelling by boat is not nearly as common as you may imagine.

You can informally hire larger *boutres* (single-masted dhows) and *goëlettes* (larger cargo vessels), or hitch a ride as a passenger on a cargo vessel which is sailing anyway. Along coastal roads, especially on the east coast, vehicles are ferried by raft across river estuaries. Occasionally, bridges are down or too dangerous to cross. This is especially true during the wet season, and travellers will have the choice of crossing by boat and continuing under their own steam, or waiting for repairs.

There are boat-cum-ferry services between the mainland and the two island resorts of Nosy Be and Île Sainte Marie (details of these boats are covered in the relevant chapters). It is not difficult to get lifts on cargo boats around the far north-east coast, especially anywhere between Île Sainte Marie and Sambava, because the roads are either bad or non-existent. All of these services are at the mercy of weather

PAUL GREENWAY

A dhow heads out for a fishing trip along the Manakara River, eastern Madagascar.

conditions and you will share the limited sleeping space with the cargo.

Trips by pirogue and luxurious boats are becoming increasingly popular along the Canal des Pangalanes in the far east, and the Tsiribihina River in far western Madagascar. To fully explore these rivers will take a lot of time or money but they are great fun. Canoe trips to pristine or culturally interesting sites such as Lokaro near Taolagnaro, and Lokobe on Nosy Be, are also becoming more popular.

LOCAL TRANSPORT
Bus
Tana has several good public bus service companies, such as ANTAFITA, FIMA and MALAKIA. Fares around town cost FMg 300 to FMg 500. A few other provincial capitals and major towns, including Fianarantsoa, Mahajanga and Antsirabe, have city bus services. However, with the overcrowded vehicles, deplorably slow traffic, central location of attractions and hotels, and the abundance of cheap taxis and *pousse-pousses* (rickshaws) local buses are rarely necessary.

Taxi
Taxis, mostly dilapidated Renault 4s and Citroëns, are limited to larger towns and cities, where they're plentiful, especially around airports, train stations and taxi-brousse stations. (The only place where tourists are found and taxis are not is the island of Île Sainte Marie.) Taxis have no meters; patrons must know the approximate fare and bargain with the drivers to obtain it. Always make sure you agree on a fare to your intended destination before you climb in. There is a surcharge after dark, but it should be factored into the agreed fare rather than tacked on after the ride.

By and large Malagasy taxi drivers are honest, but like their counterparts everywhere they won't hesitate to attempt tricks aimed at increasing the agreed fare. If you're tight on cash stay on your guard and stand your ground. The best idea is to ask for an approximate fare from a local with no vested interest.

Pousse-pousse
Pousse-pousses are actually 'pull-pull' rickshaws which provide a quick and convenient dash around most flat and spread out towns. They are a legacy of the Chinese who were brought in by the French to help build the roads and railways. These rickshaws became known as pousse-pousses, not because they scoot around like cats, but because when climbing a hill, the pilot would shout to others to get behind the cart and 'push-push'. At least that's as good an explanation as any.

Pousse-pousses still operate in some numbers in Toliara, Toamasina, Manakara and Antsirabe (but not in Tana), where these individually painted conveyances liven the street scene with bright colours. They are convenient for short-distance runs around town. Whether or not you think it's ethical to be dragged around by a human beast of burden the pousse-pousse drivers must earn a living as well as pay a daily rate to pousse-pousse owners, so they are always grateful for custom.

Locals pay around FMg 500 for a ride. Tourist rates start at about FMg 1000, although drivers sometimes charge tourists FMg 2000 to FMg 3000, and it's always very negotiable. When it's raining the price automatically doubles for everyone. If you do use a pousse-pousse, agree on a fare before you climb aboard.

Some pousse-pousse drivers, especially in Antsirabe, have a habit of driving foreigners to the brink: mobbing them at the train station, following them down the street, lying in wait outside hotels and continuing to hound even after it should be clear that the target customer would prefer to walk. But who could blame them; an unsuspecting foreigner may literally be the haul of the day, agreeing to pay five or 10 times the going rate!

Zebu Cart
In some remote stretches of the country travelling on a cumbersome wooden cart

(commonly referred to as an ox-cart) drawn by some slothful zebus is a common form of transport. For example, around the Réserve des Tsingy de Bemaraha in western Madagascar, the road is *so* bad and the rivers *so* dominant, that zebu carts are the only way for locals – and foreigners – to get around. Zebu carts are excruciatingly slow and often exceedingly uncomfortable, but they are a form of transport that is unique.

Horse

Horses generally aren't a popular form of transport for locals, so hiring a steed for any short or long-distance travel will be hard to organise. Also, the choice of horses and the quality of riding gear are poor. About the only place you are likely to find horses to rent are places frequented by tourists (eg the Parc National de Montagne d'Ambre, near Antsiranana), and prices are naturally high. Regardless of the difficulties, visitors who have hired horses for trips around the countryside rave about it as a perfect way to avoid bad roads, to go where vehicles rarely dare to venture and to meet heaps of fascinated locals.

ORGANISED TOURS

A growing number of tour operators in Madagascar offer just about anything you'd like to do, including 4WD circuits, mountain bike treks, walking excursions, bus tours, wildlife viewing trips, cultural and history tours, and so on. Furthermore, they can get you to any part of the country you care to name.

There are a number of reasons for taking a locally organised tour. First of all, if you have only limited time it will minimise the amount of time spent sorting out the logistics of public transport. Furthermore, though ready contact with the culture and people may be hindered, a tour will allow you to actually see the country, stopping for photographs or at sites of interest along the way – simple pleasures which are impossible on an Air Mad flight at 10,000m, or beneath the human crush aboard a taxi-brousse.

The hitch is that unless you're lucky with timing, it's unlikely you'll be able to front up at a travel agency in most towns and book a tour on the spot; agencies will organise a trip if you can get a group together.

For information about local companies which arrange organised tours, refer to the Travel Agencies section in the Antananarivo chapter and the relevant sections throughout the book. For details about foreign travel agencies, refer to the Organised Tours section in the Madagascar Getting There & Away chapter.

Antananarivo (Tana)

- Telephone Area Code: 2

Antananarivo's original name was Analamanga (Blue Forest). In 1610 a Merina king, Andrianjaka, conquered the Vazimba villages (the Vazimba is a general name given to the group believed to be the first settlers of Madagascar) which sat at 1300m on the *hauts plateaux*, and stationed a garrison of 1000 men to defend the area. He constructed his palace on the highest hill and renamed it Antananarivo, which means Town of the Thousand (Warriors) (it sounds better in French: La Ville des Mille). The French later changed the name to Tananarive, but after Independence the old name returned to common usage. Nowadays, locals and visitors simply call it Tana.

Tana is like many other African and Asian capital cities: crowded, polluted and noisy, but it is spectacular in places and worth exploring. Tall narrow houses with crumbling red brickwork, terracotta-tiled roofs, wooden balconies and shuttered windows climb up the various levels over the city's 12 hills. Among them rise the spires of the city's many churches, and crowning Tana are the ruins of the Rova, the former palace of Queen Ranavalona I.

ORIENTATION

Làlana is Malagasy for street; *arabe* or *araben* is avenue; and *kianja* or *kianjan* is place or square. However, street signs are scarce and those that remain are often illegible or confusing, since most of the old French street names have been changed in honour of Malagasy heroes.

The hub of Tana's lower town is Araben ny Fahaleovantena (commonly known as Avenue de l'Indépendance). At one end is the main railway station and at the other the Hôtel Glacier. At this point, it narrows and becomes Araben ny 26 Jona 1960 (or Ave 26 Juin 1960).

This district is known as Analakely, which means Little Forest – that's the name to look

HIGHLIGHTS

- The Zoma market – the world's second largest. The Zoma is a maze of colour and activity every day, but especially on Fridays.
- Parc Botanique et Zoologique de Tsimbazaza. A pleasant park for a walk or picnic, with captive lemurs and a museum.
- Lac Mantasoa, 60km east of Tana, is a popular weekend retreat where visitors can enjoy camping, fishing and swimming.

for on bus placards if you wish to take a local bus to the centre of town. The area is thronged with permanent street markets, part of the famous Zoma, and whatever trees once graced its namesake forest have long since been replaced by swarms of off-white umbrellas balanced precariously on old tyre rims.

To the south-west of Analakely a busy stairway leads to a small piece of greenery called the Kianja ny Fahaleovantena (commonly known as the Place de l'Indépendance) in the area of Haute-Ville (Upper

ANTANANARIVO

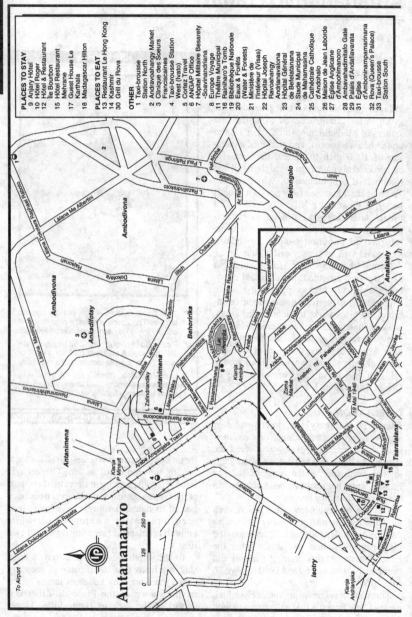

PLACES TO STAY
9 Anjary Hôtel
10 Hôtel Roger
12 Hôtel & Restaurant Ile Bourbon
15 Hôtel Restaurant Mehrane
17 Guest House Le Karthala
18 Madagascar Hilton

PLACES TO EAT
13 Restaurant Le Hong Kong
14 Kashmir
30 Grill du Rova

OTHER
1 Taxi-brousse Station North
2 Androvothangy Market
3 Clinique des Soeurs Franciscaines
4 Taxi-brousse Station West (Ivato)
5 Cortez Travel
6 ANGAP Office
7 Hôpital Militaire Besarety -Soavinandriana
8 Europe Voyage
11 Théâtre Municipal Rainiharo's Tomb
16 Bibliothèque Nationale
19 Eaux & Forêts (Water & Forests)
20 Ministère de l'Intérieur (Visas)
21 Hôpital Joseph Ravoahangy Andrianavalona
22 Hôpital Général de Befelatanana
23 Stade Municipal de Mahamasina
24 Cathédrale Catholique d'Andohalo
25 Eglise Anglicane d'Ambohimanoro
26 Maison de Jean Laborde
27 Ambavahadimitafo Gate
28 Palais d'Andafiavarata
29 Eglise d'Amboninampamarinana
31 Rova (Queen's Palace)
32 Taxi-brousse Station South

Antananarivo

To Airport

0   125   250 m

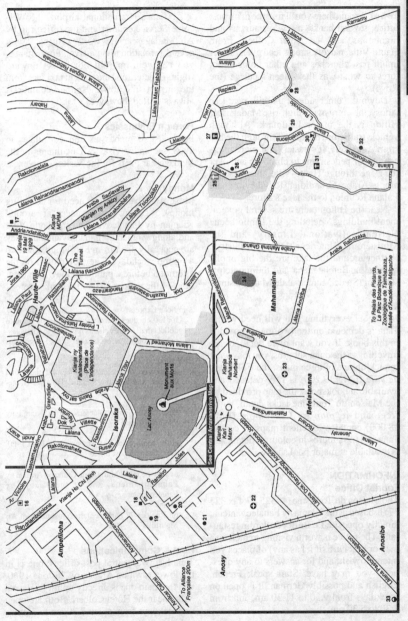

Town). Around here you'll find the main post office, several banks, a few restaurants and nightclubs, and the Hôtel Colbert. From Haute-Ville, narrow streets lead even further uphill past churches and other noble structures to what was the Queen's palace (the Rova).

Down the other side of the hill, near Lac Anosy, the obtrusively high-rise Madagascar Hilton is the major landmark. Although vehicle traffic use the tunnel through the hill from Analakely, it's easier (and more interesting) for pedestrians to climb up and over the ridge through Haute-Ville, then descend along Arabe Grandidier Rabahevitra and Làlana Réunion to the lake's shore.

Near the Hilton there are several government buildings, including the Bibliothèque Nationale (National Library) and the Ministère de l'Intérieur (Interior Ministry). Further around the lake are the big public hospital at Befelatanana and the municipal stadium (Stade Municipal de Mahamasina).

Maps

Just about everything you will need within Tana is depicted on the two maps provided in this book. If you want more detail, or are travelling to the outer suburbs, you may want to pick up one of three maps: the FTM *plan de ville* (FMg 19,200) is very detailed and available at bookshops; the map provided by the Maison du Tourisme lacks detail, but is free; and *le plan* by Carambole (FMg 18,000) contains excellent maps of central Tana and the suburbs in colourful detail, and is available at major bookshops.

INFORMATION
Tourist Office

The Maison du Tourisme (☎ 325 29; fax 325 37) is based at the Kianja ny Fahaleovantena, directly opposite Le Buffet du Jardin restaurant. The office is worth visiting to pick up a map or brochure (if it has any) of places you intend to visit, and for answers to any questions you may have. Staff speak French, English and possibly German. It is open on weekdays from 9.30 to 11.30 am, and from 1.30 to 5.30 pm.

At Tana's international airport, the Welcome Service counter and the office run by Air Madagascar are worth visiting if you need information upon arrival. For instance, you can confirm (but not book) onward flights or determine the current taxi fare from the airport into town. Neither counter is always staffed, however.

Foreign Embassies

For a list of embassies and consulates in Tana, see under Visas & Documents in the Madagascar Facts for the Visitor chapter.

Money

Most of the banks you'll need for changing money, or getting cash advances, are around Kianjan ny Fahaleovantena in Haute-Ville and along Araben ny Fahaleovantena. They are generally open from 8 to 11 am, and 2 to 4 pm on weekdays. They are closed on the afternoon before a public holiday. The locations of the major and central banks are:

American Express
  for lost cheques (but not to cash cheques) and to collect mail (Amex clients only), go to Madagascar Airtours (refer to the Travel Agencies section)
BFV Bank
  at the end of a side street behind the Hôtel Glacier; and near the Radama Hôtel in Haute-Ville
BMOI Bank
  next to the Hotel Glacier; and at Kianja ny Fahaleovantena
BNI-CL Bank
  at the southern end of Araben ny 26 Jona 1960, near the main post office
BTM Bank
  next to the Hôtel Muraille de Chine on Araben ny Fahaleovantena; and at the Kianja ny Fahaleovantena
UCB Bank
  on Rue des 77 Parlementaires, just up from Air Mauritius

Post & Communications

Tana has two central post offices: one is in the lower town on Araben ny 26 Jona 1960, and the main one is directly uphill in Haute-Ville, near the Hôtel Colbert. Both are open on weekdays from about 7.30 am to 3 pm.

The 1st floor of both post offices is open for telegrams and local, interstate and international calls from 7 am to 7 pm, Monday to Saturday, and from 8 to 11 am on Sundays and public holidays. The poste restante is at the main post office in Haute-Ville. Both sell a few souvenirs and postcards, and have an excellent array of colourful stamps for sale (as souvenirs, but rarely for placing on letters or postcards).

Travel Agencies

The capital city is full of travel agencies, but many are little more than a tiny office containing one person, a desk and a telephone. They can organise trips (if you find the people) for a commission or book and confirm flights, but you can (and should) also do this yourself.

The following agencies in Tana are reliable, and run a variety of interesting trips around the country. All staff speak French, most speak English, and sometimes some Italian and German is spoken.

Boogie Pilgrim – 40 Araben ny Fahaleovantena (☎ 258 78; fax 251 17; email bopi@bow.dts.mg). This impressive outfit runs adventurous (and slightly up-market) tours, including along the Pangalanes canal.

Cortez Travel – 25 Rue ny Zafindriandiky, Antanimena (☎ 219 74; fax 213 40; email cortezmd@bow.dts.mg). This US-based agency offers a great range of itineraries for individuals and groups year-round, and is recommended for its efficiency and reliability.

Espace 4X4 – 50 Ave Grandidier, Isoraka; BP 5154 (☎ 262 97; fax 272 96)

Julia Voyage – 7 Rue Patrice Lumumba; BP 3179 (☎ 268 74; fax 348 53)

La Caravane Malagasy – 21 Rue Rabozaka, Ankadilalana; BP 5192 (☎ /fax 355 54). It has a fascinating range of tours around Tana, southern Madagascar, Nosy Be and the Tsiribihina River by, of all things, a hydroglider.

Madagascar Airtours – 33 Araben ny Fahaleovantena (next to Air Mad) (☎ 241 92) and in the Madagascar Hilton hotel (☎ 241 92). It serves as the American Express representative, and has offices in Toliara, Fianarantsoa, Antsiranana and Nosy Be. Mad Airtours offers an impressive range of tours to most corners of the island.

Madagascar Evasion – 8 Rue Rajihanson Emile (☎ 328 47; fax 252 70)

Mad Cameleon – Lot 11 K, Rue Rasamoely, Ankadivato Ambony; BP 4336 (☎ /fax 344 20). It runs a range of tours and specialises in trekking in western Madagascar.

SETAM – 56 Araben ny 26 Jona 1960 (☎ 272 49; fax 347 02). SETAM has an imaginative range of tours focussing on birds, reptiles, culture and trekking.

Tropika Touring – 41 Lalana Ratsimilaho, Ambatonakanga (just up from the Hôtel Colbert) (☎ 222 30; fax 349 01; email tropika@bow .dts.mg). It specialises in trips around the Tsiribihina River and arranges other customised trips.

Voyages Bourdon – 15 Rue Patrice Lumumba; BP 8196 (☎ 296 96; fax 285 64). Besides offering a variety of standard tours, Voyages Bourdon is recommended for its excellent guides and packaged tours.

Bookshops

Tana boasts several decent bookshops. All sell French-language tourist publications, political works, histories, guidebooks, journals, magazines and newspapers; Malagasy dictionaries in French, English, Italian or German; and postcards and maps.

The best stocked is the Librairie de Madagascar, halfway along Araben ny Fahaleovantena. Others include the Tout pour l'École, directly opposite the Hôtel Mellis; the Espace Loisirs, opposite the Acapulco Nightclub, which often stocks novels in English; and the Champion Supermarket, which is often surprisingly cheaper than the Librairie de Madagascar. Avoid the expensive bookshop at the airport.

Libraries

The Bibliothèque Nationale, or National Library, is probably not worth visiting. The indexing is haphazard and the staff are unhelpful. The various cultural centres (see next section) are far better sources of books. The National Library is next to the Madagascar Hilton, in the Anosy district, and is open from Monday to Friday, 8 am to noon and 2 to 5 pm.

Cultural Centres

The American Cultural Center (☎ 202 38), near the tunnel entrance, has a large library and magazine section. Foreigners are welcome to come in and read whatever is on the shelves, but you must be a member to borrow anything. The library is open from 12.30 to 5 pm on weekdays. The Center also runs some films, lectures and concerts – call in for a monthly program. This is a good place to meet English-speaking locals and maybe hire a guide.

The German equivalent is the Cercle Germano-Malagasy (☎ 214 42), at the bottom of the steps leading up to Haute-Ville from Araben ny 26 Jona 1960. Besides maintaining a reading library with German magazines and newspapers, it stages theatre, film and music performances.

The French Alliance Française de Tananarive (☎ 211 07) on Rue Seimad, west of Lac Anosy, offers more or less the same programs as the Germans and Americans, but they are better organised, more frequent and presented in French and therefore attract more local people.

Check the local daily newspapers for listings of current and future activities organised by these cultural centres. Refer to the Entertainment section for details about the Centre Culturel Albert Camus (CCAC).

Film

Tana now has several good places to stock up on film, get your prints (not slides) developed and even to buy spare parts and batteries (though you should always bring your own). The best places to go are Opticam, opposite the Acapulco Nightclub; Express Photo, on the steps which lead up to Kianja ny Fahaleovantena from Analakely; Champion Supermarket in Haute-Ville; Lab Art Studio, next to La Hutte Canadienne in Haute-Ville; and the Fuji place, two doors up from the Hôtel Mellis. Prices at any place near the Hôtel Colbert are oriented towards tourists, not locals.

Medical Services

Try not to get sick in Madagascar. If you do, make sure it's in Tana where at least there are a few hospitals. The Hôpital Militaire Besarety-Soavinandriana, also known as the Hôpital Militaire d'Antananarivo (☎ 403 41), receives French government support; it has X-ray equipment and basic stocks of drugs and medicines. It employs several French doctors (doing their national service). The Clinique des Soeurs Franciscaines (☎ 235 54), also known as Clinique et Maternité St-Francais, has X-ray equipment and is reasonably clean and well run. Both of these places require payment in advance of treatment.

The Hôpital Général de Befelatanana (☎ 223 84) and the Hôpital Joseph Ravoahangy Andrianavalona (☎ 279 79) are free public hospitals with much lower standards of care and hygiene.

Local daily French/Malagasy-language newspapers list some available doctors and their contact details, as well as the location and telephone numbers of current pharmacies, dentists and hospitals.

Emergency

We hope you won't need to contact the following emergency numbers:

- ambulance (☎ 357 53)
- fire brigade (☎ 18)
- police emergency (☎ 17)

The Ministry of Foreign Affairs (☎ 211 98) is near the Madagascar Hilton Hotel and the main police station (☎ 229 72) is on Làlana Karija. Up-to-date emergency numbers are helpfully included in each of the three daily French/Malagasy newspapers and in most tourist guides available in Tana.

Dangers & Annoyances

The possibility of robbery after dark in Tana cannot be overstated. Unfortunately, there are few street lights and tragically plenty of desperately hungry and homeless people. Foreigners with bulging pockets and loosely held cameras and bags may be the targets of snatch-and-run robberies and pickpockets in the crowded streets, buses and markets. Even walking around remote suburban areas can be a bit dicey, but as long as you are careful and there are other people around you will be OK.

Be very careful walking outside your hotel after dark and before dawn, especially around Analakely, along Araben ny Fahaleovantena or near the railway station – and never use stairways at night because you will have nowhere to run if trapped. To avoid problems at night – for instance, when going to a restaurant – walk in a largish group; take a taxi; hire a guard to accompany you from your hotel; or run (this may sound silly, but it eliminates the element of surprise). Alternatively, eat a main meal at lunch and snack in your room in the evening (dial-a-pizza service is not yet available in Tana).

Another danger of walking along unlit streets at night is the possibility of falling in giant potholes – which often lead to sewers.

THINGS TO SEE & DO
Zoma Market

One of the major attractions of Tana is the massive daily Zoma market or Friday market. The thousands of stalls in the market extend off Araben ny Fahaleovantena, continue along Araben ny 26 Jona 1960 and up the stone steps on either side. The market turns into a frenzy on Friday, when all traffic is diverted; it calms down on Saturday (which is the best time to wander around); almost closes down on Sunday; and then starts to crank up again on Monday, leading to the weekly crescendo on Friday.

The Malagasy claim that the Zoma is the second largest open-air market in the world. (They never tell you which is the largest, but we'd cast a vote for Bangkok's Weekend Market). It is certainly an impressive sight, particularly when viewed from the balconies of the hotels along Araben ny Fahaleovantena.

The Zoma traders – all under octagonal white umbrellas (at eye-level, so watch out!) – are grouped according to the goods they sell. Finding what you want can be a little confusing. Generally, the best place to buy Malagasy crafts is near the Air Madagascar office and behind the burnt-out shell of the town hall (the old town hall, or Hôtel de Ville, was destroyed in riots on 13 May 1972). Beautiful flowers and pots are sold just north of Air Mad; clothing can be found all over, but vendors seem to concentrate around the Palace Hôtel; books are found at the foot of the Analakely steps; and tools, mechanical parts, automobile components and items fashioned from recycled aluminium are sold around the Hôtel Glacier.

Some locals have realised there are easier and more literal ways of grabbing a quick quid, so mind the frequent warnings about looking after your things when walking in the Zoma. Thieves are noted more for grabbing and snatching than pickpocketing, so shopping or strolling will be more enjoyable without handbags, watches, shoulder bags, wallets, cameras, etc. Carry just enough change for the day's intended purchases. If you run across something irresistible that's more expensive, it will be worth a special trip back to your hotel for additional cash.

Andravoahangy Market

Located in the north-eastern part of town, this market is where stonemasons, embroiderers, booksellers, carpenters, wood carvers and other professional craftspeople produce and sell their wares. Here you will see them at work, but the selection of finished products is better at the Zoma. The Andravoahangy market is open every day but Sunday. Be careful here too: this market is often more packed, and risky, than the Zoma. A taxi out to Andravoahangy shouldn't cost more than FMg 5000.

Churches

En route to the burnt out shell of the Rova (see the entry later in this chapter), you pass the Catholic **Cathédrale Catholique d'Andohalo** and the Anglican **Église Anglicane d'Ambohimanoro**. Their Sunday morning services and hymn-singing can be engaging, and you'll always be welcome (though stared at constantly). The churches themselves may not be so fascinating, but they are in the nicest part of the city and the views across Tana, Lac Anosy and the stadium are truly wonderful, especially at sunset.

ANTANANARIVO

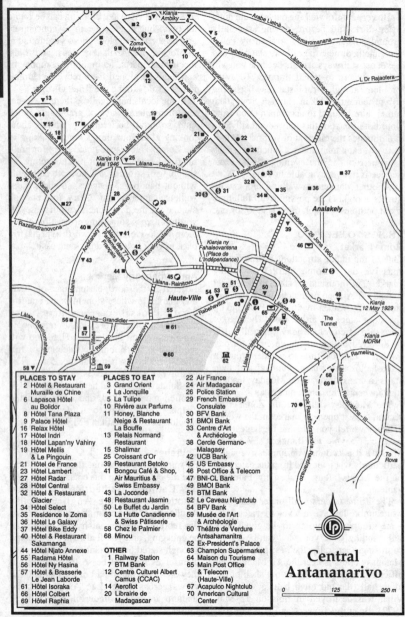

PLACES TO STAY

2 Hôtel & Restaurant
   Muraille de Chine
6 Lapasoa Hôtel
   au Bolidor
8 Hôtel Tana Plaza
9 Palace Hôtel
16 Relax Hôtel
17 Hôtel Indri
18 Hôtel Lapan'ny Vahiny
19 Hôtel Mellis
   & Le Pingouin
21 Hôtel de France
23 Hôtel Lambert
27 Hôtel Radar
28 Hôtel Central
32 Hôtel & Restaurant
   Glacier
34 Hôtel Select
35 Residence le Zoma
36 Hôtel Le Galaxy
37 Hôtel Bike Eddy
40 Hôtel & Restaurant
   Sakamanga
44 Hôtel Njato Annexe
55 Radama Hôtel
56 Hôtel Ny Hasina
57 Hôtel & Brasserie
   Le Jean Laborde
61 Hôtel Isoraka
66 Hôtel Colbert
69 Hôtel Raphia

PLACES TO EAT

3 Grand Orient
4 La Jonquille
5 La Tulipe
10 Rivière aux Parfums
11 Honey, Blanche
   Neige & Restaurant
   La Bouffe
13 Relais Normand
   Restaurant
15 Shalimar
25 Croissant d'Or
39 Restaurant Betoko
41 Bongou Café & Shop,
   Air Mauritius &
   Swiss Embassy
43 La Joconde
48 Restaurant Jasmin
50 Le Buffet du Jardin
53 La Hutte Canadienne
   & Swiss Pâtisserie
58 Chez le Palmier
68 Minou

OTHER

1 Railway Station
7 BTM Bank
12 Centre Culturel Albert
   Camus (CCAC)
14 Aeroflot
20 Librairie de
   Madagascar

22 Air France
24 Air Madagascar
26 Police Station
29 French Embassy/
   Consulate
30 BFV Bank
31 BMOI Bank
33 Centre d'Art
   & Archéologie
38 Cercle Germano-
   Malagasy
42 UCB Bank
45 US Embassy
46 Post Office & Telecom
47 BNI-CL Bank
49 BMOI Bank
51 BTM Bank
52 Le Caveau Nightclub
54 BFV Bank
59 Musée de l'Art
   & Archéologie
60 Théâtre de Verdure
   Antsahamanitra
62 Ex-President's Palace
63 Champion Supermarket
64 Maison du Tourisme
65 Main Post Office
   & Telecom
   (Haute-Ville)
67 Acapulco Nightclub
70 American Cultural
   Center

**Central
Antananarivo**

0   125   250 m

Also near the Rova, on top of the cliff, is the **Église d'Amboninampamarinana** (The Place of Hurling), constructed by missionaries on the site where Christians were martyred by Queen Ranavalona I. It's accessible from Arabe Rabozaka, the street which connects the municipal stadium to the Tsimbazaza zoo complex.

Parc Botanique et Zoologique de Tsimbazaza

The botanic park and zoo at Tsimbazaza (which means 'They are not Children') is definitely worth a visit unless you have already spent a lot of time in the forests among lemurs (it's probably best to visit the zoo before you head out to the national parks). You could easily wander around for a few hours; maybe take a picnic and have lunch in the park; or combine it with a meal at one of the restaurants near the entrance gate.

In the past, the park suffered from inexperienced management and a lack of funding, and during the 1991 strike everything went to pieces. Once the problem was settled, things improved: new cages have been built; captive breeding programs are being expanded; and the local community is taking an increasing interest thanks to school conservation education programs.

The park has several species of caged and uncaged lemurs (including aye-aye and other rare species), as well as egrets, herons (mostly caged), crocodiles, and Aldabran and Malagasy tortoises. As well, there's an array of palms and other endemic plants; some reconstructed **tombs**; and a **vivarium** with live chameleons, snakes, lizards, small lemurs and tortoises.

Also on the zoo grounds is the **Musée d'Académie Malgache** (if Madagascar is a living museum, is this place sort of redundant?) which contains some amazing natural and cultural exhibits, including the vertebrae of a dinosaur discovered near Mahajanga in 1907. There was also once a pickled coelacanth taken from the marine research station in Nosy Be, but it was so poorly preserved and maintained it eventually rotted away.

The museum also features the skeletal remains and a preserved egg of the extinct 'elephant bird' (*Aepyornis maximus*), giant lemurs, a short-tailed white hippo and a dugong. Other Malagasy animals which have been stuffed (up) for posterity include aye-aye, indri and some tenrecs (small hedgehog-like mammals). In another room there are exhibits of Malagasy funerary art and tribal village life.

If you thrive on crowds and lots of activity, go on a Sunday when half of Tana seems to descend on the place; on other days it is fairly serene. The park and zoo are open every day from 9 am to 5 pm, and cost a hefty FMg 20,000 for tourists. If you want to see the aye-ayes at night, you will need to pre-arrange a special evening visit for another FMg 25,000 per person. A few T-shirts and posters are for sale at the main office.

Keep your ticket because someone will want to see it when you leave. When you enter the park, you will be mobbed by potential guides; they are not compulsory, nor really necessary. Even if you make it clear that you do not want a guide they will follow you, point out the obvious and expect a payment. Be firm, because they are a real nuisance.

To get to the park/zoo from the centre of town, take an ANTAFITA bus No 15 (FMg 500), or, better, a taxi for about FMg 5000 one-way. If coming by bus don't get off at the green PBZT sign, but continue for two km further south. The park entrance is opposite the Restaurant Indonesia (which serves decent gado-gado and other dishes for FMg 7500 to FMg 15,000).

Museums

The museums in Tana are nothing to get excited about. The **Musée de l'Art et Archéologie** (also known as the Musée d'Art Isoraka) has some bones and egg pieces from the extinct Aepyornis, old photographs of the Rova (before the fire) and Araben ny Fahaleovantena (when it was all trees), some funerary art carvings, porcelain pots and an Indian doorway from Nosy Be –

but that's about it. The museum, which was being renovated at the time of research (so may improve), is a steep walk up from Anakely and only open on weekday afternoons. Refer to local daily newspapers for information about current exhibits. Entrance is free.

Slightly better is the **Centre d'Art & Archéologie**, on the top floor of the mustard-coloured building right in the middle of the Zoma market. It contains more exhibits on archaeology than art, but is worth a visit if you have an interest. The best part about this museum is the views of the market from the window. Entrance is free.

The **Maison de Jean Laborde**, where the famous Frenchman Jean Laborde (1803–78) once lived, has now been taken over by the French embassy for administrative purposes. There is nothing much left to see except a couple of cannons and live tortoises, but the street is pretty and offers some outstanding views across Tana.

Rova

The Rova (commonly known as the Palais de la Reine or Queen's Palace), the imposing structure which caps the highest hill overlooking Lac Anosy, was the major tourist attraction in Tana. Because of structural problems the palace was long closed to the public and only opened as recently as 1992.

Tragically, the Rova was almost completely destroyed by fire in November 1995. It occurred on the evening of the local elections and was almost certainly politically motivated arson. Another fire was deliberately started in a church on the other side of town, attracting all available fire engines, so most of the Rova burned down. Local authorities could not tell us if or when the Rova will be rebuilt; it depends entirely on the availability of funds, but in case it reopens a brief description and history is included in the aside that follows.

You cannot enter the Rova complex while it is being rebuilt, but it's still worth visiting

---

Every Inch a Rova

Just left of the entrance to the Rova were two wooden *tranomanara* (cold houses) which sheltered the Tombs of the Kings and Queens. Here the kings Andrianjaka, Radama I and Andrianampoinimerina, and queens Rasoherina, Ranavalona I, Ranavalona II and Ranavalona III were buried. The main palace, Manjakamiadana (translation: A Fine Place to Rule), was built in 1867 for Queen Ranavalona II. The outer stonework was courtesy of the Scottish missionary and architect, James Cameron, and is very solid. The outer shell covered the earlier and more appropriate wooden palace, which was built by Frenchman Jean Laborde in 1839 for Queen Ranavalona I. The linchpin of this structure was a 39m rosewood trunk which was blamed for past structural problems. It apparently took 10,000 slaves to drag this log 300km from the eastern forests, and 1000 of them succumbed to the extreme conditions along the way. It took 12 days to set the log in place.

The much simpler palace and tomb nearby belonged to King Andrianampoinimerina (the name is short for Andrianampoinimerinandriantsimitoviaminandriampanjaka), who united the Merina – and all Madagascar – at the end of the 18th century, and opened up the country to European influences. His own Rova is on a hill at Ambohimanga, 21km north of the capital (one palace is visible from the other). Andrianampoinimerina's tall and narrow cottage, Mahitsielafanjaka ('The Reign of a Righteous Spirit Endures'), contained his bed, set high above the room which he shared with the favoured one of his 12 wives. Resting in the rafters was a pirogue in which the king would hide when visitors arrived. If the guest was welcome, the king would signal to his wife by dropping pebbles on her head.

Beside this building was the Tranovola (Silver Palace), a wooden structure built in 1839 by French castaway Jean Laborde for the infamous Ranavalona I. Close by was another large palace, known as Manampisoa ('That Which Inspires Happiness'). It was constructed by British missionary William Poole for Queen Rasoherina in 1866. This contained copies of letters from the governors of Mauritius and Réunion and from various Malagasy queens. There were also gifts from the British kings and queens as well as Napoleon III, including a bible, cups, goblets and a sabre. How much of the structure and items in the Rova survived the fire is unknown, but hopefully in a few years some of it can be seen by the public again. ■

Top: Madagascar's capital, Antananarivo, is usually known simply as Tana. The city straddles several hills which afford spectacular views at sunset.

Bottom: Tana's Zoma ('Friday') market covers the main thoroughfare under a sea of white umbrellas. It operates every day, but reaches a crescendo on Friday.

PAUL SCOTT

DAVID CURL

PAUL GREENWAY

Top: The landscape between Ihosy and Fianarantsoa, central Madagascar.
Middle: Caravans carrying charcoal for sale parked outside the capital Tana.
Bottom: Pousse-pousses (rickshaws) ready to pounce on foreigners arriving by train at Antsirabe, central Madagascar.

for the views, to imagine what it may have been like, and maybe to have lunch at the fantastic Grill du Rova restaurant nearby (see Places to Eat).

To get to the Rova from the centre of Tana, catch an ANTAFITA No 21 bus, take a taxi (about FMg 6000 return) or walk. It's best to take a taxi up, and take a pleasant stroll down through the narrow twisting streets past other interesting buildings. You can also climb directly up the crag, perhaps after visiting the zoo, via paths and steps which pass between a labyrinth of Malagasy homes.

At the foot of Làlana Raonivalo, just below the Rova, the large **Ambava-hadimitafo Gate**, which once served as an entrance to the Rova, survived. A huge boulder used to be rolled in front of it as a door; the boulder now stands permanently to one side. Just above is the old residence of the Malagasy prime ministers, which is not open to the public.

Other Attractions

Tana is a city for wandering. Some of the most interesting places and situations will be chanced upon during leisurely strolls through the narrow streets and stairways which climb haphazardly over the hills.

Perhaps the most impressive building in Haute-Ville is the former **Ex-President's Palace**, which was occupied by President Didier Ratsiraka until 1990 when he moved into his brand new, North Korean-built replica of the Rova (which is along the road to Antsirabe, 13km south of Tana). The old palace was slated to become a museum to house portions of Dr John Mack's *Island of the Ancestors* relics from the Museum of Mankind (part of the British Museum), but, despite what some brochures may say, the Palace is not a museum.

Lac Anosy lies near the Madagascar Hilton in the southern part of town; it is surrounded by jacaranda trees with purple blooms. The lake is lovely in parts, scrappy in others, but is worth a walk around. On an island in the middle of the lake, connected to the shore by a causeway, stands the **Monument aux Morts** (Monument to the Dead),

an imposing WWI memorial erected by the French. Tana's other 'lake', **Lac Behoririka**, is an obnoxious collection of reeds among untreated sewage.

In a fairly grubby part of town stands **Rainiharo's tomb**. The building and tomb, dedicated to a former prime minister, are nothing to get excited about, but they're set in a pleasant garden, one of the few bits of green in the city. Entrance is free.

PLACES TO STAY

There is a wide choice of accommodation in the centre of Tana, but there is very little value for money; prices are considerably lower in the countryside.

Finding a hotel with a restaurant, or near one, is worthwhile (for security reasons) to avoid having to leave your hotel at night for an evening meal. It's a good idea to make a telephone booking (even from the airport when you arrive) for the better hotels and the middle-range places. The latter are popular with travellers, especially in the peak season (June to August). Few places of lower standard have a telephone. If you're travelling a lot around the countryside and using Tana as a base it's worth pre-booking a room in a hotel in Tana before you leave.

With a few notable exceptions, the hotels listed in the bottom-end range are dirty, noisy and usually double as brothels. If you are on a tight budget and normally stay in places listed in the bottom end, you may have to bite the bullet, pay extra for comfort (and, importantly, safety) and stay at a hotel in the middle range – then head for the countryside where prices are lower.

Prices for middle to top-end hotels are sometimes listed in French francs because that is their preferred currency, but you can always pay the equivalent in US dollars or Malagasy francs.

Places to Stay – bottom end

None of the places at the bottom end have private bathrooms (unless stated; if they do, they certainly won't have hot water unless you pay for a more expensive room).

The *Hôtel Njato Annexe* – not to be confused with the permanently full hostel Njato Hôtel, just down the street – is good value and in a nice part of town. Rooms are a bargain FMg 8000, so not surprisingly, it is often full of Malagasy guests.

On Làlana Radama I is the *Hôtel Lapan'ny Vahiny*, a Malagasy hotel with eight 'character-filled' rooms costing FMg 10,000 – it is above a bar where you can get simple meals. It may look really awful from the outside, but it's not that bad and is pretty good value in this range.

The *Hôtel Roger* (☎ 309 69), opposite a railway line, is a good choice in the upper range of the bottom-end hotels. Surprisingly large and clean rooms cost FMg 30,000, but this area of Tana is pretty noisy. The basic, but friendly, *Relax Hôtel* has reasonable rooms for FMg 20,000. It is in a central location, on a side street off Rue Rainibetsimisaraka.

The inconspicuous *Hôtel Restaurant Mehrane* (☎ 275 06), on Làlana Razafindranovona, is very clean and secure but a bit lifeless. Rooms cost FMg 36,000/40,000 for a single/double; if you want one, inquire at the restaurant next door. Recommended for its central location (just up from the petrol station) and quaint bar, the *Hôtel Bike Eddy* (☎ 211 65) is probably worth trying for FMg 35,000 per room. The surly staff refused to show us a room, but the place looked clean enough.

The most frequently recommended bottom-end hotel is the friendly *Hôtel Lambert* (☎ 229 92). Despite its dodgy location near the top of the steep steps from Analakely, the rooms (which are sometimes a bit dingy) are secure, and have hot showers (wow!). It's good value at FMg 35,000/45,000, and FMg 55,000 for a triple. There's a good restaurant attached, the hotel balcony has wonderful views of the city and it's a good place to meet other travellers.

The family-run *Lapasoa Hôtel au Bolidor* is conveniently located near the railway station – look for the sign along Arabe Andrianampoinimerina. The rooms, off a nice verandah, are basic but quiet and at FMg 35,000/40,000 they are good value for the location.

The only budget hotel in Haute-Ville is the *Hôtel Isoraka* (☎ 355 81) – formerly known as the Hôtel Valiha. It's certainly improved over the past few years, and now comes recommended by many readers. Rooms with hot showers cost FMg 35,000/45,000; snacks (including breakfast in bed for FMg 7500!) and drinks are also available. It is popular and often full, so ring ahead.

If you are desperate and everything else is full try the *Hôtel Le Galaxy*, where staff seemed surprised when we asked about the price for the night (FMg 14,000) – they normally rent rooms by the hour (or for however long it takes); or the *Hôtel Ny Hasina* for FMg 10,000/15,000, which is friendly, but noisy and opposite a makeshift garbage dump.

Places to Stay – middle
There are several very nice mid-range hotels in Tana, but few are good value. All have private bathrooms (unless stated) and for these prices they should include hot water.

Located on both sides of Rue Dokotera Ranaivo, the friendly *Anjary Hôtel* (☎ 244 09; fax 234 18) has small but clean rooms for FMg 62,000 – ask for rooms with views on the top floors.

The *Guest House Le Karthala* (☎ 248 95; fax 203 97) is not in a very safe area and up some stairs, but the management is charming and the views are superb. It is readily visible from below; just look for the reddish roof with 'Le Karthala' written across it. Unfortunately, its popularity has resulted in an unjustified increase in prices: doubles start from FMg 75,000 and go up to FMg 90,000 for a room with a view. There is also a pricey restaurant.

Close to Araben ny Fahaleovantena, the *Hôtel Mellis* (☎ 234 25; fax 626 60) is very popular with travellers. Rooms are quaint, if a little old, but unfortunately there's no restaurant so you'll have to run the gauntlet at night. If you can't get a cheap single/double for FMg 45,000/55,000 without a bathroom and are forced to pay FMg 75,000 or more for a room, you will be better off trying another place. Its advantages are the friendly, English-speaking staff, good laundry service and lounge with cable TV.

Not far away, the popular *Hôtel Central* (☎ 227 94; fax 357 04) was closed for refurbishment at the time of research, which undoubtedly means that prices are likely to increase. But it will be worth checking out. The *Residence le Zoma* (☎ 231 13; fax 348 35) is not great value for single rooms, but is recommended for triples at FMg 80,000 per room. It is high above the Zoma market and has great views.

If everything is full around Araben ny Fahaleovantena, there are a few other places to try. The dingy *Hôtel Glacier* (☎ 291 04) has grubby, noisy rooms for FMg 50,000 with share toilet, and FMg 70,000 for a larger room with facilities; don't stay in the cheaper rooms (FMg 37,000) in the annexe, which is quite unsafe. The *Hôtel Select* (☎ 210 01) is friendlier than the Glacier and costs FMg 62,000 per room. The lift may not work, and the furniture should have been traded in many decades ago, but it is OK. The *Hôtel Radar* (☎ 205 55) costs FMg 55,000 for a room – and is not bad value. Directly across from the railway station, the Chinese-run *Hôtel Muraille de Chine* (☎ 230 13) has a reasonable range of rooms from FMg 40,000 to FMg 75,000 and is fairly good value for the location.

Thoroughly recommended is the new, homely and quiet *Hôtel Raphia* (☎ 253 13). It is in a great location (just off Làlana Ranavalona III) and the staff are friendly. Small rooms cost FMg 55,000, and larger ones FMg 60,000. The communal bathrooms are large and spotless, but the toilets are strangely tiny.

Also recommended – and incredibly popular – is the new *Hôtel Sakamanga* (☎ 358 09; fax 245 87). It is the only place in town which caters for budget, independent foreign travellers: there is a noticeboard, tour agency and a good restaurant, and it's a great place to meet other travellers. Pleasant rooms cost from FMg 55,000 with shared

facilities to FMg 78,000. Bookings at any time of the year are strongly advised.

For a little bit extra, the bright-orange *Hôtel Indri* (☎ 209 22; fax 624 40) is worth considering. The location is good, and the staff (who speak English, French, German and Italian) are friendly. Excellent rooms with TV cost F150, or F250 for something larger and more luxurious. Breakfast is FMg 12,000.

Another very good option is the *Hôtel Le Jean Laborde* (☎ 330 45; fax 327 94) where very agreeable rooms with a huge bathroom cost from FMg 85,000 to FMg 100,000. It is in a grimy part of town, but the rooms, service and restaurant are excellent. Also, the *Hôtel Île Bourbon* (☎ 279 42) is a marvellous, quiet place with friendly staff. Spotless, charming rooms with a large bathroom cost FMg 75,000/80,000. It is a little hard to find on 12 Rue Benyowski. An excellent restaurant is attached.

At the uppermost end of the middle range is the quiet and relaxed *Relais des Pistards* (☎ 291 34), a favourite with French quatre-quatre (4WD) and VTT (mountain bike) fiends. Small rooms in quaint surroundings (watch out for wandering tortoises) are good value at FMg 90,000/130,000 with two meals; FMg 55,000/65,000 without meals. It is in Tsimbazaza, about 300m south of the zoo entrance. A taxi from Analakely should cost FMg 5000.

Places to Stay – top end

The *Hôtel Colbert* (☎ 202 02; fax 340 12) is in the heart of Haute-Ville. It's a throwback to French imperialism at its best – or worst, depending on your perspective (non-French expats complain of surly staff). It is smaller, plusher, cheaper and more intimate than its main competitor, the Hilton. Rooms start at F550 and go much higher, but each has a small safe which is an excellent idea for security. The hotel also boasts a small casino, two bars, a pâtisserie and two restaurants.

English-speaking visitors often prefer the *Madagascar Hilton* (☎ 260 60; fax 260 51), the tallest building in Madagascar. It offers a nightclub, casino, swimming pool, business centre and an arcade with foreign exchange facilities, and expensive souvenir and clothing shops. The biggest drawback is its location, about a 20 minute walk from the centre of town, and the prices are very upmarket: F840/960 for a single/double room.

A new option is the *Radama Hôtel* (☎ 319 27; fax 353 23), in a great location in Haute-Ville. It's clean and the management is friendly, but the prices are now quite high: F320 for a room, F420 for a studio apartment and on the terrace, F520.

The *Hôtel de France* (☎ 213 04; fax 201 08), which has recently been refurbished, is where many package tourists stay. Very nice rooms (ask for one away from the busy street, though) cost F250. Under the same management, the *Palace Hôtel* (☎ 256 63; fax 339 43), near the railway station, has small/large rooms for F450/470, which is really too much – but this is Tana.

On a corner directly opposite the railway station is the recently refurbished *Hôtel Tana Plaza* (☎ 243 09; fax 218 65) (it was once the budget Hôtel Terminus). Small but luxurious rooms with cable TV cost F280; breakfast is F35 and set meals F70.

PLACES TO EAT

Tana isn't known as a gourmet's paradise, despite more than half a century of French rule, but there are several good options within a wide range of cuisines and cost. Many restaurants offer special *menus du jour* and *plats du jour*, which usually work out cheaper than ordering a la carte dishes. Be especially careful when going out at night in Tana (see the Dangers & Annoyances section).

Street Stalls

The suburban streets of Tana, and particularly the Zoma market, are lined with street stalls selling everything from yoghurt and ice cream to meat sambos (samosas) and other unidentifiable objects fried in batter. You can pick up a potato and celery broth for around FMg 750 a bowl, or soupe chinoise (vegetable, noodle and coriander soup) for FMg 1000 – but these will hardly fill you up

or satisfy the taste buds. If you're willing to take greater risks you can opt for meat and rice.

Hotelys

You'll find loads of *hotelys* of varying quality around the *taxi-brousse* stations and elsewhere outside the centre of town. Those which lack table cloths are the cheapest; here, you'll get a Malagasy meal of rice with a few tidbits of meat and boiled vegetables. Meals start at about FMg 1800. In more refined places, a similar meal will cost from FMg 3000 to FMg 4000.

Breakfast & Snacks

Along Araben ny Fahaleovantena and Araben ny 26 Jona 1960 are several *salons de thé* (tea houses) which are great for breakfast and snacks. You'll get coffee or tea for about FMg 1500 (sometimes as little as FMg 500), as well as a variety of sausage rolls, cakes, pastries, doughnuts and other confections. Unfortunately, they are often closed during the lunch hour (about 1 to 2 pm) and are rarely open in the evening.

Three of the best are in a row on the east side of the street near the burnt out Hôtel de Ville. The best is *Blanche Neige* (Snow White), complete with a mural of the famous lady. On comfy chairs inside, or on quasi-alfresco seats along the pavement, you can pig out on awesome ice cream dishes (FMg 11,000), excellent cooked breakfasts (FMg 9500) and other snacks.

Next door, the *Restaurant La Bouffe* offers less appetising but cheaper meals, such as chicken and chips (French fries) for as little as FMg 6500. However, they may not be enough to satisfy your hunger pangs. The third place, *Honey*, is recommended for ice cream, and light snacks are also available. Next to the Hôtel Mellis, *Le Pingouin* is a pleasant place for a cheap drink and pastry while you watch the manager ferociously attack flies with her flyswatter.

One of the most popular places with locals is the *Restaurant Betoko*, at the bottom of the steps from Araben ny Fahaleovantena to Haute-Ville. OK, the service is deplorable and there are more flies in the dining room than anywhere else in Madagascar (except, probably, the kitchen), but if you can get a tasty steak and salad for about FMg 5000, and a three course menu du jour for FMg 8000 in the middle of Tana you are doing very well.

Just up from the Hôtel Mellis, the *Croissant d'Or* is one of the best cafes in town. It can do a great cooked breakfast for FMg 6500 and other simple meals for about FMg 8000. Unfortunately, it is also closed in the evenings. Recommended is the *Minou*, with great views and meals for about FMg 8000. The servings are often small so you may want to start with a salad or soup.

For pastries and fresh fruit shakes, among other tasty things, try a couple of places near the Champion Supermarket: the *Swiss Pâtisserie* is very nice for a drink and snack, and next door *La Hutte Canadienne* has a great range of tempting treats.

Lunch & Dinner
Chinese Many of Tana's middle-range restaurants serve Chinese cuisine with a dash of French and Malagasy influence, such as frogs' legs and zebu. The most renowned is the *Grand Orient*, in a dodgy location just around the corner from the railway station. The rollicking atmosphere is pleasant, service is top class and the wine reasonably priced. At night, a honky tonk pianist sometimes plays traditional European, American and Malagasy tunes so it's not just another Chinese meal. One traveller remarked that the place reminded him of 'Rick's Bar' from the movie 'Casablanca'. Prices for meals range from FMg 8000 to FMg 12,000.

One of our favourites is the *Restaurant Le Hong Kong*. It has a nice decor inside and seats outside, and a large range of meals from FMg 5000 for a large Chinese soup to FMg 10,000 for main dishes. Another place is the *Rivière aux Parfums*, a highly recommended – as well as inexpensive – choice for French and Chinese cuisine. Some travellers have complained about the small portions though. You'll find it just behind the old Hôtel de Ville market area.

A nice place with a casual but sophisticated atmosphere and tasteful decor is *Restaurant Jasmin*, near the tunnel. It serves Chinese specialities from FMg 14,000 to FMg 18,000, but the value and service have been recently emulated by several other places so it's no longer a 'must'.

Other recommended places to try are the inexpensive cubbyhole restaurant *La Tulipe*, and the friendly *La Jonquille*. Avoid *La Muraille de Chine*, in the hotel of the same name, which is very poor value. The cheapest meal is fried noodles for FMg 10,000 and a large beer costs a ludicrous FMg 8000.

Indian-Pakistani There are several nominally Indian and Pakistani restaurants (which don't serve alcohol). Opposite the Anjary Hôtel, the *Kashmir* serves Indian specialities for a pricey FMg 15,000, but is good for drinks and pastries. The best place for a curry is definitely the *Shalimar*, in an unsigned green building (it is unsafe to wander there at night). Curries cost about FMg 9000, and the FMg 13,000 menu du jour, including bread, main course, rice, a lentil dish and fruit, is excellent value.

Other Cuisines One of our favourites for good value meals is the friendly Malagasy-run *Chez Le Palmier*, worth a short walk from Haute-Ville past Lac Anosy. The menu is limited, but you can get a 'steack frites' for a bargain FMg 7000 in a pleasant covered outdoor setting. Just up from the Hôtel Sakamanga is the highly recommended *La Joconde*. The friendly manager will cook up on the open fire some steak or chicken, which you can enjoy with some chips (French fries) and/or salad for around FMg 8000, or some brochettes (FMg 500 each). It also serves very cheap beer (and a lot of research was done on this topic).

The *Relais Normand Restaurant* on Arabe Rainibetsimisaraka is one of the best value places in Tana. It has an up-market appearance but reasonable prices, good food and friendly service. The creative menu includes Chinese, Indian and French cuisine. The only drawback is its dodgy location, which is also subject to flooding when it rains.

An extremely popular lunchtime venue, and a good place to meet other travellers, is *Le Buffet du Jardin* in Haute-Ville, opposite the Champion Supermarket and the tourist office. Breakfast is overpriced at FMg 9500, but the pizzas are reasonable (if small) for FMg 12,000. Although there's a nice outdoor patio seating area, drinks are expensive in order to prevent people spending too much time over a beer or coke when the tables could be occupied by diners.

Hotels The *Hôtel Glacier* serves good meals and has a view of the lively passing parade, but considering the grubby decor, meal prices (about FMg 16,000) are way too high. It is a popular place for an evening drink, but it's full of prostitutes, and beggars hover just outside.

The restaurant at the *Radama Hôtel* comes highly recommended by some travellers for decor, service and a range of meals, including tasty Malagasy dishes.

The brasserie at the *Hôtel Le Jean Laborde* has excellent French meals, including a dash of Malagasy zebu, from FMg 12,000. The *Hôtel de France Brasserie* (not its main restaurant, *O Poivre Vert)* has a good range of meals and excellent service (for which you pay an extra 6% on your bill). It is often full in peak season, so you may need to book a table. Pasta meals start at FMg 11,000 and others are a reasonable FMg 16,000. The restaurant at the *Hôtel Île Bourbon* specialises in Réunion cuisine, and often has a jazz band in the evenings. If it is a quiet night, the waiters (or customers!) may join in and sing. It is worth trying to find this place for the rôti canard à la vanille (roast duck with vanilla).

Understandably popular with guests and the public is the restaurant above the *Hôtel Sakamanga*. It is one of the very few places to really cater for foreigners and has a good range, but when it's busy service can be slow. Prices are tourist-oriented – FMg 9500 for a plat du jour (which may not be available),

other meals for FMg 12,000, and FMg 6000 for a large beer.

For a Splurge One of the top eating spots in Tana is the *Hôtel Colbert*, a favourite with the Tana business set and bons vivants. Here you can enjoy such wonders as tripe in paillarde de zebu (tripe in apple brandy sauce) and nymphes which are frogs' legs (for sentimental and environmental reasons, these aren't recommended). The *Madagascar Hilton* has an impressive range of expensive Italian, Malagasy, fish and Chinese buffets on different evenings.

For something really special take a taxi to the *Grill du Rova* (☎ 356 07), near what was the Rova palace. It has a charming outdoor setting, and the prices are quite reasonable considering the excellent location and views: main courses are FMg 6000 to FMg 10,000 and the menu du jour is worth a splurge at FMg 20,000. Ring ahead to find out what music they may have on (refer to the Entertainment section following for more details).

Self-Catering

The best-stocked supermarket is upstairs at the *Champion Supermarket* in Haute-Ville, but the prices are equally hauts. Just down from the Champion is one of the chain of health food shops, *La Hutte Canadienne*, which sells fresh organically grown farm produce, whole foods and home-made natural fruit ice cream and sorbet. Also for imported luxuries, check out the *Bongou* shop and cafe, next to Air Mauritius.

The Analakely *produce market* climbs the hill north-east of Araben ny 26 Jona 1960, and there are numerous other markets scattered all over the city and environs.

ENTERTAINMENT

To find out what is going on and where, buy one of the three French and Malagasy-language newspapers produced in Tana, or ask at the tourist office.

Cinemas

Incredibly, there are no large-screen cinemas in the whole city. They have been replaced by informal video clubs showing low-grade kung fu classics, mainly in the suburbs. For films of a higher quality, the American Cultural Center, Alliance Française, Cercle Germano-Malagasy and the Centre Culturel Albert Camus (CCAC) often show free movies in various languages.

Discos & Nightclubs

It's not Paris, but Tana offers some lively nightlife, with a reasonably good choice of dancing spots. Most are discos but some have live bands or orchestras which play a mixture of Malagasy, western rock/folk and pre-war French dance music. The admission price usually includes your first beer. Most places are in Haute-Ville, less than 200m from Hôtel Colbert.

Le Caveau Nightclub is one of the best while Le Papillon at the Madagascar Hilton is the most prestigious, with occasional live music and a superb view over the bright lights of Tana.

An extremely popular disco is the Acapulco Nightclub. It has its own jazz orchestra and is described in a tourist brochure as follows: 'You feel like being in some United States town where at the request of musicians playing Chick Corea's 'Spain' or Wayne Shorter's 'Limbo', people of pleasure jig up and down in cigarette smoke and alcoholic effluvium. No clothing requirements.'

Music & Theatre

The modern Centre Culturel Albert Camus (CCAC) (☎ 236 47) is Tana's foremost cultural venue. It has a library, and holds regular screenings of new and old French films, regular concert and theatre performances and local and international art exhibitions. You can call in for a free monthly program. You can join the CCAC if you are going to be in Tana for a while, but visitors are welcome to attend performances and exhibitions without having to join. The American Cultural Center also shows films, and hosts visiting lecturers. These are mainly for local students but foreigners are often welcome to join in.

Malagasy theatre and dance perfor-

mances, as well as pop concerts, are held regularly in the old Théâtre Municipal in the Isotry district, and at the amphitheatre at the Théâtre de Verdure Antsahamanitra. Inquire at the tourist office, or check posters and local newspapers for dates, times and locations.

Definitely worth checking out is the Grill du Rova restaurant (☎ 356 07). It regularly holds traditional Malagasy music recitals and plays, often on Sundays. You can enjoy these shows while having a great meal at reasonable prices (see Places to Eat) and admiring the views. It is worth ringing to find out what it has on, or you can pick up a pamphlet at the restaurant which lists shows for the current month.

Hira Gasy

The traditional Malagasy spectacle of acrobatics, music and speeches called a hira gasy is held most Sunday afternoons on a block of land near the new Alliance Française building. Contact the tourist office for exact details about the current location and the times of performances. Refer to the Facts about Madagascar chapter for more details about the hira gasy.

Spectator Sports

There is very little in the way of sports in the capital city; most Malagasy are more concerned about trying to earn a living than playing or watching sports. You can bet on the horses at the Bevalala Race Track about nine km south of the centre of Tana. Football (soccer) is held at the huge Stade Municipal de Mahamasina stadium on weekend afternoons, mainly on Sundays.

THINGS TO BUY

Naturally the best places to buy your souvenirs are the Zoma and Andravoahangy markets. You will be able to choose from a huge range of carvings and intricate linen, as well as plenty of tacky stuff. Of course, prices are never fixed and are highly negotiable. Competition is high, so if you stay away from a wandering packaged tour, and bargain hard, you will get something you want for a good price.

The best range of postcards and small sketches is in the same arcade as the Express Photo shop, just up from the start of the steps from Araben ny Fahaleovantena to Haute-Ville.

Around the Hôtel Colbert and Le Buffet du Jardin you will be surrounded with hawkers selling things like huge sailing boats, which can't possibly fit in a backpack or be sent home. Some of the more interesting and ecologically sound souvenirs are the figures made from recycled tin sold along the footpaths of Haute-Ville.

Refer to the preceding Zoma market section and the Things to Buy section in the Madagascar Facts for the Visitor for more suggestions.

GETTING THERE & AWAY
Air
The head office for Air Madagascar (☎ 222 22) is at 31 Araben ny Fahaleovantena. There are also special contact numbers for the times of arrivals and departures (☎ 288 65) and for long-distance reservations (☎ 331 54). If flying on an international or domestic flight with Air Mad, book and confirm as far in advance as possible. It's a good idea to get to the Air Mad office at opening time to beat the rush. Air Mad is open from 7.30 am to noon, and from 2 to 5.30 pm, on Monday to Friday; and 8 to 11.30 am on Saturday mornings.

The offices in Tana for the handful of airlines which fly into Madagascar are:

Aeroflot
  19 Làlana Mahafaka (next to the Shalimar restaurant) (☎ 235 61)
Air Austral
  represented by Air Madagascar
Air France
  29 Araben ny Fahaleovantena (next to Air Mad) (☎ 223 21)
Air Mauritius
  Làlana des 77 Parlementaires (between the Hôtels Central and Njato) (☎ 359 90)
Inter Air
  in the Madagascar Hilton arcade (☎ 224 52)
TAM
  in a new building behind the Hilton hotel (☎ 296 91); and at the airport (☎ 449 49)

For information about the cost and frequency of flights to and from Tana, refer to the relevant regional sections throughout the book. For details on international flights, and information on international arrivals and departures, see the Madagascar Getting There & Away chapter. Accommodation near the airport is outlined under Ivato in the Around Antananarivo section later in this chapter.

Taxi-Brousse
Taxis-brousse serve all towns and villages around Tana, as well as the rest of the country. There are departures about every hour to Antsirabe, Fianarantsoa and Toamasina, with connections to Mahajanga (Majunga) and Toliara (Tuléar) every day. Hardy travellers can opt for an overland adventure to Ambanja, not far from the port for the ferry to Nosy Be; and real masochists can taxi-brousse all the way to Antsiranana (Diego Suarez) or Taolagnaro (Fort Dauphin), although it would be quite punishing to do it all in one go.

There are four main stations (gares routières), which all have a chaotic plethora of taxis-brousse, minibuses, bus and taxis-be. For long distances, you can (and should) book in advance.

Taxi-brousse Station North (Gare Routière du Nord) at Ambodivona.
  Go to this station for transport to Toamasina (FMg 25,000), Mahajanga (FMg 40,000) and Antsiranana (FMg 140,000). To reach the station from the centre of town, take a MALAKIA No 4 bus, or a taxi.
Taxi-brousse Station South (Gare Routière du Sud) at Anosibe.
  This station actually has all sorts of vehicles going to all points south, and to the east and west coasts. There are regular departures to Antsirabe (FMg 15,000), Fianarantsoa (FMg 35,000), Morondava (FMg 58,000), Manakara (FMg 53,000), Toliara (FMg 55,000) and Taolagnaro (FMg 85,000). This station is about 1½ km south-west of Lac Anosy on Làlana Pastora Rahajason. Take a FIMA No 10 bus, or a taxi.

Taxi-brousse Station West (Gare Routière de l'Ouest).
  This station, several hundred metres from the railway station, is where you'll find taxis-brousse going to Ivato and the airport. You can either walk, catch a KOMAFI bus (Nos 23 or 8) or take a taxi to the station.
Taxi-brousse Station East (Gare Routière de l'Est) at Ampasampito.
  From this station in the distant suburbs of Tana, you'll find taxis-brousse and taxis-be to nearby places such as Manjakandriana, Lac Mantasoa (FMg 4000) and Moramanga (FMg 7000). To the station, take an ANTAFITA bus (Nos 1 or 2) or, better, take a taxi (about FMg 7500).

Bus

A range of public buses leave from the taxi-brousse stations to major regional towns such as Toamasina, Fianarantsoa, Toliara and Mahajanga.

The *Confo Express* leaves Tana every Tuesday for Toliara and returns from Toliara on Thursday, stopping off at any place along the main highway. Undoubtedly, this is only the first of many private, tourist-oriented, long-distance buses. Fares are about twice the price of a public bus, but you get far more comfort and security, as well as a few gimmicks like free bottles of mineral water and snacks. Bookings in Tana can be made at the Europe Voyage travel agency (☎/fax 630 49), opposite the Lac Hôtel in Behoririka. Refer to the Southern Madagascar chapter for more information about the trip from Toliara.

Train

There are two main railway lines from Tana. The track to Toamasina, with a branch line north to Ambatondrazaka from Moramanga, was damaged at the time of research but was due to reopen very soon. Normally, a train leaves Tana for Toamasina (FMg 17,500/30,500 for 2nd/1st class) on Thursday at 8 am and returns from Toamasina on Sunday morning. From Tana to Ambatondrazaka (21,500/48,500) there is normally a train on Tuesday, Thursday and Saturday mornings, which returns the next day.

A fascinating private train known as La Micheline travels between Tana and Toamasina. You may be able to buy a ticket for FMg 87,500 per person, which seems a lot, but it's great fun and worth a splurge. For more information about the magical Micheline, refer to the Toamasina section in the Eastern Madagascar chapter and the Madagascar Getting Around chapter.

From Tana, a daily train also leaves for Antsirabe at 7 am (FMg 8000/14,500). It returns from Antsirabe at about 1 pm that afternoon. This track is also subject to inoperation.

For up-to-date information, talk to the helpful staff (who speak French and English) at the Bureau d'Information et de Reception (☎ 205 21) in the terminal building at Tana. You can usually book a ticket – which is recommended, especially in peak season – the day before departure; otherwise get to the station at least an hour before the advertised departure. And expect delays and cancellations.

Car

For information about car rentals from agencies in Tana for trips around the countryside (only an idiot would hire a car to drive around Tana), refer to the Madagascar Getting Around chapter.

GETTING AROUND

Most restaurants and hotels in Tana are within a short distance of each other so it's easy enough to walk (except when it is very hot, wet or at night). To further out places like the taxi-brousse stations and zoo, and particularly up steep parts of town, such as the Rova, take a taxi. You should also consider safety when walking long distances in unfamiliar and/or remote sections of the city.

The Airport

Tana's international and domestic airport is at Ivato, 14km north of the centre of Tana. Taxis-brousse travel between Ivato village, one km from the airport, and the Taxi-brousse Station West every 15 minutes or so. Don't even consider taking this taxi-brousse after dark.

If you are not an expert on public transport in Tana, or have some luggage, you are advised to take a taxi from the airport to your hotel – even though you will be overcharged. The current 'tourist' price for a taxi *from* the airport to any hotel listed in the book will be FMg 45,000 – but if you have a little patience, and there are not many *vazahas* (tourists) on the flight, you should be able to get it for a comparatively reasonable FMg 30,000. If in doubt, check with the Air Mad or Welcome Service counters at the airport for the current taxi fares to town. Prices will stay at around FMg 45,000 if there are many vahazas on the flight and if it is dark or raining – ie, when you have less bargaining power. From the city to the airport, however, don't pay more than FMg 30,000.

For more information about arriving at, or departing from, the international airport refer to the Madagascar Getting There & Away chapter.

Bus

Most buses around the city begin and end on Araben ny Fahaleovantena and Araben ny 26 Jona 1960 in the centre of town. They usually run fully packed so try to avoid the peak periods from 7 to 8.30 am and 5 to 6.30 pm. They stop only at official bus stops so there's no need to wave, clap or whistle when you want to get on or off. Beware of pickpockets in the crush, but the threat isn't as great as other African or Asian cities. The standard fare for any distance is about FMg 500, payable to the conductor.

However, considering the abysmally slow traffic, and narrow and steep roads, it is often quicker to walk to anywhere nearby, and far more comfortable and secure to take a taxi to anywhere more than two or three km away.

Taxi

There are plenty of taxis in Tana but stick to the Citroën Deux Chevaux (2CVs) or Renault 4s because they're cheaper than other sedans. Avoid those hanging around the Hilton, Colbert and other top-end hotels. And always agree on the price before you climb into a taxi. If one taxi is no good, keep trying:

We wanted to get to an address near the Rova from around the corner from the Hilton. The first taxi we hailed was a 2CV who had to admit that he couldn't make it up the hill, and the second didn't have a clue where we wanted to go.

The loosely defined 'standard' fares (for tourists) range from FMg 2500 for a hop of a couple of hundred metres (eg, from the Hôtel de France to the railway station) to FMg 5000 to FMg 6000 to anywhere around town, including Tsimbazaza or any of the distant taxi-brousse stations. After dark, you'll pay about FMg 6000 to FMg 8000.

Taxi drivers are skilful at browbeating foreigners into paying ridiculous fares; in the interest of future taxi-tourist relations don't let them get away with it! Ask a local or someone from your hotel about the current fares around town, or ask a Malagasy to hail the taxi and negotiate a fare on your behalf.

Around Antananarivo

If the crowds, noise and pollution in Tana are starting to get you down, or you have a few days to spare, there are several excellent and easy day trips from the hustle and bustle of the capital city.

IVATO
• Telephone Area Code: 2

Ivato, 14km from the city, is where Tana's international airport is located. If you have flown back from somewhere in the provinces and have another flight to catch the next morning, and/or you want to avoid paying high taxi fares to or from the city, there are some modest hotel alternatives in and around Ivato village.

The **Parc d'Élevage des Crocodiles**, open every day from 9 am to 5 pm, is only a few km from the airport. It is pretty much like other crocodile farms around the world, but may be worth a visit if you have some time to kill between flights. A snack bar and souvenir shop sell a few things made from recalcitrant crocs.

Places to Stay & Eat

Along the main road to the airport, in an area known as Mandrosa, there are plenty of cheap but noisy places to stay – and you will still have to get a taxi to these places. The *Sitara* and *L'Emeralde* hotels are good value. Closer to the airport are the middle-range *Motel au Transit* (☎ 445 81) and the *Auberge de Cheval Blanc* (☎ 446 46), where single/double rooms cost about FMg 28,000/35,000.

The nicest place to stay near the airport – and within a 20 minute walk – is *Le Manoir Rouge* (☎ 441 04) in the village of Ivato, run by the same crowd who run the pleasant budget Hôtel Lambert in Tana. Clean and comfortable rooms (but with no hot water in the communal bathroom) range from FMg 21,000 to FMg 40,000. The good restaurant downstairs serves meals for about FMg 9000. To get there from the airport terminal, turn left at the gate to the airport, walk past the military barracks and into the village – then look for the sign to the hotel.

Getting There & Away

A taxi from the airport to Ivato will cost about FMg 5000, but it may not be worth it for drivers to go such a short distance; what they're after is a fat fare back to the centre of Tana. Perhaps ask fellow passengers if they wouldn't mind sharing a taxi for this short distance.

Refer to the Getting There & Away section for details about getting from Ivato to Tana.

AMBOHIMANGA

A popular day excursion from the capital is to Ambohimanga (Blue Hill), 21km north of Tana. This was the original capital of the Merina royal family and even when the seat of government was shifted to Tana for political reasons, Ambohimanga remained something of a sacred site. As such, it remained off limits to foreigners for a long time.

The entrance to Ambohimanga village is marked by a large traditional gateway, one of the seven gateways to the eyrie-like hilltop.

PETER PTSCHELINZEW

Roadside stalls outside Antananarivo on the road to Toamasina, eastern Madagascar.

To one side is an immense flat round stone. At the first sign of threat to the village, some 40 slaves would roll this stone and seal off the gate. Someone has been allowed to construct a ludicrous Chinese pagoda beside the gate; it provides some amusement but completely spoils the traditional ambience.

This lovely village provides a rustic contrast to the city surroundings – its brilliant red earth and eucalyptus trees may make Aussie travellers feel right at home. En route, you pass several small hamlets which may leave you with the impression that you've stepped into a Brueghel painting. The area is dotted with Merina tombs, but they are mostly undecorated cement blocks and aren't as interesting as those further south.

The Rova
A few hundred metres uphill from Ambohimanga village is the walled Rova, the palace compound of King Andrianampoinimerina, who ruled from 1787 until his death in 1810. It's spartan compared to the Rova in Tana (before the fire), but the atmosphere is quieter and the rural surroundings are lovely.

His King's Home, the Bevato, resembles a large black wooden shed with a 10m-high sloping roof supported by a rosewood pole. Spears, shields and eating utensils cover the walls. His Majesty's bed, shared with the wife of the week, is high up near the ceiling, while the beds belonging to his 11 other wives are closer to the floor.

Ambohimanga became the weekend retreat for queens Ranavalona I to III. They constructed themselves a lovely summer house inside the royal compound which still contains original furnishings. Inside are several paintings and gifts, including a wash basin, presented to the royal family by Queen Victoria.

If someone is praying inside any of the structures, don't enter until they have finished. Pilgrims from all over the country come to pray to God through the spirits of the queens, who they believe serve as messengers for their prayers.

The outside walls of the Rova are interest-ing, having been constructed using an egg-based cement. If you follow these stairs up and over the top, you'll reach an overlook with a spectacular view back to Tana. A curious depression has been hollowed out in the rocks there; women pitch pebbles into this hollow in the belief that it will help them become fertile. The Rova is open to the public from 8 to 11 am and 2 to 5 pm daily, except Mondays. The entrance fee is now FMg 10,000, which is a bit steep.

Places to Stay & Eat
About six km from Ambohimanga along the route from Tana is the *Auberge du Soleil Levant* (☎ 426 12) (yes – the House of the Rising Sun!). It's isolated and in need of some serious maintenance, but worth calling by if only to taste the *bibasy* fruit off their trees. This rustic and friendly place has electricity but no running water (the water supply comes from an open well). Double rooms begin at FMg 17,500. The Auberge has a separate restaurant.

The *Restaurant d'Ambohimanga Rova* is perfectly located beside the Rova with terrific views across the countryside to Tana. Meals aren't cheap but are well worth the splurge; otherwise, just enjoy a beer out in the flower garden. You may be lucky enough to catch a rehearsal or display of Malagasy dancing by villagers, often accompanied by live music.

Alternatively, try the simpler and cheaper *La Colline Bleue*, just uphill from the taxi-brousse stop.

Getting There & Away
Taxis-brousse leave from just outside the Taxi-brousse Station North at Ambodivona in Tana. The trip takes about an hour and costs FMg 1300. They leave at least hourly and will take you right through the gate of Ambohimanga village. You must then walk about one km up the hill to the Rova. Alternatively, if you want to take a taxi from Tana, you will be charged FMg 100,000 for the return trip including waiting – the price is hard to bargain down. Sharing with other travellers is obviously a good idea.

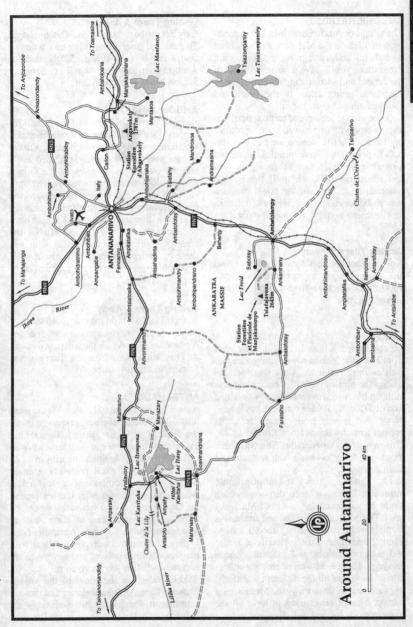

Around Antananarivo

AMBOHIDRATRIMO

The village of Ambohidratrimo, 17km north-west of Tana on the Mahajanga road, sits on a windy hill and is an agreeable place to visit. From there you'll have a beautiful view of the capital and surrounding country, including some pretty lakes to the south and south-east, just below the hill.

In the village are several **tombs**; nearby is a stone post with two carved breasts protruding from it. Sterile women used to visit this post to pray. They were blindfolded, turned around seven times, then set facing the post and instructed to touch it. If the woman touched the left breast, she could expect a son; if she touched the right breast, a daughter. Touching both breasts meant twins!

Getting There & Away

Ambohidratrimo lies on the Mahajanga road and is accessible by taxi-brousse (FMg 1000) from the Taxi-brousse Station North in Ambodivona.

ILAFY

On the sacred hill in Ilafy, 12km by road from Tana, the Merina royal family once had their country residence. Ilafy was founded around the turn of the 17th century and was built up by Andrianasinavalona, who ruled from 1675 to 1710. He built the royal residence, but it was later redesigned in its present form by Ranavalona I in the 1830s. This two-storey wooden building with three rooms per floor has been well restored and maintained.

The house, now an **ethnographic museum**, lies up a steep dirt road which might be too much for most old Malagasy taxis. The collection of relics and artefacts is worth a visit and there are model tombs, hunting and fishing tools, details of magic and religious rituals, and modern wooden carvings. There is also an interesting collection of photos of all the different traditional wigs and hairstyles worn by the Merina royal family. Merina kings used to have all the royal laundry washed in Ilafy.

Getting There & Away

Ilafy lies on the road towards Ambohimanga. To get there from Tana, either take a taxi or find a taxi-brousse (FMg 750) headed for Ambohimanga from the Taxi-brousse Station North at Ambodivona.

AMBOHIJANAKA

Just a few km south-west of Tana is the 17th century fortified village of Ambohijanaka, which means The Place of Children. Village houses bear Indonesian-style horned roofs and the old red stone gates of the village remain, along with a quiet square of red earth set with sacrificial stones. Nearby are the **family tombs** of local chieftains which are covered with small wooden huts. These have been constructed for the benefit of the *andevo* (traditional underclass) who use these structures as sites of worship in order to gain blessings from the ancestors of high-standing families.

Getting There & Away

Ambohijanaka lies on the main road south of Tana so any taxi-brousse headed for Ambatolampy or Antsirabe will pass through it. They leave Tana from the Taxi-brousse Station South in Anosibe.

ANTSAHADINTA

Antsahadinta (Forest of Leeches) is the most remote and one of the best preserved of all the hilltop villages around Tana. This extremely photogenic settlement was founded by King Andriamangarira in 1725 and the Rova, or royal precincts, contain several terraced **tombs** and a well-maintained garden. As you enter the settlement, the large tomb on your left is that of Queen Rabodozafimanjaka, one of King Andria-nampoinimerina's 12 wives. Accused of disloyalty, she had to undergo an ordeal with *tanguin*, a strong poison, and no-one today is certain whether she survived it.

You'll also see the tomb of the village founder, King Andriamangarira and there is a **museum** which explains everything (in French).

If you ask a guide, you will be directed to a small house where visitors can spend the night for a nominal, negotiable fee.

Getting There & Away

The road to Antsahadinta is poor and it takes a very long time to drive the 14km from Tana. As public transport is sparse, you may be better off walking. Turn left at Ampitatafika (not to be confused with Ampitatafika between Antsirabe and Ambatolampy) and head south-west following the only road. The road winds through hills and valleys past many village clusters of tall Merina houses. When you reach a turn-off leading up to the wooded sacred hill, you'll see a signpost saying 'Antsahadinta 1.7 km'. From here, the road is quite good.

LAC ITASY

Lac Itasy, which covers 45 sq km, was formed when the valley which contains it was blocked by a lava flow 8000 years ago. It lies near the village of Ampefy, 120km west of Tana and about 11km south of Analavory on RN1. Although the area has been completely deforested and none of the original vegetation remains, the surrounding landscape of volcanic domes is quite beautiful.

Recently the area was deemed by the WWF to be a 'sight of interest', and 3500 hectares have been allocated for research into, and preservation of, some 33 types of birds, including many migratory species.

The lake has lent its name to the entire Itasy region, which is enclosed by two ranges – the Ankaratra in the south and the Bongolava in the west. There's excellent **hiking** around the shore except in the boggy south, but swimming is precluded by both crocodiles and bilharzia. In the crater lake of **Lac Andranotoraha**, about five km south of Ampefy, there's also reputed to be a Loch Ness-type monster.

About 300m north of Ampefy a footpath turns off to the west, crosses a bridge and continues for five km to the village of **Antafofo**, where the Liliha River plunges more than 20m. In French, the falls are known as the **Chutes de la Lily** (the Malagasy name Liliha is pronounced 'lily').

Places to Stay

In Ampefy, you can stay at the *Hôtel Kavitaha* (☎ 4), pleasantly located above Lac Kavitaha, for FMg 20,000 a double, or at the cheap but very seedy *Bâtiments Administratifs*.

Getting There & Away

Take a taxi-brousse headed for Tsiroanomandidy from Tana and get off at Analavory village. From there, wait for another taxi-brousse, hitch or continue on foot south along RN43 for 11km to Ampefy.

ARIVONIMAMO

En route to Lac Itasy and 47km west of Tana, you may wish to visit Arivonimamo, the geographic centre of Madagascar. Here, there's a revered peak, **Ambohipanompo**, on which there are **sacred royal tombs** (which unfortunately were pillaged in 1988).

At the Friday **market** you can sample a local speciality known as *bononoka*, a delicious cheesy concoction made from strips of fermented manioc. This region is also known as a centre for weaving *lamba mena* (burial shrouds). Arivonimamo also serves as a starting or finishing point for treks through

---

The Menalamba

Arivonimamo was the home of Madagascar's first nationalist movement, the Menalamba. On 22 November 1895 revolutionaries attacked the compound run by the London Missionary Society, which to them represented Europe and all it stood for, and killed an English Quaker family. This incident is commemorated on a monument in the village. French troops were sent from Tana and killed 150 Menalamba before the remaining rebels retreated into the Ankaratra Massif. ■

the Ankaratra massif. If you need to stay overnight in Arivonimamo try *Chez Wilson* (☎ 10).

To get there take any taxi-brousse (FMg 3800) careering towards Tsiroanomandidy.

LAC MANTASOA

This 2000-hectare artificial lake (built in 1937) lies 60km by road east of Tana, and a little south of the Toamasina road. The pine and eucalypt-fringed mountain lake provides a popular weekend retreat for Tana folk, with opportunities for fishing, swimming and sailing. For visitors, it's a wonderful place for hiking, camping and a picnic lunch.

On the lake, the Frenchman Jean Laborde built a country palace at the instructions of Queen Ranavalona I as well as a host of manufacturing establishments: a carpentry, gunsmith shops, a pottery, glass works, tannery, cement mill, paper mill, munitions factory, iron forge and a foundry.

The primary aim was to supply the difficult monarch with swords, arms and ammunition and other nasty implements. Much of this one-man economic boom now lies beneath the waters, so apart from a few unrecognisable ruins, little evidence remains of Madagascar's industrial revolution. However, you can still see **Jean Laborde's home** in the former village of Andrangoloaka nearby, his **grave** in the local cemetery and the (signposted) **munitions factory** is worth a look around.

The lake is two to three km past Mantasoa village; follow the main path through the village.

Places to Stay & Eat

There is nothing stopping you camping around the lake for a few days as long as you check with nearby houses to make sure you are not on any private property. Bring your own food, though there are some limited supplies in Mantasoa village.

At the Swiss-owned chalet-style *Hôtel le Chalet Suisse* (☎ 20) you may be able to negotiate a bungalow for as little as FMg 15,000/20,000 for a single/double with hot water, but prices are generally a little higher. Reservations are recommended. The attached *restaurant* serves raclette (a Swiss-cheese dish) and fondue savoyarde (cheese fondue), among other Swiss treats.

With a lot more cash you can enjoy an atmospheric getaway at the legendary four-star *Hôtel Ermitage* (☎ 5). It has a tennis court and offers horse riding, but the place is really showing signs of wear and tear. It is about six km past the village; follow the signs.

Getting There & Away

One way to Lac Mantasoa is to take an early morning Tana to Toamasina train and get off at Ambatoloana, the first station east of Manjakandriana. From there, hitch or find a taxi-brousse along the rough 15km road south to the lake. The road is easy and pleasant to walk along, but save some energy for hiking around the lake.

More reliable than the train is the direct taxi-brousse from the Taxi-brousse Station East at Ampasampito, Tana, which will cost around FMg 4000 one-way to Mantasoa village. Start early from Tana if you want to get back on the same day; leave the lake by about 2 pm.

STATION FORESTIÈRE D'ANGAVOKELY

En route to Lac Mantasoa is the lovely village of **Carion** (Nandihizana) from where you can visit the 690 hectare Angavokely Forestry Station, established to preserve the original vegetation of the hauts plateaux and to plant eucalypts.

It's a great place for hiking and its two rocky peaks, including 1787m-high Angavokely, afford good views of both Tana and Lac Mantasoa. If you ask directions (and can pronounce the names) you can also visit the eerie caves of **Grotte d'Andavabatomaizina** and **Grotte d'Andavavatsongomby**.

To get to the reserve from Carion, look for a trail with the sign to Angavokely from the main road. After a 30-minute walk you come to a barrier for another trail. This will open after you buy your permit (FMg 20,000) from a hut about 10 minutes walk further along the original trail.

AMBATOLAMPY
• Telephone Area Code: 260

The flowery town of Ambatolampy lies on both RN7 and the railway line, 68km south of Tana. The main attractions are the hills of the **Ankaratra massif**, and the nominally protected Station Forestière et Piscicole de Manjakatompo, 17km west of Ambatolampy (see the following section).

If you have a vehicle you can also visit the new **Musée Privée d'Entomologie**, a private collection displaying over 5000 insects that is open to the public (no other details were available at the time of research).

Places to Stay & Eat
One of the more famous restaurants near Tana is the *Au Rendez-vous des Pecheurs* (☎ 204), 800m north of the railway station. Many expats and visitors stop here on the way south, but we were a little disappointed with the plat du jour of (stringy) duck for FMg 12,500. If you are stopping at Ambatolampy, the restaurant has rooms upstairs which are very good value: charming rooms with a balcony (overlooking the busy road) cost a bargain FMg 26,000/35,000 for a single/double.

An even better place to stay and eat is the classy *Au Gîte de France Hôtel & Restaurant* (☎ 258), about 400m north of the railway station. The menu du jour is FMg 30,000; other good meals are about FMg 12,000. It has several charming and huge, old-fashioned rooms, with shared bathrooms, for FMg 35,000/40,000 (more for the bungalow).

Up in the Ankaratra massif is the wonderful *Manja Ranch* (☎ 234). Rooms in a lovely farm house are a bargain FMg 15,000; some bungalows are due to be completed soon. If you eat at least one meal (which are excellent but pricey at FMg 20,000) you can camp there for nothing – but ring first to confirm

this. From the ranch, you can explore the hills on horseback (FMg 18,000 per hour), by mountain bike (FMg 5000 per hour) or on foot. The ranch is one km from the main road; you can see the sign along the main road near Ambatolampy. Reservations are advised.

Getting There & Away
To Ambatolampy, take the Tana to Antsirabe train and alight at Ambatolampy, which is about midway between the two cities. From the station, the two hotels in town are a short but steep walk up the hill. Alternatively, take a taxi-brousse(FMg 5500) to Ambatolampy from the Taxi-brousse Station South in Tana.

STATION FORESTIÈRE ET PISCICOLE DE MANJAKATOMPO
This new reserve, established with the help of the German development agency GTZ, is 7808 hectares of forest, plains, mountains, waterfalls and ponds with plenty of fish. There's a campground and the area offers almost unlimited off-the-beaten-track **trekking**. Unfortunately many of the trails go through degraded areas, but a reforestation scheme commenced as far back as 1926 has matured into stands of pine and cypress brought from Europe.

The reserve is bound to become a popular attraction, not least because of its accessibility from Tana. This is not lemur country, but you will see native flora and some 38 species of birds, such as the Madagascar turtle-dove.

You can walk around the reserve on a short half-day circuit, on a 'medium' (one day) or a 'grand' (two day) circuit. These trails take you past **Lac Froid** which, as the name suggests, offers cool swimming, and to the foot of the country's third highest mountain, the 2643m-high **Tsiafajavona** (Place of Perpetual Mists).

There's a particularly strong local *fady* (taboo) against pork in the Ankaratra massif so don't even think about carrying sausages on your hike. If you want some more information about the reserve, including a decent map of the area, buy the excellent tourist guide (in French) available at the bookshops listed in the Antananarivo section.

To get to the reserve, hike (17km) from Ambatolampy to the entrance (where you buy a permit) – look for the sign from the main road. Market days in the main village of **Ankeniheny** are on Monday and Thursday, which is when you are more likely to get a taxi-brousse (About FMg 1000) between the Taxi-brousse Station South in Tana and Ankeniheny, via Ambatolampy.

Eastern Madagascar

The long, eastern central coast of Madagascar is known as the Coast of Rosewood or Coast of Greenery, among other less appealing monikers such as the Cyclone Coast and Pirate Coast. The region includes the main town, Toamasina (commonly known as Tamatave); the wild Masoala Peninsula; Nosy Mangabe; the eastern rainforests; Parc National d'Andasibe-Mantadia (commonly known as Périnet Reserve); the 665km-long chain of lakes and artificial canals which form the Canal des Pangalanes system; and the former pirate sanctuaries from the Baie d'Antongila south to Île Sainte Marie (Nosy Boraha) – which is rapidly overtaking Nosy Be in popularity as a beach tourism venue.

It's said that the east coast experiences only two climatic seasons: the wet season and the season when it rains. Yes, it is wet – and from December to March, drenching wet. If that's not enough, every couple of decades it suffers a really severe blow. In 1927, the city of Toamasina was flattened by a cyclone; in March 1986, another storm caused extensive damage on Île Sainte Marie; and in February 1992, Cyclone Geralda wreaked havoc.

As sticky and unpleasant as the weather can become, the rain does make Madagascar's eastern coast the lushest and greenest on the island. Relatively extensive areas are draped in endemic rainforest and along the coastal strip there is a rich variety of palms and pandanus. The climate also aids in the production of cloves, vanilla, coffee and fruit for export. The Vanilla Coast extends from Toamasina all the way north to Iharana (Vohémar).

The people of the densely populated coastal strip belong mainly to the Betsimisaraka tribe, formed in a confederation of several tribes around 1712 and, therefore, the youngest of the 18 Malagasy tribes.

The east coast may have many fine beaches but sharks and currents will limit visitor appreciation. Some of the beaches at

HIGHLIGHTS

- Périnet Reserve, a great place to see lemurs including indri, the largest (and loudest) of them all.
- The Canal des Pangalenes, a system of artificial and natural waterways stretching over 600km along the east coast.
- The lovely beaches and relaxed atmosphere of Île Sainte Marie, a former haunt of pirates.

Mahambo, Mahavelona (Foulpointe) and Fenoarivo (Fénérive) are considered comparatively safe but it's still wise to check with locals before diving in.

The road between Tana and Toamasina is in good condition but unless you have a private vehicle or a good lift take the rail trip (if it is running), which traverses a scenic route through green hills and rainforests – it is more comfortable and rewarding. From Tana, the line goes directly east, descending and following the road for much of the way until it hits the coast just east of Vohibihony

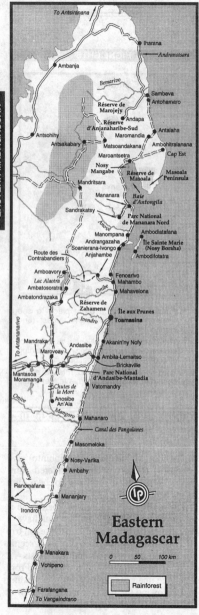

To Antsiranana
Iharana
Andranotsara
Ambanja
Bemarivo
Sambava
Antohamaro
Réserve de Marojejy
Andapa
Réserve d'Anjanaharibe-Sud
Antalaha
Antsohihy
Maromandia
Antsakabary
Matsoandakana
Ambohitralanana
Maroantsetra
Cap Est
Nosy Mangabe
Réserve de Masoala
Masoala Peninsula
Mandritsara
Baie d'Antongila
Mananara
Sandrakatsy
Parc National de Mananara Nord
Antanambe
Manompana
Ambodiatafana
Andrangazaha
Île Sainte Marie (Nosy Boraha)
Soanierana-Ivongo
Anjahambe
Ambodifotatra
Route des Contrabandiers
Amboavory
Fenoarivo
Mahambo
Lac Alaotra
Ambatosoratra
Mahavelona
Ambatondrazaka
Réserve de Zahamena
Île aux Prunes
Ivondro
Toamasina
To Antananarivo
Mandraka
Andasibe
Akanin'ny Nofy
Marovoay
Ambila-Lemaitso
Brickaville
Parc National d'Andasibe-Mantadia
Mantasoa
Moramanga
Vatomandry
Chutes de la Mort
Onive
Anosibe An'Ala
Mangoro
Mahanaro
Canal des Pangalanes
Masomeloka
Ampasimpy
Nosy-Varika
Ambahy
Ranomafana
Mananjary
Irondro
Manakara
Eastern Madagascar
0   50   100 km
Vohipeno
Farafangana
To Vangaindrano
Rainforest

(Brickaville) at Ambila-Lemaitso. There it turns sharply north and follows the coastal strip between the sea and the Pangalanes canal to Toamasina. Be warned, we have had reports of seasickness from all the rocking and rolling along the poorly maintained track!

AMBATONDRAZAKA & LAC ALAOTRA
• Telephone Area Code: 4

Lac Alaotra, Madagascar's largest body of water at 22,000 hectares, has historically been Madagascar's rice bowl and once supplied much of the national demand.

Now, however, the area serves as a microcosm of the environmental ruination which faces the country. As the population grew and the forests which once cloaked the surrounding hills were felled and converted to agricultural land, the landscape changed. Without the protective vegetation cover, the soil eroded and was sluiced into the lake. This siltation caused the lake to shrink and grow shallower. The current average depth of about 2m is maintained by a massive irrigation system installed during the colonial period.

Today, Lac Alaotra is less than 30% of its former size (which was around 75,000 hectares), expanding only after periods of heavy rain. The surrounding land is growing increasingly barren and can no longer produce enough rice.

The region's largest town and service centre, Ambatondrazaka, was once lakefront property but now lies a good 25km from the shore (less if the lake is flooded). The lake's main attraction for visitors is the 74 bird species, primarily water birds, which live around the lake. Unfortunately, the use of pesticides, the introduction of carnivorous black bass in the lake and widespread poaching have severely decimated bird populations. The only mammal species around the lake is the grey bamboo lemur which is also the victim of rampant poaching. There's good coverage of the area's problems in Gerald Durrell's book, *The Aye-Aye and I.*

Route des Contrabandiers

This five to six day trek connects the village of Imerimandroso near Lac Alaotra with Anjahambe, 48km by road from the east coast. Historically, the route was used for smuggling goods from Réunion and Mauritius into the landlocked Merina highlands, hence the name Route des Contrabandiers (Smugglers' Path).

But be warned: this is a tough trek, especially when it's raining, and is only for those who thrive on tough trekking. One reader described the eastern part of the path as 'either six inches of oozy bilharzia-infested mud, or steep steps and eroded gullies of slippery clay'. Yet just about everyone who has done the trek has been mightily impressed with the lakes, rainforests, villages and mountains along the way.

The track begins 6km north-east of Imerimandroso and heads downhill through rugged country all the way to Anjahambe. There are several villages along the way; the major ones are Sahatavy, where there's a small shop selling basic supplies, and Andasibe (not to be confused with the Andasibe on the railway line further south). A portion of the route follows the Manambato River. The trail usually ends (or starts) at Anjahambe where you can catch a *taxi-brousse* to the village of Ansikafoka on the coast just north of Mahambo.

About halfway between Anjahambe and Ansikafoka, you can stay at the village of Vavatenina where there are some unnamed *bungalows* for hire for about FMg 10,000. Some villages along the way have a small hotel, and in most villages someone will offer you a room in a local hut – but you should still take camping equipment because you'll never be able to rely on being in a village with a hotel when you want to stop for the night.

This track traverses a large and rugged tract of the eastern rainforest. It's a good idea to take a guide. You can easily hire a guide at your starting point, or along the way; they may also act as a porter and carry your gear from one village to another. Expect to pay from FMg 20,000 to FMg 30,000 per day for

a guide. A map is requisite. Pick up a detailed one from the FTM office (see the Madagascar Facts for the Visitor chapter).

You'll have the best chance of good weather between May and October. Trekkers need to bring their own food; there's normally plenty of water around but it will have to be purified.

To reach the trailhead, get off the train at Ambatondrazaka and catch a taxi-brousse north along the eastern shore of Lac Alaotra to Imerimandroso. For a more scenic route, get off the train at Vohidiala and catch a taxi-brousse north to Tanambe and thence down to Vohitsara on the lake shore (don't confuse this with Vohitsara on the coast). From there, you'll be able to find pirogues crossing the lake to Imerimandroso.

Places to Stay & Eat

The Chinese-owned *Hôtel Voahirana* in Ambatondrazaka has rooms for about FMg 15,000. The best option is the *Hôtel Max* near the railway station, which has rooms for FMg 14,000 to FMg 18,000. If you want to get an early start on the Route des Contrabandiers there's also the basic *Hotel Bellevue* in the pleasant town of Imerimandroso.

Getting There & Away

Air Air Madagascar (☎ 813 75) flies from Tana to Ambatondrazaka (US$43), and often onto Toamasina (US$32), on Monday and Friday.

Train Although the train trip between Tana and Ambatondrazaka, via Moramanga, is subject to long delays and breakdowns, it's still the nicest way to go. At the time of research, the track had been damaged yet again, and only cargo and mining trains went some of the way. Normally, the train runs about three times a week in both directions and costs FMg14,500/22,500 for 2nd/1st class betweeen Moramanga and Ambatondrazaka.

Taxi-brousse From the Taxi-brousse Station East in Tana you can travel as far as

EASTERN MADAGASCAR

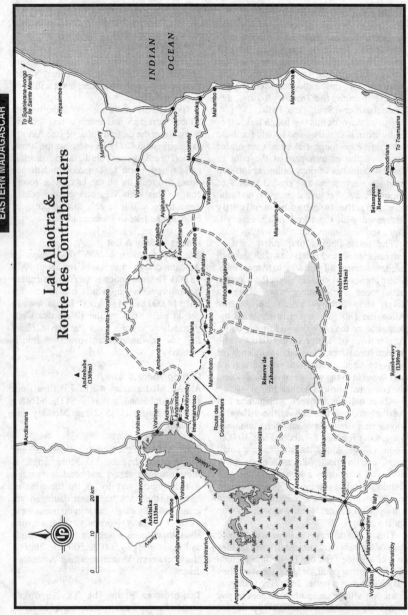

Lac Alaotra &
Route des Contrabandiers

INDIAN OCEAN

To Soanierana-Ivongo
(for Île Sainte Marie)

To Toamasina

Ambatondrazaka from where other vehicles travel to Tanambe on the far north-western edge of the lake. Tanambe is a good place to rent a pirogue across the lake.

MANDRAKA

Near Mandraka, east of Manjakandriana and along the railway line between Tana and Moramanga, is a fascinating private reserve – **Réserve de Peyrieras** – operated by author, researcher and naturalist M André Peyrieras.

Here he raises endemic plants and non-mammalian animals for study, captive breeding and export. These include butterflies and urania and comet moths; giant centipedes and pill bugs; and assorted reptiles and amphibians, such as crocodiles, geckos, chameleons and frogs. Although some of the animals go to collectors to be bottled or mounted on pins, local people do see evidence of a monetary return for preserving the forest habitat of such diverse fauna.

The reserve presents a good opportunity to see a large cross section of some beautiful Malagasy fauna and makes a rewarding day trip from the capital, especially for those with private transport. Alternatively, it's a convenient stopover between Tana and Périnet Reserve, and most organised tours heading east will stop here for lunch and a look around en route to Périnet.

If you have your own vehicle, head for the village of Mandraka and follow the signs. If travelling independently, it's best to take the Tana–Toamasina train to Mandraka from where it's about an hour's walk – follow the signs or ask directions. Guided tours in French are provided by Malagasy staff, who will allow you to handle and photograph the animals. There's a restaurant on site, but no accommodation is available.

MORAMANGA
• Telephone Area Code: 4

The town of Moramanga lies 30km west of Andasibe and is popular with Périnet-bound tour groups. It is a useful base for exploring the nearby reserve, but if you want to go on any early-morning or night walks around Périnet you should stay in or near the reserve (see Places to Stay & Eat in Andasibe).

The only sites of interest in town are the **market**; the **memorial** to the Chinese workers who built the highway; and the surprisingly good **Musée de la Gendarmerie** at Camp Tristany – the last of these is open daily (look for the signs around the market). The BTM and BNI-CL banks in town change money.

Chutes de la Mort

These large waterfalls lie 53km south of Moramanga on the road towards Anosibe An'Ala. To whet your expectations, along the way you'll pass the village of Niagarakely (Little Niagara). Taxis-brousse run occasionally but the route is passable only during the dry season.

Places to Stay & Eat

The largest and most popular hotel is the *Grand Hôtel* (☎ 325 15) opposite the market/taxi-brousse terminal. The friendly manager speaks English. Singles/doubles (some with the largest bathrooms in the country) cost FMg 35,000/42,500, while bungalows cost FMg 55,000. In the lovely restaurant, breakfast costs FMg 6500 and other meals about FMg 8500. Near the Grand, also on the main road, the *Emeraude Hôtel* costs FMg 37,000/47,000, and has a great pâtisserie downstairs.

Another good option, which has also been recommended by several readers, is the *Hotel Restaurant Mirasoa* (☎ 621 49), just back from the main road as you enter from the west. Rooms are good value and range from FMg 16,000 to FMg 20,000.

The cheapest place to stay is the *Hôtel Fivami*, opposite the Coq d'Or. It's quite basic and not the cleanest place but rooms are a cheap, and negotiable, FMg 12,000.

Some diplomats rate the garlic frogs' legs at the *Restaurant Coq d'Or* as outstanding, and even worth a day trip from Tana! Other tasty meals range from FMg 7000 to FMg 10,000. Another good place with an extensive menu is the Chinese restaurant, the *Guangzhou*, opposite the Grand Hôtel.

Getting There & Away

Train The track between Tana and Moramanga, which continues on to Ambatondrazaka, was under repair at the time of research. Normally, a train travels three times a week between Tana and Moramanga (FMg 11,500 for 1st class).

Taxi-brousse Taxis-brousse (FMg 7000; two hours) leave regularly from Tana's Taxi-brousse Station East. From Moramanga, there are regular direct taxi-brousse connections to Andasibe. Travelling between Andasibe or Moramanga and Toamasina is often a little more problematic. From Andasibe, it's best to wait along the main Tana–Toamasina road and flag down whatever comes by; from Moramanga, something will eventually leave from the taxi-brousse station.

PARC NATIONAL D'ANDASIBE-MANTADIA

This 12,810 hectare park is sometimes known as Réserve Spéciale d'Analamazaotra (after the river which traverses it), but is more popularly known simply as Périnet. This vast park lies in a region of low hills covered by degraded forest and is punctuated by a couple of beautiful small lakes. Most of the local people are Betsimisaraka and work at the graphite mine in Mantadia. The best time to visit the national park is between September and January, or in May (just before the June–September winter period). Most travellers stay in or near the village of Andasibe (see later in this chapter). If you have a tent, you can camp behind the office at the park entrance.

Permits & Guides

Like all national parks in Madagascar, you can buy a three day permit for FMg 50,000 at the ANGAP office in Tana, but it's far easier to buy it at the entrance to Périnet.

Don't hire any guide who approaches you in Andasibe, or even Moramanga – official

---

The Legend of the Babakoto

One local legend about the origin of the indri goes something like this: a man called Koto and his young son left their village to collect honey in the forest. When they failed to return, the village dispatched a search party. They were unable to find the father or the son but did find two indris gazing down from the trees. The people guessed that Koto and his son had mysteriously been transformed into lemurs, hence the Malagasy name for the indri, babakoto, which manes Papa Koto. Fortunately for this spectacular lemur, this human ancestry has rendered it *fady* (taboo) to kill or eat the indri. ■

---

guides (compulsory) will be allocated to you at the park entrance. (Every guide speaks French as well as one or more other language: English, German, Spanish, Italian or Japanese.) At the time of research, local guides had formed an association, and were not too keen about the new pricing regulations set up by ANGAP. The schedule of prices established by the guides association are listed at the entrance and start at FMg 20,000 for a two hour tour. ANGAP is planning to reduce these fees to FMg 2500 per person per visit.

Périnet Reserve

The entrance to Périnet Reserve is an easy 2km walk along a tarmac road from Andasibe. Because the reserve is small, most of it can be covered in short walks. The best time to see anything is early in the morning – from around 7 am – when it's not too hot for lemurs and visitors alike.

Before you start exploring the park, visit the ANGAP office beside the park entrance which has a small display, and some posters and maps for sale. The maps available at the park (FMg 10,000) are better than the normal ANGAP maps, and while maps are not particularly necessary (you must have a guide anyway) they do make a nice souvenir. At the park entrance there is also a small information office and a souvenir stall.

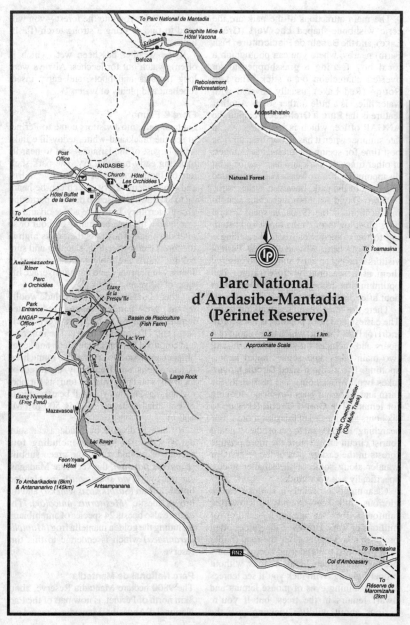

To Parc National de Mantadia

Graphite Mine &
Hôtel Vacona

Erikaná

Beloza

Reboisement
(Reforestation)

Andasifahatelo

Post
Office

ANDASIBE

Church

Hôtel
Les Orchidées

Natural Forest

Hôtel Buffet
de la Gare

To
Antananarivo

Analamazaotra
River

Parc
à Orchidées

To Toamasina

Park
Entrance

Étang
de la
Presqu'île

ANGAP
Office

Bassin de Pisciculture
(Fish Farm)

**Parc National
d'Andasibe-Mantadia
(Périnet Reserve)**

Lac Vert

0   0.5   1 km
Approximate Scale

Large Rock

Étang Nymphea
(Frog Pond)

Canal

Mazavasoa

Ancien Chemin Muletier
(Old Mule Track)

Lac Rouge

Feon'nyala
Hôtel

To Ambarikadera (8km)
& Antananarivo (145km)

Antsampanana

To Toamasina

RN2

Col d'Amboasary

To
Réserve de
Maromizaha
(2km)

The main attractions of the park are the eerie wishbone-shaped **Lac Vert** (Green Lake); and the **Bassin de Piscicuiture** (Fish Farm) nearby, where you can photograph a local boy feeding a grasshopper to an overfed chameleon on a stick. The **Lac Rouge** (Red Lake), usually covered with water lilies, is a little further south. Another feature is the **Parc à Orchidées**, behind the ANGAP office, which is less attractive in late summer when it has all but dried up. The best time for seeing the orchids is October; at other times the park and lake can be a bit disappointing for flowers. The undisputed highlight of the park, however, is the indri.

When David Attenborough came searching for indris in the 1950s, he spent several days plodding through the forest and listening to their raucous call before catching a glimpse of them. Nowadays, few Périnet visitors who get an early start fail to observe them at a reasonably close range. The optimum time to begin looking is about an hour after daybreak.

There are three organised walking trails. The easiest, and most popular, is the **Circuit Indri** (or Petit Circuit) which takes about two hours and includes only the fish farm and two main lakes, and some limited lemur-spotting. The medium-sized **Circuit Moyen** takes two to four hours and also visits the farm and lakes but goes further out looking for lemurs. The **Grand Circuit** takes up to six hours and does all of this plus more lemur searching. If you want to get off the standard tourist circuit and explore the more pristine forests in the eastern part of the reserve, or wander along some of the smaller tracks, specifically ask your guide.

Clear nights, especially in summer, can be glorious – full of eerie sounds, with towering rainforest trees set against a backdrop of millions of stars. However, the guides often prefer to take visitors along the road (rather than the forest trails) during nocturnal tours because trails can be hazardous without proper lighting. With luck you'll see tenrecs and the shining eyes of mouse lemurs and dwarf lemurs in the trees, but if you're serious about wildlife viewing, ask the guides to take you into the forest – you will need to find or bring a strong torch (flashlight).

If the weather has been wet (which is often), watch out for leeches. Always wear long trousers and boots, and carry insect repellent and plenty of water.

Flora & Fauna

Quite simply, most visitors come to Périnet to see the black-and-white, teddy-like indri – the largest of the lemurs – and to hear its haunting early-morning cry. The park shelters 62 family groups of two or five indris, and this trademark cry, which can be heard up to 3km away, is used to define a particular group's territory. Indris are active on and off throughout the day, beginning an hour or so after daybreak. They pass their days high in the forest canopy feeding, sleeping and sunbaking. Indris are monogamous, mating in January or February, and have an average life span of 80 years.

Other Malagasy favourites include woolly lemurs, grey bamboo lemurs, red-fronted lemurs, aye-ayes (which are very rarely seen) and 11 species of tenrec. The immense and colourful Parson's chameleon and seven other chameleon species are also found here. (Chameleons are frequently captured by local boys and presented to tourists for photographing. For this you will be expected to give a small donation of FMg 500 to FMg 1000.)

Birdlife is diverse by Madagascar standards with 109 species, including four species of ground roller, the green sunbird *(Cinnyrus notatus)*, the very rare Madagascar red owl *(Tyto soumagnii)*, the slender-billed flufftail *(Sarothrurus watersi)* and the brown mesite *(Mesitornis unicolor)*. The reserve also boasts 24 species of amphibians, including the golden mantella frog *(Mantella aurantiaca)* which is endemic to this tiny reserve.

Parc National de Mantadia

The 9800 hectare Mantadia Reserve, about 8km north of Périnet, is now part of the Parc National d'Andasibe-Mantadia. Created primarily to protect the indri, it has two species of lemur not found in Périnet. The park is vastly unexplored and undeveloped, and has dozens of magnificent waterfalls. With a (compulsory) guide, you can go on some extraordinary treks taking anywhere from two hours to three days, or even longer. Get your permit and guide at the entrance to Périnet.

Mantadia had been the subject of litigation between conservationists and the graphite mine, so neither party was legally able to build a main road to the park entrance (but ANGAP plans to finish one in a few years). Camping is possible at the park entrance, and at a spot about 15km north of the entrance. You can get there along the unpaved roads from Andasibe or Fanovana.

AMBARIKADERA

Ambarikadera is a new tourist restaurant and bungalow complex in a nice quiet setting between Moramanga and Andasibe. From here, there's a stimulating 16km return day walk to the lovely waterfall at **Ambodirina**. The track, known as the **Route de Lakato**, turns south 150m west of the Ambarikadera bungalows, near the bridge.

RÉSERVE DE MAROMIZAHA

This 10,000 hectare reserve, south-east of Périnet, is not yet a protected reserve, but is still relatively remote and offers the best camping in the area. It is home to 11 species of lemur, including two species not found in Périnet: the diademed sifaka and the black-and-white ruffed lemur (these species are also found at Mantadia).

There are lots of walking tracks as well as good stands of rainforest and panoramic views. The Périnet guides will also be happy to organise trips into this area.

ANDASIBE
- Telephone Area Code: 461

The former logging centre of Andasibe is frequently used by travellers as a base for visiting the world-famous Périnet Reserve. The village itself is small, pleasant and a bit medieval, and does merit a couple of hours

exploring. About 8km along the road to Toamasina is **Maromiza hill**, which provides a good vantage point over the region.

Places to Stay & Eat

For campers, the Hôtel Buffet de la Gare (see below) has a *campground* 1km from the village for FMg 10,000 per tent. It sits amid guava trees near the river, and is an ideal spot for a swim. Alternatively, if you want to be kept awake by the haunting screeches of the indri, you can camp at the park entrance – get a permit at the ANGAP office, and ask to leave your gear at the office when you are not around.

In lieu of a railway station, Andasibe has the *Hôtel Buffet de la Gare* (☎ 2) with a buffet, bar and dining room. This impressive structure, built in 1938, is reminiscent of an alpine lodge. Fairly ordinary singles/doubles in the main building cost FMg 27,000/33,000, and seven pleasant bungalows across the road cost FMg 77,000/90,000 (the older bungalows are not as good for FMg 44,000 each). Despite its mixed reviews, most people wind up eating at the restaurant, with its waiters in starched white uniforms. Malagasy meals cost FMg 7000 to FMg 9000; European food costs a little more.

Alternatively, the small, wooden *Hôtel Les Orchidées* in the village (look for the sign) costs FMg 20,000/28,000/32,500 for a comfortable single/double/triple with a communal (but very clean) bathroom. The hotel looks and feels like something out of the Wild West. The meals at the restaurant, three doors down, are a little overpriced, but good. A 'petit dejeuner complet' costs FMg 6000, but you may want to give the pizza a miss:

Les Orchidées served the most fascinating pizza we've ever had in Madagascar. It looked like a slice of bread covered with some tomatoes and an egg. Cheese was completely missing, The cook told us that he had completed a course at the Hilton in Tana to learn the art of preparing pizzas.
Sanne Freidrich, Switzerland

Only 200m from the T-junction leading to Andasibe from the Toamasina–Tana road is the recommended *Hôtel Feon'nyala* (☎ 305 18). It's in a lovely setting and a room in the hotel or in a bungalow costs FMg 28,000/35,000 for a double/twin bed with shared facilities, or FMg 45,000/49,000 with private bathroom. The restaurant, where the menu du jour costs around FMg 15,000, is very good. The kitchen will even provide sandwiches for your jungle treks.

The up-market place is the *Hôtel Vacona* (☎ 213 94), aka *Vakona Forest Lodge*, about 7km past Andasibe village. Luxurious bungalows cost F260. There is even a crocodile zoo to inspect. No public transport goes past the hotel, and it is too far to walk to Périnet, so there is no point staying there unless you have your own transport. However, it is the best place to base yourself for explorations into the undeveloped Parc National de Mantadia.

Getting There & Away

Train Andasibe lies on the railway line between Tana and Toamasina. At the time of research, the track had been damaged but once repaired, trains should run in either direction three times a week. Refer to the Moramanga section earlier for more details.

Taxi-brousse When coming from Tana, some travellers get off the Tana–Toamasina taxi-brousse at the T-junction, but from there you will have to walk (about 6km) to Andasibe, or wait for another irregular taxi-brousse. It is quicker and less hassle to get a regular Tana–Moramanga taxi-brousse, and from there get to Andasibe on a regular taxi-brousse (FMg 2000) which will drop you off at your hotel.

Coming from Toamasina, taxis-brousse rarely stop at Moramanga, and never go to Andasibe, so getting off at the T-junction for Andasibe and waiting for ongoing transport is usually the only option.

Taxi Taxis may be hired in Tana for a day trip to Périnet. It's not a good deal, however, because the trip takes at least three hours each way – and costs heaps – and you'll

arrive too late in the morning to hear the indri.

CANAL DES PANGALANES

The Canal des Pangalanes is a collection of natural rivers and artificial lakes which stretches an incredible 665km along the east coast from Toamasina to Farafangana. Of this, 420km from Toamasina to Mananjary is currently navigable. Whether travelling independently or on an organised tour, you can stop along the way and explore **Lac Rasoamasay**, which is being developed for water sports; **Lac Rasobe**, which is particularly popular for swimming (the sea is full of sharks around there); the pretty traditional village of **Andevoranto**; and the main town **Akanin'ny Nofy** (Nest of Dreams). The best times to tour the region are March to May and September to December.

Do-it-Yourself

It is probably best to start in Toamasina where you are likely to get some useful advice from travel agencies, and find more regular transport. You can either travel by boat down the canal, by taxi-brousse along a road parallel to the canal, or some of the way by train. A combination of all three is best, but allow plenty of time.

For boat travel from Toamasina, start at the *gare fluviale* (river station) just west of the railway station near Maréchal de Lattre Tassigny. There's no scheduled transport along the canal, so you'll have to ask around. Take anything going to a village with accommodation (if you don't have a tent) – refer to Places to Stay & Eat later in this section. Every day keep asking about onward public boats, or pirogues or dhows which can be chartered.

To explore the region from one base on the canal, get a train to the tiny village of Andrano-Koditra from Tana (about eight hours) or Toamasina (90 minutes). From here you can rent a pirogue and/or trek around the lake, and stay at the Pangalanes and Bush-House hotels (see Places to Stay & Eat). Another option is to get off along the road between Brickaville and Toamasina and hike (at least 20km), or rent a vehicle, to the shores of the lakes and canal.

Organised Tours

Most organised tours usually just cruise from Toamasina to the Malotrando, Ampitabe or Irangy lakes, stay at a bungalow, organise a few water sports and easy treks and then return. Rarely do they travel along the canal for any great distance. Following are three reliable agencies which organise trips along the canal:

Softline (☎/fax (5) 329 75) is the best, most luxurious and most expensive option and uses the yacht *Mpanjakamena*. This allows you to water-ski and swim, and visit lemur parks and villages along the way. For departure dates and costs check ads in the newspapers in Tana, or visit Softline's office at 20 Blvd Joffre, Toamasina. It sometimes organises six-day trips from Toamasina as far as Mananjary.

Boutique Hibiscus (☎ (5) 334 03) is the best place in Toamasina to investigate organised tours down the canal.

Vanofotsy Voyages (☎ (2) 205 21 or ☎ (5) 329 06) is based at the railway station in Tana and organises train trips on the Micheline to Ankanin'ny Nofy, and boats around the canal and lakes. Prices are lower than others, but the quality and reliability may not be there.

Jardin la Mer (☎ (7) 940 80), the main hotel in Mananjary, is a good place to ask about an organised tour.

Places to Stay & Eat

If you travel along the canal yourself, you can stay at several cheap places along the way. At Ambila-Lemaitso there are rooms at the *Hôtel Relais Malaky* (☎ (540) 260 13), the *Hôtel Everglades* (☎ (540) 442 47) or the bungalows at the Cocotiers Plage. At Brickaville there's the *Hôtel Des Amis* and the *Hôtel Restaurant Le Florida*. At Vatomandary try the *Hôtel Deerien* or *Hôtel Fontsy*, and at Mahanaro the *Hôtel Huo Wai Min* is recommended.

There is also a choice of expensive places to stay on the lakes or canal but getting to them will involve some effort, or expense (if you take transfers organised by the hotels).

At Ankanin'ny Nofy, on the northern shore of Lac Farihy Ampitabe, is the friendly and pretty *Hôtel Pangalanes* (☎ (5) 334 03). Comfortable bungalows on stilts above the water cost from F200 per person for half-board; meals are F55.

The *Village Atafana* (☎ (2) 223 64 or ☎ (5) 205) is in a lovely position within walking distance of the beach and offers huge bungalows for FMg 65,000 with bathroom. However, the meals are a bit overpriced at around FMg 25,000.

The area is rich in vegetation and the hotels offer hikes in the surrounding forest. All sorts of nautical activities may be undertaken on the lake (the sea in this region is rough and full of sharks), such as sailboarding, fishing and pirogue trips.

Also on Lac Farihy Ampitabe, but not within walking distance of the beach, is the recommended *Bush-House* (☎ (2) 331 85; fax (2) 251 17) which costs F165/200 for half-board/full-board; meals are F45.

TOAMASINA (TAMATAVE)
• Telephone Area Code: 5

Toamasina (commonly known as Tamatave) is the country's largest port, responsible for 70% of all cargo traffic to/from Madagascar. With a population of nearly 200,000, the city lies on a long and scenic stretch of coastline, and is far nicer than other regional cities such as Mahajanga or Antsiranana. Most visitors will happily spend a day or two pottering around, breaking up the journey between Tana and Île Sainte Marie or organising a trip down the Canal des Pangalanes.

Toamasina is probably the favourite holiday destination of the Malagasy and is to Tana what Brighton is to London or Nice is to Paris. Unlike Brighton or Nice, however, the sea is not friendly – there's a beach, but it's unwise to swim because of high levels of pollution and because throngs of sharks are attracted by the abattoir around the corner.

The origin of the Malagasy name is disputed. One theory states that it was derived from the Portuguese name São Tomas (St Thomas), while another attributes it to King Radama I's first visit to the seaside in 1817.

EASTERN MADAGASCAR

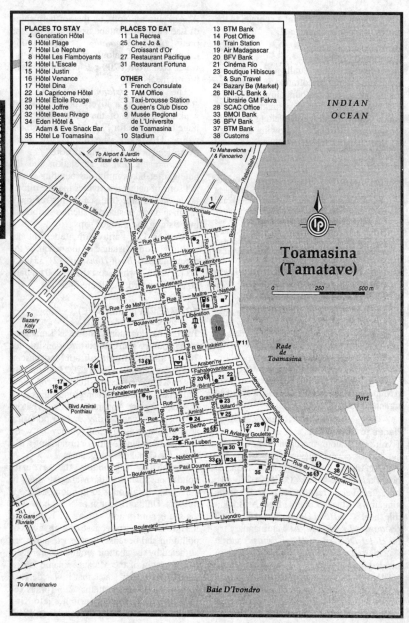

PLACES TO STAY
4   Generation Hôtel
6   Hôtel Plage
7   Hôtel Le Neptune
8   Hôtel Les Flamboyants
12 Hôtel L'Escale
15 Hôtel Justin
16 Hôtel Venance
17 Hôtel Dina
22 La Capricorne Hôtel
29 Hôtel Étoile Rouge
30 Hôtel Joffre
32 Hôtel Beau Rivage
34 Eden Hôtel &
     Adam & Eve Snack Bar
35 Hôtel Le Toamasina

PLACES TO EAT
11 La Recrea
25 Chez Jo &
     Croissant d'Or
27 Restaurant Pacifique
31 Restaurant Fortuna

OTHER
1   French Consulate
2   TAM Office
3   Taxi-brousse Station
9   Queen's Club Disco
9   Musée Regional
     de L'Universite
     de Toamasina
10 Stadium

13 BTM Bank
14 Post Office
18 Train Station
19 Air Madagascar
20 BFV Bank
21 Cinéma Rio
23 Boutique Hibiscus
     & Sun Travel
24 Bazary Be (Market)
26 BNI-CL Bank &
     Librairie GM Fakra
28 SCAC Office
33 BMOI Bank
36 BFV Bank
37 BTM Bank
38 Customs

INDIAN
OCEAN

Toamasina
(Tamatave)

0   250   500 m

To Airport & Jardin
d'Essai de L'Ivoloina

To Mahavelona
& Fanoarivo

Rue le Conte de Lille

Boulevard   Labourdonnais

Prasteur

Boulevard

Rue du Petit

Rue Victor   Hugo

Boulevard

Rue Cuyemer

Rue

Augagneur

Rue Lieutenant

Rue F de Mahy

Boulevard de la Liberté

Boulevard   de la   Convention

Boulevard

Fraternite

Thouars

Rue   Jetée

Letimbre

Noel

Maitre

Rue   de   la

Bernard

Rue   de   Saint Pierre

Liberation

R Bir Hakeim

Nativel

Quiros

O

To
Bazary
Kely
(50m)

To
Gare
Fluviale

To Antananarivo

Rade
de
Toamasina

Port

Araben'ny
Fahaleovantena

Araben'ny
Fahaleovantena

Blvd Amiral
Ponthiau

Marecal

Rue Choiseul

Foch

Rue Lieutenant

Berard

Rue   Bouvet

Grandidier

Amiral   Billard

Rue   des   Hovas

Rue   Bertho

R Aviateur Goulette

Rue Lubert

Boulevard

Nationale

Rue   Paul Dourer

Rue   Ile-de-France

Boulevard   de   Livondro

Boulevard   Ratsimilaho

Rue du
Commerce

Rue   Flacourt

Rue
Romain

Rue   Delisse

Batterie

Baie D'Ivondro

It's said that the king knelt to taste the water and reputedly stated the bleeding obvious: *Toa masina* ('It is salty').

History

Although Toamasina had its earliest beginnings as a pirate settlement, things didn't really get started until the early 19th century. In 1807, the same year that the British parliament voted to abolish slavery in its colonies, Napoleon sent a commercial agent, Sylvain Roux, to represent French trading interests on the east coast. In 1811, however, the British governor of Mauritius, Sir Robert Farquhar, sent ships to take the port for Britain and thereby halt the region's thriving slave trade.

Toamasina was placed under the protection of Mauritius and remained so until the Treaty of Paris in 1814. During that period a hearty trade was built up between the two islands and the town grew into a busy port.

Upon the involuntary departure of the British, one Jean-René, a Betsimisaraka interpreter (who had worked for Sylvain Roux), proclaimed himself ruler over the east coast and set up a residence at Toamasina. He reigned for three years before joining a confederation with the Merina king, Radama I. His tomb may now be seen near the mouth of the Ivoloina River, north of Toamasina. Sylvain Roux was buried on Île Sainte Marie.

In 1845 there was a skirmish when the British and French became unhappy about Queen Ranavalona I's imposition of trade restrictions on Europeans. In the end, the Malagasy were successful at repelling their joint attack on the port. In 1883, in an attempt to force the Malagasy to submit to the proposed treaty of protectorate, the French again bombarded Toamasina. Again, they were repelled by Malagasy forces. In 1885, the treaty was signed and Madagascar came under French rule.

During political strife in the early 1990s, the Toamasina region was the area of greatest resistance to change, maintaining support for former President Didier Ratsiraka, whose family is of Betsimisaraka origin. Militant factions were responsible for destroying the railway bridge which effectively cut the main supply lines to Tana.

Orientation

Toamasina's town planners have graced the city with wide avenues and boulevards lined with flamboyants (poincianas) and coconut trees. At times, the scale leaves the place seeming almost quiet and empty, with pedestrians and tiny *pousse-pousses* lost against the larger backdrop. The main commercial street is Blvd Joffre. The 6km-long Blvd Ratsimilaho along the coast is the favourite promenade for locals and holiday-makers. The broadest street, Araben'ny Fahaleovantena (also known as Ave Poincaré), runs east-west from the waterfront to the railway station.

Information

Money The main BTM bank is not far from the railway station; the main BFV bank is on the corner of Blvd Joffre and Araben'ny Fahaleovantena; the BNI-CL bank is also along Blvd Joffre; and the BMOI bank is a little further south along the same street. They all change money, but some travellers report less success at the main BFV bank.

There are also BFV and BTM banks in the port area, but the staff may ask you to go to the main branches to change money. The Hôtel Le Neptune will also change travellers' cheques for guests and non-guests at a reasonable rate.

Post & Communications The main post office is on Araben'ny Fahaleovantena opposite the old town hall. It's open from 8 am to noon and 2 to 6 pm weekdays, and until noon on Saturdays.

Travel Agencies Like most mid-sized towns, there are a few decent travel agencies worth approaching if you need to book flights and tours, hire vehicles, or obtain some local advice. Sun Travel (☎ 333 82), on Blvd Joffre, can book expensive packages by air to Île Sainte Marie. Boutique Hibiscus (☎ 334 03), next door, is a very good place to investigate organised tours down the Canal des Pangalanes, and to organise bookings at some hotels along the canal. It also handles other local tours, for example to Ivoloina park for F35 per person. Chez Jo (refer to Places to Eat) handles bookings for diving courses and bungalows at Mahambo.

Bookshop The only bookshop in town is the Librairie GM Fakra, right next to the BNI-CL bank. It has a reasonable range of French-language novels and magazines, and sells postcards.

Markets

Toamasina's Bazary Be (Big Market) lies between Rue Amiral Billard and Rue Bertho, and offers fruit, vegetables, snacks, exotic spices and handicrafts. Bazary Kely (Little Market) occupies the ruins of a commercial complex (which was burned out in 1973) on Blvd de la Fidelité, about 250m west of the railway station. There you can buy fish as well as a variety of local produce.

Musée Regional de l'Université de Toamasina

This is the best museum in the country, so if you have any interest in Malagasy culture make sure you visit. It contains modest but interesting displays of traditional musical, cooking and hunting implements, among other things, and a full-scale, furnished thatched hut in the grounds. The helpful guides can provide a full explanation and tour (in French). The museum is directly opposite the Hôtel Plage, and is open from 9 am to 4 pm every day but Monday; a donation in lieu of an entrance fee is requested.

Île aux Prunes (Nosy Alanana)

This small island north-east of the port is a one-hour journey from Toamasina by chartered motor pirogue. Surrounded by a coral reef, it serves as a mini marine reserve and a refuge for fruit bats. The best way out there is to take an organised tour. Ask at one of the travel agencies listed in the Information section earlier.

Jardin d'Essai de l'Ivoloina

These pretty botanic gardens are on the banks of the Ivoloina River 13km north of Toamasina. Here you'll see a small selection of the flora and fauna found in eastern Madagascar, including caged and wild lemurs (feeding by visitors is certainly outlawed). The park is a highlight of the region, and definitely worth a visit. All explanations are in Malagasy or French, but you can buy some handy notes (FMg 2500) in English which describe the zoo and its 'guests'.

The Jersey Wildlife Preservation Trust in the UK, and the Duke University in the USA, among others, have set up an education centre, captive breeding programs for endangered species and a halfway house for animals being reintroduced into the wild.

The gardens are open from 9 am to 5 pm every day and entry costs FMg 10,000. You can also hire a pirogue around the lake; or bring some food and drink from Toamasina for a picnic on the shores.

A taxi to the park entrance from town will cost around FMg 30,000 return. Funny little taxis-brousse from Toamasina to Ivoloina (FMg 1500) leave every hour or two. From Ivoloina village it is a lovely 4km walk to the park entrance.

Places to Stay – bottom end

There's a problem with mosquitoes in Toamasina; the bottom-end hotels rarely offer any protection, so bring your own mosquito coils, repellent and/or net.

On Blvd Amiral Ponthiau, near the railway station, there are three cheapies in a row – at least one sells condoms at reception, giving you some idea of the normal clientele. Women on their own may want to avoid these places. The *Hôtel Dina* (☎ 333 14), in a big old colonial-style building, has large rooms from FMg 14,000 to FMg 20,000. The rooms at the *Hôtel Justin* (which is a lot easier to say than its former name, Vakinankaratra) range from as little as FMg

DEANNA SWANEY

DAVID CURL

DAVID CURL

Top Left: Lac Tritriva, central Madagascar, is subject to numerous superstitions.
Top Right: The avenue of baobabs north of Morondava, western Madagascar.
Bottom: Parc National de Isalo, western Madagascar, protects a series of colourful and dramatic sandstone massifs.

ROBERT WILLOX

DAVID CURL

DAVID CURL

Top Left: Travel by taxi-brousse can be slow and fraught by poor roads.
Top Right: A morning wash at the village pump, Ambalavao, central Madagascar.
Bottom: Painfully slow it may be, but travel by zebu-cart is sometimes the only option
             in remote parts of the island. It's all part of the adventure of Madagascar!

11,000 to FMg 17,000. The best of the three is the *Hôtel Venance*, with a reasonable Malagasy restaurant downstairs. Rooms cost FMg 17,000 – but it's often full.

Alternatively, try the *Hôtel L'Escale*, which is handy to the railway station but in a noisy location. Singles/doubles for FMg 32,500/45,000 are overpriced, but negotiable if business is slow – which is most of the time. Rooms with two bedrooms and a kitchen for FMg 70,000 are better value.

There are two other good, cheap and central options. The *Hôtel Beau Rivage* has friendly staff and clean rooms with fan from FMg 25,000 to FMg 30,000. The *Eden Hôtel* (☎ 330 36), next to the Adam & Eve Snack Bar, has rooms for FMg 37,000 to FMg 42,000 – but the rooms at the front with a balcony are noisy.

Places to Stay – middle & top end

The *Hôtel Plage* (☎ 320 90), opposite the stadium, is a noisy, ramshackle sort of place. It has a rambling South Seas atmosphere, but at night prostitutes ply the hotel bar and terrace so it isn't for everyone. Single or double rooms cost FMg 25,000 with communal facilities. It is definitely worth paying more for a room with bathroom (and hot water) and views for FMg 37,000.

A previously popular place, the *Hôtel Étoile Rouge* (☎ 322 90), has been getting bad reviews lately. The rooms cost around FMg 50,000 and there is oodles of hot water, but some rooms are unclean and noisy.

The colonial *Hôtel Joffre* (☎ 323 90), in a great location on Blvd Joffre, has rooms for FMg 68,000 with air-con and hot water. This price is pretty good value, but for views you end up paying as much as FMg 120,000. It is regularly used by organised tours, and is often full. Book ahead.

One of the best in this range is the *Generation Hôtel* (☎ 321 05), along the northern end of Blvd Joffre. The service is good and the staff are friendly. Large, comfortable singles/doubles/triples with fan cost FMg 59,500/68,950/87,250.

Also worth checking out are the *Hôtel Les Flamboyants* (☎ 323 50), a little west of the

Hôtel Plage, with rooms for FMg 32,000/39,000 with fan/air-con; and the *Hôtel Le Toamasina* (☎ 335 49) and new *La Capricorne Hôtel* (☎ 331 66), which both have luxurious rooms with TV and air-con for about FMg 70,000.

The classiest place to stay is the *Hôtel Le Neptune* (☎ 322 26), right on the beach. This hotel boasts a casino, nightclub, swimming pool and 20 air-con rooms for F425 a single/double.

Places to Eat

Chez Jo, in a nice setting overlooking the busy Blvd Joffre, specialises in pizzas but you will need to order a large one (FMg 15,000) if you are the least bit hungry. Overlooking the unexciting port, and close to Hôtel Plage, *La Recrea* is one of the very few places in the whole country with a menu in English. Malagasy plats du jour cost FMg 7000; other meals are from FMg 8000 to FMg 12,000. It is great for breakfast, and a good place to meet other travellers.

Strongly recommended for good value and tasty food, in a place popular with locals, is the *Buffet de la Gare* in the railway station. A good zebu steak and chips (French fries) will set you back about FMg 10,000.

Of the hotels, the *Generation Hôtel* is deservedly popular. The service is excellent, as is the decor and range. Most meals cost from FMg 12,000 to FMg 15,000. You can enjoy a beer (at a reasonable FMg 6000) and other drinks in the outdoor bar (which attracts less hawkers and beggars than the Hôtel Joffre).

The *Hôtel Joffre* is a charming place with old-fashioned (ie, a little slow) service. The menu du jour is occasionally worth a splurge for FMg 25,000; other meals cost about FMg 12,000. For good-value pasta, pizza, and a reasonable cappuccino, the restaurant downstairs at the *Hôtel Beau Rivage* is recommended.

A couple of good Chinese restaurants near the Hôtel Joffre are worth checking out. The highly recommended *Restaurant Pacifique* has plats du jour for FMg 8000, while a Chinese fondue (for four people) costs FMg

La Micheline

An alternative to the ordinary train between Antananarivo and Toamasina is the privately run La Micheline. The first patent for the prototype Micheline was registered as early as 1846 by an English engineer called Robert Thomson. The design was later improved and made popular by André Michelin who wanted to create a comfortable and quiet train. The first Micheline, as the train became known, rolled off the production lines in France in 1931. Only a year later, it was being tested along the line between what was known as Tamatave (now Toamasina) and Tananarive (Antananarivo). By 1933, the Micheline was being used by the public (almost exclusively French residents). The two Michelines which remain in Madagascar – and run when possible – are the last functioning trains of this type left in the world. They are named *viko viko* and *tsikirity*, two types of Malagasy birds. ■

40,000 per person. The *Restaurant Fortuna*, just opposite the Pacifique, is not quite as good, but has a wide selection of oriental dishes at reasonable prices.

For snacks, try the *Adam & Eve Snack Bar*, close to the Hôtel Joffre. Here you can sit on strange high-chairs set around an outdoor counter and pig out on excellent samosas and milkshakes. Under Chez Jo's, the *Croissant d'Or* is the best place for pastries, and coffee or tea, as well as a few delicacies such as chocolate and biscuits (locally made and French).

Entertainment

Toamasina is the country's largest port and much of the town's nightlife is laid on for sailors. Visitors should be aware that HIV/AIDS is already a serious problem. The town lets its hair down at the *Queen's Club Disco*, next to the Hôtel Plage; the *Makoumba Club Disco*, directly opposite the Generation Hotel, which is a bit of a hangout for expats; and the *Hôtel Le Neptune*, which has an expensive nightclub and casino.

The *Cinéma Rio* looks like it has suffered the fate of other cinemas across the country: lack of demand means it barely functions.

Getting There & Away

Air Air Mad flies daily between Toamasina and Tana for US$60. Twice a week, TAM flies between Tana and Toamasina for the same price, as well as on to Île Sainte Marie. TAM also links Toamasina with Réunion for F2450 return.

The Air Mad office (☎ 323 56) is on Araben'ny Fahaleovantena; the TAM office (☎ 336 92) is along the northern end of Blvd Joffre.

Train At the time of research, the railway line between Tana and Toamasina was being repaired but was due to reopen soon. Although not as spectacular as the Fianarantsoa–Manakara line, it is still good fun.

The train normally leaves Tana on Thursdays at about 8 am and returns to Tana on Sunday morning. The 2nd/1st class fare from Toamasina to Tana (12 hours) is FMg 17,500/30,500, to Moramanga it's FMg

12,500/21,500, and to Ambila-Lemaitso FMg 4500/7500.

La Micheline A fantastic alternative to the public train is the privately run La Micheline train. Its schedule, naturally, depends on the state of the track, and on demand, but it sometimes runs from Tana to Toamasina on Thursdays and returns from Toamasina to Tana on Sundays. If it is running and you want to take a train, La Micheline is worth a splurge at FMg 87,500 per person.

For departure details and bookings contact the offices of Vanofotsy Voyages at the railway station in Tana (☎ (2) 205 21), or in Toamasina (☎ (5) 329 06). You can even hire the train for about F1000 but this would involve a lot of negotiation with railway authorities.

Taxi-brousse The taxi-brousse station at the north-western end of town serves Tana as well as all points north as far as Maroantsetra, and south to Mahanaro – roads, rivers, weather, bridges and spare parts permitting. Between Tana and Toamasina (six to eight hours) all buses, taxis-brousse (about FMg 18,000) and minibuses (FMg 25,000) leave at least every hour. You are advised to start your journey early to make sure you arrive in either town during daylight.

Taxis-brousse travel regularly to Moramanga (FMg 15,000 to FMg 20,000), for a connection to Périnet, and leave early every morning as far as Soanierana-Ivongo (FMg 15,000) for the ferry to Île Sainte Marie. Taxis-brousse only leave a few times a week to Mananara (FMg 65,000) and Maroantsetra (FMg 90,000).

Bus Due to the increasing popularity of this part of the country, a number of expensive, air-con tourist buses ply the Tana-Toamasina-Soanierana-Ivongo route. For details about what is going where and when from Toamasina, contact Transports Circuits Excursions at the Hôtel Plage, but fares are high at about FMg 45,000 from Toamasina to Mahavelona. Better is Allcars (☎ 336 33),

next to the Hôtel Les Flamboyants, which runs minibuses once or twice a week to Tana and up the east coast for less.

Boat Despite the number of boats going to and from Toamasina, very few of them carry passengers. Nevertheless, with some patience and determination you will find a lift on a cargo boat going to Île Sainte Marie, Antsiranana, or even Mauritius and Réunion – just ask around the shipping agencies in the port area. For boats to the last two islands, contact SEAL and MSC Shipping in the port. (Refer to the Madagascar Getting There & Away chapter for more details.)

The SCAC marine transport company (☎ 320 48) runs weekly ferries (currently leaving Toamasina on Tuesday evenings; 10 hours) to Île Sainte Marie. This trip isn't for everyone; the seas are normally quite rough, the boat is squalid and it's often crowded beyond reasonable capacity.

Getting Around
The Airport Taxis to and from the airport, 5km north of town, cost a standard FMg 7000 per person, regardless of how many people are squeezed in. Very little negotiation is possible.

Local Transport Pousse-pousse drivers charge from FMg 1000 to FMg 2000 per trip anywhere around the centre of town, which is a 'tourist price' – about three times what locals pay. The drivers are persistent, but not nearly as bad as they are in Antsirabe.

Around town, taxis cost FMg 2000 by day and FMg 2500 at night. This is a standard fare and there's no bargaining. A bicycle would be a perfect way to get around Toamasina, and to pedal as far as the botanic gardens at Ivoloina. Unfortunately, there is no official agency which rents bikes (budding local entrepreneurs, please take note of this serious deficiency!). You could ask around the esplanade on a Sunday afternoon when bikes are rented to locals by the hour.

Car & Motorcycle There seems little point in renting a car because the public transport and roads in this region are comparatively good. If you do, try Rabarjaona (☎ 339 58), just off the northern end of Blvd Joffre or LCR (☎ 339 04) in the main business district on the same street. The best rates are at Allcars (☎ 336 33), next to the Hôtel Les Flamboyants, where a Peugeot 405 costs FMg 120,000 per day – plus a few extras. No-one seems to rent motorcycles.

ÎLE SAINTE MARIE (NOSY BORAHA)
• Telephone Area Code: 567

The slender 57km-long granite Île Sainte Marie lies 8km off the eastern Malagasy coast. It is slowly overtaking Nosy Be as the prime tourist destination in Madagascar. (Nosy Boraha (pronounced 'noosh bor-AH') is the Malagasy name for the island, but is almost never used. Locals will rarely understand you if you use this name – probably because you will mispronounce it.

Île Sainte Marie is prettier and quieter than its west-coast counterpart, Nosy Be. It is lined with lovely coconut-rimmed beaches and offers pockets of pleasant rainforest, coral reefs, shallow seas and a heavy dose of historic interest. It's also considerably cheaper than Nosy Be. Île Sainte Marie has an excellent range of budget-style (and some more expensive) bungalows along the various beaches.

Ambodifotatra (spelt 'Ambodifototra' on some maps) is the island capital with 2500 of the island's 16,000 people, and is the only real town. There are numerous tiny villages and also a large population of mosquitoes. Although rain can be expected year-round (the island receives about 3.5m of rain annually!), your best chances of fine weather will be from late August to late November. From December to March, Île Sainte Marie is subject to violent cyclones.

History
The Malagasy name of the island, Nosy Boraha, is presumed to mean Island of Ibrahim, perhaps derived from a name bestowed by an early Arabic trader. The commonly used French name, Île Sainte Marie, is derived from Santa Maria, the name originally given by early 16th century Portuguese sailors.

The Dutch admiral Houtman reported the presence of an Arab settlement on the island as early as 1595, but the first European settlers of Île Sainte Marie were an international melange of pirates: English, Portuguese, French, American and others.

After the confederation of Betsimisaraka, the island was presented as a wedding gift to Princess Bety of Betsimisaraka by her father, King Ratsimilaho, upon her marriage to Frenchman, Jean-Onésime Filet (or La Bigorne). On 30 July 1750, Bety ceded the island to France and, in turn, the French government passed control to the French East India Company.

In 1752, two island princes, Siba and Tsifanda, revolted. As a result Bety was exiled to Mauritius and control of the island reverted to the Betsimisaraka. In 1818, the French returned, governing Île Sainte Marie first from Réunion, then Antsiranana and, finally, from Toamasina. Thanks to Princess Bety's magnanimous gift to France, the independence agreement allowed for the inhabitants of Île Sainte Marie to choose between French and Malagasy nationality. Although the majority chose Malagasy, many retain French names.

Information
Money The only place to change money on the island is the BFV bank, directly next to the small boat harbour in Ambodifotatra. It is open from about 8 am to 3 pm on weekdays. Up-market hotels on the island may change travellers' cheques for guests, but they prefer to change French francs in cash.

Post & Communications There is a small post office in the 'upper part' of Ambodifotatra, but for sending or receiving mail a larger centre such as Toamasina is far more reliable. There is no public telephone office on the island; telephone services in

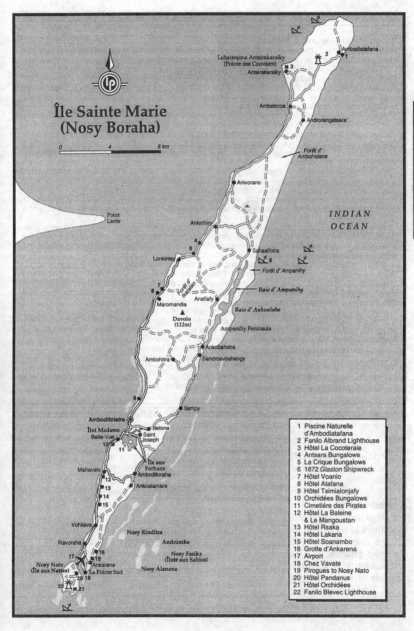

Île Sainte Marie (Nosy Boraha)

0   4   8 km

Locations on map:

- Ambodiatafana
- Lohatanjona Antsirakaraiky (Pointe des Cocotiers)
- Antsirakaraiky
- Ambatoroa
- Androrangatsara
- Forêt d' Ambohidena
- Anivorano
- Point Larée
- Ankirihiry
- Sahasifotra
- Lonkintsy
- Forêt d' Ampanihy
- Baie d' Ampanihy
- Anafiafy
- Forêt d'Ilaolao
- Maromandia
- Baie d' Ankoalabe
- Davolo (112m)
- Ampanihy Peninsula
- Ankobahoba
- Ambohitra
- Sandroavoahangy
- Ilampy
- Ambodifotatra
- Betona
- Îlot Madame
- Belle-Vue
- Saint Joseph
- Île aux Forbans
- Mahavelo
- Ambodiforaha
- Ankoalamare
- Vohilava
- Nosy Rinditra
- Andromba
- Ravoraha
- Ankarena
- Nosy Fasika (Îlots aux Sables)
- La Pointe Sud
- Nosy Nato (Île aux Nattes)
- Nosy Alanana

INDIAN OCEAN

1 Piscine Naturelle d'Ambodiatafana
2 Fanilo Albrand Lighthouse
3 Hôtel La Cocoteraie
4 Antsara Bungalows
5 La Crique Bungalows
6 1872 *Glaston* Shipwreck
7 Hôtel Voanio
8 Hôtel Atafana
9 Hôtel Tsimialonjafy
10 Orchidées Bungalows
11 Cimetiére des Pirates
12 Hôtel La Baleine & Le Mangoustan
13 Hôtel Rsaka
14 Hôtel Lakana
15 Hôtel Soanambo
16 Grotte d'Ankarena
17 Airport
18 Chez Vavate
19 Pirogues to Nosy Nato
20 Hôtel Pandanus
21 Hôtel Orchidées
22 Fanilo Blevec Lighthouse

EASTERN MADAGASCAR

Kingdom of Rogues & Pirates

At the close of the 17th century and beginning of the 18th, Île Sainte Marie and the east coast of Madagascar became the headquarters for the world's naval pirates. The once rich pickings in the Caribbean had thinned out and English and French naval policing had slowed profits to a trickle. Madagascar was an ideal base from which to ambush traders sailing around the Cape of Good Hope between Europe and the Far East, and Île Sainte Marie was a particularly inviting spot. It was within easy reach of the mainland, yet separate enough to maintain a degree of independence from mainland chiefs, and it became the pirates' centre of operations.

Many of the more prominent pirate leaders, along with their men and slaves, set up housekeeping – or in some cases miniature kingdoms – in eastern Madagascar. Among them were John Avery, William Kidd, Nathaniel North, Thomas White, David Williams, Thomas Tew, John Plantain, Olivier Levasseur (La Buse) and Captain Misson. At one stage, the pirate population of Madagascar reached nearly 1000 in all. They frequently married women from local tribes and their *mulatto* offspring came to be known as *Zana-Malata*.

One English pirate, John Avery, set up a base in about 1695 in the Baie d'Antongila, near present-day Maroantsetra. One of his raids was on the ship of a Mogul maharajah on his way to Mecca. Among the booty was the daughter of an oriental sovereign, whom Avery took as his bride. Formulating and cementing treaties with neighbouring pirate leaders, he proclaimed himself ruler of Antongila. It isn't known what eventually became of Avery but some historians believe he returned to England to live out his days incognito.

However, it was Ratsimilaho, the son of a Malagasy princess, Antavaratra Rahena, and an English pirate, Thomas White, who would have the greatest impact on Madagascar. Ratsimilaho was leader of the Zana-Malata and, thanks to a number of military successes, became founder and chief of the unified Betsimisaraka (Those Who Stand Together).

Princess Bety, Ratsimilaho's daughter and heir to the throne of Betsimisaraka, fell in love with a Frenchman from Réunion, Jean-Onésime Filet (better known as La Bigorne), who had been shipwrecked on Île Sainte Marie. The couple married just prior to Ratsimilaho's death in 1750 and as a wedding gift the king presented them with the island. After ascending to the throne of Betsimisaraka, Bety handed over sovereignty of the island to the King of France.

At this stage in the story came an eccentric Hungarian-born slave trader called Maurice-Auguste Comte de Benyowski. An officer in the Austrian army, Comte Benyowski was captured by the Russians while fighting in Poland. To cut a long but fascinating story short, he wound up in Madagascar in 1773, where he founded the community of Louisville, also on the Baie d'Antongila.

Through treaties and force Benyowski's power increased, but he went a step further than Avery and declared himself emperor of all Madagascar. However, while he was away in France negotiating with the king, his empire collapsed. In 1785, he returned in hopes of salvaging power but was killed by French Réunionnais troops at Mahavelona (Foulpointe) in 1786. Louisville disappeared and no-one has yet found a trace of either it or Benyowski's grave. ■

Ambodifotatra are very limited, and virtually non-existent around the rest of the island.

Ambodifotatra

Although there's not much to Ambodifotatra (and there is no beach), the island's largest village does boast Madagascar's oldest **Catholic church**. This dates back to 1857 and was a gift to the island from the Empress Eugénie of France. At the southern end of town, overlooking the causeway to Îlot Madame, there's an old **granite fort** which dates back to 1753. It's quite impressive but it now serves as a military post and is off limits to the public.

Just south of the fort is the **Tomb of Sylvain Roux**, France's first commercial attaché on the east coast of Madagascar. From the tomb there's nice views across the town and islands. At the northern end is the **Tomb of François Albrand**, a French military commander of the island who died in 1826 at the age of 31. His epitaph (in French) is particularly amusing.

A colourful **market** is held on Tuesdays and Thursdays, when it's considered *fady* (taboo) to work in the fields. Refer to Places

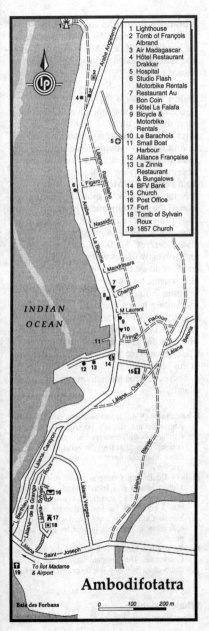

1 Lighthouse
2 Tomb of François Albrand
3 Air Madagascar
4 Hôtel Restaurant Drakkar
5 Hospital
6 Studio Flash Motorbike Rentals
7 Restaurant Au Bon Coin
8 Hôtel La Falafa
9 Bicycle & Motorbike Rentals
10 Le Barachois
11 Small Boat Harbour
12 Alliance Française
13 La Zinnia Restaurant & Bungalows
14 BFV Bank
15 Church
16 Post Office
17 Fort
18 Tomb of Sylvain Roux
19 1857 Church

INDIAN OCEAN

Ambodifotatra

To Îlot Madame & Airport

Baie des Forbans

0   100   200 m

to Stay & Eat for details about accommodation in the village.

Cimetiére des Pirates

The appropriately eerie and wildly overgrown pirate cemetery is probably the most visited attraction on Île Sainte Marie. Many of the names and epitaphs are long illegible, but given that few if any of the big-name buccaneers died a peaceful death at 'home' on the island, there are no really infamous names anyway. One stone with the skull and crossbones carved on it reads: *Joseph Pierre 1788 – par son ami Hulin. Passans priez pour lui* (Joseph Pierre 1788 – by his friend Hulin. Wayfarers, pray for him).

The cemetery lies beside the Baie des Forbans, about a 20 minute walk south-east of the southern end of the causeway. There are several tidal creeks to be crossed along the track so it's only accessible at low tide. Much of the route is over slippery stones and logs.

There is now an entrance fee of FMg 1000. Sadly, some very annoying kids may follow you all the way demanding money and gifts. Some travellers have reported feeling uncomfortable because they believed the children would steal things from them if there was an opportunity. Be careful.

Île aux Forbans

Atop Île aux Forbans, opposite the cemetery in the bay of the same name, are the ruins of an **ancient gateway**. Its significance is unknown but it's thought to have been a pirate landmark or lookout post.

Îlot Madame

The tiny island of Îlot Madame lies at the entrance to the Baie des Forbans and is connected to Ambodifotatra on the north and Belle-Vue on the south by two causeways. The island served as the fortified administration centre of the French East India Company until it was taken over by local government offices. It is also the location of a deep harbour for larger cargo boats and yachts.

Nosy Nato

Nosy Nato is a magical place to visit for a few hours, or to stay. Only a short walk from the airport runway, you can hire a pirogue to take you over to the island for FMg 3000 to FMg 5000 return – the price depends on demand and your bargaining ability. You can easily swim across, and during low tide you could even walk across at about waist or chest high.

You can walk around the island, and visit the village, in less than three hours. The **Fanilo Blevec lighthouse** is no longer used, but you can go inside and get great views of the islands. There are two hotels on the island – refer to Places to Stay & Eat for details.

Ankarena

At the island's south-eastern tip there is a fine stretch of peaceful reef-protected beach and a deep **cave** in the base of the cliffs. Not surprisingly, the cave has given rise to several pirate legends, many regarding treasure. You are likely to see hundreds of bats hanging from the ceiling. To reach Ankarena, cross the ridge from the airport.

East Coast

A good trip by mountain bike or motorcycle is along the rough road from Ambodifotatra north-east to Ankobahoba and beyond. (The correct road from Ambodifotatra to the east coast is hard to find – you will have to ask for directions.)

Some of the island's finest **beaches** are on the Ampanihy Peninsula, which is cut off from the main island by the long Baie d'Ampanihy

Piscine Naturelle d'Ambodiatafana

These glorious natural swimming holes at the remote north-eastern tip of the island are a series of hollow basins in the coastal rocks which are filled by the high tide. To get there, walk 8km north-east along the main track from Ambatoroa on the west coast. Alternatively take a motorcycle (it would be tough-going on a mountain bike because the northern road is terrible).

This track takes you via the **Fanilo Albrand**, a lighthouse atop the ridge, from where you can see as far as Maroantsetra at the head of the Baie d'Antongila. At Christmas time Ambodiatafana villagers stage an all-night festival.

Diving

Île Sainte Marie may not have all the coral it once did, but there is plenty to see and several good operators around the island. Diving is really only possible between July and February, and it's best from October to December. (Diving centres may be closed from February to May.)

Some of the best spots for diving are around the two shipwrecks in the far north, and along the east coast, not far from Sahasifotra. Prices are fairly standard for all diving centres: F200 per dive; F230 for a night dive; two dives will set you back F350; and four dives, F720. The centres below can also arrange boat hire.

Some hotels and diving centres rent snorkelling gear for about FMg 20,000 per day; try the Voanio and Lakana hotels and the Mahery Be Diving Centre. One accessible spot for good snorkelling is in front of Chez Vavate (see Places to Stay & Eat later in this section).

There are three main diving centres on the island:

Il Balemotero (☎ 48) is an Italian-run outfit based in Ambodifotatra, directly opposite the Hôtel La Fafala. It is fully equipped and runs certificate courses, as well as trips for certified divers and those who just want some underwater photographs.

Mahery Be Diving Center is based just north of Mahavelo and is a friendly outfit which runs PADI and CMAS certificate courses. There is also a cute little bar and restaurant called the Vanilla Café on the same premises. The centre also rents full snorkelling gear for FMg 25,000 per day.

St Marie Dive Centre is based at the Hôtel La Cocoteraie. The company is well set up, but caters more for the up-market crowd and package tours.

Whale-watching

Every year from July to September between

500 and 700 whales swim along the strait between the west coast of Île Sainte Marie and the mainland of Madagascar. About 100 of these stay in the strait to give birth, or look for mates. (The French word for whale is *baliene*, but curiously the French often also use the phrase 'whale-watching'.)

The diving centres listed earlier, and the better hotels, have access to decent boats and are a good place to ask about whale-watching trips. During the right season you will also see advertisements in the hotels and restaurants about these trips. Prices are high – from FMg 100,000 to FMg 150,000 per person – but it would be very hard to organise anything yourself for less. A boat trip to watch the whales is an incredible experience – locals guarantee that you will see many of these magnificent creatures.

If you are a whale enthusiast, and read French, pick up the excellent booklet, which is small but has a very long name – *Petit Guide Pratique á L'Usage des Observateurs de Baleines à Bosse à Madagascar*. It costs FMg 25,000 and is available at the Hôtel Lakana.

Organised Tours

The more expensive hotels organise tours around the island by 4WD, pirogue or boat for those with a lot of dollars or francs in their pockets. The Lakana, and its sister hotel, La Crique, as well as the Soanambo Hôtel, have a range of good tours. A day trip to Nosy Nato costs from F100 to F150 per person, including a fantastic lunch at the Hôtel Orchidées; and a trip around the east coast as far as Ampanihy (which is the only way to really see this part of the island) costs about F200 per person. Look out for other organised tours arranged by new budget hotels and bungalows, especially in the peak season (June to September).

For boat trips, the Lakana and La Crique can organise a catamaran for up to seven people for F470 per boat per day. Other boat trips, and prices for charters, are often advertised in the hotels and restaurants around the island. Any trip on a pirogue organised by a

hotel will be a rip-off – you can certainly organise that yourself for far less.

Places to Stay & Eat

The smaller and better value bungalow complexes around the island have limited space and are frequently booked out during the high season (from 15 December to 15 January, April, May, and July to October), as well as weekends and Malagasy holidays. Reserving and checking on vacancies can be a problem because only a handful have the phone connected. You will be accosted by hotel touts when you arrive by air or sea. Make sure that your rooms are mossie-free – with nets, fans or air-con – as the little buggers can be a problem.

If you are staying on the island for a while it is worth avoiding the hotel touts, spending your first night in Ambodifotatra, and then hiring a mountain bike or motorcycle to find a bungalow you really like. Then travel there later by taxi-brousse. One cheap way to explore the island is to stay in Ambodifotatra (where there is no beach, however). From there you can easily make day trips around the island by mountain bike, motorcycle or taxi-brousse.

Alternatively, leave your heavy luggage in Toamasina, Soanierana-Ivongo or Ambodifotatra, rent a mountain bike or motorcycle for a few days and 'bungalow-hop' around the island, staying at a few different places. You could 'bungalow-hop' anyway with all your luggage by using the (expensive) taxi-brousse – but this is only practical in the off-season when there are empty rooms.

There are a few locally run restaurants around the island, but unless you have transport, you are staying in Ambodifotatra or you rely on the one and only taxi-brousse, you will probably end up eating at your hotel or bungalow. There is nothing stopping you staying at one hotel and eating at another.

Places to Stay & Eat – bottom end

Ambodifotatra The cheapest place, the *Hôtel La Falafa*, on the main street, is poor value at FMg 24,000 for an airless thatched room (not a bungalow). The best place in town is the *Hôtel Restaurant Drakkar*, a short walk north of the port. A bungalow virtually on the shore (but with no beach) costs FMg 25,000; a perfectly good room with sea views costs a little less. All rooms have communal facilities. The Drakkar has an excellent restaurant with views (the breakfasts are very good, with a huge pot of tea if you want) but prices are a little high.

The only other place is *La Zinnia Restaurant & Bungalows*, virtually opposite the small boat harbour. The bungalows have been built too close to each other, but they are comfortable, have private bathrooms and cost FMg 30,000. However, the generator next to the bungalows may keep you awake at night.

A couple of restaurants in the village, *Le Barachois* and *La Zinnia*, cater for expats and tourists. They have a nice decor and a good range of meals, but the prices are way too high – for example, a large bottle of beer costs a ridiculous FMg 9000. Easily the best place for good-value meals, and cheap drinks, is the *Restaurant Au Bon Coin* on the main street.

South South of Ambodifotatra, just past Mahavelona, the friendly, Malagasy-owned *Hôtel La Baleine* has bungalows with shared bathroom for as little as FMg 15,000, but most cost a reasonable FMg 35,000 with private bathroom. A family bungalow with four beds and private facilities costs a bargain FMg 40,000. Huge fish and lobster dinners are available if pre-ordered. One reader did complain about the insect life around the hotel, however.

Close by, the cheapest bungalows on the island are at the new, very friendly and Malagasy-run *Le Mangoustan*. Basic bungalows with a shared (spotless) bathroom cost FMg 10,000. Other bungalows (with a bathroom) right on the beach cost FMg 40,000. Great fish meals can be ordered in advance for FMg 15,000; breakfast costs FMg 5000. If the La Baleine or Le Mangoustan are full, try the *Hôtel Rsaka* a little further south, where the price and standards are a little lower.

In the far south, within walking distance of the airport, is the popular *Chez Vavate*. Bungalows (which seem a bit run-down) with nice views cost FMg 30,000. Although you can get better value around the island, the location is excellent (and great for snorkelling) and the meals (FMg 23,000, and FMg 9000 for breakfast) are superb.

A couple of independent places are worth trying for meals. The *La Ravinala*, great for fish and pasta, is in the village of Vohilava. The *Il Pirata*, in Belle-Vue (3km south of Ambodifotatra), has a disco, and the pizzas (FMg 14,000) come heartily recommended.

North Only about 4km north of Ambodifotatra is the budget *Hôtel Tsimialonjafy*. It has tiny, homely bungalows on a fine beach for a bargain FMg 15,000.

A very popular place is the *Hôtel Atafana*, just past the village of Maromandia. The setting on the beach is lovely, and the outdoor restaurant and the food are very good, but the prices for the bungalows are now a little high – FMg 27,000/50,000 without/with a private bathroom. Only a few hundred metres further north, better value can be found at the *Hôtel Voanio*. Both hotels are close enough to each other to check out and then negotiate (particularly in the low season). At the Voanio, prices start from FMg 18,000 for a basic bungalow and from FMg 25,000 to FMg 35,000 for a bungalow (with bathroom) right on the lovely beach.

Another popular place in the north of the island is the *Antsara Bungalows*, about a km north of the village of Lonkintsy. Very pleasant, but basic, bungalows on the beach (which is only so-so compared to others) cost a reasonable FMg 18,000 to FMg 27,500. Other more luxurious bungalows cost FMg 60,000. The restaurant (where the menu du jour costs FMg 30,000) and office are in a huge building which looks like a barn. Lack of transport in the area is a problem.

On the east coast, at Sandroavohangy, *Le Lagon Bleu* has some pleasant bungalows and a restaurant, and organises fishing and pirogue trips. The problem is getting there:

there's no public transport, so you'll need to hire a boat, motorcycle or mountain bike.

Nosy Nato Off the far south coast of Île Sainte Marie, Nosy Nato is a gorgeous, secluded place to laze around for a few days (or weeks). Of the two places to stay, the cheaper is the *Hôtel Pandanus*, right on the beach. Basic bungalows at the Pandanus range from FMg 25,000 to FMg 40,000, all with shared bathrooms. An alternative and cheaper place to eat is *Chez Jacqueline's* in the village of Aniribe.

Places to Stay – middle & top end

South Only about 3km south of Ambodifotatra, the *Orchidées Bungalows* (☎ 54 or ☎ (2) 237 62) is a modern, friendly place on a superb beach. According to its brochure it 'is covered with falafa ... which emit benevolent freshness'. Modern air-conditioned bungalows, each with three single beds and a spotless bathroom, cost FMg 60,000/75,000 for a single/double.

Even if you are on a tight budget, it is still worth considering the magnificent *Hôtel Lakana* (☎ (5) 336 79). Built around a picturesque, shady beach, bungalows cost FMg 60,000 with bathroom. There are also gorgeous bungalows on stilts above the sea with private balconies for a bargain FMg 50,000. The bungalows are attached to a jetty, and the communal bathrooms are on terra firma. The hotel also boasts a wide range of tours, a laundry service, small lending library, lovely lounge area, and one of the best restaurants on the island.

The *Hôtel Soanambo* (☎ 40) has all the luxury, but no character, for F290/350 a single/double. Guests have access to a swimming pool and tennis court. A huge range of incongruous concrete bungalows are being built next door.

If you are staying for a while or travelling in a group, the best place to check out is the *Bungalows de Vohilava* (☎ (5) 312 98), in the village of the same name. Huge bungalows, with two bedrooms, lounge, bathroom, kitchen (with oven and fridge) and even cable TV, which can easily house six people,

cost F250 per night. The cost is less per night for longer stays.

North One of the best in the middle range is *La Crique Bungalows* (☎ (5) 336 75). Although the bungalows are too close to each other, and the place is remote (transport is a problem), the setting on the beach and the service and range of facilities are superb. Prices aren't too bad either: they start from FMg 65,000 for 'ordinary' bungalows or FMg 80,000 for a two-roomed 'family' bungalow. If you want a private bathroom with hot water, and a bit of seclusion, prices start at FMg 110,000. Breakfast is FMg 12,500, and other meals are FMg 35,000.

The most isolated of the island's hotels, *Hôtel La Cocoteraie* (☎ (5) 332 61 or ☎ (2) 461 17) is on Pointe des Cocotiers near the northern tip of the island, 35km north of Ambodifotatra. There are 50 thatched bungalows and a restaurant fronting a glorious 3km-long white-sand beach. Prices for one person are F250, and go up to F390 for four-person bungalows. Off-season discounts are possible.

Somewhere worth trying for almost absolute seclusion, way off the beaten track in the village of Anafiafy on the east coast, is the *Hôtel Paradis d'Ampany*. Large, clean bungalows cost FMg 40,000 for a double; or larger ones which can fit a family cost around FMg 80,000. From here, you can really explore the eastern coast, but getting to the hotel with the island's limited transport will be a real hassle.

Nosy Nato Arguably the nicest place around Île Sainte Marie is the *Hôtel Orchidées* (☎ (2) 356 07) – not to be confused with the bungalows of the same name near Ambodifotatra. Prices are reasonable considering the seclusion, the gorgeous setting, superb service and meals. Bungalows, which hold three people, cost F150, and a 'chalet' for two people costs a comparatively cheap F100. Breakfast costs F15; other meals are F45. It is only open from mid-July to mid-December. Bookings are essential.

Getting There & Away

Air Air Madagascar flies from Tana to Île Sainte Marie every day for US$83, often via Toamasina (US$37). The airline flies less regularly north to Sambava for US$105.

You can bypass Tana completely and fly directly to Île Sainte Marie from Réunion on TAM for about F1100 return. TAM also flies the Tana-Toamasina-Île Sainte Marie route and back twice a week for the same price as Air Mad.

Make absolutely sure that you confirm, and reconfirm, all bookings – flights to and from the island are very popular, especially in peak season (July–August).

The Air Mad office (☎ 46) is opposite the Hôtel Drakkar in Ambodifotatra; the TAM office/hut (☎ 40) is opposite the Hôtel Soanambo in the south of the island.

Boat There are two types of boat to and from Île Sainte Marie: passenger boat and cargo boat. The overcrowded wooden *Thalassa Express* or *Le Dugong* travels from Soanie-rana-Ivongo to Ambodifotatra. This is undoubtedly the biggest tourist rip-off in Madagascar: a one-way ticket costs FMg 75,000 (Malagasy people pay FMg 25,000), and FMg 120,000 return. The people who sell you tickets are so embarrassed about the price that you can easily bargain them down to FMg 45,000 (which is *still* too much). They charge from FMg 35,000 to FMg 65,000 for motorcycles (depending on their size), but there is no way they could have room on the boat.

Tickets are available from the Le Barachois restaurant (☎ 25), opposite the small boat harbour in Amdodifotatra; from the Hôtel Le Relais de Sainte-Marie in Soanierana-Ivongo; or from the Bureau Kofito at the taxi-brousse station in Toamasina (this is a useful option). The boat currently leaves Soanierana-Ivongo at 1 pm every day; from Ambodifotatra, it leaves at 7 am. Buy tickets as soon as you can: despite the price, the boat fills up quickly.

The only other alternative, the *Sirene Sofi*, apparently also travels between Soanierana-Ivongo and Ambodifotatra, but the official

told us 'it may run today; maybe tomorrow; maybe never'. If or when it starts running again, the prices and departure times should be about the same as the *Thalassa Express*. Contact the Hôtel Zanatany in Soanierana-Ivongo or the ticket office opposite the small boat harbour in Ambodifotatra.

If you have time – and an adventurous streak – ask around for a lift on a cargo boat. These generally come and go from the deep harbour on Îlot Madame, close to Ambodifotatra. The main destinations are Maroantsetra (about FMg 75,000; 16 hours), often stopping at Nosy Mangabe; Toamasina, from where the pasenger ferry *Rapiko* leaves on Tuesday evenings (about 10 hours); and Antalaha and Sambava. These boats are often not set up for passengers, so conditions – and the seas – can be rough. However, between the north-east coast and Île Sainte Marie, a boat is usually the only option.

Getting Around

The Airport Île Sainte Marie's airport consists of a concrete shed and a runway at the southern tip of the island, 13km south of Ambodifotatra. If you are coming or going on an international flight, allow plenty of time as procedures alternate between chaotic and slow.

You will be accosted by dozens of pushy hotel touts when you arrive. Most hotels send minibuses to meet incoming flights and they provide transfers to the airport, but they have no shame in charging silly prices for transfers to their hotels: for example, to the Lakana, FMg 4000; to La Belaine, FMg 7000; to the Antsara, FMg 25,000; and to La Crique, FMg 35,000.

Alternatively, take the taxi-brousse (see the following section). From the airport, it charges a ridiculous FMg 12,000 to Ambodi-fotrata and FMg 22,000 to Lonkintsy, from where it is a short walk to the Antsara or La Crique bungalows.

Taxi-brousse Incredibly, there is one – that's right, *one* – taxi-brousse on the island. It is run by an expat Frenchman; there is a certain novelty watching a *vazaha* driving Malagasy people around. Fares are a tourist rip-off, but you have little choice. The taxi-brousse runs as far north as Lonkintsy and as far south as La Pointe Sud for the airport and pirogues to Nosy Nato. It does this run five to six times a day, every day but Saturdays. Schedules are posted in hotels and restaurants.

Motorcycle A motorcycle is the perfect means of getting around – but prices are steep. A good place to pick up a motorcycle is the unnamed place opposite the small harbour in Ambodifotatra. Open every day from 6 am to 6 pm, it charges FMg 90,000/130,000 (half day/one day) for a tiny Peugeot *mobylette*. The Atafana charges the same price. Older moped-style bikes are available at the Hôtel Lakana for FMg 60,000/100,000.

For something bigger, faster and more expensive, talk to the guys at Studio Flash, along the main street in Ambodifotatra. They charge FMg 120,000/200,000, or FMg 25,000 per hour, for a Honda 200cc or Yamaha 125cc.

Bicycle The next best way to get around the island is on a mountain bike. When the badly rutted roads are muddy, however, they are slippery and difficult to negotiate (north of Lonkintsy the road is terrible all the time). The Soanambo, Voanio, Antsara, La Baleine, Atafana and Le Mangoustan hotels, and the unnamed rental agency opposite the small boat harbour in Ambodifotatra, all rent mountain bikes. The price is a standard FMg 25,000/30,000 (half day/one day), but for that price make sure you get something new and reliable.

A few local Malagasy entrepreneurs rent bikes from huts along the main road around the island for less – why not patronise these rather than the rich, expat hotel owners?

Walking For those who prefer to walk, Île Sainte Marie offers excellent opportunities to strike out on foot – the island is criss-crossed with forest tracks.

Pirogue It's also possible to hire islanders' pirogues for jaunts along the coast or trips to Île aux Forbans or Nosy Nato. Most hotels can also arrange pirogue hire but they will certainly charge more than the cost of hiring one yourself.

North of Toamasina

The road between Tana and Soanierana-Ivongo (for the ferry to Île Sainte Marie), via Toamasina, is paved and well serviced by public transport. North of Soanierana-Ivongo public transport is far more scarce, and the road gets increasingly worse. The road stops at Maroantsetra, so you cannot continue to Antalaha or Sambava by road.

One popular method of travelling in this region is to fly one-way to Île Sainte Marie from Tana and travel the other way overland, stopping off at a few places along the way. Otherwise, you can easily travel 'overland' between Toamasina and Île Sainte Marie, via Soanierana-Ivongo, in one day if you get an early start.

MAHAVELONA (FOULPOINTE)
• Telephone Area Code: 5710

Mahavelona (Where One is Reborn) – commonly known as Foulpointe – lies 58km north of Toamasina. Around this village there are some beautiful deserted white-sand beaches, but swimming anywhere away from the hotel area, which is protected by a reef, is risky. Some locals have become annoying, pleading to take vazahas out on a pirogue to the reef for swimming or snorkelling.

About 500m north of Mahavelona are the ruins of a round 19th century Merina fort known as **Fort Hova**, made from a coral, sand, shell and egg-based cement similar to that used in the walls of Ambohimanga near Tana. These walls are 6m high and between 2m and 4m thick.

Places to Stay & Eat
The best place to stay is the *Au Gentil Pêcheur*,

on the beach about 300m from the road. Clean bungalows, with bathroom and good service, cost FMg 31,000. Incredibly, this tiny place accepts Visa credit cards. The restaurant, right on the beach, is also very good.

There are a couple of other cheap bungalows along the main road in the village for around FMg 20,000, such as the *Hôtel Cristal*. The *Restaurant Riaka*, near the Au Gentil Pêcheur, is excellent value – easily the best place to eat. Great fish and rice meals cost a bargain FMg 8000.

The up-market *Manda Beach Hôtel* (☎ 322 43) is a very clean European-style beach resort with tennis courts, a swimming pool and a golf course. Prices are not too bad if you are in a group: a room for two is F250; a suite for four is F350; and a lovely bungalow, which sleeps five, costs F400. It has a special all-you-can-stuff-down-your-throat buffet on Sundays.

Getting There & Away
A comfortable minibus (FMg 10,000) leaves Toamasina every day at 6.30 am. Stand by the side of the road in Mahavelona before 9 am if you want to get a lift on a taxi-brousse to Soanierana-Ivongo (FMg 15,000), and a ticket on the afternoon ferry for Île Sainte Marie. If heading south to Toamasina from Mahavelona, most vehicles come by in the early afternoon; very few vehicles head north from Mahavelona after 11 am.

MAHAMBO
• Telephone Area Code: 5710
Mahambo, 30km north of Mahavelona and 91km from Toamasina, has a nice beach which is safe for swimming. Due to its wonderful vegetation, the area has a sort of otherworldly beauty. Many places are slowly recovering from the wrath of Cyclone Bonita in 1996. (Refer to Getting There & Away under Mahavelona for advice on travel to and from Mahambo.)

Places to Stay & Eat
On the beach there's *Le Récif* (☎ 345 25), a group of beach bungalows (complete with a frog or two in the loo!) from FMg 33,000 to FMg 50,000. The hotel continues to get rave reviews from readers, though the menu du jour at FMg 22,000 could be better value. Nearby, *Le Gîte* is a lovely, up-market version of Le Récif. Excellent bungalows with hot water range from FMg 65,000 to FMg 100,000.

Another option is *Le Dola* with 12 simple beach bungalows, about 100m south of Le Gîte. Bungalows cost FMg 40,000. Le Dola also runs diving trips and certificate courses. Bookings are possible at Chez Jo's in Toamasina (☎ (5) 327 19). Other cheaper places are being built so look around.

FENOARIVO (FÉNÉRIVE)
The largish and pleasant town of Fenoarivo (Thousand Warriors) was the first capital of the Betsimisaraka tribe; it was here in the early 18th century that the founder, Ratsimilaho, united the tribe and proclaimed himself king. At Nosy Kely there is an old **Zana-Malata cemetery**. Three km south of town are the ruins of an old **pirate fort**, Vohimasina, with its triangle-shaped water wells, and, if you ask around, you can visit a nearby **clove factory**.

If you aren't visiting these places, there is no need to stay. If you do, your best bet is the central *Girofla d'Or* for around FMg 20,000 per room, or the *Belle Rose* bungalows, on the road leading to the hospital.

SOANIERANA-IVONGO
Soanierana-Ivongo serves only as a port for boats to and from Île Sainte Marie and a place to get taxi-brousse connections further up the coast – there is no reason to stay longer here than necessary.

Taxis-brousse head to Soanierana-Ivongo every morning from Toamasina for the afternoon boat. When you arrive by boat from Île Sainte Marie, taxis-brousse will be waiting and can drop you off at places further south. For information about the boat to Île Sainte Marie, refer to the earlier Île Sainte Marie section.

If you miss the boat (so to speak) and need to stay you have two options. The *Hôtel Le*

Relais de Sainte Marie charges FMg 20,000 for a decent room; the meals are reasonable, but the drinks are the most expensive in northern Madagascar. Opposite, the very basic *Hôtel Zanatany* charges a rock-bottom FMg 10,000 per bungalow.

MANOMPANA

The road north of Soanierana-Ivongo towards Manompana soon turns nasty. There is no need to stay in Manompana unless you change your mind about going further north, and want to return to Île Sainte Marie!

The extremely basic *Hôtel Antsiraka* has no electricity or running water, but it's relatively clean and well cared for. Rooms with just a bed cost about FMg 12,500. Alternatively, try the *Bungalow Loulou* for a little more comfort and price.

A couple of taxis-brousse travel past Manompana in both directions, but the road is very poor and the trip between Manompana and Mananara will take at least five hours under optimum conditions.

MANANARA

Mananara, at the southern entrance to the Baie d'Antongila, lies an adventurous 84km drive from Manompana, and 185km from Fenoarivo. Mananara is the place to stop if you wish to explore the Mananara Nord National Park, including the tiny Aye-Aye Island (see the next section), or to break up the tough journey to or from Maroantsetra. If you are a cave freak, you can charter a vehicle to Ambalatrano, about 17km south of Mananara, and visit the **Grotte d'Andavahandrehy** which is up to 200m underground.

Places to Stay & Eat

For a long time the only accommodation in Mananara was *Chez Rogers* in the centre of town, where large bungalows cost FMg 20,000. The main competition, the *Hôtel Aye-Aye*, near the airport costs about the same – the food is highly recommended but you must book meals in advance. Another good, cheap alternative is the friendly *Tonton-galet Restaurant & Bungalows*, near the hospital, which costs FMg 10,000.

Getting There & Away

Air Madagascar (☎ 31) flies to Mananara every few days as part of a trip between Tana (US$94) and Toamasina (US$60), via Maroantsetra (US$25). Make absolutely certain that you confirm your onward flight or you could be in Mananara somewhat longer than you bargained for.

Mananara lies at least five, sometimes eight, hours from Manompana by the daily taxi-brousse (FMg 15,000). From Toamasina, a taxi-brousse only travels this far north a few times a week (FMg 65,000).

PARC NATIONAL DE MANANARA NORD

This 23,000 hectare national park comprises a large chunk of inland rainforest as well as 1000 hectares on offshore islets and surrounding reefs. The largest of these is Nosy Antafana.

The park is the only known habitat of the hairy-eared dwarf lemur; researchers are hoping to also find examples of the rarest lemur species, the broad-nosed gentle lemur. The park also protects the indri, diademed sifaka, ruffed lemur and aye-aye, as well as crocodile, dugong and reef life.

Surrounding the park, a much larger area of 140,000 hectares has been set aside by UNESCO as an International Biosphere Reserve. This reserve also includes 70km of coastline from Mananara south of the Anove River, and up to 40km inland.

To visit the park, go to the UNESCO Biosphere office in Mananara to get a permit (FMg 50,000) and a guide. To start exploring, take a taxi-brousse to Sandrakatsy. From there, you'll have to hike for around 5km to Varary, and the same distance again to the official park entrance. If you have the energy, tents, food and wet-weather gear, you can continue trekking up the coast to Maroantsetra.

Aye-Aye Island

One of the main reasons to stop in Mananara

is to visit the Rogers Reserve on Aye-Aye Island in the Manahara River. Here you have the opportunity to look in on aye-ayes in their natural environment. Tours of the island were once run only by the Chez Rogers hotel in Mananara, but now you don't have to stay at that hotel to visit the island. Contact the UNESCO office in Mananara for information about getting to the island, permits and so on.

MAROANTSETRA

The next major town north of Mananara is the dreary river port of Maroantsetra, between the Antainambalana River and the Baie d'Antongila. The town suffers from an undeniable surfeit of rain – over 3000mm annually – but it is nevertheless attracting more and more visitors. Most of them come to visit the Réserve de Nosy Mangabe (see the next section) just offshore, while others are hoping to set out on the increasingly popular, but tough, trek across the Masoala Peninsula to Antalaha or Cap Est (see the Masoala Peninsula Trek section later in this chapter).

If you have a fine day, perhaps take a leisurely four hour walk east along the coast to **Plage Navana** beach. Along the way there are several waterways which must be crossed by pirogue.

Places to Stay & Eat

The cheapest place in town is the dilapidated *Hôtel Antongil*, with rooms at around FMg 15,000. Another grubby place is the *Hôtel Vatsi*, with rooms for FMg 10,000, and bungalows for FMg 15,000.

A new and popular place, across from the market, is the *Hôtel du Centre* (aka *Chez Cyrille*). It has rooms with a private shower, but shared (and often filthy) toilets, for FMg 20,000. The hotel rents mountain bikes for FMg 15,000 per day, and it's a good place to start organising a visit to Nosy Mangabe Reserve or a trek across the peninsula. However, some women have complained about the sleazy activities of some hotel staff.

The *Bar Calyspo* is a great place to meet locals. The best place to eat is the *Restaurant Le Pagode de Chine* – no prizes for guessing the main type of cuisine.

Getting There & Away

Maroantsetra lies 112km north of Mananara. Although it is now more or less accessible by a very rough road from Mananara and points south, most visitors arrive by air. Every few days tiny Air Mad planes fly north to Sambava (US$37) and on to Antsiranana (US$94), and south to Manara (US$25) and on to Tana (US$105).

Hitching a lift on a cargo boat to/from Maroantsetra may be quicker than using the road, but it will still be as uncomfortable. If you ask around the port, and can wait a day or two, you will find a boat going to Antalaha and Sambava; to Toamasina (about FMg 90,000); and, more regularly, to Île Sainte Marie via Nosy Mangabe (FMg 75,000; 16 hours).

RÉSERVE DE NOSY MANGABE

The area's most renowned attraction is the idyllic, thickly forested 520 hectare island nature reserve of Nosy Mangabe. This is a truly enchanting island and one of the last pockets of untouched rainforest left in the country; a visit may be one of the highlights of your trip to Madagascar.

The island is in the Baie d'Antongila 5km offshore from Maroantsetra. The aye-ayes, which were introduced in 1966 and are flourishing, are the major drawcard. You'll also see several species of lemur – dwarf, mouse, brown, and black-and-white ruffed (which have been introduced) – as well as the bizarre leaf-tailed gecko (*Uroplatus fimbriatus*), one of nature's most accomplished camouflage artists; several species of chameleon, one of which is an incredible bright pink; and lots of frogs. There's even a harmless snake, *Pseudoxyrohopus heterurus*, which is found nowhere but on Nosy Mangabe.

The island lacks visitor facilities, but there is an established campground for those who have camping equipment and wish to spend more than one day exploring the island's many forest tracks. If camping, take your

Vanilla

Madagascar is the world's largest producer of vanilla, which accounts for about 20% of the country's exports; it also earns a large percentage of the Comoros' export income. The vanilla plant was introduced to Madagascar from Mexico by French plantation owners and grows most abundantly in the north-eastern part of the country, particularly around Sambava and Andapa where the hot and wet climate is perfect. Vanilla is a type of climbing orchid, known scientifically as *Vanila planifolia*, which attaches itself to trees. The vanilla seeds, which contain the substance of interest to manufacturers, are found in a longish pod hanging from the plant (the word vanilla comes from the Spanish *vainilla*, or little pod. In French it is *vanille* and in Malagasy *lavanila*).

Vanilla is used in the flavouring of ice cream and chocolate, and for perfume; dark brown or black pods are preferred because they have a stronger aroma. The thousands of seeds in the longish pod are collected and cured in factories which you may see dotted around the north-east coast. If you ask, you will normally be able to visit a factory and watch this complicated process.

You can buy samples of vanilla at souvenir shops and around the Zoma market in Tana. If you have a specific interest, you could contact the Institut de la Vanille de Madagascar (aka Ivama), BP 804, Antananarivo (☎ (2) 221 90; fax (2) 249 72). ■

own food from Maroantsetra, and charcoal to burn for cooking. Be sure you're well equipped for rain (thunderstorms are frequent, year-round) and be prepared for intolerable sandflies.

Transport to the island is by chartered pirogue from Maroantsetra (only 5km) – but this is only feasible in good weather. Any of the hotels in Maroantsetra can arrange day trips, guides (about FMg 25,000 per day), and possibly rent you some camping equipment.

One great option is to charter a pirogue from Maroantsetra to Nosy Mangabe, and arrange for one of the regular Maroantsetra–Île Sainte Marie cargo boats (which often stop at Nosy Mangabe because of tides) to pick you up a day or two later then continue to Île Sainte Marie.

For more information about permits, guides and camping, visit the Nosy Mangabe information office behind the market in Maroantsetra.

MASOALA PENINSULA TREK

One of Madagascar's premier treks connects Maroantsetra with the town of Antalaha or Ambohitralanana (aka Cap Est). It goes over the Beanjada massif, traversing the wild and rugged Masoala Peninsula, now part of the Réserve de Masoala (see below). It's a good, hot and sticky slog made even more challenging for the morale by incessant rain, leeches and knee-deep mud. Although the trail is very tough at times you may go through some of the last unexplored rainforests in Madagascar and, if you are lucky, see plenty of lemurs.

The main route begins at the village of Mahalevona, 22km east of Maroantsetra, or at Maromandia, 23km south-west of Antalaha. Including the approaches on either end, which you will probably have to walk, the route is 111km long and takes at least five days. This is a more established path, connecting the numerous villages and settlements along the route. For the most part, the path sticks to the rice paddies bordering the Sakafihitra River and does not traverse a lot of rainforest.

A better start (or finish) is at the village of Ambohitralanana – but getting there or back is a problem (see the Cap Est section). This trek (also about five days) gives you more opportunity to trudge through the rainforest, and to admire the flora and fauna (if you have the energy). From Cap Est, hire a pirogue upstream for six hours along the River Onive, and then trek almost directly west. By about the third day, you join the main path at the village of Ampakafo and continue to Mahalevona or Maromandia.

You must pick up a detailed map from the FTM office in Tana. A guide is absolutely essential, and is available in Maroantsetra, Sambava or Antalaha. They charge about FMg 35,000 per day. Porters (around FMg 15,000 per day) are an excellent idea for carrying your luggage and food. Camping spots are few, so most trekkers wind up staying in villages. You should bring your own food, though you can buy bananas and rice (but nothing else) along the way. The trek can also be organised through Sambava Voyages in Sambava (see the Sambava section later in this chapter).

RÉSERVE DE MASOALA

This new 210,000 hectare reserve (which will be later upgraded to a national park) contains one of the best rainforests in the country, and is home to lemur (red ruffed and white-fronted) and several species of tenrec and mongoose. There is also a marine reserve to protect the mangroves, lagoons and coral reefs, as well as the occasional whale. It rains a helluva lot around here – less so from September to December – but be prepared for a lot of rain, all the time.

At the time of research, there was no further information about the reserve. ANGAP plans to open an office for visitors in Antalaha and Maroantsetra. Access to the reserve is basically on foot, starting from Maroantsetra.

ANTALAHA
• Telephone Area Code: 8

Antalaha is another outpost on the Vanilla Coast, with another fantastic beach. It is a lovely, laid-back town. The only problem is the lack of reliable and regular transport – but that is almost an advantage because it puts off a lot of other vazahas.

Places to Stay & Eat

The unsigned *Hôtel La Plage* (☎ 812 05), right on the beach, has some nice bungalows for FMg 40,000 with bathroom. Rooms at the homely *Hôtel du Centre* (☎ 811 67) for FMg 18,000 are better value. This hotel serves a tasty menu du jour for FMg 15,000 in the evening. You can also hire mountain bikes here.

Also cheap and friendly are the *Hôtel Florida* and the handful of *bungalows* (☎ 811 33) behind the Chamber of Commerce in the centre of town. The only restaurant in Antalaha is the *Fleur de Lotus* (look for the sign).

Getting There & Away

Air Mad flies to Antalaha several times a week as part of a Twin-Otter run which links it with Sambava (US$25) and, sometimes, other places in the north-east of the country.

Every day, several buses leave at around 7.30 am for the trip along the sandy track from Sambava (at least three hours). Ask the driver to drop you off at your hotel or bungalow.

For information about boats, ask around the tiny jetty/port. You are more likely to get some luck hanging around Sambava.

CAP EST

One of the most incredible and remote parts of northern Madagascar would have to be the region known as Cap Est – the easternmost point in Madagascar. The coral here, and especially further south at the bottom of Masoala Peninsula, is pristine and arguably the best in Madagascar. Expensive trips for diving and deep-sea fishing can be organised here, and the cape is the best place to start or finish a trek across the Masoala Peninsula.

Another reason to come – and the only place to stay – is the magnificent *Le Residence du Cap* (aka *Residence Cap Est*), about 1km south of the tiny village of Ambohitralanana. Supreme isolation and exquisite service cost FMg 65,000 per bungalow; magnificent three-course fish meals range from FMg 20,000 to FMg 35,000.

The problem is getting there: there's no public transport, so you have to hire a vehicle, go by mountain bike (about six hours from Antalaha) or hitch a ride on an infrequent cargo boat (about FMg 10,000).

SAMBAVA
• Telephone Area Code: 885

The garden city of Sambava, more or less orphaned between Antsiranana and Maroantsetra on the wild north-east coast, lies between the sea and the soaring Marojejy Massif. This town of 20,000 considers itself the vanilla capital of Madagascar.

Sambava is growing in popularity as a cheaper and more secluded beach destination than Île Sainte Marie. The beaches are gorgeous, but we are unsure about the sharks: locals say they are far from the shore (or are they waiting for tasty vazahas?). If you're craving a swim, it may be safer to try the lovely palm and casuarina-lined **Lac d'Andohabe** at the fishing village of Antohamaro 9km south of Sambava, near the airport. Oh, yes ... watch for crocodiles.

All four major banks are represented in the centre of town and will change money. About 3km south of the airport you can visit the **Germoir Pepiniere**, a coconut tree nursery, or the **Lopat Vanilla Factory**.

Organised Tours

The best (and only) travel agency on the east coast north of Toamasina is the impressive *Sambava Voyages* (☎ 110; fax (2) 413 94). The English-speaking staff can arrange a number of (expensive) day trips by 4WD and boat, from about FMg 140,000 per person, visiting vanilla and cocoa plantations and local villages, and exploring nearby rivers. It also arranges guided treks across the Masoala Peninsula.

Places to Stay & Eat

The large *Hôtel Carrefour* (☎ 60), right on the beach, is a charming old place with a wide range of rooms. Prices start at FMg 51,000 for a room with a fan in the annexe, to FMg 77,000 for air-con and views. Beware of the restaurant, however, which has no set menu and may overcharge on an agreed meal and price.

The *Hôtel Esmeralda* (☎ 63), formerly known as the Hôtel Orchidea Beach, is in a gorgeous setting only metres from the beach. Bungalows cost FMg 40,000; less exciting rooms, a little less. The restaurant is very good, and it's a superb place to have a drink in the evening. Next door, *Las Palmas* (☎ 87) is a little nicer and more expensive at

FMg 75,000 for a bungalow – meals are only available for guests.

Further south along the beach, the friendly *Hôtel Le Club* (☎ 64) is worth checking out. It has a pool and a great range of bungalows from FMg 50,000 to FMg 85,000 (with a fridge and lovely bathroom).

There are a couple of cheaper alternatives a short walk from the beach. The *Hotel Pacifique* (☎ 124), opposite the southern taxi-brousse station, has rooms from FMg 25,000, while the *Hôtel Calypso* (☎ 108), on the main road, has rooms from FMg 25,000 to FMg 35,000.

You can eat in your hotel, but the best restaurant in town is the *Restaurant Étoile Rouge* along the main street, not far from Esmeralda's. Also along the main street are two recommended Chinese restaurants: *Mandarin* and the *Hôtel Restaurant Le Cantonnais*. Le Cantonnais also rents out cheap rooms.

Getting There & Away

Air Air Mad flies to Sambava several times a week from Tana (US$139), usually via Maroantsetra (US$37) and Toamasina (US$71). The flights then go on to Antsiranana (US$60). Air Mad (☎ 37) is on the main street, close to Esmeralda's. The chaotic little airport is a few km from town by chartered taxi.

Taxi-brousse Sambava has two taxi-brousse stations: to places on the east coast, such as Andapa and Iharana, take a local share-taxi to the northern station (which doubles as a huge market on Saturday). To Antalaha and Andapa, there is another taxi-brousse station at the southern end of town. During February and March it's almost impossible to travel overland to Sambava.

ANDAPA

The dusty, unexciting town of Andapa is south-west of Sambava. It lies in a lovely agricultural valley in the largest rice-growing area in northern Madagascar. Beyond, the greatest tracts of remaining primary forest in the country offer challenging trekking opportunities. If you ask directions in town, you can walk about 45 minutes up the top of what looks like a white hill for fantastic **views** of the region.

During the drier months of September and October (which are nevertheless still rainy), it's possible to trek through the rainforest from the Andapa Valley to the Andranofotsy River above Maroantsetra in six or seven days. From there, you must hire a pirogue downstream to the coast. This route served as the venue for the 1992 Mada-Raid. This is an arduous trip, not to be taken lightly. A guide and detailed FTM map are essential.

Places to Stay & Eat
The only hotel in town is the *Hôtel Vatosoa* (aka *Hôtel Crystal*). Clean rooms range from FMg 32,000 to FMg 37,000 with hot water and toilet. Nice bungalows, a short ride from the hotel, will cost FMg 50,000 if/when they are ever completed. The restaurant at the Vatosoa is very good, and even worth a day trip from Sambava (if the bus doesn't spend too long looking for passengers). A three course menu du jour, in a lovely setting with soothing background music, costs FMg 20,000.

Getting There & Away
Andapa lies 109km from Sambava along an asphalted, but winding road. The daily bus (FMg 15,000) leaves Sambava at around 7 am and can take up to five hours (mainly to look for passengers), so a day trip is a little impractical.

RÉSERVE DE MAROJEJY-ANJANAHARIBE-SUD
The rugged and precipitous Marojejy Massif, with an area of 60,150 hectares, rises north of the road between Andapa and Sambava. It protects a vast and remote wilderness, with over 200 types of plants, which harbours diverse species of lemur, frogs, chameleons and birds. At lower elevations the landscape is dominated by thick rainforest; above 800m the rainforest is replaced by highland forest; and at the highest elevations (up to the peak of Mt Marojejy at 2133m) the primary vegetation cover is comprised of heaths, mosses and lichens. It is also one of the wettest places in the country (3000mm per year).

The Réserve de Marojejy is officially closed to tourists, but you can visit the reserve known as Anjanaharibe-Sud, 40km south of Andapa. There isn't any public transport, nor any decent roads to this reserve, so you'll have to trek or ask about a lift at the WWF office. In the reserve, a lovely trail through the rainforest leads to the **Ranomafana thermal baths**.

If travelling independently, get your permit – and ask about any transport going to the reserve – at the World Wide Fund for Nature (WWF) office in Andapa. Guides are not compulsory, but are still a good idea. Camping is allowed in the reserve. Sambava Voyages in Sambava can arrange trips.

IHARANA (VOHÉMAR)
• Telephone Area Code: 840
Iharana (commonly known as Vohémar) is 153km north of Sambava along a rough but mostly asphalted road. It is the last stop north on the east coast before the long and difficult trip across to Ambilobe and Antsiranana. Like the towns further south on the east coast, it's a centre of vanilla production. It is thought to be the 9th century landing site of the Zeïdistes, descendants of the Prophet Mohammed. In this area archaeologists have uncovered 12th century Chinese artefacts.

Lac Andranotsara
The main site of interest for visitors is Lac Andranotsara 7km south of Iharana. In French it's known as Lac Vert (Green Lake) because of its colouration by algae.

Legend has it that there was once a village at Andranotsara. One night, however, an irritable seven-headed monster curled up for a sleep in the village. Unfortunately, he was quite heavy and the ground beneath him subsided. This incident was followed by seven days of rain which left the village resembling a sort of Malagasy Atlantis. Locals believe the crocodiles which inhabit the lake are the villagers reincarnated and whenever the crocs appear dissatisfied a zebu sacrifice is organised to appease them. Several fady are in effect so inquire before visiting or making assumptions.

Places to Stay
The main hotel in Iharana is the *Sol et Mar* aka *Motel Solymar* (☎ 45). Nice bungalows cost FMg 35,000 and rooms are FMg 23,000. One reader claimed that the hotel served the best punch drinks in the country. Other choices are the *Hôtel Railovy* and the cheap and simple *Poisson d'Or*, which costs FMg 10,000 per room and serves really top-notch food. Another good place for a feed is the *La Cigogne*.

Getting There & Away
Air Mad (☎ 31) occasionally flies between Iharana and Antsiranana for US$37. This is especially useful during the wet season when the roads may be impassable.

Taxi-brousse transport is easy and regular between Sambava and Iharana (FMg 15,000; five hours). The road between Iharana and Antsiranana, however, is very rough and not recommended. By taxi-brousse it can be as much as 30 hours of serious bumping and grinding, but if the road is good you can get from Ambilobe to Iharana in as 'little' as 12 hours (FMg 30,000). One reader claimed that it took him five days to get from Ambilobe to Iharana in the wet season – so be warned!

Southern Coast

MANANJARY
• Telephone Area Code: 7

Mananjary, sliced in two by the Canal des Pangalanes, is a vanilla, coffee and pepper producing community about 177km north of Manakara. It is a pleasant, laid-back place but not on the way to anywhere else, so getting there involves a lot of backtracking unless you fly in or out.

It is here that the small Antambahoaka tribe holds mass circumcision ceremonies known as *sambatra* every seven years. The actual operations are now performed in the hospital. The next ceremony will take place in the year 2000. (They are also held in other Malagasy villages; see Festivals in the Madagascar Facts for the Visitor chapter.)

North of Mananjary is the locally revered **White Elephant** sculpture at Ambohitsara. This relic is attributed to the Zeïdistes, descendants of the prophet Mohammed who first landed at Iharana on Madagascar's north coast and then moved south. It bears strikingly little resemblance to an elephant, however. The Hôtel Jardin de la Mer runs trips to the sculpture.

Places to Stay & Eat
Mananjary has the small *Solimotel* (☎ 942 85) on Blvd Maritime, on the ocean side of the canal. Rooms cost around FMg 20,000 and there's a good restaurant.

The nicest place is the *Hôtel Jardin de la Mer* (☎ 940 80) with singles/doubles from FMg 25,000/30,000.

Getting There & Away
Air Mananjary is usually (but not always) part of the run up and down the south-eastern coast. Air Mad flies from Tana for US$71, and then goes on to Manakara, Taolagnaro and Toliara.

Taxi-brousse From Fianarantsoa, taxis-brousse (FMg 22,000) travel every day. It's also an easy four to five hour trip (FMg 15,000) along the good road to Manakara, but you may need to get off at the junction village of Irondro and wait for a connection.

Getting to Mananjary from Toamasina and points north is another story, however, and will require determination and creativity. By using a combination of methods you should be able to do the trip in a week, depending on your luck. It will probably begin by connecting with the occasional taxi-brousse which runs from Toamasina to Mahanaro, 255km to the south. From there, you'll have to rely on coastal boats from Mahanaro to Nosy Varika and hitching or walking from Nosy Varika to Mananjary.

MANAKARA
• Telephone Area Code: 7

Because of its long beach and easy rail access from Fianarantsoa, the lovely town of Manakara is becoming an increasingly popular travellers' destination. Beachcombing and sun-worshipping are possible, and hiring a pirogue around the lagoon is a great idea. Unfortunately, nautical activities are thwarted by the presence of large and nasty sharks in the sea.

The sprawling town is divided in two parts. In the centre, known as Tanambao, are the railway station, taxi-brousse station, market and several hotels. Across the lagoon-like estuary of the Manakara River is the old seaside district of Manakara-be. In this area are the BTM and BFV banks, post office, a couple of hotels and beach.

Places to Stay & Eat
The cheapest place to stay is the *Hôtel Tsy Manavaka*, opposite the railway station. Rooms cost FMg 15,000 and would be quite acceptable except for the state of the toilets. It is handy for a late-night arrival by train, however.

Although a bit run-down, the colonial-style *Hôtel de Manakara* (☎ 211 41) is probably the best place to stay. It serves good meals (especially at breakfast), has a nice terrace, and is close to the beach. Large, dusty rooms at the front cost FMg 20,600; worse rooms at the back cost less.

Right on the beach, several hundred metres from the Hôtel de Manakara, the *Parc du Parthenay* is a large, rustic place with bungalows for FMg 30,000. It also has a nice saltwater swimming pool (often empty), which may be used by non-guests for FMg 1500 per day.

Another alternative which is central, but a little overpriced at FMg 38,000, is the *Hôtel Morabe* near the market; you may be able to get a cheaper room at the back for FMg 20,000. The restaurant is probably the best in town with an excellent range of meals from FMg 7000.

At the large and soulless *Hôtel Sidi* (☎ 212 02), most rooms cost FMg 53,000 including breakfast; a few downstairs cost FMg 38,000 with shared facilities. The Sidi also boasts a nice restaurant and an excellent salon de thé.

For a bit of a splurge, the *Restaurant La Chalet Suisse* (☎ 231 89), between the taxi-brousse and railway stations, serves a range of Chinese, Malagasy and Indian meals for FMg 12,000 plus. It also has a couple of nice bungalows for rent at FMg 50,000.

Getting There & Away
Air Once or twice a week, Air Mad flies from Tana to Manakara (US$94), often via Mananjary, and then to other places along the south-east coast. The Air Mad office (☎ 212 04) is in the Hôtel Sidi complex.

Train The vast majority of travellers prefer to travel at least one way on the rollicking train from Fianarantsoa. Tickets cost FMg 20,500/34,500 for 2nd/1st class to Fianarantsoa. Trains officially depart Manakara early on Mondays and Thursdays, but delays are normal. Refer to the Fianarantsoa section in the Central Madagascar chapter for more details about this great train trip.

Taxi-brousse Taxis-brousse travel between Manakara and Fianarantsoa (FMg 25,000) several times a day, but to other places (including Mananjary), they only leave when there is enough demand. There are daily servies (depending on demand) south to Vohipeno (FMg 4500) and Farafangana (FMg 10,000), sometimes continuing as far as Vangaindrano and the pleasant village of Manombondro (dry season only).

Overnight minibuses (FMg 53,000) leave Manakara for Tana on most afternoons. The taxi-brousse station is a long pousse-pousse trip north of all hotels.

Getting Around

Manakara is one of several Malagasy towns with pousse-pousses, and you will need one to get to or from the train and taxi-brousse stations. A ride from the railway station to anywhere near the beach should cost about FMg 2500 (more at night), but you will probably be asked for three times more.

VOHIPENO

Vohipeno lies on the Matitanana River about 27km south of Manakara. This small town is at the heart of the Antaimoro culture area. There are no hotels or restaurants in Vohipeno so you'll have to consult with the mayor about a place to stay or camp.

The daily taxi-brousse from Manakara costs about FMg 4500 each way. The trip is through mostly empty countryside. Although the road turns horrid about 5km south of Vohipeno, these overloaded vehi-cles continue to Farafangana, 109km to the south from Manakara.

FARAFANGANA

• Telephone Area Code: 7

Farafangana is at the southern extreme of the Canal des Pangalanes and is 109km by road south of Manakara. It is a quiet, laid-back little place without much to recommend it except its friendly atmosphere and easy-going ambience.

The favourite hotel in Farafangana is the *Tulipes Rouges* (☎ 911 86). Alternatively, try the cheaper *Rose Rouge* (☎ 911 54) which costs just FMg 7000 for a room. The only restaurant is *La Palmiers* near the market.

Most days, depending on demand, taxis-brousse travel from Manakara to Farafangana (FMg 10,000) often continuing on to Vangaindrano. The only way to con-tinue south to Taolagnaro is on the once-weekly Air Mad flight (US$70) or by mountain bike along the rugged but beautiful 315km track.

Central Madagascar

South of Tana, the *hauts plateaux* stretch southward to Antsirabe, Fianarantsoa and beyond until the rolling hills, plains and rice paddies give way to the dry country of the far south. Antsirabe, which lies in southern Antananarivo province, is a primarily Merina town, while the eastern central province of Fianarantsoa is the heart of Betsileo territory. The Betsileo are experts at cultivating rice, laying out and irrigating terraced fields and, with the assistance of Swiss settlers, they've also taken to producing wine.

ANTSIRABE

• Telephone Area Code: 4

The beautiful town of Antsirabe, at an altitude of 1500m, lies 169km south of Tana. (The name Antsirabe means 'where there is much salt' but should probably be renamed 'where there is much *pousse-pousse*'.) This primarily Merina town of 100,000 people serves as an industrial centre, a sort of thermal spa resort and Madagascar's preeminent trading centre for semiprecious stones and minerals. Antsirabe is well worth a few days' exploration and makes an excellent stopover along the road between Tana and Fianarantsoa.

The town was founded by Norwegian Borgen and Rosaas missionaries in 1872 as a health retreat and later became popular with French colonials as both a spa town and hill station. It was, and still is, a cool retreat from the rigours of Tana or the feverish east coast. During the winter months it can even get quite cold.

Orientation

Antsirabe actually has three distinct areas. One is the lower, dusty and bustling Malagasy town which contains the daily market and most of the shops and businesses. North of the cathedral lies another world. This elegant and sprawling French creation is a large, open grid of flowering avenues and resembles a cross between suburban upstate

HIGHLIGHTS

• The pretty spa town of Antsirabe, which is also the centre for trade in semiprecious stones.

• The Zafimaniry villages for their wonderful wood carvings. Take a guide to get the most out of a visit and observe local *fady*.

• The train journey from Fianarantsoa to Manakara – the most exciting and interesting in the whole country.

New York and perhaps a turn-of-the-century French housing estate. At its heart is Grande Ave, a broad ceremonial axis dominated at one end by the railway and at the other by the immense and once very grand Hôtel des Thermes. The hotel overlooks lily-filled Lake Ranomafana, where the thermal bathhouse is located.

The third area, west of Lac Ranomafana, is one of Madagascar's major industrial zones, boasting the Star Brewery (producer of Three Horses Beer, among other bottled treats), a cotton mill and a tobacco factory.

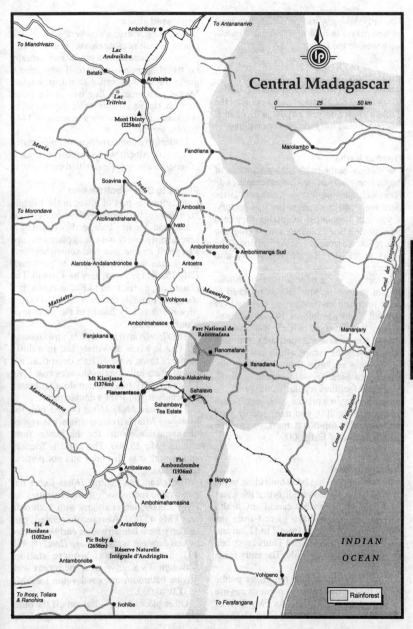

Central Madagascar

0   25   50 km

The daily Asabotsy market (which is biggest on Saturdays) is held in this area, immediately west of the lake.

Information
Money The BTM, BFV and BNI-CL banks, all next to each other and opposite the Baobab and Soafyel hotels, will change money without too much fuss or waiting.

Thermal Baths
The thermal baths (with the grand name of the Centre National de Crenotherapie et de Thermoclimatisme) have changed little since their construction earlier this century. If you can bear a bit of grunge they're a worthwhile visit, especially after a gruelling hike to Lac Tritriva or Lac Andraikiba. (The baths at nearby Betafo are better and cleaner.)

Immersion in the mineral-rich water from the hot springs in Antsirabe is believed to assist in curing rheumatism as well as liver and gall bladder problems. Beside the baths is Lac Ranomafana which was created mainly for ornamental purposes, but also helps prevent the escape of thermal gases.

The baths are open from 7 am to 1 pm, Monday to Saturday – but opening times, prices and facilities regularly change. A 20-minute lounge in a private cubicle still costs a bargain FMg 200; you must supply your own towel. A top-notch massage (for the tourists) will cost FMg 5000.

Swimming Pool
A swimming pool has been built close to the thermal baths; the downside is that the water conditions will probably cancel any health benefits you might have gained from the baths. The pool is open from 7 to 11 am and 2 to 5 pm weekdays (except Thursdays); and on Saturdays to 11 am only. The entry fee is FMg 200.

If you can't quite face the grimy public pool at the thermal baths, non-guests can use the pool at the Arotel Hôtel for FMg 4000 or at the Hôtel des Thermes for FMg 4500.

Organised Tours
Considering there are several interesting places to visit near Antsirabe, it is very surprising that there are few guides and virtually no travel agencies in town. If you need a guide, or want to organise a trip, contact Michel (who speaks English) at the Hôtel Baobab. He can arrange a half-day trip to the two lakes and Betafo for a reasonable FMg 80,000 per car.

Under no circumstances use a guide called Tamimy or Albert: we have received dozens of letters from *very* dissatisfied customers.

Places to Stay – bottom end
In the grubbier part of town, in the triangle bordered on two sides by Rue le Myre de Villers and Ave de l'Indépendance, there are several dirty, noisy but cheap places to stay. Just stroll around and find somewhere less grimy than the others; expect to pay about FMg 10,000 for a very, very basic room. The *Hôtel Lito*, on the road to Fianarantsoa, is a cheap but bearable option at FMg 10,000 per person and is very handy to the main *taxi-brousse* station.

The *Hôtel Niavo* (☎ 484 67), up a laneway off Rue le Myre de Villers and in a dusty corner of town, is now a little overpriced but is still often full. Singles/doubles cost FMg 15,000/30,000, but you can do a lot better, especially if you want a double room.

The *Cercle Mess Mixte* (☎ 483 66), the Malagasy Army's living quarters, has a range of reasonable rooms for the public from around FMg 25,000. The place is friendly and central; it is also busy and not particularly relaxing.

The clean and central *Hôtel Rubis* has good-value rooms with shared facilities for FMg 35,000; larger rooms with bathroom cost FMg 45,000. Also recommended, particularly for a late arrival or early departure by taxi-brousse, is the *Manoro Hôtel* (☎ 480 47), next to the taxi-brousse station. Although it's a noisy area, the rooms with private bathroom are good value for FMg 35,000/40,000.

Other places to try – but only if the other places are full – include the average *Hôtel*

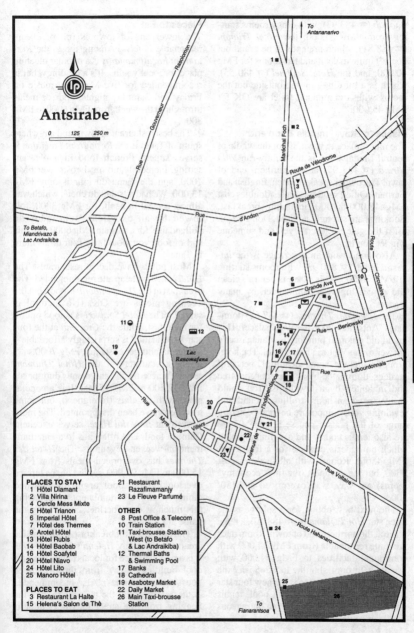

CENTRAL MADAGASCAR

Antsirabe

0   125   250 m

To Antananarivo

To Betafo, Miandrivazo & Lac Andraikiba

Lac Ranomafana

To Betafo & Lac Andraikiba

To Fianarantsoa

PLACES TO STAY
1 Hôtel Diamant
2 Villa Nirina
4 Cercle Mess Mixte
5 Hôtel Trianon
6 Imperial Hôtel
7 Hôtel des Thermes
9 Arotel Hôtel
13 Hôtel Rubis
14 Hôtel Baobab
16 Hôtel Soafytel
20 Hôtel Niavo
24 Hôtel Lito
25 Manoro Hôtel

PLACES TO EAT
3 Restaurant La Halte
15 Helena's Salon de Thè

21 Restaurant Razafimamanjy
23 Le Fleuve Parfumé

OTHER
8 Post Office & Telecom
10 Train Station
11 Taxi-brousse Station West (to Betafo & Lac Andraikiba)
12 Thermal Baths & Swimming Pool
17 Banks
18 Cathedral
19 Asabotsy Market
22 Daily Market
26 Main Taxi-brousse Station

Baobab (☎ 483 93), with dingy rooms starting from FMg 25,000; the *Hôtel Trianon* (☎ 488 81), which pretends to be grand but doesn't quite make it and has rooms for FMg 40,000; and the *Hôtel Soafytel* (☎ 480 55), which is a bit dingy on the outside but the rooms with a communal toilet are OK for FMg 45,000.

Places to Stay – middle & top end

The nicest place in town, if not the whole of central Madagascar, is the family-run *Villa Nirina* (☎ 485 97) at the northern end of town. The owner speaks French, English and German. Quiet, spotless singles/doubles cost FMg 40,000/60,000, including breakfast. Bookings are strongly advised. Don't be put off if the gate is closed – yell and someone will let you in.

Also good value in this range is the *Imperial Hôtel* (☎ 860 93) with rooms starting at FMg 70,000. This place is central, clean and comes highly recommended by many readers.

The *Hôtel des Thermes* (☎ 487 61) dominates Antsirabe like a royal palace. This grand old colonial building is Madagascar's answer to the Victoria Falls Hotel. The hotel grounds include some beautiful, peaceful gardens, dominated by an ancient cedar tree and inhabited by a few birds. You could easily spend an hour strolling around and regaining your composure beyond pestering range of the pousse-pousse brigade. There are also tennis courts and a swimming pool which non-guests can use for a fee (about FMg 4500). Rooms with all facilities cost F300, but the cheapest (the tiny 'economy' rooms) are way, way overpriced at F150/ 200.

The next best option for a splurge is the three star *Hôtel Diamant* (☎ 488 40), a huge place at the northern end of town. Room rates are quite reasonable (from FMg 34,000 with communal facilities to FMg 54,000 with private bathroom), but the location isn't the best. The top of the range is the new four star *Arotel Hôtel* (☎ 481 20) with pool, tennis court and so on. Rates start at an outrageous F400 per room.

Places to Eat

The lower end of town is full of cheap, reasonable *hotelys*. Among these, the *Restaurant Razafimamanjy* is a popular meeting place for local youths. It's a bit dingy, but is recommended for live Malagasy music on Friday and Saturday nights, and for meals throughout the week from FMg 6000 to FMg 8000.

The best restaurant in town (and anywhere south of Tana) is the *Restaurant La Halte*. It serves superb French food in a pleasant setting. Incredibly, no meal costs over FMg 7000, and the menu du jour is only FMg 13,000. We had a 'salad du chef', which was almost a meal in itself, for FMg 3000, followed by an excellent 'tournedos de hollandaise' for a bargain FMg 6000. For this sort of food you would pay four times more in Tana.

Most hotels have decent restaurants. The *Hôtel Niavo* is cheap and recommended. The breakfast at the *Hôtel Baobab* is poor, but the evening meals are OK. (No alcohol is served.) The *Hôtel Soafytel* is a good option for breakfast, while the *Croc Inn* at the four star Arotel Hôtel is surprisingly affordable – a tasty hamburger costs just FMg 7000.

The restaurants at the *Hôtel Diamant* serve Chinese meals, and menus du jour for FMg 12,500 to FMg 15,000. It is a popular place with *vazahas* (foreigners), but some travellers have been disappointed. The more convenient *Imperial Hôtel* serves excellent Chinese food, and often has live entertainment on weekend evenings. The *Hôtel des Thermes* has overpriced meals from FMg 15,000 to FMg 25,000, served on the terrace overlooking the pool or in the elevated dining room. It is certainly not worth paying this much at des Thermes considering the value at La Halte.

The best place for breakfast, cakes and ice creams is definitely *Helena's Salon de Thé*. It is a popular place for locals and is in a nice cool building (away from those damned pousse-pousse drivers). Also recommended is the *restaurant* at the railway, though the begging from the street kids next door is heartbreaking. *Le Fleuve Parfumé* continues to get mixed reviews from travellers – from 'tasty food and reasonable prices' to 'we found a large insect in our wonton and a fly charred to an eggroll'.

Entertainment

The places to be seen in Antsirabe are the lively *Night Club Le Tahiti* in the Hôtel Diamant, and the *Palace Night Club* at the Imperial Hôtel. In the evening, the Hôtel des Thermes has the tiny *Royal Casino* (where shorts and sandals are not the permitted style of dress).

Things to Buy

Antsirabe is a centre for selling and trading tourmaline, beryl, aquamarine, amethyst, zircon, rose quartz and other indigenous stones. There are several lapidaries in town where you can watch the cutting and polishing process, examine the goods and perhaps pick up a souvenir.

You will be regularly approached in the streets to buy gemstones, which are often packaged in attractive boxes. There is also an excellent selection of gemstones at the stalls at Lac Andraikiba. Bargain hard, and make sure the stones are not antique or truly precious, otherwise you will need to obtain Customs clearance and pay tax (refer to Things to Buy in the Madagascar Facts for the Visitor chapter).

Getting There & Away

Train If you're going from Tana to Antsirabe, or points between, the train is best for comfort, speed and scenery. The narrow-gauge railway line provides an amazing roller-coaster ride as the train gallops along the rails, stopping at 12 stations along the 159km track. There is no food service on the train but you'll find a variety of snacks for sale on the platform during the stop at Ambatolampy.

The train should leave Tana every day at 7 am, and return from Antsirabe after about 1 pm. (Always check the current schedule at the railway the day before you want to leave.) The price is FMg 8000/14,500 for 2nd/1st class to Tana; and FMg 5000/8000

to Ambatolampy. Get to the railway an hour before the arrival of the train from Tana (usually about 12.30 pm). Tickets aren't on sale until the train arrives.

Taxi-brousse From the main taxi-brousse station in the south of town, taxis-brousse and *taxis-be* run every hour or two to Tana (FMg 15,000), and several times a day to Fianarantsoa (FMg 17,500). Antsirabe is the junction for all daily public transport to western Madagascar – to Miandrivazo (FMg 15,000/16,000 by taxi-brousse/bus) and to Morondava (FMg 35,000/42,500).

Another taxi-brousse station, lost among the Asabotsy market in the western part of town, serves local villages including Betafo.

Getting Around

Bus Antsirabe's recently acquired bus fleet, courtesy of Japanese aid, serves surrounding towns and villages, including Betafo. It's well-organised with drivers and conductors wearing similar uniform overalls. Buses depart from the taxi-brousse/bus station at the Asabotsy market. You won't need a bus within Antsirabe, which is small enough to walk around, but try convincing a pousse-pousse driver that.

Pousse-pousse If there is one thing you will remember about Antsirabe, it is the pousse-pousse. They reign in this town, a legacy of Chinese coolie labour imported to work on the Tana–Antsirabe railway. They are brighter, more plentiful, more decorative – and far more annoying – in Antsirabe than in any other Malagasy town.

The pousse-pousse drivers were a nightmare. No 30 attached himself to us for the three days we spent in Antsirabe, and tried to scare us with tales of bandits etc. I *think* they were just tales.
Rachel Andrews, UK

If you arrive by train prepare to be mobbed by pousse-pousse drivers, who fight among themselves for newly arrived foreigners (who don't yet know what the going rate is).

Vazahas will have to pay at least FMg 1500 for each ride.

There are three ways to ensure that the pousse-pousse drivers do not make your stay in Antsirabe a complete misery: (a) walk quickly, shaking your head vigorously, and shout 'Non! Non! Non!; (b) hire a bike, and outrun the pests; or (c) bow to their demands and hire one for the length of your visit – he will make sure you are not pestered by other drivers.

Bicycle Thankfully, Antsirabe is flat and ideal for bikes. It is not too difficult to cycle to the Andraikiba and Tritriva lakes (but it can be slow-going in places, with mud, ruts and patches of sand). It's also an easy ride to Betafo. Hiring a bike will ensure that you do not have to battle with the pousse-pousse drivers around Antsirabe.

You can rent bikes at the Restaurant La Halte (see Places to Eat earlier). The prices seem to be quite negotiable – we were offered different prices by the waiter and the manager. Expect to pay FMg 30,000/40,000 for a half day/day. For the same prices, you can rent bikes from the friendly fellow based near Helena's Salon de Thé (he speaks English); or try the Baobab and Soafytel hotels.

Horse Another way to avoid the pousse-pousse drivers is to rent a horse for a very negotiable FMg 25,000 per day, or FMg 6000 per hour from along Grand Ave.

AROUND ANTSIRABE
Lac Andraikiba & Lac Tritriva

In the hills west of Antsirabe there are two attractive and interesting lakes, both of volcanic origin. Either or both make a fantastic day trip from town. The larger of the two, Lac Andraikiba, lies 7km west of Antsirabe just off the Morondava road. During the 19th century it was a favourite retreat of Queen Ranavalona II, and later the French turned it into a holiday aquatic centre. The once lively Club Nautique now sits deserted and empty. You can swim if you don't mind everyone watching you and the shores of the lake are great for hiking.

Lac Andraikiba is said to be haunted by the ghost of a pregnant girl who drowned in a swimming competition with another girl for the prize of marriage to a Merina potentate. Villagers say that each day at dawn she may be seen resting for a few minutes on a rock by the lake shore. There are plenty of gemstones for sale by the lake.

Probably more interesting is Lac Tritriva, which lies in the hills about 18km south-west of Antsirabe. This deep-blue lake can appear beautiful or forbidding, depending on the weather. It's a bit eerie even when the sun is shining and it's said that the lake level inexplicably falls during the rainy season and rises in the dry season. It's shaped a bit like Africa or Madagascar – if you squint and adjust your head.

Lac Tritriva is surrounded mostly by a sheer cliff and a pleasant, easy walk circles the lake. Locals have seen the advantages in living near such a pretty lake and now charge a hefty FMg 10,000 to enter; the fee includes a French-speaking guide and a couple of bored kids trailing along.

As with Lac Andraikiba, a tragic legend surrounds Lac Tritriva. The waters are supposedly cursed by two star-crossed lovers – a local version of Romeo and Juliet – who leapt from the cliff edge when they were refused permission to marry. Their affection lives on in two intertwined thorn trees above the lake. At the lake is a tomb of a Chinese man who was dared to swim across the lake, but drowned. There are two local *fady* (taboos): do not take pork to the region, and do not swim in the lake.

Places to Stay & Eat There are no hotels in the villages near the lakes but if you ask around, someone will put you up. Local 'authorities' allow visitors to camp alongside Lac Tritriva, which would be excellent except for the annoying kids and the sound of the locals chopping down the forest. There is no-one to stop you camping anywhere around the magical Lac Andraikiba.

Getting There & Away Antsirabe to Lac Tritriva is 18km, Lac Tritriva to Lac Andraikiba is 12km and from Lac Andraikiba back to Antsirabe is about 7km. Apart from a small bush shop there are no real facilities along the way, so carry food and water if you're travelling on foot or by pedal power.

Most people visit both lakes in a combined day trip, but if you're going on horseback or under your own steam there is a considerable distance to cover and you'll need to get an early start. You may want to consider using a combination of walking, horse riding, taxis and public transport. A very pleasant, and easy, option would be to hire a taxi to Lac

Tritriva, walk the 12km from there to Lac Andraikiba, and flag down a passing bus or taxi-brousse for the trip back to Antsirabe. The cheapest way to Lac Andraikiba is on a taxi-brousse going towards Betafo or Talatakely from Antsirabe. The lake lies approximately a km south of the main road.

Many readers recommend taking a mountain bike (though, depending on the season, the sandy or muddy roads can be tough) or a horse. See the earlier Getting Around section under Antsirabe for hire details.

Lac Tritriva is a three hour walk from

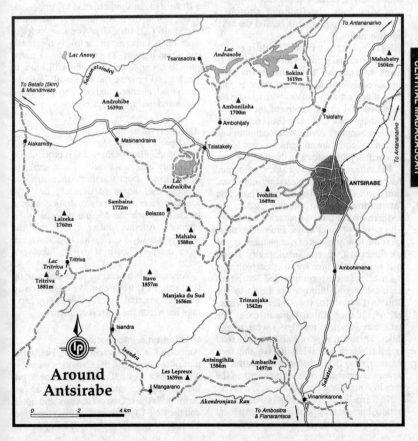

Antsirabe but you may be lucky and get a lift from a passing taxi-brousse or local car. A more interesting option would be to hire a guide from Antsirabe who can lead you along short-cuts using smaller paths and tell you about the local fady.

Betafo

The typically red-brick Merina village of Betafo (Many Roofs) lies 22km west of Antsirabe and makes another worthwhile day trip from Antsirabe. Architecturally, Betafo is one of the nicer highland towns, with lovely arcades and intricate wrought-iron trimmings; the **Catholic church** is particularly inspiring (it is behind the taxi-brousse station).

Between the various buildings are **vatolahy**, raised stones with carved inscriptions honouring past chieftains who displayed exceptional military prowess. One particularly ornate vatolahy, which is erected on a pedestal in the centre of the market-place, dates back to the late 19th century and stands in memory of one Rainihasimbola. In the same vicinity are numerous others; locals are normally happy to point them out for you.

The village is divided into the commercial district and the more interesting old town, 1km north, dominated by the crater lake, **Lac Tatamarina**. A short circular road at the northern end of the lake passes a **cemetery** with tombs of local kings. From here there are some lovely views of rice paddies. If you ask directions, several small, pretty waterfalls north of the lake are worth exploring.

From the lake, a recommended 5km return walk takes you through the fields to the **Chutes d'Antafofo**, a two-level, 20m waterfall which slices through basalt rock. The track can get quite muddy so wear proper shoes. Three km west of Betafo, on the road to Morondava (turn left before the sign 'Miandrivazo 195'), the **hot water baths** are cleaner, quieter and more authentic than the ones in Antsirabe.

No formal accommodation is available in Betafo, but you may be able to stay in a local house if you ask around. It is easy enough to

get there and back in a few hours from Antsirabe.

Getting There & Away From Antsirabe, buses and taxis-brousse leave hourly from the Asabotsy station in the west of town. One excellent way to Betafo from Antsirabe is by mountain bike. Unlike the trails to the nearby lakes, the road to Betafo is flat and paved. Refer to Getting Around in the previous Antsirabe section for information on bike hire.

Mont Ibinty

Just west of the southern road to Ambositra, about 25km from Antsirabe, is the Ibinty mountain (2254m). Here you can look for gemstones and camp in the lovely forest and mountain regions. There is no direct transport to the mountain, so you will have to catch a taxi-brousse and then walk from the main road, charter a taxi or try to arrange an organised tour from Antsirabe.

AMBOSITRA
* Telephone Area Code: 7

Ambositra (Place of Eunuchs) is pronounced uncannily like 'ambushed'. There seems to be a dispute about whether Ambositra was named after some particularly healthy-looking steers or a mass castration after a battle in which the Merina defeated their enemies. Another source claims that the word is actually a corruption of a Malagasy word meaning 'town of roses'. Take your pick!

Ambositra is a peaceful place to break up the journey between Antsirabe and Fianarantsoa, and a great place to buy carvings for which the town is renowned.

Orientation & Information

Ambositra is a sprawling place. The upper part of town, around the Catholic church, is a nice place to stroll around and check out the carvings for sale. The BTM bank, just down from the L'Oasis restaurant and hotel, and the BNI-CL bank, just up from the Hôtel Violette Annexe, will change money.

Places to Stay & Eat

The friendly and recommended *Hôtel Violette Annexe* (☎ 710 84) is 700m up from the Taxi-brousse Station South. Rooms with a shared bathroom and balcony overlooking the (noisy) street cost FMg 25,000. The restaurant is popular with vazahas passing through (avoid the stringy chicken).

Just 500m up from the Taxi-brousse Station North (ask directions), the only place to stay in this part of town is the original *Hôtel Violette* (☎ 711 75). It has seen better days; ordinary rooms cost FMg 30,000. The Annexe is better.

The *Grand Hôtel* (☎ 712 62) – which is not so grand – is in the older, nicer part of town, about halfway between the two taxi-brousse stations. Small, quaint singles/doubles with private bathroom cost FMg 30,000/45,000. The old restaurant still carries some fading flashes of grandeur. It serves French meals for FMg 9000 to FMg 12,000, and breakfast for FMg 7500, often with some entertainment:

The Grand Hôtel dining room provides unscheduled evening entertainment by the owner's dog, Frou-Frou, which resembles a little heap of old knitting wool ends. As the food arrives, the dog does slightly inadequate turns on its hind legs – not easy on a highly polished rosewood floor. Failure to provide tidbits results in a disgusted look and on one occasion he resolutely lifted his hind leg and peed against the table leg. This spectacle is repeated at every table, every night.

Clare & Johan Hermans, UK

The best place to eat is *L'Oasis* (☎ 711 13), just a little south, and opposite, the Hôtel Violette Annexe. It is above a nice pâtisserie. The Oasis has a small selection, but the service and food is good; meals cost from FMg 6000 to FMg 8000. Behind the restaurant, the manager rents some clean, quiet *rooms* which range from FMg 25,000 to FMg 40,000 for a 'family room' with a private bathroom.

Things to Buy

Ambositra is justifiably noted for its wood carvers and furniture manufacturing. Even the balustrades on the verandahs of homes are decorated with ornately carved designs. The town has several good souvenir shops selling quality carvings.

Just up from the Hôtel Violette Annexe is the *Arts de Tropiques*, and a little further up again is the *Galerie des Arts Zafimaniry*. Both have a good range of carved bowls and figures, as well as a few tacky souvenirs, all at reasonable prices. There are a couple of other souvenir shops around the Grand Hôtel.

Getting There & Away

To make it a little confusing, Ambositra has two taxi-brousse stations. The station for places to the north, eg Antsirabe (FMg 6000) and Tana (FMg 15,000), is a junction at the far northern end of town. So if you are coming from the north, you will need to get a local taxi (around FMg 2500) from the station to your hotel. If coming from the south, eg Fianarantsoa (FMg 15,000), you can walk to most hotels from the Taxi-brousse Station South.

For all forms of transport going in both directions, start at about 7 am to allow plenty of time to get a ride.

ANTOETRA & THE ZAFIMANIRY VILLAGES

Out in the forests east of Ambositra is a cluster of villages inhabited by the master wood carvers, the Zafimaniry people. The homes in these villages are veritable works of art whose shutters and walls are carved in geometric designs.

The main village is Antoetra, which is linked to other villages higher on the massif by a good system of forest tracks (distances are approximate): Ifasina (4km from Antoetra), Ankidodo (8km), Ambohimanarivo (12km), Ambatolahy (17km) and Faliarivo (22km).

Accommodation or camping in or around the villages will be possible only with permission from village chiefs. The market days in Antoetra are Tuesday and Saturday – but double check the dates before going out there if you want to see the market.

CENTRAL MADAGASCAR

This is a sensitive area, and we strongly recommend you visit only with a guide who can help you communicate with the villagers and make suggestions which will minimise your impact. Inquire about local fady, do not indiscriminately distribute gifts (especially to children) and tread as lightly as possible.

Getting There & Away
The most accessible Zafimaniry village, Antoetra, lies 23km south-east of Ivato (which is 10km south of Ambositra). Antoetra is accessible by taxi-brousse from Ambositra on Tuesdays and Saturdays. Otherwise, you can walk along the road from Ivato to Antoetra in a day.

Again, an experienced guide will do wonders to make your visit more interesting and help you to avoid many of the problems which arise when tourists invade such traditional areas.

FIANARANTSOA
• Telephone Area Code: 7

Fianarantsoa (population 150,000), capital of the province of the same name, is the academic and intellectual centre of Madagascar. Thanks to heavy missionary activity, it's also the country's Catholic centre. Fianarantsoa (Place Where Good is Learned) was founded on 1 June 1830 after Queen Ranavalona I decided to build an intermediate capital between Tana and the remote southern provinces.

It lies at the heart of Madagascar's most productive agricultural region and is renowned for its production of wine and tea. Fianar, as the town is often called, also has a surprisingly good selection of cheap and comfortable accommodation – which is probably reason enough to base yourself here for a while.

To the west, Fianarantsoa's backdrop is dominated by 1374m Mt Kianjasoa. The city has a chilly, high-country feel to it and, like Antsirabe, can get quite nippy in the evening. Bring a jumper or jacket, or resort to the Malagasy style of dress and wrap up in a thick *lamba* or blanket.

Orientation
Like Antsirabe, Fianarantsoa has three parts. Basse-Ville (Lower Town) is the poorest but liveliest area, with the main post office and the train and taxi-brousse stations. Some of the restaurants and hotels (including Madagascar's most bizarre place to stay, the Hôtel Soafia) are here. Nouvelle-Ville (New Town) is the business area, with the banks and several good hotels.

The most beautiful district is Haute-Ville (Upper Town) which sits atop a hill overlooking the other two districts and is marked from below by a cluster of church spires. Haute-Ville has many lovely narrow streets, a quaint atmosphere and picturesque views across Lac Anosy and the surrounding rice paddies. To save your knees, take a taxi up to Haute-Ville and stroll down at your leisure.

Information
Tourist Office The Syndicat d'Initiative, or tourist office (☎ 506 67), is in an unsigned white building with red shutters behind the Hôtel Moderne. The staff are more involved in implementing policy and generating a bureaucracy, so they leave it to Stella from Stella Tours (see Organised Tours) to provide information and arrange tours. In fact, you won't be able to get past Stella anyway.

Money All the banks are along the same street in Nouvelle-Ville. They're open from 8 to 11 am and 2 to 4 pm on weekdays.

Post & Communications The main post office and Telecom office is opposite the railway. There's another post office in Nouvelle-Ville.

Dangers & Annoyances
As a large Malagasy city, Fianarantsoa has a lot of child beggars – street kids who have no family, home or regular meals. They hang around Basse-Ville, particularly the taxi-brousse and railways. At times, they can be very distressing and annoying.

Organised Tours

Several recommended tour guides/travel agencies can organise basically the same sort of day trips for the same sort of price. A day trip to Ambalavao via some vineyards and a tea plantation (see the Around Fianarantsoa section) costs about FMg 100,000 per person. A trip to Ranomafana National Park costs around FMg 200,000/250,000 for a one/two day trip per person, and a two day pirogue trip down the Matsiatra River is FMg 200,000 per person.

Angelo (☎ 508 15) speaks French and English and is based at the Hôtel Moderne/Chez Papillon. The effusive Stella from Stella Tours, based at the Syndicat d'Initiative (☎ 506 67), speaks French and English and charges a reasonable FMg 25,000 to FMg 30,000 per day as a guide. The Tsara Guest House and Arinofy Hôtel also have resident guides.

Places to Stay

Fianar has a great range of value accommodation. Nouvelle-Ville is a far nicer place to base yourself, but it's a steep walk from there

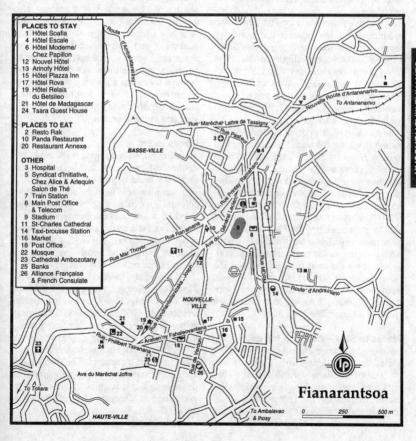

PLACES TO STAY
1 Hôtel Soafia
4 Hôtel Escale
6 Hôtel Moderne/ Chez Papillon
12 Nouvel Hôtel
13 Arinofy Hôtel
15 Hôtel Plazza Inn
17 Hôtel Rova
19 Hôtel Relais du Betsileo
21 Hôtel de Madagascar
24 Tsara Guest House

PLACES TO EAT
2 Resto Rak
10 Panda Restaurant
20 Restaurant Annexe

OTHER
3 Hospital
5 Syndicat d'Initiative, Chez Alice & Arlequin Salon de Thé
7 Train Station
8 Main Post Office & Telecom
9 Stadium
11 St-Charles Cathedral
14 Taxi-brousse Station
16 Market
18 Post Office
22 Mosque
23 Cathedral Ambozotany
25 Banks
26 Alliance Française & French Consulate

BASSE-VILLE

NOUVELLE-VILLE

HAUTE-VILLE

To Toliara

To Ambalavao & Ihosy

To Antananarivo

Fianarantsoa

0   250   500 m

CENTRAL MADAGASCAR

to Basse-Ville. If you stay in Nouvelle-Ville, you will need to catch a few taxis and local buses to save your aching knees.

Places to Stay – bottom end

Although a bit grubby, there are a couple of real bargains at the bottom end of the scale. The *Nouvel Hotel* (☎ 510 55) has reasonable rooms for about FMg 20,000, but is often full. The *Hôtel de Madagascar* (☎ 511 52) is excellent value at FMg 11,500 per room (some have awesome views of the rice paddies). It is in a great location in Nouvelle-Ville. If you want a room, you may have to wake up the receptionist in the restaurant/bar next door.

The dusty *Hôtel Rova* (☎ 505 19) is also in a nice spot. It has quaint rooms (curiously named, rather than numbered) for FMg 15,000/20,000 for a single/double. The *Hôtel Relais du Betsileo* (☎ 508 23) is recommended for small groups or families: large rooms with several beds and a private bathroom cost about FMg 42,500, and some rooms have wonderful views.

Just a short walk up from the taxi-brousse station (look for the signs) is the very good *Arinofy Hôtel* (☎ 506 38). It boasts a cheap laundry service, TV lounge, good local information and a friendly, English-speaking manager. Clean rooms with communal bathrooms cost FMg 25,000/50,000; FMg 36,000 for better rooms upstairs. You may be able to get a bunk bed for FMg 20,000, and if the place is full, you are usually allowed to pitch your tent in the gardens for FMg 5000.

Just down the road from the railway, the *Hôtel Escale* (☎ 500 31) may not look much from the outside, but the largish rooms, with shared facilities, have charming furniture and cost a reasonable FMg 35,000.

Places to Stay – middle & top end

In a bright orange building in Nouvelle-Ville, the excellent *Tsara Guest House* (☎ 502 06) is definitely worth a splurge – but bookings are advisable. It provides very useful information for visitors, staff speak English, and there's a cheap laundry service. Spotless rooms cost FMg 38,000/50,000 for a double/triple with private toilet and communal showers. A double with private facilities costs FMg 52,000.

Directly opposite the railway, the *Hôtel Moderne* (☎ 508 15) aka *Chez Papillon* is better known as a restaurant than a hotel. Well-furnished rooms with a bathroom cost FMg 40,000, and up to FMg 90,000 with a sitting room and TV. The new *Hôtel Plazza Inn* (☎ 515 72), next to the market, is one of the best in this range and pretty good value for F90/110.

At the far northern end of town is the unique *Hôtel Soafia* (☎ 503 53). There's nothing else like it in Madagascar, and it's worth a look even if you're staying elsewhere. It's constructed in the form of a rambling Chinese temple with convoluted walkways and hallways between various segments. Even if you take a cheap room for F125 you can use the tennis court and pool (apparently clean: a glowing water analysis report from the Pasteur Institute in Tana is pinned to the bedroom door!) – but use of the gym and sauna are extra.

Places to Eat

The *Chez Papillon* has long had a reputation as the best restaurant in Madagascar, but sadly it's steadily going downhill. Still, if you want French food in some decaying colonial elegance, with waiters in clean, starched white jackets behaving as they would in a Paris restaurant, the meals start at about FMg 16,000. The terrace is a good place to enjoy a bottle of something and watch Fianar go about its business.

Of the hotels, the food and setting at the *Tsara Guest House* is very good; a full breakfast costs FMg 11,500 and other, lighter, snacks FMg 6000 to FMg 8000. The meals at the *Arinofy Hôtel* are also very good; a menu du jour costs FMg 12,000 and breakfast is FMg 7000. The spaghetti is constantly recommended by readers. The restaurant at the *Hôtel Escale* may look a bit grimy from the outside but it is quiet, clean and serves good food at a bargain FMg 3500 to FMg 5000.

In the centre of town is another very

>=0>=0>=0>=0>=0>=0>=0>=0>=0>=0>=0>=0>=0>=0>=0>=0>=0>=0>=0>=0>=0>=0>=0>=0>=0>=0>=0>=0>=0<

The Fianarantsoa-Manakara Rollicking Train
The best train ride in Madagascar is undoubtedly the 170km trip between Fianarantsoa and Manakara (that is, if the train is running and the track is not damaged).

The train usually only has three carriages, two of which are 2nd class. These are comfortable enough, but also cheaper than 1st class, so are very crowded – a sort of railway-taxi-brousse. The train stops 17 times (almost every 10km) at tiny villages where you can (quickly) stretch your legs and buy something from the frantic sellers. There is always plenty of eggs, fried bananas and bread for sale, though strangely no drinks (except possibly some warm beer) – so bring your own.

Always have plenty of time up your sleeve. You can count yourself lucky if the train leaves an hour after the scheduled departure and is not delayed by breakdowns along the way by two hours longer than the normal eight hour trip. (Officially, the train takes 15 minutes longer from Manakara to Fianar because it's uphill all the way.) Cancellations of 24 hours are not unusual.

If travelling from Fianar to Manakara sit on the left side (the right-hand side from Manakara to Fianar) for the best views of rock cliffs, misty valleys and waterfalls. (However, the most spectacular waterfall is on your right if going from Fianar to Manakara; it is just after Madporano, about two hours from Fianar). Sadly, you will also see plenty of examples of slash-and-burn agriculture. ■

>=0>=0>=0>=0>=0>=0>=0>=0>=0>=0>=0>=0>=0>=0>=0>=0>=0>=0>=0>=0>=0>=0>=0>=0>=0>=0>=0>=0>=0<

popular spot: the *Panda Restaurant*. Good-value Chinese meals from the extensive menu cost from FMg 10,000 to FMg 15,000. Another recommended Chinese place is at the *Hôtel Soafia*; it has an extensive menu and, as you expect in the Soafia, interesting decor. The *Chez Alice* is recommended for pizzas from FMg 7000 to FMg 10,000, and Malagasy meals for about FMg 7000. You can even become an honorary member of the Fianar Darts Club inside.

The salon de thé in the Hôtel Soafia compound serves freshly baked cakes and bread – try the 'pain au chocolat' (a chocolate-filled croissant). The unassuming *Arlequin Salon de Thé*, opposite the tourist office, is a quiet place for pastries and hot or cold (soft) drinks.

Finally, a couple of unassuming and cheap places for Malagasy food are the *Resto Rak* in Basse-Ville, and the *Restaurant Annexe* (though it seems to have no name outside), next to the Hôtel de Madagascar.

Entertainment
Surprisingly, there isn't a great deal to do in Fianar. The best place to enjoy a drink is the terrace bar at the Chez Papillon, but there are no nightclubs or other places to go in the evening.

For something sophisticated, such as films and concerts, the tourist office may have an idea of what is going on – but probably not. The combined Alliance Française and French Consulate often arranges something cultural, but you will have to call in to find out. On Sunday afternoon, spirited games of football (soccer) are played at the stadium near the railway.

Getting There & Away
Air Because there is regular road transport to and from Fianar, and a very good road from Tana, there are few flights. Air Mad flies between Tana and Fianar (US$83), with connections to Toliara (US$94), at least twice a week. Air Mad (☎ 512 52) is in the Madagascar Airtours office in the Hôtel Moderne building.

Train The train between Fianar and Manakara (FMg 20,500/34,500 for 2nd/1st class) is the most exciting and interesting train trip in the country, and is definitely recommended unless you are in a real hurry, or prone to 'seasickness'. The train officially leaves Fianar at 7 am on Tuesdays and Saturdays, and returns from Manakara the next day. However, delays and cancellations caused by a damaged track are not uncommon – and the trip does take a rough-and-ready 10 or so hours.

Get to the amazing, Swiss-style station in Fianar at least an hour before the train is due to depart and scramble to get your tickets when the doors to the ticket office open.

Taxi-brousse Fianarantsoa's lack of air connections isn't too serious because the road from Tana is good and there are plenty of taxis-be and taxis-brousse from Antsirabe (240km away) and Tana (410km).

Although the route south-west to Ihosy and Toliara has been vastly improved in recent years, there are still a few rough bits. The road to Ihosy runs through lovely open country punctuated by hulking whaleback peaks; the road from Ihosy directly south to Taolagnaro (Fort Dauphin), however, is an assault course.

Every day, taxis-brousse go to Antsirabe (FMg 17,500), Tana (FMg 35,000), Ihosy (FMg 18,000), Manakara (FMg 25,000; about nine hours) and Ranomafana (FMg 10,000; 90 minutes). To Toliara (FMg 30,000), Taolagnaro (FMg 70,000) and Morondava (FMg 70,000), a bus or taxi-brousse leaves Fianar two or three times a week. For long distances, it's best to book at least the day before you want to leave.

Fianarantsoa's taxi-brousse station used to get our vote as the most unfriendly and chaotic station in the country, but things have improved a little. You will still be besieged by taxi-brousse touts, but you will probably have to rely on them to lead you to the area where booths sell tickets to your destination.

Getting Around
If you stay in Nouvelle-Ville or you're doing a bit of exploring in Haute-Ville you may wish to take a local taxi around town for about FMg 2500 a trip, or a local bus. Bus No 2 marked 'Anjoma' goes to the market, and Nos 3 and 6 go to Haute-Ville via the market.

AROUND FIANARANTSOA
The guides and travel agencies in Fianarantsoa will readily arrange trips to the places listed in this section (except the two mountains). Refer to Organised Tours in the previous Fianarantsoa section for some recommendations.

Iboaka-Alakamisy
About 16km north of Fianar, and a good stop on the way to Ranomafana if you have your own vehicle, is Iboaka-Alakamisy. It hosts a lively daily market, which starts early and is generally over by mid-afternoon. You can easily get a taxi or taxi-brousse there from Fianar.

Vineyards
In the 1970s, a Swiss corporation saw the wine-growing potential in the Betsileo country, so it set up an association and provided funding to promote wine production. Today, Fianarantsoa is Madagascar's wine-making centre.

Several of the largest vineyard estates lie north-west of town along the route to Isorana, or north along the road to Ambositra. Another is the Soavita vineyard, only a few km north of Ambalavao. The most popular and accessible vineyard is Lazan'i Betsileo (☎ 502 75), 15km north of Fianarantsoa. You can phone to arrange a visit to the estate or go on an organised tour.

Even if you don't visit these vineyards, try to sample a bit of the product while you're in town. It goes down well with the menu du jour at Chez Papillon.

Sahambavy Tea Estate
The Sahambavy Tea Estate produces high-quality tea for export and a lesser grade for local consumption. It lies near the village of Ampaidranovato about 22km east of Fianarantsoa, and along the railway line to Manakara.

If you'd like to visit, you can either go on an organised tour or find a taxi-brousse headed towards Sahalavo, get off at the obvious turn-off and get another vehicle heading to the estate. Alternatively, you can take the train towards Manakara and get off at Ampaidranovato near Sahambavy. The train is often delayed, however, so it's generally quicker by taxi-brousse. For private visitors, the estate is only open on Fridays from about 8 am to 3.30 pm.

Ambalavao

• Telephone Area Code: 763

Ambalavao (The New Valley) is worth a visit: it's an easy day trip from Fianarantsoa, or you can stay in Ambalavao and break up the journey between Ihosy and Fianarantsoa. This lovely and friendly town has an attractive complement of intriguing **Betsileo architecture** (lots of those wonderful carved balcony balustrades) and a unique highland atmosphere. It also hosts an incredible **zebu market**. The day of the market changes, so ask around in Fianar or Ambalavao.

Famadihana (second burial ceremonies), which were adopted from the Merina after the unification of Madagascar, are common. The town is also known for the production of elegant traditional *lamba arindrano* (woven handspun silk) and used as burial shrouds or as fine dress for the living.

Papier Antaimoro Factory Most people visit Ambalavao to see the factory which makes Ambalavao's famous Antaimoro paper. You can see the products being made (ask for a free, quick tour) and buy some products in the shop. The prices are not open to bargaining: eg notepaper costs around FMg 9000; lamp shades (a little hard to squeeze into a backpack) cost from FMg 20,000; and intricate (easier-to-fold) tablecloths cost from FMg 14,000 to FMg 225,000.

The factory is in the upper part of town next to the taxi-brousse station for Fianarantsoa, so it is easy to find if you're coming from Fianar. Get to the factory early – by about 8 am many sheets of paper are already drying in the early morning sun.

Places to Stay & Eat The cheapest place to stay in Ambalavao is the reasonable *Resto Stop Hôtel* where rooms cost a bargain FMg 10,000. You must book at the *Stop Restaurant* on the main street, though the rooms are about 400m away in a quieter part of town. The Stop Restaurant can also rustle up some decent brochettes.

A better place to stay is the friendly *Hôtel Snack Bar Aux Bougainvillees* (☎ 1) in the grounds of the Antaimoro paper factory. Quaint, clean and quiet bungalows with shared but spotless bathrooms cost a reasonable FMg 25,000. The prices for food – about FMg 7000 for an omelette and FMg 12,500 for a 'steack frites' – are too high, but the service and setting are very pleasant. Cheap hotelys along the main street serve basic Malagasy meals.

Getting There & Away Ambalavao lies 56km south of Fianarantsoa, a few km off the winding main road. The town is only directly accessible by taxi-brousse to Fianar (FMg 5000), so to places north of Fianar you will have to go to Fianar first. If you arrive from the south on a taxi-brousse from Ihosy, for example, you will be dropped off at a junction from where it is a steep 3km to 4km walk

---

Antaimoro Paper

Antaimoro paper originated from the Antaimoro tribe on the east coast of Madagascar, who were influenced by the Arabs marooned there in the 8th century.

The handmade papyrus-like sheets were originally made from a bush called *havoha* and were used by the *katibo*, the aristocratic scribes who copied verses from the Koran in Arabic script. The result was known as Sorabe (Great Writings). Later the paper was used by astrologers to record their predictions and by *ombiasy* (healers) for writing down the formulae for their potions.

In 1936 the art of making Antaimoro paper was bought to Ambalavao by a French planter called Pierre Mathieu. He established the factory which you can still visit. The paper, which is now more often made from pounded sisal, uses pressed dried flowers in fanciful combinations for menus, books, stationery and even lamp shades. ■

to Ambalavao. Taking another local share-taxi will save you this walk.

Around Ambalavao

Not far south of Ambalavao, watch for the twin peak formation known as **Varavarana 'ny Atsimo** (Gate to the South). When approached from the south, it resembles a pair of rabbit ears and is visible for about 75km. Still farther south, immediately northwest of the road about midway between Ambalavao and Ihosy, you'll see another imposing monolith (you can't miss it). It has a large amphitheatre on top and a **waterfall** issues from solid rock on the side facing the road.

Pic Ambondrombe

The Ambondrombe Peak (1936m) is 42km east of Ambalavao along a well-defined track. The peak, which towers over the village of Ambohimahamasina, is both the

Valhalla and the Elysian fields of the Betsileo ancestors. In the village, strange and haunting echoes and voices are heard constantly. Numerous fady are in effect so if you go there, be extremely careful to toe the line and don't assume anything without consulting with a local.

Pic Ifandana

Another traditional site near Ambalavao is Ifandana Peak (1052m), which is visible from the main road. This outcrop was the site of a mass suicide in which people threw themselves from the cliffs rather than submit to the troops of Radama I; it is said that bones can still be found there. According to some sources it is forbidden to even point at the peak.

To visit either of these mountains, you must seek permission from the *fokonolona* (local council) in Ambohimahamasina and Ambalavao, respectively. Inquire about local fady and take heed of them when visiting. In any case, access to these areas is quite difficult.

RÉSERVE NATURELLE INTÉGRALE D'ANDRINGITRA

The 31,160 hectare Andringitra Reserve lies near the village of Antanifotsy about 50km south of Ambalavao. This beautiful plateau area of bald granite domes is one of Madagascar's few high massifs. Significantly, the eastern part of the reserve protects one of the last remaining vestiges of primary forest on the hauts plateaux. The reserve is home to a rich variety of endemic flora and fauna, including seven species of lemur and 22 species of frogs and toads.

The World Wide Fund for Nature (WWF), which has conducted local development studies, has recommended that this reserve should eventually be elevated to national park status and be developed for tourism. This is yet to happen. Andringitra is still technically classified as a 'special reserve' (which by definition is open only to research personnel). Contact the ANGAP office in Tana if you wish to visit.

PAUL GREENWAY

A typical Betsileo house at Ambalavao, central Madagascar.

Getting There & Away

There are two very basic roads leading into the Andringitra vicinity but neither is passable in the wet season. Under normal conditions, a 4WD vehicle or a good mountain bike will be necessary. The better of the two roads goes via the village of Antanifotsy (where guides may be hired, if you have permission to visit the park), 50km due south of Ambalavao. The other access is from the Farafangana road 109km east of Ihosy. No public transport goes along either route.

RANOMAFANA

• Telephone Area Code: 7610

The village of Ranomafana (Hot Water) is one of the more pleasant places in Madagascar, with friendly, relaxed people and a lovely setting. Like Antsirabe, it long served as a thermal bath centre and was quite an attraction during the colonial era.

These days, nearly all the attention is focused upon the Parc National de Ranomafana which has been established nearby. This park is truly one of the wonders of Madagascar, a beautiful spread of rainforested hills with plenty of wildlife. Ranomafana's national park and village are now one of the country's requisite visits.

Thermal Baths

The thermal baths, for which the town is named, are about 150m behind the Hôtel Thermale (see Places to Stay & Eat). The path to the left of the bridge leads to the place where you can get a massage (FMg 6000 for 15 minutes), or take a private bath (FMg 200) which is meant to cure rheumatism, asthma, tension, stomach ailments and even sterility. The baths are far cleaner and better managed than the ones at Antsirabe. The large, hot pool at the bridge costs FMg 200.

The baths and pool are open from 7 am to 11.30 am, and 2 to 4 pm every day except Friday, when they are closed for cleaning – so Saturday will be the healthiest day to visit.

Places to Stay & Eat

You can stay either in Ranomafana village, from where it is a fair walk uphill to the park, or stay at the park (see the Parc National de Ranomafana section). In the village there are four places to choose from.

The least expensive is the homely *Hôtel Ravinala* on the western side of the village as you come from Fianarantsoa. It doesn't look much from the outside, but the clean singles/doubles, some with stunning views, cost a reasonable FMg 12,500/20,000. It also has a basic restaurant.

For a touch of (very) faded grandeur, the *Hôtel Station Thermale de Ranomafana* (☎ 1) is in the centre of the village. Very ordinary rooms are FMg 30,000/35,000 with communal facilities. The huge restaurant, with waiters in white uniforms, is worth visiting for some colonial-style service; plats du jour cost FMg 12,000, and omelettes and salads about FMg 4500.

The best place to stay is the *Manja Hôtel*, 400m past the eastern end of the village. Set across the road from a pretty river, the small but clean wooden bungalows are good value at FMg 33,000. Buckets of hot water are available on request. It is also one of the best places to eat, with tasty Malagasy meals for a bargain FMg 4000 or FMg 5000.

The new *Hôtel Domaine Nature* (☎ (2) 310 72) is the new bungalow complex in a gorgeous jungle setting about halfway between the park and village. Bungalows with good facilities cost F180. Excellent meals are available to guests and the public in the restaurant.

The *Hotely Kavana*, next to the taxi-brousse stop in the village, serves basic Malagasy food – small, fresh crayfish are a local delicacy. You can also pick up some fruit, bread and other basic supplies in the village market.

Getting There & Away

The only direct access to Ranomafana village is along the rough road from Fianarantsoa; the trip by taxi-brousse takes about 90 minutes and costs FMg 10,000. Coming from the east coast, just get off at the village or park. Heading back down to the east coast from Ranomafana you will have to jump on whatever vehicle is going through the village.

PARC NATIONAL DE RANOMAFANA

About 6km from Ranomafana village, the 39,222 hectare Ranomafana National Park lies at an altitude of 800m to 1200m. It is mainly comprised of rainforested hills carved by numerous small streams which plummet down to the beautiful white-water Namorona River. Although much of the region has been logged in the past, the easternmost part of the park retains relatively large areas of primary forest.

Ranomafana National Park was created in 1991 with the aim of establishing a structure that is friendly to wildlife, tourists and local residents. Locals are being encouraged to participate in park operations and establish businesses which profit from tourism.

Centre de l'Environnement

Before you visit the park make sure you go to the excellent environment centre and museum in the western part of Ranomafana village, not far from the Hôtel Ravinala. Open every day from 8 am to 5 pm, the centre has several stimulating displays (in French and English) about the park and general Malagasy culture.

There is also a gift shop and snack bar. Entry is free, but you are asked to leave a small donation. The centre has one or two bikes for hire at FMg 10,000/15,000 for a half day/full day, but the roads are so steep in the area that you will also need to hire the appropriate leg muscles. Permits for the park are available at the park entrance.

Flora & Fauna

Ranomafana National Park is home to 29 species of mammal, including 12 lemurs. On an average day walk, you'll easily see red-bellied lemurs, diademed sifakas and red-fronted lemurs. If you're very lucky, you'll glimpse a golden bamboo lemur (first discovered in 1986), which is unique to the park. It will probably be happily munching away at a stand of bamboo.

Even rarer is the broad-nosed gentle lemur, also partial to bamboo, which was thought to be extinct until it was rediscovered in Ranomafana in 1972; it was observed again in the late 1980s. This species remains on the verge of extinction, however, and is rarely observed. For the whole story, see the special Wildlife section at the beginning of the book.

On a night walk, there's a good chance of seeing woolly, mouse and sportive lemurs (but some will unfortunately require a bit of banana baiting to draw them into range). During the summer months, there's also a chance of spotting fat-tailed dwarf lemurs, which hibernate in winter, living on fat stored in their large tails.

Another frequently observed night creature is the striped civet (*fossa* in Malagasy), which is also normally baited into photo range. Local agriculturalists complain frequently about the much larger fosa (*Cryptoprocta ferox*), a puma-like creature which is blamed for night raids on stock and all sorts of other mischief. These are also rarely sighted.

Birdwatchers will have some of their richest Madagascar pickings here, with 96 species representing 38 different families of birds. Of these, 68 species are found only in Madagascar. The forests also abound with geckos, chameleons and some beautifully coloured frogs.

Although most visitors come for the animals the flora is just as incredible, with orchids, tree ferns, palms, mosses, a variety of flowering plants and stands of giant bamboo. In all there are 278 species of trees and bushes (81 of which are endemic) and numerous other species of smaller plants. Anyone with an interest in the local flora will want to buy an informative booklet (in French or English) from the park entrance. The booklet contains excellent descriptions of the numbered ferns and palms.

Permits & Guides

Currently, permits cost FMg 20,000 per person but a three day permit is due to increase to FMg 50,000 in September 1997, in accordance with future ANGAP guidelines.

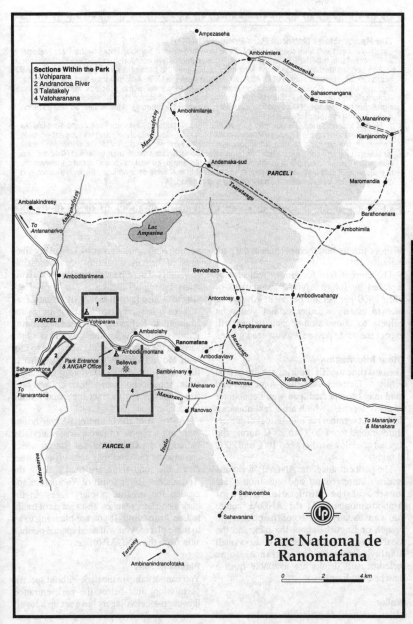

Sections Within the Park
1 Vohiparara
2 Andranoroa River
3 Talatakely
4 Vatoharanana

Ampezaseha

Ambohimiera

Mananonoka

Sahasomangana

Manarinony

Kianjanomby

Ambohimilanja

Mantranofotsy

Andemaka-sud

PARCEL I

Maromandia

Tsaratanana

Barahonenara

Ambalakindresy

Andranofotsy

Ambohimila

To
Antananarivo

Lac
Ampasina

Bevoahazo

Amboditanimena

Antorotosy

Ambodivoahangy

1

PARCEL II

Vohiparara

Ampitavanana

Ambatolahy

Ranomafana

Baralango

2

Park Entrance
& ANGAP Office

Ambodiamontana

Ambodiaviavy

Sahavondrona

3

Bellevue

To
Fianarantsoa

Sambivinany

Namorona

Kelilalina

4

Manarano

Menarano

Andranoroa

Ranovao

Irelo

To Mananjary
& Manakara

PARCEL III

Sahavoemba

Sahavanana

**Parc National de
Ranomafana**

Farony

Ambinanindranofotaka

0   2   4 km

CENTRAL MADAGASCAR

The Ranomafana National Park Project (RNPP)
Established in 1986 after the discovery of the very rare golden bamboo lemur in the Parc National de Ranomafana, the RNPP is one of the first and most impressive ecotourism projects in Madagascar.

It is coordinated by ANGAP, the Malagasy NGO, with the help of a large number of local and international agencies such as US-AID, universities from the USA, Antananarivo and Fianarantsoa, and the Missouri Botanic Garden. Together they aim to conserve the precious rainforest in the Ranomafana area which is the habitat of several species of lemur (two of which are unique), a significant percentage of Madagascar's birdlife and nearly 100 species of butterflies, as well as being a vital source of water for local rivers.

Half of the entrance fee you pay to visit the Parc National de Ranomafana helps sustainable development among the 100 or so villages in the park area. Several schools and health centres have been built; the camping ground at the park is completely owned and run by locals; a training centre for Malagasy guides and naturalists has been established; and the excellent museum at Ranomafana village is a classic example of funds used to educate visitors, as well as locals, about conservation. In the space of about 10 years the region has been able to survive economically through tourism and maintaining the forest, rather than by logging and hunting. ■

Visitors simply buy their permits at the park entrance.

The current fees for guides will also be replaced by future ANGAP regulations of FMg 2500 per person per visit. Always be sure to clarify whether or not you want helpers to come along; each helper will expect the same payment as the lead guide.

Other Information
The best time to visit is during the dry season – July to October. Although some rain and mud may be expected, you won't encounter as many leeches (which are a real nuisance during wet weather) or mosquitoes. Temperatures range from 20°C to 25°C during the day but cool down to between 10°C and 20°C at night.

The park entrance, the ANGAP 'welcome centre', campground and guesthouse are located at the minuscule village of Ambodiamontana. At the ANGAP centre you can usually buy some pamphlets (in French or English) about the park and the local flora and fauna, and there is also a small display. Opposite the entrance, some welcome soft drinks are available from a thatched outdoor kiosk.

Walks
Most visitors concentrate on the small section of the park known as Talatakely since most of the park is off limits or inaccessible to visitors. There are only two major walking trails through Talatakely. The short **Petit Circuit** – also known as the Ala Mando Trail – takes a leisurely two hours as far as the lookout at Bellevue and back, including lemur-spotting along the way. This is the same as the nocturnal walk. The three to four hour **Moyen Circuit** goes a little further in the search for lemurs. If you go on a night walk, some zebu meat will be cooked on a fire at Bellevue to attract the usually timid fossa.

Upstream of the Namorona River bridge there are a couple of impressive waterfalls, including the **Cascades del Riana**, which can also be factored into your visit. Further down the road there are tracks along the Andranoroa River south of Vohiparara and around the pristine primary forest in the park's northern reaches, and a series of tracks to **Lac Ampasina**. If you are planning to go to these places, you will need special permission from the ANGAP office.

Places to Stay
You cannot camp in the park without specific permission. Just below the park entrance, however, local villagers have set up a lovely *campground* where you can pitch your own

Tavy

A staggering 25% to 30% of the countryside of Madagascar is set on fire each year to clear the landscape for grazing, rice farming and urban development. This slash-and-burn type of farming is locally known as *tavy*.

Malagasy farmers believe that nutrients in grass will increase after the landscape has been burned. However, in a year or two the grasses regrow with less nutrients and are unwanted by zebu. The farmers must then look elsewhere for grass, and start the tavy process again. Local farmers also believe that tavy helps to improve the irrigation of their rice farms, but it actually causes soil erosion and does not improve rice yields. Some observers also believe that fires are deliberately lit by some Malagasy to antagonise unpopular governments which plead for the farmers *not* to burn the countryside.

From the west coast of Île Sainte Mare you will often see incredible smoke from fires burning along the eastern coast of the mainland. You will see tavy at its worst when travelling by road or train between Fianarantsoa and Manakara.

Some environmental organisations such as the Ranomafana National Park Project are desperately (but often unsuccessfully) attempting to reduce tavy by helping farmers to change rice farming methods; improve animal husbandry by breeding less destructive animals such as pigs, chickens and ducks; and to seek alternative types of fuel and building materials. ■

tent under a thatched roof for FMg 5000 per tent, or rent a tent from the ANGAP office for FMg 10,000.

The *guesthouse* next to the park entrance is a charming, rustic place with a few bunk beds (FMg 20,000 per person), a shared bathroom, and a basic kitchen where you can cook your own food. This is one of the very few parks where you can virtually stay in the park – particularly useful if you want to go on a nocturnal walk. You may be disappointed in the peak season as this place will be popular and you can't book ahead.

Getting There & Away

If you start early enough you could easily, but briefly, see the park on a day trip from Fianarantsoa (FMg 10,000 by taxi-brousse along a rough road). Just get off at the park entrance, take the short or medium walk, hike down to the Ranomafana village for lunch and/or a thermal bath, and catch whatever is going back to Fianar.

Any of the travel agencies in Fianarantsoa (see under Organised Tours in that section) will organise day trips to the park for about FMg 200,000 per car. This is far too much considering how easy it is to visit the park yourself.

Apart from the taxis-brousse between Ranomafana village and Fianarantsoa, no public transport is available from the village to the park, so you'll have to hitch a ride on whatever is going past, or walk the 6km – and it's a steep climb. The environment centre in Ranomafana village may have a vehicle going to the park – it is worth asking. If coming from Manakara or Mananjary on the east coast by taxi-brousse, just get off at the village or park.

Along the road between the park and Fianarantsoa, you will see Tanala (Forest People) by the roadside selling charcoal, honey (the Tanala are renowned for making and eating honey) and woven bags full of local crayfish. The Tanala also have a reputation for their extensive *tavy* (slash-and-burn) methods of farming.

Southern Madagascar

Southern Madagascar actually begins somewhere south of Ambalavao, around where the road emerges from the domed granite mountains and issues onto a high grassy plain. As one continues south of there, the climate becomes drier and the land more parched. In the heart of this semi-desert lies the magnificent Isalo Massif, an otherworldly area of stark beauty preserved as a national park.

The southernmost tip of the island, south of the Tropic of Capricorn, is the driest and wildest region of the country. Here one finds Madagascar's most startling flora, including stands of baobabs and the renowned spiny forest, a fantasy land of thorns where buggy-whip stalks of *Alluaudia* and *Didierea* thrive amid succulents such as aloes and several species of *Euphorbia*.

The south-west and central-south regions are home to three of Madagascar's 18 tribes: the Bara around Ihosy and Isalo campground; the Mahafaly south of Toliara; and the Vezo clan of the Sakalava on the southwest coast. The latter two are known for their funerary art – the Mahafaly particularly for their elaborately decorated tombs and the Vezo for erotic tomb carvings.

The south-east region is the home of another two Malagasy tribes. The Antanosy live in the far south-eastern corner of the country while the Antandroy occupy territory west of Taolagnaro (Fort Dauphin) to a point about midway between the east and west coasts.

Noting the resemblance between southern Madagascar and the North American deserts, the French based at nearby Réunion introduced the Mexican prickly pear cactus and cultivated it into natural fences as defence barriers. It's now very well established in southern Madagascar and the Antandroy, who use it for cattle feed, know it as *raketa*.

Unusual flora endemic to the cooler and wetter Taolagnaro area include the rosy periwinkle, which became famous as a

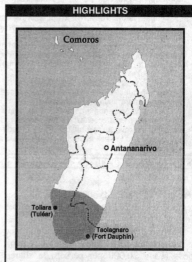

- The privately-run Berenty Reserve, which hosts an excellent variety of wildlife.
- Taolagnaro, a pleasant coastal town with a great climate and spectacular scenery.
- World-class diving at Ifaty, a sleepy village north of Toliara.
- Trekking through the rugged sandstone massifs of the Parc National de Isalo.

treatment for leukaemia; the carnivorous pitcher plant; and the bizarre three-cornered palm. Sisal is grown in commercial quantities and used for making rope. The industry is slowly dying out, but there's still a factory near Taolagnaro and vast sisal plantations around Berenty.

IHOSY
- Telephone Area Code: 740

The small town of Ihosy (pronounced 'ee-oosh') serves as the capital of the Bara tribe. Unlike other Malagasy, the Bara practise polygamy. However, zebu get a higher profile than wives in the Bara men's book, which holds that a man's worth is judged by the number of zebu he possesses – regardless of how they have been acquired. Because zebu numbers have diminished considerably in the past 15 years, customary rustling has taken on a more serious nature.

Ihosy is at its loveliest later in the year when the jacarandas are blooming, but you'll enjoy the dramatic scenery along the five to seven-hour trip (sometimes rough) between Ihosy and Fianarantsoa in any season. Ihosy

is worth a stop if you just want to take a break, or you may need to come here from Ranohira for a connection further north.

Information

The BTM bank beside the central market changes money. The post office is near the courthouse, not far from the *taxi-brousse* station. Electricity only works in Ihosy from 5.30 pm to midnight.

Places to Stay & Eat

There are several dirt-cheap ('dirt' is the

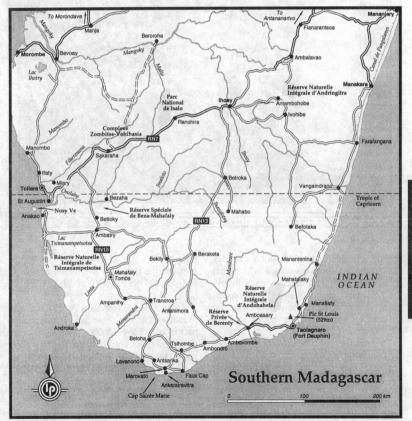

Southern Madagascar

Zebu

The zebu would have to rate with the lemur, chameleon and ravinala (or travellers' palm) as the most identifiable symbols of Madagascar. Zebu indicate wealth and power; they are used for dowries and transport; and are sacrificed during major ceremonies (particularly by the Vezo people). But they are less popular for milk and meat. Zebu are herded (and rustled) in vast numbers by the Mahafaly people of the south and the Bara in central Madagascar.

Zebu are sometimes known as a brahman in Australia or North America and are virtually identical to the domesticated cattle commonly seen throughout India. A zebu is recognisable by a large hump on its back and loose skin under its throat – this increases surface area, thereby allowing better regulation of heat. They are also particularly hardy and often resistant to diseases which affect other livestock. ■

DAVID CURL

appropriate description) wooden cubicles around the taxi-brousse station which cost about FMg 10,500 each; these are primarily for Malagasy people waiting for connections. Opposite the terminal, the *Hôtel La Galaxie* (☎ 65) is slightly better at FMg 12,500.

Two km west of the taxi-brousse station, the comfortable *Zahamotel* (☎ 83) is worth a splurge if you have had a rough time along the bumpy road between Fianarantsoa and Toliara. Although its location is a little inconvenient, very nice rooms with a bathroom (and sporadic hot water) are good value at

FMg 47,500. It also has the best restaurant in town; the menu du jour is reasonable at FMg 20,000 but the price of drinks is a little high.

At the *Hôtel Relais Bara* (☎ 17), near the roundabout as you come from Fianarantsoa, rooms cost FMg 35,000. This is another clean and quiet option; it has a pretty good restaurant too. The last option is the spartan but homely *Hôtel Ravaka* (☎ 12) – look for the sign from the road to Fianarantsoa. Rooms cost FMg 25,000 and are set around a pretty garden.

If you prefer not to eat at the hotels, there's

a line-up of good-value Malagasy hotelys around the taxi-brousse station – the best is probably the *Manambitsoa Hôtel*.

Getting There & Away

Air Ihosy's small airport lies 3km north of the town. It is used by government officials, construction managers and the occasional package tour, but is not currently available for commercial flights. If Air Mad starts to fly here again, the agency for tickets and information is at the Zahamotel.

Taxi-brousse Although the 206km road from Fianarantsoa (FMg 18,000) to Ihosy has been improved over the past few years, it isn't yet a silken surface. The journey can take up to seven hours and there's still a bit of shaking going on.

Taxis-brousse run along the good road between Ihosy and Toliara (FMg 25,000) at least daily, and three times a week to Taolagnaro (FMg 70,000). If you get stuck try hitching from the taxi-brousse station hotely, which lure truckers in for a break. Expect to pay the same as you would for a taxi-brousse.

To see a good cross section of southern Madagascar try the rough and remote RN13 from Ihosy to Ambovombe and on to Taolagnaro, but don't be in too much of a hurry. Normally, there's at least one taxi-brousse in either direction every day. The trip takes two to three days and stops are usually at Betroka (118km from Ihosy) or Berakata (243km), where rudimentary hotel accommodation is available. One survivor of this route likened the road to a solidified mountain torrent.

Unfortunately, the recent drought and resulting famine in southern Madagascar has seriously affected this area so you may want to check the current situation before you set out. Living conditions are appalling in places and robberies of both foreign and Malagasy travellers are not uncommon.

Finally, there is also a 284km road connecting Ihosy with Farafangana on the east coast. However, this route is usually impassable to 'normal' motor vehicles.

RANOHIRA
• Telephone Area Code: 742

The dusty 'one-horse' town of Ranohira lies 91km west of Ihosy. Most travellers use it as a base for exploring Isalo National Park, so it has become a bit like a highway service centre. When the road came through, the population centre that sprang up near the base of the Isalo massif adopted the name of the tiny village of Ranohira near the mouth of the Canyon des Singes, 10km from the new Ranohira.

Unfortunately, a couple of foreigners have recently had stuff stolen from their hotel rooms while they were exploring the park. It may be a good idea to leave your valuables with the hotel manager (if you trust them); take your important items with you; or use your own padlock, if possible. And be careful about the occasional thief if you are camping in the park.

More information on visiting Parc National de Isalo follows this section.

Places to Stay & Eat

As demand sometimes exceeds supply, and there are only a handful of choices, prices for accommodation in Ranohira are too high. If you're going into the park and plan to stay overnight in Ranohira after you return, it's a good idea to make a reservation. Only the Hôtels Berny and L'Orchidée de L'Isalo have electricity; in other places, you'll be provided with hurricane lamps and candles.

The cheapest place, at FMg 20,000 per room, is the basic but reasonable *Chex R Thomas*, on the southern side of the village. The popular and homey *Hôtel Les Joyeux Lemuriens* is a ramshackle but clean hotel. Prices for the rooms are now way overpriced at FMg 35,000, especially as there is no electricity and some rooms are stuffy. It does serve good meals, as well as a decent breakfast with lots of tea, but they are also overpriced.

Just across the street, the *Hôtel Berny* (☎ 6), with a shop, petrol station and half-decent restaurant, is a better option. This place has a few rooms, rather like staff quarters, surrounding a nice courtyard at the back of the shop for FMg 31,000/37,000 a single/double. If they're full, you will probably be able to pitch a tent in the peg-resistant courtyard; use stones from the rock garden to keep your tent in place.

The best place in town is the new *Hôtel L'Orchidée de L'Isalo* (☎ 14) – bookings are recommended. The modern, clean rooms for FMg 40,000 with shared bathroom and FMg 50,000 with private facilities are good value. More rooms were being added at the time of research. The busy restaurant serves tasty French and Malagasy food for around FMg 10,000, though servings are sometimes small.

A stay at *Le Relais de la Reine*, about 9km south of the village, is highly recommended if you have the money or inclination for a splurge. Refer to the following section for details.

It's easy enough to stock up on a few basic supplies, such as bread, fruit, vegetables and bottled water, in the village – except in the peak season (July-August) when stocks may be stretched to the limit.

Getting There & Away

The road to Toliara has been undergoing massive reconstruction as far as Sakaraha, 110km south-west of Ranohira, and is now in excellent condition. The same can't be said about the road north to Fianarantsoa, which is rough in places though improving every day.

Ranohira is directly connected to Ihosy only by a couple of daily taxis-brousse which cost the '*vazaha* price' of FMg 10,000. To anywhere north of Ihosy or anywhere south towards Toliara you will need to hitch a ride on anything that is going past. This may be time-consuming, but a few vazahas will probably get off the bus or taxi-brousse at Ranohira and create some room.

Public transport from Toliara often comes

PAUL GREENWAY

A typical busy street in the centre of Ihosy, southern Madagascar. The journey between Fianarantsoa and Ihosy is spectacular, if rough at times.

past Ranohira between 9 and 11 am, and from 2 pm onwards vehicles come from the north and go towards Toliara. Check with your hotel about current departure times of public transport, and don't be afraid to ask for a lift on any passing vehicle: one lucky traveller talked her way into an air-conditioned 4WD all the way to Toliara!

PARC NATIONAL DE ISALO

Isalo National Park, established in 1962, covers 81,540 hectares of the wildly eroded Jurassic sandstone massif of the same name. This is a magical place of extraordinary landscapes and worth a few days' exploration on foot. To give you some idea of the dramatic increase in Isalo's popularity: in 1986 just 62 people visited the park officially. In 1992 there were over 1000, and a staggering 7000 people visited in 1995, according to ANGAP statistics.

Park topography is characterised by alternating flat grassy plains and sandstone ridges, sculpted by wind and water into fanciful hoodoos – eye-sockets, ears, noses and beaks. In French it is known appropriately as *ruiniforme*.

As you might expect of such a haunting place, there is a host of local *fady* in effect. One tradition requires the placing of a stone on existing cairns to appease ancestors who guard the paths. The rocks shelter lots of old concealed Sakalava tombs; understandably, local guides are often reluctant to indicate them or explain anything about them. If you spot one and your guide seems uneasy about it, drop the subject.

Flora & Fauna

Although animal life isn't the park's most prominent feature, there are a few species to look out for: grey mouse, ring-tailed and brown lemurs, Verreaux's sifaka; and, at night, the nocturnal Coquerel's dwarf and red-tailed sportive lemurs. There are also 55 species of birds, including the rare Benson's rock-thrush, a grey bird with a reddish breast which inhabits the lichen-stained rocks.

Most vegetated areas of the park are covered with dry grassland or sparse, low deciduous woodland. Near streams and in the microclimates of the deeper canyons, there are ferns, pandanus, and feathery palm trees. At ground level in drier areas look for the beautiful yellow flowering *Pachypodium rosulatum* (especially beautiful in September and October), which resembles a miniature baobab tree and is often called an 'elephant's foot'.

Unfortunately, fires are an ongoing problem and large swathes of Isalo are subject to intentional (illegal) or accidental burning. Poaching and hunting are also rampant, and greatly affect the local ecology.

Permits & Guides

Like all national parks, you must buy a permit for FMg 50,000 (valid for three days) from the ANGAP office in the nearby village of Ranohira. If you are trekking for more than three days, you will need to negotiate a special, higher-priced permit with the ANGAP office.

Unofficial guides will probably approach you when you arrive in Ranohira, or while you are at your hotel. You must use a guide within the park but they must be authorised and allocated by ANGAP, which takes the training of its guides seriously: posters around the ANGAP office indicate which guides have recently been banned. You can choose a guide who speaks English, Italian, German or French; and some are apparently 'specialists' in flora or fauna.

Current fees for guides are about FMg 30,000 per day, but this is due to decrease to FMg 2500 per person per visit; how the guides will take to this is unclear. In any case, prices will be listed in the ANGAP office and are non-negotiable.

If you are travelling in a group of more than five or six people and the guide will be cooking and setting up camp, it's only fair to take two guides. Most are willing to carry their own gear, but you may also hire porters for the official (current) rate of FMg 10,000 per day. A porter is a good idea because trekking is hot and includes a fair bit of scrambling and climbing, and a porter can act as a guard for your tent and backpack if

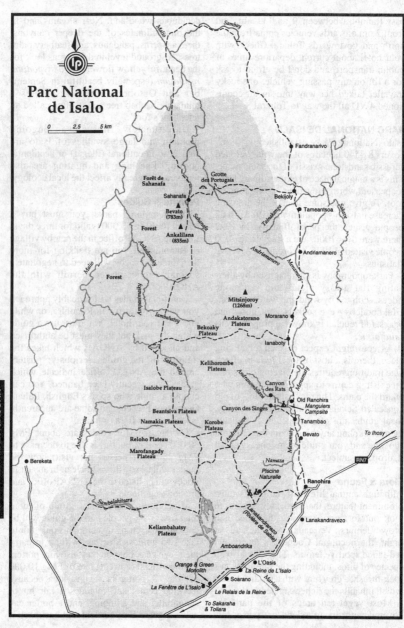

Parc National de Isalo

0   2.5   5 km

you are camping. You will be responsible for buying food for your guide or porter.

Visiting the Park

Before you start any trek, or hire a guide, visit the ANGAP office next to Hôtel Berny in the village of Ranohira – look for the sign 'Accueil du Parc'. Here you must pay for your permit and choose a guide. The friendly staff (some speak English) can provide information about trekking; and there's also a small library and some souvenirs for sale. The office is open from about 7 am to 6 pm every day, though you may have some difficulty finding anyone around (or awake) during the heat of the day.

There are several organised trails to follow, all starting and finishing at Ranohira. (More information about the attractions themselves follows.) On longer treks you can camp along the way.

One-day walks
  (a) The Piscine Naturelle – 6km one way on foot (about 90 minutes), or 3km by car and then 3km on foot.
  (b) The Canyon des Singes and Canyon des Rats – 9km one way on foot (about two hours), or 16km by car then 1km on foot.
Two to three day trek
  Hike to the Piscine Naturelle and on to the Canyons des Singes & des Rats – about five to six hours – then return to Ranohira; camp overnight at either place.
Five day trek
  Hike to the Grotte des Portugais – about 45km – and back, via the canyons. Allow three days if you have a vehicle which can take you as far as Tameantsoa, from where it is another two day walk to the caves and back.
Six to seven days
  The 'Grand Tour'; hike to the Grotte des Portugais, via the canyons then take the long way round (along the western side of the park) to the Piscine Naturelle and back to Ranohira.

You will always need to carry a lot of water – don't underestimate how hot and unshaded this particular park is. The best time to visit is from April to October. If camping, be careful because some light-fingered locals may ransack your possessions. If you have hired a porter (and you trust him), he can guard your tent and possessions while you are doing some short hikes or swimming.

Canyon des Singes & Canyon des Rats

The tightly constricted Canyon des Singes ('Canyon of Monkeys', also known as Canyon Andranokova) makes an interesting return day walk from Ranohira. It's better, however, to make it an overnight trip and leave time for exploration. From Ranohira the track winds slowly down the slope into the valley, where it crosses the Menamaty River then strikes off to the village of old Ranohira. The village is surrounded by rice paddies and in the cliffs above are the **tombs** of past village leaders.

Several hundred metres from the canyons is the official campground, known as *Manguiers campsite* because it's sheltered by a long grove of mango trees. From here it's just a few minutes walk to the mouth of the Canyon des Singes and slightly longer into the neighbouring canyon, Canyon des Rats (also known as Canyon Andranoavo). There's an idyllic campground farther up Canyon des Singes, but villagers discourage its use because the river is their source of drinking water.

In Canyon des Singes you'll have a good chance of seeing sifakas leaping through the trees. After a rather rough hour on foot, you'll reach a boulder field and on the far side, a sandy wadi. Take the right fork here and continue up to the end of the canyon.

Most guides need a bit of encouragement to enter the neighbouring, thickly vegetated Canyon des Rats. Ask your guide to show you the **Bara Zafimagnely tombs**.

Canyon des Singes to Piscine Naturelle

Another popular excursion is from the campground at Canyon des Singes through the Isalo massif to the Piscine Naturelle. It's a hot and thirsty five to six hour walk with lots of ascents and descents, but the landscape along the way is even more breathtaking: there are hidden canyons, brilliantly coloured ranges, bizarre strata and the chance of observing sifakas as well as ring-tailed lemurs.

SOUTHERN MADAGASCAR

The walk finishes along a stream bed known as **Rivière de Sable** where there are several specimens of *Pachypodium rosulatum* (which all the guides will point out). When the Rivière de Sable turns into an increasingly lush palm-lined stream, you'll know the Piscine Naturelle isn't far away. After another 250m upstream – or on the high route along the rock rim – you'll arrive at the natural pool.

At Piscine Naturelle there's a natural stone cave which overlooks a waterfall. This in turn tumbles into a deep green pool surrounded by overhanging pandanus trees. It's ideal for swimming, especially after a long hot grunt over the massif from Canyon des Singes. There is a wonderful official *campground* (which can be a little busy in peak season).

In the same area are rectangular collections of small holes on flat rock bases. These were made long ago by cattle herders, who would while away the time playing a game which uses pebbles and is similar to draughts (chequers) or solitaire.

Grotte des Portugais The Grotte des Portugais, known in Malagasy as Zohin'y Taniky, lies at the northern end of the park. It is quite a large cave, about 30m long by 3m high, with unmistakable signs of habitation.

The cave isn't much to look at and is full of zebu shit and detritus from nearby communities. However, the surroundings are worthwhile and in the nearby **Forêt de Sahanafa** there are natural water sources and quite a few lemurs.

Trekking to the Grotte des Portugais is more of an expedition than visiting other park attractions. Unfortunately, there's no direct access from Ranohira over the massif itself. The trip begins with a 33km walk or ride along the front range of Isalo to the villages of Tameantsoa and Bekijoly. From Bekijoly a track heads 19km west to the cave. This return trip will take five days on foot, or three by car and foot.

L'Oasis About 10km south-west of new Ranohira another Eden-like natural swimming hole, L'Oasis, lies only 250m off the Toliara road.

Look for a lush green oasis backed by a convoluted pile of standing rocks. It's a superb (unofficial) campground and the rocks behind are quite unusual.

La Reine de L'Isalo The rock formation known as the Queen of the Isalo lies about 2km south-west of L'Oasis. As you're heading south, she stands about 10m from the road on the left. Oddly, the stone resembles a queen from any direction. As you pass by, her position seems to change and you can imagine she's dancing. Well, almost.

La Fenêtre de L'Isalo As its name implies, La Fenêtre is a natural 'rock window' which lies about 4km from Soarano. Speckled with brilliant green and orange lichen, it affords a vista over a palm-studded plain punctuated by misfit rocks. It's best viewed from below in the afternoon sun.

The track to La Fenêtre can be driven on under some conditions. To get there go to the milestone reading 'Fianar 295/Sakaraha 93' on RN7. About 500m towards Toliara turn right on a track which follows the road for a way, then angles right past an immense orange and green monolith. La Fenêtre lies about a km further along this track. For hikers there's a short-cut to La Fenêtre from Soarano which cuts at least a km off the route.

Places to Stay

You can camp at two official campgrounds in the park: *Manguiers* at the Canyon des Singes, and the unnamed one near the Piscine Naturelle. These sites are becoming a bit polluted, so please do not leave any rubbish behind. You can camp elsewhere in the park if you are going on a longer trek and first obtain permission from the ANGAP office in Ranohira. Isalo is so well set up that you may be able to hire tents and sleeping bags from the ANGAP office or a guide, though the quality may be wanting.

>€0€0€0€0€0€0€0€0€0€0€0€0€0€0€0€0€0€0€0€0€0€0€0€0€0€0€0€0€0€0€0€0€0€0€0€0€0€0€0€

La Grotte des Portugais

Some historians and a few archaeologists think the cave served as a shelter for 16th century Portuguese sailors – hence the name – who had supposedly been shipwrecked off Morombe on the west coast in 1527. The cave provided a safe haven during their overland journey to the more hospitable country around present-day Taolagnaro, where another group of Portuguese shipwreck victims had constructed a fort. However, there's not much evidence to support this theory and the local Malagasy say they couldn't fathom any *vazaha* staying in a cave by choice!

Because the fortress-like shelter is oriented toward Mecca, suggesting Islamic influences, another theory ventures that the cave dates back to the 11th century and its original inhabitants were of Arabic origin. The Malagasy, on the other hand, maintain that it was inhabited by the legendary Vazimba or Kalanoro people, whom they believe were Madagascar's first inhabitants. (However, anthropologists don't believe such tribes ever existed.) ∎

>€0€0€0€0€0€0€0€0€0€0€0€0€0€0€0€0€0€0€0€0€0€0€0€0€0€0€0€0€0€0€0€0€0€0€0€0€0€0€0€

ANGAP also plans to build some huts at Andriamanero in the north of the park for visitors – inquire at the ANGAP office about these huts and any other new camping sites.

For something extraordinary, you can stay at the expensive but wonderful *Le Relais de la Reine* at Soarano. Soarano is 2km south-west of La Reine and about 9km south of Ranohira. The magnificent three star hotel has bungalows, a restaurant and – you guessed it – a piscine naturelle. If you are thinking about splurging on one great hotel during your visit to Madagascar this is probably the place to do it. The backdrop is very impressive: a jumble of wildly sculpted standing rocks and silent valleys ripe for exploration (It's very easy to become lost so if you do go walking, note your progress carefully.) with lots of *Pachypodium*.

The immaculate rooms are not worth the price, but the setting certainly is; rooms cost F320, breakfast F20 and meals F60. Bookings are highly advisable and can be made at Madagascar Discovery Agency in Tana (☎ (2) 351 65; fax (2) 351 67).

SAKARAHA

The small community of Sakaraha lies 110km south of Ranohira, about halfway along the excellent road between there and Toliara. It's a useful place to break the journey (but there seems little need because the road is so good) or to explore the nearby Zombitse forest.

Complexe Zombitse-Vohibasia

The 21,500 hectare Zombitse-Vohibasia complex is two small areas of forest. It is mainly of interest to birdwatchers, who are likely to see various species of sunbirds, greenbuls, couas and vangas. The most accessible section, Zombitse, stretches across the main road nearly 25km north-east of Sakaraha.

In the future the forest may become a national park with guides and visitor facilities. Get your permit (FMg 50,000) at the ANGAP office in Tana, or at the WWF forest station at the park entrance.

Places to Stay & Eat

The best place to stay in Sakaraha is the *Hôtel Edena,* along the main road, where rooms cost about FMg 15,000/20,000 for a single/double. For a half-decent meal of chicken and fried potatoes eat at *Le Buffet Resto Hôtel*, where your bus may stop for a rest and meal anyway.

Getting There & Away

From Toliara to Sakaraha (FMg 5000), get on any taxi-brousse heading to Ihosy. Along the way you'll pass several impressive Antanosy and Mahafaly tombs. From Sakaraha to anywhere north or south, you will have to flag down anything going your way. A taxi-brousse to Ranohira costs FMg 5000.

TOLIARA (TULÉAR)
• Telephone Area Code: 9

A dusty town of 60,000 people, Toliara – also known as Tuléar – came into existence in 1895 and is the most recently established Malagasy provincial capital. It supposedly got its name when a European sailor arrived and asked where he could tie up his boat. A local apparently pointed and replied, '*Toly eroa*' ('Tie up down there'). Well, it's as good an explanation as any.

Toliara's architecture, or rather what is left of it after the race riots of March 1987, is not particularly prepossessing. Nor are the 'beaches' along the promenade, Blvd Lyautey, which most people would refer to as mangroves and mudflats. Toliara certainly lacks the charm and beaches of Taolagnaro.

Most of the commerce is controlled by Indo-Pakistani traders who bore the brunt of Malagasy violence in the 1987 riots. On one street, a Chinese store escaped untouched to continue business while the Indian premises on either side, along with most of the central area, was gutted.

The town itself is like an Australian Outback town or a Wild West 'Laredo by the Sea'. The central area is lethargic (the town seems to completely close down between 11.30 am and 3 pm) with lots of dust, dry heat and broiling sun. However, there are several worthwhile attractions in the area, including the beach and diving at Ifaty, the Beza-Mahafaly Reserve and the St Augustin area south of town.

Information
Tourist Office Along the esplanade there's a funny place with a couple of friendly old men which serves as the tourist office or Delegation Regionale du Tourisme (☎ 414 59). It provides scant local information but no maps or brochures, and is probably only worth a visit if you speak French and badly want some information.

Money All banks change money and are open during normal working hours. The most convenient are the BTM bank in the market area and the BNI-CL bank on Rue du Lieutenant Chanaron near the Air Mad office.

Post & Communications The tiny post office and Telecom office, along Blvd Gallieni, are chaotic, but they somehow function reasonably normally. Their hours are not long: 7 to 11.30 am and 3 to 5.30 pm, Monday to Friday.

Museums
The **Musée d'Art des Traditions Populaires du Sud Malgache** (aka Musée Mahafaly-Sakalava) was temporarily closed at the time of research, but next door the **Musée Regional de L'Université de Toliara** was open. It contained a small collection of local cultural exhibits, as well as an egg from the prehistoric 'elephant bird', *Aepyornis*. Either museum is worth visiting; the entrance fee for each is FMg 5000.

The **Musée Rabesandratana** or Ocean Museum (signposted as the 'Station Marine') is strictly for a-fish-ionados. The displays of pickled fish, coral and shells (as well as butterflies) are mildly interesting, but you may be forced to pay the absurd 'vazaha entrance fee' of FMg 20,000. (No ticket is issued, and change is obtained from a staff member's handbag ...) The museum is near the Solima petrol station on the causeway which leads to the port. It is normally open from 9 am to noon, and 3 to 4 pm, Monday to Saturday. Even when officially open someone may need to find the key anyway.

Organised Tours
Several travel agencies can organise tours in and around Toliara. The prices per person (minimum of four) charged by each agency are fairly standard: for a tour around the town, FMg 40,000 to FMg 56,000; to the caves at Grottes de Sarodrano, FMg 100,000 to FMg 150,000; and to St Augustin FMg 120,000 to FMg 140,000. Don't expect any tour to be instantly available; you will probably have to organise a group yourself.

Some of the better agencies to contact are: Air Fort Services (☎/fax 426 84) in the Hôtel Sud building; Madagascar AirTours (☎ 411 73)

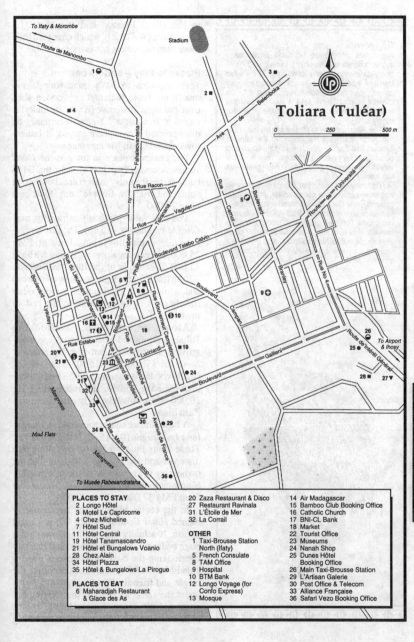

PLACES TO STAY
2 Longo Hôtel
3 Motel Le Capricorne
4 Chez Micheline
7 Hôtel Sud
11 Hôtel Central
19 Hôtel Tanamasoandro
21 Hôtel et Bungalows Voanio
28 Chez Alain
34 Hôtel Plazza
35 Hôtel & Bungalows La Pirogue

PLACES TO EAT
6 Maharadjah Restaurant
& Glace des As

20 Zaza Restaurant & Disco
27 Restaurant Ravinala
31 L'Étoile de Mer
32 La Corrail

OTHER
1 Taxi-Brousse Station
North (Ifaty)
5 French Consulate
8 TAM Office
9 Hospital
10 BTM Bank
12 Longo Voyage (for
Confo Express)
13 Mosque

14 Air Madagascar
15 Bamboo Club Booking Office
16 Catholic Church
17 BNI-CL Bank
18 Market
22 Tourist Office
23 Museums
24 Nanah Shop
25 Dunes Hôtel
Booking Office
26 Main Taxi-Brousse Station
29 L'Artisan Galerie
30 Post Office & Telecom
33 Alliance Française
36 Safari Vezo Booking Office

Aepyornis

Aepyornis were large flightless birds, commonly known as 'elephant birds', and have been extinct for many centuries. They were usually about the size of a modern-day ostrich, but one species was thought to be over 4m high and laid eggs measuring roughly 30cm by 20cm (about the size of a rugby ball!).

The Aepyornis was thought to be the inspiration for the giant roc (found in the tales of Sinbad the Sailor) which was able to swoop down and carry off elephants. This is highly fanciful, however, because the Aepyornis was too heavy to fly.

You may see some fragments of Aepyornis eggshells along the south coast, particularly around Faux Cap, or be offered some for sale, but please remember that the shells are important for research and should not be moved. It is also illegal to take shells or shell fragments out of Madagascar, and if you are caught you will be penalised by Customs officials. ■

in the Hôtel Plazza; and the Motel Le Capricorne (☎ 426 20), which charges a little more than the others but is more reliable.

Places to Stay – bottom end

Toliara seems to have gone 'bungalow-mad': any basic thatched or wooden shed overlooking a mangrove (if you are lucky) is called a 'bungalow'. You will certainly be disappointed if you have stayed in bungalows elsewhere in Madagascar.

The cheapest place in town is the *Hôtel Tanamasoandro* (☎ 41 246), near the BTM bank. It is in the noisy market area but is good value and friendly. Simple bungalows cost FMg 20,000.

The best-value place is the friendly, new *Chez Micheline* (☎ 415 86). The tiny bungalows are a bit dingy but cheap at FMg 25,000; larger bungalows with a fan are FMg 35,000. It is handy to the Ifaty taxi-brousse station (look for the signs to the hotel nearby) and while it's a good place to meet other travellers, it is inconvenient to the rest of town.

Along the esplanade, overlooking Toliara's renowned M & M (mud and mangroves), is the basic but friendly *Hôtel et Bungalows Voanio* (☎ 416 60). It has a dozen small wooden bungalows with shared facilities for FMg 25,000, and rooms for FMg 30,000. Unfortunately, it is near the noisy Zaza disco.

A little further south, the *Hôtel & Bungalows La Pirogue* (☎ 415 37) is slightly better. These funny little bungalows are falling into disrepair and are popular with ants, but the owners try to keep ahead of the patching up. Single or double bungalows with a toilet cost from FMg 37,000 to FMg 42,000.

In the centre of town, the appropriately named *Hôtel Central* (☎ 428 80) is a good option. It actually has no bungalows, but a huge bedroom with a bathroom and balcony overlooking the busy street costs a reasonable FMg 40,000. Just around the corner, the bright and friendly *Hôtel Sud* (☎ 415 89) is about the same standard as the Central, but costs a little more. Single/double rooms (some are smallish) with bathrooms are FMg

45,000/60,000. The advantages are that the reception can provide good local information and it's a handy place to meet other travellers.

Places to Stay – middle & top end

Inconveniently located in the north-east of town is another outpost of the de Heaulme empire (see the Taolagnaro section), the luxurious *Motel Le Capricorne* (☎ 426 20) – so named because the Tropic of Capricorn passes just south of Toliara. Many packaged tours stay here. Air-con rooms cost F310, a studio apartment is F400 and an extra bed is F60.

Not quite in the same league as the Capricorne, but cheaper, is the *Hôtel Plazza* (☎ 419 03). The drawcard is the superb garden setting; it's a wonderful place to watch the sun set (over the mudflats). Air-con rooms with full facilities are F200/250 for a single/double.

Down a small lane near the main taxi-brousse station, the best bungalows in town are set among a shady grove of coconut palms (though nowhere near the sea) at *Chez Alain* (☎ 415 27). Spartan but comfortable bungalows with a bathroom cost from FMg 55,000, or FMg 35,000 without a bathroom. Plenty of good information about local tours is available to guests, but travellers continue to complain about the unfriendly and lazy staff.

Although inconveniently located, with no restaurant, the peaceful *Longo Hôtel* (☎ 421 07) is pleasant enough. Nice bungalows with a bathroom cost FMg 49,000 and a room with a bathroom costs FMg 60,000. The comfortable tourist bus, the Confo Express, leaves from here.

Places to Eat

The cheapest place to pick up a tasty filling meal for FMg 2000 to FMg 4000 is around the *market* during the day, and at *stalls* set up along the esplanade in the evening. A couple of Indo-Pakistani salons de thé are definitely worth trying. The best is the *Maharadjah Restaurant*, which has a good selection of French dishes, and Indian and Pakistani

curries (too hot to try during the day) for FMg 8000 to FMg 10,000. The English-speaking manager is friendly. Next door, the *Glace des As* is popular for a cold drink and (safe) ice cream.

For cheap meals, the restaurant at *La Pirogue* bungalows is worth a visit – though the views may be more enjoyable than the food. If you are around the main taxi-brousse station, the *Restaurant Ravinala* can provide some tasty Malagasy food at good prices.

Along the esplanade, the *La Corrail* is currently the trendiest place in town for French expats. The pizzas are cheap at about FMg 10,000, but we thought they were only average. Next door, the spacious *L'Étoile de Mer* costs a little more, but the service is good (mainly because it is usually empty). Fish meals cost about FMg 13,000, Malagasy meals FMg 10,000 and vegetarians will love the huge salads on offer for FMg 7000.

Of the hotels, the *Hôtel Sud* does a good breakfast. The *Hôtel Plazza* has a surprisingly limited menu, but for FMg 15,000 to FMg 18,000 a dish, the food, service and setting is very nice. Also on the esplanade, the *Zaza Restaurant & Disco* has good Malagasy meals for FMg 10,000 and reasonable pizzas for FMg 12,000. Your bill entitles you to a free ticket to the 'happening' disco next door in the evening.

Even if you are not staying at *Chez Alain*, the outdoor restaurant is certainly worth a visit. The menu du jour is FMg 13,000 to FMg 15,000 and other tasty dishes cost about FMg 13,000. The cheap food at *Chez Micheline* is also recommended: when asked what was on the menu, the landlady replied: 'Everything. I am the cook!' (Don't take her word literally, mind you.)

Entertainment

Among expats *La Corrail* is the most popular place in town for a drink and a chat. For a drink at surprisingly reasonable prices the outdoor bar at the *Hôtel Plazza* is definitely the best place to watch the magical sunsets.

Some of the best places to find live music, or dance away the night at a disco or nightclub, are the *Zaza Restaurant & Disco*, *La Corrail* and the *Feelings* disco in L'Étoile de Mer. They 'happen' nightly, but most of the action takes place on weekends.

The Alliance Française, along the esplanade, is particularly well set up in Toliara, and is a great place to catch up on some (French) newspapers and magazines. The noticeboard lists whatever concerts and films are on in town.

Things to Buy

Toliara is one of the better places to shop around for a souvenir or two. Opposite the enormous unfinished stadium, the *Nanah Shop* has a range of agreeable, locally made clothes, carvings from FMg 10,000 and large drums for about FMg 90,000. Also check out *L'Artisan Galerie*, along the lane behind the post office. It is especially good for carvings.

You will be able to buy some gorgeous shells, and souvenirs made out of shells, from around the streets, and particularly at a small informal market opposite the post office. Before buying anything containing shells, please consider the ecological damage caused by the collection of these creatures and by the tourists who contribute to the demand. If your conscience doesn't stop you, stringent Customs regulations may.

Getting There & Away

Air Air Mad flies between Toliara and Tana (US$150) at least four days a week; to Taolagnaro, there are several flights a week from Toliara for US$83. Air Mad also flies a few times a week from Toliara to places in southern Madagascar such as Morombe (US$49) and Ampanihy (US$43). Twice a week, TAM flies between Toliara, Tana and Taolagnaro for the same price as Air Mad. This flight either starts or finishes in Réunion.

If you want to book or confirm a flight out, the busy but helpful Air Mad office (☎ 415 85) is open normal working hours though closed on Friday. The TAM office (☎ 410 63) is next to the Hôtel Sud.

Taxi-brousse There are two taxi-brousse

stations in Toliara. For transport along the rough route north to Manombo and Ifaty use the Taxi-brousse Station North on the appropriately named Route de Manombo. A few taxis-brousse and trucks go to Manombo and Ifaty between 6 am and the early afternoon every day. You will probably end up waiting a few hours for a vehicle; be prepared for a rough ol' ride.

The well-organised main taxi-brousse station, which caters for transport to everywhere else, such as Taolagnaro, Fianarantsoa and Tana, is in the far eastern part of town. To Taolagnaro (FMg 42,500), via Betioky, Ampanihy and Ambovombe, a bus leaves four days a week, and takes at least 40 hours – but allow another 15 to 20 hours for breakdowns and bad roads. For more details about this trip refer to the Toliara to Taolagnaro section later in this chapter.

Public transport leaves several times a day along the northern road towards Tana. The cost for a taxi-brousse/minibus to Ranohira is FMg 15,000/24,000; to Ihosy, FMg 20,000/30,000; to Fianarantsoa, FMg 30,000/40,000; and to Tana, FMg 55,000/65,000. If you book ahead you may be able to get on a more comfortable, and slightly more expensive, long-distance public bus.

If you are heading towards Morondava (FMg 60,000), a taxi-brousse leaves from Toliara three or four times a week. The very rough road passes Bevoay (Big Crocodile) – get off here for a short connection if you are going to Morombe. If things go according to schedule (which is not often), the taxi-brousse to Morondava stops overnight at Manja and continues north along the excruciating road the following morning. From there, it takes anywhere from 24 to 36 hours to reach Morondava.

Private Bus The *Confo Express* is a private bus which travels all the way between Toliara and Tana, and the first of several that will probably run in future. The quality of bus, seating and service is far nicer than the normal public bus, and there are a few gimmicks like free bottles of mineral water, but

>0<>0<>0<>0<>0<>0<>0<>0<>0<>0<>0<>0<>0<>0<>0<>0<>0<>0<

Mangroves

The dictionary defines mangroves as 'any tropical evergreen tree or shrub of the genus *Rhizophora* having stilt-like intertwining aerial roots and forming dense thickets along coasts'. They are much maligned by many – the word that usually follows mangrove is 'swamp' and the image conjured up is of something dark, muddy and smelly that is humming and crawling with insects, and generally most unattractive.

In fact, mangroves form an extremely interesting ecosystem whose vital importance has only been recognised comparatively recently. Mangroves are the advance troops, the first plants to reclaim land from the sea. While salt water kills most plants, mangroves are remarkably resistant to it; in fact, they thrive in it. This is possible because they can either restrict entry of salt through their roots or expel the excess through their leaves. Their extensive root system helps to stabilise tidal mud and as a mangrove colony grows the coastline becomes sheltered.

Gradually mangroves create new land, but in the process they provide an environment for a host of other living things from oysters, crabs and snails to mudskippers (fish that prefer to scamper and leap around in and on the mangrove mud rather than swim in water). They also serve as sheltered nurseries for young fish and shrimps, which in turn become valuable food for humans and other life forms. ■

>0<>0<>0<>0<>0<>0<>0<>0<>0<>0<>0<>0<>0<>0<>0<>0<>0<>0<

you pay about double the normal bus fares: it's FMg 35,000 to Ranohira, FMg 78,100 to Fianarantsoa, FMg 112,600 to Antsirabe and to Tana it costs FMg 130,000.

The *Confo Express* leaves from the Longo Hôtel every Thursday morning and from Tana on Tuesday. Bookings should be made as soon as possible at Longo Voyage (☎ 412 68) in Toliara, or Europe Voyage (☎ (2) 630 49) in Tana.

Boat Refer to the Morondava section in the Western Madagascar chapter for information about the possibility of travelling between Morondava and Toliara by boat.

Getting Around

The Airport A taxi between the Ankorangia airport, 7km east of Toliara, and the centre of town costs a standard, non-negotiable FMg 10,000. Only if you pre-book with an up-market hotel in Toliara, or with a resort in Ifaty, will a hotel bus be waiting at the airport. There are surprisingly few hotel touts at the airport – a reflection of the lack of tourist interest in Toliara.

Car There are very few places near Toliara which you can reach by a normal vehicle (such as the sandy trail to Ifaty), so hiring a car seems pointless. And rental prices are very high: FMg 250,000 per day from Ravel Tour (☎ 416 54) and Air Fort Services (☎ 426 84), and if you go to Ifaty you may be charged another FMg 100,000 per day! L'Étoile de Mer advertises cars from FMg 150,000 to FMg 225,000 per day.

Taxi Within town, taxis charge a standard rate of FMg 2500.

Pousse-pousse The pousse-pousse drivers can be annoying at times, but you will probably be forced to use them – for example, to go to the taxi-brousse stations. The standard rate for a pousse-pousse is FMg 500 but foreigners will normally have to pay at least FMg 1000.

AROUND TOLIARA
Miary

The village of Miary, about 10km north-east of Toliara, is known for its interesting and unusual stands of **banyan trees**. One tree in particular, enclosed in a high wall, is considered sacred and it is fady to damage it in any way. To visit the sacred tree on your own, you'll need to secure permission from the local *fokonolona* (local community council).

Auberge de la Table

This lovely private desert garden lies about

17km east of Toliara. The Swiss owner conducts tours (in French), and afterwards his wife usually provides a *table d'hôte* lunch. To get there, catch any bus or taxi-brousse from the centre of Toliara towards Befety and ask to be dropped off. Or you can charter a taxi from Toliara – the return fare should be about FMg 30,000 plus waiting time. The garden is just a few hundred metres from the main road.

IFATY
On the coast, 22km north of Toliara, Ifaty is a soporific village which is becoming justifiably popular for its world-class diving. In fact, most of Toliara's visitors wind up there.

Here you can walk along gorgeous beaches which literally stretch away to the horizon past tiny Vezo fishing villages. The area has been experiencing a drought for many years now, but although the hinterland is an inhospitable looking place it still has an unearthly beauty. Not far inland from the village is a fascinating **spiny forest** where you will see plenty of baobabs – but the walk is hot, so take a hat and water. In July and August you will probably see **migrating whales** pass through the Mozambique Channel.

Be especially careful with water; all the hotels provide an adequate supply for their guests, but please don't waste it or use it unnecessarily.

Dangers & Annoyances
Because the diving equipment used at several of the Ifaty diving centres doesn't comply with international certification restrictions, it's not always in top shape and there are often risks involved. Ask to look at the equipment and check it out before you commit yourself to a diving trip. If in doubt, go to another diving centre; the places listed here should be OK.

And one more thing ... the Mozambique Channel is one of the world's most shark-infested areas. To minimise the danger, avoid swimming in the late afternoon, and if you're away from the shallow area near the beach don't thrash about on the surface.

Diving & Water Sports
Experienced divers mention the quality of diving at Ifaty in the same breath as the Red Sea, the Great Barrier Reef and the Maldives, so if you have a hankering for some scuba diving or snorkelling you shouldn't be disappointed.

Most Ifaty hotels have centres for divers and other water sports enthusiasts. At both the full and new moon, Ifaty experiences dramatic tidal variations so diving trips and other activities must be timed accordingly. The prices, which are high compared with other places in Madagascar, are fairly standard among the diving centres in Ifaty: about F200 per dive, a night dive for F210 and six-day courses for F2800. You may be able to rent a hobie cat for F150 per hour, and fishing trips will cost a hefty F600 per person for the half-day.

The main diving centres are:

Bamboo Club (☎ 427 17)
    This place also rents full snorkelling gear for FMg 20,000 per day and can arrange snorkelling trips for FMg 50,000 per person.
Blue Moon Bay
    Based at the Dunes Hôtel in Ifaty; diving trips can be pre-booked at the Safari Vezo booking office in Toliara (☎ (9) 413 81).
Club Nautique (☎ 421 59)
    This outfit is based at the Mora Mora bungalows; it can also organise boat trips, and rents snorkelling gear.
Deep Sea Club
    This is one of the better organised centres. It can arrange windsurfing and fishing trips and just about any other water sport imaginable. Snorkelling equipment can also be rented for about FMg 18,000 per day. The booking office (☎ (9) 426 20) is in the Motel Le Capricorne in Toliara.

Places to Stay & Eat
Most places listed here have a booking office in Toliara and you are strongly recommended to make arrangements with them before heading out to Ifaty. Checking out each bungalow complex is hard work and the one you prefer may be booked out, closed, have inadequate food and so on. You will probably also need to arrange a transfer from Toliara to Ifaty, unless you stick with the

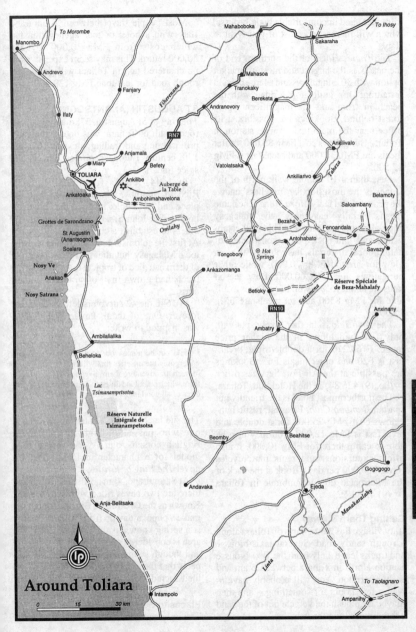

Around Toliara

0   15   30 km

infrequent and uncomfortable taxis-brousse, which will increase the cost of your visit to Ifaty.

The *Dunes Hôtel*, at the northern end of the beach, is the largest and most up-market option with 30 bungalows and a large bar and restaurant. It's built atop a dune with the beach in front and the magnificent spiny forest behind. Bookings are possible at its office near the main taxi-brousse station in Toliara. Bungalows cost FMg 85,000, buffet meals are FMg 30,000 and breakfast is FMg 12,500.

Less than a 10 minute walk north of the Dunes is the most popular travellers' haunt, the peaceful and leafy *Mora Mora*. The name means literally 'easy easy', the Malagasy equivalent of 'hang loose'. This well-established and laid-back place, constructed of natural local materials, has rooms with a sea view for around FMg 70,000, while other bungalows are FMg 60,000. Low season rates are about 15% lower. Breakfast is available for FMg 8500 and set meals are FMg 15,000.

The *Vovo Telo* is another lovely spot with only five bungalows in the higher price range: F160/210 for a double/triple; breakfast is F20 and other meals F65. Bookings are possible at the Air Fort Services office (☎/fax (9) 426 84) in the Hôtel Sud, Toliara.

The northernmost hotel is the friendly but spartan *Bamboo Club*. Pleasant, rustic bungalows cost FMg 75,000 for a double and breakfast is FMg 12,000. You may also be able to camp there for FMg 10,000. It also offers excursions, and rents motorcycles (FMg 200,000 per day). Book at the back of the Pharmacie du Mozambique in Toliara (☎ (9) 427 17).

Getting There & Away

Ifaty village lies 22km north of Toliara along a rough sandy road. Several taxis-brousse and trucks leave daily from the Taxi-brousse Station North in Toliara between 6 am and early afternoon. You will probably have to wait a few hours for something – and then maybe help push the vehicle out of the sand a few times along the way.

Most people travel between Toliara and Ifaty with a hotel or tour agency transfer, which costs from FMg 30,000 to FMg 50,000 return. This may seem expensive but no chartered taxi in Toliara will go on that rough road for less than FMg 120,000!

ST AUGUSTIN (ANANTSOGNO)

The Bay of St Augustin, 37km along a poor road south of Toliara, was one of the early provisioning and trading sites for 16th and 17th century European pirates, slavers and spice traders.

In 1644, reports from English sailor Richard Boothby, who was taken with the place and its people, inspired the less-than-honourable John Smart and a group of 120 others to establish a colony at St Augustin. At first the colonists dealt and traded with the local Malagasy, but after two years over half of them had died of tropical maladies and the locals had grown tired of strangers in their midst.

In 1646 the 12 survivors left Madagascar forever. One of them, Powle Waldegrave, was inspired to write:

I could not but endeavour to dissuade others from undergoing the miseries that will follow the persons of such an adventure themselves for Madagascar ... from which place God divert the residence and adventures of all good men.

The site later became a haunt of pirates and one who passed through, the infamous English corsair John Avery, served as a model for a character in Daniel Defoe's novel *The King of Pirates*.

At Sarondrano, 4km north of St Augustin, there are two caves filled with sweet water. Known as the **Grottes de Sarondrano**, they make a popular day tip from Toliara. Nearby is a spring known as the **Source Bina**. The area is considered sacred to the Vezo people and though swimming is possible, one suspects that the locals would prefer not to see their sacred spot used as a swimming hole.

Places to Stay & Eat

The only accommodation in the area is *Les*

Mangroves Chez Alain, 20km south of Toliara, which serves as a sort of beach annexe for the landlocked Chez Alain in Toliara. Bungalows, which are starting to look shabby and neglected, cost FMg 45,000/55,000 for a single/double. Set meals are pricey at FMg 25,000. You should be able to camp at the complex (but with no access to shower facilities) for FMg 10,000 per tent. If you are looking for a beach setting you will be disappointed: this place is called 'The Mangroves' for a reason.

Getting There & Away

There is now a daily taxi-brousse to St Augustin (FMg 2500) from Toliara. Most people use the easier – but more expensive – option of going on an organised tour from Toliara (see under Organised Tours in the Toliara section), or on the 'unimog' which normally leaves Chez Alain in Toliara every day for FMg 30,000 return. Alternatively, you can try hitching; head about 15km east of Toliara on RN7 then turn south and continue for 14km more to Sarondrano. St Augustin lies 4km farther south.

ANAKAO & NOSY VE

The beach village of Anakao lies about 22km south of St Augustin. The reef area is good for swimming and diving, and is the departure point for trips to the paradisiacal island of Nosy Ve. Be careful because it is *very* hot around here, and you will soon turn red and crispy without protection. There is very little else to do, so if you are not into swimming and diving Anakao and Nosy Ve may not be worth the effort.

The first European to 'discover' Nosy Ve was the Dutch pirate Admiral Cornelius de Houtman in September 1595. The island became a haunt of pirates and is still littered with their bones. Nosy Ve is now considered one of the world's finest diving sites; it is hard to decide whether or not Ifaty is better.

Organised Tours

Safari Vezo in Anakao organises half-day/one-day trips to Nosy Ve for F50/75; excursions on the Onilahy River; and, best

of all, camping trips to the remote Tsimanampetsotsa Reserve. It also arranges diving for F200 per dive, or F1200 for seven dives, and rents snorkelling gear for F25 per day.

Places to Stay & Eat

The only accommodation is *Safari Vezo* at Anakao – bookings are possible at its office behind the post office in Toliara (☎ (9) 413 81). Simple, pleasant bungalows cost F100 and an extra bed is F40. Awesome meals, which naturally go heavy on the seafood, are F35 and breakfast is F15. If you have a tent, and get permission from the local council chief, you can camp anywhere near Anakao or on Nosy Ve for nothing.

Getting There & Away

The Safari Vezo transfer (by pirogue) from Toliara (F150 return) can add substantially to the cost of your stay. From Les Mangroves bungalows at St Augustin, a boat (with a minimum of three people) costs ·FMg 75,000/90,000 per person one way/return. Don't pay the ridiculous prices (FMg 200,000 return per person) asked by some hotels in Itafy. During rough weather, the trip to Anakao by boat can be quite an adventure.

RÉSERVE NATURELLE INTÉGRALE DE TSIMANAMPETSOTSA

The centrepiece of this 43,200 hectare reserve is the large shallow Lac Tsimanampetsotsa, 7km from the coast and about 40km south of Anakao.

Because of the chalky bottom the lake's waters are oddly white and opaque, and in them lives a species of blind white fish. The reserve is also inhabited by 72 bird species, including plovers, couas, rock-thrushes and immense numbers of flamingos, and also sustains a large population of ring-tailed lemurs. You'll also have the opportunity to see the radiated tortoise in its natural habitat.

There are still no facilities in the reserve so visitors must be completely self-sufficient. It's OK to camp, but get permission from the local villagers.

Getting There & Away

If you have access to a 4WD vehicle, a rough and sandy 130km track leads to the reserve from Betioky. The easiest access, however, is with a tour organised by Safari Vezo in Anakao – see under Anakao & Nosy Ve in the preceding section.

MOROMBE

• Telephone Area Code: 980

Along a very rough and sandy 284km road from Toliara is the coastal town of Morombe. Although there's not a great deal to do or see in the place, Morombe ('Vast Beach') has long been expected to become a popular beach destination. However, the town is in the middle of a rough overland trip between Morondava and Toliara, so is rarely on the tourist trail. (For more information about Morondava, how to get there and the west coast in general refer to the Western Madagascar chapter.)

Lac Ihotry

An interesting excursion from Morombe is to a shallow saline lake, Lac Ihotry, accessible along a very poor 20km secondary road that turns south from the village of Tanandava, about 60km from Morombe. There are a few lemurs in the area – including ring-tailed and brown lemurs and Verreaux's sifakas – and there are also fosas. But the major attraction is the birdlife: at different times of the year one can observe over 100 species of forest and water birds, and migratory birds from the northern hemisphere. Excursions to the lake can be arranged at the Hôtel Baobab in Morombe.

Places to Stay & Eat

The cheapest place to stay is the strangely named *Hôtel Koweit City*, which charges FMg 11,000 for very basic reed bungalows. Only a bit higher up the scale is the austere concrete *Hôtel Datier*, which begins at FMg 17,500 for a room with shared facilities. Moving slightly up-market, the *Hôtel/Restaurant Croix du Sud* (☎ 18) charges FMg 35,000/45,000 for a single/double. The French-run *Hôtel Baobab* has pleasant bungalows and a sea view; doubles cost FMg 65,000 and the staff can also arrange excursions to nearby locations.

Apart from the restaurant at the Croix du Sud, you can eat at the *Brillant* across the street.

Getting There & Away

Air Every few days Air Madagascar links Morombe with Morondava (US$49) and with Toliara for the same price. Its office (☎ 54) is in a bizarre building in the centre of town.

Taxi-brousse Every day there is a taxi-brousse, or some sort of vehicle, heading to Toliara and Morondava, though you may need to get a short taxi-brousse connection to the junction of Bevoay and hitch a ride on whatever is going your way.

Boat You can also charter boats and pirogues from Morombe to Toliara or Morondava. For more information refer to the Morondava section in the Western Madagascar chapter.

TOLIARA TO TAOLAGNARO

The route between Toliara and Taolagnaro passes through archetypal southern Madagascar, with its parched landscapes and whimsical vegetation. This is the land of the Vezo (a subgroup living in the Sakalava territory) and the Mahafaly.

Between Betioky and Ampanihy, the **tombs of the Mahafaly** are large buildings about a metre high and up to 15m square, painted with scenes from the life of the deceased and often showing details of the actual death and funeral. These tombs are often adorned by *aloalo*. Aloalo consist of a carved pattern of geometric figures crowned by a pertinent and often amusing item or scene representing the life of the deceased. These can be family scenes or events from daily life, including games, transport, work and so on.

Mahafaly tombs also bear a number of zebu skulls, which correspond to the number of cattle sacrificed upon that person's death. Extremely important figures in Mahafaly society may merit as many as 100 bovine victims, but the majority of the tombs are adorned with 10 or fewer.

The Antanosy and the Antandroy, who inhabit the country east of the Malafaly, are two of the country's poorest tribes. Many of the villagers eke out a meagre living producing charcoal from the few remaining trees. The tombs and funerary art of these two tribes are also renowned.

If you travel across this rough but fascinating road by taxi-brousse, you are advised to do it in stages, staying at Betioky, Ampanihy and Ambovombe. Transport between these towns isn't too difficult to find, though it can be time-consuming; several trucks and taxis-brousse go through in both directions every day. If you do the 650km trip between Toliara and Taolagnaro nonstop, it takes at least 40 hours (and possibly 55 to 60 hours). Don't expect to travel more than 25 km/h along the way. And we will warn you again: this is a rough ol' ride.

Betioky & Bezaha

Betioky (Where the Wind Blows), and Bezaha on the Onilahy River, lie in the heart of Mahafaly country. The main objective of most visits to the area is to see the bizarrely decorated tombs which are the Mahafaly's trademark, and to arrange a trip to the Beza-Mahafaly Reserve.

On the road into Betioky from Toliara is the **Exposition des Arts Mahafaly**, but it's more a marginal sort of crafts shop than anything interesting. Nearby are the **tombs** of a former village chief and his wife with some particularly nice aloalos. At Ambatry, not far from Betioky, is a good stand of **spiny forest** with *Didierea*.

Places to Stay & Eat The best place to stay in Bezaha is the *Teheza Hôtel* (☎ (950) 19) which costs FMg 20,000 for fairly clean rooms. In Betioky, there's the filthy *Hôtel Mamy Rano* which costs FMg 5000 per bungalow and FMg 10,000 for a room, or the *Hôtel Mahafaly* which is marginally better for FMg 15,000 per room. The Hôtel Mahafaly is the best place to try for meals.

Getting There & Away To get to Bezaha, 129km east of Toliara, travel 70km northeast on RN7 then turn south on RN10. After 42km head south-east and continue 17km to the village. Betioky lies along RN10 about 46km south of the Bezaha turn-off.

There are two daily direct taxis-brousse between Toliara and Bezaha (FMg 7500) and one daily between Toliara and Betioky (FMg 10,000). Either trip takes six to seven hours. From Betioky to Ampanihy or Toliara, flag down any vehicle going along RN10. Along the way you'll see some of the best and most interesting examples of **Mahafaly tombs** in the area. There may be occasional flights on Air Mad between Toliara and Betioky (US$25) – but don't count on it.

Réserve Spéciale de Beza-Mahafaly

The Beza-Mahafaly Special Reserve consists of two parcels of land 3km apart – Parcel I consists of 100 hectares of sand and forest and Parcel II 480 hectares of spiny desert. During the dry season the rivers are beds of sand, but when it rains they can flood and inundate the entire area – including the research camp in the reserve.

The normal objective of most visitors is to observe lemurs: ring-tailed, fat-tailed dwarf, mouse and sportive lemurs, and Verreaux's sifaka. Other mammals include the rare large-eared tenrec. Beza-Mahafaly is also one of the remaining habitats of the radiated tortoise. The most interesting of the 61 species of birds are the sickle-bill vanga, which scurries around the gallery forest, and the hoopoe, which is at home in the dry spiny forest.

Permits to visit the reserve should be obtained at the ANGAP office in Tana.

Places to Stay Accommodation is available in Parcel I, 17km north-east of Betioky, but it is mainly reserved for students, researchers and staff. Although there are occasional vacancies, casual visitors should be self-sufficient with food and camping equipment.

Getting There & Away Beza-Mahafaly lies 17km east of Betioky, a few km from – but not accessible by road from – the village of Bezaha. The reserve can be reached along a poor road from Betioky but the route is confusing so you'll need a guide. The journey is much better in the dry season; if it has been raining, check conditions before setting out.

Alternatively, you may be able to catch a lift in with reserve employees, but that could entail long waits in Betioky. It's also possible to walk but it's a long, hot grunt, and, again, a guide will be requisite. Otherwise, locals can arrange to take you in by zebu cart (in this case, a long hot crawl). For the easy option, you can arrange an expensive overnight trip with a travel agency in Toliara (refer to Toliara's Organised Tours section earlier in this chapter for details).

Ampanihy
Five to seven hours by taxi-brousse from Betioky, Ampanihy is a sad and uninspiring place.

Between Ampanihy and Tranoroa (whose name means 'Two Houses'), at the western edge of Antandroy country, the road hits rock-bottom and the 41km trip can take about three hours.

Places to Stay & Eat The clean and comfortable *Hôtel Relais d'Ampanihy* is a welcome place to stay after the hard slog across the desert. Rooms should cost FMg 32,000, but we subsequently heard of visitors being charged a ridiculous F125/150 for a single/double. Bargain them down or go to the *Hôtel Chez Tahio* where rooms cost FMg 15,000/25,000.

Getting There & Away Ampanihy lies 283km from Toliara and 224km from Ambovombe. All traffic between Toliara and Taolagnaro stops in Ampanihy, so it is a matter of flagging down anything going your way. There may be occasional flights to/from Toliara (US$43) on Air Mad (☎ (960) 10), but don't hold your breath.

Réserve Spéciale de Cap Sainte Marie & Faux Cap
Cap Sainte Marie is the southern tip of Mada-

gascar, just over 200km from Taolagnaro. It is difficult to reach unless you take a tour, have access to a mountain bike or a strong 4WD vehicle – or have plenty of stamina, time and creativity at your disposal. Then prepare yourself for an expedition.

Some of the area has recently been allocated as a small (1750 hectares) special reserve to protect 14 bird species and two rare species of tortoises.

In addition to the bizarre vegetation and the opportunity to stand at the 'land's end', the area attracts people because it once was the habitat of Aepyornis, which has been extinct for over 2000 years. Eggshells still cover the sands as if they had been smashed yesterday. Although there are lots of fragments, in the interests of future visitors and research, please resist the temptation to collect them as souvenirs. It is also highly illegal to take Aepyornis eggs or fragments of eggs out of the country.

Getting There & Away If you don't have a 4WD vehicle, or a sturdy mountain bike, and lots of supplies, access to Madagascar's 'Patagonia' will be quite difficult unless you opt for an expensive tour. Some of the travel agencies listed under Organised Tours in the Taolagnaro section organise trips to the cape and reserve; expect to pay about FMg 540,000 per person for a two day trip.

To reach the region from Taolagnaro on your own, take a truck or taxi-brousse towards Toliara and get off at Tsihombe, from where it is a hot 30km slog to Faux Cap. To reach Cap Sainte Marie is more difficult – from Faux Cap, it is accessible via Marovato, which is 30km from Faux Cap along a basic track and 18km from Cap Sainte Marie.

Alternatively, get a taxi-brousse to Beloha, from where Faux Cap is 35km along a rough track to the coast at Lavanona; from there it is another 30km to Cap Sainte Marie.

Ambovombe
The large dusty town of Ambovombe lies 110km west of Taolagnaro on a good tarred road. On Monday the town holds a large

zebu market, as well as an ordinary market, from dawn until mid-morning. If you wish to visit the markets, especially from Taolagnaro, get a very early start or you'll miss the action – or stay the night in Ambovombe.

If you're heading west from Ambovombe, note the **Mahafaly tombs**; one tomb, about 20km west of Tsihombe, is capped by a replica of an aeroplane.

Places to Stay & Eat Very few travellers bother staying in Ambovombe because it is not far from Taolagnaro (and along a good paved road), but a couple of hotels cater for local travellers. The most convenient, the *Hôtel L'Oasis* has clean rooms for FMg 25,000 and a good restaurant, or try the *Hôtel Relais des Androy* for about the same price.

Getting There & Away Taxis-brousse run between Ambovombe and Taolagnaro (FMg 7500) at least twice a day. All traffic between Toliara and Taolagnaro passes through Ambovombe, so you may be able to jump on any vehicle heading your way. The town is also the terminus for the very rugged trip along RN13 to Ihosy. Public transport travelling between Ihosy and Taolagnaro is likely to be full.

Taolagnaro to Ambovombe

The paved road from Taolagnaro to Ambovombe is definitely worth exploring; if you are going to Berenty or Kaleta reserves from Taolagnaro on an organised tour you will certainly stop at most of the attractions along the way anyway.

Beginning in the lush and rainy eastern climate around Taolagnaro, you travel west over the hills into the dry country that dominates southern Madagascar. The first stop is at a small swampy area to see a stand of **pitcher plants**, whose pitcher-like yellow-green flowers contain a sticky liquid which attracts and digests insects. These plants are most prominent on the island of Borneo (where immense specimens have been known to digest rats), but there are also two

species in the western Indian Ocean – one in Madagascar and one in Seychelles.

Farther west is another oddity, a **forested hillside** dotted with the world's only specimens of the bizarre three-cornered palm *(Neodypsis decary)*. In fact, nearly the entire range of the species is visible from this one roadside stop. The palm is especially significant because it represents the only example of three-way symmetry in the plant kingdom.

Near the village of Ranopiso, you'll visit the most photographed **tomb** in Madagascar, which isn't actually a tomb at all, but a site where the Antanosy commemorate their dead with aloalos and zebu skulls. Look carefully at what's going on in these masterfully carved aloalos – they recall all sorts of events from the mundane to the grisly. The most renowned is by the Antanosy sculptor Fesira and probably dates back to the 1930s. It portrays a boatload of people who were drowned in a canoe accident.

As you head west from Ranopiso, the landscape begins to flatten and dry out, and enters the formidable **spiny forest**. Most of the spiny forest is comprised of several species of baobabs, the spiral-spined *Alluaudia*, the randomly spined *Didierea* and the cactus-like woody succulent *Euphorbia*. You'll have to go for a close-up view of the *Didierea* and *Alluaudia* before their differences become obvious. The largest species is *Alluaudia ascendens*, which can reach a height of 15m.

The dusty village of **Amboasary**, 75km west of Taolagnaro, is the site of a hospital and a headquarters for international drought aid to southern Madagascar. Here you cross the bridge over the broad but often bone-dry Mandrare River. You can stay at the extremely basic *Hôtel Mandrare* (☎ 27). The road to the Berenty and Kaleta reserves turns north here, passing through **sisal plantations** as far as their entrances.

RÉSERVE PRIVÉE DE KALETA

The Kaleta Private Reserve (also known as the Réserve d'Amboasary-Sud) opened in 1988 as the Hôtel Kaleta's budget answer to the expensive, up-market Berenty Reserve (see next section). The Kaleta Reserve continues to get mixed reviews: some claim it to be a highlight of their trip – possibly someone who has not been to any other park and is impressed by how close you can get to the lemurs.

Frankly, we consider Kaleta Reserve to be a poor, contrived and ecologically unsound imitation of Berenty, and not nearly as good as other, more accessible reserves in Madagascar. Even if your means won't stretch to a visit to Berenty you are still better off going to other parks to see lemurs, such as Périnet or Ranomafana, unless you are visiting only southern Madagascar.

The advantage of Kaleta is that you can see – and feed – many ring-tailed lemurs and sifakas. Banana feeding may be great for photos, but it isn't sound practice because the lemurs come to depend upon it, become tame and may even jump up on you to look for food while you walk along the trail. (The feeding of lemurs is banned in many other parks.)

Some unfortunate snakes, tortoises and crocodiles are kept in tiny pools in the reserve (they don't respond to banana-baiting).

Although most people visit on a day trip from Taolagnaro, camping is permitted in the reserve for FMg 20,000 per tent. You can also hire a tent for FMg 20,000 – but don't turn up expecting one to be available. If you have your own tent it's better to camp discretely outside the reserve for nothing, but bring your own food and water. Bungalows are still being built in the reserve. Alternatively, you can stay in Amboasary and hitch a ride to or from the park.

The entrance fee is FMg 20,000 (but this may go up when entrance fees to ANGAP parks increase to FMg 50,000). Guides, who are not needed along the blindingly obvious 20 to 30 minute trail, will cost a ridiculous FMg 20,000. No meals are available (unless you are on an organised tour), only warm drinks.

Getting There & Away

Most agencies in Taolagnaro (see Organised Tours under that section for details) can organise trips to Kaleta for about FMg 140,000 per person, which includes the entrance fee of FMg 20,000. (Berenty Reserve is virtually off limits to any agency not associated with the up-market de Heaulme hotels in Taolagnaro.)

The only way to get there on your own is to charter your own taxi-brousse (about FMg 200,000 for the day) from Taolagnaro, or take any taxi-brousse heading towards Amboasary and ask to be dropped off at the laneway (which is not signed) to the park. If you go by public taxi-brousse from Taolagnaro you will miss all the great attractions along the way, so it's worth chartering a vehicle or going on a tour. Refer to the Taolagnaro to Ambovombe section for information about this route.

RÉSERVE PRIVÉE DE BERENTY

Whatever you think of the private reserve concept, Berenty is an undeniably magical place. Together with its small companion reserve Bealoka, 7km to the north, it contains nearly one-third of the remaining tamarind (or *kily*) gallery forest in Madagascar. Vaguely reminiscent of the African bush, the forest area of Berenty lies between the arms of a former oxbow lake on the Mandrare River.

The reserve was established in 1936 by a sisal planter, Henri de Heaulme, who felt that a stand of gallery forest along the banks of the Mandrare River was worth preserving for its own sake. The reserve, as well as the surrounding sisal plantation, has now passed to his son, M Jean de Heaulme.

In 1962 Dr Alison Jolly of Princeton University came to Berenty to study its healthy population of ring-tailed lemurs; since then Berenty's relative ease of access has lured numerous other researchers and naturalists from diverse fields of study. Berenty was first opened to tourists in the early 1980s and it has since become one of Madagascar's best known and most visited reserves. In 1985 the WWF awarded Jean de Heaulme the Getty Prize for nature conservation.

Berenty is one of the three areas of focus

for the Wildlife Preservation Trust International, which has been working with the owner to set up a long-term management plan for the reserve. Banana-feeding of lemurs has been stopped in the forest and greatly restricted around the compound. In addition, forest tracks are no longer swept daily; there has been a census of wildlife; Bealoka is being set up as a reserve; and teams have begun to remove such bothersome non-endemic plant invaders as sisal, raketa and the rubber vine.

Flora & Fauna

Although small, the Berenty forest contains over 115 plant species, which serve as habitat for a surprising variety of wildlife. The forest, which is dominated by the tamarind, is a 265 hectare oasis enclosed by spiny desert, sisal plantations and the beautiful Mandrare River.

Most visitors come to see the lemurs, of which the ring-tailed are most prominent. Many lemurs still have fond memories of unrestrained banana feeding by tourists and in the compound it's still not unusual to see a visitor struggling beneath a tackle of hopeful beasts.

Among the best times to visit Berenty is in late September and October, just after the young are born. In late September the baby ring-tailed lemurs are clinging to their mother's undercarriage, but after a couple of weeks they climb up onto her back and hold on for dear life as she goes about her daily business. Males are normally relegated to the sidelines and, except during breeding season in April or May, are largely exempted from ringtail social life.

Then there are the Verreaux's sifakas, large white lemurs which are among nature's most accomplished acrobats. You'll never forget the sight of sifakas hurling themselves across vast distances between tamarind trees

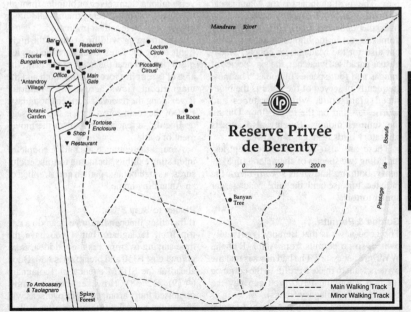

Réserve Privée de Berenty

Mandrare River

Bar
Research Bungalows
Tourist Bungalows
Office
'Antandroy Village'
Main Gate
Botanic Garden
Tortoise Enclosure
Shop
Restaurant
Lecture Circle
'Piccadilly Circus'
Bat Roost
Banyan Tree
Passage de Boeufs

To Amboasary & Taolagnaro
Spiny Forest

0   100   200 m

- - - - Main Walking Track
- - - - Minor Walking Track

or dancing their way across open ground on two legs.

Also abundant is a subspecies of the brown lemur, the red-fronted lemur *(gidro)* transplanted to Berenty from Analabe Reserve in western Madagascar; this reserve also belongs to M de Heaulme (see the Western Madagascar chapter).

You'll also see two species of nocturnal lemurs: the sportive lemur *(songiky)*, which is normally known as lepilemur, and the grey mouse lemur *(tsidy)*.

Other mammals include the tenrecs, fossas (striped civets) and flying foxes or *fanihy*. Unfortunately, the local Malagasy believe that these large fruit bats make excellent eating. The main roost, which centres on one immense tamarind tree in the heart of the reserve, has been closed to visitors in order to protect the remaining population and confine them to the reserve.

Berenty is one of the best birdwatching sites in Madagascar; 83 bird species have been recorded, nine of which are birds of prey. The most abundant is the Madagascar buzzard, which is frequently seen hovering over the tamarind trees and occasionally comes to rest in the highest branches. Look out also for the Madagascar coucal, Madagascar paradise flycatcher, the six species of vangas and four species of couas. The most frequently observed of the latter is the blue-faced giant coua, which scratches and scurries around on the forest floor. During the summer months, Berenty also attracts migratory birds from eastern Africa.

There are also 26 species of reptiles, including two species of chameleon (in Malagasy, both are known as *sokorokotra)*, the radiated tortoise and the rare Madagascar spider tortoise.

Guides & Permits

The good news is that Berenty is privately owned, so no permits from ANGAP or the WWF are necessary. The bad news is that the owners want to make a profit, so the entrance fee is a whopping F100 (you can pay the equivalent in Malagasy francs).

Guides aren't strictly necessary (nor are they compulsory) because the trails are easy enough to follow. However, a good guide will help you to spot birds by day and lemurs, chameleons, tenrecs and fossas by night.

Visiting the Reserve

The greatest joy at Berenty is to wander the many forest paths at different times of the day, observing the changing scene. The most memorable times are early morning before breakfast, late afternoon and just after dark, though the overwhelming silence of midday in the forest is also a worthwhile experience. The most magical time is often from 5 to 6 am – you may see a troop of ringtails devouring the huge flowers of a large cactus, their heads disappearing inside the flower to lick up the nectar.

While walking in the forest, especially on night walks, it's important to move as quietly as possible. Although the sifakas and ring-tailed lemurs long ago ceased to be wary of visitors, the nocturnal lemurs and smaller creatures are still skittish. Those who converse among themselves or blunder through the forest will miss seeing them – and other visitors will be less than impressed.

Apart from the wildlife, some of the highlights along the forest tracks are the tangled **giant banyan** near the heart of the park, the area of true **spiny forest** in the south and the magnificent views across the Mandrare River along the reserve's northern boundary. East of the main forest area is the 'Passage de Boeufs', a fenced corridor for the movement of cattle.

Around the entrance area are a couple of interesting exhibits, including tortoise enclosures, a small botanic garden and a replica of an Antandroy home.

Places to Stay & Eat

If travelling independently you can do a day trip from Taolagnaro, but if you have the time staying overnight is a good idea. *Bungalows* cost F310 and breakfast is F30. Book ahead at the SHTM agency in Taolagnaro (☎ (9) 212 38). However, because most organised tours arranged from overseas will stay at the bungalows they are often full. If you are discreet, there is nothing to stop you walking out of the reserve and camping nearby so that you can visit the park in the early morning or late at night. Alternatively, stay in Amboasary and hitch a lift to and from the park.

A *restaurant* in the compound for guests serves up ordinary but well-prepared set meals. Near the bungalows, a great *open-air bar* serves drinks and snacks. There's also a small gift shop opposite the dining area.

Getting There & Away

Nearly all visitors to Berenty take a de Heaulme (SHTM) tour (see under Organised Tours in the Taolagnaro section), but there are no restrictions on those who prefer to make their own arrangements. At the SHTM agency adjacent to Le Dauphin hotel in Taolagnaro, you can join a very expensive day trip – F950 per car for one to three people, or F380 per person if there is at least four people in the group.

To do the trip on your own, take a taxi-brousse (80km) to Amboasary and look for another headed north. Tell the driver you're headed for Berenty (though it will probably be obvious) and he'll drop you within about 500m of the entrance. But if you go to Berenty by public taxi-brousse you will miss all the great attractions along the way, so it is probably worth considering chartering a taxi or going on a tour.

TAOLAGNARO (FORT DAUPHIN)

• Telephone Area Code: 9

Taolagnaro (far more commonly known as Fort Dauphin) is a small, pretty and isolated town of about 25,000 people. Even though it is remote it is a popular destination and one of our favourite places in Madagascar. Its attractive location – backed by windswept green hills, blue seas and fine beaches – and the myriad of surrounding sights justify a detour.

Much of Taolagnaro is under the control of M Jean de Heaulme, who owns the up-market hotels in town, a sisal plantation, the private estate of Berenty, 80km to the west, and various and sundry bits in between.

Taolagnaro enjoys the most pleasant climate on the east coast of Madagascar, lying just east of the mountain range which prevents nearly all moisture from reaching the interior. Although Taolagnaro catches frequent rainstorms and lashings from the wind, the temperatures and humidity are lower than farther north. From September to December the winds can be fierce, so hang onto your hat.

History

If Toliara is the youngster of Madagascar, Taolagnaro is the grand-daddy. The first European settlers in the area were a group of Portuguese sailors who had been shipwrecked offshore in 1504. They constructed a fort near the Ambinanibe River and remained there until 1527, when the local Antanosy decided it was time for them to leave. After much bloodshed the surviving Portuguese fled into the hills, where they eventually fell victim to the elements and continuing Antanosy resentment.

In 1642 a Société Française de l'Orient expedition, led by a rogue of a governor called Sieur Pronis, arrived at Baie Sainte Luce (north of present-day Taolagnaro) to establish trade and claim Madagascar for the King of France. However, this site was abandoned the following year for the more favourable peninsula 35km to the south where there was already an established Malagasy village called Taolankarana (Place of Dreams).

At Taolankarana the colonists constructed Fort Flacourt and named the surrounding settlement Fort Dauphin, after the six-year-old dauphin who was later crowned Louis XIV. In 1646 Pronis exiled 12 mutineers to the then uninhabited island of Réunion, which is now a full French *départemente*. Like the Portuguese, the French met resistance from the local Antanosy and there were frequent skirmishes. The colony survived until 1674 when, facing further war, disease and treachery, it was abandoned.

Some years later, the French returned to dabble in slave trading and used Fort Dauphin as a port. At the end of the 19th

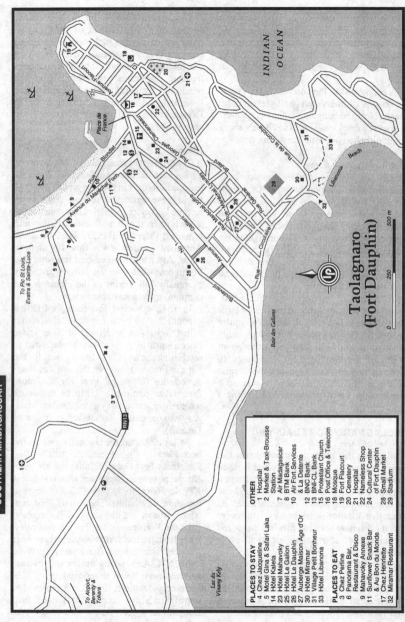

SOUTHERN MADAGASCAR

INDIAN OCEAN

Libanona Beach

Baie des Galions

Lac du Vinany Kely

To Pic St Louis,
Evatra à Sainte-Luce

To Airport,
Berenty &
Toliara

RN13

Taolagnaro
(Fort Dauphin)

0   250   500 m

PLACES TO STAY
4 Chez Jacqueline
5 Motel Gina & Safari Laka
14 Hôtel Kaleta
23 Hôtel Mahavoky
25 Hôtel Le Galion
26 Hôtel Le Dauphin
27 Auberge Maison Age d'Or
30 Hôtel Miramar
31 Village Petit Bonheur
33 Hôtel Libanona

PLACES TO EAT
3 Chez Perline
6 Panorama Bar,
   Restaurant & Disco
9 Mahavoky Annexe
11 Sunflower Snack Bar
   & Au Bon du Monde
17 Chez Henriette
32 Miramar Restaurant

OTHER
1 Hospital
2 Market & Taxi-Brousse
   Station
7 Air Madagascar
8 BTM Bank
10 Air Fort Services
   & La Detente
12 BNC Bank
13 BNI-CL Bank
15 Protestant Church
16 Post Office & Telecom
18 Mosque
19 Fort Flacourt
20 Cemetery
21 Hospital
22 Nameless Shop
24 Cultural Center
   of Fort Dauphin
28 Small Market
29 Stadium

century it was incorporated into the united French colony of Madagascar.

Information
Money The banks – BTM, BNI-CL and BNC – which are along or just off Ave du Maréchal Foch (which is basically the main street), are open from 8 to 11 am and 2 to 4 pm, Monday to Friday.

Post & Communications The post office, which faces the scruffy Place de France, is open from 8 am to noon and 2 to 6 pm Monday to Friday, and on Saturday from 8 am until noon. The Telecom office is next door.

Cultural Center of Fort Dauphin The Cultural Center of Fort Dauphin, next to the Hôtel Mahavoky, is run by the (American) Peace Corps. It was established to teach English to local Malagasy and welcomes the occasional English-speaker to help local students practise their language. The center also has a library and occasionally shows English-language films.

Things to See & Do
Taolagnaro has several places to explore. **Fort Flacourt**, built by the French in 1643, has almost completely disappeared, though a few cannons remain. If you want to see what is left, and admire the view from the cape, negotiate a 'fee' with a soldier at the gate who will show you around. Photos of the fort (but not the barracks) are allowed.

A lovely, blustery stroll along the Rue de la Corniche from the Hôtel Miramar to the fort passes a small overgrown **cemetery**. The northern bay is dotted with **shipwrecks** (reportedly dumped there by foreign governments for a fee). We saw at least four – but the sea is too rough to go snorkelling.

The small beach called **Libanona**, near the Hôtel Miramar, is one of the prettiest and cleanest in Madagascar, and the best place to swim in Taolagnaro. There is a strong current and occasionally rough seas, so snorkelling is out. The beach along the **Baie des Galions** on the other side of the small pen-

insula is tempting, but the water is shallow and it's only used as a landing site for fishing pirogues.

Around September, dolphins and whales are visible offshore from Taolagnaro. You may be able to get on an organised boat trip to see them.

Organised Tours
Taolagnaro is well set up with travel agencies. These can organise tours to anywhere in the region (refer to the Around Taolagnaro section for some ideas about nearby attractions), and as far as the Kaleta and Berenty reserves. You will probably have to get a group together yourself if you want to cut costs, but Safari Laka runs a lot of tours so you can probably join one at short notice.

Air Fort Services (☎ 212 34; fax 212 24) This well set-up firm rents cars, 4WD vehicles, mountain bikes, pirogues, launches, catamarans and even aeroplanes, as well as camping equipment.

Hôtel Kaleta (☎ 213 87) Though there isn't an agency as such, the hotel can arrange inexpensive excursions, catering for down-to-earth travellers. This is the natural place to organise a tour to the Kaleta reserve (which the hotel owns).

Safari Laka (☎ 212 66) Based at the Motel Gina, this excellent outfit offers something wild and different – regular mountain bike excursions, mountain climbing, trekking, canoeing. You name it, Safari Laka probably does it.

SHTM (☎ 212 38) This is the up-market tour company based at Hôtel Le Dauphin. It caters for packaged holidays and cost more than the competition, but SHTM is the only option for visiting Berenty – a trip which you should not miss if your funds stretch that far.

Places to Stay – bottom end
In addition to the usual national tourist tax calculated per night, there is an additional FMg 2500 tax per person per stay at any hotel in Taolagnaro.

The cheapest places to stay are a couple of dives around the busy (and at night, very dark) market and taxi-brousse station. These places should only really be used if you are desperate to save money; otherwise there is good value in the far nicer older part of town, nearer the beach.

In 1888, the Norwegian-American

Lutheran Society of Minnesota established a church and school in Taolagnaro which has now been converted into the *Hôtel Mahavoky* (☎ 213 32). This quiet, well-organised place is now immensely popular with travellers, so bookings are advised in peak season. Gigantic rooms leading onto a huge balcony cost FMg 30,000 with shared facilities (though the toilets and taps are tiny – they were set up for children). It also has a cheap laundry service.

Chez Jacqueline (☎ 211 32), convenient to the market and the airport but to nothing else, is essentially a Chinese restaurant. At the back, it has six singles/doubles with hot showers for a reasonable FMg 25,000/40,000, but the bungalows for FMg 60,000/80,000 are overpriced.

The homey *Auberge Maison Age d'Or* gets mixed reviews – look for the large sign 'Recommended by Lonely Planet' on the outside written in a couple of languages. Small, often noisy, rooms with a bathroom are a bargain at FMg 18,000/20,000. The new rooms at *Safari Laka*, next to – but not part of – Motel Gina (see Places to Stay – middle & top end), are good value at a negotiable FMg 35,000, but they are inconvenient for the rest of town.

Places to Stay – middle & top end

The *Motel Gina* (☎ 212 66) has large bungalows with four beds (two downstairs and two in the loft) for F103/129 a single/double. Across the road, the *Gina Village* has so-so double rooms (some without mosquito nets) for F67/84. Unfortunately, it is not a great part of town and going to restaurants may involve a bit of a stroll (which is not that pleasant at night because there are very few street lights).

Despite its scruffy location, the large and stark *Hôtel Kaleta* (☎ 212 87) is a good option. Prices start at FMg 65,000 for rooms with private bathrooms, and peak at FMg 80,000 if you want a balcony with views. A package deal including three meals for an extra FMg 25,000 seems good value, but there are some great restaurants in town to try.

The *Hôtel Libanona* (☎ 212 87) serves as an annexe for the Hôtel Kaleta. The bungalows are a bit run-down, but are reasonably priced at FMg 50,000 and the location and views are excellent. The meals and drinks in the restaurant are a little expensive.

If you are after a large bungalow near (but not overlooking) the beach, the new *Village Petit Bonheur* (☎ 212 74) is probably better. Clean new bungalows cost FMg 65,000, and a little more for views. The pet lemur tied to a tree in the grounds is not an attraction, however.

The remaining three hotels in Taolagnaro are part of the SHTM company: *Le Dauphin* (☎ 212 38); its annexe, *Le Galion*, just across the street; and the *Hôtel Miramar* (☎ 211 92), in a lovely hillside setting (but not actually overlooking the beach). The Miramar restaurant is across the road about 150m away; it has a wonderful terrace which overlooks the Baie des Galions and affords the best sunset view in town. The prices for all rooms for the three hotels are F310; a studio apartment, if there is one, will cost F400 and breakfast is F30.

Places to Eat

Taolagnaro arguably has the nicest range of restaurants in the country, and if you are into seafood, especially lobster, you will be delighted. Unusually, several restaurants have translated their menus into English (or rather a sort of MalaFrenGlish).

The cheapest places are inconveniently near the market/taxi-brousse station: *Chez Jacqueline* is good for Chinese food, but don't get stung by the unrealistic prices for drinks and extras. *Chez Perline* is another hotely-style place recommended for its inexpensive food. Down in the backstreets, just down from the post office, is another 'chez': *Chez Henriette*. It is a bit flyblown, but the friendly family can rustle up some fried cutlets and potatoes, or fried rice, for a bargain FMg 5000.

The restaurant in the *Motel Gina* is nice, but caters exclusively for up-market tourists and prices are way too high. Pizzas start at a ridiculous FMg 25,000; fish and meat dishes are FMg 17,000 to FMg 25,000. The restaurant at the *Hôtel Libanona* is recommended for its setting, and good food, but the prices for drinks and meals (FMg 15,000 to FMg 20,000 for main dishes) are also high.

There's a good hotel restaurant at the *Hôtel Mahavoky* which is gaining a reputation as an excellent option for tasty and inexpensive meals, particularly seafood. Breakfasts are great, and include large pots of tea and huge omelettes (what do they feed their chickens with?).

The best restaurant in town is a toss-up between the unassuming *Mahavoky Annexe* and the *Panorama*. The former, at the northern end of town and associated with the Hôtel Mahavoky, serves excellent, good-value meals (fish, naturally, is a specialty) for about FMg 11,000. It is also good for breakfast.

Our favourite restaurant in town, and probably the best south of Antsirabe, is the *Panorama* – you can sit at the informal front bar, or the pleasant restaurant at the back. While service could improve (the waitress obviously hasn't smiled for years), outstanding meals cost FMg 8000 to FMg 10,000. We just couldn't go past the tasty tuna steaks for FMg 10,500.

Also recommended is *La Detente*, above the Air Fort Services office. It has a pleasant decor and views, and serves pasta and other dishes for FMg 12,000 to FMg 15,000; the drinks are a little pricey. The best place for a snack, coffee, beer (FMg 4500) or breakfast (FMg 6000 FMg 10,000) is an outdoor cafe called the *Sunflower Snack Bar*. The choice is limited and if you want to order any substantial meals you must give 12 hours' notice.

Entertainment

Taolagnaro is the sort of place where locals let their hair down once a month rather than every night or weekend. If there's anything happening, you'll see it advertised on posters. The *Panorama Bar & Disco* is open on weekends and often has a few 'ladies of the night'. You can try a (genuine) massage at the hut along Blvd No 1 towards Le

Dauphin hotel, or if you are desperate, go to one of the video clubs around town which show French-dubbed kung fu classics for FMg 300.

For something a little more sedate, have a beer at the bar at *Le Dauphin* or better, at the terrace at the *Miramar Restaurant*. English-speakers may want to check out the Cultural Center of Fort Dauphin (see under Information) to see if there are any concerts, films or exhibitions in town.

Things to Buy

A few small huts sell a few tacky souvenirs around the up-market hotels. In the same building as the Sunflower Snack Bar, Au Bon du Monde has one of the best selections of mementos in the country. Run by a gang of giggling girls, the shop sells carvings, raffia products and other locally made southern Malagasy gear, as well as postcards.

A nameless shop near Chez Henrietta's has a surprisingly good range of drinks, postcards, French magazines and souvenirs.

Getting There & Away

Air Air Madagascar flies directly between Taolagnaro and Tana every day for US$150, and also to Toliara (US$83). Taolagnaro is also the start or finish of the run up and down the east coast through Farafangana (US$71), Manakara (US$83) and Mananjary (US$105), and then on to Tana.

The Air Mad office (☎ 211 22), on a hill overlooking the coast not far from the Panorama, is open Monday to Friday from 7.30 am to noon and 2.30 to 6 pm; and from 8 to 11 am on Saturday.

Alternatively, you can fly with TAM: twice a week it flies to Réunion for F2920 return, and to Tana and Toliara for the same price as Air Mad. The TAM representative is Air Fort Services (☎ 212 34).

Bus If you are going towards Tana via Ihosy (ie, not through Toliara), the more comfortable Sonatra bus leaves Taolagnaro every Tuesday, Wednesday and Friday evening. For tickets (FMg 85,000) and departure details go to Chez Henrietta's.

Taxi-brousse Taolagnaro's taxi-brousse station is near the market in the western part of town. Travelling anywhere by road from Taolagnaro (except for the short paved stretch to Ambovombe) is not for the faint-hearted.

Taxis-brousse and Mercedes trucks travel from Taolagnaro to Toliara (FMg 42,500) four days a week and take at least 40 hours, often far longer. You are advised to break up the journey and spend some time exploring the attractions along the way. Refer to the Toliara to Taolagnaro section for more details about this route. To Ihosy, Fianarantsoa (FMg 70,000) and Tana (FMg 85,000), the route turns off at Ambovombe and heads north along the rough RN13.

Taxis-brousse occasionally head north along the coast to Sainte-Luce or along the road farther inland to Ehazoambo, but you will have to do a lot of waiting and asking.

Getting Around
The Airport The airport is 4km west of town. The standard 'official' (ie non-negotiable) taxi fare between the airport and the centre of town is FMg 10,000. You may be able to talk yourself on to (for a small fee) the Air Fort Services bus which is used mainly for transporting airport staff.

Most middle to top-range hotels offer a useful airport transfer service for their guests – and if business is slow, non-guests can also use this service. The Hôtels Kaleta and Libanona charge FMg 8000 one way (which is cheaper than a taxi), and will even take your luggage to the airport beforehand and check it in.

Car Air Fort Services seems to have the monopoly on local car hire. The prices are way over the top at FMg 350,000 per day, plus tax and the cost of fuel. If you want a driver you are slugged even more.

If you are flush with funds, or have a few people to share the costs, you can hire a 4WD at Air Fort Services for FMg 2,000,000 for a two day trip to Toliara, or a more reasonable FMg 2,900,000 for a three-day trip to Tana. In either case, the trip will be rushed and you won't have much time for sightseeing along the way.

You can always hire a taxi-brousse with a driver for the day, but you will naturally have to negotiate hard. A day trip to Berenty or Kaleta and back, with stops along the way, should cost no more than FMg 200,000 per car – not bad if you have three or four people to share the cost. To visit a lot of places around Taolagnaro you will need a very expensive 4WD, unless you go on an organised tour or love tough trekking.

Taxi Taxis aren't generally needed except to or from the airport or taxi-brousse station. They cost from FMg 2500 to FMg 3000 per trip around town.

Bicycle Getting around Taolagnaro's sandy streets is best done on foot or by bicycle. You can hire bicycles (often old and run-down) at the garage run by Air Fort Services for FMg 35,000 per day (FMg 30,000 for half-day). Inquire and pay at the Air Fort Services office; they will take you to the gargage. Otherwise, ask around town if you can rent one privately for about FMg 20,000 per day. If you have the fitness and determination, there is no reason why you can't reach and explore many of the small lakes in the region on bike.

AROUND TAOLAGNARO
Any of the travel agencies in town can arrange trips to the following places. You can organise trips yourself by taxi-brousse anywhere along the paved Taolagnaro-Ambovombe road; to anywhere else the roads are sandy and/or muddy and public transport is very rare, so an organised tour may be your only option.

Ambinanibe
Not far from the airport, at the village of Ambinanibe, there is a small, new **botanic park** and some bungalows which cost FMg 50,000 per night. If you have your own surfboard (you may be able to hire something from the village in the future), the beach is often great for surfing.

To get there, join a half-day trip (FMg 65,000) from Air Fort Services, charter a taxi-brousse, or ask about infrequent public taxis-brousse. Refer to the later Tranovato section for information about trekking, or taking a bike, to Ambinanibe.

Parc Saiadi

Only 10km from Taolagnaro on the way to Sainte Luce, Saiadi botanic park is home to a reasonable collection of palms, orchids, ravinala palms and eucalypts. SHTM seems to organise the only tours out there, other-

wise charter a taxi-brousse for an hour or two.

Pic St Louis·

From the summit of 529m-high Pic St Louis, which dominates Taolagnaro, you'll have a grand view of the city's magnificent environs. From the base, strong hikers should allow about 1½ hours for the ascent and one hour for the descent. A dawn climb would be ideal, before the going gets too hot or windy.

To get started, follow the sandy road north from the Panorama Bar. After 3km, past a

SOUTHERN MADAGASCAR

Around Taolagnaro

Rainforest

0   25   50 km

fuel base and military camp, you'll reach a modern-looking sisal factory (signposted 'Usine Sifor') on the left. Many travellers have trouble finding the path, so ask directions if in doubt; once found, the path is easy to follow. The going is easy enough, but there are some overhanging bushes to contend with. At the summit is a huge rock from which you'll get great views over the town and surrounding countryside, as well as miles of beaches running north along the coast.

If you want one, a guide is easy to arrange for about FMg 30,000 for a half-day. Ask at your hotel or a travel agency.

Evatra & Lokaro

Lokaro is an area of idyllic inland waterways, green hills, barrier beaches and natural swimming holes. It lies about 12km (as the crow, or Madagascar turtle-dove, flies) north-east of Taolagnaro along the coast – but a lot further by road.

Trips offered by the major travel agencies cost about FMg 100,000 per person per day for a two-day trip, sleeping in a Malagasy village. The trip begins with a 3km drive from Taolagnaro to the shore of **Lac Lanirano**, then continues by boat down the lake and through the marshy passage which connects it to the next lake, **Lac Ambavarano**. At the north-eastern end of this lake is the tiny fishing village of Evatra. From there it's only 20 minutes on foot over the hills to a glorious beach. It's also possible to travel by pirogue to nearby Île Lokaro.

If you'd prefer to go solo, you'll have to either hire a pirogue from a local or forego the chain-of-lakes approach to Evatra. If you're doing it without a pirogue, head north-east on foot from the customs yard along the eastern beach, Anse Dauphin, for about 12km. At Evatra, you can hire a pirogue to take you across to Île Lokaro, though reaching the island isn't essential – the beautiful Lokaro Peninsula alone is worth the trip. On foot, it will take a good long day and you will need to be self-sufficient with food, water and camping equipment.

Manafiafy (Baie Sainte-Luce)

Baie Sainte-Luce was the original site of the first French colony in Madagascar. Now called Manafiafy, it was abandoned when Taolagnaro was built in 1643.

It's a magical spot with an idyllic beach and M de Heaulme has established a small nature reserve to protect one of the last strongholds of humid coastal forest in Madagascar. He's also built a *bungalow complex*; prices (F310 per room) are the same as for the de Heaulme hotels in Taolagnaro.

If you have a vehicle, drive 35km north of Taolagnaro to the village of Mahatalaky, then continue 4km farther and turn right; from there it's 11km down to Manafiafy. Alternatively, you can either opt for the occasional taxi-brousse from Taolagnaro to Manafiafy (a three-hour trip), or take a day trip – expect to pay about FMg 110,000 per person (minimum of five).

Tranovato (Ilôt des Portugais)

Little is known about the Portuguese occupation of Madagascar in the 16th century, but they left at least one substantial structure: an island fort known as **Le Fort des Portugais**. It was built in 1504 by shipwrecked sailors near the mouth of the Ambinanibe River and is thought to be the oldest building in Madagascar. The Malagasy name, Tranovato, means House of Stone; three ruined, 1m thick, 3.5m high and 10m long walls stand atop a grassy, tree-studded knoll. There is a good view across rice paddies, zebu, rivers and out to sea, and it's also home to some beautiful butterflies.

To reach the island, take a taxi-brousse or cycle west of Taolagnaro on RN13. At the bar-cum-grocery store, just beyond the 10km mark, turn south along a track and follow it for 3km from where a track takes off for the small Antanosy village of Ambinanibe on **Lac Andriambe** (the walk will take about half an hour). There, the villagers will help you hire pirogue pilots to take you across the lake to the island, 1km away. The trip across the lake takes about 15 minutes; haggling about the price will take a lot longer.

Much easier but much, *much* more expensive is to visit the island on a tour arranged by one of the de Heaulme hotels in Taolagnaro.

Réserve Naturelle Intégrale d'Andohahela

Also known as the Manangotry Rainforest, this 76,020 hectare zone of humid tropical forest in the mountains is partially open to the public, but ANGAP is still waiting for authorisation from the government to develop the reserve into a national park. It is divided into three parcels and includes Trafonomby, Andohahela and Vohidagoro mountains; the latter is the source for 10 rivers.

Andohahela has some of the last remnants of rainforest in southern Madagascar, and includes spiny forest. There are possibilities for some rough but enjoyable trekking along boulder-strewn forest streams. With a good guide you can spot some of the 13 species of lemurs (one of the largest selections in the country).

It's possible, but not easy, to reach the reserve on your own. It lies 37km north of RN13 along a bad road which turns off near the small roadside market 20km west of Taolagnaro. By taxi-brousse you can get as far as Ehazoambo, about 10km short of your goal, but beyond there you'll have to walk.

The impressive, new and accessible **Centre d'Interpretation** has been built along RN13 about 30km west of Taolagnaro – it is impossible to miss. The centre, which was not open at the time of research, but should be by the time you go there, is the best place to get information, guides and permits, and to arrange a trip. Plenty of taxis-brousse go past the centre.

Lac Anony

The 2350 hectare lake and beauty spot, Lac Anony, lies 15km south of Amboasary and 75km west of Taolagnaro. This shallow lake, part of the estuary of the Mandrare River, is just a km or so from the sea. It's known for its populations of water birds and is now an ANGAP 'site of biological interest'.

If you're going from Taolagnaro to Berenty with the SHTM tour, you can visit Lac Anony for an additional F100 per person.

Cap Andavaka

One of the most amazing day trips from Taolagnaro is to Cap Andavaka (75km west of Taolagnaro) where there's an incredible otherworldly cave beside the sea. After passing through the cave you arrive in a 30m-deep sinkhole that is full of lush vegetation and inhabited by lemurs. It is bizarre and in fact looks a bit prehistoric.

Getting There & Away Cap Andavaka is quite a way from the main road and there's no public transport in the area. Safari Laka in Taolagnaro organises day trips for about F250 per person, or F450 if you include a side trip to Kaleta Reserve.

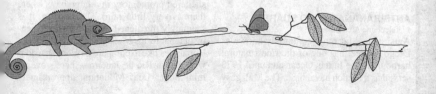

Northern Madagascar

Climatically, Madagascar's northernmost tip enjoys relatively pleasant conditions, with distinct wet and dry seasons and more sunshine than the east coast. Thanks to the Tsaratanana Massif, Madagascar's highest range, the Nosy Be region captures more precipitation than more southerly areas on the west coast.

The north is also one of the more cosmopolitan regions of the country, with a large Muslim community; descendants of African slaves, Indian traders and Arabic sailors; a contingency of French expats; and more recent arrivals like itinerant western aid and diplomatic workers. The dominant Malagasy tribe in the region, the Antakàrana (Those from the Cliffs), was one of the last tribal groups to be incorporated into the Malagasy confederation by Radama I.

The main area of interest for visitors is along the relatively accessible north-west route between Antsiranana and Nosy Be. The Malagasy have christened the Antsiranana Province the 'Coast of Undiscovered Islands' for the tourist trade, but in fact most of the islands have already been well and truly discovered. Here, as nowhere else in Madagascar, tourism, which is relatively heavy, has had dramatic effects on the local demeanour and prices.

Fortunately, the mainland remains relatively untouched and it would be a shame to embark on a hedonistic rush to the beaches of Nosy Be and miss its other attractions. These include the sacred Lac Antanavo, Montagne d'Ambre National Park and its up-and-coming counterpart, the magnificent Ankàrana Reserve.

ANTSIRANANA (DIEGO SUAREZ)
- Telephone Area Code: 8

Antsiranana, far more commonly known as Diego Suarez, has one of the finest natural harbours in the Indian Ocean and until 1973 served as a French naval base. The Malagasy

HIGHLIGHTS

Comoros
Antsiranana (Diego Suarez)
Antananarivo

- Parc National de Montagne d'Ambre has great walks, beautiful scenery, camping and even horse riding.
- Sacred Lac Antanavo, inhabited by crocodiles which locals believe are reincarnations of drowned villagers.
- Nosy Be for lazing on tropical beaches, and snorkelling and diving over superb coral reefs.

name means simply Where There is Salt, but to add to the name confusion it is sometimes spelt Antseranana (Where There is a Port); either name is appropriate. In any case, most people just refer to it as Diego.

This town of around 75,000 sits on a small sheltered promontory in a large bay (where there is very little rain). On the map, it is seemingly threatened by the fish-hook peninsula that forms Madagascar's northern tip. Romantics like to compare its scenic harbour with that of Rio de Janeiro – there's even a mini Sugar Loaf Mountain, appropriately

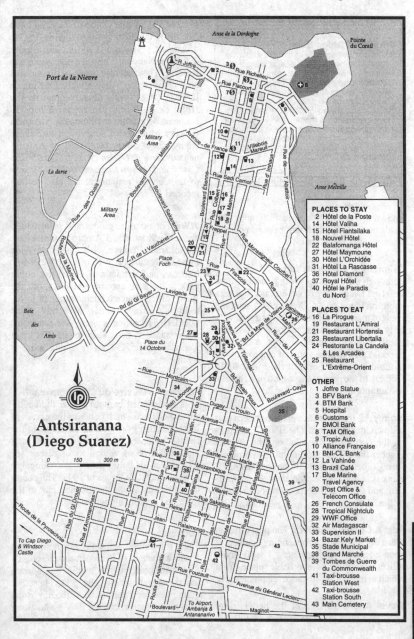

Antsiranana
(Diego Suarez)

0   150   300 m

PLACES TO STAY
2 Hôtel de la Poste
14 Hôtel Valiha
15 Hôtel Fiantsilaka
18 Nouvel Hôtel
22 Balafomanga Hôtel
27 Hôtel Maymoune
30 Hôtel L'Orchidée
31 Hôtel La Rascasse
36 Hôtel Diamont
37 Royal Hôtel
40 Hôtel le Paradis
   du Nord

PLACES TO EAT
16 La Pirogue
19 Restaurant L'Amiral
21 Restaurant Hortensia
23 Restaurant Libertalia
24 Restorante La Candela
   & Les Arcades
25 Restaurant
   L'Extrême-Orient

OTHER
1 Joffre Statue
3 BFV Bank
4 BTM Bank
5 Hospital
6 Customs
7 BMOI Bank
8 TAM Office
9 Tropic Auto
10 Alliance Française
11 BNI-CL Bank
12 La Vahinée
13 Brazil Café
17 Blue Marine
   Travel Agency
20 Post Office &
   Telecom Office
26 French Consulate
28 Tropical Nightclub
29 WWF Office
32 Air Madagascar
33 Supervision II
34 Bazar Kely Market
35 Stade Municipal
38 Grand Marché
39 Tombes de Guerre
   du Commonwealth
41 Taxi-brousse
   Station West
42 Taxi-brousse
   Station South
43 Main Cemetery

NORTHERN MADAGASCAR

▶◀◀▶◀◀▶◀◀▶◀◀▶◀◀▶◀◀▶◀◀▶◀◀

Origins of Diego Suarez
There are two schools of thought about the origin of the name Diego Suarez. Some historians believe it comes from an amalgamation of the names of two Portuguese sailors – Diego Dias, who first landed on Madagascar in August 1500, and Fernan Soares, who arrived in 1506. The other, more likely explanation is that another Portuguese sailor, Diego Suarez, who arrived from India in 1543, modestly named the bay after himself and his name was used for the subsequent settlement. ■

▶◀◀▶◀◀▶◀◀▶◀◀▶◀◀▶◀◀▶◀◀▶◀◀

known as Pain de Sucre, just offshore. But don't be fooled – the town bears no resemblance to the Brazilian city.

Orientation & Information
Although the city is sprawling, most visitors will find Diego easy to get around. The area south of Place du 14 Octobre is a seething mess of markets, shops and dirty streets, with only the *taxi-brousse* stations and a few cheap hotels to interest visitors. A far more pleasant area to base yourself and to explore is the thin stretch north of the Place du 14 Octobre to the port, along which most hotels, restaurants and offices are located.

Money All the banks are in the northern part of town, near the port. The BNI-CL Bank is on the corner of Rue Colbert and Ave de France; the BTM Bank is on the corner of Rue Colbert and Rue Richelieu; the BFV Bank is in a great location along Rue Richelieu; and the BMOI Bank is one block south of the BFV.

Post & Communications The post office at Place Foch is reliable for sending mail and is open normal working hours. The Telecom office next door is a reliable place from which to make long-distance telephone calls.

Travel Agencies One of the better travel agencies around is *Blue Marine* (☎ 221 89;

fax 294 15) on Rue Colbert. They run tours (see the Around Antsiranana section) to Cap d'Ambre, Windsor Castle, Montagne d'Ambre National Park and the Ankàrana Reserve. They can also organise diving trips around the region. Alternatively, Le King de la Piste (☎ 225 99), directly opposite the *Hôtel de la Poste*, can organise trips to Ramena, Montagne des Français, Ankàrana Reserve, Montagne d'Ambre and the Baie de Rigny, about 50km south-east of Antsiranana. *Nature & Ocean* (☎ 22 632) at 5 Rue Cabot, and *Quatro Evasion* (☎ 21 955), next to La Candela restaurant, are also recommended for tours.

WWF For permits, guides and information about the Montagne d'Ambre National Park or Ankàrana Reserve, visit the World Wide Fund for Nature (WWF) office (☎ 219 57). You can get permits and guides for either park at the park entrances anyway, but the WWF office is an excellent source of information where you can also buy some booklets. The office is along Ave Sourcouf; the entrance is on a side street. It is open weekdays from 7.30 am to 12 pm, and 2 to 6 pm.

Tombes de Guerre du Commonwealth
This well-signed cemetery is at the south-eastern end of town. It contains the graves of British soldiers (as well as others from the British colonies of the subcontinent and mainland Africa) who died of disease or were killed in battle during the campaign against the Vichy forces in 1942. The cemetery is small, but it's the greenest part of the town and is probably worth a quick look.

Lookouts
There is nothing spectacular about the Joffre Statue at the end of Rue Joffre itself, but it's a pleasant place to stay awhile and admire the view over the bay and port. The other quiet place for a panorama of the bay is the decaying rotunda near the BFV bank, along the esplanade.

Places to Stay – bottom end

The two cheapest places to stay are in the less salubrious part of town, but they are close to the taxi-brousse stations and markets. The *Hôtel Diamont* is good value at FMg 26,000/30,000 for a clean, if a little noisy, single/double with shared facilities. Nearby, the *Royal Hôtel* (☎ 228 15) is identical in price and has very similar standards – but is often full. The rambling *Hôtel le Paradis du Nord* (☎ 214 05), around the corner and opposite the Grand Marché, has a wide range of rooms, but it is in a poor location and no longer good value at FMg 60,000/65,000.

The popular *Hôtel Fiantsilaka* (☎ 223 48) is in a central position along Bde Étienne and has a reasonable restaurant. However, the rooms – FMg 35,000 with shared bathroom and FMg 60,000 with fan and hot water – are close to the noisy TV lounge. Central and good value, but also a little noisy, are the rooms at the back of *Les Arcades*. They cost FMg 40,000/60,000 without or with a private bathroom. They also have a couple of basic rooms for as little as FMg 25,000.

The *Hôtel Maymoune* (☎ 218 27) is clean, comfortable and central, but now a little overpriced. Rooms cost FMg 47,000 with a fan and communal toilet, and considerably more for air-con and a private bathroom. The *Nouvel Hôtel* (☎ 222 62) is in a great position and has decent rooms, with a shared shower but private toilet, for FMg 40,000. The place may look abandoned during the day; the restaurant opens up at about 6 pm, so you may have to wait until then to organise a room.

Two recommended places are next to each other in a handy location on the Place du 14 Octobre. The quiet *Hôtel L'Orchidée* (☎ 210 65) has rooms for FMg 42,000 with a fan and a bathroom with hot water, or FMg 55,000 with air-con. Next door, the *Hôtel La Rascasse* (☎ 223 64) has identical prices, and is popular with foreigners, but the service continues to be exceedingly poor.

Pleasant, cheap and laid-back alternatives to the high prices in Antsiranana are the hotels at Ramena beach, a short taxi-brousse ride away, and Ambohitra (aka Joffreville).

See the Around Antsiranana section for details about accommodation at these places.

Places to Stay – middle & top-end

The *Hôtel Valiha* (☎ 221 97) is in a good central location. It charges FMg 77,000 for rooms which are fan-cooled, and FMg 87,000 with air-conditioning. It is better known for its food than its hospitality – the staff seem to be more concerned with restaurant patrons than room guests, and the rooms can be dirty. Try to get a room away from the main road.

Some travellers have recommended the new *Balafomanga Hôtel*, which is managed by a friendly French couple and has a great restaurant attached. Rooms range from FMg 46,000 to FMg 76,000, but they have no hot water or air-con and can be noisy.

The most expensive place to stay is the colonial-style *Hôtel de la Poste* (☎ 220 44) which overlooks the bay from the top of Rue Joffre. It's extremely poor value at F250 per room. Some rooms have no views and are tiny, but you may stay there if you are on an organised tour.

At the time of our research, a new hotel called the *Triskell Hôtel* was due to open near the hospital sometime in 1997 – but we could find no signs of construction. The hotel plans to be an alternative to the Hôtel de la Poste, which could certainly do with the competition.

Places to Eat

Diego has a range of interesting (but generally not cheap) places to eat and drink. One of the best in the lower range is the *Restaurant Hortensia* near the post office. The service is deplorable and the decor is unsavoury, but the meals, such as omelettes (FMg 5000) and steak and chips (FMg 10,000), are tasty and the drinks are cheap.

One of the all time favourites for budget-minded travellers is the *Restaurant Libertalia*, right on Place Foch. The menu is limited, but the meals are excellent value at FMg 5000-7000; the 'poisson en sauce' (fish in sauce) is superb and good value for FMg 6000. Another cheapie but goodie is the *Res-*

>‹0›‹0›‹0›‹0›‹0›‹0›‹0›‹0›‹0›‹0›‹0›‹0›‹0›‹0›‹0›‹0›‹0›‹0›‹0›‹0›‹0›‹0›‹0›‹0›‹0›‹0›‹0›‹

Joseph Jacques Joffre (1852-1931)

It won't take long to notice the name Joffre when you are in Antsiranana. There is a large statue of the man at the end of Rue Joffre, and he also lent his name to the nearby village of Joffreville. (This former French name is still commonly used, though the official Malagasy name is Ambohitra.)

Général Joseph Jacques Joffre had an unremarkable start to his career, serving as a French representative and commander in remote posts like Timbuktu. After serving as a military commander of Diego Suarez in the late 1890s, his career seemed to blossom: he became chief of general staff in 1911 and commander-in-chief of the French forces on the Western Front between 1914 and 1916. He did not distinguish himself in the unsuccessful Plan XVII in 1914, in which outnumbered French forces where slaughtered by German troops; he is best remembered for his brilliant strategies, which brought victory on the Western Front and earned him the moniker 'Victor of Marne'. Joffre resigned in 1916 after further French casualties, was created *Maréchal-de-France*, and later became Ambassador to the United States. ■

>‹0›‹0›‹0›‹0›‹0›‹0›‹0›‹0›‹0›‹0›‹0›‹0›‹0›‹0›‹0›‹0›‹0›‹0›‹0›‹0›‹0›‹0›‹0›‹0›‹0›‹0›‹0›‹

taurant L'Extrême-Orient for Chinese meals, though the Kenny Rogers music in the background wasn't a highlight.

Of the hotels, the *Hôtel L'Orchidée* is small but recommended – breakfasts can be particularly good. Next door, the *Hôtel La Rascasse* is one of the best in town: there's a good range of meals, costing from FMg 7000 to FMg 10,000, and a popular outdoor bar. Some of the best pizzas and fish dishes north of Tana can be found at the *Nouvel Hôtel* – the large pizza should satisfy most hungry troopers. Dishes cost about FMg 10,000, but it is only open in the evenings. The *Hôtel Valiha* has pizzas for about FMg 12,000 and other dishes, such as fried rice (which we thought was so-so), for FMg 10,000.

There are also many up-market places, catering mainly for French expats and the tourist crowd. The *Restaurant L'Amiral* serves pizzas and other dishes for around FMg 12,000 in an agreeable, nautical-style setting, but we thought the pizzas weren't particularly good. *La Pirogue*, along Rue Colbert, is very cosy but expensive; and upstairs, opposite the Place Foch, the *Restorante La Candela* is heartily recommended for pricey, but very tasty, pizzas and pasta – worth a splurge.

The only supermarket outside of Tana is along Rue Colbert, just south of the Nouvel Hôtel. The *MAGRI Supermarket* is a good place to stock up on a few 'necessities' like chocolate bars; you can also buy recent French magazines and newspapers, and other personal items.

Entertainment

Diego has a clutter of Friday and Saturday night 'hot spots', such as the *Hôtel le Paradis du Nord,* the *Tropical* (one block behind the Hôtel L'Orchidée) and the *Nouvel Hôtel*.

For a drink in the evening (or at any time), *La Vahinée*, opposite the BNI-CL bank, is a popular outdoor bar and a good place to meet other travellers. (Unattached males may soon find themselves hustled by 'working ladies'.) Just around the corner, the incongruous-sounding *Brazil Café* promises, and delivers, 'ambiance tropicale' in the midst of a tiny jungle setting.

Like many mid-sized towns in Madagascar, the impressive *Alliance Française* organises films and concerts, and has a well-stocked library. Check out their noticeboard for information about what is going on and when. It is now housed in the old market building, and worth a visit (open 9 to 11.30 am and 5 to 7 pm, Tuesday to Saturday) if only to see how they converted the place.

Diego is almost unique in Madagascar because it actually has a large, functioning cinema. *Supervision II*, on the Place du 14 Octobre, shows the usual kung fu action flicks (in French) – but they pass the time at FMg 1000 per ticket. Spirited football (soccer) games are held in the Stade Municipal late on Sunday afternoons.

Getting There & Away

Air Air Madagascar flies daily between Diego and Tana (US$162), often via Nosy Be (US$37) and Mahajanga (US$116). The Air Mad office (☎ 293 75), directly opposite the Hôtel L'Orchidée, opens from 8 am; queue up before opening time if you want to book or confirm your ticket. Just about everyone flies in and out of Diego, so this is a very busy office.

TAM (☎ 210 16), on Rue Flacourt, links Diego with Réunion; it also flies four times a week between Diego and Mahajanga and Nosy Be for the same price as Air Mad.

Taxi-Brousse Curiously, Antsiranana has three tiny taxi-brousse stations, all literally on the side of the road. And to make it more difficult, most taxis-brousse, which are generally unmarked, may not be at the station when you arrive because they are circling the town busily looking for passengers.

The Taxi-brousse Station South is the one to use for destinations anywhere south of Antsiranana (which includes most of Madagascar). The small Taxi-brousse Station West covers routes west, and north of town up towards Cap D'Ambre. Another makeshift station, known as the *gare routiére Sonatra* (named after a bus company, not the singer), outside the Supervision II cinema, also has taxis-brousse going to Ambanja, Mahajanga, and even to Tana (good luck!) for FMg 140,000.

If you're travelling overland from Antsiranana to Nosy Be you must first take a taxi-brousse to Ambanja. To get to places on the east coast, mainly Iharana (Vohémar) or Sambava, it is quicker to get a taxi-brousse to the junction town of Ambilobe, from where vehicles regularly head east.

Road travel between Tana and the far north is restricted to the dry winter months between April and November. Even when the roads are passable, however, the trip will require several days and will carry you over unimaginable stretches of road, particularly the bit between Antsohihy and Ambanja.

Sea Only those who love long, uncomfort-able boat trips would contemplate travelling to or from Antsiranana by sea. There are no organised passenger boats, so you'll have to travel on a cargo boat from Mahajanga, Sambava or, possibly, the Comoros islands. To inquire about boats from Antsiranana visit Somacram (☎ 331 83) on Ave Sourcouf, or Valiha Voyages (☎ 215 31) at 41 Rue Colbert.

Getting Around

The Airport Antsiranana's Arrachart airport is six km south of the town centre. The taxi-drivers have a cartel and refuse to take less than FMg 10,000. To avoid paying this, just walk a few metres out onto the main road near the airport and hail a passing taxi-brousse, which will take you to one of the taxi-brousse stations in town. From there, you can walk or take a short taxi ride to your hotel.

Car & Motorcycle A 4WD at Le King de la Piste (see the preceding Travel Agencies section) costs F150 per day plus F2 per km, or F400 per day for unlimited km for a minimum of six days.

Renting a motorcycle is the ideal way of exploring the attractions around Diego. At Le King de la Piste, a Honda 125cc will cost FMg 125,000 per day. Nearby, Tropic Auto (☎ 229 21) rents a Yamaha 600cc for FMg 250,000 per day, and a Yamaha 125cc for FMg 160,000 per day.

Taxis Plenty of tiny Renault 4TL taxis ply the streets. They are worth taking to the taxi-brousse stations, especially if you have any luggage. They cost a negotiable FMg 1000 to FMg 3000 per trip around town, which is one of the cheapest taxi rides in the country.

Share-taxis, known as *taxis spéciales*, also travel around the streets, and go to nearby towns. Taxis can be chartered for trips to the national parks and beaches – refer to the Around Antsiranana section for details about fares.

Bicycle The Blue Marine and Le King de la

>⬦<⬧>⬦<⬧>⬦<⬧>⬦<⬧>⬦<⬧>⬦<⬧>⬦<⬧>⬦<⬧>⬦<⬧>⬦<⬧>⬦<⬧>⬦<

Libertalia

Legend has it that for 35 years during the 17th century the region around Antsiranana was known as the pirate republic of Libertalia, and flew the banner *A Deo a Libertate* ('For God and Liberty')...

Because there is no physical evidence of this first communist-cosmopolitan state, some historians have relegated the story of Libertalia to the realms of fantasy. The first formal account was in a book published in 1726 entitled *Lives and Actions of Famous Highwaymen, Robbers and Pirates* by Daniel Defoe writing under the *nom de guerre* Captain Charles Johnson. Libertalia sceptics argue that the man who created Robinson Crusoe could have easily invented a pirate republic, even in a purportedly factual work.

The pirate republic, the story goes, was founded by a French adventurer called Captain Misson (his Christian name has escaped record). Like his notorious counterpart, Olivier 'La Buse' Levasseur, Misson was a well-educated man. But his motives were more humanitarian and revolutionary than selfish and anarchic. This seagoing Robin Hood freed slaves and avoided bloodshed where possible.

He teamed up with a defrocked Dominican priest, Father Caraccioli, and decided to apply the socialist principles of Jean-Jacques Rousseau from scratch – away from France and the much slower route to revolution. After a period of troubleshooting and fund raising around the Comoros, they set up their Utopia in Antsiranana around the Baie des Français.

They began building with the help of 300 Comorans, who were a gift from the Sultan of Anjouan, as well as assorted African slaves, and British, French, Dutch and Portuguese sailors. A parliament was formed, a printing press was started, crops were planted, stock was reared, and some sort of integration with local or captive women was attempted. Even a new international language was established. The pirates were Misson and Caraccioli's emissaries, importers and immigration service.

All seemed to be going well until the Malagasy tribes surrounding the 'International Republic of Libertalia' descended en masse from the hills and massacred the Libertalian population. Caraccioli was killed, but Misson either escaped to sea or was already at sea when the attack occurred. His eventual fate remains a mystery. ■

>⬦<⬧>⬦<⬧>⬦<⬧>⬦<⬧>⬦<⬧>⬦<⬧>⬦<⬧>⬦<⬧>⬦<⬧>⬦<⬧>⬦<⬧>⬦<

Piste travel agencies rent mountain bikes for FMg 24,300/40,500 for a half/full day. Antsiranana is somewhere to consider hiring a bike – the town is big, and you can visit a couple of nearby attractions with pedal power.

AROUND ANTSIRANANA
Nosy Lonja

The small island of Nosy Lonja is off-limits to foreigners. It is considered sacred by the Malagasy, who use it for *fijoroana* ceremonies in which they invoke the ancestors. In French the island is called Île de le Pain de Sucre or 'Sugar Loaf Island'

Ramena

This attractive beach, adorned with a collection of ramshackle bungalows, lies 18km east of town across the Baie des Français and makes an ideal day trip from Antsiranana (you can also stay there). If you have your own vehicle, Ramena can be combined with visits to Baie des Dunes or the **lighthouse** which guards the harbour entrance at Cap Miné.

At the time of research, *Les Ecuriers D'Archirs* stables were being established along the main road, about one km before Ramena. Make inquiries there if you wish to hire a horse.

Places to Stäy & Eat Staying at Ramena is a cheaper, quieter and far more relaxed alternative to Diego, but the hotels do have problems with unreliable running water. One budget place, which costs FMg 40,000 for a comfortable room, is the *Hôtel L'Oasis*. It is right on the beach with a great outdoor bar and restaurant. Also recommended is the *Badamera*. It has rooms at the same price and standards as L'Oasis, but is not quite on the beach. The *Mora Mora Plage Snack Bar*, on the sandy beach, is probably the best place to eat.

The *Hotel Ramena Nofy* (☎ (8) 228 62) has built clean and modern bungalows in a spartan, shadeless area 200m up from the

Around Antsiranana

0   10   20 km

Cap D'Ambre
(Tanjon'ny Bobaomby)

Lotsohina

Bobahala
(235m)

Andranovondronina

Le Coq
(273m)

Vohilava

Nosy Hao

Anjiabe

Andohonko

Nosy Antaly Be

Nosy Vaha

Tsararano

Nosy Fasy

Nosy Suarez

Nosy Diego

Baie des
Courriers

Anoronjia

Nosy Faty

Nosy Foty

Windsor
Castle
(391m)

Nosy
Famaho

Andramahimba

Ramena

Cap Miné
Baie de Dunes

ANTSIRANANA

Nosy Hara

Nosy Lakandava
Nosy Anjombavola

Ampasindava

Ankorikakely

Baie des Sakalava

Nosy Lonja
(Pain de Sucre)

Mangoaka

Namekia

Montagne
des Français

Nosy
Manonoka

Nosy Valiha

Antsahampano

Antanamitarana

Nosy
Tango

Baie
d'Befotaka

Forêt D'Ambre
Reserve (2 Parcels)

RN6

Nosy Tendro

Nosy
Mandazona

Sakaramy

Mahavanona

Andranofanjava

Ambohitra
(Joffreville)

Andrafiabe

Nosy Bory

Montagne
d'Ambre
(1475m)

Anjavinihavana

Antsalaka

Sadjoavato

Nosy Lowry

Bobakilandy

Ankarongana

Irodo

Baie de Rigny

Nosy Lava

Antsalaka Sud

Menagisy

Parc National
de Montagne d'Ambre

Anivorano
Nord

Lac Antanavo

Bobasakoa

Tsarakibany

Réserve
d'Analamera

Matsaborimanga

Réserve Spéciale
de L'Ankàrana

Antsatrobonko

Andrafiabe

Mahamasina

Nosy Mangího

Antsaravibe

Ambararata

Maromokotra

Sirama

Ankàrana

Tanambao-
Marivorahona

Antsohimbondrona

Mantaly

Isesy

Anjiabeambony

Ambilobe

To Andoany (Hell-Ville)
& Ambanja

To Iharana
(Vohémar)
& Sambava

beach. What it lacks in character it makes up for in luxury. Bungalows cost FMg 95,000/ 120,000 for a double/triple.

Getting There & Away To get to Ramena, catch a taxi-brousse or taxi spéciale heading the fishing villages of Ramena or Anoronjia (FMg 3500). The flat, boring trip is possible by mountain bike, but it's a hot ride. Chartered taxis from Antsiranana cost about FMg 50,000 return. You can arrange for them to pick you up later, or just catch anything going along the main road from Ramena – every vehicle will be going back to Antsiranana.

Baie des Dunes

This bay is not far from Ramena and has a deserted and unsheltered beach. Its location, on the windy east coast of the peninsula, provides an alternative for those who want a quieter and more relaxed scene. Nearby are some unusual **rock formations**. Camping is possible, but bring all your own food and water.

Coming from Antsiranana, head north along the road towards Ramena, then turn right on a meandering dirt track just south of the village. From there, the walk takes about two hours. There's also a more direct route but you'll need a local guide to find it.

Farther south along this coast is the idyllic beach on the **Baie des Sakalava**. It may be reached by the five-km track which leads east from Ankorikakely, a village 13km from Antsiranana along the road to Ramena.

Montagne des Français

Just seven km from Antsiranana, and an excellent day trip, is the Montagne des Français. This lovely pocket of wilderness was named in memory of the Malagasy and French forces killed in 1942 in Allied resistance to the pro-German Vichy French forces. There are **caves**, the remains of a **fort**, lots of birds, interesting vegetation and a magnificent view across the bay. The track to the peak is clearly marked with the Stations of the Cross.

To get there, take a taxi to the start of the route (seven km south-east of Antsiranana). Ask the driver to return for you at an agreed time. The walk to the peak takes about an hour each way but you'll want to leave time for exploring and to enjoy the view. Several travel agencies, such as Le King de la Piste can organise trips for a reasonable FMg 48,600 per person (minimum of two).

Windsor Castle

This impressive squarish-looking 391m rock formation lies about two km north of the village of Andramahimba, north-west of Antsiranana. It first served as a French fort and lookout, but after the German occupation of France the rock was appropriated by the Vichy forces as an observation point. In 1942 it was taken by the occupying British. A decaying stairway leads to an awesome view from the top out over the Baie des Courriers.

Windsor Castle is best reached by 4WD vehicle; during very dry weather an ordinary taxi may possibly get through. Follow the route west along the bay for 20km and turn north at Antsahampano. At Km 32 from Antsiranana (which is 12km beyond Antsahampano) you'll see a track turning west towards the imposing bulk of Windsor Castle, five km away.

If you wish to press on towards Madagascar's beautiful northernmost point, **Cap d'Ambre**, also known as Tanjon'ny Bobaomby, you should either have access to a boat or a sturdy 4WD vehicle. Some travellers have tried to ride a mountain bike all the way from Antsiranana, but it is a long (40km) and hot trip, and you may be stopped by local military along the way and asked what the hell you are doing. Just explain your destination, show them your passport and carry on.

The easiest way to Windsor Castle or the Cap d'Ambre is on an organised tour from Blue Marine travel agency (refer to the Antsiranana section for details). It won't come cheap – FMg 243,000 per person (minimum of four) for a day trip to Windsor Castle, and an overnight trip to the cape for FMg 470,000 per person.

PARC NATIONAL DE MONTAGNE D'AMBRE

Northern Madagascar's most visited natural attraction, Montagne d'Ambre National Park, covering 18,200 hectares of a prominent volcanic massif, lies just 40km south of Antsiranana. It was created in 1958 to 'preserve the regions' biological treasure' of unique flora and fauna, as well as the massif. The altitude ranges from around 850m to the peak of Montagne d'Ambre at 1475m. All of the tourist development is in the accessible northern area of the park. Unfortunately, the remote and less protected southern reaches of the park are suffering from clearing by fire and illegal logging.

Flora & Fauna

When it comes to flora and fauna, Montagne d'Ambre is more or less an extension of the eastern rainforest, though it does have several endemic species not found farther south. Extensive rain (3585mm per year) also makes the rainforest lush – and the leeches voracious.

The lemurs at the park are rather shy and retiring because of a history of unpleasant experiences with humans, but few visitors fail to see at least one group. Of the seven species of lemurs, most notable are the crowned lemur and Sanford's brown lemur. Other species which have been spotted in the park include the northern sportive, rufous mouse and dwarf lemurs – as well as the aye-aye and the local Amber Mountain fork-marked lemur. Among other mammals the ring-tailed mongoose is probably the most frequently observed.

The reptile and amphibian life includes a variety of frogs, geckos, chameleons and snakes. You'll see these hopping, slithering and sliding through the trees and along the dark forest floor. Look especially for the bizarre-looking blue-nosed chameleon (Chamaeleo boettgeri), which is fairly common, and the stump-tailed chameleon.

Keen birdwatchers will have the chance to see the crested wood ibis and the malachite kingfisher, as well as 71 other bird species.

Permits & Guides

The WWF virtually took over the running of the park in 1985. Their office in Diego is definitely worth visiting if you are preparing to go, or even thinking about going, to the park. Permits (FMg 50,000) are available at the office or at the park entrance.

At the office you can buy an excellent booklet Discover ... Amber Mountain: its Park and People (FMg 10,000). It is written in English or French, and includes maps and outstanding information on local and national flora and fauna. Bird enthusiasts can also pick up Olivier Langrand's Check List of the Birds of Amber National Park in English or French for FMg 6000.

Like all national parks, a guide is compulsory – and essential anyway if you are doing any serious trekking. Currently, guides cost FMg 40,000 for the three- to four-hour circuit; FMg 50,000 per day for longer treks. A porter costs about FMg 20,000 per day. These costs will change, however, from September 1997 following a restructuring of fees. WWF plans to charge visitors FMg 2500 per person per visit for a guide.

Horse Hire

Montagne d'Ambre is the only park in Madagascar which you can visit and travel around on horse. This is obviously far more ecologically sound than tearing around in a car, though watch where you step if you are hiking!

Prices for hiring horses depend on how many people are in your group. Costs are FMg 25,000 per hour per horse if three people rent horses or FMg 40,000 if there is only one of you. Longer hire costs FMg 85,000 per person for a half-day if going alone, or FMg 85,000 per person if in a group of three. For the whole day, the cost is FMg 150,000/110,000 per person for one person/group of three.

Inquire and book at La Glace Gourmande (☎ 228 58) snack bar and ice creamery, just south of Nouvel Hôtel on Rue Colbert in Antsiranana. Alternatively, ask around the tiny village of Ambohitra (aka Joffreville).

Parc National de Montagne d'Ambre

0   2   4 km

To Antsiranana
(Diego Suarez)

Ampompotra
(440m)

Forêt D'Ambre
Reserve

Sakaramy

Makis

Antongombato

Les Fleurs
(619m)

Pic Janson
(598m)

Ambibaka
(612m)

Sakaramy

Andranofanjava

See Enlargement

Joffreville
(Ambohitra)

National Park Entry

Besokatra

Grande Cascade

Cascade Touristique

Petite Cascade

Pic Badens
(1119m)

Petit Lac

Andavakoera
(570m)

Ankijahabe
(693m)

Roussettes Research Station

Anjavy

Pic Jordan
(1354m)

Ambihivahikely

Lac Maudit

Sommet d'Ambre
(1475m)

Grand Lac

Saharenana

Ambibaka
(833m)

Anjavinihavana

Antsalaka
(703m)

Lac Texier

Ambohimarirana

Antsalaka

Antsakoakely

Bedingadingana
(1234m)

Antsalaka Sud

Ambohitrasorolava
(1215m)

Ampondrabe
(1001m)

Lac Fantany

Ambiloby

Andrafiabe

Marovato

Anivorano Nord
To Ambilobe

Lac Antanavo

Enlargement

Joffreville
(Ambohitra)

National
Park Entry

Grande
Cascade

Cascade
Touristique

Pic Badens
(1119m)

Petite
Cascade

Research
Station

Petit Lac

0   1   2 km

NORTHERN MADAGASCAR

Visiting the Park

During the dry season the park is ideal for walking, with about 20km of well-maintained tracks, but if you are feeling a little lazy you can take a vehicle along some of the trails. In fact, taking a vehicle will save you the long walk from Ambohitra – but the trails will become impassable after heavy rain. Inquire at the park entrance before taking any vehicles into the park. The biggest nuisance when getting around the park will be leeches, which seem to come out in force after wet weather. And remember that this is a particularly wet region – always carry wet weather gear, proper shoes and mosquito repellent.

The first place of interest is the serene and pretty **Petit Lac**, a crater lake also known as the Lac de la Coupe Verte. There is a steep descent to the lake, but it is not too daunting. During the dry season the water recedes sufficiently to provide a nice spot for a picnic on the shore. We spotted some lemurs near the lake, but this is unusual.

The **Petite Cascade** is a small, lovely waterfall flowing into a paradisiacal pool surrounded by fern-covered cliffs. If you are there at dusk, you may witness the incredible (and a little scary) sight of dozens and dozens of bats zooming around, often within inches of your face.

Nearby is the path known as **Jardin Botanique** – not really a botanic garden but rather a forest track with a good sprinkling of interesting and bizarre vegetation, including orchids, palms, lianas and bromeliads. Not far away, another trail leads to the smaller but lovely **Cascade Touristique** aka Antakarana waterfall – a sacred place where locals often cleanse themselves.

Another, longer track leads to the viewpoint over the **Grande Cascade**, a thin ribbon of water majestically plunging 80m into a forest grotto. From the viewpoint there's a steep and rather slippery descent to the base of the cascade. Here you'll see a variety of butterflies attracted by the water and have a good chance of observing crowned lemurs.

A southern trail leads about 11km to the summit of the 1475m **Montagne d'Ambre** – its a fairly easy three-to four-hour hike from the research station, and less than an hour to the summit from the base. You can also visit **Lac Maudit** ('Damned Lake'), just below the peak. Beyond the peak to the south-east is a larger **Grand Lac** (at 1445m), where you are allowed camp.

An easy one-day trip of about 10km (starting at the research station) takes in the Grande and Petite Cascade, Jardin Botanique, research station and the Petit Lac. If you have more time and proper hiking and camping equipment, you can take a leisurely two or three days and visit the above sights, as well as the summit of Montagne d'Ambre, Grand Lac, Lac Maudit (no swimming – it is *fady*) and **Lac Texier** (known as the 'Lake of Rough Waves' in Malagasy), about two km south of Montagne d'Ambre.

With a guide, proper equipment and heaps of determination, you could do an excellent 10-day trek that takes in the highlights of the Amber National Park and the Ankàrana Reserve. From Mt Amber, trek to the sacred lake of Antanavo via Anjavinihavana, Antsaiaka Sud and Anivorano Nord. From the lake, flag down a taxi-brousse to Mahamasina then walk into Ankàrana. You can camp along the way, or your guide will arrange for you to stay in local villages. Book guides and make inquiries at the WWF office in Antsiranana before you go.

Places to Stay & Eat

This park is also one of the few in Madagascar where you can officially camp. You may pitch your tent at a pretty spot next to the abandoned Rousette Research Station – though the toilets seemed to have had the same lack of maintenance as the crumbling 60-year old research station. You can also camp at the Grand Lac in the south of the park. Camping is free and permission is not needed, but let the guides at the park entrance know that you intend to camp, where and for how long.

In Ambohitra (more commonly known as Joffreville), which was built in 1902 as a resort for the French military, there are two nice places to stay. *Chez Henriette*, next to the long-abandoned Hôtel Joffre, has four rooms for FMg 20,000 and is an excellent alternative to Antsiranana, even if you are not visiting the park. Eighty metres down the street from Henriette's, the unsigned *Balafomanga* costs FMg 30,000 per room. Meals are available at both places.

The quaint village store called, in English, 'The Village Store', sells basic supplies, but if you're camping for several days in the park it's wise to bring food from Diego.

Getting There & Away

Taxis-brousse run every hour or so along the good tarred road from the Taxi-brousse Station West in Diego to Ambohitra (about FMg 4500), 32km to the south. You can also hire a taxi from Diego for the day for around FMg 80,000 including waiting time – there will be nothing in Ambohitra to charter.

The road to Ambohitra is smooth. The final seven km track into the park is passable by normal vehicles (in the dry), but can be long and hot if you walk. You may be exhausted before you even start exploring the park, which is a good reason to camp there overnight or charter a vehicle. If you're walking look for chameleons along the track.

You can always go on an organised tour, but these are unnecessary because it is easier and cheaper to do it yourself. Le King de la Piste agency in Antsiranana has 4WD trips for FMg 283,500 per person (two to four per vehicle).

RÉSERVE D'ANALAMERA

Although a visit to this 34,700-hectare reserve will be possible for very few, it's worth mentioning because the Analamera Plateau (along with Ankàrana Reserve) is the only habitat of Perrier's diademed sifaka, also known as the black sifaka (not to be confused with the black lemurs, which inhabit Nosy Komba near Nosy Be and surrounding areas). It's estimated that 2000 remain in this reserve, which is currently receiving special attention and funding from WWF.

Now part of the Amber Mountain Project established between the WWF and local conservation authorities, the reserve currently has no visitor facilities and access is possible only from June to October. If you have your own 4WD vehicle it's fairly easy to reach from the turn-off at Sadjoavato, 52km south of Antsiranana. From there go to Menagisy (near Ankarongana) or Irodo, from where you can hire guides to take you onto the plateau. Talk to the staff at the WWF office in Antsiranana before venturing into the reserve.

ANIVORANO NORD & LAC ANTANAVO

The people living around Anivorano Nord believe that Lac Antanavo – also known as the Sacred Lake or Lac Sacré – lies on the site of a village which was inundated after its inhabitants refused to offer water and hospitality to a wayfarer. The crocodiles which inhabit the lake are believed to be reincarnations of the unfortunate villagers.

Minor feeding rituals and offerings take place each Saturday, and the people occasionally stage elaborate ceremonies with much dancing, beating of drums and hand clapping. Heaps of zebu meat is tossed around to attract all the crocs on shore. You can read more about this ritual in David Attenborough's book *Journeys to the Past*.

Getting There & Away

To get there, take a taxi-brousse to Anivorano Nord 75km south of (and on the main road from) Diego, or stop off on the way north from Ambilobe. From Anivorano Nord, you must walk an easy four km to the lake. You can also visit the lake as part of an excellent 10-day or longer hike from the Montagne d'Ambre National Park to the Ankàrana Reserve.

RÉSERVE SPÉCIALE DE L'ANKÀRANA

The spectacular Ankàrana massif, about 100km south-west of Antsiranana, is an undeveloped region of bizarre *tsingy* formations, and also part of the WWF's Amber Mountain project. These formations are intersected by hidden forest-filled canyons and underlain by a honeycomb of caves and subterranean rivers containing crocodiles and freshwater shrimp. The massif is also considered sacred by the local Antakàrana people, who have buried several of their kings in one of the caves – they continue to hold traditional rites there.

Flora & Fauna

The vegetation could hardly be more varied; on the high, dry tsingy, succulents such as *Euphorbia* and *Pachypodium* predominate, while the sheltered canyons in between are choked with leafy cassias, figs, baobabs and other trees typical of dry deciduous forest.

Of the six species of lemurs the most abundant are crowned, Sanford's brown and northern sportive. There are also woolly (*avahis*), rufous mouse, fat-tailed dwarf and fork-marked lemurs, Perrier's diademed sifakas and aye-ayes. Other common mammals include tenrecs, fosa and ring-tailed mongooses. (The latter have been known to visit campsites at night in search of food; and don't pat them because they may have rabies.) There are also nine species of bat.

Birds are also abundant and 83 species have been spotted, including some of the country's most interesting: the orange and white kingfisher, crested coua, Madagascar fish-eagle, crested wood ibis and banded kestrel.

A large range of chameleons and geckos are outmuscled by a few crocodiles which live in rivers in the underground caves – you are very unlikely to come across one (or so you hope). However, beware of scorpions if you are camping.

Permits & Guides

Foreigners must obtain permits to the reserve; they cost a regulation FMg 50,000 per person for three days. It is better and easier (especially if you are coming from Diego) to get a permit at the WWF office there, although you can also get one at the main park entrance at Mahamasina. Guides are compulsory and can be found at Mahamasina.

Visiting the Reserve

So strange and isolated is Ankàrana that visitors with time to explore will begin to feel they've entered an alternative universe. Ankàrana's higher elevations are characterised by tsingy formations, impenetrable 'forests' of sharp limestone pinnacles. The terrain limits exploration to the forested canyons, the perimeter or the extensive cave system.

One relatively accessible cave, the **Andrafiabé Cave**, is 11km long and has over

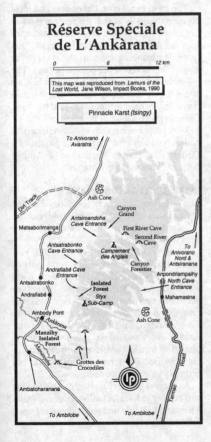

Réserve Spéciale de L'Ankàrana

0   6   12 km

This map was reproduced from *Lemurs of the Lost World*, Jane Wilson, Impact Books, 1990

Pinnacle Karst *(tsingy)*

To Anivorano Avaratra

Dirt Track

Ash Cone

Antsiroandoha Cave Entrance

Matsaborimanga

Canyon Grand

First River Cave

Second River Cave

Antsatrabonko Cave Entrance

Campement des Anglais

Andrafiabé Cave Entrance

Antsatrabonko

Andrafiabé

Ambody Pont

Manzihy Isolated Forest

Grottes des Crocodiles

Ambatoharanana

To Ambilobe

Isolated Forest

Styx

Sub-Camp

Ankàrana

Mananjeba

Canyon Forestier

Anpondriampaihy

North Cave Entrance

Mahamasina

Ash Cone

Tarmac Road

To Anivorano Nord & Antsiranana

To Ambilobe

>O<O<O<O<O<O<O<O<O<O<O<O<

Tsangatsaina Rituals

The ritual called Tsangatsaina involves a re-enactment of the return of the ancestors from Nosy Mitsio (near Nosy Be), where they'd fled in the early 1700s to escape the marauding Merina in Ankàrana. The ritual starts every five years with a visit to royal tombs to secure royal sanction to proceed with the ceremonies. The next stage takes place a year later in the village of Ambotoharanana where a sacred pole, made from trunks of the *hazoambo* tree, is raised above the tombs of later Antakàrana political leaders. These rites are intended to honour the unity of Antakàrana past and present and the continuing role of the monarchy. ∎

>O<O<O<O<O<O<O<O<O<O<O<O<

100km of passages. The cave is undeveloped so you'll need a good guide, caving lights – preferably headlamps – and some sort of backup light source before venturing inside. Other caves which will need expert guides to find and explore properly include the multiple **Grottes des Crocodiles** – the inhabitants are mostly underground, thankfully, and you are more likely to see chameleons, lemurs and mongooses. Another day can be spent exploring the incredible tsingy formations.

A couple of the sacred caves may be visited only with local guides who are members of the local royal family. There are numerous *fady* in effect in and around these caves so visitors must be sensitive and respectful.

Places to Stay & Eat

There are plenty of good camping spots around the reserve, but it's better to base yourself at recognised camping spots: *Campement des Anglais* and *Styx Sub-camp*. If camping, be especially alert for the dangerous scorpions which may find their way unnoticed into clothing or camping equipment.

Very limited supplies are available at the shop in Mahamasina, so carry all the food and equipment you'll be needing as well as a hefty receptacle for carrying your water

supply. All permanent water in the massif is in underground rivers coursing through the caves. The water is drinkable after you have purified it.

Getting There & Away

There are three main entrances to the reserve. The main one is at Mahamasina village, which is easy enough to get to on the taxi-brousse route between Ambilobe and Antsiranana. The other two entrances are on the western side, at Ambatoharanana and Matsaborimanga, but they are really only accessible in normal vehicles between June and October.

The most expensive, but easiest and most comfortable, way to visit the reserve is on an organised tour. A couple of travel agencies (see the Antsiranana section for details) run three-day camping tours to the reserve for about FMg 200,000 per person per day. The all-inclusive trips run by Le King de la Piste come highly recommended by one German traveller, who commented that it 'was German organisation at its best'.

With proper equipment and some determination, you can visit the reserve as part of a 10-day trek from Montagne d'Ambre National Park via Lac Antanavo.

NOSY BE TO ANTSIRANANA

The 'overland' trip between Nosy Be and Antsiranana (Diego) is easy, and can be managed in one day; it is one of the better trips in northern Madagascar.

From Nosy Be, ferries (FMg 3000; two hours) leave every few hours to the port of Ankify. They normally leave between 6 am and 1 pm, depending on the tide; it's best to get there early to beat the heat and the crowds. A sturdier and larger boat, the *Fivondronana*, sails between Nosy Be and Ankify every two days – its schedule is pinned up in many hotels and travel agencies on Nosy Be. The ferry is more regular but certainly more overloaded.

As soon as the ferry arrives in Ankify, you will be dragged – or, actually, *squeezed* – into a Renault 4TL (we had nine people in ours!) for Ambanja. From Ambanja, it is easy to get a taxi-brousse immediately to Diego, via Ambilobe, which is the junction for vehicles heading to the east coast.

From Ambanja you can also get on a taxi-brousse (FMg 110,000) to Mahajanga – but this road is rough, and often impassable in the wet season. A taxi-brousse (FMg 40,000) to Antsohihy (183km), where there are several reasonable hotels, takes at least ten hours and possibly two days in the wet.

Ankify

Around the port of Ankify, there are a few expensive resorts, but you will need your own transport to get to them. The best is *Le Baobab*, about 500m from the ferry landing, though it is expensive at FMg 80,000 for a comfortable bungalow.

Ambanja
• Telephone Area Code: 850

Ambanja is a pleasant, tree-lined town. It is situated on the Sambirano River and there are some pleasant walks near the estuary and the bridge just south of town. Around **Benavony**, about four km upstream, you have a good chance of observing black lemurs.

You would only need to stay in Ambanja if you are late for the ferry to Nosy Be. If you have arrived from Nosy Be it's best to keep going, but if you want to stay there's a limited choice of accommodation. The *Hôtel Roxy* and *Chez Sachine* (☎ 32), both opposite the taxi-brousse station, are very basic but very cheap. Better are the *Étoile de Mer* (about 300m from the taxi-brousse station), at about 25,000 a room, or the *Hôtel Patricia* (☎ 73) (ask for directions), for the same price.

Ambilobe
• Telephone Area Code: 837

If coming from the south, the dreary junction town of Ambilobe is the nearest place to stock up on supplies for visits to Ankàrana Reserve. It is also of interest to travellers looking for a truck or taxi-brousse to Iharana (on the east coast) or anyone wishing to break the trip between Ambanja and Diego.

You'll need to ask for directions to the friendly *Hôtel L'Escargot* (☎ 8). It rents out rooms in a different building – pink and unsigned – two blocks west of the street where the taxis-brousse stop. For FMg 20,000, with a mosquito net and fan, these rooms are not bad value.

If coming from the north, get off at the *Golden Night Hôtel* (FMg 25,000 a room) next to the *La Valley Rose* restaurant – otherwise it is a long walk to these places from the taxi-brousse station. If coming from the south look for the sign to the *Lotus Bleu*, which has bungalows for FMg 18,000 and excellent meals.

Sirama Estates If you're in Ambilobe it's worth hopping on a taxi-brousse out to Sirama, the immense sugar estates which provide most of Madagascar's sugar supply (3000 tonnes of cane is processed each day, and distilled into 60,000L of alcohol.) It was originally constructed by the French in the 1950s as the archetypal company town, complete with hospitals, shops, housing, transport and a garden atmosphere. Although it has changed considerably since colonial times, it's still operating and visitors are welcome. The factory is open every day but Saturday from May to November. Take a taxi-brousse to Ankàrana village (FMg 5200; one hour) then walk a couple of km north to Sirama.

Nosy Be & Other Islands

• Telephone Area Code: 8

In the waters north-west of Ambanja lie Nosy Be, Madagascar's premier tourist resort island, and several smaller islands including Nosy Komba, Nosy Tanikely, Nosy Sakatia, Nosy Mitsio and Nosy Iranja. Nosy Be is a popular island, but probably more suited to someone who wants resort-style accommodation, plenty of restaurants and nightspots. If you are looking for a similar sort of island, with great beaches, diving and hiking, but with budget accommodation

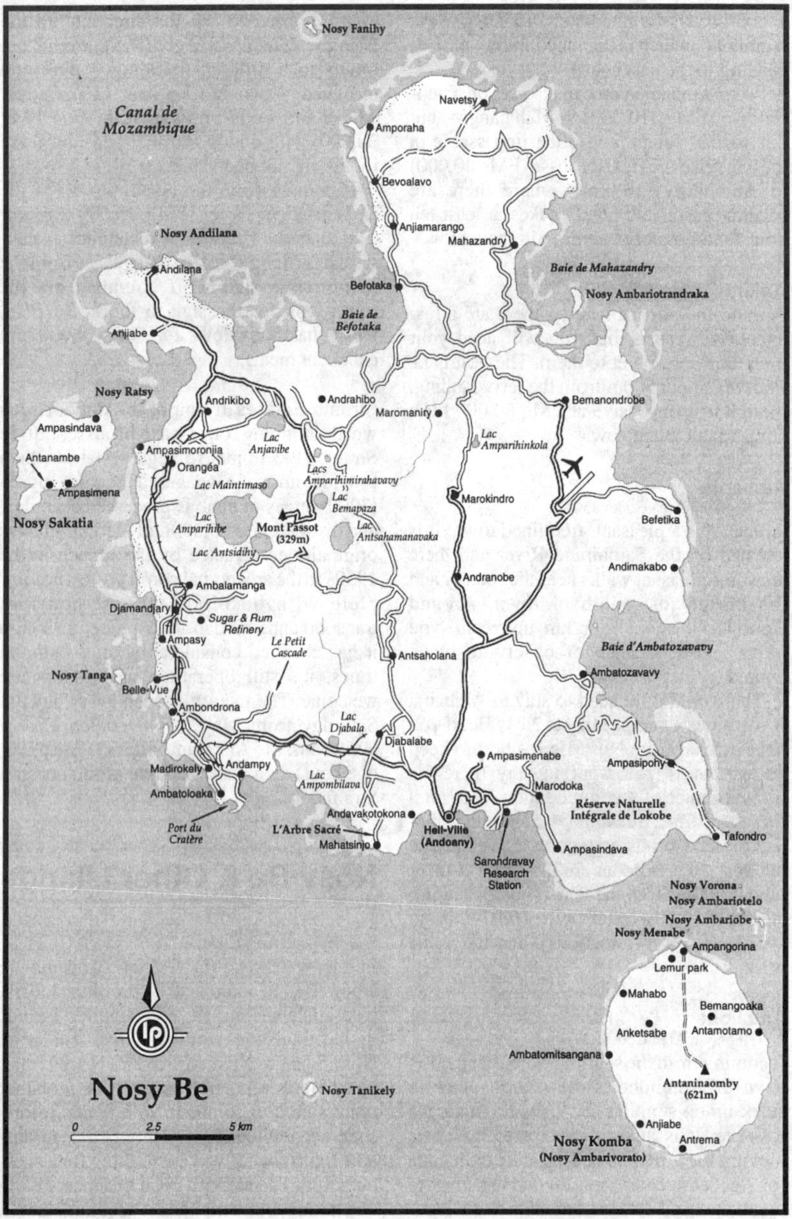
Nosy Fanihy
Canal de Mozambique
Navetsy
Amporaha
Bevoalavo
Anjiamarango
Mahazandry
Nosy Andilana
Andilana
Befotaka
Baie de Mahazandry
Nosy Ambariotrandraka
Baie de Befotaka
Anjiabe
Nosy Ratsy
Andrikibo
Andrahibo
Bemanondrobe
Maromanitry
Ampasindava
Lac Anjavibe
Lac Amparihinkola
Ampasimoronjia
Antanambe
Orangéa
Lacs Amparihimirahavavy
Lac Maintimaso
Ampasimena
Lac Bemapaza
Marokindro
Befetika
Nosy Sakatia
Lac Amparihibe
Mont Passot (329m)
Lac Antsahamanavaka
Lac Antsidihy
Andimakabo
Andranobe
Ambalamanga
Djamandjary
Sugar & Rum Refinery
Ampasy
Le Petit Cascade
Baie d'Ambatozavavy
Antsaholana
Nosy Tanga
Ambatozavavy
Belle-Vue
Ambondrona
Lac Djabala
Djabalabe
Ampasimenabe
Ampasipohy
Madirokely
Andampy
Lac Ampombilava
Marodoka
Ambatoloaka
Réserve Naturelle Intégrale de Lokobe
Andavakotokona
Port du Cratère
L'Arbre Sacré
Mahatsinjo
Hell-Ville (Andoany)
Tafondro
Ampasindava
Sarondravay Research Station
Nosy Vorona
Nosy Ambariotelo
Nosy Ambariobe
Nosy Menabe
Ampangorina
Lemur park
Mahabo
Bemangoaka
Anketsabe
Antamotamo
Ambatomitsangana
Antaninaomby (621m)
Nosy Be
Nosy Tanikely
0
2.5
5 km
Anjiabe
Nosy Komba (Nosy Ambarivorato)
Antrema

and less development, head for Île Sainte Marie (refer to the Eastern Madagascar chapter). Make no mistake, Nosy Be is a comparatively expensive place to visit and stay.

Boating & Fishing

With so many fantastic places to dive and swim, organised boat trips are a popular, and easy, way to explore the islands. But because they cater for the up-market tourist crowd they are expensive. Motor-boats *(les bateaux a moteur)* or sailing boats *(les voiliers)* regularly leave for day trips. You can also charter these boats for an horrendous price, but smaller six-person boats cost a more affordable FMg 250,000 per boat. For information about chartering boats, or getting on a boat trip, check out the tourist office in Andoany (Hell-Ville), inquire at a travel agency or souvenir shop, or ask at your hotel.

One very popular day trip is on the catamaran *Daniel* (☎ 614 31), which travels to Komba and Tanikely islands, and includes an outstanding fish and salad lunch. BYO snorkelling gear. One definite advantage is that the *Daniel* leaves every day; it costs FMg 90,000 per person, including return taxi fare to/from your hotel anywhere on the island. The boat can drop you off at Komba and/or Tanikely islands, and pick you up one or more days later, and you can continue on the trip for no extra cost.

Another similar trip is organised by the Hôtel Le Robinson at Ambatoloaka. For a day trip to Tanikely, Komba and Sakatia islands they charge FMg 80,000 per person, including lunch, but you will have to get together six people to obtain this price. Up-market hotels, such as the Residence d'Ambatoloaka, can organise tours around Nosy Be for FMg 97,000 per person, to Komba and Tanikely islands for FMg 120,000, and around the Baie des Russes for the same price. For fishing enthusiasts, a chartered boat for the day will cost FMg 125,000 per person – but you will have to get twelve people together to share the cost.

For additional information about fishing and boat hire and trips, contact the Centre de Pêche Sportive de Madagascar (☎ 613 66) in Hell-Ville, and Nosy Be Game Fishing (☎ 610 13) in Ambondrona.

Diving & Snorkelling

The sea life around Nosy Be is quite varied and a bit of underwater exploration is likely to reveal an array of species: boxfish, surgeonfish, triggerfish, damselfish, clownfish, yellowfin tuna, barracuda, eagle rays and even manta rays, and the odd whale, not to mention sea urchins, starfish, eels and anemones. Around Nosy Sakatia, expect to see clownfish, barracudas and turtles; and the dolphins around Sakatia may be a bit friendlier than the whale sharks.

Superb diving is available in a few places around the islands, particularly Ambatoloaka on the western shore of Nosy Be and Nosy Sakatia. The best months for diving are from April to July and September to November. For snorkelling, the best spots are around Nosy Tanikely and Nosy Komba.

There are three major diving centres; it's probably best to use the one at or near your hotel to save you travelling around the island. Prices (payment is usually required in French francs) – which include equipment hire – are standard between each agency: F200 for the first dive, F170 per subsequent dive, F190 for a night dive, two dives in a day F325, F810 for five dives and F1550 for ten.

Courses for NAUI, PADI, CMAS and ETDS certificates are conducted in French or English – and some staff speak Italian and German. Courses cost about F1200 for five dives and five hours' tuition, or F1500 for six dives and 10 hours' tuition. You can also hire snorkelling gear, but it is expensive: flippers (F90 per day), snorkel (F45) and mask (F20).

Madagascar Dive Club (☎ 614 18) – based at Madirokely (north of Ambatoloaka), this Italian-run outfit arranges certificate courses, as well as diving trips for experienced divers.

Oceane's Dream (☎ 614 26) – based at Ambatoloaka, this company offers certificate courses and multiple-day diving/camping excursions to Nosy Iranja, Nosy Mitsio and Nosy Sakatia, as well as Baie des Russes on the mainland. All divers must

Sea Urchins

The spiny sea urchins are members of the echinoderm group, which includes starfish and *bêches-de-mer* ('sea cucumbers'). With a spherical body covered in spines, it is the sea urchin which gives the name to the entire group: from the Greek for spiny *(echino)* and skin *(derm)*. The spines can vary considerably from the short blunt spines of the slate-pencil urchin to the long sharp black spines of *Diadema* urchins. These spines will easily penetrate skin if the urchin is trodden on or handled; once broken off they are difficult to remove and frequently cause infections.

When an urchin dies the spines fall off and the round 'sea egg' which remains makes a fine, if fragile, ornament. It's easy to see the five-armed star pattern on the casing, which is evidence of the urchin's relation to starfish. The sea urchin's complex mouth structure at the bottom, known as Aristotle's lantern, allows it to graze as it creeps over the sea floor. Despite the formidable protection afforded by their spines, sea urchins shelter during the day and only come out to feed at night. Spines or not, some triggerfish will eat sea urchins and they are a popular ingredient in the diet of coastal people. ∎

be certified but non-divers are also welcome to join excursions.

Sakatia Dive Inn (☎ (2) 258 78) – based on Nosy Sakatia, this Swiss-owned place runs diving courses and a host of excursions. They operate a hotel on the island (see the Nosy Sakatia section). For local bookings, contact the Au Coin de la Plage bungalows, about three km north of Djamandary, which serves as a launching point for boat trips to Nosy Sakatia.

Organised Tours

Nosy Be is small and well set up so you can easily organise your own trips around the island. Travel agencies and hotels on Nosy Be organise trips, such as a boat cruise around Nosy Komba and Tanikely (FMg 160,000 per person); a tour of the island by road (FMg 150,000); and trips to Lokobe Reserve (FMg 162,000).

Some unusual trips are organised by *La Caravane Malagasy* which has an office in Tana (☎ (2) 355 54; fax (2) 343 74) and Madirokely (☎ 614 11) on Nosy Be. Besides having an impressive array of motor boats for hire, they can also arrange trips by hydroglider.

Accommodation & Food

Most accommodation is on Nosy Be, and it isn't cheap. As usual the good hotels have their pick of the best beaches, but there is nothing to stop outsiders wandering in and sharing them. The larger tourist hotels split their tariffs into high and low season; the high seasons are from 20 July to 15 September, 10 December to 15 January, and 10 days before and after Easter. Make sure your room has mosquito nets or staff can guarantee that the rooms are mosquito-free – the blighters, known locally as *moka fohy*, can be fearsome.

Restaurants are also expensive and in the off-season (November to April) some places may even be closed during the day. Many hotels include breakfast, so it is hard to find somewhere which serves breakfast to the public. Only at Ambatoloaka will you be able to buy any cheap Malagasy food.

NOSY BE

Nosy Be ('Big Island') is the largest island (321 sq km) lying off the Malagasy coast. In tourist brochures, it is known as the Île aux Parfumée and, like the nearby Comoros, is a centre for the production of perfume essence from the bizarre *ylang-ylang* tree. Other island products include sugar cane, coffee, vanilla, pepper, saffron and other spices.

Nosy Be is Madagascar's tourist trump card, self-proclaimed as a 'tropical island paradise' to lure big-spending overseas visitors (about 15,000 per year). Thankfully, a combination of competition from other Indian Ocean islands and Madagascar's economic ills have prevented anything developing on Nosy Be on the scale of

Mauritius or the Seychelles. Nosy Be's internationally-owned hotels are essentially tourist capsules away from population centres. As a result there are few groups of scantily-clad package tourists to contend with.

For the majority of visitors, the most visible signs of Nosy Be's status as a holiday island are the negative effects of tourism: high prices, a relatively disinterested populace and a mob of small-time unsavouries with fingers in as many pies as possible.

History

Nosy Be's first inhabitants were probably 15th century Swahili and Indian traders, who would certainly have found the island an agreeable site to settle for awhile. Several centuries later a boatload of Indians were shipwrecked here; they settled in and constructed the now ruined settlement of Marodoka on the Baie d'Ambanoro seven km east of Hell-Ville. Later, Nosy Be attracted refugees, merchants and settlers of all descriptions.

During King Radama I's confederation efforts in the late 1830s, the Sakalava royalty petitioned help from the Sultan of Zanzibar. The sultan apparently didn't realise the highland nature of the Merina enemy because he sent a warship to discourage any attempt at naval conquest!

In 1839 the Sakalava queen Tsiomeko fled to Nosy Be and turned to the French for help in resisting the highlanders. Seeing an opportunity, Captain Passot dispatched a message to Admiral de Hell in Réunion and the good admiral, also aware of the opportunity he was being offered, signed a treaty of protectorate with the Sakalava royalty. In 1841 the Sakalava ceded both Nosy Be and neighbouring Nosy Komba to France.

Perhaps the most bizarre story, however, is that of the Russian warship which was dispatched by the czar to Nosy Be during the 1904-5 Russo-Japanese War – its orders were to protect the Mozambique Channel from Japanese incursion. Unfortunately, once the war ended, the contingent was forgotten and the men were left stranded awaiting further orders, unaware that Russia was at peace. And so they remained on Nosy Be where most of them eventually succumbed to malaria, typhoid and other tropical diseases, and were buried in a corner of the vast Hell-Ville cemetery (opposite the Air Madagascar office).

Nosy Be's most obvious recent development is the growth in tourism (25% of the inhabitants work in the tourist industry). Its population is also increasing, and rampant burning of the vegetation for crops, settlement and tourist development goes on at an alarming rate. Deforestation and the resulting siltation have had devastating effects. The magnificent coral reefs which once fringed Nosy Be and some surrounding islands have all but disappeared and, at the present rate of destruction, it's estimated that the island's once luxuriant forests will be gone within 10 years.

Special Events

A new initiative from local tourist authorities is the Music Festival held each May on Nosy Be. Musicians and dancers come from the Indian Ocean region – Madagascar, the Comoros, Mauritius and Réunion. In addition, canoe races and exhibitions of handicrafts and art are held. (The dates and location of this festival may change, so it's best to confirm things with the tourist department in Tana or Nosy Be, or contact ☎ (2) 417 15; fax (2) 417 16.)

Hell-Ville (Andoany)

Despite the implications of its French name, Nosy Be's capital (population 30,000 – two-thirds of the island's total) and port is quite a bright and pleasant little town. Like Hell-Bourg in Réunion, it was named after Admiral de Hell, a former governor of that island. The official Malagasy name, Andoany, is rarely used, even by locals.

Little seems to have changed in Hell-Ville since the French vacated the country – or since they occupied it for that matter. Cannons overlook the port and the walls leading up from the pier are inlaid with the initials 'HV'. In the town itself there are some fascinating colonial buildings, including the **old prison**, built in 1855, on the broad avenue, Rue Passot.

Money The places to change money are the BFV Bank in the old part of town, opposite L'Oasis restaurant; the BTM Bank, just up from Chez Nana; and the BNI-CL Bank, opposite the Chamber of Commerce building.

Post & Communications The post/telephone office is on the corner where Boulevard de l'Indépendance meets Rue

Passot. It is open normal hours, but it is not reliable and lacks modern facilities.

Tourist Office An unofficial (non-government) tourist office (☎ 614 39) has opened up along the main street in the old part of town, not far from the port. Run by the local hoteliers association, they offer a few free brochures and maps in French and English (as well as German and Italian), and the staff speak French and English. If you are staying awhile on the island, or want any specific information about boats, hotels, diving etc, it is worth paying them a visit.

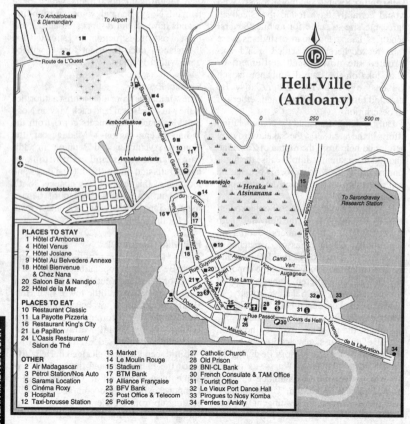

Hell-Ville (Andoany)

PLACES TO STAY
1 Hôtel d'Ambonara
4 Hôtel Venus
7 Hôtel Josiane
9 Hôtel Au Belvedere Annexe
18 Hôtel Bienvenue & Chez Nana
20 Saloon Bar & Nandipo
22 Hôtel de la Mer

PLACES TO EAT
10 Restaurant Classic
11 La Payotte Pizzeria
16 Restaurant King's City
21 Le Papillon
24 L'Oasis Restaurant/ Salon de Thé

OTHER
2 Air Madagascar
3 Petrol Station/Nos Auto
5 Sarama Location
6 Cinéma Roxy
8 Hospital
12 Taxi-brousse Station
13 Market
14 Le Moulin Rouge
15 Stadium
17 BTM Bank
19 Alliance Française
23 BFV Bank
25 Post Office & Telecom
26 Police
27 Catholic Church
28 Old Prison
29 BNI-CL Bank
30 French Consulate & TAM Office
31 Tourist Office
32 Le Vieux Port Dance Hall
33 Pirogues to Nosy Komba
34 Ferries to Ankify

Places to Stay There are plenty of places to stay in Hell-Ville – look out for the sign *chambres à louer* (rooms to rent). However, the only reason to stay there is to connect with an early ferry to the mainland, or to save some money by staying in the cheapies in town and visiting the beaches and other attractions by taxi-brousse (if you can find one).

The two cheapest places on the island probably also double as brothels. The *Saloon Bar* has a couple of cheerless rooms with a fan around the corner from the bar (inquire at the bar first) for FMg 20,000. The *Hôtel Venus*, along the busy main road, has very noisy rooms for FMg 16,000 – try to get a room at the back if you want any sleep.

The *Hôtel de la Mer* (☎ 613 53) continues to get bad reports, but it really isn't that bad – and it is central. The wide range of rooms start from a reasonable FMg 26,000, but go much higher if you want air-con, views or something a bit cleaner.

If you can get a room at the back and commandeer a fan the *Hôtel Bienvenue* is worth trying for FMg 35,000, but otherwise the rooms are very noisy and very hot. It is almost next door to Chez Nana, at the back of another nameless restaurant. If you can't get enough of staying in a bungalow, one excellent option is the *Hôtel d'Ambonara*, just up from the Air Mad office on the way out of town. Pleasant bungalows in a nice garden cost FMg 75,000, and they are quiet and comfortable.

Just off the Boulevarde Général de Gaulle, the *Hôtel Au Belvedere Annexe* is vastly overpriced at FMg 75,000 per room. Though it has a nice lounge area, which is great if you're travelling in a group, contrary to its promise it has no hot water. Nearby, the *Hôtel Josiane* (☎ 610 97) has been recommended by a couple of readers. Rooms cost FMg 65,000, but we found the staff really surly and they refused to show us an empty room.

Places to Eat The *Restaurant King's City*, one block off the main street, is one of the best in town. It has a lovely setting and good

Chinese dishes starting at FMg 15,000 (which is a little pricey). An excellent choice for light meals is *L'Oasis Restaurant/Salon de Thé* on the Boulevard de l'Indépendance. It has an outdoor setting and serves breakfast for FMg 3500, including fresh fruit juice. Just up the street, one of our favourites, if only for the cosy atmosphere, is *Chez Nana*.

Around the corner from the market, one of the better pizzas in the region can be found at the *La Payotte Pizzeria*. Small (snack-size) pizzas cost FMg 7000-10,000, while large ones (enough for one hungry person) are FMg 15,000-20,000. The beer is cheap but the service is very ordinary. Also heartily recommended is the covered outdoor restaurant at the *Hotel d'Ambonara*. Meals range from FMg 13,000 to FMg 20,000 and, if you are lucky, you may be offered a free glass of local (ie, very strong!) rum by the management.

Strongly recommended and popular with locals is the *Restaurant Classic*, also along Boulevard Général de Gaulle. Pizzas cost FMg 13,000 to FMg 15,000, and the tuna steak for FMg 15,000 is excellent. Good value meals are also possible at the *Saloon Bar* for about FMg 10,000-12,000, and the beer is reasonably priced. The current trendy place is the *Le Papillon*, which serves expensive French food.

Just east of town, near the Sarondravay Research Station, is Hell-Ville's classiest restaurant, the *Blue Fish*. It has reasonable prices and serves excellent seafood meals. To get there, hire a pirogue from just north of the Le Vieux Port Dance Hall.

Entertainment The *Saloon Bar*, with its Wild West-type theme, is good for a cheap drink, but it seems to have been overtaken as the place to be seen by the *Nandipo*, immediately around the corner. This new place is full of expat French rugby fans playing pool, and has a very handy noticeboard for travel-related information.

The *Hôtel de la Mer* is a cool and breezy spot to linger over a beer or two and contemplate the wonderful view out to sea. On weekend evenings, it has a raucous disco-cum-bar (known as the *No 1 Night Club*). *Le Moulin Rouge*, near the market, is a new and trendy place to hit the dance floor.

Le Vieux Port Dance Hall and bar near the port has live bands on weekends playing modern Malagasy favourites. Unfortunately, it's full of prostitutes and foreign men are considered prize catches. One locally-made tourist brochure summed it up: 'In the heat of the night with Afro-Jamaican and Malagasy rhythms, allowing you to dance with the most beautiful girls of the island who have the rhythms in them'.

In Hell-Ville there is a cinema, *Cinéma Roxy* (tickets FMg 1500), which shows kung fu 'classics'. Impromptu band and song contests are held at the *Hell-Ville Theatre Municipal* in the market.

Things to Buy Hell-Ville's colourful market is one of the friendliest spots on the island and bustles from dawn until just before dusk. It's an excellent spot to pick up spices – vanilla beans, black and green pepper, cloves, saffron, cinnamon and so on – for very reasonable prices. In most cases, prices are marked on the items but the vendors are still happy to negotiate.

The best place to pick up a souvenir – especially some ylang-ylang – is *Chez Abud*, along Boulevard Général de Gaulle and close to the Restaurant Classic.

Around Nosy Be

Sarondravay Research Station Along the coast road three km east of Hell-Ville is the marine research base, Centre National de Recherches Océanographiques de Sarondravay. Under the French it was known by the acronym OSTROM, but it is now operated locally (with the help of UNESCO).

The centre was once intended to be an aquarium with a display which would include a preserved coelacanth. Alas, the coelacanth went to the Tsimbazaza museum in Tana (and subsequently decomposed!) and the aquarium has dried up. In its place, there's a **marine museum** full of more commonplace fish, either stuffed or pickled in formaldehyde. It's open Monday to Friday from 8 am to 2 pm.

Marodoka If you walk or drive six km east along the coastal road from Hell-Ville, you'll reach some marginally impressive sand and coral cement ruins in the process of reclamation by luxuriant vegetation. This is Marodoka, which legend attributes to a shipwrecked boatload of 17th or 18th century Indian sailors but whatever its origin this ruined settlement is a little-known highlight of Nosy Be.

Réserve Naturelle Intégrale de Lokobe Lokobe Reserve (740 hectares) contains most of what is left of Nosy Be's endemic vegetation. It also protects black lemurs and chameleons, and vital water sources for the flora and fauna.

With luck you'll see boa constrictors and the giant but harmless Madagascar hognosed snake, which can be identified by its intricate chequerboard markings. You should also encounter four species of lemurs including black and sportive; in case you're interested, the latter is the only subspecies (*Lepilemur mustelinus dorsalis*) which snoozes the day away in vines and branches rather than in tree hollows. Of the 42 species of birds recorded in the reserve, you could see Madagascar paradise flycatcher and pygmy kingfisher.

In the tiny village of Ampasipohy, the new *Jungle Village* bungalows are the best place to base yourself during an organised trip around the reserve. The comfortable bungalows are overpriced at FMg 70,000 including breakfast (a meal is FMg 30,000), but there is no alternative accommodation on that part of the island. The problem is getting there: you will need your own 4WD vehicle or to charter a boat.

Currently, you must enter the reserve as part of an organised, guided tour – and you will need guides to show you around anyway. Contact a travel agency in Hell-Ville, such as Crossiers (☎ 613 51), next to the Hôtel Bienvenue; ask at the Jungle Village; or check around Ambatozavavy or

Ampasipohy. Organised day trips from the villages in the reserve cost about FMg 100,000 per person – with a minimum of three. Trips organised by your hotel or a travel agency will cost considerably more – up to FMg 162,000 per person per day.

Port du Cratère Port du Cratère, a harbour formed by a half-drowned natural crater, isn't overwhelming but it is an interesting natural feature. To get there, follow the Route de l'Ouest from Hell-Ville towards Ambatoloaka. Six km west of Hell-Ville,

veer left and continue past Andampy to the end of both the road and the sugar railway which runs parallel to it.

Mont Passot & The Crater Lakes Mont Passot, Nosy Be's loftiest point at a modest 329m, lies 30km north of Hell-Ville. It's a good spot to await the sunset or just take in the far-ranging view, including many other islands – though in the wet season thick fog may spoil your view.

The mountain is surrounded, clockwise from the north, by the beautiful blue sacred

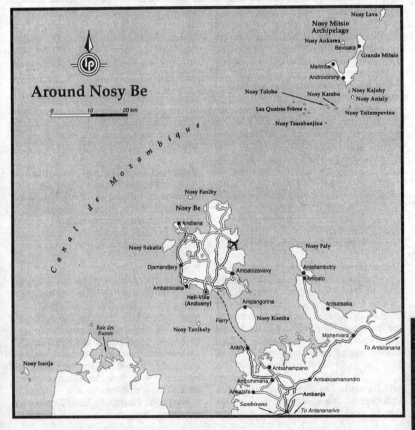

>◁0>◁0>◁0>◁0>◁0>◁0>◁0>◁0>◁0>◁0>◁0>◁0>◁0>◁0>◁0>◁0>◁0>◁0>◁0>◁0>◁0>◁0>◁0>◁0>◁0>◁0>◁

Ylang-ylang

The most amazing thing on Nosy Be (besides the prices charged by the hotels and restaurants) is the 'upside down' tree of the ylang-ylang (pronounced e-lang-e-lang). These low, gnarled trees are known to scientists as *Cananga odorata* and their scented green or yellow flowers are used for perfumes, giving the island the moniker *L'Île Parfumée*. They are deliberately stunted and pruned like grape vines to picking height. The flowers bloom most of the year, but particularly during the humid and wetter season from November to April, and are stripped by hand daily. About 100kg of flowers are needed to make about 2.5kg of ylang-ylang oil. The oil is then cured and exported to the west for perfume.

Ylang-ylang is one of Madagascar's vital export crops; it is also grown in the Comoros, where it covers about one-third of arable land, and on Mayotte. Around Nosy Be you will see a few alambic, or ylang-ylang, distilleries, including a couple along the airport road. The large distillery just inland from the Sarondravay Research Station is open to the public Monday to Friday from 8 am to 3.30 pm, and Saturday from 7.30 am to 2.30 pm, but you can only see the ylang-ylang being distilled on Monday, Wednesday and Friday. Entry is free. ■

>◁0>◁0>◁0>◁0>◁0>◁0>◁0>◁0>◁0>◁0>◁0>◁0>◁0>◁0>◁0>◁0>◁0>◁0>◁0>◁0>◁0>◁0>◁0>◁0>◁

lakes of Anjavibe, Amparihimirahavavy (actually two small lakes), Bemapaza, Antsahamanavaka, Antsidihy, Amparihibe and Maintimaso.

The larger hotels arrange sunset minibus tours to the summit (via the good road from near Andilana). One good way to visit the area is to hire a taxi (about FMg 30,000 one-way) to the top, and walk back down (eight km) to Djamandjary, where you can get public transport back to your hotel. If you are fit, a sturdy mountain bike would make it up the good (northern) road, but it's probably a fair way to the start of the road from your hotel. A motorcycle would be perfect.

There is actually a restaurant at the top called *Coucher du Soleil* ('Sun Setting'), but it seems to be permanently closed.

L'Arbre Sacré If you have a motorcycle, or have chartered a vehicle, make a short detour between Hell-Ville and Ambatoloaka towards Mahatsinjo. You will pass a tiny forest in which there is one enormous banyan tree, known as L'Arbre Sacré or the Sacred Tree. No-one around could really explain why it is sacred – you may have better luck getting an explanation from someone.

Petit Cascade Just north of the turn-off to Ambatoloaka, this small waterfall is a little like the ones in the Montagne d'Ambre

National Park in the far north of the country. You may be charged FMg 5000 by some locals to get close enough to look at the waterfall.

Ambatoloaka The southernmost beach at the tiny fishing village of Ambatoloaka, 10km from Hell-Ville, is the undeniable focus for the budget to mid-range beach brigade.

Places to Stay The best value place in Ambatoloaka, and on all of Nosy Be, is the *Authentique* bungalows, about 30m above the village centre – look for the sign next to Chez Angeline. Simple bungalows, with shared facilities, are noisy, but they are clean and have mosquito nets. The cost is a comparatively reasonable FMg 35,000 per bungalow.

Right at the southern end of the village are two good choices. The bed and breakfast-style *Chez Gerard & Francine* (☎ 614 09), right at the road's dead end, has spotlessly clean and airy colonial-style rooms with hardwood floors and a covered verandah opening onto the beach. With breakfast, they cost FMg 150,000 for air-con rooms and FMg 120,000 with fan. Bookings are strongly recommended.

Next door, the friendly *Hôtel Tropical* has bungalows, which also face onto the beach, with shower and toilet for FMg 66,000 including breakfast and afternoon tea. This place is popular, and therefore often full, but travellers have reported that some rooms can be dirty and showers non-functional.

Next up the beach is the relaxed, but poorly-signed, *Motel Coco Plage* (☎ 613 53). The rooms are quite acceptable – most have a shower and toilet – but at FMg 91,000, including breakfast, they are grossly overpriced. The attached restaurant, which is open to the public, serves good French and Malagasy cuisine.

The *Hôtel Le Robinson* (☎ 614 36), also known as *Chez Joel*, is the first place you'll pass as you approach the village by road. The bungalows are cosy and quiet, and the staff are friendly, but the place overlooks a mangrove rather than a beach. They are overpriced – FMg 75,000 with breakfast – but so is just about everything on Nosy Be.

Further up the price range, the limestone and thatch *Résidence d'Ambatoloaka* (☎ 610 91) overlooks the beach and costs F177/185 for a single/double. The *Hôtel Restaurant L'Espadon* (☎ 614 28) has excellent, modern bungalows overlooking the sea for FMg 300,000; those about 50m from the beach cost a little less: FMg 250,000. The small *Hôtel Ylang-ylang* (☎ 614 01) costs a surprisingly reasonable FMg 145,800. It is in a superb setting, and the room and restaurant service is excellent.

The *Soleil et Découverte* (☎ 614 24) is a great spot for a drink overlooking the beach, but the airless, noisy concrete rooms are poor value for a negotiable FMg 80,000.

Places to Eat The only way to eat cheaply is to sit at one of the few stalls along the main street where you can get a hearty meal of fish, rice, vegetables and fresh tropical fruit for as little as FMg 5000.

La Saladerie (look for the sign from the main street) has one of the best settings in the village, and offers an extraordinary range of meals – Italian, Chinese, Mexican; the list goes on and on. In the village centre (if it can be called that), the *Dauphin Blanc* has one of the best outdoor settings for watching everyone go by. Fish meals cost FMg 15,000, but you pay extra for chips or salad.

One recommended place, which is surprisingly poorly patronised, is *La Ravinala*. Great fish and Chinese meals costs a little less than other places – about FMg 12,000 a dish – and it's quieter and has a nice setting.

The *Karibo* serves passable pizzas for FMg 15,000-18,000, but it has a damned karaoke machine. For some nightlife, the *Turquoise Café*, at the entrance to the village, has been recommended by some travellers, particularly for its homemade punches. It also claims to be a casino, with blackjack and roulette.

A little more expensive, but worth a splurge for service and decor, is the restaurant in the *Hôtel Ylang-ylang* where meals cost from FMg 18,000. For a drink and a beach-side setting it is hard to go past the *Soleil et Découvetre*. You can enjoy a reasonably priced drink with a free bowl of nuts, and chat with all sorts of interesting characters at the bar.

Madriokely The beautiful beach at Madriokely, just a short walk north of Ambatoloaka, is quieter, and not nearly as developed (yet) as Ambatoloaka. The main place to stay is the ultra-expensive *Le Marlin Club* (☎ 610 70) – a lovely, quiet place which costs F680/780 in the low/high season, including breakfast.

Ambondrona The next bay north of Ambatoloaka, Ambondrona has a perfect little curved beach and is the site of a growing string of hotels and restaurants. To walk there from Ambatoloaka, follow the road north to the sugar cane railway then turn left at the first motorable track and strike out over the hill through the cane fields; otherwise just follow the coast around from Ambatoloaka. You'll soon see the grove of coconut trees that shelters both the beach and all the action.

Places to Stay & Eat Coming from the south, the first hotel is the *Palm Beach* (☎ 612 84). It is a bungalow resort with 60 rooms, a swimming pool and tennis court. They have 1001 different rates for rooms/bungalows, singles/doubles, high/low seasons, breakfast, half board, or full board and so on; reckon on a minimum of F380/500 for a single/double on a half-board basis.

The other major resort here is the *La Villa Blanche Hôtel Restaurant* (☎ 610 85), with 38 bungalows. This is an older, charming place and worth a splurge. Rooms with breakfast cost FMg 175,000/259,000/336,000 for a single/double/triple. The meals in the large outdoor restaurant are very good.

Next door, the *Tsara Loky* (☎ 610 22) – which means 'bon cuisine' in Malagasy – has six very pleasant little bungalows right on the beach for FMg 150,000. Meals have been particularly recommended by travellers who have been lucky enough to stay there. The management sometimes allows travellers to pitch a tent on the grounds for FMg 15,000 per tent.

One of the cosiest and friendliest places on the island would have to be the *Au Rendez-vous des Amis* – one of the very few Malagasy-owned places on the island. The manager was away when we visited, and the old man there couldn't tell us the price – but it is unlikely to be more than FMg 50,000 per bungalow. The rustic restaurant serves French and Malagasy food.

Belle-Vue A little further north, at the beach known as Belle-Vue, *Les Cocotiers* (☎ 613 14) has 26 bungalows which occupy a dreamy beach. Prices start at F300/500 for a low/high season single and F500/850 for a double. The complex also offers expensive tours and excursions. A little further north, along the same beach, is the superb *Hôtel La Belle Plage* (☎ (2) 351 23) where the standard, luxurious air-con brick bungalows cost a little less than at Les Cocotiers.

Djamandjary The Sirama sugar and rum refinery (which produces 900,000L of rum a year) is at the west coast town of Djamandjary, Nosy Be's second largest community. The factory is open to visitors and is an interesting place to walk around. Bring your own bottle and you can buy the locally distilled rum for a pittance.

Just east of town is the sugar mill, which is worth visiting to see two decaying but functional 1903 steam locomotives. These are still occasionally used during the cutting season (May to August) to transport cane along part of Nosy Be's (mostly-abandoned) 37km of rail line.

Places to Stay & Eat North of Djamandjary, just seaward of where the railway line crosses the main road, is *Au Coin de la Plage*. It's mainly a bar and restaurant, but they also have three bungalows to rent for about FMg 60,000. The setting is idyllic, but the place is scruffy and the staff are not particularly friendly. It also serves as the booking office for the Sakatia Dive Inn (see the Diving and Snorkelling, and Nosy Sakatia, sections for details) and as the dock for boats going to the island.

Andilana Few travellers venture as far out as Andilana, at the north-western corner of the island 27km from Hell-Ville. It's primarily a resort for the relatively well-to-do but the new inexpensive guesthouse may start to shift the tourist demographics a bit. This is probably the best beach on the island – but it is remote.

Places to Stay & Eat The most imposing place to stay is the *Andilana Beach Hotel* (☎ 611 76), formerly the Holiday Inn, complete with a casino, nightclub, tennis courts and 120 rooms. This was eerily closed at the time of research, and no-one was sure if, or when, it would reopen. If it does, rooms will cost F275/350 for a single/double.

Far more down to earth is the *Chez Loulou*, also known as the *Belvedere*, which sits on a hilltop and affords a wonderful view over the beach. Bungalows are good value from FMg 100,000 to FMg 120,000, including breakfast.

The local village restaurants, *Chez Louisette* and *Chez Ernesto*, serve as alternative places to eat and drink in the area. If you have chartered a taxi to Andilana, your driver may suggest that you eat at Ernesto's because the drivers get a kickback from the restaurant owners.

Getting There & Away

Air Air Madagascar flies between Tana and Nosy Be (US$150) every day, often via Mahajanga (US$83). Flights often go on to Antsiranana (US$37). Air Mad (☎ 613 57) is on the Route de l'Ouest at the crest of the hill just opposite the cemetery at Hell-Ville.

The new airline, TAM (☎ 613 92), is in the Chamber of Commerce building on Rue Passot. TAM links Réunion with Nosy Be, and travels to Tana, Mahajanga and Antsiranana from Nosy Be four times a week for the same price as Air Mad.

The other Réunion-based airline, Air Austral, in conjunction with Air Mad, flies once or twice a week (depending on the season and demand) between Nosy Be and Mayotte (the independent island close to the Comoros) as part of its flight between Réunion and Moroni (the capital of the Comoros). Refer to the Madagascar and Comoros Getting There & Away chapters for details.

Taxi-Brousse For information about travelling 'overland' between Nosy Be and Antsiranana, refer to the Nosy Be to Antsiranana section earlier in this chapter.

Ferry Small and large passenger and cargo boats operate daily between Hell-Ville and Ankify, the nearest port on the mainland to Nosy Be. For information about these boats, see under Nosy Be to Antsiranana earlier in this chapter.

Cargo Boat As an alternative to the gruelling taxi-brousse ride, gruelling coastal cargo boats travel from Hell-Ville to Mahajanga and, to a lesser degree, from Hell-Ville to Antsiranana. These trips can take anywhere from 24 to 72 hours and while some boats can be relatively comfortable with passenger cabins and food provided, the smaller ones are often a nightmare.

All the cargo offices which arrange bookings for passengers are in Mahajanga or Antsiranana, so its very hard to organise a trip from Nosy Be. For more details, see Getting There & Away under Mahajanga in the Western Madagascar chapter.

Yacht Nosy Be is certainly the best hunting ground if you're hoping to crew a yacht to Mayotte, Mahajanga, South Africa or elsewhere. The yachting season in the Indian Ocean falls between August and November, before the onset of the cyclone season. Because of the prevailing winds, nearly all the yachts will be coming from the north or east and heading south or west. Very few sailing boats set out from Madagascar for Mauritius, Réunion, Seychelles or Australia.

Many of the Australian and English yachts calling in at Nosy Be are on around-the-world runs. The French and South African boats are generally doing shorter hauls. Check out the travel agencies, ask boat owners at the port in Hell-Ville and look at the noticeboard at the Nandipo bar in Hell-Ville for information about crews.

Getting Around

The Airport Nosy Be's Fasrene airport, which is something of a showcase, lies about 12km from Hell-Ville on the eastern side of the island. When you arrive you will be overrun by hotel touts and taxi-drivers, who can all be a little overwhelming at first. As there is very little public transport on the island, you have virtually no choice but to take an overpriced taxi.

One way to cut costs is to share a taxi with a fellow passenger – most budget-minded travellers head for Ambatoloaka anyway. The current taxi fares from the airport are: to Hell-Ville, FMg 17,500; Ambatoloaka, Ambondrana or Djamandjary, FMg 30,000; and Andilana, FMg 40,000. Transfers organised by your hotel will cost about the same – they are not free.

Taxi-Brousse Very few taxis-brousse travel around the island, which is remarkable considering the number of them around the rest of the country. This is probably because Nosy Be is a tourist island and 'tourists can afford taxis'.

The cheapest form of public transport is the share-taxis, the tiny Renaults into which about six people are squeezed. You are more likely to get public transport *from* Hell-Ville if you hang around the taxi-brousse station there. Around the island, you could wait a long time for any public transport with room to come by.

Taxis Whether you like it or not, taxis are the normal mode of transport for visitors. Taxi rates on Nosy Be are standardised, but that doesn't stop them trying to overcharge and all rates double after 8 pm. Fares around the island and the costs for chartering are often displayed in the reception areas of hotels. Taxi-drivers can be quite annoying at times and any foreigner who dares to walk will be regularly hassled for fares.

One excellent way of seeing the island if you are in a hurry, or you have some people to share the cost, is to hire a taxi with driver. The current rate is FMg 85,000 for a half-day (ie, from about 7 am to midday), or FMg 135,000 for the whole day (from about 7 am to 7 pm).

Car & Motorcycle The best place to hire a car is Sarama Location (☎ 610 50), opposite the Cinéma Roxy in Hell-Ville. Prices for a small vehicle of variable quality range from FMg 120,000 to FMg 155,000 per day. You could try Nos Auto (☎ 611 50) at the petrol station in Hell-Ville, but the quality and reliability may not be there, and you should always be on the lookout for hidden extras.

Most up-market hotels can arrange car hire, but you will pay about FMg 350,000 per day for a 4WD with driver. A 4WD is not necessary unless you visit Lokobe Reserve, where hiking is a better way of getting around anyway. For ordinary vehicles hotels will charge about FMg 250,00 per day.

Renting a motorcycle is the perfect way to get around. Sarama Location, as well as several other places such as Location Jeunesse (☎ 614 08) in Ambatoloaka, rent motorcycles. Expect to pay about FMg 80,000/150,000 for half-day/one-day rental for a Honda 125cc; less for a Suzuki 50cc.

Bicycle If you're fed up with the lack of taxis-brousse and can't afford to hire a car or motorcycle, a mountain bike is the way to go. The southern road around most of the island – ie from the airport to Andilana, via Ambatoloaka – is paved and quite flat; other internal roads are rougher and steeper. Mountain bikes can be hired from Sarama Location and Location Jeunesse (see the preceding section) for about FMg 25,000 per day. (Negotiable discounts are possible for longer use.) From up-market hotels the rental will be higher.

Boat For information on travelling by boat between Nosy Be and neighbouring islands, see the following sections covering the various islands.

NOSY KOMBA

Nosy Komba, sometimes known as Nosy Ambarivorato, is a small, round, volcanic island lying midway between Nosy Be and the mainland. It's a magical place where you can laze about for many days without doing very much at all.

The landing site for ferries, and the largest village, is Ampangorina at the island's northern tip. Here the villagers, by now well acquainted with the tourist scene, sometimes mob visitors in an attempt to sell handicrafts and local produce.

Bathing is possible but not really recommended around Ampangorina since the beach serves as a public toilet and the water is polluted. The best snorkelling area is near the village of Mahabo, south-west of Ampangorina. The water is fairly clean and as long as one is sensible sea urchins aren't a problem.

For those with more time, a good day **hike** leads up the track from Ampangorina to the summit of the 621m volcano, Antaninaomby. Those of average ability should be able to do the return trip in five or six hours. The highly motivated will find lots of tracks connecting the interior villages. Note that there are no tracks around the coastline so trips between Ampangorina and other coastal villages will either require climbing over the mountain or somehow finding a pirogue. **Anjiabe**, on the south-west coast, has a particularly nice beach.

The real attraction of Nosy Komba, however, are the semi-tame black lemurs which frolic around a park set aside for their protection. These fortunate creatures are the beneficiaries of a local fady which deems them sacred and safe from hunters. That, combined with the attention and bananas they receive from locals and photo-hungry tourists, makes for a right spoilt mob! (The feeding of any lemurs outside the park is strictly forbidden.) This is one of the best places to get some good photos of these normally shy creatures. Admission to the compound is FMg 2500.

Places to Stay & Eat

There are now a few collections of bungalows on the island within easy walking distance of the harbour at Ampangorina. They are fairly similar in price and standard, but you'll soon forget about the lack of comfort and wallow in the hospitality, tranquility and gorgeous beaches. The best of the lot is the *Hôtel Les Lemuriens*, run by a friendly German and Malagasy couple. Simple but very pleasant bungalows cost from FMg 35,000 to 40,000.

A *restaurant* has been set up at the end of a beach at Ampangorina. It is in a stupendous position, but seemed to be closed at the time of research; otherwise, you can eat well at your bungalow. Not suprisingly fish and fruit feature heavily on the menu.

Getting There & Away

Most visitors come to Nosy Komba on an expensive day trip run by the hotels on Nosy

Be. Unless you charter your own pirogue, or take the boat trip on the *Daniel* (refer to the preceding Boating & Fishing section) you will need to arrange a transfer by boat from Hell-Ville. This is easier said than done because none of the places on Nosy Komba have telephones. All bungalow complexes on Komba charge about FMg 20,000/30,000 per person one-way/return for this service.

NOSY TANIKELY

Tiny Nosy Tanikely (Little Land Island) is 10km west of Nosy Komba. As an officially protected marine reserve it is one of the best remaining snorkelling and diving sites in the area, with coral, lobsters, eels, myriad colourful fish and, occasionally, even marine turtles. Organised day tours sometimes provide snorkelling equipment; independent visitors will have to bring their own.

Even if you're not getting wet, the beaches and tide pools are beautiful and you'll certainly see flying foxes and red-billed tropicbirds. On foot, the entire island can be explored in an hour or so, including an easy climb up to the lighthouse which is home for Nosy Tanikely's sole human inhabitants, the lighthouse keeper and his family. You can camp there easily enough – but take your own food and water, and take everything out with you. And watch out for the rats which may nibble through your tent if you leave any food around.

Getting There & Away

Most organised day tours combine Nosy Tanikely with Nosy Komba, commandeering the beach on Nosy Tanikely for an elaborate picnic at lunchtime. If you're going via this route, please encourage (and help) the organisers clean up the mess and discourage attempts to toss used papers and empty tins into the bushes.

Locals, as well as the hotels, on Nosy Komba can arrange day trips by sailing pirogue to Nosy Tanikely for about FMg 50,000 per person (including a picnic if you wish). It takes two hours each way so bring a hat and sunscreen. If the wind doesn't cooperate, you may have the opportunity to contribute your biceps to the cause of loco-motion.

NOSY SAKATIA

Nosy Sakatia, just off the west coast of Nosy Be, is quiet and tiny (3 sq km). Its appeal lies mainly in the opportunity to wander the forest tracks, see lots of wild orchids, fruit bats, chameleons and other wildlife, and partake in some excellent diving.

Places to Stay & Eat

There are two accommodation options. The *Sakatia Passions* (☎ 612 53) has 12 rooms (no prices were available at the time of research) and several boats for hire.

The main resort is the one run by Sakatia Dive Inn. (Refer to the preceding Diving & Snorkelling section for more information.) The resort caters primarily for people taking diving courses, but is open to anyone when there's space available. Tents can also be hired. Bookings are recommended. Some travellers have complained that there is nothing at all to do during the evenings but discuss the day's diving – but this sounds fairly idyllic to us.

NOSY MITSIO

Nosy Mitsio (Unknown Island) is actually an archipelago lying 55km north-east of Nosy Be, another of those elusive – and tragically short-lived – tropical island paradises.

For a while, these privately owned islands reigned as the area's last truly unspoilt corner. Unfortunately the largest island, Grande Mitsio, which has an established beach campground on the south-west coast, is already in the process of being trashed. The culprits, mainly yacht charters, continue to leave the beaches covered in tins, bottles, plastic and other garbage. In addition, the island's handful of inhabitants have already begun setting bush fires and the process of destruction that plagues other islands in the area is well underway.

Having delivered that depressing news, the Nosy Mitsio archipelago remains beautiful if not entirely pristine. Grande Mitsio is large enough to offer several days of exploration on foot but the smaller islands are absolute marvels. Nosy Tsarabajina has a wonderful white sand beach and on another island, Nosy Antaly, you can see the impressive natural basalt formation known as Les Cannes d'Orgues (The Organ Pipes). However, the big attractions are underwater and the diving is superb.

Getting There & Away

The trip between Nosy Be and Nosy Mitsio takes an average of about four to six hours. If you are in a group of at least three people, any of the Nosy Be hotels (eg Hôtel L'Espadon in Ambatoloaka) will organise trips to Nosy Mitsio for around FMg 280,000 per person per day in the high season. Alternatively, you can make your own arrangements through private boat owners on Nosy Be, many of whom live in Ambatoloaka, but you will need to muster a large group to avoid horrendous charter prices.

If you're interested in diving, Oceane's Dream in Ambatoloaka offers complete five-day packages around Mosy Mitsio. For more information see the Diving & Snorkelling section earlier in this chapter.

NOSY IRANJA & OTHER ISLANDS

The lovely island of Nosy Iranja (Island of Turtles) lies around the corner from Nosy Be, just beyond the entrance to Baie des Russes (also known as Baie d'Ambavatoby). Nosy Iranja actually consists of two islands, one of which is inhabited. The islands are connected by a two-km long sand bar, negotiable on foot at low tide. On the uninhabited island there is an established beach campground set amid coconut palms and casuarina trees.

The remote Nosy Radama islands, still farther afield but accessible by charter from Nosy Be, also offer snorkelling and diving opportunities. The largest island, Nosy Betafia, lies 60km south of Nosy Iranja.

Getting There & Away

Charter details to Nosy Radama are essentially the same as for Nosy Mitsio. The trip from Nosy Be to Iranja takes four to six hours, and on an organised tour expect to pay around FMg 220,000 per person per day. Along the way, watch for the amazing flowerpot rock which pokes dramatically out of the sea.

Western Madagascar

The western coastal region from Mahajanga south to Morondava is the homeland of the Sakalava tribe. Historical differences have managed to divide the Sakalava into two segments: the Menabe in the south and the Boina in the north. Because of its proximity, African influences have been greater in western Madagascar than in other parts of the island. In general, this is reflected in the darker skin and more animistic religious beliefs of the Sakalava; and their burial practices are less elaborate than those of other Malagasy.

The wild west is Madagascar's least populated region, with large uninhabited tracts interspersed with light settlement. The wide alluvial plains along the rivers support large herds of cattle and the area surrounding Mahajanga is one of Madagascar's most agriculturally diverse, producing tobacco, cotton, peanuts, coconuts, cashews, rice, manioc, fruit, sugar cane and raffia.

The climate is dry from April to December and temperatures are considerably higher than on the east coast. Nevertheless, the low humidity makes it much more comfortable. In early 1991 Cyclone Cynthia struck the west coast of Madagascar and caused widespread damage, but things have settled down and homes and businesses have been rebuilt.

Although the west is well off the beaten tourist track – mainly because it lacks decent roads – interest in the area is growing. More and more travellers are using Mahajanga, Morondava and smaller centres as staging points for trips into the magnificent hinterland: to the Ampijoroa Forestry Reserve, along the Tsiribihina River and the incredible Tsingy de Bemaraha Reserve.

MAHAJANGA (MAJUNGA)
• Telephone Area Code: 6

Mahajanga (often called Majunga), on the Baie de Bombetoka and at the mouth of the Betsiboka River, is Madagascar's second port (after Toamasina). It is a *very* hot, dusty

HIGHLIGHTS

Comoros

Mahajanga
(Majunga)

✛ Antananarivo

• Cruising down the Tsiribihina River over several days in a pirogue, watching for wildlife and visiting villages.

• The incredible canyons, pinnacles and caves of eroded karst in the Tsingy de Bemaraha Reserve.

• Morondava's fine climate and nearby attractions, such as the Avenue of Baobabs and Sakalava tomb carvings.

and *very* lethargic place with long, wide promenades – a crumbling frontier town of interesting architecture, shady arcades and rambling bougainvilleas. Apart from a number of religious buildings – there are numerous churches and at least 20 mosques – there's precious little in the town itself. Mahajanga is often ignored by travellers because getting there involves a lengthy and uncomfortable detour by road, or a relatively expensive trip by air.

There are two explanations regarding the origin of the name. One proposes that it was

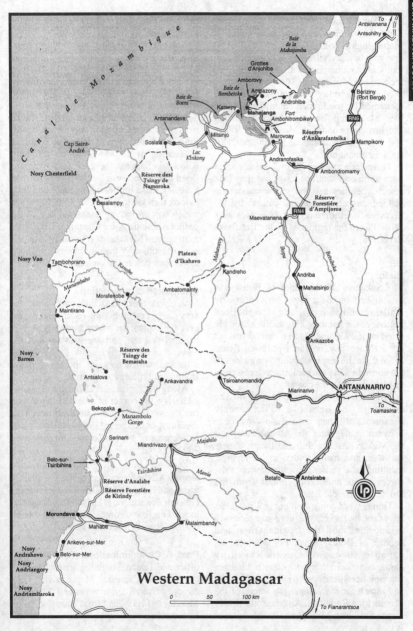

Western Madagascar

named by the founder of the Boina kingdom, King Andriamandisoarivo, who called it Maha Janga (The Cure), presumably after its dry and healthy climate. The other, more likely, explanation is that it was derived from the Swahili Mji Angaîa (Town of Flowers).

Much of today's town sits on land reclaimed by the French colonists from the bay. Mahajanga has the largest Comoran Muslim community in Madagascar and is also home to a substantial Indian and Pakistani merchant class.

There are a number of good, safe beaches both north and south of town, but they lack resort amenities and the sea hereabouts is stained an eerie blood-red caused by the massive haemorrhage of lateritic soils carried from the highlands by the Betsiboka River.

History

The Sakalava sub-kingdom of Boina was established in the early 18th century by Andriamandisoarivo, the disinherited brother of the Menabe king in the south. He ruled until 1712 and his first capital was set up at Marovoay on the Betsiboka River. From there, he set about conquering lands to the north. In 1745 the capital was transferred to Mahajanga on the coast.

The new capital, well placed on the estuary of the Betsiboka River, quickly became established as a trade crossroads between Madagascar, the African coast and the Middle East. Swahili and Indian traders called in and many settled in Mahajanga, resulting in a thriving commerce in cattle, slaves, arms and exotic goods from the Orient and Middle East.

Things were going well but in 1780, after 25 years in power, the king mysteriously disappeared and the fragmentation and decline of Boina began. For a while, his capable successor Queen Ravahiny managed to hold things together but neither she nor her successor, Andriansouli, were any match for the conquering forces of the Merina king Radama I. Andriansouli finally conceded, but Mahajanga's inhabitants

resisted, rioting and setting one section of the town on fire.

Because of its viability and strategic location, the French also saw opportunity in Mahajanga and in 1895 selected it as the base of operations for their expeditionary forces. In 1897 these forces successfully turned Madagascar into a French protectorate.

In 1977 Mahajanga experienced racial riots against the Comoran population, resulting in the deaths of over 1000 people and the evacuation of 16,000 Comoran refugees. Known as Sabenas (because they were airlifted to the Comoros by the Belgian airline Sabena), these unfortunate people had little to look forward to in the Comoros Republic, which was crumbling under the rule of the despot Ali Solih. Some Comorans have since returned and Mahajanga remains a Comoran outpost, although their numbers are much lower than before the violence.

Orientation & Information

Mahajanga is divided into two areas: the very sleepy and crumbling older part of town near the esplanade, where most hotels, restaurants and the port are located; and the newer (but still sleepy) area to the east of the cathedral, which contains the *taxi-brousse* station but little else of interest.

Along the esplanade (also called La Corniche), on the corner of Ave de France, you can't miss the grand **old baobab** tree. This specimen of *Adansonia digitata* has a circumference of 14m and is thought to be over 700 years old.

Money All the banks change money quickly and readily: the BNI-CL bank is opposite the Hôtel de France; the BTM bank is centrally-located on Rue Georges; and the BFV bank is along Rue du Maréchal Joffre.

Post & Communications The main post office and Telecom building are easy to find, opposite the Cathedral Majunga Be. They are open from 8 am to noon and 2 to 6 pm Monday to Friday, and from 8 am until noon on Saturday.

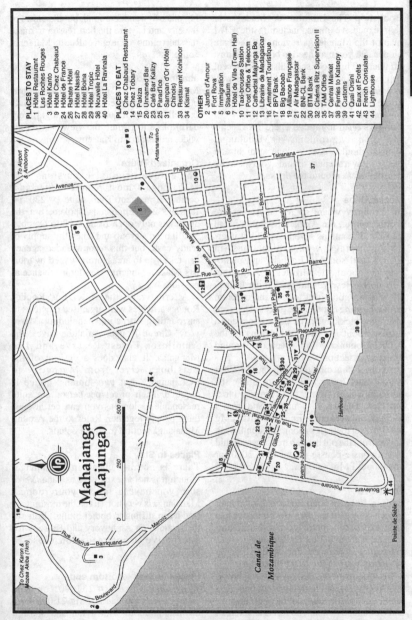

Mahajanga (Majunga)

PLACES TO STAY
1 Hôtel Restaurant
1 Les Roches Rouges
3 Hôtel Kanto
9 Hôtel Chez Chabaud
24 Hôtel de France
26 Rahate Hôtel
27 Hôtel Nassib
28 Hôtel Boina
29 Hôtel Tropic
36 Nouvelle Hôtel
40 Hôtel La Ravinala

PLACES TO EAT
8 Chez Chabaud Restaurant
14 Chez Tobany
15 Pakiza
20 Unnamed Bar
23 Café Bar Kalizy
25 Paradlce
31 Sampan d'Or (Hôtel Chinois)
33 Restaurant Kohinoor
34 Kismat

OTHER
2 Jardin d'Amour
4 Fort Rova
5 Immigration
6 Stadium
7 Hôtel de Ville (Town Hall)
10 Taxi-brousse Station
11 Post Office & Telecom
12 Cathedral Majunga Be
13 Librairie de Madagascar
16 Armement Touristique
17 BFV Bank
18 Big Baobab
19 Alliance Française
21 Air Madagascar
22 BNI-CL Bank
30 BTM Bank
32 Cinéma Ritz Supervision II
35 TAM Office
37 Central Market
38 Ferries to Katsepy
39 Customs
41 Quai Orsini
42 Eaux et Forêts
43 French Consulate
44 Lighthouse

Bookshop The Librairie de Madagascar sells expensive maps, including the FTM map of the Mahajanga region, but they are hidden and you may need to blow some dust off them. This bookshop also sells recent copies of *Le Monde* and *Le Figaro*, as well as postcards and daily French/Malagasy-language newspapers from Tana.

Dangers & Annoyances There have been a few security problems in Mahajanga. Women shouldn't walk alone at night and even by day travellers should avoid the more deserted areas around the docks.

Mozea Akiba

In a country where so few museums are worth visiting, the Akiba museum is a real treasure. It contains several small but interesting displays, with explanations (in French, and some in English) and photographs, about the Grottes d'Anjohibe, Ampijoroa Reserve and the Cirque Rouge. It's a damn good idea to visit the museum before heading out to these places. There are also some pickled fish, dinosaur bones and a display about the fascinating ruins of the Ambohitrombikely fort – see the Around Mahajanga section.

About 200m directly up from the Chez Karon hotel (refer to Places to Stay), the museum is open from 9 to 11 am and 3 to 5 pm, from Tuesday to Thursday, and from 3 to 5 pm on weekends. Entrance costs FMg 5000. To get there, it's a long, hot uphill walk 2.5km from the old baobab tree, or you could take a pousse-pousse (about FMg 3000) or taxi (about FMg 5000).

Fort Rova

Built in 1824 by King Radama I to counter French control of the area, the Fort Rova had a moat about four metres deep with a circumference of about 800m. The whole place was extensively damaged during the French-Malagasy wars of the late 19th century.

Restoration of the Bishop's Palace, hospital and government building is continuing, a joint effort of the universities of Mahajanga and Gotland, Sweden. The fort is an interesting place to wander around, but the views of the city and bay are the best reason to make the short climb to the end of Rue du Maréchal Joffre.

Jardin d'Amour

Maybe this was a garden once upon a time, but it's no longer there. As for amour (love) ... well. This is a quiet (and at night, very dark) place to admire the views across the wide, red estuary to Katsepy.

Organised Tours

For unique original excursions into Mahajanga's most remote hinterland, contact Armement Touristique (☎ 220 54; fax 293 21). English is spoken, but the agency is only open from April to October. You'll need a group and a healthy supply of ready cash, but this recommended agency can take you to areas rarely visited by tourists. Make arrangements as far in advance as possible.

Alternatively, the Hôtel Les Roches Rouges arranges well-organised day trips to surrounding attractions, including Marovoay, Cirque Rouge, Anjohibe caves, the Ampijoroa Forest Reserve and Lac Mangatsa. It also does a descent of the Betsiboka River from Marovoay to Mahajanga – but two months' notice is required. Their prices per person are quite reasonable as long as you can get at least three people together. Refer to the Around Mahajanga section for more details.

Places to Stay

There is nothing cheap in Mahajanga, though it is not as expensive as Tana. Make sure you have a fan in your room – Mahajanga is *very* hot. (Even the mosquitoes find it too stifling to bother biting.) Refer to the sections on Ambovory and Katsepy for alternative accommodation close to Mahajanga.

Places to Stay – bottom end

The *Hôtel Nassib* (☎ 231 90) on Rue Georges isn't too bad at FMg 21,000 for a downstairs room with a fan and shower.

Cooler upstairs rooms cost FMg 26,000. The disadvantages are that the toilets are generally grubby and some staff don't even speak French.

Behind the Nassib, on Rue Flacourt, the *Hôtel Boina* (☎ 224 69) is a bit seedy and is poor value at FMg 40,000/50,000/70,000 for a single/double/triple with fan and bathroom. Another rock-bottom choice is the gloomy *Rahate Hôtel* in the 'Muslim quarter' on Ave Gillon. Rooms have air-conditioning, but few have outside windows. Prices for depressing, airless rooms start at FMg 25,000.

One of the best in the bottom range is the *Hôtel Tropic* (☎ 236 10), next to La Ravinala. The rooms with fan and communal toilets are a bit small but they are reasonably priced at FMg 35,000. With air-conditioning the cost per room is FMg 55,000.

The *Hôtel Chez Chabaud* is some distance from the centre of (the old) town but is handy to the taxi-brousse station. The clean upstairs rooms are the best value in Mahajanga at FMg 40,000, but avoid the dumpy annexe rooms which are overpriced at FMg 30,000.

The *Sampan d'Or* Chinese restaurant (☎ 233 79) – also known as the *Hôtel Chinois* for obvious reasons – has a couple of reasonable rooms upstairs for FMg 42,000 with air-con and private bathroom.

Places to Stay – middle & top end

With sea views across the red waves, the best value in this range is certainly the friendly and quiet *Hôtel Kanto* (☎ 229 78), about 800m north of the big baobab tree. Rooms range from FMg 30,000 with a fan to FMg 40,000 for a room with fan, shower and toilet. For air-con, which is always welcome in this climate, they charge FMg 65,000 per room. A pleasant outdoor restaurant and bar is attached.

Not far away, at the end of Rue Marius Barriquand, the *Hôtel Restaurant Les Roches Rouges* (☎ 238 71) has singles/doubles with shower, toilet and air-con (but you may need to ask the reception to turn on the power supply for the air-con) for FMg 65,000. Bungalows with fan and bathroom

are a very reasonable FMg 35,000. However, half-board and full-board are ridiculously overpriced – eat out. The hotel also offers a number of excursions to sites around Mahajanga (see under Organised Tours).

The *Nouvelle Hôtel* (☎ 221 10) – aka *New Hotel* – has been recently renovated and now charges a fair bit for rooms with air-con: FMg 65,000 to FMg 110,000. The rooms with fan in the annexe, across the road, are better value for FMg 45,000. The popular, colonial-style *Hôtel de France* looked like it had been burnt down; repairs are busily underway.

The clean and central *Hôtel La Ravinala* (☎ 229 68), near the harbour, has also gone up-market after recent renovations. The hotel is pleasant enough, but you may get some unwanted noise from the nightclub downstairs and the price per room (FMg 72,000) is too much.

North-west of town is the recommended *Chez Karon* (☎ 226 94), sometimes known as the *Hôtel de la Plage*. Large, comfortable rooms right on the beach are FMg 70,000 to FMg 80,000. It's down a back street about three km from the centre of town. Take a taxi – it is worth the effort for the seclusion and beach.

Places to Eat

The best places to eat are the tiny *food stalls* which come out of nowhere when the heat starts to subside and are set up along La Corniche. You can pick up some tasty brochettes and rice-based meals for around FMg 2500.

It is hard to beat any of several small Pakistani-run salons de thé for value. The *Kismat* is friendly but watch the temperature of their chilli dressing. Its main competitor, the popular *Pakiza*, has a cool outdoor setting at the top of Ave de la Republique. Plats du jour cost FMg 12,000, and tasty samosas are FMg 500 each. Another great place for a curry menu du jour is the *Restaurant Kohinoor* – but watch out for a little furtive overcharging.

For snacks, breakfast (FMg 9000) and (so-so) ice cream, the niftily-named

Parad'Ice, near the Rahate Hôtel, is worth trying. A great outdoor place – especially recommended for a cooked breakfast (FMg 5500) with a fresh fruit shake – is the *Café Bar Kalizy*. In the newer, unexciting suburbs, the *Chez Chabaud Restaurant* is a treat if you are keen on genuine French food; courses cost around FMg 12,000 to FMg 16,000.

Set up especially for the limited tourist and expat trade is the excellent outdoor *Chez Tobary*. Prices for a good steak and salad, and other meals, cost a surprisingly reasonable FMg 8000; a large beer is FMg 3500. For excellent and cheap Chinese food, the *Sampan d'Or* is heartily recommended.

The restaurants in the following hotels are also worth trying: *La Ravinala* has a large, breezy restaurant with meals from FMg 12,000; the restaurant at the *Hôtel Kanto* has great views and cool breezes (a real selling point) with surprisingly reasonable prices; and if you are craving a pizza, try the *Nouvelle Hôtel* – though they are pricey at FMg 15,000 for a big 'un.

Entertainment

During the long hot days, sheltered doorways and sidewalks are littered with dozing bodies. This doesn't mean the locals have had a wild night, but if they did it would likely have been at *La Ravinala Disco* in the hotel of the same name, or the *San Antonio Nightclub* at the Les Roches Rouges, which promises (but rarely delivers) 'cabaret shows'. The *Cinéma Ritz Supervision II* looks permanently closed.

Just down from the *Alliance Française* – which is the only place to inquire about any local cultural activities – is an unnamed, lively outdoor Malagasy bar. It is a perfect (and very cheap) place to have a beer, eat some food from the roadside stalls outside and watch the sun set – a great way to finish off a hot day.

Getting There & Away

Air Every day Air Mad flies between Mahajanga and Nosy Be (US$83), Tana (US$94) and Antsiranana (US$116). Mahajanga is also the transit point for local flights to tiny, remote settlements around the west coast, such as Besalampy and Soalala.

In conjunction with the Réunion-based Air Austral, Air Mad flies between Mahajanga and Moroni, the capital of the Comoros, every Friday; and to Dzaoudzi, on the independent French island of Mayotte, on Thursday and Saturday. Refer to the Madagascar Getting There & Away chapter for details.

The other Réunion-based airline, TAM, also links Mahajanga with Réunion, and with Nosy Be and Antsiranana, four days a week. TAM charges the same fares as Air Mad.

The Air Madagascar office (☎ 224 21), along Ave Gillon, opens at 7.30 am every day but Sunday. Get there early to beat the crush. The TAM office (☎ 231 64) is not far from the Nouvelle Hôtel.

Taxi-Brousse Surprisingly, the taxi-brousse station is little more than a wide shoulder along Ave Philibert Tsiranana. There are really only two main routes out of Mahajanga: to Tana and to Antsiranana (FMg 130,000), via Ambanja for Nosy Be. Neither road is great for overland travel because they are rough and boring, and there is nowhere the least bit exciting to stay along the way.

Competition on the run between Tana and Mahajanga is fierce so you'll have a choice of taxis-brousse (FMg 40,000), taxis-be, Mercedes truck-buses and more comfortable minibuses (FMg 45,000). Most leave Mahajanga early in the afternoon and arrive at the Taxi-brousse Station North in Tana early the next morning.

If you're travelling from Mahajanga to Tana, the temperature drop is dramatic as you climb onto the *hauts plateaux*, so carry some warm clothing. The landscape along the way is a vision of environmental apocalypse, but the road has improved over the years so the trip is not the nightmare it once was. About 12 to 15 hours is fairly normal these days, but it may take a lot longer in the wet season:

From Tana to Mahajanga, I needed seven days and six nights (about four nights travelling on the road). When the taxi-brousse got stuck in the mud and broke, me and another *vahaza* marched through the jungle. After one hour, we reached the truck we had seen four hours before on the horizon from another road. It had needed four hours to travel four km...

Daniel Muller, Germany

The 218km between Antsohihy and Ambanja (see the Mahajanga to Nosy Be section later in this chapter) can take as long as 36 hours, so be prepared for a great deal of shake, rattle and roll.

It isn't really practical or even possible to travel overland along the coast to Morondava. In the dry season you'll make it as far as Soalala, Besalampy and perhaps even Maintirano, but it's a long and very difficult trip with next to nothing in the way of transport. To continue farther south, you'll either have to fly or backtrack through Tana and Antsirabe.

Boat Travellers can avoid the uncomfortable taxi-brousse ride between Mahajanga and Ambanja (for Nosy Be) by taking the uncomfortable (and slower) cargo boats. These carry mainly rice and sugar, and operate at least weekly between Mahajanga and Hell-Ville on Nosy Be. Less frequently, there are also boats from Mahajanga to Antsiranana.

Most boats depart from Quai Orsini, but check carefully because they sometimes load up around the dhow port farther east. On a large boat the trip to Nosy Be will take anywhere from 24 to 36 hours. On the smaller boats – which are not recommended – it can take up to 72 hours. There are no passenger cabins, but if you're lucky there'll be space to throw out a sleeping bag on deck. In most cases, passengers must bring their own food and water.

Between Mahajanga and the Comoros, contact the TRIN agency, opposite the Quai Orsini, which has cargo boats going to Mayotte, Anjouan, Moroni and as far as Zanzibar and Dar es Salaam in Tanzania. TRIN had a nice office when we visited but the staff were as lethargic as the rest of the city. Refer

to the regional Getting There & Away chapter for more information about travelling to or from Madagascar via Mahajanga.

Getting Around

The Airport Amborovy airport lies six km north-east of town, near the coast. Taxis into town charge a non-negotiable and 'official' FMg 15,000, but if you walk outside the airport you will be able to catch an Amborovy taxi-brousse to the main taxi-brousse station in Mahajanga for a fraction of this.

Car The Hôtel Les Roches Rouges (see Places to Stay) rents cars for an overpriced FMg 350,000 per day. Try Maki-Loc car hire (☎ 231 21), on the way to the airport, which should be cheaper.

Pousse-pousse The pousse-pousse drivers in Mahajanga must be the most lethargic and least bothersome in Madagascar. This is probably because of the heat, and one would hesitate to ask them to burn their bare feet on the hot tarmac during the middle of the day anyway. They charge tourists between FMg 2500 and FMg 4000, but one or two may ask – with a huge toothless grin – for FMg 10,000. Ask one or two locals about the proper pousse-pousse fare.

AROUND MAHAJANGA

If you can't be bothered with the hassle of organising a trip to the following places by yourself, the Hôtel Les Roches Rouges can organise something at a reasonable price (refer to Organised Tours).

Katsepy

The small fishing village of Katsepy (pronounced 'catsup') lies across the estuary from Mahajanga. Although the ruddy sea is uninviting in these parts, the lonely beaches stretch into the distance and provide pleasant walks in the strong sea breeze.

Most people come for the restaurant run by the French-trained chef, Madame Chabaud, whose incredible lunches and dinners cost from around FMg 15,000 – and are worth it. Go for the seafood in general and the oysters in particular, which are renowned as some of the best in Madagascar. If you can't get enough of Madame Chabaud's cooking in a single visit, she also rents out basic *bungalows* for a negotiable FMg 40,000 to FMg 50,000. There is no reason why you can't camp along the beach if you have a tent – but having said that, one reader had a very unpleasant experience with a local thief.

Ferries (FMg 2500) officially leave Mahajanga from the bottom of Ave de la Republique at 7.30 am and noon, and leave Katsepy at 10 am and 3 pm – but they are almost always late. Take the 7.30 am ferry if you hope to make it to Katsepy and back in one day. Ask the ferry office for latest departure times.

Mitsinjo

From the ferry landing at Katsepy you'll find taxis-brousse (FMg 10,000) heading south towards the pleasant and welcoming village of Mitsinjo, four hours away on the Mahavavy River. There is no accommodation to speak of so camping or asking for a room in a local house is the only option. Mitsinjo is the best place to arrange a trip to Lac Kinkony.

Lac Kinkony

With a bit of effort you can visit the semi-protected wildlife reserve at the 15,000 hectare Lac Kinkony, 30km from Mitsinjo. There are Verreaux's sifakas and brown lemurs, but the major drawing card is the birdlife. This includes myriad water birds, as well as birds of prey and migratory species. It is truly a magnificent place and well worth the effort.

As visiting the lake becomes more popular, it may be easier to find someone in Mitsinjo or Katsepy to take you there. The area has no facilities so visitors must be self-sufficient. Neither is there any public transport. Hitching is a possibility but there's very little traffic; it may be better to wait for a taxi-brousse heading towards Soalala from

Katsepy and ask to be dropped at the point nearest the lake.

Amborovy

Near the airport and six km from Mahajanga is the relaxed beachside village of Amborovy, a quieter and cooler alternative to staying in Mahajanga.

The most up-market option is the *Zahamotel* (☎ 223 24), located on the nicest stretch of beach. With TV and air-con, the lovely rooms cost F250, while bungalows are considerably more at F390. There is even a sparkling swimming pool, but the place needs a lot more trees. Not quite on the beach, but certainly close enough to walk, *Transmad* (☎ 236 22) has bungalows for about the same price. Cheaper bungalows are being built around the village so look out for these alternatives.

A return taxi from Mahajanga costs an 'official' FMg 30,000, but you should be able to bargain for less. You can easily get a taxi-brousse from Mahajanga to the village of Amborovy, from where it's a 30 minute walk to the beach.

Ampazony

If you *really* want to get off the beaten track, but not be too far from Mahajanga, go to the secluded beach at Ampazony. There is a circuitous trail there for 4WDs or motorcycles; otherwise head north along the beach from the airport terminal for about eight km. You will need to take all your own camping equipment, food and water.

Cirque Rouge

If you're hankering after a pleasant desert hike visit Cirque Rouge, a colourful natural amphitheatre just north of the airport. The wildly eroded rock is tinted in rainbow hues, including every conceivable shade of red. If you squint a bit, you could almost imagine being lost somewhere in Arizona. At the head of the cirque, you'll find a stand of ravinala palms and other greenery surrounding a perennial **freshwater spring**. The best time to visit is from May to November.

Taxi drivers initially ask FMg 20,000 for

the 12km return trip, but FMg 12,000 is more realistic. Arrange for the taxi to pick you up later, allowing about two hours for a good look around. Taxis-brousse from the station in Mahajanga regularly go to Amborovy, from where it is a 45 minute walk to the cirque via a lovely ravine heading inland from the coast.

Lac Mangatsa

Another interesting site near the sea north of Amborovy is the tiny sacred Lac Mangatsa (aka Lac Sacré), 18km from Mahajanga. Here, locals come to give thanks or to petition the help and favour of the Boina royal ancestors, reincarnated in the form of immense tilapia which inhabit the clear lake. The best time to visit is from May to October.

Strict *fady* (taboos) prohibit fishing and bathing, and the lake's fish are left to grow to maximum size. The surrounding green belt also harbours wildflowers and interesting lizards, chameleons and spiders; all of these are also protected by fady.

Getting There & Away Access isn't easy. From the airport, continue one km along the asphalted road, then turn right onto the rough track (which begins by following an old airstrip) and continue for 11km to the lake. Unless you're up to a long walk, you'll either need your own vehicle or will have to pay through the nose for a taxi. Visitors *must* remain sensitive to the local fady which are taken extremely seriously; you'll get much more out of your visit with a local guide.

Fort Ambohitrombikely

About 20km south-east of Mahajanga, in the midst of a dense forest, lay the ruins of the 19th century Ambohitrombikely fort. It was built by the Merina, but very little else is known about it. There are plenty of cannons, cannonballs, cooking utensils and other implements scattered around.

The display about the fort at the Mozea Akiba museum in Mahajanga is about as close as most travellers will get. To get to the fort, you will need to take a taxi-brousse or private vehicle along the road towards Marovoay and then find a guide because very few people in the area know much about it.

Marovoay

Marovoay was the original Boina capital but in 1745 it lost out in favour of Mahajanga which lies nearer the sea. The name means Many Crocodiles, but most of the crocs have fallen victim to enthusiastic hunters. There's nothing special about the town itself; the real appeal is to organise a **pirogue trip** from Marovoay to Mahajanga, weaving along the lovely convoluted channels and marshes of the broad red Betsiboka estuary. There is an interesting **zebu market** on Fridays.

If you wish to stay in Marovoay, the *Hôtel Tina* (☎ 61) has basic singles/doubles for FMg 9000/12,000 with shared facilities.

One interesting way to travel is to take a taxi-brousse (FMg 6000) to Marovoay and return to Mahajanga by river. Ask in Marovoay about hiring a pirogue and guide, but you may not be able to get anything for less than FMg 250,000 all-inclusive per boat for the two day trip.

Grottes d'Anjohibe

Some of the most impressive caverns in Madagascar are the remote Zohin' Andranoboka, whose name, not surprisingly, means the Big Caves (they are also known as the Anjohibe caves, after a nearby village). Long known to local people, they were first 'discovered' by Europeans in 1934.

Beneath two small hills wind a series of subterranean rooms and galleries; the most extensive stretches over five km. This impressive underground world is eerily adorned with stalactites, stalagmites and other cave decorations but, sadly, many have been damaged by witless visitors.

Getting There & Away With a 4WD vehicle, access is straightforward. Follow the main southern road from Mahajanga for 10km, then turn north on a seasonal track which leads 63km to the caves. The route is passable only between April and October. By taxi-brousse, you can only go as far as Androhibe, which is a walkable 15km short of the caves. Look for guides either there or at Anjohibe itself.

RÉSERVE FORESTIÈRE D'AMPIJOROA

The 20,000 hectare Ampijoroa Forestry Reserve (sometimes referred to as a forestry station) is the only readily accessible portion of the 60,520 hectare Réserve Naturelle Intégrale d'Ankarafantsika, which occupies a separate parcel farther north. These reserves are the only fully protected example of dry western deciduous forest in Madagascar, and they protect a vital and vulnerable watershed.

Ampijoroa is best known for a centre jointly established by the Malagasy government and the Jersey Wildlife Preservation Trust for the breeding of two threatened tortoise species, the flat-tailed tortoise *(Pyxis planicauda)* and the very rare ploughshare tortoise *(Geochelone yniphora)*. The ploughshare, or *angonoka*, is currently being reintroduced to its native habitat around Soalala, south-west of Mahajanga. The unusual mating habits of these tortoises are hilariously described in the book *The Aye-Aye and I* by Gerald Durrell (see under Books in the Madagascar Facts for the Visitor chapter).

Flora & Fauna

At Ampijoroa, you'll have no problem observing wildlife. It is home to seven lemur species and around the campground you're sure to see the acrobatic Coquerel's sifaka – look in the prominent mango tree. These black, white and chocolate-coloured lemurs are good for hours of entertainment.

Tortoise Love

When you're as endangered a species as Madagascar's ploughshare tortoise, people are bound to be interested in your love life. In fact, at the Réserve Forestière d'Ampijoroa the Jersey Wildlife Preservation Trust has set up a research and breeding centre to encourage and promote tortoise courtship and mating. The latter follows quite an unusual procedure, which Gerald Durrell described in his book *The Aye-Aye and I*:

Each pen was spacious and could be made three or five times the size to help with the mating procedure by the simple expedient of moving a few logs. The strange protuberance of the shell under the animal's head (which bestows on it the name Ploughshare) called an *ampondo* is the animal's fighting gear. It is essential, apparently, for the males to fight in order to be roused to such a pitch that they are overcome with emotion and can mate with the females. A lone male kept with any number of luscious, buxom and voluptuous females (by tortoise standards) just tends to wander round forlornly, ignoring the wiles and manifold attractions of the females, simply because he has no one to fight. To be the only male surrounded by attractive and willing females is a situation, you would have thought, that would bring out the Don Juan in any tortoise worth his salt, but the Ploughshare needs fisticuffs as an aphrodisiac. When the situation is right, however, battle commences and it is a fascinating contest to watch.

The two males, rotund as Tweedledum and Tweedledee dressed for battle, approach each other at what, for a tortoise, is a smart trot. The shells clash together and then the Ploughshares' *ampondo* comes into use. Each male struggles to get this projection beneath his opponent and overturn him to win a victory in this bloodless duel. They stagger to and fro like scaly Sumo wrestlers, the dust kicked up into little clouds around them, while the subject of their adoration gazes at their passionate endeavours, showing about as much excitement and enthusiasm as a plum pudding. Finally, one or the other of the suitors gets his weapon in the right position and skidding along and heaving madly he at last overturns his opponent. Then, he turns and lumbers over to gain his just reward from the female, while the vanquished tortoise, with much leg-waving and effort, rights himself and wanders dispiritedly away. Like so many battles in nature, it is merely a stimulus, a trial of strength in which no one is hurt and no gore is shed.

The actual mating process begins with the male turning the female over a couple of times, perhaps to keep her humble after the potentially ego-inspiring battle for her attention, and culminates with the big event, which will hopefully result in the propagation of this species, the world's most threatened reptile.

(Reprinted from *The Aye-Aye and I* with permission from Gerald Durrell and Harper-Collins Publishers.) ∎

You're also likely to see brown lemurs and four nocturnal species: sportive, woolly, grey mouse and fat-tailed dwarf lemurs. More elusive is the rare mongoose lemur, which is observed almost exclusively in Ampijoroa. The best chance of seeing one is at the onset of the wet season, when it is active during the day. As at Périnet Reserve, near Tana, hearing the lemurs screeching in the forests will probably be a highlight of your trip around the reserve. Other mammals include two species of tenrecs and the grey long-tailed mouse *(Macrotarsomys ingens)*, which is found nowhere else but in the higher elevations of this reserve.

Ampijoroa is one of Madagascar's finest birdwatching locations and 101 species have been recorded. Perhaps the most exciting to see is the rare Madagascar fish-eagle, while the noisiest is the raucous sicklebill vanga.

There are at least 32 species of reptiles, including large iguanas, a rare species of leaf-tailed gecko *(Uroplatus guentheri)* and the rhinoceros chameleon *(Chamaeleo rhinoceratus)* – the male sports a bizarre bulb-like proboscis.

Vegetation at Ampijoroa consists mainly of relatively low and scrubby deciduous forest with pockets of such dry-country plants as aloe and the *Pachypodium* or 'elephant's foot'.

Permits & Guides

The best place to get your permit is from the Circonscription des Eaux et Fôrets (District Water and Forests Department) (☎ 2644), opposite the French consulate in Mahajanga. This department is nowhere near as well organised as the usual ANGAP office, and trying to organise a trip to the reserve can be a bit time consuming and frustrating. Three-day permits currently cost FMg 20,000, but are likely to rise to FMg 50,000 like the permits issued by ANGAP.

If you are coming overland from the south, say on the long haul from Tana, you can buy your permit at the park entrance rather than going to Mahajanga first. Guides are compulsory and easy to pick up at the park entrance.

Visiting the Reserve

At the present time, only the Ampijoroa Reserve is open to tourists and, in any case, the main body of Ankarafantsika Reserve is remote and difficult to reach. The best time to visit is between May and November. Rainfall is still relatively light during the December to April wet season, when you'll have the best chance of seeing the rare mongoose lemurs.

A visit is just within the realms of a day trip from Mahajanga, but it won't leave much time for looking around. To fully appreciate the site you'll need at least two days. If you're pressed for time, day tours (combined with a visit to Marovoay) are available through the Hôtel Les Roches Rouges for FMg 120,000 per person, including the FMg 20,000 entrance fee – but it will only be at this price if you can get five people in a group.

Places to Stay & Eat

There are no formal visitor facilities so unless you opt for a whirlwind day trip from Mahajanga, bring your own tent. Camping is allowed at the park office and someone there will even cook you something. There is a small store at the campground which may have some very welcome cold drinks, but it's best to bring your own supplies from Mahajanga. There are a couple of basic *hotelys* (roadside stalls) in Andranofasika village, four km along the road towards Mahajanga. Drinking water may be found in the reserve, but for washing use the pond across the road.

Getting There & Away

Happily, access is not difficult. The reserve and campground lie near RN4 about 114km south-east of Mahajanga, four km south-east of Andranofasika village and 455km from Tana. Direct taxis-brousse from Mahajanga (about FMg 16,500) take about two hours and leave at around 8 am. Taxis-brousse coming from Tana tend to arrive in the middle of the night so don't sleep through the stop (you'll have to pay the full Tana-Mahajanga fare of FMg 40,000).

MAHAJANGA TO NOSY BE

The 624km 'overland' route between Mahajanga and the tropical paradise of Nosy Be is fairly interesting, but more suited to those who want to save money on a flight or have an adventurous (ie masochist) streak. You are strongly advised to do the trip in stages.

Firstly, the 153km road from Mahajanga to Ambondromamy, past the Ampijoroa Reserve, is fairly good, but it gets gradually worse as you approach Mampikony. Depending on the state of the road, you will probably have to stay the night in Mampikony (where there doesn't seem to be a hotel) or in Boriziny (also known as Port Bergé). Here you can stay at the *Hôtel Zinia* (☎ (680) 22) or the *Hôtel Restaurant Le Monde*.

A slightly better road takes you further north to the junction of Antsohihy, where you can stay at the *Central Hôtel* (☎ (680) 710 96) for about FMg 17,000 a room, or the *Hôtel de France* at FMg 15,000 a room. From Antsohihy bad roads lead to several other villages such as Béalanana (134km to the north-east) or Befandriana Avaratra (87km to the south-east), or you can charter a pirogue along the river Loza. (Around these places a white face is so rare that kids may go screaming to their mothers. There is also some fady in the region, so be careful.)

To 193km stretch from Antsohihy to Ambanja (FMg 40,000; 10-12 hours) is woeful at best – and impassable in the wet season. If you get through to Ambanja, a taxi-brousse takes you to the port of Ankify for the regular boat to Nosy Be.

MIANDRIVAZO

• Telephone Area Code: 458

The normally broiling and rather nondescript town of Miandrivazo serves as a convenient halfway break on the long haul between Antsirabe and Morondava, and as the place to organise a trip along the Tsiribihina River (see the next section). These trips, which are being offered by an increasing number of agencies, take a minimum of three days at a wonderfully lazy pace.

Places to Stay & Eat

One of the most popular places to stop is the *Chez La Reine Rasalimo* (☎ 38), overlooking the Majahilo River. Rather stuffy bungalows cost around FMg 35,000 for a single or double. The food is generally pretty good, but the pizzas are fairly awful.

Less expensive is the *Relais de Miandrivazo* (☎ 3), with spartan rooms and communal facilities for FMg 25,000 to FMg 30,000. Other reasonable options are the *Hôtel Bemaraha*, which has rooms with fan for FMg 12,500, and the *Hôtel Restaurant Masoandro* (☎ 27), which costs a little more.

A nice place to eat is the *Palais de la Reine* – though one reader commented that there was a 'fascinating variety of insects falling on us during dinner; not for the faint-hearted'.

Getting There & Away

There are infrequent Air Mad Twin-Otter flights from Tana (US$60) to Miandrivazo via Ankavandra (US$25). Most people take a taxi-brousse because the Tana-Miandrivazo road, through Antsirabe, is good and has regular transport; taxis-brousse leave for Antsirabe (about six hours) and Morondava (about eight hours) on most days.

TSIRIBIHINA RIVER

A boat trip 145km downstream from Miandrivazo to Belo-sur-Tsiribihina is increasingly popular among those on organised trips and for the independent traveller. It is a very slow, relaxing ride, where you will visit local villages, see an endless variety of wildlife such as bats (hopefully not crocodiles) and birdlife such as storks, herons and ducks (which whistle).

Trips can be organised through agencies abroad, or in Tana or Fianarantsoa. Alternatively, the well-motivated can make their own informal arrangements easily with an increasing number of keen pirogue owners in Miandrivazo. Motorless pirogues are slower (allow about four to five days), but naturally they are quieter and do not disturb the wildlife.

Do-It-Yourself

By travelling independently the trip will naturally be cheaper and more flexible. In Miandrivazo, a trip is very easy to organise through your hotel or with anyone who approaches you. Expect to pay about FMg 80,000 per person per day for a three to five day trip by motorless pirogue. This price should include a reliable boat, food, guide(s) and transport from Belo-sur-Tsiribihina to Morondava; you may need to supply your own tent. And bargain hard.

It is always a good idea to bring a sleeping bag. You will spend most of the day in the baking sun, or pouring rain, cramped in a small boat, so bring a hat, sunscreen, something to sit on and protection from the rain. Otherwise ask the boat owners to erect a simple shelter over the pirogue. And mosquitoes can be awesome, so be prepared. Few of the boatmen speak French. Please take out all your rubbish with you and ask your guide and boatman to do the same.

Organised Tours

Organising a trip down the Tsiribihina River may be the sort of tour best left to someone who knows what they are doing with regards to equipment, boat hire, cooking, visiting villages and so on. Naturally, you will pay more on an organised tour, but being on a reliable boat, sheltered from the elements and with a knowledgeable guide is important. The following agencies are recommended:

La Caravane Malagasy (π/fax (2) 355 54) – this impressive outfit runs fascinating seven-day trips from Tana partly by, of all things, a hydroglider. But you will pay heavily for the excitement: about F890 per person per day.

Mad Cameleon (π/fax (2) 344 20) – this agency is good for boating and trekking trips in the general Tsiribihina area. Prices are available if you ring them.

Madagascar AirTours (π (2) 241 92; fax 343 70) – it organises an exciting trip around the river and to the Tsingy de Bemaraha Reserve over eight days. Prices were not available at the time of research, but are likely to be reasonable.

Sakamanga – this excellent hotel in Tana also organises three-day trips. Refer to Places to Stay in the Antananarivo chapter for contact details.

Tropika Touring (π (2) 222 30; fax 349 01; email tropika@bow.dts.mg) – this agency has reasonably priced six-day tours on board the fully equipped barge *Renala I*, starting from US$355 per person (depending on the number of passengers).

BELO-SUR-TSIRIBIHINA
* Telephone Area Code: 454

Belo-sur-Tsiribihina (also known as just Belo), lost in the vast marshes, mangroves and barrier islands of the Tsiribihina delta, is the finishing point for most trips down the Tsiribihina River, and the starting point for trips to the Tsingy de Bemaraha Reserve. At Serinam, about 15km east of town, you can find some wonderful examples of **Sakalava tombs**.

Belo's main hotel and restaurant is the comfortable *Hôtel du Menabe* (π 10). Single/double rooms with shower cost FMg 20,000 to FMg 30,000. Staff can prepare some decent meals, but you have to order in advance.

The two to three hour trip between Belo and Morondava is served by frequent taxis-brousse (FMg 20,000). There are occasional flights by Air Mad (π 37) between Belo and Morondava (US$25) – more in the peak (tourist) season in mid-year.

RÉSERVE NATURELLE INTÉGRALE DES TSINGY DE BEMARAHA

Ever since *National Geographic* published an awe-inspiring two-page photo spread of the Tsingy de Bemaraha in their February 1987 issue, travellers and tourists have been working out ways to reach this once practically inaccessible wonderland. It has since become a UNESCO World Heritage site and is featuring in more and more tour itineraries.

Tsingy de Bemaraha covers 152,000 hectares and is the largest protected area in Madagascar. The highlight is the vast forest of eroded karst pinnacles, which are even more rugged than those at Ankàrana Reserve in northern Madagascar. Unfortunately the main region of the reserve known as the

Grand Tsingy is currently off limits to tourists, but you can explore the Petit Tsingy which is almost as good as the real thing and certainly still worth a look.

Many species of wildlife are presumed to live in the reserve, but because of its remoteness few have been officially recorded. So far there are 53 species of birds, eight species of reptile and six species of lemur: grey mouse, fork-marked, grey bamboo, sportive and brown (or red-fronted) lemurs and Decken's sifaka. Independent travellers should get a permit from the ANGAP office in Tana.

Organised Tours

A number of companies (mainly those listed under the Tsiribihina River section) have recognised the appeal of the Tsingy de Bemaraha and include the reserve in their itineraries. These trips may include a canoe trip down the Manambolo River from Bekopaka. Visiting the reserve is only possible from April to November. If going on an organised tour with a tour operator or guide from Belo-sur-Tsiribihina or Morondava, make sure the road from Belo to Bekopaka, the nearest village to the reserve, is passable before you set off in any vehicle; some guides take your money knowing the road is impassable anyway.

Places to Stay

If you are on a package tour you will probably stay at *Gîte de Mr Bora* or *Ibrahim Cottages* in Bekopaka. If not, you may be able to stay at either place anyway, but in peak season accommodation is scarce so you may have to camp.

Getting There & Away

Reaching Bekopaka and the Tsingy de Bemaraha on your own is very difficult. In the wet season it will be almost impossible;

DAVID CURL

Parson's Chameleon (*Chamaeleo parsoni*) is one of two species that could claim to be the largest in the world. Although measuring up to 60cm in length, it is completely harmless.

DAVID CURL

DAVID CURL

Top: Rice was introduced by Malay-Polynesian seafarers who settled Madagascar nearly 2000 years ago. Today rice paddies dominate the landscape of Imerina.

Bottom: A baobab tree grows in a sea of sisal in southern Madagascar. Sisal is grown for its tough fibrous flesh, which is used in the manufacture of rope.

PAUL SCOTT

DAVID CURL

Top: The pirogue is a traditional means of getting about in coastal areas, such as here at Nosy Tanikely in northern Madagascar.

Bottom: Ramena Beach, near Antsiranana (Diego Suarez) in northern Madagascar, is among the many unspoilt and tranquil beaches that await the visitor.

in the dry season, take one of the occasional taxis-brousse from Belo-sur-Tsiribihina heading towards Bekopaka, 80km away. The vehicle will continue until the road becomes impassable – normally about 20km short of Bekopaka. At this stage, you'll have to walk and/or take a zebu cart across a few rivers – which is not always a lot of fun, as one reader told us:

We bartered for two ox-carts. The first river crossing meant standing up in the cart, rucksacks above our heads, as the ox swam and the whole cart disappeared under water. After four hours our guide gleefully pointed out a village 100 yards away. We assumed we had reached our destination, only to be told that this was the village we had left some four hours ago. We had just done a *grande diversion*. It was now pitch black and we were hungry. The cart drivers soon became lost and we ploughed on through thorny scrub in only shorts and T-shirts, mosquitoes enjoying the feast. At midnight our cart suddenly lurched sideways and fell down an eight-foot hole. Fifteen hours from anywhere, one member of our party collapsed with possible cerebral malaria. At this point the heavens opened up...

Once in Bekopaka, you're within easy reach of the Petit Tsingy (or at least the southern end of it) and the spectacular **Manambolo Gorge** where you will see waterfalls, lemurs and untouched forests. To explore the incredibly convoluted landscape to the north, you'll need to hire a guide in Bekopaka – but this area is probably off limits, so check before organising any major expeditions. Carry all the supplies you'll be needing.

RÉSERVE D'ANALABE

Analabe, sister reserve to Berenty in south-eastern Madagascar, occupies 4000 hectares of flat coastal plain near Beroboka Avatra about 55km north of Morondava. Most of the vegetation consists of dry deciduous forest plus marshes and mangroves. Like Berenty, Analabe is owned by M Jean de Heaulme.

Analabe is one of Madagascar's few birdwatching paradises – 113 species have been recorded to date – and is one of the best places to observe the fosa. Analabe supports six species of lemur, none of which have yet been spoilt by soft touch tourists. This is one of the only habitats of a subspecies of the sportive lemur, *Lepilemur mustelinus ruficaudatus,* and there's also a healthy population of Verreaux's sifakas. Berenty's ever-present brown lemurs were transplanted there from Analabe.

The reserve may be reached by taxi-brousse along the Morondava to Belo-sur-Tsiribihina route, but reservations will probably be required. Before you go, check at the Hôtel Les Bougainvilliers in Morondava for the latest news about the park and hiring bungalows.

RÉSERVE FORESTIÈRE DE KIRINDY

The 10,000 hectare Kirindy Forestry Reserve, 50km north of Morondava, is an experiment in sustainable logging and forest management set up by the Centre de Formation Professionelle Forestière (CFPF). It's commonly known as the Swiss Forest because it's being managed and logged by the Corporation Suisse.

The idea involves selective logging in which only larger or older trees are felled. To minimise damage when the tree is subsequently dragged away, CFPF is experimenting with different methods. The forest is divided into a chequerboard with the squares of forest separated by clearways (rides) for the removal of cut trees. To reduce the width of these rides, the zebu carts used to transport the logs are being redesigned. To regenerate the forest in the long term, every tree felled is immediately replaced with saplings of the same species from the CFPF nursery in Morondava. Once the timber is sawn into lumber at the CFPF mill in Morondava, the leftover scraps are turned into charcoal.

Amid all this human activity, the Kirindy Reserve supports six species of – mainly nocturnal – lemurs, including the fat-tailed lemur. There are also 45 bird species and 32 species of reptile; among the latter are the rare Madagascar flat-tailed tortoise, which is found only in the forests around Morondava, the side-necked turtle *(Erymnochelys*

The Menabe Clan

The Menabe clan of the Sakalava tribe was founded in the Morondava region during the 14th century. During most of the 17th century, the Menabe were ruled by Andrianahifotsy, the White King, who moved the capital from Mahabo to Maneva (both east of present-day Morondava) and proceeded to conquer surrounding lands using firearms acquired from traders.

His ambition was to create a grand Sakalava kingdom which would take in all of Madagascar, but upon his death a quarrel between his two sons resulted in the splitting of Sakalava into the Menabe in the south and the Boina in the north. ∎

madagascariensis), Madagascar's only freshwater turtle, and plenty of chameleons to look out for. Other creatures include the giant jumping rat and several species of tenrec and mongoose.

Permits & Guides

Thankfully, the park has been recently opened to tourists and is now one of the best places in western Madagascar for flora and fauna. The entrance fee is FMg 20,000, payable at the campground. There are no official guides as such, but if you are genuinely interested, and speak French, some of the researchers at the reserve may provide some information about the park and its inhabitants. There are several paths with well-marked trees – a list is available at the park entrance identifying the trees.

Places to Stay & Eat

You can camp (FMg 5000 per site), or stay in some basic huts (FMg 6000). It is best to get permission from the CFPF office in Morondava before you take your tent out there. You may be able to get some simple meals at the campground, but it's always a good idea to bring your own food from Morondava.

Getting There & Away

Kirindy lies 50km north of Morondava along the route to Belo-sur-Tsiribihina; along the way you'll pass the magnificent Avenue du Baobab, the most photographed trees in the country. The reserve can be easily reached by using the taxi-brousse between Morondava and Belo-sur-Tsiribihina – ask your driver to let you off. From the road, it's a five km walk to the campground (where you get your permit).

You could do a day trip from Morondava quite easily, but most of the lemurs in the park are nocturnal so staying overnight is a good idea. The best time to visit is late in the year, around October and November.

MORONDAVA

* Telephone Area Code: 4

Morondava, in the heart of Sakalava territory, is known for the erotically sculpted tombs of the Menabe ancestors. It is a decaying town of interest mainly to those wishing to explore the parks, rivers and beaches in the region. Morondava also has one of the finest climates in Madagascar – 10 months of hot, dry sunny days, tempered by sea breezes.

In spite of its appeal to tourists and professional fisherfolk, the sea is rapidly eroding this sandy coastline. During the 19th century at least two nearby coastal villages were overtaken by the surf and the process continues. It's estimated that since 1900 several km have been shaved away. Stone breakwaters have had little effect and seaside neigh-bourhoods are often forced to relocate away from the advancing shoreline.

Information

The BTM Bank on Rue Lille, and the BFV Bank on the Place de L'Indépendence, will change money.

Avenue du Baobab

One of the most photographed and picturesque places in Madagascar is the avenue of

Adansonia grandidieri baobabs, about 15km north of Morondava. Try to be there at around sunset to watch the colours of the trees change and the long shadows move, or at dawn. Either time is magical for photos.

There are several ways to see the baobab: on foot – though it is not a great walk, especially around Morondava; by mountain bike – although currently there is nowhere to rent one (budding entrepreneurs take note!) and your muscles may not appreciate the sandy roads anyway; on a frequent taxi-brousse which goes through the avenue; by chartered taxi – expect to pay about FMg 20,000 return, plus waiting and photography time; or by motorcycle, which can be rented in Morondava.

Sakalava Tombs & Funerary Art
The Sakalava dead are both entombed and enshrined in *fasambezo* (cemeteries), in which the tombs are encircled by well-executed, and often erotic, funerary carvings representing life and fertility. Many take the

The carvings on Sakalava tombs usually depict scenes from the life of the deceased.

form of fanciful birds while others portray men and women with exaggerated sexual organs.

In cases where male and female figures are juxtaposed, the female is normally disproportionally large, perhaps in honour of the female role in the rebirth of the ancestors. Interspersed are carvings representing the life of the deceased.

Unfortunately, past visitors have included imbeciles who have desecrated the tombs and carvings for the sake of souvenir collection. As a consequence, these sacred sites were only open to outsiders if they were accompanied by a guide. Recent research, however, indicates that some tombs have been closed permanently, so ask around Morondava about the current situation. If open to tourists, the nearest tombs to Morondava lie at Mangily, Antalitoka and Ankirijibe – all out in the never-never northeast of town – and at Marovoay south of town.

Some travellers find the tombs fairly uninteresting, however, so you may not want to make the effort unless you have a special interest.

Organised Tours
The tour company Espace 4x4 (☎ (2) 262 97), based at the Hôtel Les Bougainvilliers, organises tours to Belo-sur-Mer and other sites of interest, and expensive deep sea fishing and diving trips.

Places to Stay
Thanks to a tourism boom a number of hotels have sprung up in recent years. Things still tend to fill up in July and August so reservations are recommended.

The old Morondava favourite, *Hôtel Les Bougainvilliers* (☎ 521 63), south of town, is not the value it once was. Bungalows cost FMg 62,000/88,000 for a single/double; for those on a budget, basic rooms are available for FMg 30,000. The beachside restaurant has good food, but the service could be improved.

The *Hôtel de la Plage* (☎ 521 30) is an amenable, basic place to crash for FMg 21,000 a single or double. Also south of town, not far from the beach, is the *Hôtel L'Oasis* (☎ 521 60), which charges FMg 34,000 for a bungalow. A good choice is the *Hôtel Menabe* (☎ 520 65), near the taxi-brousse station in the town centre. Its spacious upstairs rooms, complete with hot showers (which suffer from a lack of pressure on the upper floors) and air-con, cost FMg 28,500. Downstairs, there are budget rooms for just FMg 16,500. It's very popular with travellers.

Another possibility is the appealing *Hôtel Central* (☎ 523 78), where rooms with shower and toilet cost FMg 40,000. Guests are expected to adhere to Muslim dietary codes – no pork or alcohol are permitted in the building.

Places to Eat

Morondava's food scene is memorably heavy on the seafood and there are several outstanding restaurants. Those who enjoy eating may want to settle in for a while! This is one place where you can probably afford to buy lobster.

The *Chez Coco* or *Chez Cuccu*, attached to the Nosy Kely bungalows two km south of the town centre, is consistently recommended for excellent (but relatively pricey) meals. For a portion of fish that buries the plate you'll pay about FMg 13,000, more if you add vegetables and rice. Like other places in town it may close for the day at 2 pm, unless there is enough demand. *La Cantonaise* serves delicious Chinese food (as you would expect).

Farther north, right on the waterfront near the centre of town, is the recommended and more down to earth *Restaurant Le Renala*, which serves superb seafood as well as Malagasy specialities.

If you prefer a trendy taste of Europe, visit the praiseworthy *Carré d'As* at the Village Touristique south of town. The restaurants at *Les Bougainvilliers* and *Hôtel L'Oasis* are also recommended, but they may not be open at night. The only place which is reliably open all day and in the evening for a meal is

DAVID CURL

Moonrise over a Sakalava coastal village near Morondava, western Madagascar. Great seafood is one of the many reasons to visit; it's one place where you can probably afford to buy a lobster.

La Mozambique; it is in the town and very easy to find once you are there.

Entertainment

Morondava's position as a seaside holiday spot is taken seriously and the town supports two discos: *My Lord* and *Harry's*. The latter makes excellent 'punch coco' but unfortunately keeps a couple of captive lemurs. Unaccompanied women may want to bear in mind that both are favourite haunts for prostitutes. For snacks and a real beach-hut atmosphere try *La Mozambique* for an evening drink.

Getting There & Away

Air Air Mad flies several times a week from Tana to Morandava (US$94); and often from Morondava to Toliara (US$83), via Morombe (US$49). These flights have an annoying habit of showing up permanently full on the Air Mad computers in Tana. If you are going to fly one-way and return overland, fly to Morondava first from Tana.

Taxi-brousse The regular taxi-brousse between Antsirabe and Morondava, via Miandrivazo, takes at least 15 hours and costs FMg 35,000. Most days there is also some form of public transport going all the way to Tana for FMg 38,000; and three times a week a minibus or taxi-brousse goes to Fianarantsoa (FMg 70,000).

Every week, four taxis-brousse travel along the west coast from Morondava to Toliara, usually via Morombe – but be warned, this is another of Madagascar's torture trips. It takes at least two days (FMg 60,000), but there is some interesting landscape to admire along the way.

To break up the journey to Morondava, and to experience the exotic Tsiribihina River, it's a great idea to get off at Miandrivazo and take a pirogue down to Belo-sur-Tsiribihina. Refer to the relevant sections for details.

Boat Morondava is connected with villages south by short-haul cargo and fishing boats, which stop at each village along the way to deliver food and supplies. For the 40 hour trip to Morombe, which lies a day from Toliara by taxi-brousse, there are coastal cargo boats departing at least weekly. Facilities are very basic, so carry a supply of sunscreen and all the food and water you'll be needing.

Alternatively, charter a sailing pirogue along the coast between Morondava and Morombe, or even to Toliara (but this may be too far for the boat owners, and it would test your threshold of discomfort). From Morondava to Belo-sur-Mer, a chartered sailing pirogue holding two or three people will cost about FMg 150,000 and take one day; from Morondava to Morombe allow FMg 350,000 per boat and three days. However, strong winds may thwart your plans at any time. It is quicker and more comfortable to use the winds from the south and sail from Morombe to Morondava, but it is probably more difficult to organise a boat in Morombe.

Getting Around

You can rent motorcycles for FMg 70,000/120,000 for the half-day/full-day from next to the Jirama plant. This is a great way to visit the sites around Morondava.

BELO-SUR-MER

Belo-sur-Mer is a beautiful little village with a sandy breakwater which makes ships at sea seem like they are floating on sand.

The place to stay and eat is the *Campement Espace 4x4* which, despite the name, is actually a bungalow complex operated by the tour company Espace 4x4 in Morondava. It is superb, but mighty expensive at FMg 125,000 per bungalow in low season, including meals. It organises fishing and catamaran expeditions as well as windsurfing and snorkelling excursions. Catamaran transfers between Morondava and the campement will cost an additional bundle of Malagasy francs; prices vary considerably, depending on season, number of passengers and how long you intend to stay.

Getting to Belo-sur-Mer will involve waiting around for an irregular taxi-brousse to fill up, or talking your way onto any vehicle heading towards Morombe or Toliara. A better way is by boat (as mentioned earlier).

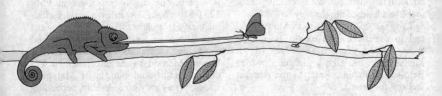

Facts about the Comoros

Early seafaring Arabs called these islands Djazaïr al Qamar (Islands of the Moon), which was massaged over the centuries into the modern name Les Comores in French and the Comoros in English. Once you've arrived it won't take long to discover the inspiration for the name. The moon hangs brilliantly behind the palm trees, turning crumbling and labyrinthine old Swahili towns and waterfronts into images conjured up by Scheherazade in the *Arabian Nights*. Conveniently, the moon also symbolises the Muslim faith which strictly governs life on the islands. The crescent moon and stars appear throughout the Comoros on seals, stamps, insignia and flags.

The Comoros, like Korea and Samoa, is in effect a single nation with two separate governments. The République Fédérale et Islamique des Comores (Federal Islamic Republic of the Comoros) consists of three islands – Grande Comore (also known as Ngazidja), Anjouan (or Ndzuani) and Mohéli (Mwali or Moili).

The fourth island in the group, Mayotte (or Maore), is a Collectivité Territoriale of France. This designation lies between a French Département d'Outre Mer (DOM – an overseas department, like Guyane, Martinique, Guadeloupe and Réunion) and a Territoire d'Outre Mer (TOM – overseas territory, such as French Polynesia, New Caledonia and Wallis & Futuna). This gives Mayotte the same status as St-Pierre et Miquelon off the Newfoundland coast. Mayotte is geographically, but not politically, a part of the Comoros.

The Comoros, while still heavily dependent on France, is hoping to claim Mayotte; the Mahorais (people of Mayotte) are struggling to strengthen their Comoran identity under French rule while exercising their rights as citizens of a European power. During France's referendum to ratify or reject the Maastricht Treaty in 1992, the Mahorais voted overwhelmingly in favour

---

COMOROS FACTS

Official Name: Federal Islamic Republic of the Comoros; Mayotte
Capital: Moroni (Comoros); Mamoudzou (Mayotte)
Head of State: President Mohammed Taki Abdul Karim (Comoros); French President Jacques Chirac (Mayotte)
Official Languages: Arabic, French (Comoros); French (Mayotte)
Official Religions: Islam (Comoros); Christianity and Islam (Mayotte)
Currency: Franc Comoran/CF (Comoros); Franc Français/FF (Mayotte)
Exchange Rate: approx. CF372 = US$1 (Comoros); approx. FF4.96 = US$1 (Mayotte)
Area: 2230 sq km (Comoros); 375 sq km (Mayotte)
Population: 550,000 (Comoros); 88,000 (Mayotte)
Population Growth Rate: 3.56% pa (Comoros); 3.8% pa (Mayotte)
Time: GMT/UTC +3 (Comoros & Mayotte)
Per Capita GNP: US$510 (Comoros); US$600 (Mayotte)
Inflation: 15% pa (Comoros); n/a (Mayotte)

---

of European unity and the opportunities it would afford them.

There is a saying in the Comoros: 'Mohéli sleeps, Anjouan works, Mayotte plays and Grande Comore complains'. While each island has its own distinct character (and Grande Comore isn't that bad!), all offer a variety of appealing opportunities for visitors, ranging from lovely mountain walks and crater lakes to white sand (as well as black lava) beaches where marine turtles lay their eggs, and maze-like villages and markets reminiscent of Zanzibar. Superimposed on all this is the mysterious appeal of the Swahili culture, derived from the Arab, Persian, African and Portuguese seafarers and traders who plied these coasts five to 10 centuries ago.

HISTORY

For an overview of the pre-colonial history of the Comoros, including Mayotte, refer to the general Facts about the Region chapter at the beginning of the book.

The French Takeover

Over the centuries the island of Anjouan had been the domain of two sultanates, one based at Mutsamudu and one at Domoni. Occasionally one sultan conquered the other's realm and united the island under a single regime. In 1782 Sultan Abdallah of Mutsamudu did just that and took the name of Abdallah I. In order to maintain power Abdallah sought aid and protection from the British, who provided arms and enough money to build the citadel at Mutsamudu. Once, while Abdallah was away travelling, a challenger took the opportunity to seize the throne and took the name Allaoui I. Later, the

throne was passed peacefully to his son, who took the name of Allaoui II, but he was forcibly dethroned by Salim, a new Sultan of Domoni.

During the mid-19th century the French were scrambling for African colonies. In April 1841 the Sultan of Mayotte, Tsy Lavalou Andriansouli, who had been rather ruthless in coming to power and had quite a few enemies, formed an accord ceding the island to the French in exchange for protection from his rivals, an annual rent of FF5000 and a French education for his sons.

Mayotte had traditionally been considered a dependency of Anjouan, but Salim, the new sultan, didn't protest because France had officially recognised his jurisdiction over the entire island of Anjouan. The official transfer of Mayotte took place in May 1843 and the island was transformed from a sultanate into a haven for French planters and slaveholders who established sugar cane estates. Sultan

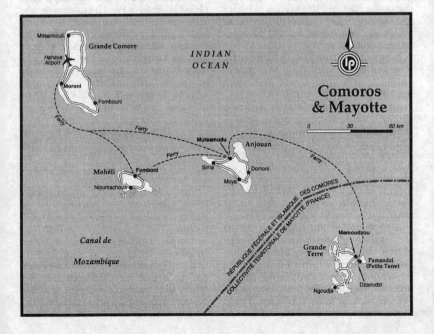

Andriansouli died on the islet of Dzaoudzi in 1846.

Meanwhile the former Sultan of Anjouan, Allaoui II, pleaded with the British for help in securing the throne for his sons, Saïd Hamza and Aboudou. The British refused to interfere so the boys went to the French island of Réunion to petition for French intervention in the matter – again without success. To stir things up, Salim invited the British to set up a trading house on the island. When the boys returned to Anjouan, the British, to demonstrate gratitude to Salim, refused to allow them to land and confiscated the French boat on which they were travelling. France sent a warship to recover its property. The British also sent a ship and tensions ran high. In 1848 Abdallah III, the son of Salim, took over the throne of Anjouan.

Abdallah III met with problems when the British became upset about his continued holding of slaves. When he agreed to halt the practice landholders revolted. In April 1886 the ageing Abdallah III travelled to France and signed a treaty that ceded Anjouan to France as a protectorate. In 1912 the island became a full colony.

In 1830 the Malagasy prince Ramanetaka, who had been exiled from Madagascar, arrived in Mohéli and staged a coup which left him sultan of the island. He was succeeded by his young daughter, Djoumbé Fatima I, whose Malagasy mother acted as regent until she came of ruling age. In 1852 Fatima married Saïd Mohammed, an exiled Zanzibarian prince, but thanks to an affair with a French trader, Joseph François Lambert, much of Mohéli was passed into French hands. With his British partner, Sunley, Lambert set up plantations on the island and became its primary landowner.

After the affair had cooled off Fatima abdicated the throne in favour of her 10-year-old son, Mohammed. The island of Zanzibar, sensing a vulnerable period, seized the opportunity to peacefully bring Mohéli under its protection. The following year the French were able to encourage Sultan Mohammed to proclaim independence and

on 26 April 1886, Sultan Marjani signed the treaty that turned Mohéli into a French protectorate. Shortly thereafter, French planter and slave-owner Léon Humblot purchased the bulk of Mohéli from Lambert's partner, Sunley, who had inherited the land from Lambert after his death in 1873.

On Grande Comore in 1861, Msafumu, Sultan of Itsandra, ascended to the throne. In a war over succession in the sultanate of M'bude, a one-time friend, Ahmed, Sultan of Bambao, took his revenge, and passed the sultanate of Itsandra to his brother-in-law and M'bude to his mother. In 1880 Msafumu, then *tibé* (Grand Sultan) of Grande Comore, was challenged by the younger brother of the new sultan on Anjouan, Saïd Ali, who had formed a coalition with a number of other sultans as well as the French (apparently eager to get a foot in the door). They succeeded in ousting Msafumu and eventually installed Saïd Ali as tibé.

In January Saïd Ali signed a treaty making Grande Comore a French protectorate, and in November 1885 was somehow coerced into signing a commercial treaty with Humblot, allowing Humblot to dispose of land on Grande Comore in any way he wished. After just a few years, half the island was in the hands of French planters. Outraged by the devious French, Hachim, Sultan of Badjini, led an insurrection that was put down only after repeated displays of French military strength. In January 1890 the ambitious Humblot, and another civilian insurrection, sent Saïd Ali packing to the island of Mohéli. In 1908 Grande Comore was formally annexed by France.

The Comoros were important strategically to the French as a counterweight to the British colony and base in Zanzibar. Mohéli became a French protectorate in 1886 after its capital, Fomboni, had been bombarded periodically by French warships. In 1912 Grande Comore and Anjouan capitulated. All the islands were declared a French colony and later placed under the control of the federal government in Madagascar. They were to remain as such for almost 50 years.

French Rule & the Road to Independence

Despite numerous peasant revolts, the French maintained their grip on the islands for nearly a century. Political organisations and newspapers were banned, revolts were suppressed with unrestrained military efficiency, and no-one was permitted to enter or leave the islands without permission from the colonial authorities. In the early days the colony was administered from Madagascar, but in 1947 it became a separate territory and in 1948 the Comoros voted to remain within the French community. In 1961, after the independence of Madagascar, the Comoros was granted a form of internal autonomy, although French rule continued.

Seven years later, a strike by local students (influenced no doubt by the Paris riots) led to mass demonstrations. The French Foreign Legion and paratroopers were called in to quell the unrest, but the French allowed the formation of political parties. Numerous parties sprang up representing various factional interests, ranging across the political spectrum from those demanding immediate and unconditional independence to those who vigorously supported French rule.

Over the next few years tensions grew steadily between the various political parties, and in an attempt to avoid violence the French held a referendum in 1974. Overall, 94% of the population favoured independence, with Grande Comore, Mohéli and Anjouan voting an overwhelming 'yes'. However, 64% of Mahorais were against it. Less than a year later, Ahmed Abdallah Abderemane announced a unilateral declaration of independence, while Mayotte's deputies cabled France requesting French intervention on their behalf. Just two weeks later, the Federal Islamic Republic of the Comoros, without Mayotte, was admitted to both the United Nations and the Organisation of African Unity (OAU).

In December 1975 France recognised the new government, then withdrew its US$18 million subsidy and 500 technicians. The French then stood back and waited for the fireworks, which began almost immediately.

Even before the French economic withdrawal, the islands were barely ticking over on a subsistence economy and a threadbare administration. There were few auspicious signs to encourage optimism, but the real crunch came in January 1976 when Abdallah was overthrown by mercenaries in a coup engineered by one Ali Solih.

A Rough Start

When he first came to power, Solih, an atheist despite his Islamic background, appeared to be a relatively normal leader – if a bit power-hungry. Solih zealously set out to drag the islands kicking and screaming into the 20th century and away from the old colonial attitudes. He imposed a form of Maoist-Marxist socialism and set about destroying the past. French citizens were expelled and their property nationalised, feudal institutions were attacked, women were unveiled, traditionally elaborate and costly marriage and funeral arrangements were abolished, and the privileges of ancestry based on dubious claims of direct descent from the Prophet Mohammed were likewise attacked.

The biggest problem was Solih's intolerance to opposition. He used a rabble of illiterate youths bearing the euphemistic title of Jeunesse Revolutionnaire (Revolutionary Youth) to enforce his edicts. He dismissed the 3500 members of the civil service and turned it over to the youth brigade who destroyed all public records. Anyone with the intelligence or courage to speak out against his excesses was immediately imprisoned. Needless to say, the economy went into a nosedive and so did the government's popularity.

Petty criminals and anyone who could be labelled (correctly or incorrectly) as counter-revolutionary were dressed in sacking, had their heads shaved and were beaten through the narrow streets accompanied by megaphone announcements detailing their alleged crimes. No-one, including children and elderly people, was immune from the brutality. Any ideology which Solih might once have held turned into little more than the power of the weapons brandished by his teenage thugs.

Solih quickly turned into the embodiment of the adage: 'Absolute power corrupts absolutely'. He had himself declared a prophet and was heard to tell his people at a rally: 'I am your god and teacher. I am the divine way, the torch that lights the dark. There is no god but Ali Solih'. He was clearly bonkers; towards the end he refused to leave his palace for lengthy periods, during which he went on whisky-drinking binges and watched films in the company of young girls drawn from the Revolutionary Youth.

Meanwhile on Mayotte, the French took advantage of the turmoil in the Comoros and on 8 February 1976 held another referendum on the question of independence – a whopping 99% of the population voted to stay with France. *Restez Français pour Rester Libre* (Stay French to Stay Free) remains a slogan on the island.

In 1977 there were other problems, including an eruption of Mt Karthala on Grande Comore. More serious, however, was the evacuation of 16,000 Comoran refugees from Mahajanga, Madagascar, where more than 1000 people had been killed during race riots. These hapless people, known as 'Sabenas' because they were airlifted out of Madagascar by the Belgian airline Sabena, seemed to be jumping from the frying pan into the fire.

Fall of Solih

Back in Moroni the situation was becoming unbearable. Although the Comoran people took it all with remarkable restraint, something had to give. Relief came in the form of 29 French mercenaries led by a Frenchman, Bob Dénard (who had also been involved in coups in Nigeria, Angola, Yemen and Zaire, to name just a few). Dénard had been recruited by Ahmed Abdallah, the former president, and Mohammed Ahmed, a wealthy Comoran businessman, both of whom were living in exile in Paris.

The mercenaries arrived on Grande Comore at dawn on 13 May 1978 while most of the 2000-strong army were in Anjouan.

Within a few hours, Solih's reign was over. The army surrendered and people took to the streets to celebrate. Abdallah returned to the island two weeks later to a rousing welcome and Ali Solih was shot to death by the mercenaries for allegedly 'trying to escape'. His body was dumped in his mother's garden on the slopes of Mt Karthala.

The OAU reacted with outrage, and refused to accept the new Comoran delegation to its summit conference that year. But that was the least of the Comoros' problems: although Solih had been in power for only 33 months, the country was in a shambles. Dénard's mercenaries saw to the running of the key ministries, such as defence and communications, and began to get the country back on the rails. The economy was denationalised, relations with France were re-established, French aid was resumed and children returned to school. A new constitution envisaged the eventual return of Mayotte to the fold.

Dénard hung up his gun, took a Comoran wife and settled down to what he thought would be his permanent home. But his plan didn't last long. Although Abdallah had agreed to allow him to remain in the Comoros, Dénard's presence was blocking the recognition of the new government by mainland African states. In the end, Dénard was persuaded to leave, although many of his fellow mercenaries remained, a factor which did not go unnoticed in places like Madagascar, the Seychelles and Tanzania. Eventually, Abdallah discreetly permitted Dénard to return to the Comoros.

Assassination of Abdallah

In an attempt to silence opposition, Abdallah declared a one-party state. In 1985 a coup attempt was uncovered in the early stages of planning when the Australian Federal Police caught three men trying to recruit mercenaries on behalf of Saïd Ali Kemal, a former Comoran diplomat. Later that year, a coup attempt by 20 of Abdallah's 700 presidential guards was also nipped in the bud.

In March 1985, 128 countries at the United Nations General Assembly supported the Comoros' claim to Mayotte. Only France voted against the motion. During the same month, while Abdallah was visiting France, another coup attempt by presidential guards failed. Later that year 67 people, mostly members of the banned opposition movement Front Démocratique (FD), were imprisoned, though many were granted amnesty over the following two years.

In March 1987 Abdallah held elections for the country's ruling Federal Assembly, with opposition candidates permitted to stand in only a handful of seats. Abdallah was re-elected, but allegations of fraud and intimidation tactics by the government resulted in numerous arrests of opposition leaders and members of parties opposed to Abdallah.

In November of that year, again while Abdallah was visiting France, 14 former officers of the presidential guard, aided by local troops, staged another coup attempt. Three of the rebels were killed in an attack on the main barracks and some civilians perished in the crossfire, but the mercenary-backed defences held the fort.

In 1989 Abdallah's rule came to an end when he was assassinated by his presidential guard. Dénard, suspected of complicity in the assassination, was deported for the second time in December 1989 along with the entire mercenary guard.

After two rounds of voting, on 4 and 11 March 1990, Saïd Mohamed Djohar was declared winner of the Comoros' first free presidential elections since Independence in 1975 and was installed as the new president.

Djohar, previously unknown outside the Comoros, pledged to abolish Abdallah's one-party state, announce a general amnesty for political prisoners and hold a constitutional conference to which all opposition parties would be invited.

For a while it looked as though things would improve, but Djohar failed to gain the confidence of the body politic and, in the worsening economic climate, opposition leaders began to jockey for his position. On 3 August 1990, an attempted coup was staged by Ibrahim Ahmed Halidi, who

briefly declared himself president. Within two days the coup was declared illegal; Djohar was reinstated and immediately appointed a new cabinet of ministers. Unrest and dissatisfaction continued, however, and in early 1992 he announced dissolution of the administration and scheduled a referendum.

In that referendum, 74% of the electorate voted for a new constitution which stipulated a five year presidential term and a four year term for cabinet ministers. The post of prime minister would be held by a member of the majority party in the assembly. Djohar infuriated many of the country's 24 political parties by imposing restrictive conditions for the participation of the next elections, which the majority of parties announced they would boycott. Order quickly broke down and on 26 September a group of soldiers backed by two sons of assassinated president Abdallah, and a character known as Captain Combo, a close friend of Dénard, took over the airport and radio station.

The rebels gave themselves up the following day, but the situation continued to decline. Between 13 and 21 October, fighting between rebel soldiers and forces loyal to President Djohar resulted in 22 deaths and over 100 other casualties in Moroni, northern Grande Comore and Anjouan.

When the elections were eventually held the Comoros' 245,000 voters chose from a field of 320 candidates representing 21 parties. The poll predictably suffered disruption by rioting and boycotts from the opposition. In Moroni and Mbéni, youths set fire to ballot boxes and wrecked polling stations. Djohar was re-elected, with the main opposition party, led by Mohammed Taki Abdul Karim, close behind.

The Return of Dénard

Not to be deterred, the ageing Dénard returned in late September 1995 for another try. With the aim of releasing Combo, captured during the 1992 coup, and displacing the unpopular President Djohar, Dénard sailed to Grande Comore with a motley bunch of 29 French, and one Belgian, mercenaries.

Prime Minister Mohammed Caabi El Yachroutu knew where to run: directly to the French Embassy. Djohar was captured, and Saïd Ali Kemal and Taki Abdul Karim were declared joint presidents by Combo, who became head of the Transitional Military Command. Djohar was soon released and sent to Réunion for 'medical reasons' (though he claimed he wasn't that unwell). Interestingly, the French kept Djohar there after the coup was crushed.

After some dallying, 600 heavily armed French commandoes (with some reported South African assistance) flew to Grande Comore, and about 40 arrived on inflatable rafts. The commandoes immediately overcame some limited resistance, leaving a few dead, and then surrounded the mercenaries who were at the President's Palace. A week after arrival, the mercenaries surrendered. Dénard and his men were expelled and sent back on a chartered flight to Paris.

Security officials in France almost certainly knew of Dénard's intentions and, according to some reliable reports, he must have had the tacit approval of some French authorities. The fact that Dénard was able to plan the coup, leave France, and sail unhindered for 43 days to the Comoros created severe backlashes within security and political circles in France. And Dénard was able to do all this while on probation in France for his involvement in the 1989 coup in the Comoros, the assassination of Abdallah and a coup in Benin in 1977.

There was yet another aborted coup in December 1995 – this time without the involvement of Dénard. But don't be surprised if he turns up again: recent reliable media reports indicate that Dénard has again had meetings with mercenaries and arms dealers. Ironically, Dénard's Comoran-born son still lives in Moroni and runs, of all things, a 'security company'.

In the most recent elections, held in December 1996, Mohammed Taki Abdul Karim was elected president. He choose an 11-member cabinet under Prime Minister Ahmed Abdou, the 60-year-old former finance minister.

GEOGRAPHY

The Comoros lies at the northern entrance to the Mozambique Channel nearly 500km north-west of the northern tip of Madagascar, and about the same distance from the Mozambique coast. The four islands are the summits of a volcanic ridge which rises from the channel.

The archipelago stretches over 300km from north to south; Moroni on Grande Comore lies 248km from Dzaoudzi, Mayotte, 136km from Mutsamudu on Anjouan and 85km from Fomboni on Mohéli. The islands have a combined land area of 2605 sq km and a coastline of 525km; the largest island is Grande Comore, followed by Anjouan, Mayotte and Mohéli.

All the islands are predominantly mountainous without any sizeable areas of level land. Anjouan is the most rugged and precipitous of the islands; Mohéli has been the least disturbed by humans.

GEOLOGY

The volcanoes which formed the Comoros islands began to emerge from the sea about 15 million years ago, well after the break-up of the ancient continent of Gondwanaland (when Madagascar split from mainland Africa). But the islands didn't appear simultaneously: Mayotte, which is now characterised by relatively low, rounded hills, was the first to emerge, followed by Anjouan, Mohéli and, finally, Grande Comore. The last of these features the only active volcano – and the country's highest point – 2361m Mt Karthala.

Mayotte, the oldest island, is the only one with an encircling coral reef. Anjouan and Mohéli have only fringe reefs, and the youngest, Grande Comore, still hasn't developed an extensive reef system (though diving is a main attraction for visitors to Grande Comore).

The porous rocks of the Comoros hold vast quantities of rain. A well, or *foumbou*, can be easily dug around the lower-lying coastal areas (but not in the middle of the islands, which is volcanic) to obtain vital water. This is particularly important on Grande Comore, which is more arid than the other islands.

CLIMATE

As with most tropical places, the Comoros experiences only two seasons. The hot, wet and extremely humid period falls between November and April, and the rest of the year may be described as *fraîche* (cool). This is certainly the best time to visit.

Temperatures and rainfall vary only slightly from island to island. The average year-round coastal temperature is 25°C and it rarely varies more than 4°C higher or lower. The greatest temperature variations are found on Grande Comore and Anjouan, the islands with the highest relief. In the highlands mean temperatures are as low as 22°C.

During the hot and wet season the monsoon winds, called the *kashkazi*, blow from the north-west. In the cool, drier season the islands are swept by the trade winds from the south-east, known as the *koussi*. The Comoran 'winter' occurs between these two seasons, in April and May, and is known as *nyombéni*.

The Comoros lies wholly within the cyclone belt and every three to four years, between November and April, the islands receive a severe blow. Anjouan and Mohéli were badly hit in December 1980; in January 1983 Cyclone Elinah caused havoc on Mohéli; and in April 1984 Cyclone Kamisy ravaged Mayotte, leaving 20,000 homeless and destroying 80% of the crops. Early in January 1987 another cyclone devastated villages and crops on Mayotte.

ECOLOGY & ENVIRONMENT

Because of the volcanic nature of the islands there is plenty of arable land in the Comoros. About one-third of this is used for the principal cash crop, ylang-ylang; more is needed to grow coffee, cloves and vanilla, and villagers need still more land to grow rice and breed livestock. Deforestation, caused by slash-and-burn farming and burning (for firewood, building materials and grazing crops) has resulted in severe soil erosion, especially on overpopulated Anjouan. Only about 15% of the islands retain pristine tropical forest, most of it growing around Mt Karthala and on Mohéli.

Although deforestation continues, the islands' small population and limited development ensures that most of the hills and some of the remaining forests, especially on Mohéli, will remain relatively untouched. On Grande Comore it is more often that the forces of nature – primarily the mighty Karthala volcano – make the greatest impact on the local ecology. On Mayotte tourism and development have resulted in pollution, deforestation and urban sprawl.

FLORA & FAUNA

For details about the flora and fauna of the Comoros, including Mayotte, refer to the special wildlife section in the Facts about the Region chapter earlier in this book.

National Parks

Until very recently, the only national park in the Comoros was a marine reserve established for the protection of sea turtles and other marine life around the islets south of Mohéli. Very few resources have been allocated to the protection of the turtles, but some have been saved because of an education campaign among local villagers. You can visit the islets, and hopefully see some

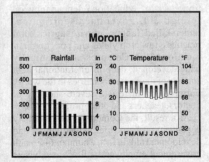

Moroni

turtles, by boat from the village of Niou-machoua.

In 1992 persistent lobbying by the diving school at Le Galawa Beach Hotel, on the coast of northern Grande Comore, resulted in the declaration of a new marine reserve, just offshore of the hotel. With the aid of the JBL Smith Institute in South Africa, a marine education program has been established for the Comoran public. It shows videos and provides courses in conservation and environmental awareness in local schools. (See also the Activities section in the Comoros Facts for the Visitor chapter.)

A permit is needed for the marine reserve near Mohéli and is available in the capital, Fomboni; the reserve off the coast of Grande Comore is only accessible through organised diving trips from Le Galawa Beach Hotel. The government agency in charge of national parks for the three islands of the Comoros is the Ministère du Développement Rural et de L'Environnement, based in Moroni (☎ 74 46 30). On Mayotte the relevant department is the Direction de l'Agriculture et de la Fôret (☎ 61 12 13).

GOVERNMENT & POLITICS
The three northern islands of the Comoros, Grande Comore, Anjouan and Mohéli, comprise the République Fédérale et Islamique des Comores. Known as the RFI des Comores, it is an officially theocratic state with government policy generally following Koranic direction.

The Comoran government continues to claim Mayotte as part of a four island nation. In fact, the four stars on the Comoran flag represent each island, including Mayotte. France, however, and most people on Mayotte, strongly reject these claims – though a minor nationalist movement among some Mahorais seeks unification.

In theory, the president of the Comoros is elected by the people, while legislative power rests in the hands of the 42-member Federal Assembly. The president appoints an 11-member cabinet, as well as a prime minister, who rarely gets time to warm his seat: 15 different PMs were appointed by Presi-

dent Djohar in the space of a few years. Each island has a governor who is appointed by the president as head of that island's council. Normal political processes are regularly interrupted, however: there have been 17 coups or attempted coups since Independence in 1975.

The ruling coalition, dominated by the Rally for Democracy and Decentralization (RDR) party, won 36 seats in the 1996 election, mainly because the opposition coalition, dominated by the Comoran Union for Progress (UDZIMA) party, boycotted the elections. This boycott paved the way for several independent candidates to win seats. Also, for the first time, the fundamentalist Islamic Party, led by Ahmed Abdullah Mohammed (the self-proclaimed 'Ayatollah') from Anjouan, won three seats, and claimed to be the main opposition party.

Mayotte, a Collectivité Territoriale of France, is under the jurisdiction of the Ministère d'Outre-Mer in France. The head of government is a *préfet*; the chief of state is the French president. Twelve of the 19 seats of the General Council are held by the ruling Mahoran Popular Movement (MPM). Given the volatility of the islands, it is not surprising that Mayotte is heavily guarded by a detachment of troops of the French Foreign Legion.

ECONOMY
Unfortunately, the news about the Comoran economy (but to a much lesser extent the economy on Mayotte) is not good. Thanks to a dearth of natural resources, overpopulation, lack of education, dependency on foreign aid, government corruption, underskilled labour, unwise agricultural practices, low crop yields and poor communications, the Comoros is chronically underdeveloped, deep in international debt and one of the poorest countries in the world. Furthermore, there is a severe shortage of doctors, teachers and other professionals.

As a result, the Comoros remains largely dependent on France for skilled labour and development aid. In fact, a number of French government employees still act as advisers in several Comoran governmental departments. The Comoros is overwhelmingly dependent on two countries for its exports – France (41% of all exports) and the USA (53%). Over half of the Comoros' imports (mostly subsistence food staples, but also building materials and transportation equipment) come from France.

France runs the Mayotte government, and local French expats control most of the economy. The dependency on France for exports and imports is very high.

Foreign aid is a huge component of the economy of the Comoros (minus Mayotte) and comprises 40% of the Gross Domestic Product (GDP). Aid mainly comes from France, and oil and building materials (mainly for mosques) are provided by fellow Islamic countries. Support from former communist allies has completely dried up.

Agriculture & Fishing

Agriculture comprises the primary economic sector of the Comoros (minus Mayotte): it employs 80% of the population and makes up 40% of the GDP. Much of the land, however, has been severely degraded and yields are becoming increasingly low. The Comoros and Mayotte must still import almost 50% of their food, including rice, to meet demand (up from 40% about four years ago). Food makes up a staggering 90% of all imports for all four islands.

The Comoros and Mayotte supplies 80% of the world's ylang-ylang, a crop which occupies a third of the arable land. The

industry has suffered from dramatic drops in prices (reduced by 42% in 1995), climatic anomalies, increasing distillation costs and competition from a cheaper Indonesian substitute known as *canaga*. Other vital exports are cloves and vanilla. The Comoros and Mayotte are the world's second largest exporter of vanilla (the first is Madagascar), but prices have also drastically decreased (by 21% in 1995). Crops grown primarily for domestic consumption include rice, maize, manioc, sweet potatoes, bananas and citrus fruits.

In coastal villages, most male villagers own *galawas* (outrigger canoes) and fishing plays a major role in the subsistence economy. The European Community (EC) has realised that Comoran waters are rich in tuna and has negotiated fishing rights for 40 French and Spanish tuna boats in exchange for development aid. As a result, the government is now concentrating on improving the public health system, food production, housing, water and energy supplies, as well as tourism.

Tourism

Only about 8000 visitors arrive in the Comoros (excluding Mayotte) each year, and of these, fewer than 2500 are actually tourists – an extremely low number compared with nearby islands such as the Seychelles and Mauritius. The 'busiest' seasons are December to January and July to September, and the greatest number of visitors are French and South African.

The Comoros is desperately trying to improve and market its tourism appeal with more hotels, which it is hoped will attract package groups from South Africa, Italy and France. Tourism authorities are also developing diving as a major attraction, on top of the usual 'tropical paradise' drawcard. The main drawbacks are lack of regular flights from Europe and mainland Africa, the poor range of hotels of any standard, and the high cost of travel because of the overvalued Comoran franc, which is linked to the French franc. (The Comoros is three times more expensive for travellers than Madagascar, next door.)

On Mayotte, tourism is an important and well-developed industry that brings vital currency to the local economy. However, all of the hotels, and just about every restaurant, diving centre and other tourist-oriented company, is owned by a French resident. Very little of the benefits of foreign tourism reaches the indigenous Mahorais.

POPULATION & PEOPLE

Most Comorans are descended from slaves from the African mainland who mixed with various groups of people passing through the region: Malay-Polynesians (including Malagasy), Arabs (mainly traders from Yemen and Oman) and Shirazi Persians who resettled in the islands from Tanzania. Other ethnic minorities include the Antalote, Sakalava, Oimatsahe and Cafre; and on Mayotte, there is a substantial French community. The words Comoran and Mahorais are used to describe the people, as well as the food, language and so on, of the Comoros and Mayotte, respectively.

Recently, the population of the islands has exploded, increasing by more than 150,000 in the past 15 years to 638,000 (including Mayotte's 88,000). By 2001 the population is expected to pass the million mark. Nearly half of all Comorans are under the age of 14; the increase is clearly caused by a rocketing birth rate rather than immigration (which is officially listed as 'zero'). Grande Comore is the most populated island, followed by Anjouan (the most densely populated), Mayotte and Mohéli.

It would be inappropriate to trot out the cliche 'warm and friendly' to describe the people of the Comoros and Mayotte. They're certainly a polite, honest, charming and hospitable people, but, by western definitions, their demeanour is not open and welcoming; they rarely smile or convey any great sense of excitement by western standards.

In Moroni and other large towns where a white face is a common sight there seems to be little curiosity about outsiders and most

people tend to keep a polite distance; several generations of French occupation has left them accustomed to foreigners. However, on Mohéli, and in remote areas of other islands, visitors are liable to be stared at, pointed out, discussed, followed and besieged with questions at every turn! Light-skinned visitors will undoubtedly be haunted by the word *mzungu* (European), which will seem to reside permanently on every lip.

EDUCATION

The Comoros government is perpetually broke, and unfortunately education is often seen as an easy place to cut costs. At the time of research, teachers, especially on Mohéli, had not been paid for almost a year – but they continued to teach. In Moroni strikes were being held by teachers, who threatened to stop teaching until they were paid.

Literacy rates on the Comoros (excluding Mayotte) are 56% for males and 40% for females. This is very poor by international standards and rated in the bottom 15% of the world's countries. Rarely does any child go past primary school, and schools are not equipped to do more than teach basic health and rudimentary reading and writing skills.

On Mayotte there is a diversity between the accessibility and levels of education between French residents and indigenous Mahorais. Some French send their children to France or Réunion, or to local private schools run by teachers from France. The Mahorais have to rely on the public education system, which is not nearly as good as the private system used by many French, though certainly far better than what is available in the rest of the Comoros.

ARTS

For in-depth information and displays on the arts and culture of the Comoros and Mayotte, visit the Centre National de Recherche Scientifique (CNDRS) museum and library, and the Alliance Franco-Comorienne (AFC), both in Moroni. The Centre Mahorais d'Animation Culturelle (CMAC), which has offices in Dzaoudzi and Mamoudzou, both on Mayotte, is also worth contacting. The CMAC and AFC regularly screen films and host art exhibitions, theatre productions and music performances, as well as run their own cultural shows and displays. The CMAC centre in Mamoudzou also has a library.

Dance

Comorans, it seems, love dancing more than anything else. This is especially so on Mayotte, where the community of Kaouéni, close to Mamoudzou, claims to be the source of the best dances and dancers.

Dancing forms an integral part of every Muslim festival and there are innumerable variations. One of the most popular is the *mougodro*, a circular dance with African and Malagasy origins in which men, women and children all participate. Other popular dances include the *m'biou* (bamboo dance), which is performed by women; *tam tam*, which uses drums; and *danse de mouchoirs* (handkerchief dance). Others include *garasisse*, *biyaya*, *shenge* and *mdandra*.

On Mayotte the most popular dance is the *wadaha* (or *danse de pilon)* in which women and young girls dance in a circle around a mortar filled with rice, to the rhythm of drums, guitars and popular songs, simulating the pulverisation of the rice with pestles. It also serves as a prenuptial dance. Performers sing and dance without ceasing for two nights and days in preparation for the fasting

month of Ramadan, and also stage street pageants and pantomimes which mock the French colonials. You may see similar dances on Nosy Be, off the western coast of Madagascar, where there is a Comoran community.

Music

Most of the music that is considered Comoran has been derived from a blend of reggae and African rhythms. It's mostly good and quite danceable, with driving, repetitious rhythms and lyrics. In general, the Comorans have stuck with traditional instruments, including drums of varying sizes, ukelele-like guitars and a variety of native percussion instruments. Some Comoran groups and singers are gaining international recognition, mainly in French-speaking Europe, such as Nguaya and Salim Ali Amir.

On Mayotte groups have adopted more western ways and produce their music and rhythms with synthesisers, modern wind instruments and electric guitars. Musicians have a fair shot at international recognition through the French market, which has long appreciated and promoted music from many of its former African colonies. Groups to look out for include Kilimanjaro International, Timmy's, Joestar and New Galaxy.

Cassettes and compact discs (CDs) of traditional music are available in Mayotte and at the CNDRS museum in Moroni. Modern Comoran and Mahorais music can be purchased in Mayotte and in Moroni at several shops near the Restaurant Almadad, as well as a few CD shops around the old market.

Crafts

Comoran artisans produce superb work in the form of wood inlay boxes, Koran holders, wooden furniture and carved doors and shutters, as well as excellent traditional silver wedding jewellery.

Beautifully embroidered festive clothing is also a speciality. For everyday use, there are baskets and hats made from raffia palm leaves; raffia dolls are made in Mutsamudu and Domoni, both on Anjouan. Also on Anjouan is a factory which is believed to be the world's only producer of furniture from coconut wood. See under Things to Buy in the Comoros Facts for the Visitor chapter for further information.

Literature

Most of the literature of the Comoros derives from oral tradition which has been passed down through the generations in the form of *hali* (folk tales). These are similar to fables and normally end with a moral. But this oral tradition isn't restricted to stories, and also includes poetry, hymns, proverbs, songs and riddles.

The first literature in the Comoros was the work of princes, sultans and others of the aristocracy. It was originally laid down in the Arabic language, or in Swahili with the Arabic script. Most of it recorded genealogies and memoirs; chronicled historical events such as battles and the lives of the sultans; or comprised apocryphal tales such as the acts of the *djinn* (evil genie), or the relationship between King Solomon and the Queen of Sheba.

In the book *Mémoires*, Saïd Hamza, son of Sultan Allaoui II of Anjouan, traces the history of that island and its warring sultans between the late 18th and early 19th centuries. One of the most comprehensive historical works on Grand Comore is *Histoire et Sociologie de Ngazidja* by Saïd Husseun, son of the last sultan of Grande Comore. It begins with the legends of the djinn who many Comorans still believe were the islands' first inhabitants.

Architecture

Most of the architecture in the Comoros (but not Mayotte) is of Swahili origin. Towns are laid out haphazardly, in the manner of Zanzibar in Tanzania or Lamu in Kenya, and feature maze-like narrow streets and two-storey buildings with lots of arcades, intricate balustrades fringing porches and roofs, and meticulously carved, wooden lattice-work doors and shutters. These beautiful touches lend an intensely exotic air to the general atmosphere and for most visitors are one of the highlights of the Comoros.

Although most dwellings in the islands are constructed of coral or wood, mud and thatch, public structures and finer homes, most of which were originally white, are constructed primarily of a cement produced from crushed coral, sand and shells.

In many villages and towns you'll notice what appear to be half-built or half-destroyed homes. Most are *maisons des filles*, homes which families begin building as soon as a daughter is born. This home is presented to the daughter upon her marriage and she is permitted to keep it if her husband dies, leaves or renounces her. Therefore, the man who has several wives also has several homes to live in, but none to call his own.

Mayotte is naturally more influenced by France, and has wide streets, parks, causeways and European-style homes. The exception are the Mahorais *banga* homes (see under Society & Conduct).

SOCIETY & CONDUCT
Traditional Marriage

Marriage customs vary from island to island. Polygamy is still practised, mainly by the wealthy, and nearly 20% of Comoran (but not Mahorais) men have multiple wives. One unique tradition is the *grand mariage*, which is still practised occasionally, especially on Grande Comore. These immense, overblown weddings and feasts are always considered a major event in Comoran village or town life. The most elaborate sometimes require three years of careful and expensive planning and organisation.

Ali Solih and his juvenile delinquents (see under History) tried to do away with the traditional Comoran grand mariage, but the practice hasn't entirely disappeared. However, it's not nearly as popular as it was in the past because few can now afford to foot the bill.

In most cases it is an arranged affair, usually between an older, wealthy man and a young bride, who is often selected when she is still just a child. Not only must the man pay for the elaborate two to nine day public festivities (known as *toirab*), catering for the entire village, he must also present his fiancee with a dowry of precious clothing, gold and jewellery, which she is entitled to keep in the event of a divorce.

A grand mariage costs a man the amount of money he is likely to earn in his entire working career and it often ruins him, but wisdom is attached to the man who finances one. Like some initiation ceremonies in mainland Africa, the ceremony entitles him to wear a special *m'ruma* (sash) which signifies his status as a *wandruwadzima (grand notable* in French).

Each village has an outdoor council area, known as a *bangwe*, marked by two high gateways. Only men who have gone through a grand mariage may participate in these village councils. Women, youths and those who can't afford the ceremony are forever excluded from village decision making.

If you hope to attend a toirab, your chances will be best in July and August. They certainly aren't exclusive affairs – normally everyone is invited – but obvious outsiders shouldn't just barge in. It's probably best to wait around looking curious about what's happening; you're almost certain to be invited to join in (one of the joys of low tourist numbers). However, *do not* attempt to take photos (or even carry a camera) without asking permission.

Bangas

Especially on Mayotte, secondary school boys and young men construct small homes for themselves on the outskirts of towns and villages. This setup allows them freedom and the opportunity to live away from their parents and siblings, and to prepare for life as men. The exterior painting and decoration of these bangas is up to the young man. The results are always amusing and creative, normally including slogans, philosophies and illustrations which reveal the individuality of the occupant. In hopes of preserving the tradition, each year in September, Mayotte holds a competition for the most originally decorated banga homes.

Dress & Decoration

Even in the religiously stricter islands of Grande Comore and Anjouan, some traditions of Islam have been abandoned. For example, *purdah*, the custom of keeping women veiled and in seclusion, is observed by very few. It has been replaced by the *chiromani* (or *leso*), an all-purpose wrap. Many women on all four islands drape themselves in these brightly coloured wraps, which are worn like a versatile sari, using one of the tails as a head covering. In most coastal villages the chiromani are black and known as *bui bui*. In Anjouan they are predominantly red and white.

One practice by many young women on the four islands, which has no religious significance, is application of the *m'sidzanou* (yellow beauty mask). The paste is made from sandalwood ground on coral and mixed with water, and, like any mud pack, is applied exclusively for beautification. It's normally caked on with only holes for the eyes and mouth, but sometimes is only dappled or spread over half the face. It is said to keep the skin looking young and provide protection from the sun and mosquitoes.

Most men in the republic's three islands wear the *kandzou* (long white cotton shirt) and often the white *koffia* (skullcap). However, the younger Mahorais are more into western clothes and fashion.

LANGUAGE

Comorian belongs to the Bantu family of African languages, but has borrowed many words from Arabic (about 30% of its vocabulary), as well as from Swahili. Today, Comorian is spoken by about 600,000 people. Outside the Comoros, considerable Comorian-speaking communities are found in France, Tanzania, Kenya, the Gulf States and even the USA, where a fraternal organisation has recently been formed.

The Comoros have three official languages: French, Arabic and Comorian. Whereas the use of French is widespread, Arabic is known to only a tiny minority. Comorians are delighted by visitors' attempts to speak Comorian, and they will patiently help and encourage their efforts.

There are four Comorian dialects; each

corresponds to a certain island: Shingazidja is spoken on Grand Comore, Shimwali on Mohéli, Shimaore on Anjouan and Shindzuani on the island of Mayotte. The words and phrases here are Shindzuani, as it is the dialect most likely to be understood throughout the archipelago. For several expressions, however, we have included the equivalent in Shingazidja (Shg).

Pronunciation

Comorian still has no official alphabet. Traditionally, Comorians have used Arabic script to transcribe their language. In the past few decades, however, the use of Latin characters has become more commonplace, especially in the media. Here is the semi-standardised transcription which has begun to emerge, with some minor alterations for ease of use by non-Comorian speakers.

a	as the 'a' in 'father'
i	as in 'street'
u	as in 'tool'
e	as in the French *clé*
o	as in 'so'

In some words, vowels are nasalised. These are indicated here by a circumflex: â, î, ô and û. Many of the consonants are pronounced as in English. Others have special sounds:

bh	like a regular 'b' but with a puff of air
dh	like a regular 'd' but with a puff of air
g	always hard, as in 'good'
j	as the 's' in 'pleasure', or the French *je*
r	always rolled

Combinations are pronounced as follows:

DH	'th' as in 'that'
dj	as in 'jack'
dr	as in 'dream'
ny	as in 'canyon'
pv	between a 'b' and a 'p'
sh	as in 'shoe'
th	as in 'thin'
tr	as in 'tree'
tsh	'ch' as in 'cheek'

Basics

Yes.	*Ewa; êê.*
No.	*Â â; â'â.*
Maybe.	*Labhda.*
	Ambhese. (Shg)
Please.	*Tafadhwali.* (sg)
	Namtafadhwali. (pl)
Thankyou.	*Marahabha.*
You're welcome.	*Karibhu.* (sg)
	Namkaribhu. (pl)
Excuse me/	*Niswamihi.* (sg)
I'm sorry.	*Namuniswamihi.* (pl)
	Samahani. (Shg)
Hello.	*Jeje?; Habhari?*
	Edje?; Barza? (Shg)
Good morning.	*Habhari za asubhwihi.*
	Barza husha. (Shg)
Good evening.	*Habhari za jio.*
Goodbye.	*Kwaheri.* (sg)
	Namkwaheri. (pl)
	Lala unono. (Shg)

Civilities

How are you?	*Jeje?*
I'm fine, thanks.	*Ndjema, marahabha.*
What is your name?	*Dzina laho dheni?*
My name is …	*Dzina langu …*
	Mi … (Shg)
Where/What country are you from?	*Ulawa havi?; Wawe wa shihavi?*
	Ula ndha? (Shg)
I'm from …	*Tsilawa …*
Are you married?	*Ulola?* (for men)
	Ulolwa? (women)
Not yet.	*Raha.*

Language Difficulties

I understand.	*Tsielewa.*
I don't understand.	*Tsaelewa; Tsisielewa.*
	Ndjaelewa. (Shg)
Do you speak English?	*Wawe ulagua shingereza?*
Please write it down.	*Tafadhwali unangishieyo.*

Getting Around

I want to go to …	*Nisitsaha nendre …*
Where is the bus stop?	*I mzio wa bisi ya havi?*

Where is the ticket office?	Vwa hununua zibiye dhe havi?
What time does the … leave/arrive?	Sa ya ngavi dhe … itsolawao/itsojao?
bus	bisi
boat	djahazi (no motor) shitrima (with motor)
airplane	âviyo
one-way ticket	biye ya hwendra
return ticket	biye ya hurudi
I'd like to hire a …	Natsovendza tsadjiri …
bicycle	biskileti
motorcycle	bekani; moto
guide	mtembeza; mntru wa hutembeza

Directions

How do I get to …?	Nitsofanya jeje ata niwaswili …?
Is it near/far?	Hoho mbali/karibhu?
(Go) straight ahead.	Nyongoa sawasawa.
(Turn) left.	(Bhuza) potroni.
(Turn) right.	(Bhuza) kumini.
at the next corner	harimwa inyonga yadhunga
north	kibhulani
south	swihilini
east	jua la uhea
west	jua la hutswa

Around Town

Where is the/a …?	I … ya havi?
tourist information office	djumba la matembezi
What time does it open/close?	Sa ya ngavi dhe wabhuao/wabhayao?
CLOSED	HUBHALWA
INFORMATION	MAELEDZO
OPEN	HUBHULWA/
PROHIBITED	HUBALIDZIWA
TOILETS	USHONI-MRABANI MSHANANI (Shg)

Accommodation

ROOMS AVAILABLE.	MAFUKO KAYASINA WANTRU

I'm looking for a …	Nisizunguha …
hotel	loteli
guesthouse	nyumba ya wadjeni
bed	ulili-shitrandra
cheap room	fuko la rahisi
How much is it per night?	Uku umoja, kisaje?
How much is it per person?	Mntru umoja, kisaje?
Can I see the room?	Nitsojua nione lifuko?
Where is the toilet?	Sho sha havi?

Food & Shopping

food stall	pvwa hudza zahula mavareni
market	bhazari shindho (Shg)
restaurant	loteli
I am vegetarian.	Wami tsili shireo.
How much is it?	Kisaje? Riali nga? (Shg)

Time & Dates

What time is it?	Ra sa ya ngavi?
When?	Lini?
today	Leo
tonight	uku vani
tomorrow	meso

Numbers

1	moja/montsi	8	nane
2	mbili	9	shenda
3	ntraru	10	kumi
4	nne	100	mia; jana
5	ntsanu	1000	alfu
6	sita	10,000	alfu kumi
7	saba		

Emergencies

I need a doctor.	Nisitsaha twabhibhu.
diarrhoea	wendro; diare
dizzy	udhu
vomiting	maraviha
Help!	Wanyawee!
Go away!	Endra dzaho!
I've been robbed.	Tsihibhiwa.
I'm lost.	Tsilatsiha.

Facts for the Visitor

PLANNING
Maps
The maps in this book of the four islands and capital cities are more than enough for the general visitor who wants to see the main sights and stay for a week or two. If you want more detail, perhaps for trekking or cycling, excellent 1:50,000 maps are published under the series *Archipel Comores* by the Institut Géographique National in France for each of the three Comoran islands and for Mayotte. We could find no single map which covers all three or four islands.

The problem is that these individual maps are hard to find in the Comoros. You can find the map for Mayotte, and probably the other three maps, in Mayotte – but many travellers bypass Mayotte because it's expensive. These maps cannot be found on Anjouan or Mohéli, but you can buy any of the four at the Nouveautés bookshop in Moroni. They are very expensive at CF4700 each.

TOURIST OFFICES
Watch out for characters with official-looking badges who pounce upon innocent, and invariably tired, foreigners at the airport at Moroni claiming to be tourist information officers. They are in fact touts for local hotels and guesthouses, hoping for commissions from guesthouse owners (which you pay, incidentally).

There is a tourist information booth at the international airport at Moroni, but it probably won't be staffed. No information is available for tourists at the airport at Mayotte.

Local Tourist Offices
Comoros At last there is a dedicated tourist office. Part of the Ministère des Transports et du Tourisme, the Direction du Tourisme, BP 97, Moroni (☎ 74 42 43; fax 74 42 42) is helpful but hopelessly inconvenient – it's along the esplanade a couple of km north of the centre of Moroni.

The particular office you want is at the back of the ministry building. Most staff speak a modicum of English (as well as fluent French), and can hand out some lists of hotels, and general brochures in French, English, Italian and German. However, it is only worth the effort of getting out to the tourist office if you have a serious complaint, or want some specific information not included in this book or available from your hotel. It is open normal government hours.

Mayotte The Comité du Tourisme, BP 1169, Mamoudzou (☎ 61 09 09; fax 61 03 46) is definitely worth visiting as soon as you arrive in Mayotte – and it is very handy. The office is located about 100m up Rue de la Pompe; look for the sign as you get off the ferry at Mamoudzou.

The helpful staff (who speak English) can hand out plenty of brochures, pamphlets and booklets. If you are staying awhile, ask for a copy of the free *Plan Guide Pratique Mayotte* which contains detailed information about local hotels, restaurants, diving centres, tourist attractions and travel agencies, among other things. They also provide free maps of the island – the colourful one entitled *Mayotte: Île à Découvrir* includes the two islands (Grande Terre and Petite Terre) and Mamoudzou.

The office is open from 8 am to 4.30 pm, Monday to Friday, and from 9 to 11.30 am on Saturdays. Opening times regularly change slightly, but they follow fairly standard business hours.

Tourist Offices Abroad

Comoros You could try to contact the small number of embassies or consulates belonging to the Comoros (or even Senegal – refer to the Embassies section following) for information, but they are unlikely to be of much help.

One option is the Indian Ocean Regional Tourist Commission, Box 903, Victoria, Mahé, Seychelles (☎ (248) 22 53 33; fax (248) 22 59 19). It should be able to provide some booklets and other information about the Comoros (but not Mayotte), as well as other islands in the region including Madagascar.

Mayotte Your local French embassy or consulate is unlikely to have anything about Mayotte. If you live in France, contact the relevant department responsible for Mayotte at 1 Ave Foch, 10 Rue de Présbourg, 75116, Paris (☎ 05 45 01 28 30).

VISAS & DOCUMENTS
Visas

Comoros Every visitor to the Comoros needs a visa. This includes French people, even from Mayotte, much to their chagrin. However, the good news is that you don't have to apply for a visa: they are issued at the international airport at Moroni as soon as you arrive – or probably a day later, if you arrive by sea at Anjouan or Moroni (see the following section).

The costs for visas, regardless of where and how you arrive, are: 24 hour transit: free; two to five days: F40; six to 15 days: F80; 16 to 45 days: F133 for one entry, F200 for two entries; and a one year multiple-entry, mainly for business people and diplomats: F267.

You can pay for your visa in French or Comoran francs. It is vital to note, however, that there are *no* money-changing facilities at any airport in the Comoros (including Mayotte) so you must have enough French

francs to pay for your visa on arrival – unless you already have some Comoran francs, which is likely to cause the immigration officer to frown and ask where you got them. At a pinch you may find someone to change some US dollars into French francs, but don't count on it.

Arrival by Sea If you arrive by sea, for example by ferry to Anjouan from Mayotte, or to Moroni from mainland Africa, your passport will be kept by the boatman. He will organise your departure from the other country with the immigration officials and keep your passport for the duration of the boat trip (double-check that he hasn't left it behind!). The boatman will then hand over your passport to the Comoran immigration official at the port. Or so the theory goes.

Depending on the time of your arrival by boat, and the number of passengers, you may be able to get your visa at the port. It is more likely that your passport will be taken, and you have to front up the next day to pick it up, get your stamp and pay for your visa.

If so, you need to go to the Ministère de l'Intérieur in Moroni or, on any other island, the local police and immigration office – refer to the individual chapters for details. The immigration official may ask you to collect your passport a few hours later. If this is inconvenient (for instance, you desperately need your passport to change money), they should be able to issue the visa on the spot.

If leaving the Comoros by sea you will have to get an exit stamp. Ask the boatman; he should be able to arrange this as part of his duties.

Mayotte Mayotte has the same entry regulations as France. Citizens of the USA, Canada, most European countries and a handful of other countries may enter France for up to three months without a visa. Australians, on the other hand, must have visas which can be valid for stays of up to three months.

Those who require French visas can apply for one at a French embassy or consulate in their own country – or collect one along the way, for instance in South Africa, Kenya, Mauritius, Madagascar or the Comoros. Make sure you tell the consular official you are travelling to Mayotte not France.

In Moroni or Mutsamudu, the application for a French (ie Mayotte) visa can take a week to process; in Antananarivo, Madagascar, the visa can be issued on the same day. The visa can cost as much as F200, depending on your nationality. You will probably have to show an onward ticket, but a flight out of Moroni will normally suffice. If you are coming to Mayotte by boat, you may have difficulty convincing the French immigration authorities that this is a valid way of arriving on the island.

EMBASSIES
Comoran Embassies & Consulates Abroad
The Comoros has very few diplomatic representatives around the world. You probably won't need to bother them because they won't have much, if any, tourist information and you can get a visa on arrival anyway.

Belgium
    27 Chemin des Pins 1180, Brussels (☎ (02) 218 6984; fax (02) 218 4143)
France
    20 Rue Marbeau 75016, Paris (☎ 02 40 67 90 54)
Germany
    Loewenburgstrasse, 50939, Cologne (☎ (221) 46 21 61; fax (223) 45 44 44)
Japan
    PO Box 66, Hogashi, Osaka (☎ (06) 203 32319)
Kenya
    (☎ (02) 222 564; fax (02) 222 964)
Madagascar
    Lot VK63 AC, Ambohitsoa, Antananarivo (☎ (2) 296 37)
USA
    UN Mission – 2nd floor, 336 45th St East, 10017, New York (☎ (212) 972 8010; fax (212) 983 4712)

You may be able to get travel information about the Comoros from a Senegalese embassy or consulate. They often represent the Comoros in countries and cities where there is no Comoran representation; for example in Washington, go to the Embassy of Senegal, 2112 Wyoming Ave NW, Washington, DC 20008 (☎ (202) 234 3712).

In the unlikely event you will need to contact a Comoran embassy or consulate elsewhere, there are also Comoran diplomatic missions in Jeddah (Saudi Arabia) and Dakar (Senegal).

Foreign Embassies in the Comoros
Only two countries have diplomatic representation in the Comoros – even the Americans and South Africans recently pulled out because of the unstable political climate, and the fact that most countries are well represented by embassies and consulates in nearby South Africa, Mauritius or Madagascar.

France
    The embassy (☎ 73 06 15) is along Ave de Republic Populaire de China, behind the Hôtel Karthala in Moroni. If you are going to Réunion or Mayotte, and come from a country which requires a visa for France, this embassy can issue you a visa – but it may take up to a week to obtain. The French consulate in Antananarivo, in Madagascar, is far better.
Madagascar
    The Malagasy Consulate (☎ 73 22 90) is opposite the Volovolo market in Moroni. For a visa to Madagascar, you will need to fill out two forms and provide two passport photos. A visa can be issued within 48 hours. A one month visa costs CF10,000 and for three months it's CF15,000. The consulate is open Monday to Thursday from 7.30 am to 2.30 pm; on Fridays from 7.30 to 11 am; and on Saturdays, from 7.30 am to noon. Remember that there is no Malagasy consulate on Mayotte; you will have to get your Malagasy visa in Moroni or somewhere else, like Réunion.

CUSTOMS
Foreigners are allowed to bring to both the Comoros and Mayotte 200 cigarettes or 100 cigars; two litres of wine, one litre of liquor or two bottles of whisky; and 50cl of perfume or aftershave.

As much as you may be tempted to buy seashells and stuff made from pretty coral, please do not buy these things, because it encourages the destruction of precious marine life. If your conscience doesn't stop you, the purchase of coral and seashells is illegal and Customs officials do spot checks on foreigners for these products.

MONEY
Currency

There are no current import or export restrictions on the amount of currency you can bring into, or take out of, the Comoros or Mayotte. Neither place has a black market.

Comoros The Comoran franc is tied to the French franc as part of the Communauté Financielle Africaine (CFA) currency union. It is usually written as the CF (Comoran Franc) – and is throughout this book – though sometimes the local currency is also written as KMF or FC. The colourful notes come in denominations of 500, 1000, 2500 (rare) and 5000, and coins come in denominations of five, 10, 25, 50 and 100. The CF5 coin is also known as a *ryali* and the CF50 piece is known as *ryali kume* or '10 ryali'.

The French franc and Comoran franc are virtually interchangeable (at the going exchange rate) and you can pay for major items like accommodation, air tickets and boat fares in either currency. For smaller items like taxi-brousse rides, and things at the market and shops, the local currency is preferable.

You can reconvert unused Comoran francs into French francs at the bank. Keep your bank receipt to show that you changed the money properly in the first place.

Mayotte On Mayotte only French francs are used. Comoran francs are no good whatsoever.

Currency Exchange

Comoros From 1948 to 1994 the Comoran franc was fixed to the French franc at the rate of 50:1, making the Comoros one of the most expensive countries in this part of the world. The local currency was devalued in 1994 and is now better value at 75:1, meaning that you get 75 Comoran francs for every French franc. Prices went up after the recent devaluation, and while costs are lower than before, they are still artificially high.

The exchange rates increase regularly and will be quite different by the time you read this. At the time of writing the rates for Comoran francs and French francs were:

Country	Unit		CF	FF
Australia	A$1	=	279	3.72
Canada	C$1	=	271	3.61
France	FFr1	=	75	
Germany	DM1	=	241	3.21
Italy	ItLir1	=	24	0.32
Japan	¥100	=	322	4.29
Switzerland	SwF1	=	277	3.69
UK	UK£1	=	631	8.41
USA	US$1	=	372	4.96

Changing Money

Comoros The only bank in the Comoros which changes cash and travellers' cheques is the efficient Banque pour l'Industrie et le Commerce (also known as Banque Internationale des Comores – it's BIC either way). It has branches in Moroni and in Mutsamudu on Anjouan. There is no permanent bank on Mohéli (though there is a BIC bank building at Fomboni); the 'bank' arrives in a satchel on a private plane every second Monday!

The BIC accepts all the major currencies listed above, but the best to carry around and the easiest to exchange are French francs, followed by US dollars and pounds sterling. The BIC banks are open Monday to Thursday from 7.30 am to 1.30 pm, and on Fridays from 7.30 to 11 am. During the month of Ramadan they close an hour earlier.

Le Galawa Beach and Itsandra Sun hotels, both on Grande Comore, also change money, but at lower rates than the banks. There is no after hours automatic withdrawal banking system and, except for the very few upmarket hotels and airlines, credit cards are next to useless in the Comoros.

Mayotte The only place to change money is the Banque Française Commerciale Océan Indien (BFC-OI). The main office is in Mamoudzou and there's also one in Dzaoudzi. Better restaurants, most hotels and travel agencies, the airline offices and all car hire firms accept credit cards – normally

American Express, MasterCard, Visa and Diners Club.

If you have the right sort of credit card linked with the right sort of bank account, you may be able to withdraw money from a 24 hour automatic teller machine at either BFC-OI branch – but don't rely on it.

POST & COMMUNICATIONS
Postal Rates
Comoros Items posted from Moroni often arrive in Europe within a few days (however, at the time of writing we had been waiting about nine months for postcards sent to Australia). Posting anything from elsewhere in the Comoros is risky.

The standard price for postcards is CF200, but the price seems to vary from island to island and even between staff at the same post office. For standard-sized letters, the price is CF125 within the Comoros, CF250 within the Indian Ocean region, CF300 to France, the Middle East and Africa, CF350 to Europe and the Pacific, and CF400 to the rest of the world. The current postal rates are usually listed in the post offices, and also included in the handy Comoros-Mayotte telephone book.

Post offices in the Comoros are generally open Monday to Thursday from 7 am to noon, and 3 to 5 pm; on Fridays to 11.30 am; and on Saturdays from 7 am until noon.

The poste restante service in Moroni is a bit quirky; if you're looking for post, write your name on a scrap of paper (with the surname capitalised) and give it to the clerk. They'll then dispatch someone to the mail room to search for your post. As you may suspect, this system isn't always reliable. You pay a small fee for each item received.

Mayotte The postal system from Mayotte is reliable, especially to Europe. The price for standard-sized letters is F5 to France and most European countries; to the rest of the non-European world the price is F7. The price of postcards is marginally less. There is only one post office – in Mamoudzou – and it is open from 7 am to 5 pm on weekdays, and 7 to 11 am on Saturdays.

Telephone
The Comoros and Mayotte are linked as part of the modern Societé Nationale des Postes et Télécommunications (SNPT) which publishes a useful telephone book (combined for the Comoros and Mayotte) listing postal and telephone rates, as well as other important contact numbers.

On both islands, the best way to normally get a direct and clear line is to buy one of the colourful telephone cards (*telecarte*), which can be used at most public telephone boxes. Otherwise, waiting to connect a call through the post office can take an eternity.

Comoros The Comoros has recently been tied into international satellite telephone services. Direct access dialling is now possible and it's no longer necessary to follow the tedious procedure of telephoning through multiple operators. There are still bugs in the system, however, so don't expect miracles; it can still take a while to get an international line.

If you need any information about telephone codes and costs contact the information desk (☎ 12). If you don't have a telecarte you can make international telephone calls from the post office in Moroni (expect waits of at least 30 minutes to get through). The Telecom offices in the other islands are less reliable.

To reach a number in the Comoros (including Mayotte) from outside the country, dial the international access code followed by the country code (269). The numbers for Grande Comore start with 73, 74, 77, 78 or 79; for Anjouan 71; and for Mohéli 72. The number for the international operator is 10.

The cost for calls within the Comoros and Mayotte is CF75 for each 30 seconds. The cost of international calls per minute is quite high: CF900 to France; CF1500 to CF2250 to other European countries; CF1500 to South Africa and nearby mainland Africa; and to Australasia and North America, CF2250.

Mayotte There are no problems telephoning

to or from Mayotte. To phone a number on Mayotte from anywhere outside the three islands of Comoros, dial your international access code followed by the country code (269) and the number desired – but don't forget to add 0269 (rather than 269) if calling from France in accordance with new changes to the French telephone numbering system. All numbers in Mayotte start with 60, 61 or 62. To dial out from Mayotte, prefix the desired number with 19.

There are a few public telephones that take a telecarte in the main towns, or you can make a call at the France Telecom office in Mamoudzou. The best rates are during evenings and weekends (when France Telecom is not open!).

BOOKS
People & Society
There aren't many publications on the Comoros in English. One, *Let's Visit the Comoros* by DE Gould, is a general introduction to the islands for secondary school students. Another is *The Comoros Islands: Struggle Against Dependency in the Indian Ocean* by Malyn Newitt.

If you read French, then you may wish to consider *Géographie des Comores* by René Battistini & Pierre Vérin. It is a colourful and well-presented study on the geography and economy of the four islands, and is occasionally available in Moroni or on Mayotte.

Available on Mayotte is *La Vie Quotidienne à Mayotte* by Sophie Blanchy-Daurel – a description of the daily lives and traditions of the Mahorais.

Two books which have been recommended by a reader (unfortunately, these titles are very hard to find) are *Human Spirits* by Michael Lambek and *Marriage in Domoni* by Martin Ottenheimer. They both offer perspectives on traditional life in the islands.

History
There's a chapter on the Ali Solih regime and the coup which brought Abdallah to power in the very readable *Africans* by David Lamb, the South African correspondent for the *Los Angeles Times*.

The best historical treatise about the Comoros is *Comores: Quatre Îles Entre Pirates et Planteurs* by Jean Martin, a two-volume work in French which covers the history from the 18th century to 1912. It's available at the Librairie Shopping bookshops on Mayotte.

Other books in French which are sometimes available – more so in Mayotte – include *Traditions d'une Lignée Royale des Comores* by Boulanier, Damir & Ottino; *L'Archipel aux Sultans Batailleurs* by Urbain Faurec; and *Mayotte, les Comores et la France* by Jean Fasquel. The most recent addition to the store of information on the islands is Martin Ottenheimer's *The Historical Dictionary of the Comoro Islands*, which is in English.

Natural History & Field Guides
The best source of information for birdwatchers in the Comoros (but you must read French to get much out of it) is *Les Oiseaux des Comores* by Michel Louette. Your best chance of finding a copy is in one of the Librairie Shopping bookshops on Mayotte. A 62-page preliminary study for this book has been published in English as *A Survey of the Endemic Avifauna of the Comoro Islands*.

For titles relating to marine life in the Indian Ocean, and other wildlife in the Comoros, see under Books in the Madagascar Facts for the Visitor chapter.

Guidebooks
Depending on which language you speak, you may want to pick up one of several useful little pocket guides while in the Comoros and Mayotte. Free from the Indian Ocean Regional Tourist Commission (IORTC), and possibly from the tourist office in Moroni, the IORTC *Directory* lists hotels, diving centres and important contact details of all Indian Ocean countries, including the Comoros (excluding Mayotte); it is available in English or French. At Le Galawa Beach Hôtel, the pocket-sized *Tourism*

Guide to Comoros, published for the English-speaking South African tourist crowd, is full of interesting tidbits about the islands, but has little practical information and is overpriced (CF3500).

On Mayotte, the useful *Mayotte en Poche*, written in French, is widely available. It contains good photos, and interesting local information, but nothing very practical.

Dictionaries
The Nouveautés bookshop in Moroni is the only bookshop on the four islands where you can buy a French-Comoran dictionary.

Bookshops & Libraries
Comoros The only bookshop in the Comoros is Nouveautés in Moroni. It sells a selection of French-language newspapers and magazines and occasionally a few English-language publications, such as *Time*, *Newsweek* and *The Economist*. It sells postcards, as well as film and expensive maps of all four islands. The best selection of English-language magazines and books, catering for South African tourists, is at the gift shop in the Le Galawa Beach Hôtel on northern Grande Comore.

If you wish to investigate a particular subject, the CNDRS museum and the Alliance Franco-Comorienne, both in Moroni, have reference libraries.

Mayotte The three branches of the Librairie Shopping bookshops sell a very good selection of French-language books, newspapers and magazines. The choice is far better than in the Comoros, but prices are naturally high.

There is also a lending library at the Centre Mahorais d'Animation Culturelle (CMAC) in Mamoudzou.

NEWSPAPERS & MAGAZINES
Comoros
The sober (but by no means dull) newspaper *Al-Watwan* (CF200), written in French and Comoran, comes out each week. It is really only available in Moroni, though we saw copies at the Hôtel Al-Amal in Mutsamudu

on Anjouan. Don't expect to buy a newspaper (or anything much else, for that matter) on Mohéli.

Its main competitor, the hand-stapled *L'Archipel*, has been going for several years and costs CF300. Another French-language monthly paper, which details recent political and economic issues, is *Le Tribune de Moroni*. The irregular French-language *Le Tambour* focuses on local art, science and culture.

Mayotte
On Mayotte, the bright community newspaper *Le Journal de Mayotte* comes out on Fridays and costs F6. This caters more for French residents; most local Comorans probably read *Kwézi*, also in French (F5), which comes out on Tuesdays.

RADIO & TV
Comoros
The only radio station is the government-run Radio Comores. The news is broadcast in Comoran, and in French three times daily: early in the morning, at noon and during the evening.

TV in the Comoros is nothing to get excited about. The only station, M TV (not to be confused with the famous US cable music channel), shows local and international music and sport, as well as films dubbed into French. Some up-market hotels pick up cable TV from France and the USA.

Mayotte
Several radio stations broadcast in French and Mahorais, such as Radio Hippocampe on FM99.1. République Française Outre-Mer (RFO) French TV services operate during most of the day and evening.

PHOTOGRAPHY & VIDEO
For general information on photography – including what not to photograph and how to get the best shots – see under Photography & Video in the Regional Facts for the Visitor chapter at the beginning of this book.

Comoros

There is now a film and processing shop in Moroni (see the Grande Comore chapter). It sells Kodak 36 print (no slide film is reliably available) for CF2600, and Fuji 36 for CF2500. It does, however, sell an impressive range of spare parts and batteries. Processing is not cheap, nor reliable, so it's best to wait until you get home or go to Madagascar.

Mayotte

Understandably, the range of print, slide and polaroid film is far better on Mayotte than the rest of the Comoros – but prices are way too high. Expect to pay about F84 for Kodak Ektachrome 24 slides (which includes processing), F44 for Fuji 36 prints and F55 for Kodak Gold 36 prints.

There is no competition to keep down the cost of processing, so unless you are dying to see that snap of the sunrise from the top of Mt Karthala wait until you get home.

HEALTH

The following brief section is specific to the Comoros and Mayotte. For a run down of general travellers' health concerns in this part of the world, see the Health chapter at the end of the book.

Water

Tap water is safe to drink at places like hotels and restaurants in Moroni, Fomboni and on Mayotte (though, tragically, only 47% of the population of the three islands of the Comoros have access to safe drinking water). The exception is anywhere on Anjouan, where the water is almost permanently undrinkable, even when boiled. (Indeed, the author became very sick after

---

Fruit

Madagascar and the Comoros are a paradise for lovers of tropical fruit: rambutans, papayas, raspberries, pineapples, guavas, bananas, mangoes and lychees are everywhere. In the Comoros, you can also try local types of breadfruit and custard apples. In some parts, particularly around the north-west coast of Madagascar, thousands of mangoes literally drop off the trees along the streets late in the year – so watch out when you're walking!

Lychee One very common fruit is the lychee. Often spelt 'litchi' or 'leechee' in other countries, it is the fruit of the *Litchi chinensis* tree, which, as the name suggests, is native to China. The lychee is grown wild throughout Madagascar, particularly in the north where there is a long dry season. The Malagasy seem to be able to eat lychees by the dozen – or two. They expertly discard the red shell, suck on the juicy grey fruit, and then spit out the seed as loudly as possible.

The hard, spiny outer skin of the lychee hides the pale, succulent fruit inside.

Guava The guava *Psidium cattleianum* was introduced into the region from South America. The fruit is well liked by lemurs, which spread the plant through its faeces. However, the guava tree adversely affects native plants in the rainforests, and is particularly intrusive in Ranomafana. Locals usually pick and eat the guava fruit in January or February, though lemurs like them riper and wait until around March. ■

drinking purified tap water from the best hotel in Mutsamudu – before he was warned not to drink the water!)

Hospitals

Comoros Unfortunately, health care in the Comoros is rudimentary at best: there are very few doctors, and life expectancy, infant mortality and calorie intake are rated in the lowest 25 countries in the world – and sinking lower.

There are hospitals in the three main towns on each island, but conditions and facilities are very poor. (Refer to the individual island chapters for locations and contact numbers.) For advice on treatment in the Comoros, contact the French embassy or consulate if you are French; your hotel, if you're lucky enough to be staying at an up-market hotel; or, as a last resort, one of the relief agencies such as the United Nations or CARE. If it is serious, but you can still get on a plane, it's best to go somewhere like South Africa, Mayotte, Mauritius, Réunion or the Seychelles, where facilities are far better (but never cheap).

There are several pharmacies in Moroni, including the Pharmacie des Comores in the northern Magoudjou district and the Pharmacie de la Corniche on Blvd de la Corniche. Mutsamudu on Anjouan has two chemists.

One disease which was fairly common on Grande Comore at the time of research (and one which should not be underestimated) is whooping cough.

Mayotte If you're going to fall ill or be injured while in the Comoros, try to do it on Mayotte where the health system is of a high standard. The main hospital is in Dzaoudzi on Pamandzi. There are also several well-stocked pharmacies. Not surprisingly, health care on Mayotte is very expensive.

BUSINESS HOURS
Comoros

Government and business offices are usually open Monday to Thursday from 7.30 am to 2.30 pm, and on Fridays, the holy day, to 11 am. Generally shops are open from 8 am to noon, and 2 to 4 pm, and on Fridays from 7.30 to 11 am, though some open earlier in the morning, close later in the afternoon, or are open a half-day or all day on Saturdays. Thanks to French influences, most businesses are closed on Sundays. Office hours are shortened or altered during Ramadan, when many shops take a long midday siesta and stay open till late at night.

Mayotte

Mayotte follows both the Comoran and French system of business hours; it can't quite decide which to use. Government offices are generally open to the public on weekdays from 8 am to noon, and from 3 to 5 pm; shops open from about 8 am to 4 pm on weekdays, and on Saturday mornings from about 8 am until noon. All shops and businesses are closed on Sundays, and it is hard to get anything done by devout Mahorais on Friday afternoons or during Ramadan.

PUBLIC HOLIDAYS & SPECIAL EVENTS

The main holidays for Comorans and Mahorais (but not French residents) are Islamic and based on the lunar calendar, so the dates change each year. The most important annual Muslim event is the 30 day dawn-to-dusk fast of Ramadan, commemorating the month the Koran was revealed to the Prophet Mohammed. Hotel restaurants and some shops remain open, but nearly everything else stops during the day and tempers tend to be on a short fuse. Businesses which do remain open extend their midday break and remain open later into the night. Naturally, non-Muslim travellers (as well as French residents) may find this inconvenient.

As one might expect, then, the biggest celebration of the year is Id-ul-Fitr, which marks the new moon – the end of Ramadan. It is in the ninth month of the lunar year. Generally, Ramadan and Id-ul-Fitr fall between January and March.

Other changeable Islamic holidays (which don't necessarily entail a day off work) include Hegire (the first day of the Muslim

DAVID CURL

A Tomb Away from Home

The Malagasy regard the dead with awe and reverence. To them the afterlife is as important as the present life – if not more so – and dead ancestors play a role in the society of the living that is rarely seen in other lands. Complex and often elaborate rituals are enacted at funerals and if it is deemed that the dead are displeased, restless or feel neglected, further ceremonies are held to appease them years and even generations later. The most famous of these rituals is the *famadihana* (turning of the bones), when the dead are exhumed, entertained, talked to and reburied with gifts and new shrouds.

PAUL GREENWAY

To the Malagasy it is only natural that the dead are housed in quarters befitting their importance. Tombs can range from sacred caves housing generations of ancestors to substantial structures of brick, concrete or stone. The siting of a tomb is subject to strict rules and can dictate the position of dwellings inhabited by the living, since it is believed these can be directly influenced by the dead. Tomb decorations can be elaborate and range from collections of zebu skulls to obelisks, such as those shown in the small photograph above, and wood carvings (those of the Sakalava tribe can be explicitly erotic). The walls may be gaily painted with scenes from the life of the departed or show how they died; for example, some show boat accidents or crocodile attacks. Large and impressive tombs such as those shown above can be seen dotted over the *hauts plateaux*. Strict *fady* (superstitions) govern tombs and visitors should not even contemplate trying to touch or photograph one without permission.

As the Malagasy say: a home is for a lifetime but a tomb is for eternity. ∎

DAVID CURL

DAVID CURL

DEANNA SWANEY

Top Left: A pousse-pousse driver at Mahajanga harbour, western Madagascar.
Top Right: Mahajanga, western Madagascar.
Bottom: Galawas on Chindini Beach, Grande Comore. Beaches in the Comoros are
             usually tucked away between headlands of volcanic rock.

New Year); and Id-ul-Adha (Feast of the Sacrifice), which commemorates the willingness of Abraham to sacrifice his son Isaac. This is followed by Id-el-Kabir, which marks the beginning of the pilgrimage to Mecca; Id e Milad un Nabi or Maoulid, celebrating the anniversary of the Prophet Mohammed's birth; Leilat ul-Miradj, commemorating Mohammed's ascension to heaven; Muharram, the Islamic new year; and Ashoura, commemorating the martyrdom of Imam Hussein.

Comoros

The following four dates are designated public holidays, ie businesses are generally closed: 1 January (New Year's Day); 1 May (Labour Day); 25 May (OAU Celebration Day); and 6 July (Independence Day).

Mayotte

In addition to the Muslim holidays, Mayotte also celebrates the main French and Christian holidays, including Bastille Day (14 July), Christmas Day and New Year's Day.

ACTIVITIES
Diving & Snorkelling

Comoros Like the Seychelles and Mauritius, the Comoros is promoting diving and snorkelling as principal attractions, but the range of diving centres and quality of diving doesn't rate nearly as high as its neighbours.

Currently, the only diving centre in the Comoros is Island Ventures (☎ 73 81 18) at the Le Galawa Beach Hôtel, in the north of Grande Comore. This outfit is very well set up and highly professional; the staff speak English, French, Italian or German; and there are off-season discounts in December and January.

For beginners, a four day PADI certificate course with five dives costs F2200 (equipment provided). Snorkellers aren't forgotten, with a cruise and dive for F33 per person plus equipment hire. Qualified divers are charged F230 for each dive (with equipment); or if you bring your own gear, you can save F30

per dive. Night dives cost F240/280 without/ with rented equipment. A package deal including five dives is F950/1100 and 10 dives is F1700/2000.

There are several good diving spots, including a designed marine nature reserve in front of the hotel; Black Coral Cave has an excellent reef which includes fan coral, a dramatic drop-off and a small coral cave; Hahaya Wall is a vertical wall dropping off into 'infinity' with excellent coral and reef life, including sponges and anemones; and Coral Garden and Treasure Cove cater more for beginners.

One definite drawback to diving in the Comoros, which you are regularly warned about, is the sea urchins which are prevalent at low tide on certain stretches of the coast. They are nasty, so watch out.

Mayotte The diving industry on Mayotte is well established and popular among tourists and locals alike. The best dive sites are found in the channels of the reef breaks. Because of river effluent the lagoon water around Mayotte is muddy red most of the time, especially during the rainy season from November to April.

If you are staying at an expensive resort around the island you can use the Centre de Plongée (☎ 60 14 19) at the Jardin Maoré Hôtel; or Mayotte Lagoon (☎ 60 13 83; fax 60 11 71), based at the Trévani Village Hôtel.

If your budget won't stretch that far, and you're based in or around Mamoudzou or Dzaoudzi, the best place to contact is Le Lambis (☎ 60 06 31; fax 60 08 45); it is based at the friendly Hôtel Lagon Sud, along the main road between the airport and the ferry terminal at Dzaoudzi. It charges F200 per dive; beginner courses are F1500 for eight dives and one hour of instruction, or F2000 for 10 dives and 10 hours of instruction. For snorkellers it rents the full gear – snorkel, flippers and mask – for around F30 per day.

Other places in the Mamoudzou port area (known as Kawéni) rent diving and snorkelling gear for slightly less, but they are inconvenient if you don't have your own vehicle, and they may not be reliable.

Boating & Fishing

The best time for fishing is from November to May, but please remember that spear-fishing is forbidden on both Mayotte and the Comoros.

If you want to rent a cheaper and more authentic boat you can always negotiate a rental fee for a *galawa* or pirogue, though, of course, you can't go far unless it has a motor.

Comoros Big-game fishing is another drawcard for wealthy South Africans and French, and the main victims are yellowfin tuna, wahoo, sharks and black marlin. The only place to organise deep-sea fishing trips is Island Ventures (see under Diving & Snorkelling). It charges F250 per person for a three hour excursion, or F380 per person for six hours.

The same outfit also has the monopoly on boat hire. A speedboat costs F250 per hour; and larger boats, suitable for deep-sea fishing, cost a whopping F1000/1520 for three/six hours per boat. Island Ventures also arranges cruises around the island, including to Lac Salé, for a more reasonable F60 per person; others cruises are organised on glass-bottomed boats from F33 per person.

Mayotte For anyone with loads of money, there are several fascinating boat trips to choose from. The *Paprika* leaves Mamoudzou every Sunday for a day trip around the island for F100 per person; bookings are advisable (☎ 60 02 44). The incredible *Visiobul* (☎ 60 02 44 for bookings) is a sort of underwater boat from which you can view fish and coral. A 40 minute trip costs F85 per person. You will see plenty of ads about these and other boat trips around Dzaoudzi and Mamoudzou, and brochures are available at the tourist office and various travel agencies.

At a few places around the island you can hire catamarans (carrying about eight passengers in four cabins) for F550 per person per day; hobie cats cost about F200 per person per day. For details, contact the travel agencies listed in the Mayotte chapter, or the tourist office.

Expensive fishing trips are also available from the travel agencies on Mayotte. The best place to make inquiries about fishing (and boat) trips, or to hire any equipment, is *Pêche & Yachting* (☎/fax 61 03 41) in the Place du Marché, near the Hôtel Caribou.

Swimming

Comoros The Comoros has a few beaches, but, disappointingly, much of the coast is volcanic and overrun by black lava. The best beaches on Grande Comore are at Itsandra on the west coast and Ngalawa on the north coast, but both have been commandeered by two exclusive and very expensive hotels. Their guards don't let just any ol' Tom, Dick or Abdul use the beaches, unless you can convince them that you are a client of the hotel or restaurant.

Other public beaches, which cost nothing to enjoy, are the Itsandra village beach (not the one used by the Itsandra Sun Hôtel), Chomoni and Bouni on the east coast, and Chindini in the south. The southern and eastern coasts of Mohéli offer some excellent beaches and, on Anjouan, Moya (where there is a quaint hotel) is one of the prettiest around.

Mayotte Mayotte has plenty of pretty white sand, and black volcanic, beaches. The problem is getting to them using public transport. The more accessible are also the busiest; try to avoid these on Sundays when half the island may invade a tiny stretch of sand.

The pick of the bunch is arguably Moya on the north-east coast of Petite Terre (Pamandzi) and N'Goudja in the south of the island. For snorkelling, try Longoni Bay.

Water Sports

Comoros Le Galawa Beach Hôtel on Grande Comore has the monopoly on all things to do with water and sports in the Comoros. Parasailing costs F120 per day and something called a 'wakensnake' (not sure what that is, but it sounds frightening!) is F20 per 10 minutes. A package deal, including all the basic watersports (though not parasailing) you can possibly squeeze into a half/full day costs a reasonable F40/80.

Mayotte There is no shortage of places around the islands to hire gear – as long as you are willing to part with loads of French francs. The up-market hotels rent all sorts of boats, windsurfing gear and so on to guests. If you're staying in or around Mamoudzou inquire at the travel agencies mentioned in the Mayotte chapter and the tourist office, or check out the ads plastered around the town or in the two weekly newspapers.

Whale-watching

Although it's not well known, during the months of May and October it's possible to see migrating whales passing through the channel between Grande Comore and Mohéli, about 10km offshore. While diving or on a boat trip, it's not uncommon to witness the magical sight of dozens of frolicking dolphins.

Hiking & Trekking

Hiking and trekking opportunities abound in the Comoros, and there are so few takers that every foray into the interior of the islands will seem like a mission of discovery. The most popular trip is the climb up the formidable Mt Karthala but, even so, only a small fraction of the Comoros' handful of visitors even attempt it.

Some of the best possible treks are on Mohéli, where a good network of tracks, superb scenery and lots of relatively pristine mountain country combine to offer enthusiastic trekkers days of wandering opportunities. Both Mayotte and Anjouan also offer several days' worth of scenic mountain hiking.

For far more information about hiking and trekking in the Comoros and Mayotte, refer to the special Trekking in the Comoros section.

ENTERTAINMENT

The attractions of the Comoros and Mayotte are outdoor; unless you are staying in an up-market hotel you will have to organise most of your own entertainment.

Comoros

The Alliance Franco-Comorienne (AFC) (☎ 73 10 87) in Moroni is the main source of entertainment for local expats; visitors are usually welcome if they ask first. Moroni has a few video clubs, but no cinema, and only a few up-market hotels sell alcohol so an evening drink is often not possible. Bring a good, long book.

Mayotte

In Mamoudzou and Dzaoudzi, the Centre Mahorais d'Animation Culturelle (CMAC) (☎ 61 11 16) shows a great range of recent and old films in French. There are considerably more places to enjoy a meal and drink on Mayotte than the rest of the Comoros, but things like an evening drink in a place with a view are pricey (about F12 for a can of beer).

SPECTATOR SPORTS

The main spectator sport on the Comoros and Mayotte is football (soccer). There is no organised competition between the islands, but the well-organised Mayotte Football League has a large number of teams playing during the dry season. Teams from Mayotte also often play against Réunion. You can catch up with the results and match programs in the weekly newspaper *Kwézi* on Mayotte.

THINGS TO BUY

Look out for finely carved wooden Koran holders, ceremonial and decorative silver jewellery, leather, sisal or raffia hats, mats and basketry (this is a speciality of Itsandra, north of Moroni), model galawas, naturally glazed pottery, dolls and puppets in traditional clothing, and colourful cotton *chiromani* robes. Spices such as pepper, nutmeg, vanilla and cloves are quite inexpensive and make excellent gifts. Colourful and diverse Comoran stamps may be purchased at the philatelic bureau across the square from the Mosquée du Vendredi (Friday Mosque) in Moroni.

It's also possible to buy beautifully and expertly embroidered *koffia*, the caps worn by Comoran men, which normally require at least a month of intricate work to make. The best prices are on Mohéli, where an elaborate cap will cost up to CF30,000.

If you have a bit of space in your luggage, you can purchase wooden doors and window shutters, intricately carved in mango, breadfruit, camphorwood and other woods, with Arabic script and geometric designs. These are specialities on Anjouan, where there's a long tradition of coconut wood carving and furniture making.

Please remember that it's illegal to collect, buy or sell shells, coral or turtle products in the Comoros and Mayotte; this includes picking up dead shells on the beach. On Mayotte, you will be offered pretty coral and shell products to buy. Please don't support this ecologically destructive market, and don't be fooled by people claiming the items they're trying to sell originate elsewhere; what's the point in destroying one country in order to keep another one pristine?

Trekking in the Comoros

Every one of the volcanic Comoros islands (and the French independent territory, Mayotte) has several excellent hikes. None of them are particularly long or difficult, mainly because the islands are small, and there is only one high mountain (Mt Karthala, a volcano).

The Accommodation section of the Regional Facts for the Visitor chapter (at the beginning of the book) has advice about camping in the Comoros, plus some tips on how to lessen your impact on the environment. The Hiking section gives some hints on what to take.

GRANDE COMORE
Mt Karthala

Mt Karthala on Grande Comore has the largest volcanic crater in the Indian Ocean region. The volcano last erupted on 5 April 1977 and, in the process, buried the village of Singani in the southern part of the island. Although it's possible to climb Mt Karthala in a very long day, it's a much better idea to carry camping equipment and spend a day or two exploring around the summit. The trek should only be attempted during the dry season, between April and November.

We went up and down Karthala in one day: we took five hours to the summit from Boboni, and five hours to return to M'vouni. It was absolutely exhausting, and we are fit.

Darren Hincks & Alex Oldroyd

Routes There are actually several options for reaching the summit: two from M'vouni (northern and southern routes) 5.5km from Moroni; one from Boboni, 10km from Moroni, at 650m elevation; and one from Dembéni (just inland from Mindralou), via Kourani. The last of these trails is the hardest; it is less used and hard to find, so you will definitely need a guide.

The most popular routes begin at **M'vouni** or further up at **Boboni** – however, the road between M'vouni and Boboni is almost impassable by normal vehicle, so you will have to take a 4WD or trek there. In a forest clearing at 1760m on the Boboni route are the ruins of a hut called **La Convalescence** which was destroyed by fire. In this area the open ground makes the routes difficult to follow; if you run into problems, head uphill and you'll eventually come to a defined route.

Just a few hundred metres above the ruins the Boboni route joins the southern route from M'vouni. From here, it's five uphill km to the summit at 2361m. The climb begins in rainforest, which diminishes in size, and eventually gives way to mountain heather and ferns near the summit.

It takes at least seven hours to climb from M'vouni to the summit and about five hours to the summit from Boboni. Although the summit and the crater are frequently clear, the slopes are normally blanketed in thick

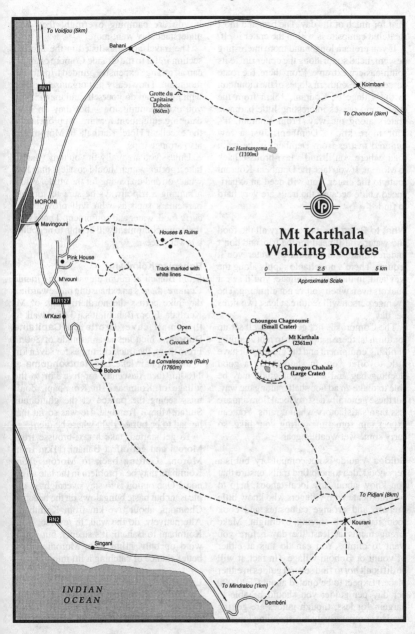

To Voidjou (5km)

RN1

Bahani

Grotte du
Capitaine
Dubois
(860m)

Koimbani

To Chomoni (3km)

Lac Hantsangoma
(1100m)

MORONI

Mavingouni

Mt Karthala
Walking Routes

0   2.5   5 km

Approximate Scale

Pink House

M'vouni

Houses & Ruins

RR127

Track marked with
white lines

M'Kazi

Open

Ground

Choungou Chagnoumé
(Small Crater)

Mt Karthala
(2361m)

La Convalescence (Ruin)
(1760m)

Choungou Chahalé
(Large Crater)

Boboni

To Pidjani (8km)

RN2

Kourani

Singani

To Mindralou (1km)

INDIAN
OCEAN

Dembéni

mist for much of the day. The best and most sheltered campsite is within the crater itself.

If you prefer a longer and more interesting descent, head south along the crater rim to its south-eastern extreme. From there, the route descends the southern slopes of the mountain to the village of Kourani, 15km from the crater, and passes interesting little barnacle craters along the way. From Kourani, it's four more km to Dembéni. Just a few hundred metres from Dembéni is the main road, where you'll find a taxi-brousse back to Moroni. If you take the Dembéni-Kourani route *to* the crater, you will need an experienced guide because the trails are very hard to find.

What to Bring Be sure to carry all the food and water you'll need for the trip, and don't underestimate the amount of water you'll require. There's no reliable supply along the way and, in the humid climate, you'll sweat buckets even when you're not climbing. The average person will require at least two litres per day.

The Comoros is not generally well set up for tourists: there is nowhere to rent camping or hiking equipment and the guides will have little to offer you. In short, bring a good sleeping bag and tent. Your guide may be able to make an ad hoc shelter along the way, but these generally destroy local flora and are less than satisfactory when it rains. You can expect rain sometime during your hike, so carry some wet weather gear.

Guides A guide is not compulsory, but is a very good idea to help find trails, ensure that you know about any local taboos, help to communicate with villagers who know little French, and arrange campsites and cook food if you are staying overnight. Make arrangements at least the day before you want to climb. You can do this at either M'vouni or Boboni village. (In fact, it will be difficult *not* to find several guides in either place.) Expect to be quoted about CF20,000 per day per guide; you should be able to bargain for less, though guides are getting used to comparatively big-spending tourists.

If you are camping overnight they will understandably want more.

The travel agencies listed in the Moroni section (refer to the Grande Comore chapter) can all arrange expensive, guided trips up the mountain. They really just organise a guide, which you can do yourself, and then charge you extra commission – but they do have camping equipment for hire. Appropriately, the excellent Hôtel Karthala in Moroni can also arrange trips.

Unless you are really fit you may want to take a porter, which should cost less than half what you end up paying for the guide. When arranging a trip always be sure to sort out particulars such as who will provide and carry food, water and equipment. Those with their own equipment will be able to negotiate a lower price.

Bahani to Koimbani
From Bahani at 600m elevation on Grande Comore, there's an exhausting but rewarding day hike across the northern flank of Mt Karthala. From Bahani, it's a 3.5km walk to the small cave, **Grotte du Capitaine Dubois**, which lies at an altitude of 860m. From there, the track continues for seven km to the mountain lake, **Lac Hantsongoma**, at 1100m, then descends for five km to the village of Koimbani. In Koimbani, don't miss seeing the **palace** of the gluttonous Sultan Mbaye Trambue. He was so fat that he had to be buried right where he died!

To get started, take a taxi-brousse from Moroni and get off at Bahani. Getting back to Moroni from Koimbani may be a problem in the late afternoon. One option is to stay overnight in the pleasant but basic bungalows on the beach at Chomoni, about five km from Koimbani. Alternatively, do the walk in reverse, from Koimbani to Bahani; it's steeper, but you'll wind up only 11km from Moroni with a better chance of catching a lift into town.

La Grille
La Grille, the northern massif of Grande Comore, also offers a couple of hiking options. From the villages of Ivembéni and

Simboussa Maouéni in the heights above the west coast village of N'Tsaoueni, walking tracks lead up and over the massif to the east coast.

The northern route begins in Simboussa Maouéni at an old French inn, Le Filao (long out of use), and climbs through low forest and past small volcanic cones to the pass at about 900m. It then begins its descent to the villages of Dimadjou and Bambadjani before meeting up with the RN3 at Moidja, just above Bouni. The southern option begins in Ivembéni and climbs to the summits of Bangohozi at 830m and Touadzaha at 860m. The track then descends for five km, through the village of Touaifa, to the RN3 at M'béni.

A circuit of the two routes, beginning at M'béni, following the southern route to Ivembéni and returning via Simboussa Maouéni and the northern route, is a 26km trek which is best done in two days.

MOHÉLI

Our favourite place for hiking is the tiny undeveloped island of Mohéli. The centre of the island is full of outstanding hiking opportunities and some of the nicest areas may be reached in day walks from Fomboni, the capital. There are lots of tracks so it's best to have a guide, but the island is so small that it would be difficult to become truly lost.

Hikes from Fomboni

A particularly fine walk begins along the Mru Déwa (Déwa River) east of Fomboni, where Persian pottery shards have been uncovered and suggest that the valley was inhabited as early as the 9th century. After a few hundred metres, the track turns sharply right (south) and begins to climb steeply, striking an even more prominent track which continues up to the interior of the island and eventually to the south coast a couple of km east of Nioumachoua. If you have a guide, ask to be taken to the lovely **waterfall** near the headwaters of the Gnombéni River.

Another route strikes out directly behind Fomboni and climbs to Bandalankoua ridge between the island's highest peak, Mt Koukoulé, and 765m Mt Kibouana. From

there you can head east to Château St-Antoine (where you can stay if it's empty) and Miringoni, or continue towards M'boinifoungue near the south coast. From Fomboni to M'boinifoungue is 12km.

Eastern Mohéli

To the eastern end of Mohéli, home of the sulphurous **Lac Dziani Boundouni**, is a great day walk. To get there, take a taxi-brousse to Wanani, 14km from Fomboni on the Plateau de Djandro, and strike off on foot eastward, past the agricultural station, along the three km track to Kangani. From there the route begins to descend and after five km arrives at the village of Iconi near the shore. Immediately beyond the village the track to Lac Dziani Boundouni strikes off to the left.

If you're heading for the beach at the fishing village of Itsamia, continue for about five km past the lake, steeply downhill to the shore. Just offshore from Itsamia is an attractive island, Chissioua Mbouzi, home to colonies of seabirds.

You can either go back the way you came or return to Iconi and follow the track above the southern shoreline for six km to Sambia, the site of another fine beach. From there, flag down a taxi-brousse back to Fomboni or on to Nioumachoua.

Southern Mohéli

A short hike west from Iconi, or a taxi-brousse ride from Fomboni, is Moihani, a bay beach near the main road about two km west of Sambia and eight km east of Nioumachoua. It affords a good view of the islands and a **shipwreck** which belonged to South African mercenaries called in to assist with the 1978 coup that toppled the tyrant Ali Solih.

Western Mohéli

At the western end of Nioumachoua are the intriguing **ruins** of a home which locals say belonged to a resident foreigner (probably Joseph François Lambert, but no-one could confirm it).

Just north-west of the ruins, beyond the inhabited area of town, is a small and quiet beach which marks the beginning of a great hike. The track strikes off from here, following the south-west coast and occasionally venturing up into the hills, before eventually reaching Miringoni at the opposite end of Mohéli's paved road. It's a beautiful coastline and a worthwhile hike, especially if you have camping equipment and make a two day trip out of it. It would be fantastic to combine the hike with a visit to Chissioua Ouénéfou just off Nioumachoua (see the Mohéli chapter for details). Between M'boinifoungue and Miringoni the route crosses a succession of ridges and valleys.

Along the way, you can make side trips to two superb beaches, Miremani-Trandrama, a small, sheltered bay beach lying between two hills (it's easily accessible by pirogue from Nioumachoua) and Miremani-Sambadjou, just over the headland from Miramani-Trandrama.

ANJOUAN
The Lakes
The small Rivière Tatinga tumbles out of the interior and powers a small hydroelectric station north of Bambao at the point where the road crosses the **Chutes de Tatinga**, a pretty 5m waterfall. The pool at the foot of the waterfall is inhabited by eels which are considered sacred by local people.

In the upper cirque are two crater lakes, **Lac Dzialaoutsounga** at 697m elevation and **Lac Dzialandzé** at 910m, on the slopes of Mt Ntingui. Together, they make a nice day trek from Bambao. Lac Dzialaoutsounga lies in a deforested area and has begun to dry up, but the area is beautiful and offers some nice picnic sites.

Begin by walking from Bambao (or finding a 4WD vehicle) to Dindi village, about seven km west of Bambao: follow the serpentine route uphill and take a left at the fork, towards Tsembehou and Dindi (the right fork will take you to Ouani and Mutsamudu). From Dindi you must go on foot. The track climbs, passing Lac Dzialaoutsounga on the left, and after two km arrives at the Col de Pomoni. The track to the right climbs for one km through a semi-wooded area to Lac Dzialandzé. This divide lake is filled only with rain water, and is the source for both the Rivière Tatinga on the east coast and the Rivière Lingoni on the west coast.

Southern Anjouan
In M'rémani (a taxi-brousse trip from Mutsamudu), ask for the route to M'rijou and continue south along it (past M'rijou) for about eight km to the village of Bouédjou, trending downhill all the way and passing plantings of ylang-ylang, clove, bananas and other crops. Turn right where the route divides and continue to descend for about five km, through Bandamadji, to the shore – where you'll feel positively alien. This was a favourite landing site for Malagasy pirates who'd finished raiding on Mayotte and were ready to have a go at Anjouan.

For the return trip, either go back the way you came and hail a taxi-brousse at M'rémani or Carrefour; or backtrack just as far as the route division at Bouédjou. Then take the right fork and follow it north-east to meet up with the road at Papani, three km south of Domoni. Along the way, note the lovely peninsula formed by a **volcanic crater** at M'ramani. The entire distance from Chiroroni back to Domoni by this route is about 30km.

Mt Ntingui
It's a steep but rewarding climb from Lac Dzialandzé up to the normally cloud-covered summit of 1595m Mt Ntingui, the highest point on Anjouan. On a rare clear day, it affords a view over all four islands of the archipelago. At this point, you can either descend to Mutsamudu or return to the Col de Pomoni, where you can decide to return the way you came or descend through the village of Lingoni to Pomoni on the west coast. For a pleasant side trip, visit the **Chute de Lingoni** waterfall a couple of km inland from Pomoni. For more information, see under Pomoni in the Anjouan chapter.

Alternatively, you can walk into the interior from Mutsamudu, following the route across the Hombo Plateau and up to the summit of Mt Ntingui. There it connects with the Bambao and Pomoni routes.

Jimilimé & the North-East Walking Routes

The far north-east of Anjouan, accessible only on foot or by boat, offers another option for exploration off the beaten path. The walk begins at the Col de Patsi at 700m (not to be confused with the village of Patsi, where the Comoros' Coca-Cola supply is bottled), about 11km above Ouani, the site of Anjouan's airport. The trekking route begins by ascending 1090m **Mt Djadjana**, then following the ridge down through inhabited areas to the badly eroded terrain around the traditional village of Jimilimé.

MAYOTTE

Authorities in Mayotte do not actively encourage camping, except at designated campsites. These are very few, however, and there was only one at the time of research (refer to the Mayotte chapter for details). You will probably have to limit your hiking on Mayotte to day hikes – which is easy enough anyway.

Mt Mtsapéré

A good day circuit from Mamoudzou will take you to the summit of 572m Mt Mtsapéré, the highest point in northern Mayotte. Begin by heading west out of Mamoudzou along Rue de la Convalescence and climb to the tiny village of Majimbini, four km from Mamoudzou. Keep going until you arrive at the summit, just a little more than one km from the village.

Once you've admired the predictably vegetated peak, either return the way you came or bear south and follow the ridge route, which descends through the village of Vahibé and meets the coast about three km south of Mamoudzou.

Saziley Peninsula

From the village of Mtsamoudou at the south-eastern corner of the island, there's an eight km circuit track which takes in the little visited beach of Saziley and colourful dunes of Magikavo. Just offshore is the lovely exposed sand bar known as Msanga Tsoholé or Îlot du Sable Blanc. This is a popular destination for day trips (you'll need to hire a boat to get there) but be warned that this treeless beach, however glorious, is exposed to the full wrath of the sun!

It can easily be walked in a couple of hours, excluding stops, but access to Mtsamoudou can be a problem so allow all day for the trip. To get there from Mamoudzou, look for a taxi-brousse going directly to Mtsamoudou. If you're unsuccessful, take one going to Chirongui via Mtsatoundou and get off at Bambo-Est. From there, it's five km walking or hitching to Mtsamoudou and the start of the circuit. Connection to Msanga Tsoholé by boat will be most convenient at weekends.

Mt Choungui

There are two routes up the formidable looking bald knob of 594m Mt Choungui, forming a traverse across the seahorse's head between the villages of Kani-Kéli and Chirongui. This is an all-day trip so begin as early as possible. Because the peak is bare of vegetation, from the summit you'll have a grand view across all of southern Mayotte.

Unless you're staying at the Jardin Maoré Hôtel, it's best to begin at Kani-Kéli (a taxi-brousse trip from Mamoudzou) and finish at Chirongui, from where it will be relatively easy to find transport back to Mamoudzou or elsewhere.

You can easily hike to the top yourself without a guide, but if you want some security and luxury, Mayotte Aventures Tropicales (see Travel Agents in the Mayotte chapter for details) can arrange a two day trip, combined with some fishing and snorkelling, for F800 per person.

Getting There & Away

This chapter deals with ways of getting to the Comoros directly from Europe, Africa and the Indian Ocean region. For general information about coming to the region from other parts of the world, particularly Australasia and North America, and finding a good deal, refer to the Regional Getting There & Away chapter at the beginning of this book.

AIR

A few obscure airlines with interesting connections often come to the Comoros and try to make some money, but they soon realise that lack of tourism and a very poor economy mean that many flights are unprofitable. For example, Sudan Airways recently ceased flights between Moroni and Khartoum via Nairobi. Ask your travel agent about some other fascinating ways of travelling by air to or from the Comoros.

Most visitors to the Comoros arrive by air to Grande Comore. The main airport is at the village of Hahaya, 19km north of Moroni. This new international airport, built with French aid, replaces the airfield at Iconi, which is now only used for private and presidential flights.

For a list of the offices for international airlines which fly to the Comoros, ie to Moroni, refer to the Getting There & Away section in the Grande Comore chapter. For contact details of the two international airlines – Air France and Air Austral – which fly to and from Mayotte, refer to Getting There & Away in the Mayotte chapter.

Europe

Comoros Until very recently, Air France was the sole carrier between France (and all of Europe) and the Comoros. These flights have now been taken over by Corsair, a subsidiary of the French charter airline service Nouvelles Frontiéres.

At the time of research flight times, as well as details of airline offices, were in a state of total confusion, but it seems that Corsair will fly from Paris to Moroni, via Antananarivo (in Madagascar) and Réunion, on Mondays. Fares are currently unknown, so contact your travel agent.

Mayotte The only flight between Europe and Mayotte is on Air France. It normally starts and finishes in Paris, but some flights will go to or from Lyon and Marseilles, depending on the season and subsequent demand. This France-Comoros flight stops in Nairobi (though, like the Air France flight between Paris and Antananarivo, you may not be able to get off or on in Nairobi) then proceeds to the Seychelles before arriving in Moroni.

Most French people and other Europeans fly on an Air France flight between Paris and Réunion which leaves daily (more often in summer), and then get a daily connection between Réunion and Mayotte on Air Austral (see the following section).

Indian Ocean

Refer to the Regional Getting There & Away section earlier in the book for details about the Indian Ocean pass issued by Air Austral.

Comoros The Comoros is reasonably well connected with other islands in the region. This is handy because you can combine a trip to the Comoros with a stop over in, for example, Mauritius.

The Réunion-based Air Austral flies from Moroni to Mauritius via Mayotte and Réunion on Fridays, returning on Mondays. Air Mauritius also flies between Moroni and Mauritius via Réunion and Mayotte on the same days. The return fare on either the Air Austral or Air Mauritius flight between Moroni and Mauritius is US$722 (there is no one-way fare). Between Moroni and Réunion, both airlines charge US$456/502 for a one-way/return flight. These are the only flights between Mayotte and Moroni –

in fact, they are the only flights between Mayotte and any other island in the Comoros. The Moroni-Mayotte fare with either airline is US$108/211.

Air Madagascar flies between Antananarivo, the capital of Madagascar, and Moroni every Friday, via Mahajanga, on the west coast of Madagascar. The one-way fare from Moroni to Mahajanga is US$223, and it's US$262 to Antananarivo. The internal Comoran airline, Amicale Comores Air, also plans to fly between Moroni and Mahajanga, via Fomboni, each Monday. These flights have yet to eventuate – probably because of underwhelming demand – but the fares will be US$228/309.

At the time of research yet another internal Comoran airline, Comores Sans Frontiéres (CSF), plans to fly between Moroni and Mahajanga for US$269 return, but flights haven't yet commenced for the same reason.

Mayotte Air Madagascar, in conjunction with Air Austral, flies between Antananarivo and Dzaoudzi (ie Mayotte) every Thursday and Saturday, via Mahajanga on the west coast of Madagascar. Air Mad (as it is affectionately known) and Air Austral also fly in conjunction between Dzaoudzi and Nosy Be (with easy connections to Antananarivo) on Fridays (sometimes on Tuesdays, also). The cost for one-way/return flights between Dzaoudzi and Nosy Be or Mahajanga is US$185/310. Leaving from Nosy Be or Mahajanga is a great way to combine a trip to Madagascar with a side trip to Mayotte, and subsequently, the Comoros.

Air Austral flies between Réunion and Dzaoudzi every day for US$550 return (the fare is sometimes as low as US$322 return). During the European summer, when hordes of French tourists flock to the islands, Air Austral usually adds one or two flights to its daily schedules. Because Réunion is well connected to France, flying from Paris to Réunion on Air France and then from Réunion to Mayotte on Air Austral is a popular and easy way to travel between the Comoros and Europe.

Air Austral also flies between Mayotte and the Seychelles on Saturdays for a standard fare of US$544 return; a discounted fare of US$473 return may be possible in the off-season. The same airline also offers flights between Mayotte and Mauritius for US$671 return – usually with a connection in Réunion.

Africa
Comoros The small South African airline, Interair, is a great way to get from southern Africa to the Comoros. It flies from Johannesburg to Moroni every Sunday; from Jo'burg, Interair has some connections to fascinating places like Uganda and Cameroun.

The other airline linking Moroni with Johannesburg is Emirates airline. It flies from Dubai to Moroni via Johannesburg – and back – on Thursdays and Saturdays. Its fares are a bit hard to fathom, though: US$531/923 one-way/return between Moroni and Dubai, and US$564/982 between Moroni and Jo'burg. So, for some reason, it's cheaper to fly from the United Arab Emirates to the Comoros than it is from South Africa.

One of the quirky little airlines which travels around the Comoros, Amicale Comores Air (ACA), has scheduled flights each Friday between Moroni and Zanzibar, off the coast of Tanzania, for US$134/201 – but don't count on them. ACA sometimes has charter flights from Moroni to Nairobi or Mahajanga, especially around the time of Christmas/New Year and Ramadan/Id-ul-Fitr. Look out for ads plastered around the streets of Moroni and in newspapers; the fare from Moroni to either place is US$188 return.

Another internal Comoran airline, Comores Sans Frontiéres, also plans to fly between Moroni and Zanzibar for the same price, but flights had not commenced at the time of research.

Mayotte Air Austral flies between Mayotte and Nairobi on Fridays, and back on Saturdays, with connections on Air France to or from Paris. The normal return flight between Mayotte and Nairobi costs US$1290; you could find discounted fares for US$845 if you look around or if you're lucky.

Arrival & Departure

Comoros Arriving by air in Moroni – the only international airport among the three islands of the Comoros – is a breeze. The first thing you need to do is fill out an arrival/disembarkation card, and possibly a health form – so have a pen ready. Neither are complicated (unless you don't speak French). Don't worry too much about the standard questions; none of the officials will pay much attention to what you write.

You then pay for your visa (refer to the Visas & Documents section in the Comoros Facts for the Visitor chapter) at the immigration counter; you will receive your visa on the spot. Then simply collect your luggage. The hard part is dealing with the persistent and unscrupulous taxi drivers who know that you will probably have no local currency, nor much of an idea about the proper taxi fare. Refer to Getting Around in the Grande Comore chapter for details about how to cope with these men, and how to get away from the airport in one piece.

Departing Moroni by air is also painless, if a little chaotic. You will have to fill out another form (which is the same as the one you filled out when you arrived). You get this form at the counter marked *attribution des siéges*, which, despite the name, has nothing to do with seat allocation. Try to find the correct check-in counter (which may not be marked), and then wait outside at the snack bar or viewing platform, where it is a little less chaotic, before going through immigration.

Mayotte The small and efficient airport on Petite Terre (Pamandzi) is easy enough to get through. If you have arrived from another developing country, like Madagascar, you will need to fill out a health form – so have a pen ready. This basically asks if you are taking any malaria tablets (which the French government recommends), and, if so, which type. You do not have to prove that you are taking tablets, but if you write 'no' on your form officials may give you some tablets (which may cost a few francs).

If you are French or a European citizen, you will breeze through immigration in less than a second. If you are not, but you still don't need a visa for France (and, therefore, Mayotte), immigration procedures may take five seconds while the official checks that you do not need a visa.

If you *do* need a visa, for example if you're an Australian, you will anger the passengers behind you while the immigration official laboriously triple-checks that rare French (ie Mayotte) visa. While this is happening, you will also have to fill out a special disembarkation form, which asks you to list the name of your hotel. If you haven't decided on one yet, just pick a hotel from this book; the immigration official will be too busy staring at your visa to take any notice, anyway.

No proof of an onward ticket or money is required (these sort of questions may be asked when you apply for your visa in the first place, though). Make sure that you have enough French francs to get you to a hotel, and to last until a bank opens because there are *no* money-changing facilities at the airport in Mayotte.

SEA

The following section contains details on how to travel to the Comoros and Mayotte from regional countries, mainly eastern and southern Africa, Madagascar, Mauritius and Réunion. For information about getting to the Comoros and/or Mayotte, and the general Indian Ocean region, on cargo boats and yachts from more distant countries, refer to the Regional Getting There & Away chapter. For specific details about travelling between the Comoros and Mayotte by boat, refer to the Comoros Getting Around chapter.

Comoros

Cargo boats and other types of vessels often stop at the Comoros, usually at Moroni, when sailing between Madagascar and mainland Africa. Passengers can often hitch a ride, or even rent a cabin (if there is one), but you will need lots of patience: waiting for something to come along, and then organising visas with immigration officials who are unused to foreigners travelling by sea, can take a long time. Added to that, the conditions on the boats, and on the seas, are usually rough; and prices quoted for foreigners are often as high as the cost of flying (unless you are able to bargain successfully).

The two places you are most likely to get a lift to or from Moroni are Mombasa (Kenya), the largest port in East Africa, and Zanzibar, the island off the Tanzanian coast with which the Comoros has a strong historical and religious link. Dar-es-Salaam, the capital of Tanzania, and Maputo, the capital of Mozambique, are hopeless for finding boats to the Comoros. Some travellers have suggested that some boats to Moroni may start or finish in Durban and Cape Town, both in South Africa. Refer to the Regional Getting There & Away section for more details.

Always be prepared for a long wait:

When I arrived in Zanzibar I got to know the Comoran community living on the island. They told me it would be just a matter of days before the boat turned up. Quickly days turned out to be weeks and I found myself waiting for ... two months with no boat in sight at all. The Comoran are the most optimistic people I have ever met!

Yves Périsse, France

There are no regular schedules, but usually there should be a boat from Zanzibar or Mombasa to Moroni about every two or three weeks; you may be lucky and find something in a week. Foreigners will be charged about US$120 one-way between Zanzibar or Mombasa and Moroni, which is only marginally cheaper than an airfare. If you add the time it will take to find a boat and the rough conditions, you may want to think twice about sailing and take the easy option of flying.

Between the Comoros and Madagascar, the best places to start asking around are Mahajanga, the major port on the west coast of Madagascar, and Anjouan, the major port in the Comoros. About every seven to 10

days, some sort of boat on which you can hitch a ride will sail between Anjouan, or possibly Moroni, and Mahajanga. However, between Moroni and Mahajanga you may be asked to pay a ridiculous US$221 one-way, which is about the same fare as the flight.

Mayotte

Owners of cargo boats sailing to or from Mayotte are a little more reluctant to take passengers, but it's certainly not impossible to hitch a ride between Dzaoudzi and Mahajanga or Nosy Be, the island off the north-west coast of Madagascar.

The easiest way to get a lift on a boat, especially to or from mainland Africa, is on a yacht or private sailing boat, which are often owned by wealthy French or South Africans. You may have to pay for the ride, or work on the boat in lieu of paying a fare. One traveller only had to pay for his food and water (and he was able to take his mountain bike on the boat without a hassle).

For information about what boat is going where from Mayotte, ask around at the yacht terminal at Dzaoudzi, or the main port of Longoni. Also check out the local weekly newspapers, which list incoming and outgoing boats. The best source of information is one of the following major cargo services on Mayotte:

AGS – Rue Mahabou (☎ 61 17 17; fax 61 12 45)
Mayotte Transit – RN Kawéni (☎ 61 10 49)
Transit Mahorais – Rue Mamoudzou, Kawéni (☎ 61 16 15; fax 61 03 69) and Longoni (☎ 62 06 07; fax 62 06 08)
Transmart, also known as SMART – Place de France, Dzaoudzi (☎ 60 10 24; fax 60 19 57) and Longoni (☎ 62 11 67)

ORGANISED TOURS

Most of the foreign visitors to the Comoros travel to Grande Comore on a packaged tour. They usually stay at one of the two up-market resorts around the coast, spend most of their time enjoying the beach and the various water sports, and visit the major attractions on day trips – but they see very little of the Comoros.

If you prefer to leave little to chance and

avoid the uncertainties of travel in this part of the world, and you don't speak French, an organised tour may be the way to go. Some of the major travel companies around the world which offer packaged deals to the Comoros are listed below. A few of the many agencies which organise trips to Madagascar also run occasional trips to the Comoros – refer to the agencies listed in the Madagascar Getting There & Away chapter.

There are very few organised packaged tours to Mayotte because the local tourist industry is well set up, and it's easy enough to get around the island independently.

Australia
    Far Horizons – George St, PO Box 96, Truro, SA 5356 (☎ (085) 864 0255; fax (085) 864 0065)
France
    Africatours – 32 Rue Linois, 75724 Paris (☎ 03.44.37.21.09)
Germany
    Feria – Frankfurter Ring 243/D – 80807 Munich (☎ (89) 323790)
    Trauminsel Reisen – Summerstrasse 8, 82211, Herrsching (☎/fax (08152) 93 19 20)

South Africa
    Wizard Tours – Victory House, 4 Herman Rd, Harmelia, Germiston (☎ (11) 392 5910)
Spain
    Gobeires – 21-10, URB La Flordia 28023, Madrid
UK
    Sunset Travel Ltd – 306 Clapham Rd, London SW9 9AE (☎ (0171) 622 5466)
    Kuoni – 33 Maddox St, London W1 (☎ (0171) 499 8636)
    Hays & Jarvis – Hayes House, 152 King St, London W6 OQV (☎ (0181) 748 0088)

DEPARTURE TAX

Currently, you do not have to pay any international departure tax when you leave the Comoros or Mayotte by air or by sea. The tax is now included in the price of your airline ticket, and authorities don't bother collecting the tax from foreigners leaving by sea because it is so rare. However, these regulations have a habit of changing back and forth, so it's best to double-check this while you are in the Comoros or Mayotte.

Getting Around

AIR

Following the demise of the former national carrier, Air Comores, in late 1995, the skies of the Comoros have been 'opened up' to foreign competition. As a result, four quirky little airlines, with only one or two planes each, now fly between the three islands – but not to or from Mayotte.

All four airlines fly between Moroni, on Grande Comore, and Mutsamudu, on Anjouan, every day, stopping off at Fomboni, on Mohéli, two or three times a week. And there is often a lot of confusion, as we noticed:

The departure and arrival times for all four airlines are almost identical, so the slightest delay can cause havoc. While waiting at the minuscule Fomboni airport, which seems crowded when two cows stroll across the runway, one plane could not depart because of fog at Mutsamudu. A few minutes later, another plane from another airline arrived, also unable to continue its flight to Mutsamudu. Within an hour, the airport was bursting beyond its seams: four planes from three airlines – representing four-fifths of all planes flying around the Comoros – were at Fomboni airport. The fog at Mutsamudu had long ago lifted, but none of the planes had enough room for a take-off!

The least organised of the four airlines, Air Archipel, leases a Twin-Otter. Amicale Comores Air (ACA) uses two old Russian workhorses with the words 'Belavia' written on the side. The pilots are Russian and speak no French, and barely passable English, and all safety instructions (if there are any) are in Russian.

The third airline with the snappy title of Comores Sans Frontiéres (Comoros Without Borders), or CSF, uses a 48 seat Russian plane with similarly incomprehensible writing inside and outside. The airline is also known as the Oriole Express, simply because that is the name written on the one and only plane; the words Comores Sans Frontiéres are nowhere to be seen. CSF does have one definite advantage over the other three airlines in that it allows passengers to carry 40kg of luggage – very useful for divers. The fourth airline is called Aeromarine.

Being a very poor country with a negligible tourist industry, it is difficult to believe that all four airlines will survive simply by travelling around the three islands. Most intend to link the Comoros with mainland Africa (particularly Zanzibar, off the coast of Tanzania), and the west coast of Madagascar (refer to the Comoros Getting There & Away chapter for details), but these flights will be irregular and were still in the planning stages at the time of research. Don't be surprised if one or two of the airlines are no longer flying around the Comoros by the time you read this book.

Air Pass

One great idea is the circular air pass offered by CSF. This allows you to visit all three islands – for instance, from Moroni to Fomboni and Mutsamudu, and back to Moroni. By using the air pass, which costs CF50,000, you will save a few CF1000 by not organising individual tickets yourself.

Fares

Fares for all flights between the three capitals on the three islands for the four airlines are basically the same, give or take about CF500 on the one-way fare. As an example, the current one-way/return fares for Comores Sans Frontiéres and Amicale Comores Air are:

Route	CSF	ACA
Moroni-Anjouan	CF21,000/37,000	CF20,500/35,850
Moroni-Mohéli	CF17,000/35,000	CF16,500/30,100
Mohéli-Anjouan	CF16,500/32,500	CF16,000/29,500

Bookings

Each airline has a proper office in, or near, Moroni (refer to the Grande Comore Getting There & Away section for details of the main offices). In the two capital cities on the other two islands, the airlines may have an office, but usually you will have to book at a hard-to-find shop or independent travel agency.

It comes as no surprise that the airlines have no computer system. Sometimes, representatives of the airlines will be at the airport when the plane arrives and can sell you an onward or return ticket. You can usually buy a ticket at the airport just before departure because there are four airlines and the planes are always half empty. You may be able to buy a ticket in Moroni for a flight from Mutsamudu to Fomboni, but you will certainly have to tell the airline office in Mutsamudu about your ticket as soon as you get there; the office in Mutsamudu won't have a clue about your booking until you tell them.

Checking-in, getting a seat, and finding the right plane can be confusing. Don't be surprised if your ticket on a flight with Amicale is stapled with a baggage label from the old Air Comores (never waste a perfectly good label!), with the word 'Mayotte' printed on and your destination scribbled over the top. Most of the planes are not marked with the name of the airline on the outside, so keep asking officials, and anyone else at the airport, to make sure that you – and your luggage – get on the right plane going to the right place.

Departure Tax

Normal departure taxes are included in the price of your ticket. The exception is at Fomboni, where you will be hit for a *redevance passagers & redevance sureté aréoportuaire* (which is a fancy way of saying 'departure tax'). Only foreigners (of which there are very, very few on this island) pay the tax (CF 1200).

Fomboni is also the only airport on the three islands where you will probably be asked to show your passport and to fill out an arrival form – after a domestic flight.

Mayotte

As a way of curbing the number of Comorans travelling to Mayotte and immigrating illegally, all internal flights between Mayotte and the other three islands have been stopped. None of the four internal airlines flying around the Comoros fly between Mayotte and the other three islands. This usually means taking a rough, and expensive, boat between Mayotte and, normally, Anjouan.

However, the flights between Réunion or Mauritius and Moroni offered by Air Mauritius and Air Austral, stop at Mayotte. The fare for either airline between Mayotte and Moroni is US$108/210 one-way/return. For more details see the Getting There & Away chapter.

TAXI-BROUSSE

If you have travelled independently around Madagascar, you will be well acquainted with the *taxi-brousse*, or bush-taxi. The taxi-brousse is a generic term to describe Comoran (and Mahorais) covered Peugeot 404/504 pick-ups, and any other vehicle which takes passengers around the islands.

These taxis-brousse travel along the main road which circles, or almost circles, each island. However, the regularity of the vehicles depends on the size and location of the various villages, and the quality of the roads. The taxis-brousse are generally uncomfortable and overcrowded, and breakdowns are common. They leave when they are full (or as full as the driver thinks they're going to get).

The waiting can be very tiresome. Drivers will wait an hour or more for an extra one or two passengers. If you pay for the one or two extra fares, rather than wait for the passengers, you will become an instant friend to everyone else in the taxi-brousse for the rest of the trip, and you may even be offered the prized seat in the front.

For more general information about the ubiquitous taxi-brousse, you may wish to refer to the Madagascar Getting Around chapter. However, there are some major differences between travelling on a taxi-brousse in the Comoros (including Mayotte) and around Madagascar:

- As the islands are so small, no trip lasts more than an hour – if you have travelled much in Madagascar, you will appreciate this!
- The Comoros are sparsely populated, so taxis-brousse leave less frequently and take longer to fill up.
- Taxi-brousse stations are little more than stops on the side of a road, rather than designated terminals.

Comoros

On Grande Comore it's relatively easy to get around using the taxis-brousse, and lots of vehicles run up and down the west coast road. In the interior of Grand Comore and along its wild east coast, however, services thin to a trickle, so if you're venturing in that direction allow yourself plenty of time.

There are also taxi-brousse services on Anjouan and Mohéli, but the roads can be reasonably rough and the services are not frequent.

Mayotte

In Mamoudzou, taxis-brousse gather at two small terminals near the ferry port. Which terminal you want depends on whether you are heading north or south from Mamoudzou. Some vehicles have their destinations painted on the side.

TAXI
Comoros

In the Comoros all taxis are the tiny Renault 4s. They are normally share-taxis, which means that you and at least three other passengers will squeeze in. You can always charter a taxi yourself, but the fare is about three to four times more than if you share it.

In Moroni, there's a flat rate to anywhere in or around town, and as far north as Itsandra and south to Iconi. There is also a 'special' (ie, more expensive) service to the airport at Hahaya. Share-taxis occasionally operate on Mohéli between the airport and Fomboni, and they usually travel between Ouani airport and Mutsamudu on Anjouan. They also ply the streets around Mutsamudu,

looking for passengers, but rarely will you see one around the tiny village of Fomboni.

To flag down a taxi, hold your hand in front of you at waist level, palm down, and wave it up and down as the vehicle approaches. The driver will let you know whether the taxi is going your way (or is inclined to go your way).

Mayotte

The taxi system is similar on Mayotte: they are usually share or collective-taxis, but they are normally more comfortable than the Renault 4s in the rest of the Comoros. There is a flat rate for taxis going around Mamoudzou and Dzaoudzi. The fare doubles during the evening and on public holidays (which includes Sundays).

CAR & MOTORCYCLE

The main roads around the Comoros and Mayotte are generally good, but can be rough in places, especially on Anjouan. When you're driving around the Comoros, watch out for the presidential convoy, a limousine with its lights on followed by a blue guard car and a military jeep. If you see it coming in either direction, you must pull over to the side of the road and wait until it passes before continuing. If you don't, you may upset the president or his guards, and your stay on the Comoros may be in peril!

Rental

Comoros Hiring a car in the Comoros is really only possible on Grande Comore, though you could hire a private vehicle or taxi-brousse with a driver on the other islands. Hiring a vehicle through a rental company on Grande Comore is becoming easier, but the price will be prohibitive to most travellers and unnecessary because taxis-brousse are fairly regular. Hirers must hold a valid international driving licence and be at least 18 years of age.

Mayotte It is very easy to arrange the rental of a vehicle on Mayotte, but probably of little interest to most travellers because the costs of hire, petrol (F5.78 per litre for super) and the ferry between Grande Terre and Petite Terre are very high, and the public transport is fairly reliable.

If you are a French citizen you can use your French driving licence to rent a car; otherwise, you will need an international driving licence.

BICYCLE

Bicycles are rare in the Comoros, but since islands are small and the roads little-travelled the country lends itself to leisurely exploration by bike. However, on all the islands, especially Anjouan and Mohéli, the roads can be rough at times and sometimes steep; a mountain bike would still allow access to a host of wild and wonderful places which would otherwise be difficult to reach.

Unfortunately, no-one has yet set up a bicycle hire service on any of the islands, so cycling enthusiasts must bring their own equipment. Keep in mind that all internal airlines – except Comores Sans Frontiéres (CSF – 40kg) – have a baggage limit of 20kg per person. There is be no problem taking a bike on a boat between the islands.

BOAT

The four islands are well connected with each other by regular boats of all shapes and sizes, whether official passenger ferries, overcrowded motorised dhows or heavily laden cargo ships. Except for Mohéli, which is sparsely populated and is often ignored by local passenger boats, some sort of passenger boat travels every day or two between each of the three ports: Moroni (Grande Comore), Mutsamudu (the Comoros' major port, on Anjouan), and Dzaoudzi (on Petite Terre, Mayotte).

Tickets for official passenger boats can usually be bought the day before departure, but for the regular and safe vessels – which are therefore popular – you can and should pay for a ticket as far in advance as possible. Each major boat will have an agency around the port area, or you can buy your ticket at an authorised travel agency, which are mostly located around the port area.

Most boats also advertise their arrival and departure times on boards attached to the gate of the ports. In Fomboni (Mohéli) there is no gate (or even a port for that matter), so noticeboards are usually nailed to a couple of trees in the middle of the main road. Fomboni is a small town.

For cargo boats, which normally don't take passengers, you must ask around at the ports. You will probably be charged the normal fare anyway.

Of the five or six passenger boats regularly travelling around the Comoros, the safest and most reliable is the *Ville de Sima*, which travels between Grande Comore, Anjouan and Mayotte (it doesn't stop at Mohéli) every few days. A former coastal patroller from France, this boat, like all the others around the Comoros, was not built to carry a lot of passengers nor be concerned about their safety.

Conditions for passengers vary from one boat to another, so it's worth checking out a boat, if possible, before buying a ticket on it. However, you will often have to buy a ticket the day before departure (and before the boat has arrived at the port), which doesn't allow you to decide if the boat is seaworthy or not. Try to avoid an overnight trip.

For more information about boats travelling between each island, refer to the relevant Getting There & Away sections in the individual chapters.

Mayotte

Except for two international flights from Mayotte to Moroni (see under the preceding Air section), the only way to travel from Mayotte to the Comoros is by a passenger boat to Mutsamudu, on Anjouan. To stop travel and immigration from the Comoros to Mayotte the French authorities now allow only a few boats, with a small number of passengers, to sail between the two islands, and set very high fares to dissuade Comorans.

One boat which plies the Mayotte-Mutsamudu route, and is worth waiting for, is the *Tratinga*. It leaves Dzaoudzi (Mayotte) on Tuesday, Thursday and Saturday mornings, and returns from Mutsamudu on Tuesday, Thursday and Sunday evenings.

Departure delays between Mayotte and Anjouan are the norm and Customs and Immigration formalities can take a long time. If anything is not correct on the boat, or among the passengers, the wait can be hours, adding 50% to the normal travelling time (eight to ten hours). In short, never expect to leave on time, but get there at least an hour before the scheduled departure time to load up and stake your seat (if there is one).

Refer to the Visas & Documents section in the Comoros Facts for the Visitor chapter for details about some possible problems getting visas and dealing with immigration if sailing between Mayotte and the Comoros.

The only real ferry in the Comoros is the one which leaves every 30 minutes or so between Mamoudzou (Grande Terre) and Dzaoudzi (Petite Terre) on Mayotte. For further information see the Mayotte chapter.

ORGANISED TOURS
Comoros
There is a handful of local tour agencies in Moroni which do some of the leg work for foreign travel agencies and tour operators, but their tours are little more than a spin past the sights on Grande Comore in a tour bus. (For details see under Travel Agencies in the Moroni section of the Grand Comores chapter.) Virtually all foreign and local travel agencies ignore Anjouan and Mohéli, which may be reason enough in itself for independent travellers to make their way to these two islands.

A typical day trip around Grande Comore includes Iconi, Chindini fishing village, a picnic on Chomoni Beach, Lac Salé, Trou du Prophète and the fort at Itsandra. There are also half-day excursions which include visits to the market, mosque and the CNDRS museum in Moroni.

Mayotte
Mayotte is naturally better set up with travel agencies – refer to the Mayotte chapter for details. They organise half or full-day trips around the island, visiting a ylang-ylang factory and a few historical attractions, as well as the waterfalls and beaches.

The attraction of Mayotte is the sea, so most tours include boat trips, scuba diving, snorkelling or fishing. Refer to the Activities section of the Comoros Facts for the Visitor chapter for more details.

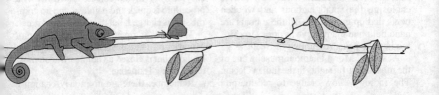

Grande Comore (Ngazidja)

Grande Comore, known as Ngazidja by the Comorans, is the largest, and geologically youngest, of the Comoros islands. It is 60km from north to south and 20km east to west, with a population of over 240,000. Of these about 10% live in the national capital, Moroni, on the west coast.

The most prominent geographical feature is 2361m Mt Karthala, the active volcano which continues to bubble away at the roof of the island. Because of the porous nature of Grande Comore's volcanic base, there are no rivers or waterways, and the water for domestic use comes from rainwater collected in cisterns and wells dug into the water table. The island is fringed by solidified lava and sandy beaches of various hues. What little agricultural land is available lies in the south, where there are banana, cassava, breadfruit, vanilla, ylang-ylang and coconut plantations.

Most of the island's population and activity is concentrated on the marginally level west coast, while the sparsely populated and dramatically beautiful east coast remains quiet and traditional, with only a few tiny thatched-hut villages.

MORONI

Moroni, also known as Port-aux-Boutres or Port of Dhows, has one of the best harbours in the country. It had its beginnings as the seat of an ancient sultanate which carried on trade within the region, primarily with Zanzibar. In Comoran the name means In the Heart of the Fire, and certainly refers to its proximity to Mt Karthala.

The waterfront itself seems more Mediterranean than African, with rock jetties enclosing the small harbour and wooden boats tied up in parallel. All these boats are hand built and many serve as dories to ships too large to squeeze through the reefs.

At sunset, Moroni harbour must be one of the most beautiful sights in the Indian Ocean. The fading yellow-orange to red-maroon light is reflected by the Mosquée du Vendredi and surrounding buildings. At dusk, there are often hundreds of men and boys swimming or fishing from ship-loading barges.

Orientation

Although Moroni is fairly spread out, it's relatively easy to find things (except in the older *medina* area). From the north, where several government offices such as the tourist office are located, a couple of main roads lead to the appropriately named Ave des Ministères, where there are even more government offices. The confusing old medina, with its maze of narrow lanes, is based around the suburbs known as Mtsangani and Badjanani, from where several roads head east towards the slopes of mighty Mt Karthala. The Ave de Republic Populaire de China, which passes the French embassy, is so named because it ends at the huge, incongruous and Chinese-built Peoples' Palace.

Information

Tourist Office There is now a helpful tourist office (☎ 74 42 42) which can provide some useful information if you can be bothered to walk or get a taxi-brousse out there. It is located along the Blvd de la Corniche, about two km north of the town centre. Refer to the Comoros Facts for the Visitor chapter for more information.

Money The only place to exchange foreign cash and travellers' cheques is the modern and impressive Banque pour l'Industrie et le Commerce (BIC) at the Place de France; it is easy to find in the middle of town. The procedure is quick and painless, and no commission is charged, but the rates are not great.

The bank is open from 7 am to 2 pm, Monday to Thursday, and 7 to 11 am on Fridays, but is closed an hour earlier on most days during Ramadan.

Remember there are no money-changing

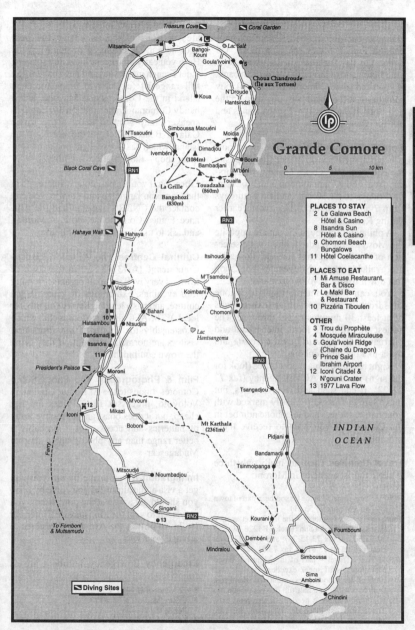

Grande Comore

0   5   10 km

PLACES TO STAY
2 Le Galawa Beach
   Hôtel & Casino
8 Itsandra Sun
   Hôtel & Casino
9 Chomoni Beach
   Bungalows
11 Hôtel Coelacanthe

PLACES TO EAT
1 Mi Amuse Restaurant,
   Bar & Disco
7 Le Maki Bar
   & Restaurant
10 Pizzéria Tiboulen

OTHER
3 Trou du Prophète
4 Mosquée Miraculeuse
5 Goula'ivoini Ridge
   (Chaine du Dragon)
6 Prince Said
   Ibrahim Airport
12 Iconi Citadel &
   N'gouni Crater
13 1977 Lava Flow

Diving Sites

facilities at the international airport at Hahaya, near Moroni, so make sure you have enough French francs (or, at a pinch, US dollars) to pay for a taxi or taxi-brousse to your hotel, and to last until you get to a bank. If you need some Comoran francs (CF), buy something at the small bar-cum-shop on the 2nd floor of the airport in French francs and ask for change in CF.

Post & Communications The main post office is at the Place de France (just opposite the BIC bank). It is open Monday to Thursday from about 7 am to noon and 3 to 5 pm, on Fridays to 11.30 am, and on Saturdays from 7 am until noon. It also closes earlier during Ramadan.

A philatelic agency in the square opposite the Mosquée du Vendredi has a wide selection of Comoran stamps for sale. Postcards are available at the Nouveautés bookshop just down from the Volovolo market.

You can make international telephone calls from the main post office (expect waits of at least 30 minutes to get through). The easiest way to make local, inter-island and international calls is to buy a *telecarte* and use it in a public telephone.

Right behind the main post office (look for the sign) is a small ACTEL agency (fax 73 22 22). It can send and receive faxes, but make sure the faxes are clearly marked with your name, address and telephone number in the Comoros if you want to receive them promptly.

Travel Agencies There are really only three reliable tourist agencies in Moroni:

Falhi Voyage – located in the far southern part of town (☎ 73 53 80; fax 73 53 81)
Tourism Services Comores – the up-market agency based at the Itsandra Sun Hôtel, BP 1226, Moroni (☎ 73 30 44; fax 73 15 33); and at Le Galawa Beach Hôtel (☎ 73 81 30; fax 73 81 32)
Tropic Tours Travel – part of the Mauritius-based Mauritours; staff speak excellent English (and French). Its various tours around the island cost from F150/305 for a half/full day per person (no minimum number is needed). It also rents cars. The address is: Place de Badjanani, BP 128, Moroni (☎ 73 02 02; fax 73 19 19).

Bookshops Nouveautés, next to the Emirates airlines office, is easily the best bookshop in the Comoros outside Mayotte. Here you can buy current local newspapers, older French magazines and newspapers, the full range of (expensive) maps for each island in the Comoros and Mayotte, and a handy Comoran-French dictionary. English-speakers may want to make a trip to Le Galawa Beach Hôtel, in the north of the island, which has an excellent book and souvenir shop – though prices are high.

Libraries If you are particularly interested in the Comoran language and culture, you can contact the CNDRS museum and the Alliance Franco-Comorienne, both in Moroni, and ask to use their reference libraries.

Cultural Centres The Alliance Franco-Comorienne (☎ 73 10 87), in the north of town, is very well set up. It organises regular film evenings, exhibitions of local art and culture, and has a lending library (mainly for locals). The AFC also has a tennis club which is ostensibly for members, but short-term visitors are normally welcome if they bring their own equipment.

Film & Photography The Photo Soleil Comores, opposite the Al Kamar Cinema in Volovolo, processes film. Prices are not cheap, but it does boast an impressive array of batteries and accessories – probably a better range than any photographic shop in Madagascar.

Immigration If you arrive by air, you will get a visa at the airport; if you come by boat, you should get a visa at the port. If not, you may need to visit the Ministère de l'Intérieur (☎ 74 46 66) on the Ave des Ministères to arrange your visa.

Emergency Emergency numbers are as follows:

- El-Maarouf Hôpital ☎ 73 26 04
- Centre Medical ☎ 74 40 77
- Police ☎ 17
- Ministère des Étrangers (Foreign Affairs) ☎ 74 41 00

GRANDE COMORE

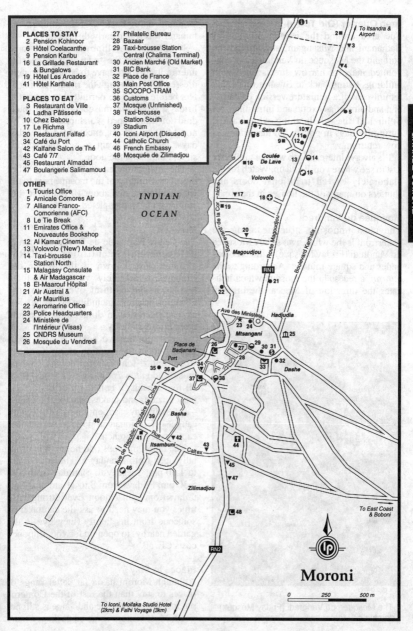

PLACES TO STAY
2 Pension Kohinoor
6 Hôtel Coelacanthe
9 Pension Karibu
16 La Grillade Restaurant
   & Bungalows
19 Hôtel Les Arcades
41 Hôtel Karthala

PLACES TO EAT
3 Restaurant de Ville
4 Ladha Pâtisserie
10 Chez Babou
17 Le Richma
20 Restaurant Falfad
34 Café du Port
42 Kalfane Salon de Thé
43 Café 7/7
45 Restaurant Almadad
47 Boulangerie Salimamoud

OTHER
1 Tourist Office
5 Amicale Comores Air
7 Alliance Franco-
   Comorienne (AFC)
8 Le Tie Break
11 Emirates Office &
   Nouveautés Bookshop
12 Al Kamar Cinema
13 Volovolo ('New') Market
14 Taxi-brousse
   Station North
15 Malagasy Consulate
   & Air Madagascar
18 El-Maarouf Hôpital
21 Air Austral &
   Air Mauritius
22 Aeromarine Office
23 Police Headquarters
24 Ministère de
   l'Intérieur (Visas)
25 CNDRS Museum
26 Mosquée du Vendredi

27 Philatelic Bureau
28 Bazaar
29 Taxi-brousse Station
   Central (Chalima Terminal)
30 Ancien Marché (Old Market)
31 BIC Bank
32 Place de France
33 Main Post Office
35 SOCOPO-TRAM
36 Customs
37 Mosque (Unfinished)
38 Taxi-brousse
   Station South
39 Stadium
40 Iconi Airport (Disused)
44 Catholic Church
46 French Embassy
48 Mosquée de Zilimadjou

INDIAN
OCEAN

Moroni

0   250   500 m

To Iconi, Moifaka Studio Hotel
(2km) & Falhi Voyage (3km)

GRANDE COMORE

Arab Quarter (Old Town)
The area around the neighbourhoods of Badjanani and Mtsangani, and around the port and the Mosquée du Vendredi, is a convoluted maze of narrow streets lined with buildings dating back to Swahili times. It's reminiscent of a miniature version of Zanzibar, and almost as exotic and intriguing. Ali Solih had the whole thing whitewashed during his days in power, but the mildew is now returning.

It's always interesting to wander aimlessly just to see where you'll end up. Watch for the elaborately carved traditional doors and shutters on many of the houses in the area.

Mosquée du Vendredi
The most imposing structure along the waterfront is the white, two storey Mosquée du Vendredi (Friday Mosque) with its colonnades and square minaret. According to the *mihrab*, a recess in the mosque which indicates the direction of Mecca, the original

PAUL GREENWAY

The Mosquée du Vendredi (Friday Mosque) dominates Moroni harbour, Grande Comore.

structure dates back to 1427 though the minaret was added early this century.

It's possible to climb the minaret for a good view over the town, but to see the interior itself you'd have to be appropriately dressed and go through the ritual washing of feet before you'd be permitted to enter. On Fridays, when the mosque fills with hundreds of white-robed worshippers, visits by non-Muslims are not encouraged. On other days, those who want to see the interior should inquire at the door.

The town is dotted with dozens of other mosques. Building of the mosque next to the Café du Port started about 10 years ago, but still hasn't been completed.

Museum
The Centre Nationale de Documentation et de Recherche Scientifique (CNDRS) museum, also known as the Musée des Comores, is definitely worth a visit for a historical and cultural overview of the Comoros islands, including Mayotte. For anyone interested in doing some research, there is also a library.

On both of the two floors, you can see a display about the eruption of Mt Karthala; some Shirazi tombs from Mohéli; clothes, music and *galawas* (outrigger canoes) from all four islands; a collection of butterflies, jars of lizards and snakes; and the showpiece – a glass display case containing a coelacanth caught off Anjouan in 1985. The detailed captions are in French.

The museum keeps odd hours. It is officially open from Monday to Thursday, 8 am to 1.30 pm; Tuesday to Saturday from 3 to 5.30 pm; Fridays from 8 to 11 am; and Saturdays from 8 am to noon. Even during these times you may need to ask the caretaker or someone from his family (they live in the garden nearby) to open up for you. Entrance costs CF750.

Places to Stay
Although Moroni has a far better range of places to stay than the rest of the Comoros put together, the choice and value is still not good. Most visitors come on packaged tours

and stay in the up-market hotels on the beaches around the island (refer to Around the Coast following). Few people bother staying in Moroni and some previously popular places have closed down; the Hôtel Ylang-ylang has now been converted into military barracks.

There are some bungalows in secluded villages around the coast, such as Chomoni, but not nearly as many as you would find in Madagascar. If you have a tent you can camp anywhere around the island.

Places to Stay – bottom end

There are a couple of comparatively inexpensive options but don't expect any sort of luxury. The cheapest is the *Pension Karibu* (☎ 73 01 17). It is very basic and stuffy with little to recommend it but the price, which is a negotiable CF4500 per room. Some hotel touts may approach you at the airport in Hahaya and recommend this place; it is not nearly as nice as they claim. The Karibu is lost in the maze downhill from the new market in the Sans Fils district – you may need to ask for directions from the Volovolo market.

Subsequent to our research, some travellers have recommended the *Pension Barakat* (☎ 73 04 36). A large sign and map next to the BIC bank indicates where it is, but the hotel may still be hard to find anyway. If in doubt, ask. It is worth finding, if only because the starting price of CF6750 per room is very reasonable for Moroni.

The friendly *Restaurant Almadad* (see Places to Eat following) has one room at the back of the restaurant. The place is noisy during the day, but the room is clean and has a fan and bathroom. Like the rest of Moroni, it is still overpriced at CF15,000 with breakfast per night per room, or CF10,000 per night for a one week stay. The owner also offers an hourly rate, which may indicate the usual type of clientele.

The best value in this range is the *Pension Kohinoor* (☎/fax 73 28 08), about 800m north of the new market along RN1. The manager promises 'a warm reception, a family atmosphere and a reasonable price',

all of which is true. The rooms, all with breakfast, range from CF9000/13,500 for a single/double room downstairs with shared toilet to CF11,250/16,125 with a bathroom and hot water upstairs. All the rooms are clean and have mosquito nets and fans, but the hotel is on a main road and is quite noisy.

Straddling the bottom to middle ranges, and worth paying extra for, is the friendly *Hôtel Karthala* (☎ 73 00 57; fax 73 02 74), opposite the disused Iconi airport. Before Independence this two storey palace, built in 1940, was *the* place to stay and be seen. Huge, spotless rooms with bathrooms and hot water cost CF15,000/22,500, which includes an excellent breakfast (but you can usually pay CF1500 less per person for the room only). An extra bed costs an additional CF6500. The higher rates for half-board (CF21,500/35,000), and full-board (CF28,000/46,500) are not worth paying for because good meals at the excellent restaurant can be had for as little as CF2000. The hotel is often used by commercial travellers from Africa and is rarely, if ever, full.

Places to Stay – middle

All places in the middle range include breakfast. The *Hôtel Coelacanthe* (☎ 73 25 75) was clearly once a nice place, but it has been sliding downhill for a long time and is now distinctly odd. There are a few air-conditioned bungalows in a nice garden, dotted by shells of other unfinished and/or abandoned bungalows, which cost CF20,000. The price is certainly open to negotiation. There's no beach (though the black lava coastline is pleasantly dramatic), and the swimming pool has been empty for many years, but it does have a nice bar and restaurant.

About 200m further south, *La Grillade Restaurant* (☎ 73 17 81) is a better option, with five modern bungalows at the back of the excellent restaurant. The bungalows are quiet and well managed, and cost F299/333 for a single/double. Like the Hôtel Karthala, the half-board (F359/440) and full-board (F405/533) is not worthwhile: you can stay at the bungalows at La Grillade and eat your meals at their restaurant (or anywhere else) for less.

If these two places are full, or aren't suitable, try the *Moifaka Studio Hotel* (☎ 73 15 56; fax 73 03 83), a couple of km south of Moroni. It would be recommended if it wasn't so far away, and is pricey at F330/440. The last resort in the up-market range is the overpriced *Hôtel Les Arcades* (☎ 73 28 47; fax 73 28 46). Its small air-conditioned rooms, some of which have a huge, pink bathroom, cost F380/460.

Places to Eat

Down Rue Caltex, the *Kalfane Salon de Thé* sells good cheap cakes and pastries to fill your face for around CF500. Two other bakeries-cum-pâtisseries are worth visiting for a snack or light meal. The *Boulangerie Salimamoud* (not to be confused with the shop of the same name, opposite Chez Babou) is good, but doesn't sell drinks. Our favourite is the *Ladha Pâtisserie*, about 200m south of the Pension Kohinoor. For lunch, you can pick up a tasty tuna and salad roll, can of Coke and pastry for a bargain CF850 in total.

Also along Rue Caltex are a few cafes, such as *Cafe 7/7*, plenty of shops selling cold drinks, and outdoor stalls for fruit and vegetables. At the end of the road (look for the sign) is the friendly *Restaurant Almadad*. It is run by an effusive Comoran who can manage some basic English. The menu has a reasonable range of Comoran food; we had a steak (which was actually liver), rice and salad, plus bread and tea for CF2000.

Another place worth checking out is the *Café du Port*. It has a fantastic location overlooking, as you would expect, the port – especially nice for sunsets. However, the staff couldn't be bothered serving anything more than beer or tea when we were there. You may have better luck at another time.

The menu du jour for CF5800 at the *Hôtel Les Arcades* is worth a splurge, except that the hotel is a little inconvenient. *La Grillade Restaurant* has an excellent selection and a superb undercover outdoor setting. It is not

as pricey as you may imagine: meals range from CF2500 to CF4000.

Our favourite restaurant is at the *Hôtel Karthala*, which is worth a walk or taxi ride if you are not staying there. The tuna and salad rolls (CF1500) and spaghetti bolognaise (CF2000) are excellent, even if they take a while to prepare. Many other meals are overpriced at CF2500 to CF3500, so choose carefully. Their cooked breakfasts, which are included in the room rate for guests but also available to the public, are excellent for CF1500. You can also enjoy a can of South African beer (CF900) while you watch satellite TV.

The friendly *Chez Babou* (also known as the Fakhri Restaurant), around the corner from the new market, serves a good range of meals including filling sandwiches for CF1000. Some of the staff (who speak English and French) can be a bit pushy because they want you to buy their expensive meals. The curries with rice are pricey at CF3500 to CF4500, but if you add some bread and excellent samosas (CF100 each), one curry meal is big enough for two people.

Along the main road, close to the Pension Kohinoor, the *Restaurant de Ville* has reasonable meals for CF2000, as long as you happen to want what they happen to have on offer. For any choice or service, you are better off going elsewhere. Another recommended option for expensive Indian and European cuisine is *Le Richma*, and the *Restaurant Falfad* is good value and popular with middle-class Comorans.

Entertainment

The *Al Kamar* cinema, not far from the new market, looks permanently closed, but it does occasionally show some films and concerts featuring modern Comoran music. Check out the noticeboard outside for details of current and upcoming performances. For something less formal, the small video cinema shed along Rue Caltex is jam-packed with locals.

The *Alliance Franco-Comorienne* (AFC) (☎ 73 10 87) is the major source of entertainment for local Comorans and the few French expats. Foreigners are usually welcome, but ring ahead to make sure. It offers a good choice of French films (or other films dubbed into French) on Tuesday and Friday evenings, as well as regular concerts and exhibitions. The library is open from 8.30 am to noon, and 3 to 7 pm on Tuesday, Thursday and Saturday, and 3 to 7 pm on Fridays. To find out what is going on, check the noticeboard outside the AFC, give them a ring or pick up their monthly booklet *Le Journal*.

For some dancing, drinking and socialising with French expats, go to the bar at *Le Tie Break*, next to the AFC. However, if you don't speak French or walk in with a tennis racquet and white shirt and shorts, you may be frowned at.

Things to Buy

The colourful old market downhill from the post office, known as *le petit marché* (or *l'ancien marché*) is the place to find fresh produce. Here, women in gaily coloured *chiromani* huddle over piles of fruit and vegetables trying to avoid being crushed by the throngs of pedestrians and vehicles squeezing through the bottleneck. It is fascinating to watch the proceedings from a spot up some nearby stairs.

Downhill from the old market along the eastern boundary of the old town is the bazaar, where you'll find clothing, pots and pans, soap and other commodities. You may also want to visit the shops of the skilled Indian jewellers who design the intricate, lace-like gold earrings, bracelets, rings and necklaces for the *grand mariage*. Look for them around the Mosquée du Vendredi. Please don't buy anything made of coral, coelacanth scales, tortoiseshell or other sensitive or endangered species.

The largest market is the new one at Volovolo in the northern part of town. Compared to the character of the old markets, this large and purpose-built covered platform is disappointing. It is a seething mass of vendors, goods and filth, as well as taxis-brousse, all sprawled across the floor and spilling onto the surrounding ground. Don't

go out of your way for this one unless you're after something specific.

AROUND THE COAST

Other than the two up-market hotels, there are very few places to stay around the island, but this doesn't matter because you can easily visit the sights around Grande Comore on day trips from Moroni using public transport. For example, one day you may wish to visit Itsandra and Iconi; another day, you can see Mitsamiouli, Le Galawa Beach Hôtel, Bangoi-Kouni, Lac Salé and the Chaine du Dragon (Goula'ivoini Ridge); and on another, travel south to Singani, Chindini and Foumbouni. Always try to get an early start, because you will spend a fair part of your day waiting around for onward transport.

After a short while travelling around Grande Comore, you will notice one annoying factor: almost no village and attraction along the main road, nor any important turn-off from the main road, is signed in any way. To know where you are, where you are going and where to get off, you will have to guess, follow a detailed map or keep asking someone on the taxi-brousse.

Itsandra

Itsandra, sitting on a rocky promontory about four km north of Moroni, was the seat of one of the most powerful sultanates on Grande Comore and, indeed, in the entire archipelago. The local tourist authority plans to develop Itsandra as a beach, as well as an historical village of 17th century Arab-influenced mosques, houses and shops of artisans. These sights will be identified and signed in a few years, but at the moment you will have to ask around the village to see anything interesting.

For most people the centrepiece of Itsandra is its clean, 200m-long white sand beach, the only really nice beach within easy reach of Moroni. It was here that Bob Dénard's mercenary forces landed on 12 May 1978, resulting in the fall of Ali Solih. (Refer to the Facts about the Comoros chapter for details about the exploits of Dénard and his merry mercenaries.)

You can try to rent a windsurfer or small catamaran at the Twamaya Nautical Club based in Le Tiboulen Plage snack bar/restaurant on the beach. The place is run by the local tourist authority, which doesn't seem to have much of an idea (yet) about the rental of beach equipment or provision of facilities, such as a kiosk or toilets, for visitors. Hopefully, things will improve soon.

This beach should not be confused with the beach belonging to the Itsandra Sun Hôtel and Casino, which lies about three km north of Itsandra village and beach. To use the beach owned by the hotel you will have pay or convince the guard at the hotel gate to let you pass.

Sultan's Fort & Palace On the crest of the hill a few hundred metres south of the village beach, the very limited ruins of a 15th century fort stand beside the road. It was here in January 1883 that Sultan Msafumu was defeated and overthrown by the young Saïd Ali. The original entrance was through a walled passageway, but is now blocked so you must walk around the side. The lava rock walls of the structure are still standing, though the area between is overgrown. Apparently, this area once contained the sultan's office, dining room and bathroom.

Uphill across RN1 from the main town are the ruins of **Hereza**, the palace of the sultan Fimnau who ruled in the late 18th century.

Places to Stay & Eat The only place to stay in or around Itsandra is the very expensive *Itsandra Sun Hôtel and Casino* (☎ 73 23 16; fax 73 23 09). It is located on a nice but tiny beach (which non-guests have to pay CF1000 to use), about three km north of Itsandra village and its public beach.

Standard rates for the Itsandra Sun are a whopping F1150/1700 for a single/double. If you are a diplomat or business person, you will 'only' pay F825/1100. On Saturday night, the price is an almost affordable F400/550. All prices include breakfast. If you are planning a splurge, or coming to

Grande Comore as part of a packaged tour, the price, setting and facilities at Le Galawa Beach Hôtel are better.

On the Itsandra public beach, *Le Tiboulen Plage* looks like a western surfing bar-cum-shop, but is virtually closed on a permanent basis, except for special functions. For a snack or a cold drink, go to the *Le Funtastic*, a few minutes' walk uphill along the road from the Itsandra public beach.

Getting There & Away Itsandra is a quick and easy taxi-brousse trip (CF200) from the Taxi-brousse Station North. You can even walk to the village and beach along a pleasant shaded road in about 40 minutes from the Volovolo market.

Ntsudjini

Just a little north of Itsandra and less than one km inland is the village of Ntsudjini, formerly the capital of the sultanate of Itsandra. Its walls were originally constructed in the late 14th century by the *tibé* (Grand Sultan) Wakandzou. Inside you can visit the **mosque** he constructed.

You can also see the **tomb of Fumnau**, who served as sultan of Itsandra during the late 18th century and ushered in the power struggles which marked 19th century Ngazidja. The tomb is marked by a three metre stone column signifying that he died in office. In the early 19th century, the city was ransacked by Malagasy pirates and most of the buildings which survived that raid were finished off in the name of French modernisation in 1921. There's nothing else startling here, but the village is still worth a visit if you have time.

Hatsambou

On the coast immediately west of Ntsudjini is the village of Hatsambou, visible from RN1 about 20m lower than the road. The Comoros is the world's second-largest producer of vanilla (after Madagascar) and here, on the inland side of the main road, is a small shed where vanilla beans are graded and sorted. The workers can explain the vanilla producing and sorting processes (in French).

Hatsambou itself is a friendly and interesting village of fisherfolk. From here you can arrange fishing trips in local galawas: it's about CF10,000 per day plus petrol for up to four people in a motorised galawa, or about CF 1500 for half a day or so in a simple two-person, human-powered galawa. If the sea is rough, however, the latter option won't be possible.

N'Tsaouéni

The village of N'Tsaouéni, once the home of the sultanate of M'bude, lies midway between the airport at Hahaya and Mitsamiouli. In the 18th century, a substantial wall was constructed around the village to protect it from the Malagasy pirates who had a penchant for raiding Comoran villages. Remains of the wall can still be seen.

N'Tsaouéni is also believed to be the final resting place of Caliph Mohammed Athoumani Kouba, a cousin of the Prophet Mohammed and one of the founders of Islam in the Comoros. The location of his tomb is the subject of some dispute, but the best case can be made for the recently renovated **tomb** beside the Mosquée du Vendredi.

In the village you can also see the **Mosquée Dalao**, which locals will tell you was built by Caliph Kouba himself in the 7th century. This mosque is in fact the Comoros' oldest, but it was constructed much more recently (probably in the early 14th century) on the site of Kouba's 7th century Mosquée Mitsuamuvindja. The rose-coloured 14th century **Mosquée Djumbe Foumou** is also worth a look.

Mitsamiouli

Mitsamiouli, near the northern tip of the island, has a population of about 4500 and is the second-largest town on Grande Comore. It also has a long, sandy beach, **Planete Plage**, which serves as a popular venue for football games. However, like Itsandra, the beaches are a bit public for sunbathing or relaxing, and there isn't a lot of shade to protect you from the fierce Comoran sun.

The village itself is very pleasant, but sees very few visitors. The main attractions are the traditionally carved wooden doors and shutters along the laneways, the lively **daily market**, and the nearby beaches. If you have your own vehicle, or you're on an organised tour, you can continue on to a **ylang-ylang distillery**. Ask for directions from Mitsamiouli if you are on your own.

Three km north-east of Mitsamiouli is the magnificent Le Galawa Beach Hôtel and Casino, on the Ngalawa beach. This beach is probably the island's finest, but non-guests who enter from the main road, through the gate, will be charged a crazy CF5000 to use the beach.

Places to Stay The only place to stay on this part of the island is the mega-expensive and very luxurious *Le Galawa Beach Hôtel and Casino* (☎ 73 81 18; fax 73 82 51). The general public (that is, anyone not on an organised tour) must pay the 'standard rate' of F1550/1700 for a single/double. Anyone with a diplomatic or business connection (and people on packaged tours) are charged F825/1100. If you just stay for a Saturday night, the price drops to a comparatively reasonable F400/550. All prices include breakfast and dinner which, with the excellent facilities, makes it a far better option than its counterpart, the Itsandra Sun Hôtel.

If you can get past the guard and convince him that you want to buy a meal, or something from the shop, the hotel is worth a look around. It boasts an excellent diving centre (refer to the Activities section in the Comoros Facts for the Visitor chapter for full details), and a good bookshop, casino, tennis court and so on. One definite advantage for English-speakers is that the regular South African clientele ensure that English is the main European language in this microcosm of South Africa.

Places to Eat The cheapest place to find a meal in Mitsamiouli village is the no-frills restaurant in the *market*, where you can wash down a plate of rice or cassava and meat with tea, coffee or Nesquik.

Practically opposite the entrance to Le Galawa Beach Hôtel is the *Mi Amuse Res-*

taurant, Bar & Disco, which advertises 'soirées volcaniques' and dancing on weekends.

Le Galawa Beach Hôtel itself has a very nice but very expensive restaurant – *Bahari Seafood Restaurant* – with à la carte lunches, as well as buffet breakfasts and dinners. There is also *Blackbeard's*, a pool bar serving salads, sandwiches and snack meals. Soft drinks, beer, juice and other drinks are available all day.

Getting There & Away Regular taxis-brousse run between the Taxi-brousse Station North in Moroni and Mitsamiouli (or Le Galawa Beach Hôtel) for CF350 per person. To Le Galawa Beach Hôtel, ask the driver to let you off or just look for the huge sign by the side of the road, next to a magnificent baobab about three km north-east of Mitsamiouli.

Trou du Prophète

Also known as Zindoni by the locals, the sheltered bay of Trou du Prophète (Hole of the Prophet) is less than two km east of Ngalawa beach. Legend has it that the Prophet Mohammed once made landfall in this safe harbour, but it almost certainly once served as a haven for 17th century pirates. It's now a popular leisure spot bordered by a few French holiday villas (including the former home of Bob Dénard) and is inviting when the tide is in. The bay is also the unlucky location of a shipwreck.

Bangoi-Kouni

In the small village of Bangoi-Kouni, about five km east of Le Galawa Beach Hotel, is the so-called **Mosquée Miraculeuse** (Miracle Mosque). No-one in the village knows anything of its origins and it's reputed to have constructed itself in a single night. Nearby are the greying **tombs** of several anonymous Shirazis.

Lac Salé

If you can't make it up to Karthala volcano, Lac Salé provides an easily accessible glimpse of the volcanic element on Grande

---

Legend of Bangoi-Kouni

According to local legends the crater with Lac Salé once contained a village, but when Prophet Mohammed himself came visiting the inhabitants refused to offer hospitality to the unknown stranger. Finally, an old woman gave him water and he instructed her to take her family into the hills. As soon as she did, the village was swallowed up by the sea. Now villagers in nearby Bangoi-Kouni are obliged to offer passing travellers a coconut or other refreshment, lest a similar fate befall their village. ■

Comore. This saltwater lake sits in a deep crater between the shore and RN3, about a km or so east of Bangoi-Kouni.

Lac Salé is similar to, but smaller than, Lac Dziani on Pamandzi (Petite Terre), Mayotte. The waters of both are said to be rich in sulphur and good for treating skin ailments or wounds. It's an easy walk around the rim of the crater, and you'll get good views of the coast, but it is difficult to reach the lake's shore. Although it looks easy to toss a stone into the lake, legend has it that stones thrown from the crater rim near RN3 are deflected by some unseen force and never reach the surface of the water.

Between the crater and the shore there are a few picturesque **baobab trees**, and below, on the shore, a sea wall and a small **beach** which leads back to the village of Bangoi-Kouni. Even in the afternoon there are lots of fruit bats flapping around and roosting in trees, and it makes for a very pleasant atmosphere.

Goula'ivoini Ridge

Three km south-east of Lac Salé is the eroded volcanic crater of Goula'ivoini, which now forms a peninsula jutting into the sea. This small but dramatic ridge of rocks resembles the backbone of a dragon (indeed, the French name is 'Chaine du Dragon'), or perhaps an immense jawbone with a row of jagged teeth.

The ridge can easily be seen from the main

road, and is worth getting off the taxi-brousse and exploring. It is a regular stop on any local tour.

Getting There & Away Direct taxis-brousse from the Taxi-brousse Station North in Moroni to Bouni and the north-east coast are infrequent, so it's probably easier to go to Mitsamiouli first, have a look around there, and get a connection further on.

East Coast Beaches

If you remain only on the west coast of Grande Comore you'll miss the greater part of the island's appeal: the wilder and more spectacular east coast, with its rambling and dusty traditional villages, thirsty slopes studded with baobabs, white coconut-lined beaches and opal-coloured seas. Here, you can fall in love with the Comoros before you set off for the outer islands.

The beaches on the east coast are all exposed to the south-west trade winds for most of the year and are much wilder than their western counterparts. The best beaches are at N'Droude, Hantsindzi, Bouni and Chomoni.

N'Droude & Île aux Tortues

Near N'Droude is a small offshore islet, Choua Chandroude or Île aux Tortues, which can be reached on foot at low tide. Sea turtles come to lay their eggs here between November and March.

Bouni Heading south, the coastal slopes become steeper and the road climbs further up the mountainside. Once the capital of the sultanate of Hamahame, the village of Bouni lies about 1500m down a steep hill from RN3. It has two stunning beaches.

If you are discreet, there is nothing to stop you camping anywhere near the beach. Maybe you could leave your gear in Moroni and camp for a night or two at Bouni. There are some basic supplies in the village, but it's a long walk from the beaches so bring your own food and water.

If you arrange it with your taxi-brousse driver, he may detour via Bouni especially.

Alternatively, he may have to go by to drop off or pick up other passengers. If not, it's a long hot walk from the main road down to the beach. Every day a few taxis-brousse leave from the Taxi-brousse Station North in Moroni and go as far as Bouni on the way to the final stop at M'béni.

Chomoni Chomoni, about halfway down the east coast, is probably the nicest beach along this part of the island because of its position beside a sheltered bay. It is a fascinating mixture of black lava and white sandy beach. Chomoni lies near the intersection of RN3 and the only cross-island road, which connects Moroni with the east coast. On weekends, the beach fills up with expats from Moroni and takes on a real holiday atmosphere.

There are some *bungalows* on the beach which cost a reasonable CF5000 (try to get the green one). Facilities are basic and there is no running water, but the meals for CF4000 are excellent and the bar also serves welcome cold drinks.

Transport by taxi-brousse (CF500) to that part of the island from Moroni is not easy to find (neither is the Taxi-brousse Station Central in Moroni), but if you wait and wait – and ask and ask – you will get there. Hitching a ride on a Sunday may be the easiest way there.

Foumbouni

The town of Foumbouni on the south-east corner of Grande Comore is the island's third-largest community, with more than 3000 inhabitants. Whiter and brighter than Moroni, Iconi or Itsandra, little-touristed Foumbouni has a more exotic feel than the west coast towns, and local people appear truly stunned at the sight of visitors.

Foumbouni was the former capital of the Sultan of Badjini. Now noted for its pottery working, it is also the site of the Comoros' largest Muslim secondary school, where young men are given religious instruction in the Koran, Islamic tradition and the Arabic language.

Along RN3, 12km north of Foumbouni,

lies the village of **Bandamadji** where several historic **tombs** have been discovered. It is believed that they date back to the early 16th century and contain the remains of early Portuguese navigators and traders who followed in the wake of Vasco da Gama. You can get there by taking another taxi-brousse from Foumbouni.

Foumbouni has a couple of stores and basic *restaurants* for lunch, but if you are camping in the area take your own food.

Getting There & Away Taxis-brousse to Foumbouni leave every hour or so from the Taxi-brousse Station South in Moroni.

Chindini

More open and airy than the beaches and villages further north, Chindini is a lovely spot, and the beach immediately west of town is idyllic. Sometimes there are a few basic *bungalows* for hire, but there are plenty of spots to pitch a tent anyway.

From the beach there's a view across to this unusual looking village, which sits on a very exposed, nearly treeless expanse of coastline, and a shipwreck rusting on the rocks. When the weather is clear, you can see Mohéli across the channel. If you're hankering to get across speak with local dhow owners, who occasionally make the 50km trip to the neighbouring island.

Getting There & Away Every hour or so, taxis-brousse to Foumbouni leave from the Taxi-brousse Station South in Moroni and will drop you off, or pick you up, at Chindini.

Singani

The village of Singani, on the way to Foumbouni, likes to think of itself as the Pompeii of the Indian Ocean. And with pretty good reason: during the eruption of Mt Karthala in April 1977 the lava flow swept through the village, destroying everything in its path; only the school was spared.

Two weeks before the eruption, a mad man in the village had taken to running through the streets, warning people of an impending eruption and bidding them to

leave the town before it was destroyed. No-one listened, but three days before the eruption the earth began to quake and the warnings were taken more seriously. After the initial eruption, the village was evacuated before the lava reached the inhabited area and no-one was threatened except the mad man himself, who elected to remain in the school. Strangely enough, the stream of lava parted and spared the building. There he remained for several days until rescuers managed to dig through the lava. By that time, he'd completely lost his grip on reality. Or so the story goes...

The only benefit the volcano had on Singani was to the local football team. The ash has been levelled into a large and particularly nice playing field.

Mitsoudjé

The village of Mitsoudjé, six km north of Singani, is a centre for **wood carving** in the Comoros. The artisans specialise primarily in decorative doors, shutters, boxes and furnishings, but they also do more portable items like candle holders and small plaques.

The area around Mitsoudjé and Singani further south is also the primary producer of ylang-ylang in the country, and in some places the plantations border RN2.

The inhabitants of Mitsoudjé believe that they are protected from evil djinn by the spirit of an aged holy man from Iconi, who had promised that whichever village constructed his tomb would be forever safe from the forces of evil. Mitsoudjé took his words to heart, and when he died they stole his body from Iconi and brought it to Mitsoudjé, building many new tombs in order to confuse anyone hoping to return him to Iconi.

Iconi

Iconi is the oldest settlement on Grand Comore and was the original capital, the seat of the Sultan of Bambao. It suffered badly at the hands of Malagasy pirates from the 16th to early 19th centuries. In 1805 a particularly determined wave of pirates sent many of the inhabitants of Iconi fleeing into the heights to hide in the crater of N'gouni. Before long, many of the men decided to return and defend their town. However, when their leader Mbangoue was killed by the invaders, the women of Iconi threw themselves off the cliffs into the sea rather than face capture.

In March 1978 a second tragedy took place in Iconi when Ali Solih's youth gangs massacred unarmed citizens who dared to protest against his policies forbidding Comoran tradition and religious fervour. Now the beach, and the area around it, is run down and rubbishy, but still worth a visit.

The most imposing buildings in Iconi, both worth a look, are the 16th century **Palais de Kaviridjeo** (the former home of the sultans of Bambao), and the **Mosquée du Vendredi** with its square six storey minaret. It's also worthwhile exploring the old town and seeking out interesting carved doors and windows. Have a look at the several residences dating back to the times of the sultans; these include the ruins of **La Fortaleza**, which is a palace attributed to early Portuguese sailors. Another interesting site in the old city is the **Place de la Cuisine des Yeux**, a public square which once served as a venue for royal meetings, festivals and spectacles.

The Citadel Upon entering Iconi from the north, look to the right and you'll see the remains of the fort wall along the rim of the extinct crater of N'gouni. It's not the Great Wall of China, but there's enough remaining for an interesting walk along the top. Inside the crater is a large oasis of palms.

The climb up is not for the weak of heart or knees, but those who do make it are rewarded by great views of Moroni and surrounding craters. It's also a good idea to take a guide because the path becomes steep and confusing in parts. Local children are keen to guide you, but ignore demands for extortionate amounts of money and please don't hire them during school hours, thereby encouraging truancy.

Getting There & Away Iconi lies just six km south of Moroni, a short walk from town, and within the standard CF200 fare from Moroni.

The Interior
Most of Grande Comore's population is scattered around the coast, leaving the highland centre sparsely inhabited and, in places, somewhat wild. If you want to see another side of the islands or just escape the heat and humidity for a couple of days, you may want to take one of several treks into the interior. For information on climbing Mt Karthala and other hikes around Grande Comore, refer to the special Trekking in the Comoros section earlier in this book.

GETTING THERE & AWAY
Air
As the capital and major city, Moroni is understandably the hub for all international flights to the three islands of the Comoros. For information about international flights to/from the Comoros (which all land in Moroni), refer to the Comoros Getting There & Away chapter.

The four airlines which fly around the Comoros are based in Moroni. They each fly between Moroni and Mutsamudu, on Anjouan, just about every day for about CF20,500/35,850 one-way/return, and about two or three times a week to Fomboni, on Mohéli, for CF16,500/30,100.

The main offices for the few local and international airlines which travel to, and around, the Comoros are:

Aeromarine
    Blvd de la Corniche (☎ 73 32 38)
Air Archipel
    Itsandra (we never found the office, and no-one could confirm its existence!)
Air Austral
    Route Magoudjou (☎ 73 31 44; fax 73 31 45)
Air Madagascar
    Villa Bouelambauba, Route Magoudjou (☎/fax 73 22 90). It is in the same building as the Malagasy consulate.
Air Mauritius
    It is in the same office as Air Austral (☎ 73 31 47)
Amicale Comores Air
    The office is in the suburbs east of Volovolo; look for the sign opposite Chez Babou (☎ 73 22 37)

GRANDE COMORE

Comores Sans Frontiéres (CSF)
    Hôtel Les Arcades complex (☎ 73 28 47)
Emirates Airlines
    Next to the Nouveautés bookshop, on Route
    Magoudjou (☎ 73 50 30)

Details about the offices of the South African airline, Interair, and of the French airline, Nouvelle Frontiéres, were not available at the time of research, but it was reported that the latter was to be located somewhere near the Café du Port.

Boat

The port is located just west of Place de Badjanani. A boat leaves just about every day to Anjouan for about CF7650 per person, and every few days as far as Mayotte (CF37,500). Far less frequently are there boats directly to Mohéli (about CF6000) – you will probably have to go to Anjouan first and get a connection.

The best boat linking all the islands (except Mohéli) is the *Ville de Sima*, which has a well-organised agency (☎ 73 11 07) next to the Café du Port. There are other agencies near the port and around the medina for other boats, such as the *Fraha*, which goes to Anjouan; the *Tratinga* (☎ 73 19 21) to Mayotte; the *Safina II* (☎ 73 01 62) to most islands; and the *Aranta* to Mayotte, and Mahajanga on Madagascar.

The place to get information about boats to other islands around the Comoros, and to places like Zanzibar, off the coast of Tanzania, and Mahajanga, are the noticeboards pinned to the wall at the port. The friendly guys at SOCOPO-TRAM (☎ 73 00 08) at the port are also a good source of information.

Refer to the Comoros Getting There & Away chapter for more information about boats to the Comoros which come through Moroni.

GETTING AROUND
The Airport

The taxi drivers at the Prince Said Ibrahim Airport are notoriously unscrupulous. They initially ask a ludicrous F100 for a fare to Moroni, and are very reluctant to bargain for less; the best fare we could get was US$10. Any major foreign currency is gleefully accepted – and no amount of chastising will dampen their enthusiasm about ripping off foreigners.

If they won't lower their price, or you want to save money, simply walk a few metres directly out of the terminal and hitch a ride on any public transport heading south to Moroni. (Threatening to do this will probably result in a lower taxi fare!) A taxi-brousse between the airport and the Taxi-brousse Station North in Volovolo only costs CF300, and you can be dropped of at the Pension Kohinoor if want to stay there.

Getting from Moroni to the airport is far easier. Just go to the Taxi-brousse Station North and get on any vehicle going north. If you have any gear, it's best to take a share-taxi for CF1000 which leaves when it's full (about every 15 minutes). A chartered taxi to the airport will cost CF3000 (but costs two to three times more *from* the airport).

Car & Motorcycle

If you are thinking about hiring a car somewhere in the Comoros, Grande Comore is obviously the place to do it, because it's the biggest island and it has the best roads and the most to see.

The charges at Avis (☎ 73 30 44), based at the Tourism Services Comores office at the Itsandra Sun Hôtel, start from F500 per day for a Suzuki jeep. Petrol and various taxes and insurance costs will bolster the daily charge by another F200 per day. A driver will cost a further F120 per day.

Far better value can be found at Tropics Tours & Travel (see under Travel Agencies). It hires out small Peugeot 205s for F420 per day (for a minimum of three days) all inclusive except for a driver, which will cost an extra F150 per day. It also organises cheaper rates for longer hire and more expensive rates for better cars.

Taxi

Around Moroni, and as far as Hahaya to the north and Iconi to the south, you can take a share-taxi, usually four passengers plus driver squeezed into a Renault 4. These are more comfortable than taxis-brousse and usually leave more often, but they are more expensive. One advantage is that you can admire the scenery, which you can't do while squashed into the back of a taxi-brousse.

There is no need to ask the fare – if you do, some drivers may take advantage of your lack of knowledge and charge you two or three times more. Find out the local fare as soon as you can, and simply pay the standard fare each time. The current fare is CF200.

Taxi-brousse

The Route Nationale which encircles Grande Comore is divided into three numbered routes. Between Moroni and Mitsamiouli it's called RN1; from Mitsamiouli to Foumbouni it's RN3; and from Foumbouni back to Moroni it's RN2.

Long-distance routes (inasmuch as there are long-distance routes on Grande Comore) are served by taxis-brousse. They leave from three stations which are, frankly, a mess – just sidings on the road, not the sort of terminals you would expect in Madagascar.

For destinations to the north and north-east, taxis-brousse gather at the Taxi-brousse Station North, near the new market in Volovolo. They go to Hahaya (for the airport), Mitsamiouli and Le Galawa Beach Hôtel, and as far as M'béni on the north-east coast. For destinations in the central part of Grande Comore, mainly Chomoni, taxis-brousse leave from the Chalima Terminal, which is lost in the old town. Ask for directions; you are unlikely to find it otherwise.

To the south, taxis-brousse leave from the Taxi-brousse Station South at Place Cobadjou, near the unfinished mosque. These taxis-brousse also pass by the shop on Rue Caltex, just in front of the Hôtel Karthala, to pick up passengers.

Other places where you can probably just stand and wait for a taxi-brousse to come by are the port, especially when boats arrive, outside the BIC bank and the Place de Badjanani.

Because the east coast is so sparsely-populated, very few taxis-brousse travel between M'béni and Chomoni or between Pidjani and Chomoni. Circling the entire island by public transport is very difficult but not impossible. Like the rest of the island, public transport seems to slow down between 11.30 am and 3 pm; after dark it virtually stops.

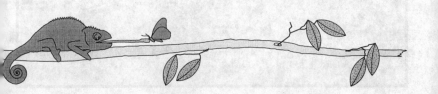

Mohéli (Mwali)

Mo! Mohéli (also called Mwali or Moili) is the smallest, wildest, least populated and least developed island of the Comoros. Because the government is in Grande Comore and Anjouan is heavily populated, Mohéli tends to be at the rear of the queue when it comes to government attention, and it is ignored by just about every Comoran and foreign travel agency.

In spite of this (or because of it) Mohéli is, for many travellers, the most interesting, pleasant and inviting of all the islands. However, transport to and around the island is very limited, and you may have to stay a few days waiting for onward transport. This wouldn't be a problem if the choice of restaurants and hotels wasn't so poor.

Mohéli is the most fertile island in the Comoros, with several substantial watercourses, lots of forests and a number of fine beaches. The island measures 30km from east to west and 15km from north to south at its widest point, and covers a total of 290 sq km. A ridge running east-west, the Mledjélé, forms the island's spine and Mt Koukoulé, which rises behind Fomboni, is its highest peak at 790m.

The people of Mohéli remain closer to their African roots than to Arabic Islam, and religion isn't stressed as much as it is on Grande Comore and Anjouan. Mohéliens also seem to be the most straightforward and melancholy of the Comorans, often apologising to visitors and pointing out all the things that their island lacks: industry, investment, development, consumer goods

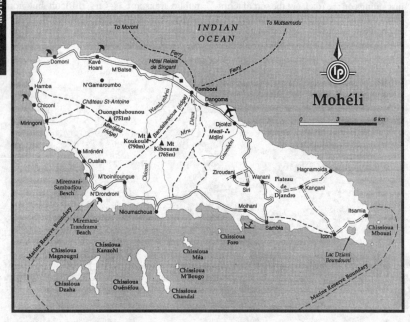

388

and attention from their government in Moroni. At times it's difficult to feel good about the quiet and solitude!

On a brighter note, several Livingstone's bats, thought to have been wiped out on Mohéli by cyclones in 1983 and 1985, have been observed on the island and two specimens have been taken to England for captive breeding. Mohéli also has the healthiest population of nocturnal *makis* (the local name for mongoose lemurs) in the Comoros.

History

The first conquerors of the island were Shirazis who came from the Persian Gulf in 933 AD; subsequent waves of Persians arrived until the middle of the 15th century.

In 1830 the Malagasy prince Ramanetaka, who had been obliged to clear out of his homeland, arrived on the island (up to that time a dependency of Anjouan) and staged a coup which left him in power as sultan. He took the name Sultan Abd El Ramane, and was succeeded by his young daughter, Djoumbé Saoudy, who took the name of Fatima I.

The French, chuffed by their 1841 success in taking over Mayotte, saw a hope of gaining a foot in Mohéli's door and sent a governess, Mme Droit, to see to the young sultana's education. In 1852 a peasant revolt resulted in Mme Droit's expulsion from the island, and the marriage of Fatima to Saïd Mohammed, an exiled prince from Zanzibar. Fatima later became enamoured of a Frenchman from Madagascar, Joseph François Lambert. A trader, adventurer and ship owner from Mauritius, he had been made the Duke of Imerina by the queen of Madagascar. Fatima and Lambert became lovers, and through the sultana Lambert was able to gain control of great tracts of land on Mohéli and set up plantations with his British partner, William Sunley.

In 1867, after the affair had begun to wane, Fatima abdicated the throne in favour of her 10-year-old son, Mohammed, and fled the Comoros with a French gendarme. At this point, the island of Zanzibar saw an opportunity and brought Mohéli and its young

sultan under its official protection. The following year, the French countered by successfully encouraging Mohammed to proclaim the independence of Mohéli and sever ties with Zanzibar.

In 1880 Sultan Mohammed was forcibly replaced by Sultan Abd El Ramane II. On 26 April 1886, he in turn was succeeded by the Shirazi prince Marjouni, who signed the treaty that turned Mohéli into a French protectorate. Sultan Marjouni's successor, Mahamoud, the second son of Djoumbé Fatima, assumed the sultanate, then fled to Zanzibar with the royal jewels and treasury. By this time the heir to the throne, Salima Machamba, was a pensioner in Réunion and never returned to Mohéli. Thus the age of the sultans on Mohéli came to a tidy end.

FOMBONI

Fomboni, the capital of Mohéli, has a population of about 6000 and lies on the central north coast. Nothing much happens in Fomboni (and even less happens around the island) as will be obvious on first contact. In fact it's little more than a village, but for those who thrive on lassitude Fomboni is the place to be. It's ideal for just wandering and observing daily life, but since the island has seen very few travellers you can expect some reciprocal attention – you will hear endless screams of *bonjour*!!! and *ça va*???

Information

Probably because so little happens on Mohéli, and a foreigner is so rare, we were stopped three times in 24 hours, including once at the airport, for a passport check. (This only happened once more during three months of research throughout the rest of Madagascar and the Comoros.) The checks were perfunctory and more of an excuse to socialise with the *étranger* (foreigner).

Electricity around the island, and in Fomboni, is sporadic, and blackouts are common, so have a candle and torch (flashlight) handy. If you plan to stay awhile, it is definitely worth bringing tinned and prepackaged foods from elsewhere, because

MOHÉLI

there are only two restaurants on the island and the shops are poorly stocked.

Money There is no permanent bank on Mohéli. If you're desperate to change money, you'll have to wait until the 'bank' arrives. It's brought to Mohéli on a private plane every second Monday.

Post & Communications Fomboni has a post office, as well as a public telephone service – look for the building with the satellite dish along the street towards the port. Don't send anything from here, though; you will almost certainly get home quicker than any letter or parcel you send.

Emergency Emergency numbers are as follows:

- Fomboni Hospital ☎ 72 03 73
- Police ☎ 72 01 37

Police & Immigration The immigration office and police station are along the main street, next to the market-cum-taxi-brousse terminal. If you pass by the police station, the bored officials may want to look at your passport. If you want to visit the islands in the marine reserve off the coast of Nioumachoua, you need a permit from the immigration office. (Refer to the Nioumachoua & Marine Reserve section following for details.)

Tombs

Near the sports ground, along the main road, you can see several very poorly maintained Shirazi tombs. In the Christian cemetery, on the other side of the sports ground, are the tombs of Joseph François Lambert and his British business partner Sunley.

Beaches

On a clear day from the shore at Fomboni,

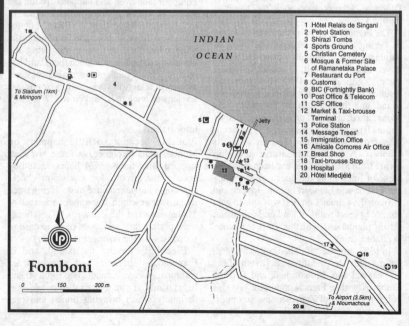

1	Hôtel Relais de Singani
2	Petrol Station
3	Shirazi Tombs
4	Sports Ground
5	Christian Cemetery
6	Mosque & Former Site of Ramanetaka Palace
7	Restaurant du Port
8	Customs
9	BIC (Fortnightly Bank)
10	Post Office & Telecom
11	CSF Office
12	Market & Taxi-brousse Terminal
13	Police Station
14	'Message Trees'
15	Immigration Office
16	Amicale Comores Air Office
17	Bread Shop
18	Taxi-brousse Stop
19	Hospital
20	Hôtel Mledjélé

INDIAN OCEAN

To Stadium (1km) & Miringoni

Jetty

Fomboni

0   150   300 m

To Airport (3.5km) & Nioumachoua

you can see Grande Comore and the mighty Mt Karthala volcano. There is a rocky beach directly in front of the Hôtel Relais de Singani, just west of Fomboni, but it's not good for swimming. There's a much better beach about 1½ km further west.

Along the shore in Fomboni proper and in the port area you can watch dhow construction and see fishing vessels bringing in their catches.

When the tide is out, boats often have to ignore the jetty and unload their cargo manually. Porters are loaded with anything from cartons of canned sausages to battered old refrigerators, then wade through the water, and load up a waiting tiny Renault 4 parked on the beach. This is fascinating to watch, and about the only entertainment on the whole island.

Places to Stay

There are only two places to stay on the whole island: one is terrible, the other is expensive. Taking a tent and camping anywhere on Mohéli, particularly on the islands south of Nioumachoua, is a far better alternative.

In Fomboni, the *Hôtel Mledjélé* gets our vote as the worst hotel in the Comoros, if not the whole of the Indian Ocean region. The staff are often drunk, inquisitive and light-fingered (a small camera went missing from our room); the toilets have to be seen to be believed; the rooms are disgustingly filthy; and there is no running water. If staying there, bring your own sheets, mosquito net and pillow. For all this 'luxury' they have the gall to charge CF7500 a room. It is an unmarked, white building, just up from the hospital; if in doubt ask directions.

The only other hotel in town, the *Hôtel Relais de Singani* (☎ 72 02 49), is worth using simply because it is a far better alternative, and has a restaurant. It is set in a nice garden (though not on a beach); and the staff are friendly. The rooms, with fan, hot water and, sometimes, views, seem palatial compared with the Mledjélé. They cost CF11,500/ 13,500 for a single/double; CF15,000/

20,500 for half-board; and CF18,500/27,500 for full-board.

Places to Eat

Getting something to eat, let alone finding a restaurant, in Fomboni is difficult. The Mledjélé has no restaurant. The outdoor bar and restaurant at the *Hôtel Relais de Singani* is normally open for guests only, but if you give them some advance notice, or plead, they may cook you something for a set CF3500.

The only restaurant (if you can call it that) is the *Restaurant du Port*, a small, unmarked hut near the port. If you give them a few hours' notice, they may drum up a passable fish meal, but they also may not be bothered. We were lucky: a local family took us under their wing and cooked us a great, varied meal of several courses for CF2000. Ask at your hotel if a local family can do this for you, too.

Frankly, it's best to self-cater. Bring your own food, otherwise you can buy a few tinned goods in shops along the street. The only two things for sale at the shops and market seem to be Coke and bananas, but a place just down from the Mledjélé sells fresh bread.

Entertainment

If you're ready for 'video night in Fomboni', the mobile *video cinema* cranks up between 8.30 and 9 pm nightly. The double features normally range from kung-fu to commando pictures dubbed in French. They are always well attended, and watching the people (who will probably be watching you, rather than the film) is entertaining in itself.

Otherwise, there's always the open air bar at the *Hôtel Relais de Singani*.

MWALI-MDJINI

About five km east of Fomboni, in the hills above the airport, is Mwali-Mdjini, the remains of a village that was first inhabited in the 10th century but was destroyed in the 18th century in a raid by Malagasy pirates. You can still see the remains of **stone houses**, a **mosque** and quite a few **tombs**.

MOHÉLI

The Green Turtle

A local taste for turtle meat has ensured that two species of turtle have all but vanished. The green turtle *(Chelonia mydas)*, which used to live in waters surrounding all three islands, now survives only near several small islands off Mohéli. Fortunately, recent conservation efforts have successfully educated locals, particularly in Nioumachoua, about the need to protect the turtles; there are beach patrols during the egg-laying season and stealing eggs is now illegal.

An adult green turtle is over a metre long and can weigh 130kg to180kg. The female hauls herself ashore on a remote stretch of beach and laboriously digs a hole to lay her eggs in the sand. Although the eggs are then buried the same female returns to the exact spot two or three times, at intervals of about two weeks, to lay more eggs. She can lay up to 200 eggs during one season.

The best place to start organising a trip to the islands (ask locally if it is the right time to watch the turtles lay their eggs) is at Nioumachoua, an easy taxi-brousse trip from Fomboni. You can hire a pirogue to Chissioua Ouénéfou and camp at the beach at the southern end. Bring your own food and water, and please be very careful of the turtles and the local environment. ■

The ruined village stands atop a hill on the Gnombéni River, above the village of Djoiézi.

LAC DZIANI BOUNDOUNI

Mohéli's wild eastern end is accessible only on rough tracks and trails. Perhaps the island's most interesting natural feature is the sulphurous crater lake, Lac Dziani Boundouni, near the south-eastern tip. Mohélians believe that bathing in the lake or washing in its water will cure a variety of maladies and conditions, including baldness and dandruff!

Even if you don't suffer from either affliction, a visit to the lake makes an agreeable day walk. You may be able to arrange a guided tour with the Hôtel Relais de Singani in Fomboni, or you can do the trip independently. Refer to the special Trekking in the Comoros section earlier in the book for more details.

NIOUMACHOUA & THE MARINE RESERVE

Nioumachoua is a beautiful village of thatched huts and friendly, inquisitive people on the far southern coast. The name of the village means Behind the Islands and it's easy to work out why. Nioumachoua's crowning feature is its broad, sandy beach which serves as departure point for fishing boats and trips into the island-studded marine reserve, established to protect the green turtles in the area.

It's possible to visit the village on a day trip from Fomboni using public transport. If you want to go to the islands, however, you will have to stay the night in Nioumachoua; ask around the village and someone will put you up for the night for a small fee. If you have camping equipment, you can camp near the village or, better, on the islands. You will have to be completely self-sufficient with food and water. Some very basic supplies are available at the village shop in Nioumachoua.

For further information about walks from, and around, Nioumachoua refer to the special Trekking in the Comoros section earlier in the book.

Permits

The bored immigration officials in Fomboni 'insisted' that foreigners going to the islands and marine reserve (but not just to the village) need a 'permit'. The form is especially typed while you wait, duly signed and stamped, and costs CF1000. Though this seems more of an exercise in making money and keeping busy than anything else, you will probably still need the permit before you can get on a boat to the islands from Nioumachoua. Pop into the immigration office in Fomboni and ask what the current situation is regarding the permit.

Marine Reserve & Offshore Islets

The small islands off Nioumachoua provide some of the best diving locations and most pristine environments in the Comoros. One of them, **Chissioua Ouénéfou**, which once served as a leper colony, has an appealing white sandy beach at the southern end. The beach is a favourite spot for green sea turtles and is great for camping. The most magic time to go is during the full moon, spending a couple of nights camping on the beach. You can swim, fish, explore on foot and perhaps see what is reputed to be the Comoros' densest population of green turtles. Fresh water is usually available on the island, but you'll need someone to point out the source. Otherwise carry water from Nioumachoua.

As you approach the village by taxi-brousse, the driver will stop, and magically a local 'tour operator' will appear. Before committing yourself, ask other people about boats and guides. However, there aren't that many for hire, so you will probably have to take whatever boats and boatmen you can find.

Naturally, the price is negotiable, and it depends whether you want to go for the day, or you want the boatman to return later to pick you up. Ask at the immigration office in Fomboni, where you need to get a permit, for their opinion about the current cost of chartering a boat to the islands from Nioumachoua.

You can also hire a boat to the other islands from Nioumachoua. However, most don't have beaches, nor are they as idyllic as Chissioua Ouénéfou for camping. For these islands, you will have to be self-sufficient with food, water and camping equipment.

Divers will revel in the coral and fish around most islands, but it is very difficult and/or expensive to organise any diving. There is certainly nowhere to hire equipment on Mohéli and the diving centre on Grande Comore is unlikely to allow you to take diving equipment there. You will have to bring your own.

Getting There & Away

From the terminal in Fomboni a taxi-brousse travels to Nioumachoua when it is full (every hour or two), and costs CF500 one-way. Even if you do not have the time, equipment or inclination to visit the islands, the taxi-brousse trip to the village is worthwhile. The road goes through some lovely dense forested areas, which you may want to explore yourself – just get off and on the taxi-brousse. But you will need to start early: you could spend most of the day waiting for the taxi-brousse then making detours for other passengers.

THE WESTERN BEACHES

At the extreme west end of the island you'll find a couple of good walks and more wonderful beaches, especially those at Kavé Hoani, Domoni and Miringoni. For more information about hiking in this area, see under Trekking in the Comoros.

Kavé Hoani

The beach immediately west of Kavé Hoani is a favourite site for female green turtles who come in at night to lay their eggs in the sand. Sometimes there's a guard posted to collect money from foreigners and prevent children sneaking in to collect the eggs.

The problem is transport. The turtles arrive at night long after the taxis-brousse cease running so you must either find a place to camp, or ask what the Hôtel Relais de Singani has in the way of (expensive) day trips.

Château St-Antoine Trek

A steep four km walk along the track inland

from Miringoni, or a five-km route from Hamba, will bring you to a forest hut high on the ridge known as Château St-Antoine (where you can stay if it is unoccupied). From this 690m point, there's a fine view down to the coast over one of the Comoros' greatest expanses of primary forest. The government is still considering turning this area into a national park and wildlife reserve.

If you don't want to back-track, continue east along the ridge to Mt Kibouana. From there, you can descend to Fomboni on the north coast or to M'boinifoungue (five km west of Nioumachoua) near the south coast, where ylang-ylang essence is distilled.

GETTING THERE & AWAY
Air
Most flights just link Mutsamudu (on Anjouan) with Moroni, and only detour via Fomboni two or three times a week. But there are currently four internal airlines so something will be going to Anjouan (about CF16,000) or Moroni (about CF16,500) every day or two.

For reasons unclear, Fomboni is the only one of the three islands where a foreigner has to fill out a disembarkation form after arriving on a domestic flight. It is painless, and only takes a couple of minutes to fill in – the local policeman will probably help you. You must also pay a local departure tax of CF1200 at the airport when you check in.

The local representatives for Amicale Comores Air (ACA) and Comores Sans Frontiéres (CSF) are usually at the airport when you arrive, so you can purchase an onward or return ticket immediately. ACA has an office on the main street; CSF bookings are possible at a shop along the main street; Aeromarine has an agency nearby (which was closed at the time of research); and no-one could tell us where to book seats for the unreliable Air Archipel airlines.

Boat
Because Mohéli is so small and sparsely populated it is not nearly as well connected by boat as the other islands. Normally, boats from Mohéli only go to Anjouan. The *Ville*

de Fomboni sails between Fomboni and Mutsamudu (about CF 5500), but irregularly; the *GS Benara* also sails to Mutsamudu every week from Fomboni; and the *Wemani* sails between the two towns when there is enough demand. Boats sailing directly to Moroni (about CF 6000) are irregular. For Mayotte, you will have to go to Anjouan first and get a connection.

For information about what boats are going where, check the notices nailed on to the 'message trees' in the median strip, opposite the police station. An empty building or two around the jetty area may also have a notice indicating the movement of local boats.

GETTING AROUND
The Airport
The Mohéli airport is about four km east of Fomboni. From the airport, you will have to hitch a ride on anything that is going into town. We managed something unique: a *free* lift on the back of a truck. To the airport, wait for something heading that way from the taxi-brousse stop near the hospital. Otherwise, it will take an easy 40 minutes to walk from the Hôtel Relais de Singani to the airport; it's 30 minutes from the Hôtel Mledjélé.

Taxi & Taxi-brousse
There are very few taxis on the island, so you must rely on infrequent taxis-brousse to get around. (You can circle all of Fomboni on foot in about 10 minutes.) The taxis-brousse seem to take an eternity to fill up because there are so few people on the island. They congregate at the main market, or at the stop near the hospital. Usually, the taxis-brousse are continually plying the streets looking for passengers, so it's a matter of asking and waiting.

The only tarred road on the island runs from Fomboni to Mirénéni, via Nioumachoua, and around the west coast to Miringoni. Unfortunately, no tarred road or public transport links Mirénéni and Miringoni, so you cannot completely circle the island. Occasionally, a taxi-brousse from

Wanani will go as far as Kangani. Public transport slows down considerably by around 3 pm, so late day-trippers may have to hitch or walk back to town.

Car & Motorcycle

From the Hôtel Relais de Singani, you can hire a car for CF15,000 per day, including a driver, which is not too bad. Hiring a car seems a little pointless, however: you cannot circle the island because of the incomplete road, so you do a lot of back-tracking; and visiting everything there is to see on the island takes about two hours.

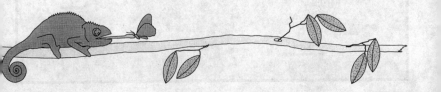

Anjouan (Ndzuani)

With several lakes and mountains in the heart of the island, steep coastlines and plunging valleys, Anjouan is topographically the most varied of the islands. Its highest peak, Mt Ntingui, rises to 1595m.

There are a few forested areas remaining on the steepest slopes, but around the coastline and in level areas deforestation is fairly common. The resulting slope erosion has caused soil to be deposited in the sea and coral reefs are being choked. The main reason for the environmental degradation is overpopulation and unsustainably intensive farming; this small island supports a rapidly increasing population.

Despite the crowding, Anjouan remains a quiet and personable island, the Comoran equivalent of a 'small town' society. As one

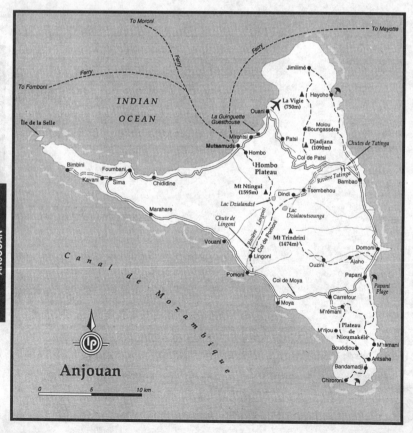

Peace Corps volunteer put it, 'If you don't remember what you had for breakfast, just ask anyone on the street'. There are only a few beaches to recommend on Anjouan, but the profusion of lakes, waterfalls, rivers, valleys and peaks in the interior are still worth visiting.

Many of the Anjouanais are Makoas, descended from slaves imported from Mozambique in the 15th century, or Wamatsaha, whose roots probably go back to the original Malay-Polynesian groups that first settled Madagascar. The island produces a great deal of ylang-ylang and vanilla, particularly on the east coast around Bambao and Domoni, the home town of the assassinated president Ahmed Abdallah.

One word of warning, which locals may give you (although it may be too late by then): the water in Anjouan is not fit to drink, even with purification tablets. You must boil the water for a lengthy period, or drink bottled water or soft drinks.

MUTSAMUDU

Mutsamudu, with its shabby buildings and maze-like streets, is one of the Comoros' most picturesque, yet grimy, urban centres. Founded in 1482, this town of 17,500 residents is the capital of Anjouan and the major port in the Comoros. Mutsamudu is more developed than Fomboni (but most places are), and easier to cope with than Moroni. The major drawback is the polluted shoreline, which stretches from the port to the closest swimmable beach at the Hôtel Al-Amal.

Orientation & Information

Most of Mutsamudu stretches along two parallel main streets, from the port area to the Hôtel Al-Amal about 750m away. Between the two streets is a fascinating maze of lanes and shops in the 'Arab quarter' or *medina*. Only one block south of the medina, the urban sprawl is halted by steep hills, from which you can get great views of the town and island. Next to the port is the town square. Here you will find most of the main offices, taxis-brousse and unemployed men.

Money The only bank on the island is the BIC Bank, on the southern side of the town square. It's open on weekday mornings from about 8 to 11.30 am, and closes a little earlier on Fridays. There's no problem changing travellers' cheques and the procedure is quite efficient.

Post & Communications The post office, where you can send mail (if you want to risk it) and make local, inter-island and international telephone calls is just west of the town square, only a few metres from the BIC bank.

Emergency Emergency numbers are as follows:

* Mutsamudu Hospital ☎ 71 00 34
* Police ☎ 71 02 00

Police & Immigration If you arrive by sea, you should be met at the port by an immigration official. He will probably take your passport, which you will have to collect the next day. The police/immigration office is along a winding street about 150m above the Hôtel Al-Amal. It is difficult to find and you will have to ask directions.

Things to See

Overlooking Mutsamudu, up a steep stairway from the medina, is a cannon-laden **citadel**, which was constructed with British money by Sultan Abdallah I in 1860 to defend the town against Malagasy pirates. The citadel was damaged in the 1950 cyclone, but still affords great views across the town and the new harbour (which was financed by Arab interests).

Beside the **Mosquée du Vendredi** in the town centre is the **Sultan's Palace**. There's also a nice and easy walk from Mutsamudu up the river gorge to the **Dziancoundré Waterfall**. The only decent beach within walking distance of town is run by the Hôtel Al-Amal. Non-guests are welcome to use it for a small fee.

Near the airport at Ouani, six km from town, is a 17th century **palace**. Although it has long been abandoned it is still in a relatively good condition and worth wandering around.

Places to Stay

Easily the cheapest place to stay is the basic *Motel Restaurant du Port*, which is not much of a hotel and less of a restaurant. It is in a noisy area, and the rooms, with shared facilities, are spartan, but the beds are comfy enough. It costs CF5000 per person.

The best value place is the *Hôtel Restaurant La Paillotte*, though it's a little hard to find in the eastern part of town. Clean and quiet rooms with a bathroom and fan cost CF9000/12,000 for a single/double.

The recognised 'tourist' hotel is Comotel's friendly *Hôtel Al-Amal* (☎/fax 71 15 80). It is set among lovely gardens with great views over the sea, a reasonable beach (marred only by heavy dumping of trash from the rocks above) and a swimming pool. The rooms, which have private balconies, fan and hot water, are as grubby as the pool,

and not really worth the official price of CF15,000/20,000, including an excellent breakfast, and CF22,000/33,000 for half-board. The prices are negotiable in the off-season and if you can wrangle a 25% discount they would be good value.

About halfway along the main road between the airport and Mutsamudu, overlooking the sea, is *La Guinguette* (☎ 71 05 85), a guesthouse above a bar and restaurant. It has a handful of nice rooms starting at CF11,250/15,000, including breakfast, complete with private bathroom, fan, desk, mosquito net and a great view over the island's north coast. It is inconvenient to town, but you can hitch a ride on passing taxis-brousse with ease.

Other inexpensive accommodation is springing up in towns and villages around the island as local families realise they can earn extra cash by renting out rooms in their homes. However, there are no listings so these places can only be found by asking

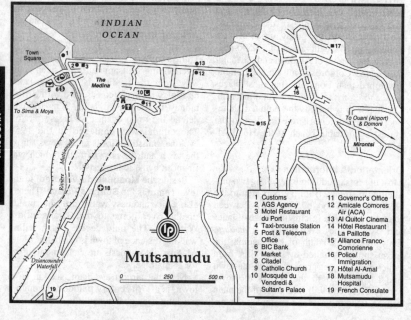

INDIAN OCEAN

Town Square

The Medina

To Sima & Moya

Rivière Mutsamudu

Dziancoundré Waterfall

Mutsamudu

0   250   500 m

To Ouani (Airport) & Domoni

Mirontsi

1 Customs	11 Governor's Office
2 AGS Agency	12 Amicale Comores
3 Motel Restaurant	Air (ACA)
du Port	13 Al Quitoir Cinema
4 Taxi-brousse Station	14 Hôtel Restaurant
5 Post & Telecom	La Paillotte
Office	15 Alliance Franco-
6 BIC Bank	Comorienne
7 Market	16 Police/
8 Citadel	Immigration
9 Catholic Church	17 Hôtel Al-Amal
10 Mosquée du	18 Mutsamudu
Vendredi &	Hospital
Sultan's Palace	19 French Consulate

around villages such as Mirontsi (just east of Mutsamudu), and Foumbani and Sima in the far west.

The only official hotel outside Mutsamudu is at Moya, on the southern coast. See the relevant section for details.

Places to Eat

There is nowhere cheap to eat around town. If price is more important than taste, you can pick up something edible at the *stalls* next to the port and town square, and along the esplanade. Because Mutsamudu is a major port, the many shops are quite well stocked so you can self-cater reasonably well.

Hôtel Restaurant La Paillotte has one of the best restaurants in the Comoros (see under Places to Stay) and is a must for anyone in need of a decent meal. Every time we went there, the staff claimed they had no set menu, but they offered tasty chicken, zebu or fish, with chips (french fries) and salad for CF3000. It has a nice outdoor-style setting, the staff are friendly and you can buy (expensive) beer or wine.

The restaurant at the *Hôtel Al-Amal* has one of the best views on the island and it serves alcohol, but unfortunately most visitors find that the quality of food is not great, and prices are high. If you stay there you are entitled to an outstanding free breakfast of fresh fruit.

La Guinguette, a pleasant stroll (or easy taxi-brousse trip) east of town, has an excellent restaurant and a bar stocked with beer. Drop by in the afternoon to order the speciality of the house: lobster in coconut cream.

The *Restaurant du Port*, in the 'motel' of the same name, has a reasonable setting and a cheap menu, but every time we tried to eat there the staff came up with a multitude of excuses for why they couldn't be bothered. Maybe you will have better luck.

Entertainment

Not surprisingly, there isn't a great deal to occupy the evenings. The *Al Quitoir* cinema looked permanently closed at the time of research, and if it ever reopens it is only

likely to show Islamic-influenced films in French. The *Alliance Franco-Comorienne* is usually a good place to ask about local cultural activities, but the range of things to do is far fewer than its counterpart in Moroni.

The only knees-up in town is the Saturday evening dinner-dance at the *Hôtel Restaurant La Paillotte*, which costs CF1000 to enter. An evening drink is available at La Paillotte or the *Hôtel Al-Amal*, but you will pay high prices.

Things to Buy

The bustling market is worth wandering around if you don't mind being stared at. There are a lot of household items and food to buy, as well as a few souvenirs such as clothes and carvings. It is just up from (and south of) the town square.

AROUND THE ISLAND

Although the interior of Anjouan is populated and well cultivated, there are a few remaining wild areas which are accessible to energetic trekkers. Wherever you go in the interior, keep a lookout for the rare and immense Livingstone's fruit bat, which is found only here and on Mohéli.

There are lots of opportunities for interesting walks. If you're feeling energetic, take camping gear and turn any combination of the three main routes (west of Bambao, north of Pomoni and south of Mutsamudu) into a cross-island trek. If the route descriptions seem a bit confusing, the map in the book should help you sort things out. Locals are always happy to show you the way.

For more information about hiking around Anjouan, refer to the Trekking in the Comoros section earlier in the book.

Bambao

The town of Bambao lies on the east coast at the mouth of the Cirque de Bambao.

Sultan Abdallah III, who ruled Anjouan from 1855 and introduced sugar cane to the island, set aside a garden for the cultivation of flowers and fragrances. He also constructed an immense white palace, **Bambao Mtsanga**, which dominates the area. The

ANJOUAN

Coelacanth

The prehistoric-looking coelacanth is a primitive fish related to the coelacanthini, which are known to have lived around 350 million years ago. Their fins were so much like limbs that researchers believe the fish used to crawl along the bottom of swamps and mangroves. They differed from most other fish by the shape of the jaw, an 'extra' tail and overlapping scales, and may, in fact, have been the ancestors of land vertebrates. This much has been surmised and shown by well-preserved fossils, and the coelacanth was long thought to have died out with the dinosaurs about 70 million years ago.

It is not surprising, then, that when a specimen of the coelacanth was discovered washed up near East London, South Africa, in 1938, it caused a furore among scientists. The fish was 1.5m long and identified by a South African professor, JLB Smith, who wrote of his subsequent discoveries in *Old Four Legs: The Story of the Coelacanthe*.

After a determined search a second coelacanth, complete with dozens of fish eyeballs in its stomach, was caught on a fishing line off Papani, Anjouan, in December 1952. It was given the scientific name *Malania anjouanae*. Naturally, Comoran fisherfolk had long been aware of the large fish they call the *gombessa* and had hauled them up regularly in Comoran waters. ∎

palace is worth a visit to see its masterfully carved wooden doors and the view from the terrace. The **sultan's tomb** lies along the approach to the palace.

Bambao is also one of the centres of ylang-ylang production and has a **ylang-ylang distillery** for perfume oils from such plants as orange flower, clove, geranium, frangipani and, of course, ylang-ylang. If you ask politely, visitors are normally welcome to tour the factory and learn about the blend of traditional and modern distillation processes in use.

Hayoho

The immense Hayoho beach on the northeast coast is one of the finest beaches on Anjouan, but it is only accessible by boat or on foot from Bambao. If you want to get away from it all, make arrangements with boat owners in Domoni, Bambao or Mutsamudu.

Domoni

Approximately nine km south of Bambao, Domoni, Anjouan's most interesting town, was the original capital of the island and is now its second-largest population centre, with more than 8500 inhabitants. The local embroidery is especially masterful and Domoni is also the source of some of the Comoros' finest wood carving; as well as traditional Koran holders and spice boxes you can also purchase carved boxes designed to hold cassette tapes.

Although the area was first settled by Arab merchants and their African slaves, the first stone building in Domoni was constructed by a man called Fani Attouman Calétschipoutou in 1274 AD. Two centuries later came the first Shirazi prince, Hassani Ben Mohammed, who proclaimed himself the first sultan. It wasn't long before he'd also annexed Mayotte and Grande Comore. In 1542 Domoni was made the capital of

Anjouan by Sultan Idaroussi. The coast is guarded by an ancient fortified wall and a ruined tower, built as protection against Malagasy pirates.

Things to See There are plenty of things to see in Domoni. The **old town**, Hari ya Moudji, seems even more labyrinthine than Moroni, with tiny cramped streets and alleys losing themselves in a maze of houses and shops. You'll also find **palaces** dating from the 16th to 18th centuries, still occupied by descendants of the sultans who built them. Unfortunately, they are generally in a poor state of repair.

Around the square outside **Mosquée Ouani** you'll see fine examples of door carvings. Also of interest is the **Mosquée de Madrassah**, built in 1555, with interesting 16th century inscriptions visible above the door and in the interior. Beside the new Mosquée du Vendredi is the **Mosquée Chirazi**, first constructed by the Shirazis. The present mosque is the sixth in a series built upon the same foundations.

A new addition in Domoni is the **mausoleum** of the president who hailed from Domoni, Ahmed Abdallah Abderemane; he was assassinated in 1989 by his presidential guard. With its brilliant white walls and four high minarets, it's now the most imposing structure in town, if not the entire country.

A short walk south of Domoni is the pebble beach of **Papani**, where the second coelacanth known to the western world was caught in 1952.

Places to Stay & Eat The only hotel in Domoni is the basic and small *Hôtel Karima* (☎ 71 92 83) where you can get a room for about CF5000 per person.

Chiroroni

The easiest way to reach the far south and its main attraction, the coral reef and white sand beach at Chiroroni, is inland from Papani. Try to find a taxi-brousse going to M'rémani (not to be confused with the coastal village of M'ramani south of Papani) on the heavily populated Plateau de Nioumakélé, 15km

from Domoni. Alternatively, find one bound for Moya, get off at the junction known simply as Carrefour and either walk or hitch (an unlikely possibility) the two km south to M'rémani. This village marks the beginning of the well-populated and cultivated route to Chiroroni.

Moya

The name Moya means 'isolated' in the Comoran language, and so it is. The particularly scruffy little village, where a white face may cause a minor riot, overlooks a beautiful beach – the best on Anjouan. The beach is protected by a reef and offers excellent swimming and rock scrambling, as well as passable snorkelling when the seas are calm.

Start early if you want to take a day trip from Mutsamudu; or you can stay overnight in the local hotel, enjoy a seafood feast and watch the spectacular sunsets. The local hotel has the cheek to charge foreign non-guests CF50 to use the beach – and you are unlikely to get away with sneaking on there if you are not a guest. Anyway, it's a small price to pay for some sand and surf.

Beware of some light-fingered kids who may take a fancy to anything you leave on the beach while swimming – leave everything looked in your room, or at the hotel reception. Also please try to resist the throngs of charming children who descend upon visitors, hoping to sell seashells; the practice is illegal and visitors have a responsibility not to encourage the market.

Places to Stay & Eat The only place to stay – and the only proper accommodation outside of Mutsamudu – is the *Moya Plage Hotel* (☎ 71 14 33), set above a lovely and dramatic stretch of coastline, and privy to Anjouan's best beach. The tiny bungalows, which have communal bathrooms (someone in the family can often boil up some water for you), and mosquito nets, are nothing special – but the setting is majestic. They cost CF5000 each.

Meals are only available if you order in advance. So, unless you ring first, or get an

ANJOUAN

early start from Mutsamudu, non-guests cannot normally just turn up at the hotel and order lunch. Meals cost CF4000; if you want to pig out on one of their awesome fish dishes, it will cost CF5000.

Getting There & Away A taxi-brousse to Moya from Mutsamudu costs CF600, and takes up to two hours one-way. Add to this endless waiting time for the taxi-brousse to fill up in Mutsamudu and to return to the capital.

The village and hotel are poorly signed. Ask your driver to let you off at the hotel, otherwise the taxi-brousse will bypass the beach and hotel. It is a lovely ride to Moya, usually via Sima, and worth a day trip in itself to see some pretty villages and go through mountain, forest and jungle scenery. But getting back may take a while – we had to wait about two hours for something to return to Mutsamudu.

Pomoni

The small village of Pomoni, with its pebble and sand beach, is of little interest but is pleasant enough. Pomoni has historically been the centre of production for copra and cacao, and perfume crops such as basil, patchouli and ylang-ylang. In the last century Pomoni was used by British warships as a coal station.

For an easy day excursion, head two km inland to the village of Lingoni. From here, turn right along a small track and follow it for 600m to an impressive 10m-high waterfall, **Chute de Lingoni**. Although it's a reasonable climb, the route is obvious and not difficult to negotiate on your own; local people are normally happy to help with directions.

The Far West

Twenty km west of Mutsamudu, **Sima** is one of the oldest settlements in the Comoros and certainly the oldest on Anjouan. Its mosque, **Mosquée Ziyarani**, was constructed in the 15th century over the top of a mosque built in the 11th century. From Sima, the circle-island route splits: the main road heads south

toward Marahare and Moya, and another continues five km west through Kavani to the sheltered fishing village of **Bimbini**, beside a picturesque beach.

Foumbani, immediately east of Sima, is the site of several volcanic craters, and at **Chididine**, east of Sima, there's a nice pebble and grey sand beach.

GETTING THERE & AWAY
Air

All four internal airlines link Mutsamudu with Moroni just about every day, and with Fomboni two or three times a week. The fares for each airline are about the same: CF20,500/35,850 one-way/return to Moroni and CF16,000/29,500 to Fomboni.

The location of the four airline offices was not entirely clear at the time of research. The airport, or an authorised travel agency around the town square, is the best place to book your ticket – try the AGS Agency (where staff speak English). Next to the Motel Restaurant du Port, AGS is a representative for Air Archipel and Comores Sans Frontiéres (CSF). Aeromarine (☎ 71 01 82) has a dedicated office next to the BIC bank, and Amicale Comores Air is in the old Air Comores building (still signed as such), along the main esplanade.

Currently there is no air link between Anjouan and Mayotte. Between these two islands you will have to detour back to Moroni and fly from there to Mayotte, or take the regular but expensive boat trip between Dzaoudzi, on Mayotte, and Mutsamudu.

Boat

Despite the dominance of Moroni as the capital of the Comoros, Mutsamudu is certainly the main port, so finding a boat between Mutsamudu and the other islands, including Mayotte, is easy.

Notices about the arrival and departure of boats are pinned to the port gate, and outside shipping agencies along the esplanade and near the port. The best place to ask about boats is the AGS Agency, next to the Motel Restaurant du Port. Staff speak English (and

French). Otherwise, contact other agencies around the port such as SOCOPO-TRAM (☎ 71 06 62), and Cocona (☎ 71 01 79) which handles bookings for the *Tratinga* boat to Mayotte.

Mutsamudu is the major connection to Fomboni on Mohéli. The *Ville de Fomboni* sails between Fomboni and Mutsamudu every few days, but the schedule is not regular; the *GS Benara* comes by every week and then goes to Mayotte; and the *Wemani* also links Mutsamudu with Fomboni when there is enough demand (which isn't often). The *Fraha* is a reasonable boat for Moroni.

For the roughish eight to 10 hour trip to Mayotte, all boats from Mutsamudu cost a whopping F400 or CF30,000. Sorry folks, no bargaining is possible because this price is set by the Mahorais authorities. Besides the *Tratinga*, the small and uncomfortable *Haute Mer* plies the lucrative Mayotte-Anjouan route three times a week in either direction.

The best of the inter-island ferries, the Mutsamudu-based *Villa de Sima*, sails every few days to Mayotte (CF30,000; at least six hours), and to Moroni (CF7650; about six hours), but not to Fomboni. The agency (☎ 71 00 65) for the *Villa de Sima* is next to the BIC bank.

GETTING AROUND
The Airport
A share-taxi to or from the airport, about six km east of Mutsamudu, costs a standard CF500, or you can go on a crowded taxi-brousse for CF100. Public transport is harder to find when you're going to the airport, but from the airport to the centre of town jump on anything that is going into town and past your hotel.

Taxi
Share-taxis (or more expensive chartered ones) are useful to get around Mutsamudu, which may seem a little spread out when it gets too hot. Share-taxis cost a standard CF400, for instance from the port to the Hôtel Al-Amal. Some drivers will assume that the few foreigners who make it to the island are made of money so you may be charged more. It's best to ask a local for the current rate of a share-taxi before getting into one.

You can always charter a taxi to take you for a tour of the island. Some travellers have been charged about CF15,000 per day, which is a little too much; see if you can bargain it down to about CF12,000 per vehicle per day. However, with reasonably regular transport around the small island and the limited number of roads on which a normal vehicle can go, it is not difficult (and far cheaper) to travel around the island using public transport and your own two feet.

Taxi-brousse
Taxis-brousse are less frequent on Anjouan than on Grande Comore and slow down after about 3 pm. The roads are fairly rough, but the Anjouan-Sima-Pomoni road will soon be upgraded with a US$7 million grant to stop it collapsing into the sea from erosion.

In Mutsamudu taxis-brousse leave from the town square in front of the post office. There are regular services between Mutsamudu and Sima, Pomoni, Bambao, Domoni and Moya from early morning until mid-afternoon.

Car & Motorcycle
If you're driving around Anjouan in September, try to avoid the carpets of *girofles* (cloves) spread out to dry on the roads! The Hôtel Al-Amal rents cars for CF22,500 per day. A driver will cost an extra CF5250 per day and a guide (speaking German, English or French) another CF10,000 per day. These are ridiculous prices: you can hire your own taxi for half that. In any event, hiring a car for an entire day is a bit pointless because you can 'circumnavigate' the island by road in about three hours.

Organised Tours
The only place which organises any tours with any reliability is the Hôtel Al-Amal. It has no set prices or schedules, however, and won't be good value.

ANJOUAN

Mayotte (Maoré)

Shaped like an exuberant seahorse standing on its head, Mayotte is the most southerly and oldest of the Comoros islands. It features relatively low rounded hills and a prominent encircling coral reef. The largest hill, Mt Bénara, is a modest 660m and the island is surrounded by an array of tiny islets such as Mtzamboro, Andrema and Bouzi.

The biggest difference from the other Comoran islands, of course, is that politically, Mayotte is a Collectivité Territoriale of France and its people are citizens of the European Community. However, it would be a mistake to assume that Mayotte is just a miniature version of Réunion with European living standards. As the inhabitants are fond of pointing out, Mayotte is not just *petite*, it's *petite petite*, and very much a French backwater. Despite large infusions of francs aimed at bringing the island's economy and infrastructure into parity with the Métropole (as mainland France is known), the real Mayotte remains Comoran with only a thin European veneer.

The 'island' of Mayotte actually consists of three main islands: Grande Terre (356 sq km), the large central island which contains the largest town, Mamoudzou; Pamandzi, or Petite Terre (18 sq km), where the airport is located; and the rock of Dzaoudzi, which covers only four hectares and is linked to Pamandzi by a causeway known as the Blvd des Crabes. The last two islands are just a short ferry ride from Mamoudzou.

Mayotte's population is rapidly approaching 90,000, of which nearly half are under 14 years old. Although the Mahorais (but not French) population is 99% Muslim, the basic tenets of religion are less formally adhered to than in the Comoros.

The people of Mayotte are known as Mahorais and, materially at least, they're better off than their cousins in the Comoros; most Mahorais seem to be quite happily French (the sentiment reached an all time high during Ali Solih's regime in the Comoros). As one would imagine, there's an increasing economically inspired illegal immigration from the other three islands to Mayotte.

One does suspect that many Mahorais are distressed to see their cultural identity and traditions being slowly eroded, despite efforts to the contrary. As in France's Pacific territories, the ethnic French element mainly keeps to itself and Mayotte is not the racial melting pot of Réunion. Still, there is only a minor movement towards independence or reintegration with the Comoros. Neither are there external military threats; to discourage any such ideas a permanent detachment of the French Foreign Legion is based in Dzaoudzi.

Before you think about coming, you must be aware that Mayotte is an expensive place – and it will seem horrendously dear if you have spent time in Madagascar. Mayotte has no bottom-end accommodation, camping is virtually outlawed and the only place to eat cheaply is at the market. Local transport is reasonably priced – but everything else is not.

ACTIVITIES

For further information about the fantastic diving, fishing, boating and other water sports available on the two main islands of Mayotte, refer to the Activities section in the Comoros Facts for the Visitor chapter.

INFORMATION

The various offices and shops that you may need, as well as hotels and restaurants, are divided between Dzaoudzi, on Petite Terre, and Mamoudzou, on Grande Terre, though most are on the latter.

Tourist Office

Just up from the ferry terminal on Rue de la Pompe, in Mamoudzou, the helpful tourist office (☎ 61 09 09; fax 61 03 46) is definitely worth visiting. It can provide advice, maps

Mayotte

Chissioi Mtzamboro
Malandzamiayatsini
Malandzamiayojou
Kadijou
peninsula
Baie de
L'Andréma
Chissioi Andrema
Mtsahara
Majiméoni
Mtzamboro
Acoua
Dzoumogné
Baie
de
Longoni
Pointe de Longoni
Trévani Village
Hôtel
Trévani
Longoni
Koungou
RN1
Ferry
Mtsangamouji
Cascade de Soulou
Mt Mtsapéré ▲
(572m)
Majimbini
Baie de Soulou
Vahibé
Tsingoni
Coimbani
Mamoudzou
Mtsapéré
Ferry
Dzaoudzi
Petite
Terre
L'Abattoir
Pamandzi
INDIAN
OCEAN
▲ Mt Coimbani
(481m)
RN2
See Enlargement
Pamandzi
Chiconi
Coconi
RN2
Dembéni
Sisoi Bouzi
Chissioi Sada
Sada
Grande Terre
Mtsanga Beach
Village Hôtel
Mtsangachehi
▲ Mt Bénara
(660m)
RN3
Chissioi Bandélé
Bouéni
Baie de
Bouéni
Chissioi Caroni
Chirongui
Restaurant
Musical Plage
Mtsatoundou
Bambo-Est
Chissioi
Bambo
Jardin Maoré Hôtel
Kani-Kéli
▲ Mt
Choungui
(594m)
Mtsamoudou
Saziley
Peninsula
Ngoudja
Dapani
Msanga
Tsoholé
Mbouini

Pamandzi
(Petite Terre)

Dziani
Dzaha
Moya
Plage
Badamiers
Plage
Bagamayo
Dzaoudzi
L'Abattoir
la Vigue
Hôtels Le Royal &
Lagon Sud
Pamandzi

0   5   10 km

To Mutsamudu
& Moroni

0   1   2 km

chures and maps. For more information, refer to the Tourist Offices section in the Comoros Facts for the Visitor chapter.

Money

There are two branches of Mayotte's only bank, the Banque Française Commerciale Océan Indien (BFC-OI): one is directly opposite the ferry terminal in Mamoudzou, and the other is next to the customs office in Dzaoudzi. Both change cash and travellers' cheques, and have an automatic teller machine which may accept your Visa or MasterCard (it didn't accept ours) for after hours cash withdrawals.

Both banks are open Monday to Friday from 7.30 am to noon, and from 1.30 to 3.30 pm. Because there are only two banks, and they have limited opening hours, long lines of impatient account holders are common. For the quickest service, get to either bank about 30 minutes before opening time.

Remember that there are no money-changing facilities at the airport, so you *must* have enough French francs to last until you can visit the bank.

Post & Communications

The main post office, just above the ferry terminal in Mamoudzou, is open from 7 am to 5 pm, Monday to Friday; and from 7 to 11 am on Saturdays.

France Telecom, in the arcade of shops on Place Mariage, is only open from 7 am to 1 pm on Monday to Friday. The opening times are not very useful if you want to ring anyone keeping business hours in Europe. But it doesn't affect most local French residents, who have private telephones or use a *telecarte* in public telephones to make calls.

Travel Agencies

A number of travel agencies on Mayotte offer a range of expensive trips around the island. These often include a ride on a boat and a picnic lunch and cost about F175/250 per person for a half or full-day trip.

The two best agencies are Mayotte Aventures Tropicales (☎ 61 19 68) – you'll

have to ask for directions – and Mayotte Tourisme et Voyages on Place du Marché (☎ 61 25 50). The latter also has an office at the airport which you shouldn't confuse with the official tourist office.

To find out what other trips and tours may be on offer, check out the ads in the weekly newspapers, look at the notices pinned on the wall outside Bar 5/5 at the ferry terminal, and talk to the helpful staff at the tourist office.

For more information about diving, fishing, boating and other water sports around Mayotte, refer to the Activities section in the Comoros Facts for the Visitor chapter.

Bookshops

There are several excellent bookshops which stock a large range of French-language books, postcards, stationery, and souvenir publications about Mayotte, as well as maps of Mayotte and the rest of the Comoros. They sell plenty of French magazines and newspapers, only a few days out of date, and if you are lucky, magazines in English, like *Time*.

The two branches of Librairie Shopping, on the Blvd des Crabes about 500m from the ferry landing in Dzaoudzi, and just behind the market in Mamoudzou, are both very good. The best-stocked bookshop is the appropriately named Maison du Livre, next to France Telecom. There's nothing in English but you will find a large selection of classics in French.

Books You may want to pick up some booklets about Mayotte to help you sort out what is on and where. *Good Morning Mayotte*, written in French and English, is outdated and not as good as the others, but it is handy for English-speakers – everything else is written in French. The pocket-sized *Mayotte en Poche* (F50), available in most bookshops on Mayotte, is a handy guide to the history and regional attractions; it has some nice photos, but contains little practical information.

Emergency

Useful emergency numbers follow. Up-to-date numbers are included in the weekly newspapers.

- Customs ☎ 60 10 14
- Fire Brigade ☎ 18
- Hospital ☎ 61 15 15
- Pharmacy (Mamoudzou) ☎ 61 12 39
  (Dzaoudzi) ☎ 60 17 69
- Police ☎ 17
- Telephone information service ☎ 12

PETITE TERRE

Dzaoudzi

The island of Pamandzi, with about 15,000 inhabitants, is connected to the rock of Dzaoudzi (a sort of poor Rock of Gibraltar) by a causeway. Until the arrival of the Foreign Legion in 1962, it served as the capital of Mayotte, and still functions as its military centre. The two small islands comprise Petite Terre, which is still considered the affluent high-rent district of Mayotte and home to most of the Collectivité's European community.

While Pamandzi has a couple of interesting and worthwhile highlights, there's little to do in Dzaoudzi but take a walk, admire several old stone buildings and visit the **Old Préfecture gardens** with their two antique cannons. Higher up on the rock are larger colonial homes and gardens. Once those options are exhausted, you could hang out with the Foreign Legion!

Places to Stay Currently, there is no accommodation in Dzaoudzi. The once-popular Hôtel du Rocher building is still there, opposite the Air France/Air Austral office, but sadly it no longer functions as a hotel. Hopefully, it may get a new lease of life and reopen in the future.

Two places next to each other along the main road between the airport and the ferry to Mamoudzou – and one in the village of Pamandzi – are worth considering, espe-

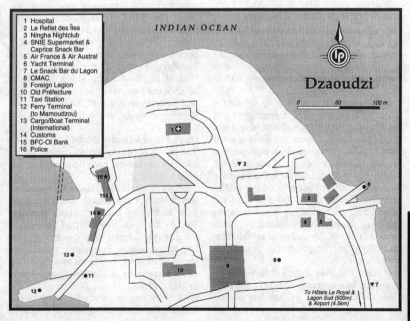

1 Hospital
2 Le Reflet des Îles
3 Ningha Nightclub
4 SNIE Supermarket &
  Caprice Snack Bar
5 Air France & Air Austral
6 Yacht Terminal
7 Le Snack Bar du Lagon
8 CMAC
9 Foreign Legion
10 Old Préfecture
11 Taxi Station
12 Ferry Terminal
  (to Mamoudzou)
13 Cargo/Boat Terminal
  (International)
14 Customs
15 BFC-OI Bank
16 Police

INDIAN OCEAN

Dzaoudzi

0   50   100 m

To Hôtels Le Royal &
Lagon Sud (500m)
& Airport (4.5km)

MAYOTTE

cially because they are the three cheapest places on Mayotte. The family-run *Hôtel Lagon Sud* (☎ 60 06 20; fax 60 17 27) is on a rocky beach (but next to a sandy one). A very pleasant single or double room with fan and hot water costs F200, and F250 for a triple. If you ask, you can get a room with a sea view. However, breakfast (F28), pre-ordered meals (there is no restaurant as such), and drinks are pricey, even for Mayotte. One advantage is that the hotel is also the centre for the impressive Le Lambis diving outfit – refer to the Activities section in the Comoros Facts for the Visitor chapter for more details.

Not quite as good value is *Hôtel Le Royal* (☎/fax 60 12 45), just a few metres south of the Lagon Sud. Le Royal has a range of rooms starting at F200 for an inside fan-cooled room with no view or outside window, to F350 for a nice room with air-conditioning and a balcony with great views. Breakfast is F25 and an agreeable restaurant is attached.

Places to Eat Of the few restaurants on this side of Mayotte, a friendly option is *Le Reflet des Îles*, right in Dzaoudzi. The poulet au coco is unbeatable; also on offer is a variety of fish dishes and a sampling of basic Chinese and Indian concoctions for F35 to F65.

For self-catering, the best place to head for is the well-stocked *SNIE Supermarket* and the *Caprice Snack Bar* which have most things you would expect to buy in a small French village shop (and at high prices). Freshly baked goodies are available in the morning from the *Boulangerie-Pâtisserie Le Lagon*, just out of Dzaoudzi on the Boulevard des Crabes about 300m west of the Hôtel Lagon Sud. Heading out towards the causeway, there is usually a portable caravan dubbed *Le Snack Bar du Lagon* selling takeaway food at comparatively reasonable prices.

If you are staying at the Lagon Sud or Le Royal hotels, it is an easy walk to L'Abbatoir. This awful sounding village has several places to eat and drink – and a couple are

comparatively cheap. Refer to the L'Abbatoir section below. Another great option for brochettes poisson (F3) and cold drinks (F6) is the unnamed house between Hôtels Lagon Sud and Le Royal – look for the notice advertising its daily specialities. *Le Royal* itself has a good restaurant with a lovely setting. The menu, which is limited, includes pork cutlets for F40 and a plate of brochettes for F45.

Many expats, French residents and visitors have access to a vehicle so they often drive to restaurants around Petite Terre. One of the best places offering expensive French cuisine and seafood in luxurious surroundings, with sea views, is *Le Tropicana*, just past the causeway towards L'Abbatoir.

Entertainment Just behind the former post office is the cinema run by the *Centre Mahorais D'Animation Culturelle* (CMAC). It screens quality films in French, or dubbed into French, several times a week. Look out for the posters next to the SNIE Supermarket advertising the films and their screening times. The CMAC is open Monday to Friday from 10 am to noon and 3 to 5 pm.

Just over the road, the *Ningha Nightclub* operates high-volume discos nightly, except Mondays. If you'd just prefer a drink in the tropical air, the Caprice Snack Bar at the SNIE Supermarket is a good place to go. You will probably meet a few characters, including some from the nearby Foreign Legion.

Moya Plage & Dziani Dzaha

The beach at Moya, and the nearby crater lake, Dziani Dzaha, each lie about two km from L'Abbatoir.

Moya Plage (Isolated Beach) is pretty and tranquil except at weekends, when it swarms with swimming and picnicking families. There's no reef, however, so the sea is rougher than around Mayotte and snorkelling is a non-starter. Fortunately, the dangers for swimmers are minimised by a sheltering cove formed by a semi-submerged and eroded volcanic crater. It's accessible by road or by crossing the ridge north of the beach in the similar crater south of Moya. To the north beyond a stand of mangroves lies yet another beach.

A short track climbs to the crater's rim at Dziani Dzaha – it's just 100m high – and an easily negotiated path down to the water's edge is lined with quicksand-like sulphur deposits. The green sulphurous waters of the lake are reputed to have therapeutic properties and to be especially effective in treating skin ailments such as psoriasis. There are several taboos associated with this lake, which is considered sacred by the Mahorais; visitors may not perform any toilet activities inside the crater and even the insects are considered revered and may not be swatted.

Getting There & Away It's easy walking along the motorable tracks to Moya Plage or Dziani Dzaha, though the route to Moya is quite steep. If you're feeling lazy, the approach to either attraction is just a short ride by taxi-brousse or share-taxi from Dzaoudzi. You are far more likely to get a lift on Sundays.

Although Moya Plage and Dziani Dzaha are quite near each other, don't be tempted to bush bash your way directly between the two; the undergrowth is quite thick and the terrain difficult. Once you've visited one, you must backtrack to L'Abattoir in order to visit the other.

Badamiers Plage & Bagamayo

Toward the north of the island, Badamiers Plage is more open and sandy than Moya Plage, but isn't as picturesque because of its proximity to the naval and fuel bases. To get there, follow the Dziani Dzaha track to the end and head west (left) down to the shore.

Near the coast, just west of Badamiers Plage, is the recently discovered archaeological site of Bagamayo. Here, researchers have uncovered pottery similar to that found on the East African coast, tombs, glass beads, spindles, a kiln and various other relics indicating what was probably a 10th century Shirazi settlement. If you want to have a look, it is also accessible from the route to Dziani Dzaha.

L'Abattoir

The village of L'Abattoir may not sound very inviting, but the village is slowly becoming urbanised by affluent Mahorais and French, though compared to places like Mauritius you could hardly call this 'urban sprawl'. The only reason to visit the village is to try one of the two good restaurants which are within walking distance of Le Royal and Lagon Sud hotels.

The cheapest restaurant on Mayotte is the friendly *Restaurant Mahorais*, along the main road. You can get an authentic Mahorais meal of beef and rice for a bargain F15, and according to its noticeboard, other meals (which may not always be available) cost F25. The food is nothing special (although they give you free cold water), but your wallet will appreciate it.

Also along the main road is the pleasant little bar patronised by expats (and mosquitoes) called *Le Triskell*. In the outdoor restaurant you can enjoy a plat du jour, such as a large hamburger and chips (french fries), for F40. Other meals start at F50.

Pamandzi

The sleepy village of Pamandzi has nothing to recommend it except that it has the cheapest accommodation on Mayotte. The friendly *Villa Raha* (☎/fax 62 03 64) is close to the airport, at 13 Rue du Smiam. The rooms, with communal bathrooms, are pleasant enough for F150 and there is a TV lounge. Breakfast costs an extra F20. Half-board, with what they promise is *cuisine typique de Mayotte*, is an extra F50 per person. The owner can also arrange the rental of cars, motorcycles and mountain bikes (known as VTTs).

GRANDE TERRE
Mamoudzou

Located on the eastern coast of Grande Terre, directly opposite Dzaoudzi, Mamoudzou (population about 34,000) is connected to Petite Terre by a regular ferry. Although Mamoudzou contains the bulk of the restaurants and businesses on Mayotte, apart from the market and the public gardens, there is little to see. The town is far more French than anywhere else in the Comoros; this may be an attraction if you are hankering for some modern European 'culture', or a disappointment if you want something more Mahorais.

Tombe d'Adriansouli Sultan Adriansouli handed Mayotte over to the French. Perhaps he is not well regarded these days, because his tomb lies in ruins. However, the expansive public garden surrounding the tomb is a lovely area of large shady trees and grass, and offers views over the pretty bay. It is worth a visit to relax, catch a breeze, and maybe have a picnic lunch. There are some walking trails which are indicated on a few maps around the park.

Musée de la Pêche If you love fish and fishing, you will probably want to visit the small Fishing Museum, also known as the Musée de la Mer (Sea Museum). It is open from 7 am to 2 pm, Monday to Thursday, and 7 am to noon on Fridays. You can find it above Banga Music along a laneway.

Places to Stay There isn't much to choose from on this part of Mayotte – and everything is expensive, or unavailable. The cheapest option seems to be the *Hôtel L'Oasis*. However, we couldn't get any information about the place because it had been temporarily commandeered by some troops. If it ever reverts to civilian use it may be worth checking out, although it is a little inconvenient.

The *Hôtel & Restaurant La Tortue Bigotu* (☎ 61 11 32; fax 61 11 35) is also inconvenient if you don't have your own vehicle. It offers nice air-conditioned singles/doubles for F350/370; or F505/680 for half-board. If you stay for seven days or more, you can save a few francs per day on the price for half-board.

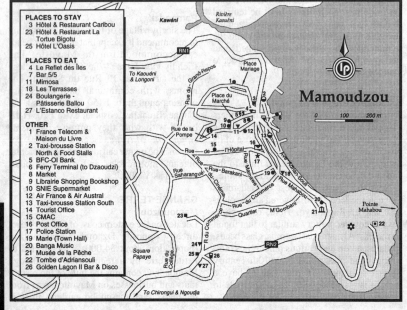

PLACES TO STAY
3 Hôtel & Restaurant Caribou
23 Hôtel & Restaurant La Tortue Bigotu
25 Hôtel L'Oasis

PLACES TO EAT
4 Le Reflet des Îles
7 Bar 5/5
11 Mimosa
18 Les Terrasses
24 Boulangerie - Pâtisserie Ballou
27 L'Estanco Restaurant

OTHER
1 France Telecom & Maison du Livre
2 Taxi-brousse Station North & Food Stalls
5 BFC-OI Bank
6 Ferry Terminal (to Dzaoudzi)
8 Market
9 Librairie Shopping Bookshop
10 SNIE Supermarket
12 Air France & Air Austral
13 Taxi-brousse Station South
14 Tourist Office
15 CMAC
16 Post Office
17 Police Station
19 Marie (Town Hall)
20 Banga Music
21 Musée de la Pêche
22 Tombe d'Adriansouli
26 Golden Lagon II Bar & Disco

Mamoudzou

MAYOTTE

The up-market place on Mayotte is the impressive *Hôtel & Restaurant Caribou* (☎ 61 14 18; fax 61 19 05), very easy to spot from the ferry terminal. The cheapest room here is F350; an extra bed is F100. The rooms, which include air-con and TV but no breakfast, are small and often noisy because of the main road below.

Places to Eat Mamoudzou has some good places to eat, but only a handful could be regarded as good value. A popular cheapie is the *Mimosa* snack bar in the market, but we found the choice very poor. They advertised omelettes for F25, but couldn't be bothered cooking one. You may have better luck. A couple of other cheap and grimy places on the perimeter of the *market* can whip up an omelette for F25 and a café noir for breakfast. For lunch the most they can do is a baked fish and rice dish, which isn't particularly tasty but cheap at F12.

The cheapest option is to pick up some tasty and filling samosas and fried bananas for a bargain F1 each from the *stalls* in front of the market. Buy them early before they start going off in the sun. In the taxi-brousse station, just north of the ferry pier, a few *food stalls* with outdoor seats are usually set up. They serve rice and fish dishes from F10. They are friendly places but the hygiene may not be up to scratch.

For a wider variety, pop into the *SNIE Supermarket*, across the street from the market. Most of the things for sale are imported from Mauritius or France, and priced to cater to well-paid French residents, so you may not save any money by self-catering. For pastries and fresh bread it is hard to beat the *Boulangerie-Pâtisserie Ballou* along Rue du Commerce.

Near the ferry terminal, are several pleasant but expensive places for a meal. Be wary: a drink could cost you the equivalent of an entire day's budget in Madagascar. The best in this area is *Bar 5/5* – the drinks and meals are not too outrageous if you stick to a hamburger for F25, or a tuna and salad sandwich, large enough for lunch, for F20. Other meals are F40 to F70. Right opposite the ferry is the classy *Le Reflet des Îles*, a popular meeting spot for trendy locals.

Other places to try around town are *L'Estanco Restaurant*, a classy grill and bar. It offers a menu du jour for a reasonable F60, a plat du jour for F40 and pizzas for F35 to F45. It holds 'le happy hour' every night from 7 to 8 pm. (It is only an hour, so drink quickly!) *Les Terrasses*, just a short walk up from the terminal, has great views of the city and esplanade and meals starting at F65. The poolside restaurant at the *Hôtel & Restaurant Caribou* has dishes such as chilli con carne for F65 and plats du jour for F60 – but other meals are expensive at F70 to F80.

For some authentic Mahorais, rather than French, food and music – at authentic Mahorais, rather than French, prices – try *Banga Music*. It has a great atmosphere and is especially lively late on weekends.

Entertainment Everything on Mayotte is expensive, so there is no such thing as a cheap night out. For a glass of beer or a shot of something stronger in the afternoon or evening, try *Les Terrasses*, which offers great views. The main 'action' night spots, apart from the hotel bars, are the *Golden Lagon II Bar & Disco* (the first Golden Lagon burned down), *Bar 5/5* and *Banga Music*, as mentioned under Places to Eat.

For French film, theatre and cultural activities, try the *CMAC* along the Rue de l'Hôpital.

Around Grande Terre
Most of the route which encircles Mayotte is paved, but the uneven coastline, especially in the north, makes for lots of twists, bends and rather slow going so don't try to cover too much ground in a day.

For information about hiking around Mayotte, refer to the Trekking in the Comoros section earlier in the book.

As you travel around Mayotte watch out for the interesting and colourful *bangas*. These are small bachelor houses, constructed by young men, which are painted with humorous sayings and philosophies such as *La vie célibataire est la vie superbe* (The bachelor life is a superb life!). Several friends often share the same banga, each encouraging the other to complete his education before marrying and starting a family. Refer to the Society & Conduct section in the Facts about Comoros chapter for more details.

Also look out for the island's subspecies of the brown lemur *Lemur fulvus mayottensis* (more commonly known as *makis*), which are relatively common on Mayotte and like to hang out in trees around hotel restaurants awaiting banana handouts.

Cascade de Soulou

On the chocolate-coloured west coast beach of Soulou is the Cascade de Soulou, an unusual 8m waterfall which plunges directly into the sea (or onto the beach at low tide). Its popularity with both locals and visitors, especially Sunday picnickers, is demonstrated by the profusion of trash left behind.

The quickest way from Mamoudzou is north along RN1 to Dzoumogné, then on the paved cross-island road which descends to the coast at the Baie de Soulou. From Mamoudzou, find a taxi-brousse headed for Mtsangamouji and ask to be dropped at the track down to the beach, two km south of Mtsangamouji.

Chissoi Mtzamboro

Off the far north-western tip is a group of islands collectively known as Mtzamboro. They are very difficult to reach but offer superb swimming and snorkelling. The travel agencies listed earlier in this chapter organise day trips by boat around the islands for about F200 to F300 per person.

Plage de Ngoudja

Near Kani-Kéli, on the south-western tip of the island, is the white sand beach of Ngoudja, reputed to be the best on Mayotte. Home of the Jardin Maoré Hôtel, it is backed by a stand of baobabs and offers good snorkelling and diving. If there's nothing going directly to Ngoudja, your best bet is probably to get a taxi-brousse from Mamoudzou to Chirongui and try to hitch from there.

Other Beaches

Good beaches include Mayotte's main port, **Longoni**, 16km north of Mamoudzou, where you'll find good snorkelling; and **Majiméoni**, 33km from Mamoudzou in the Baie de L'Andréma on the north-eastern tip of the island, which is further away and less crowded. For relatively deserted beaches go to the northern tip of the island and stroll around the Kadijou Peninsula. The black volcanic beach at **Trévani** is popular and has a hotel.

The west coast beach of **Mtsangachehi** has been recommended by some but, at low tide, the water is muddy and shallow. However, the beach affords a superb view of pinnacle-like Mt Choungui across the Baie de Bouéni.

Places to Stay & Eat

The options around the island are very expensive. The *Trévani Village Hôtel* (☎ 60 13 83; fax 60 11 71), 11km north of Mamoudzou, sits in a nice leafy setting with a swimming pool and a nice beach. Normal rates for a luxurious single/double are F420/470 and it's an extra F150 for another bed in the room. Half-board rates are F560/750. If you want a room by the sea add another F50, and if you want a lift to and from the airport you will be charged a whopping F180 return.

The hotel also organises the rental of water sports equipment, including sailboards, pedalos, water skis, glass-bottom boats, kayaks, catamarans, and snorkelling and diving equipment. For more information about the diving centre at the hotel, and diving and snorkelling in general, refer to the Activities section in the Comoros Facts for the Visitor chapter.

The most up-market accommodation on Mayotte is the *Jardin Maoré Hôtel* (☎ 60 14 19; fax 60 15 19), with many bungalows on an isolated beach in the south-western corner, 50km from Mamoudzou. The rates are bound to make independent budget-minded travellers choke on their F1 samosa: F620/1040 for half-board, or F700/1240 for full-board which is virtually mandatory as there is nowhere else to eat for a long way. These rates include access to the library, as well as archery, pétanque (bowls), mountain bikes, classical music programs and mini astronomy courses, but add on an airport transfer of F300 return!

One new place which we couldn't investigate is *Le Camping à La Plantation* (☎ 62 15 24; fax 61 21 02), a campsite set in a forest 30 minutes by car from Mamoudzou. It sounds great, and may be worth ringing and checking out for something different and hopefully reasonably priced. No other details were available at the time of research, but the tourist office in Mamoudzou should have current details.

Entertainment Apart from the hotel restaurants there's the *Restaurant Musical Plage*, which sometimes offers music, on the southeastern coast of the island. The name of the beach is reputedly derived from the celebratory songs of successful Mahorais fisherfolk.

GETTING THERE & AWAY
Air
Incredibly, there are no flights between Mayotte and the Comoros except for the flights on Air Austral and Air Mauritius between Mayotte and Moroni. For more information about these and other international flights to/from Mayotte, refer to the Comoros Getting There & Away chapter.

The two combined offices for Air France & Air Austral are near the start of the causeway in Dzaoudzi (☎ 60 10 52; fax 60 03 87); and in Place du Marché (☎ 61 10 52; fax 61 10 53) in Mamoudzou. Inquire at the tourist office for the current location of the Air Mauritius agency or office.

The internal Comoran airline, Aeromarine, has a local agency (☎ 60 07 07), though at the time of research it had no plans to fly to Mayotte –it can't because of current regulations established by the Mayotte authorities.

When leaving Mayotte for the other islands in the Comoros, or Madagascar, spend all your French franc coins, or change all your coins into notes, because coins are very difficult to use or change outside Mayotte.

Boat
Because there are no flights between Mayotte and Anjouan, boats are usually booked out in advance – and heavily loaded. All inter-island boats depart from the dock on Petite Terre, immediately next to the ferry terminal in Dzaoudzi. Buy your ticket as soon as you can at the wharf or at the offices next to the customs office. If you have any problems, ring the local boat agencies or contact the tourist office.

The two best boats to use between Mayotte and Anjouan or Moroni are the *Tratinga* (☎ 61 10 49) or *Ville de Sima* (☎ 61 35 66). The standard price for all boats travelling between Mayotte and Anjouan is a whopping F400. Try to avoid the *Haute Mer* (appropriately named the High Sea); it is worth hanging around for a decent boat otherwise the journey can be very long, uncomfortable and potentially dangerous.

Other boats which sail between Mayotte and the Comoros (mainly Anjouan) at irregular intervals are the *GS Benara*, *Vedette Chaweni*, *Aranta* (which also goes to Mahajanga on Madagascar), and *Vedette Toiwoussi*. For information about travelling between Mayotte and Madagascar, refer to the Comoros Getting There & Away chapter.

GETTING AROUND
The Airport
Getting from the airport on Petite Terre is as easy as walking out of the terminal and taking a share-taxi for F4 to anywhere along the main road as far as the ferry terminal in Dzaoudzi. If you want, you can then catch the ferry to Mamoudzou and walk, or take another taxi, to your hotel. Make sure that you do share the taxi with others – and ask what they are paying – otherwise you may be charged for a full chartered taxi.

Boat
An excellent ferry known as *le barge* for cars, motorcycles and folk who wish to walk, sails between Mamoudzou and Dzaoudzi, taking about 10 minutes. According to its schedule, the *Salama Djema I, II* or *III* leaves from both terminals on the half-hour from

MAYOTTE

Monday to Saturday, from 6 am to 9 pm; then every hour until 2 am. On Sundays, one of the boats leaves either terminal every hour from 7 am to 4 pm, and from 7 pm to midnight; and every 30 minutes from 4 to 7 pm. Check out the schedules listed at both terminals. In any event, you don't seem to have to wait long for a ferry if you just turn up, or you could enjoy a snack or drink while you wait.

One ticket entitles you to a return ride – you only pay once, ie going from Mamoudzou to Dzaoudzi. The fare per passenger is F4; for small motorcycles F10; large motorcycles F16.50; and cars F77.

Taxi
Around the immediate area of the two main towns, anywhere on Petite Terre and to/from the airport, share-taxis are the normal form of transport. The fares are comparatively reasonable: a standard F4. This goes up to F8 during the evenings and on Sundays and public holidays. There's no need to ask the fare each time, but check the current fare with a local.

Taxi-brousse
You can travel just about anywhere on Mayotte by taxi-brousse. They leave from either of the two stations next to the ferry terminal in Mamoudzou; most have their destinations painted on the side of the vehicle. Go to the Taxi-brousse Station North just north of the ferry terminal if you are heading north of Mamoudzou, and to the Taxi-brousse Station South for destinations to the southern part of the island. If in doubt, just ask. All taxis-brousse charge about 50c per km with a minimum of F4. From Mamoudzou to Longoni beach the fare is F8, and to Chirongui from Mamoudzou the fare is about F18.

Car & Motorcycle
There is no shortage of places to hire cars,

but it comes as no surprise that rental is expensive; don't forget that travelling by car on the ferry will add to the cost of your day's outing. The rental price at each agency in Mamoudzou is virtually identical, but it is a little more expensive at the up-market hotels around the islands.

Expect to pay about F300 per day with unlimited km for a Peugeot 205; F520 for a weekend; and F260 per day for a week or more. Naturally better cars, especially 4WDs, will make you open your wallet long and deep.

A few agencies to try are: Maki Loc (☎ 61 19 51), in the same shopping mall as the Maison du Livre; LMV (☎ 60 00 34) at the airport; Mayotte Location (☎ 62 03 64) in Pamandzi; and Fanny Loc (☎ 61 33 33), at the Place du Marché in Mamoudzou. Ask at least twice about any extra costs such as insurance.

Motorcycles are cheaper and a great way to get around. Expect to pay at least F130 per day for a Suzuki 125cc; F700 for a week. Contact Tirard (☎ 61 13 58) and Banga Cycles (☎ 61 06 08), both at Kawéni, the port area north of Mamoudzou.

Bicycle
A great way to get around is on a mountain bike (known in French as a VTT), but the roads are often steep and winding, especially around Grande Terre. Still, it's nice to visit the nearby areas by bike and easy enough to cycle around Petite Terre. The good news is that most roads are paved and the drivers are cautious and considerate compared to their Comoran cousins.

Surprisingly, the only places we found that rent bikes are the Hôtel Lagon Sud (see Places to Stay in Petite Terre), which charges F50/80 for a half/full-day, and Banga Cycles (see the Car & Motorcycle section above) which charges about the same price.

Glossary

Abbreviations
Com – Comoran
Fre – French
Mal – Malagasy

aka – (Englilsh) also known as
alambic – (Mal) ylang-ylang distillery
aloalo – (Mal) elaborate funereal or commemorative wood carving; normally over 1m high
andevo – (Mal) traditional underclass
asity – (Mal) small forest-dwelling bird
aye-aye – (Mal) unique nocturnal lemur with a specially adapted middle digit

baché – (Mal) bush taxi; ranges from a squarish covered van to a minibus
baie – (Fre) bay
banga – (Com) creatively decorated hut constructed and occupied by unmarried adolescent men on Mayotte
bangwe – (Com) outdoor council area, marked by two high gateways
baptême – (Fre) introductory one day diving course offered by resorts to non-divers; also known as a 'resort course'
bazary – (Mal) one of several terms for a market
bonbons – (Fre) sweets
boutre – (Mal) single-masted dhow
brochette – (Fre) skewers with small pieces of meat

cadeaux – (Fre) gifts
camion – (Fre) truck
cap – (Fre) cape or headland
car-brousse – (Mal) sturdy bush minibus
cascade – (Fre) waterfall
chiromani – (Com) all-purpose wrap; women drape themselves in these brightly coloured wraps, which are worn like a versatile sari, using one of the tails as a head covering
chute – (Fre) waterfall; short for 'chute d'eau'

cirque – mountaineering term for shallow basin with steep sides
Comoran – people of the Comoros islands; the language of the Comoros; adjective to describe anything about the Comoros
côtier – (Fre) person from the coastal regions of Madagascar
coua – any of nine species of Madagascan birds related to cuckoos

devises – (Fre) foreign currency
djinn – (Com) evil genie

fady – (Mal) taboo
famadihana – (Mal) exhumation and re-burial, literally translated as 'turning of the bones'; also known as second burial
fanafody – (Mal) herbal healing
fanorona – (Mal) popular board game
faritany – (Mal) province
fijoroana – (Mal) ceremony in which the Malagasy invoke their ancestors
firaisampo-kotany – (Mal) county
fivondron-ampokotany – (Mal) prefecture
fody – weaver bird
fokonolona – (Mal) local community council
fokontany – (Mal) people's executive committee, an arm of local or community government
fossa – (Mal) carnivorous mammal found only on Madagascar

galawa – (Com) wooden dugout canoe; identical to the *pirogue* found in Madagascar
gare routière – (Fre) *taxi-brousse* and *taxi-be* station
girofles – (Fre) cloves
goëlette – (Fre) large cargo vessel
grand mariage – (Fre) traditional wedding ceremony; still practised occasionally, especially on Grande Comore
greenbul – small Madagascan forest bird
grotte – (Fre) cave

GLOSSARY

hali – (Com) folk tale

hauts plateaux – (Fre) high plateaus; the interior highlands of Madagascar

hira gasy – (Mal) popular music, dancing and storytelling spectacle held in the highlands, and performed by a number of wildly clad troupes known as 'mpihira gasy' or 'mpilalao'

hôtel de ville – (Fre) town hall – not a hotel

hotely – (Mal) small informal roadhouse serving basic meals

Id-ul-Fitr – marks the new moon and the end of Ramadan; the biggest Muslim celebration of the year

Île – (Fre) island; a small island is called an 'îlot'

Imerina – (Mal) area of Madagascar dominated by the Merina tribe

indri – (Mal) largest of the lemurs

kabary – (Mal) highly regarded oral tradition which takes several forms, including speech-making and storytelling, often in a competition between several kabary experts

kandzou – (Com) long white cotton shirt

kapoka – (Mal) odd unit of measure; though it varies in size, it's normally defined as the amount of rice or other dry goods that will fit into a Nestlé Lait Sucre Concentré (condensed milk) tin

karatra – (Mal) ticket

kianja/kianjan – (Mal) place or square

koffia – (Com) skull cap

lac – (Fre) lake

lakana – (Mal) dugout canoe, similar to a *pirogue*

lamba – (Mal) white silk, cotton or synthetic wrap which is worn around the shoulders of women and often draped over the head, with one tail hanging behind

lamba arindrano – (Mal) woven handspun silk

lamba maitso – (Mal) 'green cloth'; when the tail of a lamba falls on the right side of the body it signifies that the wearer is in mourning (it isn't necessarily green)

lamba mena – (Mal) 'red cloth' (although it is rarely actually red); a burial shroud. On special occasions certain people wear red lambas, signifying authority.

lapan' ny tanana – (Mal) town hall

lavaka – (Mal) ugly, gaping landslip caused by erosion

lepilemur – alternative name for any of the seven species of sportive or 'weasel' lemurs

Mahorais – indigenous people from Mayotte; anyone living in Mayotte; adjective to describe anything about Mayotte

maisons des filles – (Com) homes which families begin building as soon as a daughter is born. It is presented to her upon her marriage and she is permitted to keep it if her husband dies, leaves or renounces her.

maki – (Mal & Com) a ring-tailed lemur in Madagascar; any type of lemur in the Comoros

malabary – (Mal) men's garment which resembles a nightshirt

manioc – cassava

medina – ancient quarter of Arabic settlements

menu du jour – (Fre) meal of the day, normally consisting of three courses

mesite – any of three species of birds related to rails and unique to Madagascar

moka fohy – (Mal) mosque

monnaies – (Fre) coins

montagne – (Fre) mountain

moraingy – (Mal) fights traditionally held between young men in Malagasy coastal villages; the fighting is fast and tough, with the emphasis on agility and the object of laying one's opponent out cold

mora mora – (Mal) common term meaning 'easy easy' to explain why things don't work or people are late

m'sidzanou – (Com) yellow facial treatment or beauty mask used by Comoran women

mzungu – (Com) a European

nosy – (Mal) island

ohabolana – (Mal) proverb

ombiasy – (Mal) healers who still hold considerable social status in traditional areas. Ombiasy not only prescribe herbal cures, they combine them with potions and rituals aimed at securing help from the ancestors, balancing a negative *vintana*, or banishing or communicating with a *tromba* which has possessed a person.

paillotte – (Fre) thatched beach hut
pétanque – (Fre) type of lawn bowls
pic – (Fre) peak
pirogue – (Fre) dugout canoe in Madagascar; called a *galawa* in the Comoros
plage – (Fre) beach
planche à voile – sailboard
polisy nasionaly – (Mal) national police
pourboire – (Fre) tip
pousse-pousse – (Mal) a rickshaw drawn by a person

raiamandreny – (Mal) head of the *fokontany*
Ramadan – Muslim month of sunrise-to-sunset fasting
rangani – (Mal) marijuana
razana – (Mal) ancestors, and the reverence and respect accorded to them
rova – (Mal) palace; the name of the palace which burned down in Antananarivo (Tana)

sambatra – (Mal) mass circumcision ceremony
sambo – (Mal) samosa
sifaka – widespread type of lemur
sikidy – (Mal) form of divination using seeds
sisal – Mexican plant with large fleshy leaves cultivated for its fibres, which are used in making rope

taxi-be – literally a 'big taxi'; also referred to as a 'taxi-familial'
taxi-brousse – bush taxi
taxi-spéciale – share-taxi
tenrec – small, highly diverse insect-eating mammal; some have spines like a hedgehog
tibé – (Com) historical title; grand sultan
tilapia – type of freshwater fish
toirab – (Com) two to nine day public festivities associated with the *grand mariage*

tranompokonolona – (Mal) community centre
tromba – (Mal) spirit
tsingy – (Mal) labyrinthine limestone pinnacles and caves (also known as karst)

vaky soava – (Mal) folk music
valiha – (Mal) stringed musical instrument
vanga – any of 14 species of birds with beaks adapted for different feeding habits
vazaha – (Mal) light-skinned foreigner
vedette – (Fre) small launch
vintana – (Mal) destiny or tendencies inherited through the timing of one's birth; they can be altered with the intervention of an *ombiasy*
voay – (Mal) crocodile

wagangi – (Mal) witch doctor

ylang-ylang – tree grown in the Comoros and Madagascar for its fragrant flowers, which are used in the making of perfume

Abbreviations & Acronyms
ACA – Amicale Comores Air (airline)
AFC – Alliance Franco-Comorienne
ANGAP – Association Nationale pour le Gestion des Aires Protegées; Malagasy conservation organisation
BFC – Banque Française Commerciale
BFV – Banky Fampandrosoana'ny Varotra (Malagasy bank)
BMOI – Banque Malgache de l'Océan Indien (Malagasy bank)
BNI-CL – Bankin'ny Indostria-Crédit Lyonnais (Malagasy bank)
BTM – Bankin'ny Tantsaha Mpamokatra (Malagasy bank)
CF – Comoran Franc (also KMF or FC)
CFA – Communauté Financière Africaine
CITES – Convention on International Trade in Endangered Species
CMAC – (Com) Centre Mahorais d'Animation Culturelle
CNDRS – (Com) Centre National de Documentation et de Recherche Scientifique
CSF – Comoros Sans Frontiéres (airline)

FTM – Foiben Taosarintanin'i Madagasikara; official Malagasy cartographers
LMS – London Missionary Society
RFI – (Com) République Fédérale et Islamique

TAM – Transports et Travaux Aeriens de Madagascar (airline); also written TTAM
VTT – (Fre) vélo à tout terrain; mountain bike
WWF – World Wide Fund for Nature

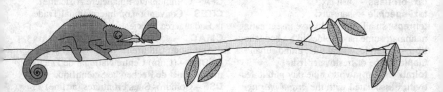

Health

Travel health depends on your predeparture preparations, your daily health care while travelling and how you handle any medical problem that does develop. While the potential dangers can seem quite frightening, in reality few travellers experience anything more than upset stomachs.

PREDEPARTURE PLANNING
Immunisations

For some countries no immunisations are necessary, but the further off the beaten track you go the more necessary it is to take precautions. Be aware that there is often a greater risk of disease with children and in pregnancy.

Plan ahead for getting your vaccinations: some of them require more than one injection, while some vaccinations should not be given together. It is recommended you seek medical advice at least six weeks before travel. Record all vaccinations on an International Health Certificate, available from your doctor or government health department.

Discuss your requirements with your doctor, but vaccinations you should consider for this trip include:

Hepatitis A The most common travel-acquired illness after diarrhoea which can put you out of action for weeks. Havrix 1440 is a vaccination which provides long term immunity (possibly more than 10 years) after an initial injection and a booster at six to 12 months.

Gamma globulin is not a vaccination but is ready-made antibody collected from blood donations. It should be given close to departure because, depending on the dose, it only protects for two to six months.

Typhoid This is an important vaccination to have where hygiene is a problem. Available either as an injection or oral capsules.

Diphtheria & Tetanus Diphtheria can be a fatal throat infection and tetanus can be a fatal wound infection. Everyone should have these vaccinations. After an initial course of three injections, boosters are necessary every 10 years.

Hepatitis B This disease is spread by blood or by sexual activity. Travellers who should consider a hepatitis B vaccination include those visiting countries where there are known to be many carriers, where blood transfusions may not be adequately screened or where sexual contact is a possibility. It involves three injections, the quickest course being over three weeks with a booster at 12 months.

Rabies Vaccination should be considered by those who will spend a month or longer in a country where rabies is common, especially if they are cycling, handling animals, caving, travelling to remote areas, or for children (who may not report a bite). Pre-travel rabies vaccination involves having three injections over 21 to 28 days. If someone who has been vaccinated is bitten or scratched by an animal they will require two booster injections of vaccine, those not vaccinated require more.

Cholera Despite its poor protection, in some situations it may be wise to have the cholera vaccine, eg for the trans-Africa traveller. Very occasionally travellers are asked by immigration officials to present a certificate, even though all countries and the WHO have dropped a cholera immunisation as a health requirement. You might be able to get a certificate without having the injection from a doctor or health centre sympathetic to the vagaries of travel in Africa. However, if you are not travelling beyond Madagascar and Comoros this should not be necessary.

HEALTH

Tuberculosis TB risk to travellers is usually very low. For those who will be living with or closely associated with local people there may be some risk. As most healthy adults do not develop symptoms, a skin test before and after travel to determine whether exposure has occurred may be considered. A vaccination is recommended for children living in these areas for three months or more.

Malaria Medication

Antimalarial drugs do not prevent you from being infected but kill the malaria parasites during a stage in their development and significantly reduce the risk of becoming very ill or dying.

Expert advice on medication should be sought, as there are many factors to consider including the area to be visited, the risk of exposure to malaria-carrying mosquitoes, the side effects of medication, your medical history and whether you are a child or adult, or pregnant. Travellers to isolated areas in high risk countries may like to carry a treatment dose of medication for use if symptoms occur.

Health Insurance

Make sure that you have adequate health insurance. See Travel Insurance under Documents in the Regional Facts for the Visitor chapter for details.

Travel Health Guides

If you are planning to be away or travelling in remote areas for a long period of time, you may like to consider taking a more detailed health guide.

Staying Healthy in Asia, Africa & Latin America, Dirk Schroeder, Moon Publications, 1994. Probably the best all-round guide to carry; it's compact, detailed and well organised.
Travellers' Health, Dr Richard Dawood, Oxford University Press, 1995. Comprehensive, easy to read, authoritative and highly recommended, although it's rather large to lug around.

Where There is No Doctor, David Werner, Macmillan, 1994. A very detailed guide intended for someone, such as a Peace Corps worker, going to work in an underdeveloped country.
Travel with Children, Maureen Wheeler, Lonely Planet Publications, 1995. Includes advice on travel health for younger children.

There are also some excellent travel health sites on the Internet. From the Lonely Planet home page there are links at (http://www .lonelyplanet.com/health/health.htm/h-links .htm) to the World Health Organisation, the US Centers for Disease Control & Prevention and Stanford University Travel Medicine Service.

Other Preparations

Make sure you're healthy before you start travelling. If you are going on a long trip make sure your teeth are OK. If you wear glasses take a spare pair and your prescription (preferably in French).

If you require a particular medication take an adequate supply, as it may not be available locally. Take part of the packaging showing the generic name, rather than the brand, which will make getting replacements easier. It's a good idea to have a legible prescription or letter from your doctor (in French) to show that you legally use the medication to avoid any problems.

Hospitals

It comes as no surprise that the hospitals in Madagascar and the Comoros (but not in Mayotte, which is part of France) are poor, and suffer from a lack of hygiene, equipment and trained doctors and nurses. These hospitals are generally adequate for emergencies, but if you need long term care go home, or at least travel to Mayotte, Mauritius, Réunion or South Africa, which are all connected by regular flights to Madagascar and the Comoros.

For more details about hospitals in Madagascar, the Comoros and Mayotte, refer to the individual chapters.

Medical Kit Check List

Consider taking a basic medical kit which includes:

- ☐ **Aspirin** or paracetamol (acetaminophen in the US) – for pain or fever.
- ☐ **Antihistamine** (such as Benadryl) – useful as a decongestant for colds and allergies, to ease the itch from insect bites or stings, and to help prevent motion sickness. Antihistamines may cause sedation and interact with alcohol so care should be taken when using them; take one you know and have used before, if possible.
- ☐ **Antibiotics** – useful if you're travelling well off the beaten track, but they must be prescribed; carry the prescription with you.
- ☐ **Loperamide** (eg Imodium) or Lomotil for diarrhoea; prochlorperazine (eg Stemetil) or metaclopramide (eg Maxalon) for nausea and vomiting.
- ☐ **Rehydration** mixture – for treatment of severe diarrhoea; particularly important for travelling with children.
- ☐ **Antiseptic** such as povidone-iodine (eg Betadine) – for cuts and grazes.
- ☐ **Multivitamins** – especially for long trips when dietary vitamin intake may be inadequate.
- ☐ **Calamine lotion** or **aluminium sulphate spray** (eg Stingose) – to ease irritation from bites or stings.
- ☐ **Bandages** and Band-aids.
- ☐ **Scissors, tweezers** and a **thermometer** (note that mercury thermometers are prohibited by airlines).
- ☐ **Cold and flu tablets** and throat lozenges. Pseudoephedrine hydrochloride (Sudafed) may be useful if flying with a cold to avoid ear damage.
- ☐ **Insect repellent, sunscreen, chap stick** and **water purification tablets**.
- ☐ **A couple of syringes**, in case you need injections. Ask your doctor for a note explaining why they have been prescribed.

Basic Rules

Food There is an old colonial adage which says: 'If you can cook it, boil it or peel it you can eat it ... otherwise forget it'. Vegetables and fruit should be washed with purified water or peeled where possible. Beware of ice cream which is sold in the street or anywhere it might have been melted and refrozen; if there's any doubt (eg a power cut in the last day or two) steer well clear. Shellfish such as mussels, oysters and clams should be avoided as well as undercooked meat, particularly in the form of mince. Steaming does not make shellfish safe to eat.

If a place looks clean and well run and the

> **Everyday Health**
> Normal body temperature is up to 37°C or 98.6°F; more than 2°C (4°F) higher indicates a high fever. The normal adult pulse rate is 60 to 100 per minute (children 80 to 100, babies 100 to 140). As a general rule the pulse increases about 20 beats per minute for each °C (2°F) rise in fever. Respiration (breathing) rate is also an indicator of illness. Count the number of breaths per minute: between 12 and 20 is normal for adults and older children (up to 30 for younger children, 40 for babies). People with a high fever or serious respiratory illness breathe more quickly than normal. More than 40 shallow breaths a minute may indicate pneumonia. ∎

vendor also looks clean and healthy, then the food is probably safe. In general, places that are packed with travellers or locals will be fine, while empty restaurants are questionable. The food in busy restaurants is cooked and eaten quite quickly with little standing around and is probably not reheated.

Water As a general rule, tap water is safe to drink in major towns in Madagascar, the Comoros (but not on Anjouan) and Mayotte. Everywhere, care should be taken immediately following heavy rain.

Reputable brands of bottled water or soft drinks are generally fine, although in some places bottles may be refilled with tap water. Only use water from containers with a serrated seal – not tops or corks. Take care with fruit juice, particularly if water may have been added. Milk should be treated with suspicion as it is often not pasteurised, though boiled milk is fine if it is kept hygienically. Tea or coffee should also be OK, since the water should have been boiled.

Water Purification The simplest way of purifying water is to boil it thoroughly. Vigorously boiling should be satisfactory; however, at high altitude water boils at a lower temperature, so germs are less likely to be killed. Boil it for longer in these environments.

Consider purchasing a water filter for a long trip. There are two main kinds of filter. Total filters take out all parasites, bacteria and viruses, and make water safe to drink. They are often expensive, but they can be more cost effective than buying bottled water. Simple filters (which can even be a nylon mesh bag) take out dirt and larger foreign bodies from the water so that chemical solutions work much more effectively; if water is dirty, chemical solutions may not work at all. It's very important when buying a filter to read the specifications, so that you know exactly what it removes from the water and what it doesn't. Simple filtering will not remove all dangerous organisms, so if you cannot boil water it should be treated chemically. Chlorine tablets (Puritabs, Steritabs or other brand names) will kill many pathogens, but not some parasites like giardia and amoebic cysts. Iodine is more effective in purifying water and is available in tablet form (such as Potable Aqua). Follow the directions carefully and remember that too much iodine can be harmful.

MEDICAL PROBLEMS & TREATMENT

Self-diagnosis and treatment can be risky, so you should always seek medical help. Although we do give drug dosages in this section, they are for emergency use only. Correct diagnosis is vital.

An embassy, consulate or decent hotel can usually recommend a good place to go for advice. In some places standards of medical attention are so low that for some ailments the best advice is to get on a plane and go somewhere else. Antibiotics should ideally be administered only under medical supervision. Take only the recommended dose at the prescribed intervals and use the whole course, even if the illness seems to be cured earlier. Stop immediately if there are any serious reactions and don't use the antibiotic at all if you are unsure that you have the correct one. Some people are allergic to commonly prescribed antibiotics such as penicillin or sulpha drugs; carry this information when travelling eg on a bracelet.

Environmental Hazards

Fungal Infections Fungal infections occur more commonly in hot weather and are usually found on the scalp, between the toes or fingers, in the groin and on the body (ringworm). You get ringworm (which is a fungal infection, not a worm) from infected animals or other people. Moisture encourages these infections.

To prevent fungal infections wear loose, comfortable clothes, avoid artificial fibres, wash frequently and dry carefully. If you do get an infection, wash the infected area at least daily with a disinfectant or medicated soap and water, and rinse and dry well. Apply an antifungal cream or powder like tolnifate (Tinaderm). Try to expose the infected area to air or sunlight as much as possible and wash all towels and underwear in hot water, change them often and let them dry in the sun.

Heat Exhaustion Dehydration and salt deficiency can cause heat exhaustion. Take time to acclimatise to high temperatures, drink sufficient liquids and do not do anything too physically demanding.

Salt deficiency is characterised by fatigue, lethargy, headaches, giddiness and muscle cramps; salt tablets may help, but adding extra salt to your food is better.

Anhydrotic heat exhaustion, caused by an inability to sweat, is quite rare. It is likely to strike people who have been in a hot climate for some time, rather than newcomers.

Heat Stroke This serious, occasionally fatal, condition can occur if the body's heat-regulating mechanism breaks down and the body temperature rises to dangerous levels. Long, continuous periods of exposure to high temperatures and insufficient fluids can leave you vulnerable to heat stroke.

The symptoms are feeling unwell, not sweating very much (or at all) and a high body temperature (39°C to 41°C or 102°F to 106°F). Where sweating has ceased the skin becomes flushed and red. Severe, throbbing headaches and lack of coordination will also occur, and the sufferer may be confused or aggressive. Eventually the victim will become delirious or convulse. Hospitalisation is essential, but in the interim get victims out of the sun, remove their clothing, cover them with a wet sheet or towel and then fan continually. Give fluids if they are conscious.

Jet Lag Jet lag is experienced when a person travels by air across more than three time zones (each time zone usually represents a one-hour time difference). It occurs because many of the functions of the human body (such as temperature, pulse rate and emptying of the bladder and bowels) are regulated by internal 24-hour cycles. When we travel long distances rapidly, our bodies take time to adjust to the 'new time' of our destination, and we may experience fatigue, disorientation, insomnia, anxiety, impaired concentration and loss of appetite. These effects will usually be gone within three days of arrival, but to minimise the impact of jet lag:

• Rest for a couple of days before departure.
• Try to select flight schedules that minimise sleep deprivation; arriving late in the day means you can go to sleep soon after you arrive. For very long flights, try to organise a stopover.
• Avoid excessive eating (which bloats the stomach) and alcohol (which causes dehydration) during the flight. Instead, drink plenty of non-carbonated, non-alcoholic drinks such as fruit juice or water.
• Avoid smoking.
• Make yourself comfortable by wearing loose-fitting clothes and perhaps bringing an eye mask and ear plugs to help you sleep.
• Try to sleep at the appropriate time for the time zone you are travelling to.

Motion Sickness Eating lightly before and during a trip will reduce the chances of motion sickness. If you are prone to motion sickness try to find a place that minimises movement – near the wing on aircraft, close to midships on boats, near the centre on buses. Fresh air usually helps; reading and cigarette smoke don't. Commercial motion-sickness preparations, which can cause

drowsiness, have to be taken before the trip commences. Ginger (available in capsule form) and peppermint (including mint-flavoured sweets) are natural preventatives.

Prickly Heat Prickly heat is an itchy rash caused by excessive perspiration trapped under the skin. It usually strikes people who have just arrived in a hot climate. Keeping cool, bathing often, drying the skin and using a mild talcum or prickly heat powder, or resorting to air-conditioning may help.

Sunburn In the tropics, the desert or at high altitude you can get sunburnt surprisingly quickly, even through cloud. Use a sunscreen, hat, and barrier cream for your nose and lips. Calamine lotion or stingose are good for mild sunburn. Protect your eyes with good quality sunglasses, particularly if you will be near water, sand or snow.

Infectious Diseases

Diarrhoea Simple things like a change of water, food or climate can all cause a mild bout of diarrhoea, but a few rushed toilet trips with no other symptoms is not indicative of a major problem.

Dehydration is the main danger with any diarrhoea, particularly in children or the elderly, in whom dehydration can occur quite quickly. Under all circumstances *fluid replacement* (at least equal to the volume being lost) is the most important thing to remember. Weak black tea with a little sugar, soda water, or soft drinks allowed to go flat and diluted 50% with clean water are all good. With severe diarrhoea a rehydrating solution is preferable to replace minerals and salts lost. Commercially available oral rehydration salts (ORS) are very useful; add them to boiled or bottled water. In an emergency you can make up a solution of six teaspoons of sugar and a half teaspoon of salt to a litre of boiled or bottled water. You need to drink at least the same volume of fluid that you are losing in bowel movements and vomiting. Urine is the best guide to the adequacy of replacement – if you have small amounts of

---

Nutrition

If your food is poor or limited in availability, if you're travelling hard and fast and therefore missing meals, or if you simply lose your appetite you can soon start to lose weight and place your health at risk. Make sure your diet is well balanced. Cooked eggs, tofu, beans, lentils and nuts are all safe ways to get protein. Fruit you can peel (bananas or lychees, example) is usually safe (melons can harbour bacteria in their flesh and are best avoided) and a good source of vitamins. Try to eat plenty of grains (including rice) and bread. Remember that although food is generally safer if it is cooked well, overcooked food loses much of its nutritional value. If your diet isn't well balanced or if your food intake is insufficient, it's a good idea to take vitamin and iron pills. In hot climates make sure you drink enough – don't rely on feeling thirsty to indicate when you should drink. Not needing to urinate or small amounts of very dark yellow urine is a danger sign. Always carry a water bottle with you on long trips. Excessive sweating can lead to loss of salt and therefore muscle cramping. Salt tablets are not a good idea as a preventative, but in places where salt is not used much adding salt to food can help. ■

---

concentrated urine, you need to drink more. Keep drinking small amounts often. Stick to a bland diet as you recover.

Lomotil or Imodium can be used to bring relief from the symptoms, although they do not actually cure the problem. Only use these drugs if you do not have access to toilets eg if you *must* travel. For children under 12 years Lomotil and Imodium are not recommended. Do not use these drugs if the person has a high fever or is severely dehydrated.

In certain situations antibiotics may be required: diarrhoea with blood or mucous (dysentery), any fever, watery diarrhoea with fever and lethargy, persistent diarrhoea not improving after 48 hours and severe diarrhoea. In these situations gut-paralysing drugs like Imodium or Lomotil should be avoided.

A stool test is necessary to diagnose which kind of dysentery you have, so you should seek medical help urgently. Where this is not possible the recommended drugs for dysentery are norfloxacin 400mg twice daily for three days or ciprofloxacin 500mg twice daily for five days. These are not recommended for children or pregnant women. The drug of choice for children would be co-trimoxazole (Bactrim, Septrin, Resprim) with dosage dependent on weight. A five-day course is given. Ampicillin or amoxycillin may be given in pregnancy, but medical care is necessary.

Amoebic Dysentery The onset of symptoms is more gradual, with cramping abdominal pain and vomiting less likely; fever may not be present. It will persist until treated and can recur and cause other health problems.

Giardiasis This is another type of diarrhoea. The parasite causing this intestinal disorder is present in contaminated water. The symptoms are stomach cramps, nausea, a bloated stomach, watery, foul-smelling diarrhoea and frequent gas. Giardiasis can appear several weeks after you have been exposed to the parasite. The symptoms may disappear for a few days and then return; this can go on for several weeks. Tinidazole, known as Fasigyn, or metronidazole (Flagyl) are the recommended drugs. Treatment is a 2gm single dose of Fasigyn or 250mg of Flagyl three times daily for five to 10 days.

Hepatitis Hepatitis is a general term for inflammation of the liver. It is a common disease worldwide. The symptoms are fever, chills, headache, fatigue, feelings of weakness and aches and pains, followed by loss of appetite, nausea, vomiting, abdominal pain, dark urine, light-coloured faeces, jaundiced (yellow) skin and the whites of the eyes may turn yellow. **Hepatitis A** is transmitted by contaminated food and drinking water. The disease poses a real threat to the western traveller. You should seek medical advice, but there is not much you can do apart from resting, drinking lots of fluids, eating lightly and avoiding fatty foods. People who have had hepatitis should avoid alcohol for some time after the illness as the liver needs time to recover.

Hepatitis E This strain is transmitted in the same way; it can be very serious for pregnant women.

There are almost 300 million chronic carriers of **Hepatitis B** in the world. It is spread through contact with infected blood, blood products or body fluids, for example through sexual contact, unsterilised needles and blood transfusions, or contact with blood via small breaks in the skin. Other risk situations include having a shave, tattoo, or having your body pierced with contaminated equipment. The symptoms of type B may be more severe and may lead to long term problems. **Hepatitis D** is spread in the same way, but the risk is mainly in shared needles.

Hepatitis C This strain can cause chronic liver disease. The virus is spread by contact with blood, usually via contaminated transfusions or shared needles. Avoiding these is the only means of prevention.

HIV & AIDS The Human Immunodeficiency Virus (HIV) develops into AIDS, Acquired Immune Deficiency Syndrome, which is a fatal disease. HIV is a major problem in many countries. Any exposure to blood, blood products or body fluids may put the individual at risk. The disease is often transmitted through sexual contact or dirty needles – vaccinations, acupuncture, tattooing and body piercing can be potentially as dangerous as intravenous drug use. Note that this includes heterosexual, as well as homosexual, contact, and in parts of Africa this is a common disease. HIV/AIDS can also be spread through infected blood transfusions; some developing countries cannot afford to screen blood used for transfusions.

If you do need an injection, ask to see the syringe unwrapped in front of you, or take a needle and syringe pack with you.

Fear of HIV infection should never preclude treatment for serious medical conditions.

Intestinal Worms These parasites are most common in rural areas and different worms infect people in different ways. Some may be ingested on food, including undercooked meat, and some enter through your skin. Infestations may not show up for some time, and although they are generally not serious, if left untreated some can cause severe health problems later. Consider having a stool test when you return home to check for these and determine the appropriate treatment.

Threadworms, or *Strongyloidiasis*, are found in low lying areas of Madagascar and Comoros; symptoms can include diarrhoea and vomiting. Avoid eating strawberries, and other uncooked foods grown in the ground, such as lettuce, spinach and mushrooms. They are often covered with fertiliser (ie faeces) from pigs, which carry the *Taenia solium* worm, or from sheep, which carries the nasty *Ecchinococcus* tapeworm.

Schistosomiasis (Bilharzia) This disease is carried in water by minute worms. They infect certain varieties of freshwater snails found in rivers, streams, lakes and particularly behind dams. The worms multiply and are eventually discharged into the water.

The worm enters through the skin and attaches itself to your intestines or bladder. The first symptom may be a tingling and sometimes a light rash around the area where it entered. Weeks later a high fever may develop. A general feeling of being unwell may be the first symptom, or there may be no symptoms. Once the disease is established abdominal pain and blood in the urine are other signs. The infection often causes no symptoms until the disease is well established (several months to years after exposure) and damage to internal organs irreversible.

Avoiding swimming or bathing in fresh water where bilharzia is present is the main method of preventing the disease. Even deep water can be infected. If you do get wet, dry off quickly and dry your clothes as well. Bilharzia is quite common in Madagascar, but is not present in the Comoros. To avoid contracting it, stay out of rivers and lakes. (No proper research has been carried out to determine which rivers and lakes are contaminated, so it is best avoid to swimming in, or drinking from, any stagnant river or lake in which livestock or people may have excreted.)

A blood test is the most reliable test, but it will not show positive in results until a number of weeks after exposure.

Sexually Transmitted Diseases Gonorrhoea, herpes and syphilis are among these diseases; sores, blisters or rashes around the genitals, discharges or pain when urinating are common symptoms. In some STDs, such as wart virus or chlamydia, symptoms may be less marked or not observed at all especially in women. Syphilis symptoms eventually disappear completely but the disease continues and can cause severe problems in later years. While abstinence from sexual contact is the only 100% effective prevention, using condoms is also effective. The treatment of gonorrhoea and syphilis is with antibiotics. The different sexually transmitted diseases each require specific antibiotics. There is no cure for herpes (although it is non-fatal) or AIDS.

Typhoid Typhoid fever is a dangerous gut infection caused by contaminated water and food. Medical help must be sought.

In its early stages sufferers may feel they have a bad cold or flu on the way, as early symptoms are a headache, body aches and a fever which rises a little each day until it is around 40°C (104°F) or more. The victim's pulse is often slow relative to the degree of fever present – unlike a normal fever where the pulse increases. There may also be vomiting, abdominal pain, diarrhoea or constipation.

In the second week the high fever and slow pulse continue and a few pink spots may appear on the body; trembling, delirium, weakness, weight loss and dehydration may occur. Complications such as pneumonia, perforated bowel or meningitis may occur.

The fever should be treated by keeping the victim cool and giving them fluids as dehydration should also be watched for. Ciprofloxacin 750mg twice a day for 10 days is good for adults.

Chloramphenicol is recommended in many countries. The adult dosage is two 250mg capsules, four times a day. Children aged between eight and 12 years should have half the adult dose; and younger children one-third the adult dose.

Insect-Borne Diseases
Filariasis, leishmaniasis, sleeping sickness, typhus and yellow fever are all insect-borne diseases, but they do not pose a great risk to travellers. For more information on them see Less Common Diseases at the end of this chapter.

Malaria This serious and potentially fatal disease is spread by mosquito bites. In Madagascar and the Comoros it is extremely important to avoid mosquito bites and to take tablets to prevent this disease. There is a risk of contracting malaria at all times of the year in Madagascar; coastal areas harbour the greatest risk. Symptoms range from fever, chills and sweating, headache, diarrhoea and abdominal pains to a vague feeling of ill-health. Seek medical help immediately if malaria is suspected. Without treatment malaria can rapidly become more serious and can be fatal.

If medical care is not available, malaria tablets can be used for treatment. You need to use a malaria tablet which is different to the one you were taking when you contracted malaria. The treatment dosages are mefloquine (two 250mg tablets and a further two six hours later) or fansidar (single dose of three tablets). If you were previously taking mefloquine then other alternatives are halofantrine (three doses of two 250mg tablets every six hours) or quinine sulphate (600mg every six hours). There is a greater risk of side effects with these dosages than in normal use.

Travellers are advised to prevent mosquito bites at all times. The main messages are:

- wear light coloured clothing
- wear long pants and long sleeved shirts
- use mosquito repellents containing the compound DEET on exposed areas (prolonged overuse of DEET may be harmful, especially to children, but its use is considered preferable to being bitten by disease-transmitting mosquitoes)
- avoid highly scented perfumes or aftershave
- use a mosquito net impregnated with mosquito repellent (permethrin) – it may be worth taking your own
- impregnating clothes with permethrin effectively deters mosquitoes and other insects

Cuts, Bites & Stings

Rabies is passed through animal bites. See the Less Common Diseases section for details of this disease.

Bedbugs & Lice Bedbugs live in various places, but particularly in dirty mattresses and bedding, evidenced by spots of blood on bedclothes or on the wall. Bedbugs leave itchy bites in neat rows. Calamine lotion or Stingose spray may help.

All lice cause itching and discomfort. They make themselves at home in your hair (head lice), your clothing (body lice) or in your pubic hair (crab lice, or crabs). You catch lice through direct contact with infected people or by sharing combs, clothing and the like. Powder or shampoo treatment will kill the lice, and infected clothing should then be washed in very hot, soapy water and left in the sun to dry.

Insect Bites & Stings Bee and wasp stings are usually painful rather than dangerous. However, people who are allergic to them can experience severe breathing difficulties and may require urgent medical care. Calamine lotion or Stingose spray will give relief and ice packs will reduce the pain and swelling. There are some spiders with dangerous bites but antivenenes are usually available. Scorpion stings are notoriously painful and in some parts of Asia, the Middle East and

Central America can actually be fatal. Scorpions often shelter in shoes or clothing.

Certain cone shells can inflict a dangerous or even fatal sting. There are various fish and other sea creatures which can sting or bite dangerously or which are dangerous to eat. Again, local advice is the best suggestion.

Cuts & Scratches Wash well and treat any cut with an antiseptic such as povidone-iodine. Where possible avoid bandages and Band-aids, which can keep wounds wet. Walking in coral will not only lead to cuts that are notoriously slow to heal, but it will also cause terrible damage to reefs. Severe pain, throbbing, redness, fever or generally feeling unwell suggest infection and the need for antibiotics promptly as coral cuts may result in serious infections. Avoid walking on coral reefs.

Leeches & Ticks Leeches may be present in damp rainforest conditions; they attach themselves to your skin to suck your blood. Trekkers often get them on their legs or in their boots. Salt or a lighted cigarette end will make them fall off. Do not pull them off, as the bite is then more likely to become infected. Clean and apply pressure if the point of attachment is bleeding. An insect repellent may keep them away.

You should always check all over your body if you have been walking through a potentially tick-infested area as ticks can cause skin infections and other more serious diseases. If a tick is found attached, press down around the tick's head with tweezers, grab the head and gently pull upwards. Avoid pulling the rear of the body as this may squeeze the tick's gut contents through the attached mouth parts into the skin, increasing the risk of infection and disease. Smearing chemicals on the tick will not make it let go and is not recommended.

Snakes There are no dangerous snakes on Madagascar or the Comoros. However, even non-poisonous snakes can inflict a nasty bite. Treat all snakes with respect and avoid handling them unless you have had previous experience. To minimise your chances of being bitten always wear boots, socks and long trousers when walking through undergrowth where snakes may be present. Don't put your hands into holes and crevices, and be careful when collecting firewood.

Snake bites do not cause instantaneous death and antivenenes are usually available. Immediately wrap the bitten limb tightly, as you would for a sprained ankle, and then attach a splint to immobilise it. Keep the victim still and seek medical help, if possible with the dead snake for identification. Don't attempt to catch the snake if there is a possibility of being bitten again. Tourniquets and sucking out the poison are now comprehensively discredited.

Less Common Diseases

The following disease pose a small risk to travellers, and so are only mentioned in passing. Seek medical advice if you think you may have any of these diseases.

Cholera This is the worst of the watery diarrhoeas and medical help should be sought. Outbreaks of cholera are generally widely reported, so you can avoid such problem areas. *Fluid replacement is the most vital treatment* – the risk of dehydration is severe as you may lose up to 20 litres a day. If there is a delay in getting to hospital then begin taking tetracycline. The adult dose is 250mg four times daily. It is not recommended for children under nine years nor for pregnant women. Tetracycline may help shorten the illness, but adequate fluids are required to save lives.

Filariasis This is a mosquito-transmitted parasitic infection that is present in Madagascar and the Comoros. Possible symptoms include fever, pain and swelling of the lymph glands; inflammation of lymph drainage areas; swelling of a limb or the scrotum; skin rashes and blindness. Treatment is available to eliminate the parasites from the body, but some of the damage already caused may not be reversible. Medical advice should be

obtained promptly if the infection is suspected.

Leishmaniasis A group of parasitic diseases transmitted by sandfly bites, found in many parts of Africa. Cutaneous leishmaniasis affects the skin tissue, causing ulceration and disfigurement, and visceral leishmaniasis affects the internal organs. Seek medical advice as laboratory testing is required for diagnosis and correct treatment. Avoiding sandfly bites is the best precaution. Bites are usually painless, itchy and are yet another reason to cover up and apply repellent.

Plague In some parts of northern Madagascar, the bubonic plague very occasionally rears its ugly head. This disease is normally carried by rodents (squirrels, rats etc) and can be transmitted to humans by bites from fleas that live on infected animals. It can also be passed from human to human by coughing.

The symptoms are fever and enlarged lymph nodes. The untreated disease has a death rate of 60%. Your chances of catching the plague are extremely slight, however, so don't panic, and there is a vaccine available. The best drug is the antibiotic streptomycin, which must be injected intramuscularly.

Rabies Rabies is a fatal viral infection found in many countries. Many animals can be infected (such as dogs, cats, bats and monkeys) and it is their saliva which is infectious. Any bite, scratch or even lick from a warm-blooded, furry animal should be cleaned immediately and thoroughly. Scrub with soap and running water, and then apply alcohol or iodine solution. Medical help should be sought promptly to receive a course of injections to prevent the onset of symptoms and death.

Tetanus Tetanus occurs when a wound becomes infected by a germ which lives in soil and in the faeces of horses and other animals. It enters the body via breaks in the skin. All wounds should be cleaned promptly and adequately and an antiseptic cream or solution applied. Use antibiotics if the wound becomes hot, throbs or pus is seen. The first symptom may be discomfort in swallowing, or stiffening of the jaw and neck; this is followed by painful convulsions of the jaw and whole body. The disease can be fatal.

Tuberculosis (TB) TB is a bacterial infection usually transmitted from person to person by coughing but may be transmitted through consumption of unpasteurised milk. Milk that has been boiled is safe to drink, and the souring of milk to make yoghurt or cheese also kills the bacilli. Travellers are usually not at great risk as close household contact with the infected person is usually required before the disease is passed on.

Typhus Typhus is spread by ticks, mites or lice. It begins with fever, chills, headache and muscle pains followed a few days later by a body rash. There is often a large painful sore at the site of the bite and nearby lymph nodes are swollen and painful. Typhus can be treated under medical supervision. Seek local advice on areas where ticks pose a danger and always check your skin (including hair) carefully for ticks after walking in a danger area such as a tropical forest. A strong insect repellent can help, and serious walkers in tick areas should consider having their boots and trousers impregnated with benzyl benzoate and dibutylphthalate.

WOMEN'S HEALTH
Gynaecological Problems
Sexually transmitted diseases are a major cause of vaginal problems. Symptoms include a smelly discharge, painful intercourse and sometimes a burning sensation when urinating. Male sexual partners must also be treated. Medical attention should be sought and remember in addition to these diseases HIV or hepatitis B may also be acquired during exposure. Besides abstinence, the best thing is to practise safe sex using condoms.

Antibiotic use, synthetic underwear, sweating and contraceptive pills can lead to fungal vaginal infections when travelling in hot climates. Maintaining good personal hygiene, and loose-fitting clothes and cotton underwear will help to prevent these infections.

Fungal infections, characterised by a rash, itch and discharge, can be treated with a vinegar or lemon-juice douche, or with yoghurt. Nystatin, miconazole or clotrimazole pessaries or vaginal cream are the usual treatment.

Pregnancy
It is not advisable to travel to some places while pregnant as some vaccinations normally used to prevent serious diseases are not advisable in pregnancy, eg yellow fever. In addition, some diseases are much more serious for the mother (and may increase the risk of a stillborn child) in pregnancy, eg malaria.

Most miscarriages occur during the first three months of pregnancy. Miscarriage is not uncommon, and can occasionally lead to severe bleeding. The last three months should also be spent within reasonable distance of good medical care. A baby born as early as 24 weeks stands a chance of survival, but only in a good modern hospital. Pregnant women should avoid all unnecessary medication; vaccinations and malarial prophylactics should still be taken where needed. Additional care should be taken to prevent illness and particular attention should be paid to diet and nutrition. Alcohol and nicotine, for example, should be avoided.

Index

ABBREVIATIONS

C – Comoros   M – Madagascar

436 Index

LONELY PLANET PHRASEBOOKS

Building bridges,
Breaking barriers,
Beyond babble-on

Listen for the gems

Speak your own words

Ask your own questions

Master of your own image

- handy pocket-sized books
- easy to understand Pronunciation chapter
- clear and comprehensive Grammar chapter
- romanisation alongside script to allow ease of pronunciation
- script throughout so users can point to phrases
- extensive vocabulary sections, words and phrases for every situations
- full of cultural information and tips for the traveller

'...vital for a real DIY spirit and attitude in language learning' – Backpacker

'the phrasebooks have good cultural backgrounders and offer solid advice for challenging situations in remote locations' – San Francisco Examiner

'...they are unbeatable for their coverage of the world's more obscure languages' – The Geographical Magazine

---

Arabic (Egyptian)
Arabic (Moroccan)
Australia
  Australian English, Aboriginal and Torres Strait languages
Baltic States
  Estonian, Latvian, Lithuanian
Bengali
Burmese
Brazilian
Cantonese
Central Europe
  Czech, French, German, Hungarian, Italian and Slovak
Eastern Europe
  Bulgarian, Czech, Hungarian, Polish, Romanian and Slovak
Egyptian Arabic
Ethiopian (Amharic)
Fijian
French
German
Greek

Hindi/Urdu
Indonesian
Italian
Japanese
Korean
Lao
Latin American Spanish
Malay
Mandarin
Mediterranean Europe
  Albanian, Croatian, Greek, Italian, Macedonian, Maltese, Serbian, Slovene
Mongolian
Moroccan Arabic
Nepali
Papua New Guinea
Pilipino (Tagalog)
Quechua
Russian
Scandinavian Europe
  Danish, Finnish, Icelandic, Norwegian and Swedish

South-East Asia
  Burmese, Indonesian, Khmer, Lao, Malay, Tagalog (Pilipino), Thai and Vietnamese
Spanish
Sri Lanka
Swahili
Thai
Thai Hill Tribes
Tibetan
Turkish
Ukrainian
USA
  US English, Vernacular Talk, Native American languages and Hawaiian
Vietnamese
Western Europe
  Basque, Catalan, Dutch, French, German, Irish, Italian, Portuguese, Scottish Gaelic, Spanish (Castilian) and Welsh

LONELY PLANET JOURNEYS

JOURNEYS is a unique collection of travel writing – published by the company that understands travel better than anyone else. It is a series for anyone who has ever experienced – or dreamed of – the magical moment when they encountered a strange culture or saw a place for the first time. They are tales to read while you're planning a trip, while you're on the road or while you're in an armchair, in front of a fire.

JOURNEYS books catch the spirit of a place, illuminate a culture, recount a crazy adventure, or introduce a fascinating way of life. They always entertain, and always enrich the experience of travel.

THE RAINBIRD
A Central African Journey
Jan Brokken
translated by Sam Garrett

The Rainbird is a classic travel story. Following in the footsteps of famous Europeans such as Albert Schweitzer and H.M. Stanley, Jan Brokken journeyed to Gabon in central Africa. A kaleidoscope of adventures and anecdotes, *The Rainbird* brilliantly chronicles the encounter between Africa and Europe as it was acted out on a side-street of history. It is also the compelling, immensely readable account of the author's own travels in one of the most remote and mysterious regions of Africa.

Jan Brokken is one of Holland's best known writers. In addition to travel narratives and literary journalism, he has published several novels and short stories. Many of his works are set in Africa, where he has travelled widely.

SONGS TO AN AFRICAN SUNSET
A Zimbabwean Story
Sekai Nzenza-Shand

Songs to an African Sunset braids vividly personal stories into an intimate picture of contemporary Zimbabwe. Returning to her family's village after many years in the West, Sekai Nzenza-Shand discovers a world where ancestor worship, polygamy and witchcraft still govern the rhythms of daily life – and where drought, deforestation and AIDS have wrought devastating changes. With insight and affection, she explores a culture torn between respect for the old ways and the irresistible pull of the new.

Sekai Nzenza-Shand was born in Zimbabwe and has lived in England and Australia. Her first novel, *Zimbabwean Woman: My Own Story*, was published in London in 1988 and her fiction has been included in the short story collections *Daughters of Africa* and *Images of the West*. Sekai currently lives in Zimbabwe.

 This project has been assisted by the Commonwealth Government through the Australia Council, its arts funding and advisory body.

LONELY PLANET TRAVEL ATLASES

Lonely Planet has long been famous for the number and quality of its guidebook maps. Now we've gone one step further and in conjunction with Steinhart Katzir Publishers produced a handy companion series: Lonely Planet travel atlases – maps of a country produced in book form.

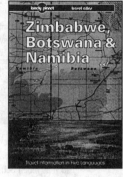

Unlike other maps, which look good but lead travellers astray, our travel atlases have been researched on the road by Lonely Planet's experienced team of writers. All details are carefully checked to ensure the atlas corresponds with the equivalent Lonely Planet guidebook.

The handy atlas format means no holes, wrinkles, torn sections or constant folding and unfolding. These atlases can survive long periods on the road, unlike cumbersome fold-out maps. The comprehensive index ensures easy reference.

- full-colour throughout
- maps researched and checked by Lonely Planet authors
- place names correspond with Lonely Planet guidebooks
  – no confusing spelling differences
- legend and travelling information in English, French, German, Japanese and Spanish
- size: 230 x 160 mm

Available now:
Chile & Easter Island • Egypt • India & Bangladesh • Israel & the Palestinian Territories •Jordan, Syria & Lebanon • Kenya • Laos • Portugal • South Africa, Lesotho & Swaziland • Thailand • Turkey • Vietnam • Zimbabwe, Botswana & Namibia

---

LONELY PLANET TV SERIES & VIDEOS

Lonely Planet travel guides have been brought to life on television screens around the world. Like our guides, the programmes are based on the joy of independent travel, and look honestly at some of the most exciting, picturesque and frustrating places in the world. Each show is presented by one of three travellers from Australia, England or the USA and combines an innovative mixture of video, Super-8 film, atmospheric soundscapes and original music.

Videos of each episode – containing additional footage not shown on television – are available from good book and video shops, but the availability of individual videos varies with regional screening schedules.

Video destinations include: Alaska • American Rockies • Australia – The South-East • Baja California & the Copper Canyon • Brazil • Central Asia • Chile & Easter Island • Corsica, Sicily & Sardinia – The Mediterranean Islands • East Africa (Tanzania & Zanzibar) • Ecuador & the Galapagos Islands • Greenland & Iceland • Indonesia • Israel & the Sinai Desert • Jamaica • Japan • La Ruta Maya • Morocco • New York • North India • Pacific Islands (Fiji, Solomon Islands & Vanuatu) • South India • South West China • Turkey • Vietnam • West Africa • Zimbabwe, Botswana & Namibia

The Lonely Planet TV series is produced by:
Pilot Productions
The Old Studio
18 Middle Row
London W10 5AT UK

For video availability and ordering information contact your nearest Lonely Planet office.

Music from the TV series is available on CD & cassette.

PLANET TALK

Lonely Planet's FREE quarterly newsletter

We love hearing from you and think you'd like to hear from us.

*When...*is the right time to see reindeer in Finland?
*Where...*can you hear the best palm-wine music in Ghana?
*How...*do you get from Asunción to Areguá by steam train?
*What...*is the best way to see India?

For the answer to these and many other questions read PLANET TALK.

Every issue is packed with up-to-date travel news and advice including:

* a letter from Lonely Planet co-founders Tony and Maureen Wheeler
* go behind the scenes on the road with a Lonely Planet author
* feature article on an important and topical travel issue
* a selection of recent letters from travellers
* details on forthcoming Lonely Planet promotions
* complete list of Lonely Planet products

To join our mailing list contact any Lonely Planet office.

Also available: Lonely Planet T-shirts. 100% heavyweight cotton.

LONELY PLANET ONLINE

Get the latest travel information before you leave or while you're on the road

Whether you've just begun planning your next trip, or you're chasing down specific info on currency regulations or visa requirements, check out Lonely Planet Online for up-to-the minute travel information.

As well as travel profiles of your favourite destinations (including maps and photos), you'll find current reports from our researchers and other travellers, updates on health and visas, travel advisories, and discussion of the ecological and political issues you need to be aware of as you travel.

There's also an online travellers' forum where you can share your experience of life on the road, meet travel companions and ask other travellers for their recommendations and advice. We also have plenty of links to other online sites useful to independent travellers.

And of course we have a complete and up-to-date list of all Lonely Planet travel products including guides, phrasebooks, atlases, Journeys and videos and a simple online ordering facility if you can't find the book you want elsewhere.

www.lonelyplanet.com
or
AOL keyword: lp

LONELY PLANET PRODUCTS

Lonely Planet is known worldwide for publishing practical, reliable and no-nonsense travel information in our guides and on our web site. The Lonely Planet list covers just about every accessible part of the world. Currently there are eight series: *travel guides, shoestring guides, walking guides, city guides, phrasebooks, audio packs, travel atlases* and *Journeys* – a unique collection of travel writing.

EUROPE

Amsterdam • Austria • Baltic States phrasebook • Britain • Central Europe on a shoestring • Central Europe phrasebook • Czech & Slovak Republics • Denmark • Dublin • Eastern Europe on a shoestring • Eastern Europe phrasebook • Estonia, Latvia & Lithuania • Finland • France • French phrasebook • German phrasebook • Greece • Greek phrasebook • Hungary • Iceland, Greenland & the Faroe Islands • Ireland • Italian phrasebook • Italy • Mediterranean Europe on a shoestring • Mediterranean Europe phrasebook • Paris • Poland • Portugal • Portugal travel atlas • Prague • Russia, Ukraine & Belarus • Russian phrasebook • Scandinavian & Baltic Europe on a shoestring • Scandinavian Europe phrasebook • Slovenia • Spain • Spanish phrasebook • St Petersburg • Switzerland • Trekking in Greece • Trekking in Spain • Ukrainian phrasebook • Vienna • Walking in Britain • Walking in Switzerland • Western Europe on a shoestring • Western Europe phrasebook

Travel Literature: The Olive Grove: Travels in Greece

NORTH AMERICA

Alaska • Backpacking in Alaska • Baja California • California & Nevada • Canada • Florida • Hawaii • Honolulu • Los Angeles • Mexico • Miami • New England • New Orleans • New York City • New York, New Jersey & Pennsylvania • Pacific Northwest USA • Rocky Mountain States • San Francisco • Southwest USA • USA phrasebook • Washington, DC & the Capital Region

CENTRAL AMERICA & THE CARIBBEAN

Bermuda • Central America on a shoestring • Costa Rica • Cuba • Eastern Caribbean • Guatemala, Belize & Yucatán: La Ruta Maya • Jamaica

SOUTH AMERICA

Argentina, Uruguay & Paraguay • Bolivia • Brazil • Brazilian phrasebook • Buenos Aires • Chile & Easter Island • Chile & Easter Island travel atlas • Colombia • Ecuador & the Galápagos Islands • Latin American Spanish phrasebook • Peru • Quechua phrasebook • Rio de Janeiro • South America on a shoestring • Trekking in the Patagonian Andes • Venezuela

Travel Literature: Full Circle: A South American Journey

ANTARCTICA

Antarctica

ISLANDS OF THE INDIAN OCEAN

Madagascar & Comoros • Maldives• Mauritius, Réunion & Seychelles

AFRICA

Africa - the South • Africa on a shoestring • Arabic (Moroccan) phrasebook • Cape Town • Central Africa • East Africa • Egypt • Egypt travel atlas• Ethiopian (Amharic) phrasebook • Kenya • Kenya travel atlas • Malawi, Mozambique & Zambia • Morocco • North Africa • South Africa, Lesotho & Swaziland • South Africa, Lesotho & Swaziland travel atlas • Swahili phrasebook • Trekking in East Africa • West Africa • Zimbabwe, Botswana & Namibia • Zimbabwe, Botswana & Namibia travel atlas

Travel Literature: The Rainbird: A Central African Journey • Songs to an African Sunset: A Zimbabwean Story